FRANK WOOD'S

Book-keeping and Accounts

FRANK WOOD'S

Book-keeping and Accounts

FIFTH EDITION

Frank Wood BSc(Econ), FCA

and

Sheila Robinson BA(Hons), Cert Ed, FMAAT

FINANCIAL TIMES
Prentice Hall

An imprint of Pearson Education

Harlow, England · London · New York · Reading, Massachusetts · San Francisco · Toronto · Don Mills, Ontario · Sydney
Tokyo · Singapore · Hong Kong · Seoul · Taipei · Cape Town · Madrid · Mexico City · Amsterdam · Munich · Paris · Milan

Pearson Education Limited

Edinburgh Gate
Harlow
Essex CM20 2JE

and Associated Companies throughout the world

Visit us on the World Wide Web at:
www.pearsoneduc.com

First edition published 1981
Fifth edition published 2001

ISBN 0 273 64619 2

British Library cataloguing-in-publication data
A catalogue record for this book is available from the British Library

10 9 8 7 6 5 4 3 2 1

Typeset by 7 in 10.5/12.5 Garamond Book
Printed and bound in Great Britain by Ashford Colour Press Ltd, Gosport

Contents

Preface vii
Matrix of subjects covered and examining bodies ix

Part 1 Introduction to double entry accounting

1 Introduction to accounting 2
2 The accounting equation and the balance sheet 6
3 The double entry system for assets, liabilities and capital 16
4 The double entry system for the asset of stock 28
5 The double entry system for expenses and revenues 38
6 Balancing off accounts 48
7 The trial balance 57

Part 2 The final accounts of a business

8 An introduction to the trading and profit and loss account 72
9 The balance sheet 87
10 Further considerations regarding final accounts 93
11 Accounting principles, concepts and conventions 110

Part 3 Books of original entry

12 Division of the ledger: books of original entry 120
13 The analytical petty cash book and the imprest system 126
14 The banking system 140
15 Two-column cash books 148
16 Three-column and analytical cash books, and cash discounts 157
17 Bank reconciliation statements 169
18 Capital and revenue expenditures 187
19 The sales day book, sales ledger, related documentation and other considerations 192
20 The purchases day book, purchases ledger and related documentation 207

21 The returns day books and documentation 215
22 Value added tax 226
23 Analytical sales and purchases day books 243
24 Control accounts 251
25 The journal 266

Part 4 Adjustments required before preparing final accounts

26 Methods of depreciation 280
27 Double entry records for depreciation and the disposal of assets 288
28 Bad debts and provisions for bad debts 296
29 Other adjustments for final accounts 308
30 Stock valuation 324
31 Accounting errors and their effect on accounting records 334
32 Suspense accounts and errors 347

Part 5 Final accounts of other organisations

33 Single entry and incomplete records 362
34 Club and society accounts 376
35 Manufacturing accounts 389
36 Partnership accounts 403
37 Limited company accounts 422
38 Analysis and interpretation of accounts 445

Part 6 Wage books and records

39 Wage books and records 468

Appendix A Glossary of accounting terms 486
Appendix B Step-by-step guides 499
Appendix C Multiple-choice questions 506
Appendix D Answers to multiple-choice questions 521
Appendix E Answers to exercises 522
Appendix F Specimen examination papers 565

Index 581

Contents

Preface vii
Matrix of subjects covered and examining bodies ix

Part 1 Introduction to double entry accounting

1 Introduction to accounting 2
2 The accounting equation and the balance sheet 6
3 The double entry system for assets, liabilities and capital 16
4 The double entry system for the asset of stock 28
5 The double entry system for expenses and revenues 38
6 Balancing off accounts 48
7 The trial balance 57

Part 2 The final accounts of a business

8 An introduction to the trading and profit and loss account 72
9 The balance sheet 87
10 Further considerations regarding final accounts 93
11 Accounting principles, concepts and conventions 110

Part 3 Books of original entry

12 Division of the ledger: books of original entry 120
13 The analytical petty cash book and the imprest system 126
14 The banking system 140
15 Two-column cash books 148
16 Three-column and analytical cash books, and cash discounts 157
17 Bank reconciliation statements 169
18 Capital and revenue expenditures 187
19 The sales day book, sales ledger, related documentation and other considerations 192
20 The purchases day book, purchases ledger and related documentation 207

21 The returns day books and documentation 215
22 Value added tax 226
23 Analytical sales and purchases day books 243
24 Control accounts 251
25 The journal 266

Part 4 Adjustments required before preparing final accounts

26 Methods of depreciation 280
27 Double entry records for depreciation and the disposal of assets 288
28 Bad debts and provisions for bad debts 296
29 Other adjustments for final accounts 308
30 Stock valuation 324
31 Accounting errors and their effect on accounting records 334
32 Suspense accounts and errors 347

Part 5 Final accounts of other organisations

33 Single entry and incomplete records 362
34 Club and society accounts 376
35 Manufacturing accounts 389
36 Partnership accounts 403
37 Limited company accounts 422
38 Analysis and interpretation of accounts 445

Part 6 Wage books and records

39 Wage books and records 468

Appendix A Glossary of accounting terms 486
Appendix B Step-by-step guides 499
Appendix C Multiple-choice questions 506
Appendix D Answers to multiple-choice questions 521
Appendix E Answers to exercises 522
Appendix F Specimen examination papers 565

Index 581

Preface to the fifth edition

This fifth edition of *Book-keeping and Accounts* continues to offer a comprehensive study text for foundation-level accountancy students. However, a substantial development has been undertaken in its content, and the book now seeks to meet the syllabus requirements of all the GCSE examining bodies.

The book is, therefore, suitable for students studying to take foundation-level examinations offered by the following:

- *London Chamber of Commerce and Industry (LCCI)*
- *Pitman Qualifications*
- *Edexcel and NVQ Level 2 Awards for Association of Accounting Technicians (AAT) and Certified Accounting Technician (CAT)*
- *Oxford, Cambridge and RSA Examinations (OCR)*
- *International Association of Book-keeping (IAB)*
- *GCSE Accounting – various examining bodies.*

In further developing the book I have added new topics, including partnership accounts and accounts for limited companies. I have also reviewed certain topics that I know from experience tend to cause students some confusion. In particular I have redrafted the chapters on control accounts, the journal, and suspense accounts in an attempt to make these easier for students to understand. In response to requests from users of the previous edition, I have included many more fully worked examples to show clearly how the theory of the relevant topic is applied. One further innovation is the inclusion of a glossary of accounting terms that appear throughout the book, listed together in Appendix A for easy reference.

A full range of exercises are provided at the end of each chapter. Many of these have been newly devised by Frank Wood and myself, and, for the others, we are grateful to those examining bodies who have allowed us to reproduce questions from their recent examination papers. Where these questions appear, the appropriate body has been acknowledged but the answers have been worked out and presented by me. Answers to most of the questions are clearly presented at the back of the book in Appendix E; answers to those denoted with the suffix 'X' are provided in a separate *Solutions Manual*, and this is available free to teaching staff who recommend this book. Multiple-choice questions are provided in three sets in Appendix C, with their answers in Appendix D. Also in this new edition is the inclusion of three complete specimen examination papers in Appendix F. Two are presented in the style of a GCSE paper and the other in the style used by non-GCSE examining bodies. These should enable teachers to test their students' progress.

As stated above, the book embraces the requirements of the various examining bodies at the accountancy foundation level. These requirements vary considerably between the bodies, and lecturers and students should be fully conversant with the syllabus of the bodies whose examinations they intend to undertake.

I would welcome any suggestions as to how the book might yet be improved. These should be sent to the publishers, who will pass them on to me.

Sheila Robinson
February 2001

Author's note

Frank Wood sadly died during the preparation of this new edition. I have been privileged to work with Frank for many years as co-author of a number of books. His contribution to accounting through his many books has been exceptional and he has had a major influence on the way in which accountancy has been taught worldwide over the last thirty years. I shall miss him but shall continue to develop the wonderful legacy he has been able to pass on.

Sheila Robinson

Matrix of subjects covered and examining bodies

Key:
✓ = included in syllabus
✗= not in syllabus

Chapters	Subjects covered	Edexcel and NVQ Level 2 AAT and CAT	GCSE (various bodies)	IAB	LCCI	OCR	Pitman qualifications
1–7	Double entry to Trial Balance	✓	✓	✓	✓	✓	✓
8–10 & 28–29	Final accounts of sole trader & adjustments	✗	✓	✓	✓	✓	✓
11	Accounting concepts & conventions	✓	✓	✓	✓	✓	✓
12	Division of the Ledgers	✓	✓	✓	✓	✓	✓
13	Petty cash	✓	✓	✓	✓	✓	✓
14	Banking system	✓	✓	✓	✓	✓	✓
15–16	Recording cash transactions	✓	✓	✓	✓	✓	✓
17	Bank reconciliation	✓	✓	✓	✓	✓	✓
18	Capital & revenue expenditure	✓	✓	✓	✓	✓	✓
19–21 & 23	Recording credit transactions	✓	✓	✓	✓	✓	✓
22	Value added tax	✓	✓	✓	✓	✓	✓
24	Control Accounts	✓	✓	✓	✓	✓	✓
25	The Journal	✓	✓	✓	✓	✓	✓
26–27	Depreciation methods & records	✗	✓	✓	✓	✓	✓
30	Valuation of stock	✗	✓	✓	✓	✓	✓
31	Trial Balance – errors	✓	✓	✓	✓	✓	✓
32	Suspense Accounts and errors	✓	✓	✓	✓	✓	✓
33	Single entry/incomplete records	✗	✓	✓	✗	✓	✓
34	Club & Society Accounts	✗	✓	✓	✓	✓	✓
35	Manufacturing Accounts	✗	✓	✗	✗	✓	✗
36	Partnership Accounts	✗	✓	✓	✗	✓	✗
37	Limited Company Accounts	✗	✓	✗	✗	✓	✗
38	Analysis & interpretation of accounts	✗	✓	✗	✓	✓	✗
39	Wages book & records	✗	✗	✓	✓	✓	✓

Note: The fifth edition of *Book-keeping and Accounts* covers the foundation level of the examining bodies listed above and also the major part of the intermediate level. As syllabuses change from time to time, it is important to check that the above details still apply to your examination.

PART 1

Introduction to double entry accounting

1 Introduction to accounting

2 The accounting equation and the balance sheet

3 The double entry system for assets, liabilities and capital

4 The double entry for the asset of stock

5 The double entry system for expenses and revenues

6 Balancing off accounts

7 The trial balance

This part of the book is concerned with the basic principles of the double entry system of book-keeping.

CHAPTER 1

Introduction to accounting

Learning objectives

After you have studied this chapter you should be able to:

- **understand the need for accounting and its importance in business management**
- **know the main users of accounting information**
- **distinguish between the different types of business organisation.**

1.1 Aims of a business

Almost every business is started with the aim of making money for its owners. To achieve this aim, they will have to trade with other people and businesses, which means selling goods and/or services.

Money is the medium of exchange used almost universally in trading, and it allows a monetary value to be given to goods or services that are offered to potential customers. It follows that the control of money in a business is vital if it is to be successful and a profit is to be made (***see*** Exhibit 1.1).

EXHIBIT 1.1 • The basis of a business

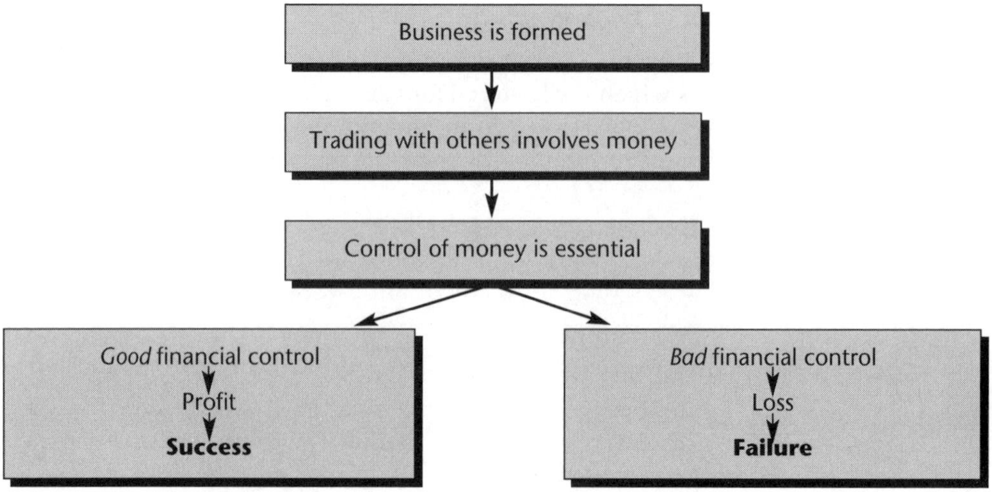

The owners of a business need to know how much money is coming into the business from the sale of goods and/or services. They also need to know how much it is costing to run the business. In other words, they need to 'account' for every pound coming into and going out of the business. This process is known as **accounting**, and keeping books provides the basic method used by accountants in the financial control of a business.

1.2 Definition of accounting

There have been a number of definitions put forward over the years but the following definition is concise and coincides with the aim of this book:

> **The skill or practice of maintaining accounts and preparing reports to aid the financial control and management of a business.**

1.3 Importance and need for accounting

As stated earlier, businesses must operate profitably otherwise they will cease to exist. The **financial statements** produced by a business's accounting department aim to show clearly the profit or loss which has been made and the financial position of the business.

The two most important statements are:

1 the trading and profit and loss account
2 the balance sheet.

Both these statements have to be checked and verified by a firm of auditors as part of the legal requirements for correct financial reporting. It is essential that accurate financial information is available to the auditors to enable them to fulfil their functions properly.

There are, however, other groups who are keenly interested in the activities of the business. These include:

- Inland Revenue – they collect employees' tax, National Insurance contributions, and tax on the profits of the business.
- Customs and Excise – they are responsible for the collection or refund of monies for a business which is registered for value added tax (VAT) purposes.
- Investors – these may be private individuals, companies or banks, any or all of which will want to monitor the performance of the business to ensure that they will get a return for their investment.
- Suppliers – this group will need to be sure of the financial stability of the business before accepting orders.
- Customers – they will need to be sure of the financial stability of the business before placing orders.

In order that the business can satisfy all these interested parties, it must follow certain accounting procedures and practices in a formal sequence. Essentially this sequence can be stated as shown in Exhibit 1.2. Each part of the sequence can be explained briefly, as set out next.

Exhibit 1.2 • The accounting sequence

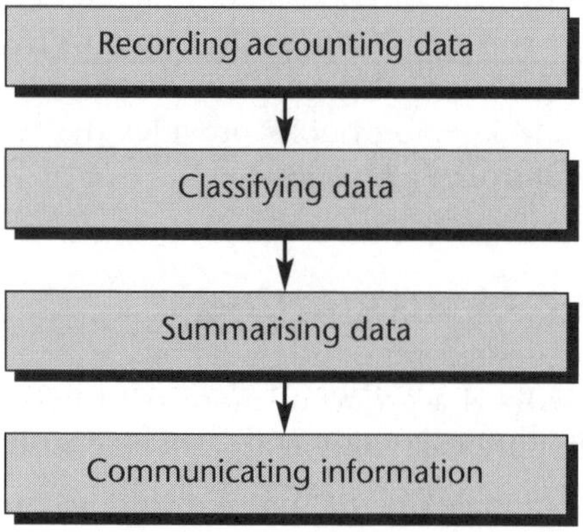

Recording accounting data

Each business must install a system to collect and record all the financial transactions that are carried out. This includes cash received and paid out, goods bought and sold, items bought for use in the business, and so on.

Classifying data

Once the data has been recorded, it has to be classified so that it can be of use to the business. For instance, if a leisure business sells both sports equipment and camping gear, it would be of value to the proprietor to know the sales figures for the separate parts of the business.

Summarising data

Summarising the data of the various financial transactions provides the managers of the business with information in a concise form.

Communicating information

When the information from the three preceding procedures has been prepared, it then needs to be presented in a formal way as the business's accounts and business reports.

1.4 What is book-keeping?

Book-keeping is the process of recording, in books of accounts or on computer, the financial effect of business transactions and managing such records.

1.5 Types of organisations

Organisations are classified according to their structure and financial make-up and are mainly classified as shown below. The classification will determine an organisation's legal status and what financial reporting is required of the organisation. Thus, we have the following:

- A **sole trader** is an individual trading alone in his or her own name, or under a recognised trading name. He or she is solely liable for all business debts, but when the business is successful the trader takes all the profits.
- A **partnership** is a group of more than two people and a maximum of twenty, who together are carrying on a particular business with a view to making a profit. This topic will be covered later in Chapter 36.
- **Limited companies**, both private and public:
  - A **private limited company** is a legal entity with at least two shareholders. The liability of the shareholders is limited to the amount that they have agreed to invest.
  - A **public limited company** is also a legal entity with limited shareholder liability, but unlike a private company it can ask the public to subscribe for shares in its business.
- **Non-trading organisations** include clubs, associations and other non-profit making organisations which are normally run for the benefit of their members to engage in a particular activity and not to make a profit. Their financial statements will take the form of income and expenditure accounts, to be covered in Chapter 34.

New terms

Accounting (p. 3): A skill or practice of maintaining accounts and preparing reports to aid the financial control and management of a business.

Book-keeping (p. 4): The recording of accounting data.

Financial statements (p. 3): Formal documents produced by an organisation to show the financial status of the business at a particular time. These include the trading and profit and loss account and the balance sheet.

Non-trading organisations (p. 5): These include clubs, associations and other non-profit-making organisations that are normally run for the benefit of their members to engage in a particular activity.

Partnership (p. 5): A group of more than two people and a maximum of twenty, who together are carrying on a particular business with a view to making profit.

Private limited company (p. 5): A legal entity with at least two shareholders, where the liability of the shareholders is limited to the amount of their investment. The public cannot subscribe for its shares.

Public limited company (p. 5): A legal entity with many shareholders since the public can subscribe for its shares. Shareholder liability is limited to the amount of their investment.

Sole trader (p. 5): A business owned by one person only.

CHAPTER 2

The accounting equation and the balance sheet

Learning objectives

After you have studied this chapter you should be able to:

- understand what is meant by assets, liabilities and capital
- understand the accounting equation
- draw up balance sheets after different transactions have occurred
- know the difference between 'horizontal' and 'vertical' styles of balance sheets.

2.1 The accounting equation

The whole of accounting is based upon a very simple idea. This is called the **accounting equation**, which sounds complicated but in fact is easy to understand.

It can be explained by saying that if a firm is to set up and start trading, then it needs resources. Let us assume that in the first place it is the owner of the business who has supplied all of the resources. This can be shown as:

Resources in the business = Resources supplied by the owner

In accounting, terms are used to describe things. The amount of the resources supplied by the owner is called **capital**. The actual resources that are then in the business are called **assets**. This means that the accounting equation above, when the owner has supplied all of the resources, can be shown as:

Assets = Capital

Usually, however, someone other than the owner has supplied some of the assets. **Liabilities** is the name given to the amount owing to this person for these assets. This equation has now changed to:

Assets = Capital + Liabilities

It can be seen that the two sides of the equation will have the same totals. This is because we are dealing with the same thing from two different points of view. It is:

Resources: what they are (Assets)	=	Resources: who supplied them (Capital + Liabilities)

It is a fact that the totals of each side will always equal one another, and that this will always be true no matter how many transactions there may be. The actual assets, capital and liabilities may change, but the total of the assets will always equal the total of capital + liabilities.

Assets consist of property of all kinds, such as buildings, machinery, stocks of goods, and motor vehicles. Also, benefits such as debts owed by customers and the amount of money in the bank account are included.

Liabilities consist of money owing for goods supplied to the firm and for expenses. Also loans made to the firm are included.

Capital is often called the owner's **equity** (or **net worth**).

2.2 The balance sheet and the effects of business transactions

The accounting equation is expressed in a financial statement called the **balance sheet**. It is not the first book-keeping record to be made, but it is a good place to start to consider accounting.

The introduction of capital

On 1 May 2007, B Blake started in business and put £5,000 into a bank account for the business. The balance sheet would appear:

B Blake
Balance Sheet as at 1 May 2007

Assets	£		£
Cash at bank	5,000	Capital	5,000
	5,000		5,000

The purchase of an asset by cheque

On 3 May 2007 Blake buys fixtures for £3,000. The effect of this transaction is that the cash at the bank is reduced and a new asset, called 'fixtures', appears.

B Blake
Balance Sheet as at 3 May 2007

Assets	£		£
Fixtures	3,000	Capital	5,000
Cash at bank	2,000		
	5,000		5,000

The purchase of an asset and the incurring of a liability

On 6 May 2007, Blake buys some goods for £500 from D Smith and agrees to pay for them some time within the next two weeks. There is now a new asset, **stock** of goods, and there is also a new liability because Blake owes money to D Smith for the goods.

A person to whom money is owed for goods is known in accounting language as a **creditor**.

B Blake
Balance Sheet as at 6 May 2007

Assets	£	*Capital and Liabilities*	£
Fixtures	3,000	Capital	5,000
Stock of goods	500	Creditor	500
Cash at bank	2,000		
	5,500		5,500

Sale of an asset on credit

On 10 May 2007, goods that had cost £100 were sold to J Brown for the same amount, the money to be paid later. This means a reduction in the stock of goods and there will now be a new asset. A person who owes money to a firm is known in accounting language as its **debtor**. The balance sheet now appears as:

B Blake
Balance Sheet as at 10 May 2007

Assets	£	*Capital and Liabilities*	£
Fixtures	3,000	Capital	5,000
Stock of goods	400	Creditor	500
Debtor	100		
Cash at bank	2,000		
	5,500		5,500

Sale of an asset for immediate payment

On 13 May 2007 goods that had cost £50 were sold to D Daley for the same amount, Daley paying for them immediately by cheque. Here one asset, stock of goods, is reduced, while another asset, cash at bank, is increased. The balance sheet now appears thus:

B Blake
Balance Sheet as at 13 May 2007

Assets	£	*Capital and Liabilities*	£
Fixtures	3,000	Capital	5,000
Stock of goods	350	Creditor	500
Debtor	100		
Cash at bank	2,050		
	5,500		5,500

The payment of a liability

On 15 May 2007, Blake pays a cheque for £200 to D Smith in part payment of the amount owing. The asset of cash at bank is therefore reduced, and the liability to the creditor is also reduced. The balance sheet now appears thus:

B Blake
Balance Sheet as at 15 May 2007

Assets	£	*Capital and Liabilities*	£
Fixtures	3,000	Capital	5,000
Stock of goods	350	Creditor	300
Debtor	100		
Cash at bank	1,850		
	5,300		5,300

Collection of an asset

On 31 May 2007, J Brown, who owes Blake £100, makes a part payment of £75 by cheque. The effect is to reduce one asset, debtor, and to increase another asset, cash at bank. This results in a balance sheet as follows:

B Blake
Balance Sheet as at 31 May 2007

Assets	£	*Capital and Liabilities*	£
Fixtures	3,000	Capital	5,000
Stock of goods	350	Creditor	300
Debtor	25		
Cash at bank	1,925		
	5,300		5,300

2.3 Equality of the accounting equation

It can be seen that every transaction has affected two items. Sometimes it has changed two assets by reducing one and increasing the other. At other times things have changed differently. A summary of the effect of transactions upon assets, liabilities and capital is shown in Exhibit 2.1.

Exhibit 2.1

Example of transaction	Effect	
1 Buy goods on credit	↑ Increase asset (Stock of goods)	↑ Increase liability (Creditors)
2 Buy goods by cheque	↑ Increase asset (Stock of goods)	↓ Decrease asset (Bank)
3 Pay creditor by cheque	↓ Decrease asset (Bank)	↓ Decrease liability (Creditors)
4 Owner pays more capital into the bank	↑ Increase asset (Bank)	↑ Increase capital
5 Owner takes money out of the business bank account for his own use	↓ Decrease asset (Bank)	↓ Decrease capital
6 Owner pays creditor from private money outside the firm	↓ Decrease liability (Creditors)	↑ Increase capital

Each transaction has, therefore, maintained the same total for assets as for capital + liabilities. This can be shown:

Number of transactions as above	Assets	Capital and Liabilities	Effect on balance sheet totals
1	+	+	Each side added to equally
2	+ −		A *plus* and *minus* both on the assets side *cancelling out* each other
3	−	−	Each side has equal deductions
4	+	+	Each side has equal additions
5	−	−	Each side has equal deductions
6		− +	A *minus* and *plus* both on the liabilities side *cancelling out* each other

2.4 Alternative form of balance sheet presentation

Earlier in this chapter you have been shown balance sheets presented in the following manner:

B Blake
Balance Sheet as at ....

Assets	£	*Capital and liabilities*	£
[*Details of all assets*]	xxx	Capital	xxx
		[*Details of liabilities*]	xxx
	xxx		xxx

This is called a '**horizontal**', i.e. side-by-side, form of presentation. There are no legal requirements saying that balance sheets have to be in a horizontal form. The authors of this book are of the opinion that (to start with) accounting is easier to learn if the horizontal balance sheet is used to explain the basic system of accounting to students.

However, a large number of lecturers and teachers prefer to start their teaching of the subject using the '**vertical**' form of balance sheet. It is simply a matter of preference, and this book will try to accommodate both methods. The reason for the common preference for the vertical method is that most modern businesses present their balance sheets in this way. In fact, once the basics of accounting have been mastered, this book will also adopt the vertical method of balance sheet presentation.

The balance sheet of B Blake as at 31 May 2007 using the vertical method of presentation would appear as follows:

B Blake
Balance Sheet as at 31 May 2007

	£	£	£
Fixed assets			
Fixtures			3,000
Current assets			
Stock	350		
Debtors	25		
Cash at bank	1,925	2,300	
Less: Current liabilities			
Creditors	300	300	
Net current assets			2,000
			5,000
Financed by:			
Capital			5,000

You will have noticed the use of the terms 'fixed assets', 'current assets' and 'current liabilities'. Chapter 9 contains a full and proper examination of these terms. At this point we will simply say that:

- **fixed assets** are assets to be kept as such for a few years at least, e.g. buildings, machinery, fixtures, motor vehicles;
- **current assets** are assets which change from day to day, e.g. the value of stock in hand goes up and down as it is bought and sold. Similarly, the amount of money owing to us by debtors will change quickly, as we sell more to them on credit and they pay their debts. The amount of money in the bank will also change as we receive and pay out money;
- **current liabilities** are those liabilities which have to be paid within the near future, e.g. creditors for goods bought.

Note: Generally, the figures used for exhibits and for exercises have been kept down to relatively small amounts. This has been done deliberately to make the work of the user of this book that much easier. Constantly handling large figures does not add anything to the study of the principles of accounting; instead, it simply wastes a lot of students' time, and they will probably make many more errors if larger figures are used. This approach could lead to the accusation of not being 'realistic' with the figures given, but we believe that it is far more important to make learning easier for the student.

New terms

Accounting equation (p. 6): The equation on which accounting is based, namely Assets – Liabilities = Capital.

Assets (p. 6): Resources owned by a business.

Balance sheet (p. 7): A statement showing the assets, capital and liabilities of a business.

Capital (p. 6): The total of resources supplied to a business by its owner.

Creditor (p. 8): A person to whom money is owed for goods or services.

Debtor (p. 8): A person who owes money to the business for goods or services supplied.

Equity (p. 7): Another name for the capital of the owner.

Horizontal balance sheet (p. 11): Side-by-side form of presentation.

Liabilities (p. 6): Total of money owed for assets supplied to the business.

Net worth (p. 7): Same as 'equity' (see above).

Stock (p. 8): Unsold goods.

Vertical balance sheet (p. 11): Modern style of presentation in column form.

EXERCISES

Note: Questions with the suffix 'X' shown after the question number do **not** *have answers shown at the back of the book. Answers to the other questions are shown in Appendix E.*

2.1 Examine the following table and complete the gaps:

	Assets £	*Liabilities* £	*Capital* £
(*a*)	34,282	7,909	?
(*b*)	276,303	?	213,817
(*c*)	?	6,181	70,919
(*d*)	?	109,625	877,138
(*e*)	88,489	?	78,224
(*f*)	456,066	51,163	?

2.2X Examine the following table and complete the gaps:

	Assets £	*Liabilities* £	*Capital* £
(*a*)	?	59,997	604,337
(*b*)	346,512	?	293,555
(*c*)	47,707	?	42,438
(*d*)	108,129	11,151	?
(*e*)	515,164	77,352	?
(*f*)	?	19,928	179,352

2.3 Determine which are assets and which are liabilities from the following list:

(*a*) Computer equipment
(*b*) Stock of goods
(*c*) Loan from H Barlow
(*d*) Motor vehicles
(*e*) What we owe for advertising materials
(*f*) Bank balance.

2.4X Which of the following are assets and which are liabilities?

(*a*) Premises
(*b*) Debtors
(*c*) Cash in hand
(*d*) Creditors
(*e*) Loan from finance company
(*f*) Owing to bank
(*g*) Machinery
(*h*) Motor vehicles.

2.5 State which of the following are shown under the wrong headings for S Murphy's business:

Assets	*Liabilities*
Cash in hand	Money owing to bank
Creditors	Debtors
Premises	Stock of goods
Motor vehicles	
Loan from C Shaw	
Machinery	

2.6X Which of the following are shown under the wrong headings?:

Assets	*Liabilities*
Cash at bank	Machinery
Computer equipment	Motor vehicles
Creditors	Loan from W Barlow
Capital	
Debtors	
Stock of goods	

2.7 Ann Wood decides to open a retail shop selling greetings cards and gifts. Her uncle lends her £30,000 to help her with financing the venture. Ann buys shop premises costing £50,000, a motor vehicle for £10,000 and stock of goods for £5,000. Ann did not pay for her stock of goods in full and still owes £2,100 to her suppliers in respect of them. After the events described above and before she starts trading, Ann has £100 cash in hand and £7,000 cash at the bank.

You are required to calculate the amount of capital that Ann invested in her business.

2.8X T Charles starts a business. Before he actually starts to sell anything, he buys fixtures costing £2,000, a motor vehicle for £5,000 and stock of goods for £3,500. Although he has paid in full for the fixtures and the motor vehicle, he still owes £1,400 for some of the goods. J Preston has lent him £3,000. Charles, after the above, has £2,800 in the business bank account and £100 cash in hand.

You are required to calculate his capital.

2.9 Draw up T Lymer's balance sheet, using the vertical presentation method, from the following information as at 31 December 2007.

	£
Capital	34,823
Delivery van	12,000
Debtors	10,892
Office furniture	8,640
Stock of goods	4,220
Cash at bank	11,722
Creditors	12,651

2.10X Draw up A Pennington's balance sheet as at 31 March 2008 from the following information:

	£
Premises	50,000
Plant and machinery	26,500
Debtors	28,790
Creditors	32,320
Bank overdraft	3,625
Stock	21,000
Cash in hand	35
Capital	90,380

2.11 Look at this list:

(*a*) We pay a creditor £70 in cash.
(*b*) Bought fixtures £200 paying by cheque.
(*c*) Bought goods on credit £275.
(*d*) The proprietor introduces another £500 cash into the firm.
(*e*) J Walker lends the firm £200 in cash.
(*f*) A debtor pays us £50 by cheque.
(*g*) We return goods costing £60 to a supplier whose bill we had not paid.
(*h*) Bought additional shop premises, paying £5,000 by cheque.

For each item shown, you are to state how it changes assets, capital or liabilities. For example the answer to (*a*) will be:

(*a*) - Assets £70
- Liabilities £70.

CHAPTER 3

The double entry system for assets, liabilities and capital

Learning objectives

After you have studied this chapter you should be able to:

- **understand what is meant by the double entry system**
- **see how the double entry system follows the rules of the basic accounting equation**
- **be able to enter the transactions using the double entry system.**

3.1 Nature of a transaction

In Chapter 2 we saw how various events changed two items in the balance sheet. Events which result in such changes are known as **transactions**. This means that if the proprietor of a business asks the price of some goods but does not buy them, then there is no transaction since no balance sheet item will have changed. If he later asks the price of some goods and then buys them, in this second case there is a transaction, since it would mean that two balance sheet items, i.e. stock of goods and cash at bank, will have changed.

3.2 The double entry system

We have seen that every transaction affects two items. If we want to show the effect of every transaction when we are doing our book-keeping, we will have to show the effect of a transaction on each of the two items. For each transaction, a book-keeping entry will have to be made to show an increase or a decrease of that item, and another entry to show the increase or decrease of the other item. From this you will probably be able to see that the term **double entry book-keeping** is a good one, as each entry is made twice.

In Chapter 2 we drew up a new balance sheet after each transaction. You can do this easily if you have only a few transactions per day. But if there are hundreds of transactions each day, it will become impossible for you to draw up hundreds of different balance sheets. You simply would not have enough time.

Instead of constantly drawing up amended balance sheets after each transaction, what we have instead is the double entry system. The basis of this system is that the transactions that have occurred are entered in a set of 'accounts'. An **account** is a place in our books where all the information referring to a particular asset, liability or the capital, is entered. Thus there will be an account for motor vehicles, where all the transactions concerning motor vehicles will be entered; likewise there will be an account for buildings, where all the transactions concerned with buildings will be shown. This will be extended so that every asset, every liability and all capital will have its own account, for transactions in that item.

3.3 The accounts for double entry

Each account should be shown on a separate page. The double entry system divides each page into two halves. The left-hand side of each page is called the **debit** side, while the the right-hand side is called the **credit** side. The title of each account is written across the top of the account at the centre – see Exhibit 3.1. Note that the word 'Debit' is often shown in a short form as *Dr*, whilst 'Credit' is often shown as *Cr*.

Exhibit 3.1

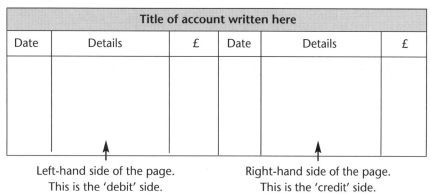

Title of account written here					
Date	Details	£	Date	Details	£

Left-hand side of the page. This is the 'debit' side.

Right-hand side of the page. This is the 'credit' side.

The words 'debit' and 'credit' in book-keeping terms do not mean the same as in normal language and should be viewed differently from the start to avoid confusion. Students new to studying double entry may find it useful to think of 'IN' when looking at the entry of a debit item, and to think of 'OUT' when looking at the entry of a credit item. We will consider this later in Section 3.5.

3.4 Rules for double entry

Double entry is relatively easy to learn and understand if the following four rules are learnt and understood:

1 Double entry means that every transaction affects two things and should, therefore, be entered twice: once on the *Debit* side and once on the *Credit* side.
2 The order in which the items are entered does not matter – although students may find it easier to deal with any cash or bank transaction first using the 'IN' and 'OUT' principle.

3 A **Debit entry** is always an asset or an expense. A **Credit entry** is a liability, capital or income.

4 To increase or decrease assets, liabilities or capital, as seen in Chapter 2, the double entry rules are as shown in Exhibit 3.2

Exhibit 3.2

Accounts	To record	Entry in the account
Assets	↑ an increase	Debit
	↓ a decrease	Credit
Liabilities	↑ an increase	Credit
	↓ a decrease	Debit
Capital	↑ an increase	Credit
	↓ a decrease	Debit

Let us look again at the accounting equation:

	Assets	= Liabilities	+ Capital
To increase each item	Debit	Credit	Credit
To decrease each item	Credit	Debit	Debit

The double entry rules for liabilities and capital are the same, but they are the opposite of those for assets. This is because assets are on the opposite side of the equation and, therefore follow opposite rules. Looking at the accounts, the rules will appear as:

Any asset account		Any liability account		Capital account	
Increases	Decreases	Decreases	Increases	Decreases	Increases
+	−	−	+	−	+

3.5 The 'IN' and 'OUT' approach

To help students having difficulty in deciding on which side of each account the items should be entered, a useful hint is for them to think of the debit side being 'IN' to the account, and the credit side being 'OUT' of the account.

To give two examples of this approach, we will use the following:

Example 1: Paid cash £200 to buy machinery

The double entry for this transaction would be as follows:

Effect	Action
(*a*) Machinery comes 'IN'	A *debit* entry in the Machinery account
(*b*) Cash goes 'OUT'	A *credit* entry in the Cash account

Example 2: Took £500 out of the cash in hand of the business and paid it into the bank account of the business.

The double entry for this transaction would be as follows:

Effect	Action
(*a*) Money come 'IN' to the bank (*b*) Cash goes 'OUT' of the cash till	A *debit* entry in the Bank account A *credit* entry in the Cash account

3.6 T accounts

The type of accounts that are going to be demonstrated are known as **T accounts.** This is because the accounts are in the shape of a T, as illustrated in Exhibit 3.3.

Exhibit 3.3

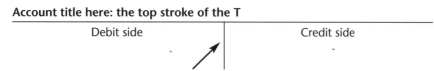

Account title here: the top stroke of the T

Debit side	Credit side

The line divides the two sides and is the downstroke of the T.

3.7 Worked examples

The entry of a few transactions can now be attempted:

Example 3: The proprietor starts the firm with £10,000 in cash on 1 August 2005.

Effect	Action
(*a*) Increases the *asset* of cash (*b*) Increases the *capital*	Debit the cash account – cash goes 'IN' Credit the capital account – cash comes 'OUT' of the owner's money

These are entered as follows:

Cash Account

Dr					*Cr*
2005		£			
Aug 1		10,000			

Capital Account

Dr					*Cr*
			2005		£
			Aug 1		10,000

The date of the transaction has already been entered. Now there remains the description which is to be entered alongside the amount. The double entry to the item in the cash account is completed by an entry in the capital account, and therefore the word 'Capital' will appear in the cash account. Similarly, the double entry to the item in the capital account is completed by an entry in the cash account, and therefore the word 'Cash' will appear in the capital account.

The finally completed accounts are therefore:

Cash Account

Dr			*Cr*
2005	£		
Aug 1 Capital	10,000		

Capital Account

Dr			*Cr*
		2005	£
		Aug 1 Cash	10,000

This method of entering transactions therefore fulfils the requirements of the double entry rules as shown in Section 3.4. Now let us look at the entry of some more transactions.

Example 4: A motor van is bought for £7,500 cash on 2 August 2005.

Effect	Action
(*a*) Decreases the *asset* of cash	Credit the cash account – Cash goes 'OUT'
(*b*) Increases the *asset* of motor van	Debit the motor van account – Motor van comes 'IN'

Cash Account

Dr			*Cr*
		2005	£
		Aug 2 Motor van	7,500

Motor Van Account

Dr			*Cr*
2005	£		
Aug 2 Cash	7,500		

Example 5: Fixtures bought on credit from Shop Fitters for £1,500 on 3 August 2005.

Effect	Action
(*a*) Increases the *asset* of Fixtures	Debit the Fixtures account – Fixtures go 'IN'
(*b*) Increases the *liability* to Shop Fitters	Credit the Shop Fitters' account – Fixtures come 'OUT' of the supplier's account

Fixtures Account

Dr			*Cr*
2005	£		
Aug 3 Shop Fitters	1,500		

Shop Fitters' Account

Dr			*Cr*
		2005	£
		Aug 3 Fixtures	1,500

Example 6: Paid the amount owing in cash to Shop Fitters on 17 August 2005.

Effect	Action
(*a*) Decreases the *asset* of cash	Credit the cash account – Cash goes 'OUT'
(*b*) Decreases the *liability* to Shop Fitters	Debit the Shop Fitters' account – Cash goes 'IN' to the supplier's account

Cash Account

Dr			*Cr*
		2005	£
		Aug 17 Shop Fitters	1,500

Shop Fitters' Account

Dr			*Cr*
2005	£		
Aug 17 Cash	1,500		

***Example** 7*: Transactions to date.

Taking the transactions numbered 3 to 6 above, the records will now appear thus:

Cash Account

Dr			*Cr*
2005	£	2005	£
Aug 1 Capital	10,000	Aug 2 Motor Van	7,500
		Aug 17 Shop Fitters	1,500

Capital Account

Dr			*Cr*
		2005	£
		Aug 1 Cash	10,000

Motor Van Account

Dr			*Cr*
2005	£		
Aug 2 Cash	7,500		

Shop Fitter's Account

Dr			*Cr*
2005	£	2005	£
Aug 17 Cash	1,500	Aug 3 Fixtures	1,500

Fixtures Account

Dr			*Cr*
2005	£		
Aug 3 Shop Fitters	1,500		

Before you read further, you are required to work through Exercises 3.1 and 3.2 at the end of the chapter.

Example 8: Now you have actually made some entries in accounts, you are to go carefully through the example shown in Exhibit 3.4. Make certain you can understand every entry.

EXHIBIT 3.4

Transactions	Effect	Action	IN/OUT
2008 May 1 Started an engineering business putting £10,000 into a business bank account.	↑ Increases *asset* of bank. ↑ Increases *capital* of owner.	Debit bank account. Credit capital account.	IN OUT
May 3 Bought works machinery on credit from Unique Machines £2,750.	↑ Increases *asset* of machinery. ↑ Increases *liability* to Unique Machines.	Debit machinery account. Credit Unique Machines account.	IN OUT
May 4 Withdrew £2,000 cash from the bank and placed it in the cash box.	↓ Decreases *asset* of bank. ↑ Increases *asset* of cash.	Credit bank account. Debit cash account.	OUT IN
May 7 Bought a motor van paying in cash £1,800.	↓ Decreases *asset* of cash. ↑ Increases *asset* of motor van.	Credit cash account. Debit motor van account.	OUT IN
May 10 Sold some of the machinery for £150 on credit to B Barnes.	↓ Decreases *asset* of machinery. ↑ Increases *asset* of money owing from B Barnes.	Credit machinery account. Debit B Barnes account.	OUT IN
May 21 Returned some of the machinery, value £270 to Unique Machines.	↓ Decreases *asset* of machinery. ↓ Decreases *liability* to Unique Machines.	Credit machinery account. Debit Unique Machines account.	OUT IN
May 28 B Barnes pays the firm the amount owing, £150, by cheque.	↑ Increases *asset* of bank. ↓ Decreases *asset* of money owing by B Barnes.	Debit bank account. Credit B Barnes account.	IN OUT
May 30 Bought another motor van for £4,200, paying by cheque.	↓ Decreases *asset* of bank. ↑ Increases *asset* of motor vans.	Credit bank account. Debit motor van account.	OUT IN
May 31 Paid the amount of £2,480 to Unique Machines by cheque.	↓ Decreases *asset* of bank. ↓ Decreases *liability* to Unique Machines.	Credit bank account. Debit Unique Machines account.	OUT IN

In account form this is shown thus:

Bank Account

Dr			*Cr*		
2008		£	2008		£
May 1	Capital	10,000	May 4	Cash	2,000
May 28	B Barnes	150	May 30	Motor van	4,200
			May 30	Unique Machines	2,480

Cash Account

Dr			*Cr*		
2008		£	2008		£
May 4	Bank	2,000	May 7	Motor van	1,800

Capital Account

Dr			*Cr*		
			2008		£
			May 1	Bank	10,000

Machinery Account

Dr			*Cr*		
2008		£	2008		£
May 3	Unique Machines	2,750	May 10	B Barnes	150
			May 21	Unique Machines	270

Motor Van Account

Dr			*Cr*		
2008		£			
May 7	Cash	1,800			
May 30	Bank	4,200			

Unique Machines Account

Dr			*Cr*		
2008		£	2008		£
May 21	Machinery	270	May 3	Machinery	2,750
May 31	Bank	2,480			

B Barnes Account

Dr			*Cr*		
2008		£	2008		£
May 10	Machinery	150	May 28	Bank	150

3.8 Abbreviation of 'Limited'

In this book, when we come across transactions with limited companies the letters 'Ltd' are used as the abbreviation for 'Limited Company'. We will know that if we see the name of a firm as T Lee Ltd, then that firm will be a limited company. In our books the transactions with T Lee Ltd will be entered in the same way as for any other customer or supplier.

New terms

Account (p. 17): The place in a ledger where all the transactions relating to a particular asset, liability or capital - whether expense or revenue item - are recorded. Accounts are part of the double entry book-keeping system. They are sometimes referred to as 'T accounts' or ledger accounts.

Credit (p. 17): The right-hand side of the accounts in double entry.

Debit (p. 17): The left-hand side of the accounts in double entry.

Double entry book-keeping (p. 16): A system where each transaction is entered twice, once on the debit side and once on the credit side.

T account (p. 19): Accounting transactions set out with horizontal and vertical ruling in the shape of a 'T'.

Transaction (p. 16): Event that results in an accounting item.

EXERCISES

3.1 Complete the following table showing which accounts are to be credited and which to be debited:

	Account to be debited	Account to be credited
(*a*) Bought motor van for cash		
(*b*) Bought office machinery on credit from J Grant & Son		
(*c*) Introduced capital in cash		
(*d*) A debtor, J Beach, pays us by cheque		
(*e*) Paid a creditor, A Barrett, in cash.		

3.2X Complete the following table showing which accounts are to be debited and which to be credited:

	Account to be debited	Account to be credited
(*a*) Bought motor lorry for cash		
(*b*) Paid creditor, T Lake, by cheque		
(*c*) Repaid P Logan's loan by cash		
(*d*) Sold lorry for cash		
(*e*) Bought office machinery on credit from Ultra Ltd		
(*f*) A debtor, A Hill, pays us by cash		
(*g*) A debtor, J Cross, pays us by cheque		
(*h*) Proprietor puts a further amount into the business by cheque		
(*i*) A loan of £200 in cash is received from L Lowe		
(*j*) Paid a creditor, D Lord, by cash.		

3.3 Write up the asset and liability and capital accounts to record the following transactions in the records of G Powell.

2008
July 1 Started business with £2,500 in the bank
July 2 Bought office furniture by cheque, £150
July 3 Bought machinery £750 on credit from Planers Ltd
July 5 Bought a second-hand van paying by cheque, £600
July 8 Sold some of the office furniture – not suitable for the firm – for £60 on credit to J Walker & Sons
July 15 Paid the amount owing to Planers Ltd, £750, by cheque
July 23 Received the amount due from J Walker, £60, in cash
July 31 Bought more machinery by cheque, £280.

3.4X You are required to open the asset, liability and capital accounts and record the following transactions for June 2008 in the records of C Williams.

2008		
June	1	Started business with £2,000 in cash
June	2	Paid £1,800 of the opening cash into a bank account for the business
June	5	Bought office furniture on credit from Betta-Built Ltd for £120
June	8	Bought a motor van paying by cheque £950
June	12	Bought works machinery from Evans & Sons on credit £560
June	18	Returned faulty office furniture costing £62 to Betta-Built Ltd
June	25	Sold some of the works machinery for £75 cash
June	26	Paid amount owing to Betta-Built Ltd, £58 by cheque
June	28	Took £100 out of the bank and put it in the cash till
June	30	J Smith lent us £500 – giving us the money by cheque.

3.5 Write up the asset, capital and liability accounts in the books of C Walsh to record the following transactions:

2007		
June	1	Started business with £5,000 in the bank
June	2	Bought motor van, paying by cheque £1,200
June	5	Bought office fixtures £400 on credit from Young Ltd
June	8	Bought motor van on credit from Super Motors £800
June	12	Took £100 out of the bank and put it into the cash till
June	15	Bought office fixtures paying by cash £60
June	19	Paid Super Motors a cheque for £800
June	21	A loan of £1,000 cash is received from J Jarvis
June	25	Paid £800 of the cash in hand into the bank account
June	30	Bought more office fixtures, paying by cheque £300.

3.6X Write up the various accounts needed in the books of S Russell to record the following transactions:

2008		
April	1	Opened business with £10,000 in the bank
April	3	Bought office equipment for £700 on credit from J Saunders Ltd
April	6	Bought motor van, paying by cheque £3,000
April	8	Borrowed £1,000 from H Thompson – he gave us the money by cheque
April	11	Russell put further capital into the firm in the form of cash £500
April	12	Paid £350 of the cash in hand into the bank account
April	15	Returned some of the office equipment costing £200 – it was faulty – to J Saunders Ltd
April	17	Bought more office equipment, paying by cash £50
April	19	Sold the motor van, as it had proved unsuitable, to R Jones for £3,000. R Jones will settle for this by three payments later this month
April	21	Received a loan in cash from J Hawkins £400
April	22	R Jones paid us a cheque for £1,000
April	23	Bought a suitable motor van £3,600 on credit from Phillips Garages Ltd
April	26	R Jones paid us a cheque for £1,800
April	28	Paid £2,000 by cheque to Phillips Garages Ltd
April	30	R Jones paid us cash £200.

CHAPTER 4

The double entry system for the asset of stock

Learning objectives

After you have studied this chapter you should be able to:

- **understand the various accounts used in recording the movement of stock, i.e. sales, purchases, returns inwards and returns outwards**
- **record the purchase and sale of goods by both cash and credit using the double entry system**
- **record the return of goods in the double entry system**
- **distinguish between the sales and purchases of goods from the sale and purchase of items that come under a different category.**

4.1 Stock movements

A business, on any particular date, will normally have goods which have been bought previously and have not yet been sold. These unsold goods are known as the businesses 'stock' of goods. The stock of goods in a business is therefore constantly changing because some of it is bought, some of it is sold, some is returned to the suppliers and some is returned by the firm's customers.

To keep a check on the movement of stock, an account is opened for each type of dealing in goods. Thus we will have the following accounts:

Account	Reason
Purchases Account	For the purchase of goods
Sales Account	For the sale of goods
Returns Inwards Account	For goods returned to the firm by its customers
Returns Outwards Account	For goods returned by the firm to its suppliers

As stock is an asset, and these four accounts are all connected with this asset, the double entry rules are those used for assets.

We shall now look at some specific entries in the following sections.

4.2 Purchase of stock on credit

On 1 August 2004, goods costing £165 are bought on credit from D Henry. First, the twofold effect of the transaction must be considered so that the book-keeping entries can be worked out. We have the following:

(*a*) *The asset of stock is increased.* An increase in an asset needs a debit entry in an account. Here, the account is a stock account showing the particular movement of stock; in this case it is the purchases movement, so that the account must be the purchases account.

(*b*) *There is an increase in a liability.* This is the liability of the firm to D Henry because the goods supplied have not yet been paid for. An increase in a liability needs a credit entry, and so in order to enter this part of the transaction a credit entry is made in D Henry's account.

Here again, we can use the idea of the debit side being 'IN' to the account, and the credit side being 'OUT' of the account. In this example, purchases have come 'IN', thus creating a debit in the Purchase Account; and the goods have come 'OUT' of D Henry, needing a credit in the account of D Henry. Thus:

Purchases Account

Dr			*Cr*
2004	£		
Aug 1 D Henry	165		

D Henry Account

Dr			*Cr*
		2004	£
		Aug 1 Purchases	165

4.3 Purchases of stock for cash

On 2 August 2004, goods costing £220 were bought, cash being paid for them immediately. As a result:

(*a*) *The asset of stock is increased.* Thus, a debit entry will be needed. The movement of stock is that of a purchase, so that it is the Purchases Account which needs debiting. (Purchases have come 'IN' - debit the Purchases Account.)

(*b*) *The asset of cash is decreased.* To reduce an asset a credit entry is called for, and the asset is that of cash so that the Cash Account needs crediting. (Cash has gone 'OUT' - credit the Cash Account.)

Purchases Account

Dr			*Cr*
2004	£		
Aug 2 Cash	220		

Cash Account

Dr			*Cr*
		2004	£
		Aug 2 Cash	220

4.4 Sales of stock on credit

On 3 August 2004, a business sold goods on credit for £250 to K Leach. Then:

(*a*) *An asset account is increased.* This is the account showing that K Leach is a debtor for the goods. The increase in the asset of debtors requires a debit and the debtor is K Leach, so that the account concerned is that of K Leach. (Goods have gone 'IN' to K Leach – debit K Leach's account.)

(*b*) *The asset of stock is decreased.* For this, a credit entry to reduce an asset is needed. The movement of stock is that of 'Sales' and so the account credited is the Sales Account. (Sales have gone 'OUT' – credit the Sales Account.)

Thus:

K Leach Account

Dr			*Cr*
2004	£		
Aug 3 Sales	250		

Sales Account

Dr			*Cr*
		2004	£
		Aug 3 K Leach	250

4.5 Sales of stock for cash

On 4 August 2004, goods are sold for £55, the cash for them being paid immediately. Then:

(*a*) *The asset of cash is increased.* A debit in the cash account is needed to show this. (Cash has come 'IN' – debit the Cash Account.)

(*b*) *The asset of stock is reduced.* The reduction of an asset requires a credit and the movement of stock is represented by 'Sales'. So the entry needed is a credit in the Sales Account. (Sales have gone 'OUT' – credit the Sales Account.)

Cash Account

Dr			*Cr*
2004	£		
Aug 4 Sales	55		

Sales Account

Dr			*Cr*
		2004	£
		Aug 4 Cash	55

4.6 Returns inwards

Returns inwards represent goods sold which have subsequently been returned by a customer. This could be for various reasons, such as:

- the goods sent to the customer are of the incorrect size, colour or model
- the goods have been damaged in transit
- the goods are of poor quality.

An alternative name for a returns inwards account is a sales returns account.

Just as the original sale was entered in the double entry system, so the return of those goods must also be entered.

On 5 August 2004, goods which had previously been sold to F Lowe for £29 have been returned by him. As a result:

(*a*) **The asset of stock was increased by the goods returned.** A debit representing an increase of an asset is needed, and this time the movement of stock is that of 'Returns Inwards'. The entry required therefore is a debit in the Returns Inwards Account. (The goods have come 'IN' – debit the Returns Inwards Account).

(*b*) **An asset is decreased.** The debt of F Lowe to the firm is now reduced, and to record this a credit is required in F Lowe's account. (The goods have come 'OUT' of F Lowe – credit the F Lowe Account.)

The movements are shown thus:

Returns Inwards Account

Dr			*Cr*
2004	£		
Aug 5 F Lowe	29		

F Lowe Account

Dr			*Cr*
		2004	£
		Aug 5 Returns inwards	29

4.7 Returns outwards

These represent goods which were purchased, and are now being returned to the supplier. As the original purchase was entered in the double entry system, so also is the return to the supplier of those goods.

On 6 August 2004, goods previously bought for £96 are returned by the firm to K Howe. Thus:

(*a*) *The liability of the firm to K Howe is decreased by the value of the goods returned to him.* The decrease in a liability needs a debit, this time in the K Howe Account. (The goods have gone 'IN' to K Howe – debit the K Howe Account.)

(*b*) *The asset of stock is decreased by the goods sent out.* A credit representing a reduction in an asset is needed, and the movement of stock is that of 'Returns Outwards', so that the entry will be a credit in the returns outwards account. (The returns have gone 'OUT' – credit the Returns Outward Account.)

K Howe Account

Dr			Cr
2004	£		
Aug 6 Returns outwards	96		

Returns Outwards Account

Dr			Cr
		2004	£
		Aug 6 K Howe	96

An alternative name for a returns outwards account is a purchases returns account.

4.8 A worked example

Enter the following transactions in suitable double entry accounts:

2004
May 1 Bought goods on credit £68 from D Small
May 2 Bought goods on credit £77 from A Lyon & Son
May 5 Sold goods on credit to D Hughes for £60
May 6 Sold goods on credit to M Spencer for £45
May 10 Returned goods £15 to D Small
May 12 Goods bought for cash £100
May 19 M Spencer returned £16 goods to us
May 21 Goods sold for cash £150
May 22 Paid cash to D Small £53
May 30 D Hughes paid the amount owing by him £60 in cash
May 31 Bought goods on credit £64 from A Lyon & Son.

The double entry accounts can now be shown as:

Purchases Account

Dr			Cr
2004	£		
May 1 D Small	68		
May 2 A Lyon & Son	77		
May 12 Cash	100		
May 31 A Lyon & Son	64		

Sales Account

Dr			Cr
		2004	£
		May 5 D Hughes	60
		May 6 M Spencer	45
		May 21 Cash	150

Returns Outwards Account

Dr			*Cr*	
			2004	£
			May 10 D Small	15

Returns Inwards Account

Dr			*Cr*
2004	£		
May 19 M Spencer	16		

D Small Account

Dr		*Cr*	
2004	£	2004	£
May 10 Returns outwards	15	May 1 Purchases	68
May 22 Cash	53		

A Lyon & Son Account

Dr		*Cr*	
		2004	£
		May 2 Purchases	77
		May 31 Purchases	64

D Hughes Account

Dr		*Cr*	
2004	£	2004	£
May 5 Sales	60	May 30 Cash	60

M Spencer Account

Dr		*Cr*	
2004	£	2004	£
May 6 Sales	45	May 19 Returns inwards	16

Cash Account

Dr		*Cr*	
2004	£	2004	£
May 21 Sales	150	May 12 Purchases	100
May 30 D Hughes	60	May 22 D Small	53

4.9 Special meaning of 'sales' and 'purchases'

It must be emphasised that 'sales' and 'purchases' have a special meaning in accounting language.

Purchases in accounting means 'the purchase of those goods which the firm buys with the prime intention of selling'. Sometimes the goods may be altered, added to or used in the manufacture of something else, but it is the element of *resale* that is important. To a firm that trades in computers, for instance, computers are purchases. If something else is bought, such as a motor van, such an item cannot be called purchases, even though in ordinary language it may be said that a motor van has been purchased. The prime intention of buying the motor van is for use by the company and not for resale.

Similarly, **sales** means the 'sale of those goods in which the firm normally deals and that were bought with the prime intention of resale'. The description 'sales' must never be given to the disposal of other items.

If we did not keep to these meanings, it would result in the different kinds of stock accounts containing something other than goods sold or for resale.

4.10 Comparison of cash and credit transactions for purchases and sales

The difference between the records needed for cash and credit transactions can now be seen.

The complete set of entries for purchases of goods where they are paid for immediately by cash would be:

(*a*) debit the purchases account
(*b*) credit the cash account.

On the other hand, the complete set of entries for the purchase of goods on credit can be broken down into two stages. First, the purchase of the goods and second, the payment for them. The first part is:

(*a*) debit the purchases account
(*b*) credit the supplier's account.

The second part is:

(*c*) debit the supplier's account
(*d*) credit the cash account.

The difference can now be seen. With the cash purchase, no record is kept of the supplier's account. This is because cash passes immediately and therefore there is no need to keep a check of indebtedness (money owing) to a supplier. On the other hand, in the credit purchase the records should show to whom money is owed until payment is made. A study of cash sales and credit sales will reveal a similar difference.

Cash Sales	Credit Sales
Complete entry: • debit cash account • credit sales account	First part: • debit customer's account • credit sales account Second part: • debit cash account • credit customer's account

New terms

Purchases (p. 28): Goods bought by a business for the purpose of selling them again.

Returns inwards (p. 28): Goods returned to the business by its customers.

Returns outwards (p. 28): Goods returned by the business to its suppliers.

Sales (p. 28): Goods sold by the business.

EXERCISES

4.1 Complete the following table showing which accounts are to be credited and which are to be debited:

	Account to be debited	Account to be credited
(*a*) Goods bought on credit from J Reid		
(*b*) Goods sold on credit to B Perkins		
(*c*) Motor vans bought on credit from H Thomas		
(*d*) Goods sold, a cheque being received immediately		
(*e*) Goods sold for cash		
(*f*) Goods we returned to H Hardy		
(*g*) Machinery sold for cash		
(*h*) Goods returned to us by J Nelson		
(*i*) Goods bought on credit from D Simpson		
(*j*) Goods returned to H Forbes.		

4.2X Complete the following table:

	Account to be debited	Account to be credited
(*a*) Goods bought on credit from T Morgan		
(*b*) Goods returned to us by J Thomas		
(*c*) Machinery returned to L Jones Ltd		
(*d*) Goods bought for cash		
(*e*) Motor van bought on credit from D Davies Ltd		
(*f*) Goods returned by us to I Prince		
(*g*) D Picton paid us his account by cheque		
(*h*) Goods bought by cheque		
(*i*) We paid creditor, B Henry, by cheque		
(*j*) Goods sold on credit to J Mullings.		

4.3 You are to write up the following in the books of account:

2004		
July	1	Started business with £500 cash
July	3	Bought goods for cash £85
July	7	Bought goods on credit for £116 from E Morgan
July	10	Sold goods for cash £42
July	14	Returned goods to E Morgan £28
July	18	Bought goods on credit £98 from A Moses
July	21	Returned goods to A Moses £19
July	24	Sold goods to A Knight £55 on credit
July	25	Paid E Morgan's account by cash £88
July	31	A Knight paid us his account in cash £55.

4.4 You are to enter the following in the accounts needed:

2006		
Aug	1	Started business with £1,000 cash
Aug	2	Paid £900 of the opening cash into the bank
Aug	4	Bought goods on credit for £78 from S Holmes
Aug	5	Bought a motor van by cheque £500
Aug	7	Bought goods for cash £55
Aug	10	Sold goods on credit £98 to D Moore
Aug	12	Returned goods to S Holmes, £18
Aug	19	Sold goods for cash, £28
Aug	22	Bought fixtures on credit from Kingston Equipment Co, £150
Aug	24	D Watson lent us £100, paying us the money by cheque
Aug	29	We paid S Holmes his account by cheque, £60
Aug	31	We paid Kingston Equipment Co by cheque, £150.

4.5X Enter up the following transactions in the records:

2005		
May	1	Started business with £2,000 in the bank
May	2	Bought goods on credit from C Shaw, £900
May	3	Bought goods on credit from F Hughes, £250
May	5	Sold goods for cash, £180
May	6	We returned goods to C Shaw, £40
May	8	Bought goods on credit from F Hughes, £190
May	10	Sold goods on credit to G Wood, £390
May	12	Sold goods for cash, £210
May	18	Took £300 of the cash and paid it into the bank
May	21	Bought machinery by cheque, £550
May	22	Sold goods on credit to L Moore, £220
May	23	G Wood returned goods to us, £140
May	25	L Moore returned goods to us, £10
May	28	We returned goods to F Hughes, £30
May	29	We paid Shaw by cheque, £860
May	31	Bought machinery on credit from D Lee, £270.

4.6X You are to enter the following in the accounts needed:

2005		
June	1	Started business with £1,000 cash
June	2	Paid £800 of the opening cash into a bank account for the firm
June	3	Bought goods on credit from H Grant, £330
June	4	Bought goods on credit from D Clark, £140
June	6	Sold goods on credit to B Miller, £90
June	8	Bought office furniture on credit from Barrett's Ltd, £400
June	10	Sold goods for cash, £120
June	13	Bought goods for credit from H Grant, £200
June	14	Bought goods for cash, £60
June	15	Sold goods on credit to H Sharples, £180
June	16	We returned goods worth £50 to H Grant
June	17	We returned some of the office furniture, cost £30, to Barrett's Ltd
June	18	Sold goods on credit to B Miller, £400
June	21	Paid H Grant's account by cheque, £480
June	23	B Miller paid us the amount owing in cash, £490
June	24	Sharples returned to us £50 of goods
June	25	Goods sold for cash, £150
June	28	Bought goods for cash, £370
June	30	Bought motor van on credit from J Kelly, £600.

CHAPTER 5

The double entry system for expenses and revenues

Learning objectives

After you have studied this chapter you should be able to:

- **understand the nature of profit and loss**
- **see the effects of profits and losses on capital**
- **record expenses using the double entry system**
- **understand the term 'revenues' and be able to record them in the double entry system**
- **understand drawings, be able to record them, and recognise the effects of drawings on capital.**

5.1 The nature of profit or loss

To an accountant, **profit** means the amount by which **revenues** are greater than **expenses** for a set of transactions. The term 'revenues' means the sales value of goods and services that have been supplied to customers. The term expenses means the value of all the assets that have been used up to obtain those revenues.

If, therefore, we had supplied goods and services valued for sale at £100,000 to customers, and the expenses incurred by us to be able to supply those goods and services amounted to £70,000, then the result would be a profit calculated as follows:

		£
Revenues	Goods and services supplied to customers for the sum of	100,000
Less Expenses	Value of all the assets used up to enable us to supply the above goods and services	70,000
Profit		30,000

On the other hand, it could also be possible that our expenses may exceed our revenues for a set of transactions. In this case the result is a loss. For instance a **loss** would be incurred given the following details:

		£
Expenses	Value of all the assets used up to supply goods and services to customers	80,000
Less Revenues	What we have charged to our customers in respect of all the goods and services supplied to them	60,000
Loss		20,000

5.2 The effect of profit and loss on capital

We can now look at the effect of profit upon capital by use of an example.

On 1 January the assets and liabilities of a firm are:

- Assets: Fixtures £10,000, Stock £7,000, Cash at the bank £3,000.
- Liabilities: Creditors £2,000.

The capital is found by the formula

Assets – Liabilities = Capital

In this case capital works out at Assets £10,000 + £7,000 + £3,000, - Liabilites £2,000 = £18,000.

During January the whole of the £7,000 stock is sold for £11,000 cash. On 31 January the assets and liabilities have become:

- Assets: Fixtures £10,000, Stock nil, Cash at the bank £14,000.
- Liabilities: Creditors £2,000.

The capital can be calculated:

Assets £10,000 + £14,000 - Liabilities £2,000 = £22,000

It can be seen that capital has increased from £18,000 to £22,000 = £4,000 increase because the £7,000 stock was sold for £11,000, a profit of £4,000. Profit, therefore, increases capital.

Old Capital + Profit = New Capital
£18,000 + £4,000 = £22,000

On the other hand, a loss would *reduce* the capital so:

Old Capital – Loss = New Capital

5.3 Profit or loss and sales

Profit will be made when goods are sold at more than cost price, while the opposite will mean a **loss**.

5.4 Profit or loss and expenses

In Section 5.1 it was shown that profit was made when the goods were sold for more than the cost price. As well as the cost of the goods, a firm incurs other **expenses** such as rent, salaries, wages, telephone costs, motor expenses, and so on. Every £1 of expenses will mean £1 less profit.

All expenses could be charged to one Expense Account, but it would then be difficult to identify specific areas of the firms expenditure, such as the amount spent on motor running costs or rent. To facilitate the need to know different types of expenses, a separate account is opened for each type of expense, for instance:

- Rent Account
- Telephone Account
- Stationery Account
- Salaries Account
- Advertising Account
- Motor Expenses Account
- Wages Account
- Insurance Account
- Postages Account

In the same way that separate accounts are opened for each type of expense, separate accounts are also opened for any additional *revenue* that the business may receive, such as rent received or bank interest received. Again, separate revenue accounts can be opened as follows:

- Rent Receivable Account
- Commission Received Account
- Bank Interest Received Account

It is purely a matter of choice in a business as to the name of each expense or revenue account. For example, an account for postage stamps could be called 'Postage Stamp Account', 'Postage Account' or even 'Communication Expenses Account'. Also some businesses amalgamate expenses – for example, 'Printing, Stationery and Advertising Account'. Infrequent or small items of expense are usually put into a 'Sundry Expenses Account' or 'General Expenses Account'.

5.5 Debit or credit?

We have to decide whether expense accounts are to be debited or credited with the costs involved. Assets involve expenditure by the firm and are shown as debit entries. Expenses also involve expenditure by the firm and therefore should also be debit entries.

An alternative explanation may also be used for expenses. Every expense results in a decrease in an asset or an increase in a liability, and because of the accounting equation this means that the capital is reduced by each expense. The decrease of capital needs a debit entry and therefore expense accounts contain debit entries for expenses.

Revenue is the opposite of expenses and, therfore, appears on the opposite side to expenses – that is, revenue accounts appear on the credit side of the books. Pending the periodical calculation of profit, therefore, revenue is collected together in appropriately named accounts, and until it is transferred to the profit calculations it will need to be shown as a credit.

Consider, too, that expenditure of money pays for expenses, which are used up in the short term, or assets, which are used up in the long term - both for the purpose of winning revenue. Both of these are shown on the debit side of the accounts, while the revenue which has been won is shown on the credit side of the accounts.

5.6 Effect of transactions

A few illustrations will demonstrate the double entry required.

Example 1: A rent of £20 is paid in cash. Here the twofold effect is:

(*a*) *The total of the expenses of rent is increased* - a benefit goes 'IN'. As expense entries are shown as debits, and the expense is rent, so the action required is the debiting of the Rent Account.

(*b*) *The asset of cash is decreased* - money goes 'OUT'. This means crediting the Cash Account to show the decrease of the asset.

Summary:
- debit the rent account with £20 - 'IN'
- credit the cash account with £20 - 'OUT'.

Example 2: Motor expenses are paid with a cheque for £55. The twofold effect is:

(*a*) *The total of the motor expenses paid is increased* - a benefit is received 'IN'. To increase an expenses account needs a debit, and so the action required is to debit the Motor Expenses Account.

(*b*) *The asset of money in the bank is decreased* - money goes 'OUT'. This means crediting the Bank Account to show the decrease of the asset.

Summary:
- debit the motor expenses account with £55 - 'IN'
- credit the bank account with £55 - 'OUT'.

Example 3: £60 cash is paid for telephone expenses.

(*a*) *The total of telephone expenses is increased* - a benefit received goes 'IN'. Expenses are shown by a debit entry, and therefore to increase the expense account in question the action required is to debit the Telephone Expenses Account.

(*b*) *The asset of cash is decreased* - money goes 'OUT'. This needs a credit in the Cash Account to decrease the asset.

Summary:
- debit telephone expenses account with £60 - 'IN'
- credit the cash account with £60 - 'OUT'.

It is now possible to study the effects of some more transactions showing the results in the form of a table. See Exhibit 5.1.

Exhibit 5.1

	Increase	Action	Decrease	Action
2006 June 1 Paid for postage stamps by cash £5	Expense of postages	Debit postages account	Asset of cash	Credit cash account
2 Paid for advertising by cheque £290	Expense of advertising	Debit advertising account	Asset of bank	Credit bank account
3 Paid wages by cash £900	Expense of wages	Debit wages account	Asset of cash	Credit cash account
4 Paid insurance by cheque £420	Expense of insurance	Debit insurance account	Asset of bank	Credit bank account

The above four examples can now be shown in account form:

Cash Account

Dr		*Cr*	
		2006	£
		June 1 Postages	5
		June 3 Wages	900

Bank Account

Dr		*Cr*	
		2006	£
		June 2 Advertising	290
		June 4 Insurance	420

Advertising Account

Dr		*Cr*	
2006	£		
June 2 Bank	290		

Insurance Account

Dr		*Cr*	
2006	£		
June 4 Bank	420		

Postage Account

Dr		*Cr*	
2006	£		
June 1 Cash	5		

Wages Account

Dr			Cr
2006	£		
June 3 Cash	900		

Sometimes the owner of a business will want to take cash out of the business for his or her private use. These are known as **drawings**. Any money taken out as drawings will reduce capital.

The capital account is a very important account. To help to stop it getting full of small details, each item of drawings is not entered in the capital account. Instead, a drawings account is opened and the debits are entered there. The following worked example illustrates the entries for drawings.

Example 4: On 25 August 2006 a proprietor takes £50 cash out of her business for her own use.

Effect	Action
1 Capital is decreased by £50 2 Cash is decreased by £50	Debit the drawings account £50 Credit the cash account £50

Cash Account

Dr			Cr
		2006	£
		Aug 25 Drawings	50

Drawings Account

Dr			Cr
2006	£		
Aug 25 Cash	50		

Sometimes *goods* (rather than money) are taken for private use. These are also known as drawings. Entries for such transactions will be described later in the book.

5.7 Revenues and double entry

We have just looked at instances of expenses being recorded. There will also be the need to record revenues. We will now look at an example.

Example 5: On 5 June 2006 it is decided that part of a firm's premises are not needed at the moment. The firm lets someone else use the space over and receives rent of £140 by cheque. Here, the twofold effect is:

(*a*) *The asset of the bank is increased* – money comes 'IN'. This means debiting the bank account to show the increase of the asset.

(*b*) *The total of the revenue of rent received is increased* – the benefit comes 'OUT' of rent received, so the action required is the crediting of the rent received account.

Summary:
- debit the bank account with £140 – 'IN'
- credit the rent received account with £140 – 'OUT'.

This will therefore appear as:

Bank

2006	£			
June 5 Rent received	140			

Rent Received

		2006	£
		June 5 Bank	140

New terms

Drawings (p. 43): Cash or goods taken out of a business by the owner for his or her private use.

Expenses (p. 38): Costs of operating the business.

Loss (p. 38): Result of selling goods for less than they have cost the business.

Profit (p. 38): Result of selling goods for more than they have cost the business.

Revenues (p. 38): Monetary value of goods and services supplied to customers.

EXERCISES

5.1 Complete the following table:

	Account to be debited	Account to be credited
(*a*) Paid rent by cash		
(*b*) Paid for goods by cash		
(*c*) Received by cheque a refund of rates already paid		
(*d*) Paid general expenses by cheque		
(*e*) Received commissions in cash		
(*f*) Goods returned by us to T Jones		
(*g*) Goods sold for cash		
(*h*) Bought office fixtures by cheque		
(*i*) Paid wages in cash		
(*j*) Took cash out of business for private use.		

5.2X Complete the following table

	Account to be debited	Account to be credited
(*a*) Sold surplus stationery, receiving proceeds in cash		
(*b*) Paid salaries by cheque		
(*c*) Rent received for premises sublet, by cheque		
(*d*) Goods returned to us by Royal Products		
(*e*) Commission received by us previously in error, now refunded by cheque		
(*f*) Bought machinery by cheque		
(*g*) Paid lighting expenses in cash		
(*h*) Insurance rebate received by cheque		
(*i*) Buildings bought by cheque		
(*j*) Building repairs paid in cash.		

5.3 You are required to enter the following transactions in the double entry accounts of B Cartwright:

2005
Jan 1 Started business with £20,000 capital, which was deposited in the bank
Jan 3 Paid rent for premises by cheque, £1,000
Jan 4 Bought goods on credit from M Parkin for £580 and J Kane for £2,400
Jan 4 Purchased motor van for £5,000, paying by cheque
Jan 5 Cash sales of £1,005
Jan 10 Paid motor expenses in cash, £75
Jan 12 Paid wages in cash, £120
Jan 17 Bought goods on credit from M Parkin, £670
Jan 19 Paid insurance by cheque, £220
Jan 25 Sold goods for £800, payment being received as a cheque, which was banked immediately
Jan 31 Paid wages in cash, £135, and electricity by cheque, £78.

5.4X The following are the transactions of G Dunn for the month of May 2007. You are required to enter the transactions in the appropriate accounts using the double entry system.

2007
May 1 Started in business with £12,000 in the bank
May 2 Purchased goods £1,750 on credit from M Mills
May 3 Bought fixtures and fittings for £1,500, paying by cheque
May 5 Sold goods for cash, £1,300
May 6 Bought goods on credit for £1,140 from S Waite
May 10 Paid rent by cash, £250
May 12 Bought stationery, £87, paying by cash
May 18 Goods returned by us to M Mills, £230
May 21 Let off part of the premises receiving rent by cheque, £100
May 23 Sold goods on credit to M Street for £770
May 24 Bought a motor van, paying by cheque £3,000
May 30 Paid wages for the month, £648, by cash
May 31 The proprietor, G Dunn, took cash for himself amounting to £200.

5.5 You are required to enter the following transactions, completing the double entry in the records of K Walsh for the month of July 2006.

2006	
July 1	Started in business with £8,000 in the bank
July 2	Paid for rent of premises by cheque, £375
July 3	Bought shop fittings for £800 paid by cheque
July 5	Bought goods on credit from A Jackson, £450; D Hill, £675; and E Frudd, £1,490
July 6	Paid insurance by cheque, £130
July 7	Bought motor van for £5,000 on credit from High Lane Motors
July 11	Cash Sales of £1,500
July 13	Paid for printing and stationery by cheque, £120
July 15	Paid wages in cash, £200
July 18	Bought goods from A Jackson, £890, on credit
July 21	Cash sales, £780
July 25	Paid motor expenses, £89, by cash
July 30	Paid High Lane Motors, £5,000
July 31	Paid wages in cash, £300, and stationery, £45, in cash.

5.6X Write up the following transactions in the books of J Blake for March 2006:

2006	
March 1	Started business with £15,000 capital in cash
March 2	Paid £14,000 of the cash into a bank account for the business
March 2	Bought goods on credit from J Paul for £592
March 4	Paid for rent of premises by cash, £250, and bought a motor van for £3,000, paying by cheque
March 5	Bought goods, paying by cheque for £2,100
March 9	Sold goods to E Ford for £323 and received a cheque
March 11	Paid for printing of stationery, £45, by cash
March 14	Cash sales of £490
March 18	Goods returned by us to J Paul, £67
March 19	Bought goods from J Paul on credit, £720
March 21	Paid for advertising, £60, by cheque
March 24	Sold goods for cash, £500
March 25	Paid the following expenses by cheque: wages, £540; motor expenses, £110; stationery, £82
March 28	Paid J Paul £1,245 by cheque
March 31	Sold goods for cash, £526.

5.7X Enter the following transactions in double entry:

2004	
July 1	Started business with £8,000 in the bank
July 2	Bought stationery by cheque, £30
July 3	Bought goods on credit from I Walsh, £900
July 4	Sold goods for cash, £180
July 5	Paid insurance by cash, £40
July 7	Bought machinery on credit from H Morgan, £500
July 8	Paid for machinery expenses by cheque, £50
July 10	Sold goods on credit to D Small, £320
July 11	Returned goods to I Walsh, £70
July 14	Paid wages by cash, £70

July 17	Paid rent by cheque, £100
July 20	Received cheque for £200 from D Small
July 21	Paid H Morgan by cheque, £500
July 23	Bought stationery on credit from Express Ltd, £80
July 25	Sold goods on credit to N Thomas, £230
July 28	Received rent of £20 in cash for part of premises sublet
July 31	Paid Express Ltd by cheque, £80.

CHAPTER 6

Balancing off accounts

Learning objectives

After you have studied this chapter you should be able to:

- **balance off personal accounts for debtors and creditors**
- **distinguish between a debit balance and a credit balance**
- **show personal ledger accounts in a three-column style, as used in computerised accounting systems.**

6.1 Accounts for debtors

Where debtors have paid their accounts

So far we have considered the recording of transactions in the books by means of debit and credit entries. At the end of each period, we will have to look at each account to see what is shown by the entries.

Probably the most obvious reason for this is to find out how much our customers owe us for goods we have sold to them. In most firms this is done at the end of each month. Let us look at the account of one of our customers, K Tandy, for transactions in August 2005.

K Tandy Account

Dr		*Cr*	
2005	£	2005	£
Aug 1 Sales	144	Aug 22 Bank	144
Aug 19 Sales	300	Aug 28 Bank	300

This shows that during the month of August we sold a total of £444 in goods to Tandy, and have been paid a total of £444 by him. At the close of business at the end of August he therefore owes us nothing; his account can be closed off on 31 August 2005 by inserting the totals on each side, as follows:

K Tandy Account

Dr			*Cr*
2005	£	2005	£
Aug 1 Sales	144	Aug 22 Bank	144
Aug 19 Sales	300	Aug 28 Bank	300
	444		444

Notice that totals in accounting are shown with a single line above them, and a double line underneath. Totals on accounts at the end of a period are always shown on a level with one another, as shown in the following completed account for C Lee:

C Lee Account

Dr			*Cr*
2005	£	2005	£
Aug 11 Sales	177	Aug 30 Bank	480
Aug 19 Sales	203		
Aug 22 Sales	100		
	480		480

In this account, C Lee also owed us nothing at the end of August 2005, as she had paid us for all sales to her.

If an account contains only one entry on each side and they are equal, totals are unnecessary. For example:

K Wood Account

Dr			*Cr*
2005	£	2005	£
Aug 6 Sales	214	Aug 12 Bank	214

Where debtors still owe for goods

On the other hand, some of our customers are likely still to owe us something at the end of a month. In these cases, the totals of each side would not equal each other. Let us look at the account of D Knight for August 2005:

D Knight Account

Dr			*Cr*
2005	£	2005	£
Aug 1 Sales	158	Aug 28 Bank	158
Aug 15 Sales	206		
Aug 30 Sales	118		

If you add the figures, you will see that the debit side adds up to £482 and the credit side adds up to £158. You should be able to see what the difference of £324 (i.e. £482 - £158) represents. It consists of sales of £206 and £118 not paid for and therefore still owing to us on 31 August 2005.

In double entry, we only enter figures as totals if the totals on both sides of the account agree. We do, however, want to close off the account for August, but showing that Knight owes us £324. If he owes £324 at close of business on 31 August 2005, then he will still owe us that same figure when the business opens on 1 September 2005. We show this by **balancing the account,** which is done in five stages:

1. Add up both sides to find out their totals. Do not write anything in the account at this stage.
2. Deduct the smaller total from the larger total to find the balance.
3. Now enter the balance on the side with the smallest total. This now means the totals will be equal.
4. Enter totals on a level with each other.
5. Now enter the balance on the line below the totals. The balance below the totals should be on the opposite side to the balance shown above the totals.

Against the balance above the totals, complete the date column by showing the last day of that period. Below the totals, show the first day of the next period against the balance. The balance above the totals is described as balance *carried down*. The balance below the total is described as balance *brought down*.

Knight's account when 'balanced off' will appear as shown in Exhibit 6.1.

Exhibit 6.1

D Knight Account

Dr			*Cr*		
2005		£	2005		£
Aug 1	Sales	158	Aug 28	Bank	158
Aug 15	Sales	206	Aug 31	Balance	
Aug 30	Sales	118		carried down	324
		482			482
Sept 1	Balance brought down	324			

Stage 5: enter balance to start off entries for following month.

Stage 4: enter totals level with each other.

Stage 3: enter balance here so that totals will be equal.

We can now look at another account prior to balancing:

H Henry Account

Dr			*Cr*		
2005		£	2005		£
Aug 5	Sales	300	Aug 24	Returns inwards	50
Aug 28	Sales	540	Aug 29	Bank	250

We will abbreviate 'carried down' to 'c/d' and 'brought down' to 'b/d' from now on.

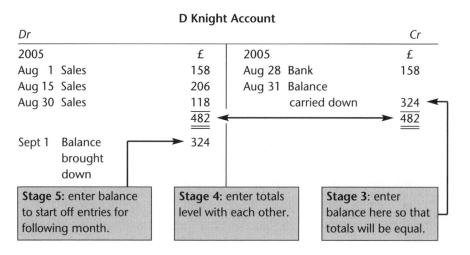

H Henry Account

Dr					Cr
2005		£	2005		£
Aug 5	Sales	300	Aug 24	Returns inwards	50
Aug 28	Sales	540	Aug 29	Bank	250
			Aug 31	Balance c/d	540
		840			840
Sept 1	Balance b/d	540			

Notes:

- The date given for the balance c/d is the last day of the period which is finishing and that for the balance b/d is given as the opening date of the next period.
- As the total of the debit side originally exceeded the total of the credit side, the balance is said to be a debit balance. This being a personal account (i.e. for a person), the person concerned is said to be a debtor – the accounting term for anyone who owes money to the firm. The use of the term 'debtor' for a person whose account has a debit balance can again thus be seen.

If accounts contain only one entry, it is unnecessary to enter the total. A double line ruled under the entry will mean that the entry is its own total. For example:

B Walters Account

Dr					Cr
2005		£	2005		£
Aug 18	Sales	51	Aug 31	Balance c/d	51
Sept 1	Balance b/d	51			

6.2 Accounts for creditors

Exactly the same principles apply when the balances are carried down to the credit side. We can look at two accounts of suppliers which are to be balanced off.

E Williams Account

Dr					Cr
2005		£	2005		£
Aug 21	Bank	100	Aug 2	Purchases	248
			Aug 18	Purchases	116

K Patterson Account

Dr					Cr
2005		£	2005		£
Aug 14	Returns outwards	20	Aug 8	Purchases	620
Aug 28	Bank	600	Aug 15	Purchases	200

We now add up the totals and find the balance, i.e. stages 1 and 2 of the five-stage process. When balanced, these will appear as shown in Exhibit 6.2.

EXHIBIT 6.2

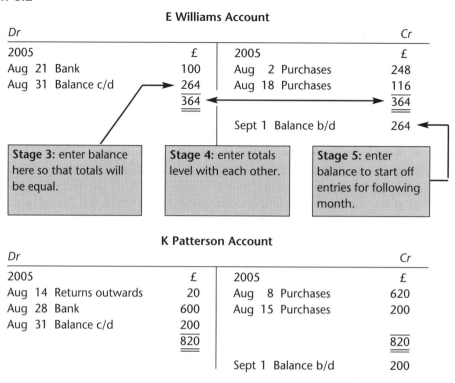

E Williams Account

Dr				*Cr*
2005	£		2005	£
Aug 21 Bank	100		Aug 2 Purchases	248
Aug 31 Balance c/d	264		Aug 18 Purchases	116
	364			364
			Sept 1 Balance b/d	264

Stage 3: enter balance here so that totals will be equal.

Stage 4: enter totals level with each other.

Stage 5: enter balance to start off entries for following month.

K Patterson Account

Dr				*Cr*
2005	£		2005	£
Aug 14 Returns outwards	20		Aug 8 Purchases	620
Aug 28 Bank	600		Aug 15 Purchases	200
Aug 31 Balance c/d	200			
	820			820
			Sept 1 Balance b/d	200

Before you read further, attempt Exercises 6.1, 6.2 and 6.3 at the end of this chapter.

The type of accounts which have been demonstrated so far are often know as 'T accounts' (see Section 3.6) since the accounts are in the shape of a letter T. The following accounts show the three-column method, which is used in computerised accounting systems.

6.3 Computers and accounts

Through the main part of this book, the type of account used shows the left-hand side of the account as the debit side and the right-hand side as the credit side. However, when most computers are used, the style of the ledger account is different. It appears as three columns of figures, there being one column for debit entries, another column for credit entries, and the last column for the balance. If you have a current account at a bank, your bank statements will normally be shown using this method.

The accounts used in this chapter will now be redrafted to show the ledger accounts drawn up in this way.

K Tandy Account

	Debit	Credit	Balance (and whether debit or credit)
2005	£	£	£
Aug 1 Sales	144		144 Dr
Aug 19 Sales	300		444 Dr
Aug 22 Bank		144	300 Dr
Aug 28 Bank		300	0

C Lee Account

	Debit	Credit	Balance
2005	£	£	£
Aug 11 Sales	177		177 Dr
Aug 19 Sales	203		380 Dr
Aug 22 Sales	100		480 Dr
Aug 30 Bank		480	0

K Wood Account

	Debit	Credit	Balance
2005	£	£	£
Aug 6 Sales	214		214 Dr
Aug 12 Bank		214	0

D Knight Account

	Debit	Credit	Balance
2005	£	£	£
Aug 1 Sales	158		158 Dr
Aug 15 Sales	206		364 Dr
Aug 28 Cash		158	206 Dr
Aug 31 Sales	118		324 Dr

H Henry Account

	Debit	Credit	Balance
2005	£	£	£
Aug 5 Sales	300		300 Dr
Aug 24 Returns		50	250 Dr
Aug 28 Sales	540		790 Dr
Aug 29 Bank		250	540 Dr

B Walters Account

	Debit	Credit	Balance
2005	£	£	£
Aug 18 Sales	51		51 Dr

E Williams Account

		Debit	Credit	Balance
2005		£	£	£
Aug 2	Purchases		248	248 Cr
Aug 18	Purchases		116	364 Cr
Aug 21	Bank	100		264 Cr

K Patterson Account

		Debit	Credit	Balance
2005		£	£	£
Aug 8	Purchases		620	620 Cr
Aug 14	Returns	20		600 Cr
Aug 15	Purchases		200	800 Cr
Aug 28	Bank	600		200 Cr

It will be noticed that the balance is calculated again after every entry. This can be done quite simply when using a computer because it is the machine that calculates the new balance.

However, when manual methods are being used, it is often too much work to have to calculate a new balance after each entry. It also means that the greater the number of calculations the greater the possibility of errors. For these reasons it is usual for students to use two-sided accounts. However, it is important to note that there is no difference in principle; the final balances are the same using either method.

New terms

Balancing the account (p. 50): Finding and entering the difference between the two sides of an account.

EXERCISES

6.1 Enter the following items in the necessary debtors and creditors accounts only; do *not* write up other accounts. Then balance down each personal account at the end of the month. (Keep your answer – it will be used as a basis for Exercise 6.3.)

2008
May 1 Sales on credit to H Harvey £690, N Morgan £153, J Lindo £420
May 4 Sales on credit to L Masters £418, H Harvey £66
May 10 Returns inwards from H Harvey £40, J Lindo £20
May 18 N Morgan paid us by cheque £153
May 20 J Lindo paid us £400 by cheque
May 24 H Harvey paid us £300 by cash
May 31 Sales on credit to L Masters £203.

6.2 Enter the following in the personal accounts only; do *not* write up the other accounts. Then balance down each personal account at the end of the month. (Keep your answer – it will be used as the basis of question 6.4X.)

2008
June 1 Purchases on credit from J Young £458, L Williams £120, G Norman £708
June 3 Purchases on credit from L Williams £77, T Harris £880
June 10 We returned goods to G Norman £22, J Young £55
June 15 Purchases on credit from J Young £80
June 19 We paid T Harris by cheque £880
June 28 We paid J Young by cash £250
June 30 We returned goods to L Williams £17.

6.3 Redraft each of the accounts given in your answer to 6.1 as three-column ledger-style accounts.

6.4X Redraft each of the accounts given in your answer to 6.2 as three-column ledger-style accounts.

6.5 Enter the following in the personal accounts only; do *not* write up the other accounts. Balance down each personal account at the end of the month. After completing this, state which of the outstanding balances represent debtors and which represent creditors.

2009
Sept 1 Sales on credit to D Williams £458, J Moore £235, G Grant £98
Sept 2 Purchases on credit A White £77, H Samuels £231, P Owen £65
Sept 8 Sales on credit to J Moore £444, F Franklin £249
Sept 10 Purchases on credit from H Samuels £12, O Oliver £222
Sept 12 Returns inwards from G Grant £9, J Moore £26
Sept 17 We returned goods to H Samuels £24, O Oliver £12
Sept 20 We paid A White by cheque £77
Sept 24 D Williams paid us by cheque £300
Sept 26 We paid O Oliver by cash £210
Sept 28 D Williams paid us by cash £100
Sept 30 F Franklin pays us by cheque £249.

6.6X

Enter the following in the necessary personal accounts; do *not* write up the other accounts. Balance each personal account at the end of the month. (Keep your answer – it will be used as the basis of question 6.8X.)

2006
Aug 1 Sales on credit to L Sterling £445, L Lindo £480, R Spencer £221
Aug 4 Goods returned to us by L Sterling £15, R Spencer £33
Aug 8 Sales on credit to L Lindo £66, R Spencer £129, L Banks £465
Aug 9 We received a cheque for £430 from L Sterling
Aug 12 Sales on credit to R Spencer £235, L Banks £777
Aug 19 Goods returned to us by L Banks £21, R Spencer £25
Aug 22 We received cheques as follows: R Spencer £300, L Lindo £414
Aug 31 Sales on credit to L Lindo £887, L Banks £442.

6.7X Enter the following, which are personal accounts only. Bring down balances at end of the month. After completing this, state which of the outstanding balances represent debtors and which represent creditors.

2006
May 1 Credit sale B Flynn £241, R Kelly £29, J Long £887, T Fryer £124
May 2 Credit purchases from S Wood £148, T DuQuesnay £27, R Johnson £77, G Henriques £108
May 8 Credit sales to R Kelly £74, J Long £132
May 9 Credit purchases from T DuQuesnay £142, G Henriques £44
May 10 Goods returned to us by J Long £17, T Fryer £44
May 12 Cash paid to us by T Fryer £80
May 15 We returned goods to S Wood £8, G Henriques £18
May 19 We received cheques from J Long £500, B Flynn £241
May 21 We sold goods on credit to B Flynn £44, R Kelly £280
May 28 We paid by cheque the following: S Wood £140; G Henriques £50; R Johnson £60
May 31 We returned goods to G Henriques £4.

6.8X Redraft each of the accounts given in your answer to 6.6X as three-column accounts.

CHAPTER 7

The trial balance

Learning objectives

After you have studied this chapter you should be able to:

- **understand why the trial balance totals should equal one another**
- **draw up a trial balance from a given set of accounts**
- **appreciate that some kinds of errors can be made but the trial balance totals will still equal one another**
- **understand what steps to take if the trial balance doesn't balance.**

7.1 Total debit entries = total credit entries

You have already seen that the method of book-keeping in use is that of the double entry method. This means:

- for each debit entry there is a credit entry
- for each credit entry there is a debit entry.

All the items recorded in all the accounts on the debit side should equal *in total* all the items recorded on the credit side of the books. We need to check that for each debit entry there is also a credit entry. To see whether the two totals are equal, usually known as seeing whether the two sides of the books 'balance', a **trial balance** may be drawn up at the end of a period.

A form of trial balance could be drawn up by listing all the accounts and adding together all the debit entries, at the same time adding together all the credit entries. Using the worked exercise given in Section 4.8, such a trial balance would appear as below. Note that it could not be drawn up until after all the entries had been made; it will, therefore, be dated as on 31 May 2004.

Trial Balance as on 31 May 2004		
	Dr	*Cr*
	£	£
Purchases	309	
Sales		255
Returns outwards		15
Returns inwards	16	
D Small	68	68
A Lyon & Son		141
D Hughes	60	60
M Spencer	45	16
Cash	210	153
	708	708

7.2 Total debit balances = total credit balances

Section 7.1 is not the normal method of drawing up a trial balance, but it is the easiest to understand at first. Usually, a trial balance is a list of balances only, arranged according to whether they are debit balances or credit balances. If the trial balance in Section 7.1 had been drawn up using the normal balances method, it would appear as below.

Trial Balance as on 31 May 2004		
	Dr	*Cr*
	£	£
Purchases	309	
Sales		255
Returns outwards		15
Returns inwards	16	
A Lyon & Son		141
M Spencer	29	
Cash	57	
	411	411

Here, the two sides also 'balance'. The sums of £68 in D Small's account, £60 in D Hughes' account, £16 in M Spencer's account and £153 in the cash account have, however, been cancelled out from each side of these accounts by taking only the *balances* instead of the *totals*. As equal amounts have been cancelled from each side, £297 in all, the new totals should still equal one another, as in fact they do at £411.

This form of trial balance is the easiest to extract when there are more than a few transactions during the period. Also, the balances are either used later when the profits are being calculated, or else they appear in a balance sheet. Trial balances, therefore, are not just prepared in order to find errors.

7.3 A worked example

The following accounts, for K Potter, have been entered up for May 2006 and balanced off.

K Potter's Books:

Bank Account

Dr			*Cr*		
2006		£	2006		£
May 1	Capital	9,000	May 21	Machinery	550
May 30	T Monk	300	May 29	T Wood	860
			May 31	Balance c/d	7,890
		9,300			9,300
June 1	Balance b/d	7,890			

Cash Account

Dr			*Cr*		
2006		£	2006		£
May 5	Sales	180	May 30	K Young	170
May 12	Sales	210	May 31	Balance c/d	220
		390			390
June 1	Balance b/d	220			

T Wood Account

Dr			*Cr*		
2006		£	2006		£
May 6	Returns outwards	40	May 2	Purchases	900
May 29	Bank	860			
		900			900

K Young Account

Dr			*Cr*		
2006		£	2006		£
May 28	Returns outwards	80	May 3	Purchases	250
May 30	Cash	170	May 18	Purchases	190
May 31	Balance c/d	190			
		440			440
			June 1	Balance b/d	190

T Monk Account

Dr			Cr
2006	£	2006	£
May 10 Sales	590	May 23 Returns inwards	140
		May 30 Bank	300
		May 31 Balance c/d	150
	590		590
June 1 Balance b/d	150		

C Howe Account

Dr			Cr
2006	£	2006	£
May 22 Sales	220	May 25 Returns inwards	10
		May 31 Balance c/d	210
	220		220
June 1 Balance b/d	210		

AB Ltd Account

Dr			Cr
		2006	£
		May 31 Machinery	2,700

Capital Account

Dr			Cr
		2006	£
		May 1 Bank	9,000

Purchases Account

Dr			Cr
2006	£	2006	£
May 2 T Wood	900	May 31 Balance c/d	1,340
May 3 K Young	250		
May 18 K Young	190		
	1,340		1,340
June 1 Balance b/d	1,340		

Sales Account

Dr			Cr
2006	£	2006	£
May 31 Balance c/d	1,200	May 5 Cash	180
		May 10 T Monk	590
		May 12 Cash	210
		May 22 C Howe	220
	1,200		1,200
		June 1 Balance b/d	1,200

Returns Inwards Account

Dr			*Cr*		
2006		£	2006		£
May 23	T Monk	140	May 31	Balance c/d	150
May 25	C Howe	10			
		150			150
June 1	Balance b/d	150			

Returns Outwards Account

Dr			*Cr*		
2006		£	2006		£
May 31	Balance c/d	120	May 6	T Wood	40
			May 28	K Young	80
		120			120
			June 1	Balance b/d	120

Machinery Account

Dr			*Cr*		
2006		£	2006		£
May 21	Bank	550	May 31	Balance c/d	3,250
May 31	AB Ltd	2,700			
		3,250			3,250
June 1	Balance b/d	3,250			

After each account has been balanced off, a trial balance can then be prepared as follows:

K Potter
Trial Balance as on 31 May 2006

	Dr	*Cr*
	£	£
Bank	7,890	
Cash	220	
K Young		190
T Monk	150	
C Howe	210	
AB Ltd		2,700
Capital		9,000
Purchases	1,340	
Sales		1,200
Returns inwards	150	
Returns outwards		120
Machinery	3,250	
	13,210	13,210

7.4 The uses of the trial balance

The trial balance may be used for the following purposes:

- to check that the books 'balance', i.e. that every debit entry has been accompanied by a credit entry
- to ascertain the amount of the error(s), should one or more have been made, and make the necessary corrections
- as a basis from which the final accounts of a business are prepared, i.e. the Trading Account, the Profit and Loss Account, and the Balance Sheet. This topic will be covered in Chapters 8, 9 and 10 in Part 2.

7.5 Trial balance and errors

With some errors, the trial balance will still balance (i.e. the total of the debit and credit balances are equal to each other). An instance of this is a credit sale of £87 which has been incorrectly entered in both the Sales Account and the Debtor's Account as £78. Since both the debit entry and the credit entry are of the same amount, then this will not affect the agreement of the totals in the trial balance.

Some errors will, however, mean that the totals in the trial balance will not agree. An instance could be where a payment of rent of £200 by cheque has been entered on the credit side of the Bank Account, but has been completely omitted from the Rent Account. Here, a credit entry was not accompanied by a debit entry for this transaction, and thus the trial balance will not agree.

Chapters 31 and 32 will deal in detail with the different types of error that may occur.

7.6 Steps to take if the trial balance doesn't balance

If the trial balance does not balance, i.e. the two totals are different, then this is evidence that one or more errors have been made in either the double entry book-keeping or in the preparation of the trial balance itself. In this case, the following eight steps should be taken to locate the error(s):

1. If the trial balance is badly written and contains many alterations, then rewrite it.
2. Add up again each side of the trial balance. If you added the numbers 'upwards' the first time, then start at the top and work 'downwards' the second time, and vice versa.
3. Find the amount of the discrepancy and then check in the accounts for a transaction of this amount and, if located, ensure that the double entry has been carried out correctly.
4. Halve the amount of the discrepancy. Check to see whether there is a transaction for this amount and, if located, ensure the double entry has been carried out correctly. This type of error may have occurred if an item had been entered on the wrong side of the trial balance.

5 If the amount of the discrepancy is divisible by nine, this indicates that when the figure was originally entered it may have had digits transposed, for example £63 entered in error as £36, or £27 entered as £72.

6 Check that the balance on each account has been correctly calculated and entered onto the trial balance in the right column using the correct amount.

7 Ensure that every outstanding balance from all the ledgers and the cash book have been included in the trial balance and tick each balance after ensuring it is entered correctly.

8 If the error has still not been identified, then the error must be sought in the accounts themselves. It may be necessary to check all the entries from the date of the last trial balance.

7.7 Skeleton trial balance

Some examining bodies provide a list of balances from which a trial balance must be drawn up, whilst other questions involve correction of a trial balance. It is essential to understand the basic principles of double entry to carry out this task, i.e. a debit balance is always an asset, expense or loss, and a credit balance is capital, a liability or income.

A skeleton trial balance is shown that will act as a guide, enabling you to answer such questions. Later in your studies you will come across other items, but we will keep it fairly simple at this stage.

Skeleton trial balance as at 31 May 2006

	Dr	Cr
*All **debit** balances will include:*		
Assets	Stock (1 June 2005) Cash Bank Machinery Motor vans Fittings Debtors Premises	
Expenses and losses	Purchases Carriage inwards and outwards Wages and salaries Advertising Rent and rates Stationery Bad Debts written off Light and heat	
Others	Drawings	
*All **credit** balances will include:*		
Capital and liabilities		Capital Creditors Loans *from* others
Income, profits and gains		Sales Commissions received Rents received

Note: Closing stock appears as a note.

7.8 Multiple-choice self-test questions

A growing practice of examining boards is to set multiple-choice questions in Accounting. This type of question certainly gives an examiner the opportunity to cover large parts of the syllabus briefly but in detail. Students who omit to study areas of the syllabus will be caught out by an examiner's use of multiple-choice questions. No longer will it be possible to say that it is highly probable that a certain topic will not be tested – the examiner can easily cover it with a multiple-choice question.

We have deliberately set blocks of multiple-choice questions at given places in this textbook, rather than a few at the end of each chapter. Such questions are relatively easy to answer a few minutes after reading the chapter, and so by asking the questions later your powers of recall and understanding are far better tested. It also gives you practice at answering a few questions in one block, as in an examination.

Each multiple-choice question has: a 'stem', namely that part which poses the problem; a 'key', which is the one correct answer; and a number of 'distractors', i.e. incorrect answers. The key plus the distractors are known as the 'options'. If you do not know the answer you should guess. You may be right by chance, or you may remember something subconsciously. In any event, unless the examiner warns otherwise, he will expect you to guess if you don't know the answer.

You should now attempt Set 1 in Appendix C, which contains 20 multiple-choice questions.

New term

Trial balance (p. 57): A list of all the balances in the books at a particular point in time. The balances are shown in debit and credit columns. These columns should balance, provided that no errors have occurred.

EXERCISES

7.1 You are required to enter the following details for the month of May 2004, balance the accounts off and extract a trial balance as at 31 May 2004.

2004		
May	1	Started in business with capital of £2,500, which was paid into the bank
May	2	Bought goods on credit from the following: D Ellis £540; C Mendez £87; K Gibson £76
May	4	Sold goods on credit to: C Bailey £430; B Hughes £62; H Spencer £176
May	6	Paid rent by cash £120
May	8	Sold goods for cash £500
May	9	C Bailey paid us £250 by cheque on account
May	10	H Spencer paid us £150 on account by cheque
May	12	We paid the following by cheque: K Gibson £76; D Ellis £370 on account
May	15	Bought stationery for cash £60
May	18	Bought goods on credit from: D Ellis £145; C Mendez £234
May	19	Paid rent by cash £120
May	25	Sold goods on credit to: C Bailey £90; B Hughes £110; H Spencer £128
May	31	Paid C Mendez £87 by cheque.

7.2 Enter up the books from the following details for the month of March, and extract a trial balance as at 31 March 2004.

2004		
March	1	Started business with £8,000 in the bank
March	2	Bought goods on credit from the following persons: K Henriques £76; M Hyatt £27; T Braham £560
March	5	Cash sales £870
March	6	Paid wages in cash £140
March	7	Sold goods on credit to: H Elliott £35; L Lane £42; J Carlton £72
March	9	Bought goods for cash £46
March	10	Bought goods on credit from: M Hyatt £57; T Braham £98
March	12	Paid wages in cash £140
March	13	Sold goods on credit to: L Lane £32; J Carlton £23
March	15	Bought shop fixtures on credit from Betta Ltd £500
March	17	Paid M Hyatt by cheque £84
March	18	We returned goods to T Braham £20
March	21	Paid Betta Ltd a cheque for £500
March	24	J Carlton paid us his account by cheque £95
March	27	We returned goods to K Henriques £24
March	30	J King lent us £600 by cash
March	31	Bought a motor van paying by cheque £4,000.

7.3X Record the following transactions in the books of C Hilton. Balance off the accounts and extract a trial balance as at 30 June 2006.

2006		
June	1	C Hilton started in business with £9,000 in cash
June	2	Paid £8,000 of the cash into a bank account
June	4	Paid rent for shop £300 by cheque
June	6	Bought goods on credit from Moorlands & Co. £675; J Swain £312; B Merton £225
June	12	Sold goods for cash £450
June	13	Bought fixtures, paying by cheque £230
June	15	Sold goods on credit T Green £180; K Wood £367; P Brown £256
June	18	Sold goods for cash £220
June	20	Paid Moorlands & Co by cheque £675 and B Merton £225
June	21	Returned goods to J Swain £112 and paid the outstanding balance on their account by cheque
June	24	Bought goods on credit from Moorlands & Co £220 and J Swain £92
June	26	Paid wages in cash £366
June	27	Cash drawings £200
June	29	Bought motor van, paying by cheque £4,000
June	30	Sold goods on credit to T Green £300; K Wood £50; P Brown £60
June	30	Received cheques from the following: T Green £180 and K Wood £367

7.4X Record the following details for the month of November 2005 and extract a trial balance as at 30 November.

Nov	1	Started with £5,000 in the bank
Nov	3	Bought goods on credit from: T Henriques £160; J Smith £230; W Rogers £400; P Boone £310
Nov	5	Cash sales £240
Nov	6	Paid rent by cheque £20
Nov	7	Paid rates by cheque £190
Nov	11	Sold goods on credit to: L Matthews £48; K Allen £32; R Hall £1,170
Nov	17	Paid wages by cash £40
Nov	18	We returned goods to: T Henriques £14; P Boone £20
Nov	19	Bought goods on credit from: P Boone £80; W Rogers £270; D Diaz £130
Nov	20	Goods were returned to us by K Allen £2; L Matthews £4
Nov	21	Bought motor van on credit from UZ Motors £500
Nov	23	We paid the following by cheque: T Henriques £146; J Smith £230; W Rogers £300
Nov	25	Bought another motor van, paying by cheque immediately £700
Nov	26	Received a loan of £400 cash from A Williams
Nov	28	Received cheques from: L Matthews £44; K Allen £30
Nov	30	Proprietor brings a further £300 into the business, by a payment into the business bank account.

7.5 Correct and balance the following trial balance.

Trial balance of P Brown as at 31 May 2006		
	Dr	*Cr*
	£	£
Capital		20,000
Drawings	7,000	
General expenses		500
Sales	38,500	
Purchases		29,000
Debtors		6,800
Creditors	9,000	
Bank balance (Dr)	15,100	
Cash		200
Plant and equipment		5,000
Heating and lighting		1,500
Rent	2,400	

7.6 Reconstruct the trial balance after making the necessary corrections.

Trial balance of S Higton as at 30 June 2005		
	Dr	*Cr*
	£	£
Capital	19,956	
Sales		119,439
Stationery	1,200	
General expenses	2,745	
Motor expenses		4,476
Cash at bank	1,950	
Stock 1 July 2004	7,668	
Wages and salaries		9,492
Rent and rates	10,500	
Office equipment	6,000	
Purchases	81,753	
Heating and lighting		2,208
Rent received	2,139	
Debtors	10,353	
Drawings		4,200
Creditors		10,230
Motor vehicle	7,500	
Interest received	1,725	
Insurance		3,444
	153,489	153,489

7.7X From the following list of balances, prepare a trial balance as at 31 December 2004 for Ms Anita Hall:

	£
Plant and machinery	21,450
Motor vehicles	26,000
Premises	80,000
Wages	42,840
Purchases	119,856
Sales	179,744
Rent received	3,360
Telephone, printing and stationery	3,600
Creditors	27,200
Debtors	30,440
Bank overdraft	2,216
Capital	131,250
Drawings	10,680
General expenses	3,584
Lighting and heating	2,960
Motor expenses	2,360

PART 2

The final accounts of a business

8 An introduction to the trading and profit and loss account

9 The balance sheet

10 Further considerations regarding final accounts

11 Accounting principles, concepts and conventions

This part of the book is concerned with the drawing-up, from double entry records, of the final accounts of sole trader.

CHAPTER 8

An introduction to the trading and profit and loss account

Learning objectives

After you have studied this chapter you should be able to:

- understand the difference between gross profit and net profit
- draw up a trading and profit and loss account from information given in a trial balance
- recognise that an adjustment is needed for the closing stock at the end of a period
- enter up the capital account after the trading and profit and loss account has been drawn up
- draw up a trading and profit and loss account using both the horizontal and vertical methods.

8.1 Purpose of the trading and profit and loss account

The main reason why people set up a business is to make profits of course, if they are not successful they will incur losses. To calculate how much profit or loss has been made over a period of time, a **trading and profit and loss account** is prepared. Normally, all businesses prepare a trading and profit and loss account at least once a year; the account could be prepared for a shorter period if required.

The main purpose of a trading and profit and loss account is for the owners to see how profitably the business is being run. It is also used for other purposes; for instance, it will be used as a basis for calculating the owners' UK income tax liability under self-assessment requirements.

8.2 Uses of the trading and profit and loss account

One of the most important uses of the trading and profit and loss account is the comparison of the results achieved with those of past periods. When doing this, it is useful – as you will see more fully later – for traders to calculate two sorts of profit. These are:

Gross profit: (calculated in the Trading Account)	This is the excess of sales over the **cost of goods sold** in the period.
Net profit: (calculated in the Profit and Loss Account	This is what is left of the gross profit after all other expenses have been deducted.

It would be possible to have one account called a **trading account**, and another called a **profit and loss account**. Normally they are combined together to form one account called the **trading and profit and loss account**.

8.3 Horizontal and vertical format for the trading and profit and loss account

In Section 8.5, we will look at trading and profit and loss accounts drawn up using the horizontal style. The left-hand side is the debit side, whilst the right-hand side is the credit side of the accounts. These accounts can therefore be seen as part of the double entry system, and students should be able to understand why each item is shown as a debit or a credit in them.

In Section 8.9, we will see how the trading and profit and loss account can be shown using a vertical style.

8.4 Preparation of a trading and profit and loss account

Exhibit 8.1

K Wade
Trial Balance as on 31 December 2003

	Dr	*Cr*
	£	£
Sales		9,650
Purchases	7,150	
General expenses	550	
Fixtures and fittings	1,840	
Debtors	1,460	
Creditors		1,180
Capital		2,800
Drawings	1,750	
Bank	820	
Cash	60	
	13,630	13,630

Before drawing up a trading and profit and loss account, you should first obtain the trial balance. This contains nearly all the information needed. (Later on in this book you will see that certain adjustments have to be made, but we will ignore these at this stage.)

Set out in Exhibit 8.1 is the trial balance for K Wade, made up to the end of his first year's trading. This information is needed to prepare his trading and profit and loss account for the year ended 31 December 2003. For now, we will assume that K Wade has no closing stock at 31 December 2003.

To calculate gross profit

Remember that:

Sales – Cost of Goods Sold = Gross Profit

We could in fact calculate this by simply using arithmetic. However, we must remember that we are using double entry methods. The answer will be the same whether normal arithmetic or proper double entry methods are used. To enable you to see fully how the calculations are performed using double entry, we will show the balances for sales and purchases, as in Exhibit 8.1, and how the entries are made to transfer these items into the calculations within the trading account.

The following steps should be carried out:

Step 1 Transfer the credit balance of the sales account to the credit of the trading account portion of the trading and profit and loss account.

Debit: sales account
Credit: trading account.

Step 2 Transfer the debit balance of the purchases account to the debit of the trading account.

Debit: trading account
Credit: purchases account.

Remember that, in this case, there is no stock of unsold goods. This means that purchases = cost of goods sold.

Step 3 If sales are greater than the cost of goods sold, the difference is gross profit. (If not, the answer would be a **gross loss**.) We will carry this gross profit figure from the trading account part down to the profit and loss part.
The double entry for gross profit is:

Debit: trading account
Credit: profit and loss account.

The above transfers are shown below in Exhibit 8.2 for Exhibit 8.1.

EXHIBIT 8.2

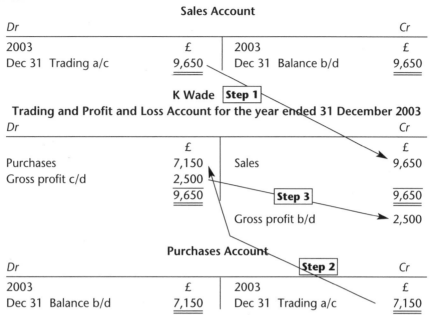

Sales Account

Dr			*Cr*
2003	£	2003	£
Dec 31 Trading a/c	9,650	Dec 31 Balance b/d	9,650

K Wade Step 1

Trading and Profit and Loss Account for the year ended 31 December 2003

Dr			*Cr*
	£		£
Purchases	7,150	Sales	9,650
Gross profit c/d	2,500		
	9,650	Step 3	9,650
		Gross profit b/d	2,500

Purchases Account

Dr		Step 2	*Cr*
2003	£	2003	£
Dec 31 Balance b/d	7,150	Dec 31 Trading a/c	7,150

Notice that, after the trading account has been completed, there are no balances remaining in the sales and purchases accounts. They are now said to be 'closed'.

To calculate net profit and record it

Remember that:

Gross Profit - Expenses = Net Profit

Remember also (from Chapter 5) that:

Old Capital + Net Profit = New Capital

Double entry needed to carry out these calculations:

Step 1 Transfer the debit balances on expenses accounts to the debit of the profit and loss account.

Debit: profit and loss account
Credit: expenses accounts.

Step 2 Transfer the net profit, when found, to the capital account to show the increase in capital.

Debit: profit and loss account
Credit: capital account.

The results are shown in Exhibit 8.3.

EXHIBIT 8.3

K Wade
Trading and Profit and Loss Account for the Year ended 31 December 2003.

Dr			*Cr*
	£		£
Purchases	7,150	Sales	9,650
Gross profit c/d	2,500		
	9,650		9,650
General expenses	550	Gross profit b/d	2,500
Net profit	1,950		
	2,500		2,500

Step 1

General Expenses Account

Dr			*Cr*
2003	£	2003	£
Dec 31 Balance b/d	550	Dec 31 Profit and loss a/c	550

Capital Account

Step 2

Dr			*Cr*
		2003	£
		Dec 31 Balance b/d	2,800
		Dec 31 Net profit	1,950
			4,750

Note: See Section 8.5 for completion of this account.

8.5 Completion of capital account

You have seen that we credit the capital account with the amount of net profit. We have, therefore, recorded the increase in capital.

In the trial balance, Exhibit 8.1, we can see that there are drawings of £1,750. Drawings means withdrawals of capital.

After entering the net profit in the capital account we can now complete the account. To do this we transfer the drawings to the capital account. Thus:

Debit: capital account
Credit: drawings account.

The completed capital and drawings accounts are as follows:

Drawings Account

Dr			*Cr*
2003	£	2003	£
Dec 31 Balance b/d	1,750	Dec 31 Capital	1,750

Capital Account

Dr					*Cr*
2003		£	2003		£
Dec 31	Drawings	1,750	Dec 31	Balance b/d	2,800
Dec 31	Balance c/d	3,000	Dec 31	Net profit	1,950
		4,750			4,750
			2004		
			Jan 1	Balance b/d	3,000

8.6 Stock of unsold goods at end of period

We have already seen that gross profit is calculated as follows:

Sales – Cost of Goods Sold = Gross Profit

However, purchases only equals cost of goods sold if there is no stock at the end of a period. We can calculate cost of goods sold as follows:

What we bought in this period:	Purchases
Less Goods bought but not sold in this period:	Closing Stock
	= Cost of Goods Sold

Remember, we are concerned here with the trading and profit and loss account of a business, as drawn up in its first year of trading when there is no opening stock. In Section 10.4 we will look at the later years of a business.

Now let us look at the drawing-up of a trading and profit and loss account for B Swift. His trial balance is shown as Exhibit 8.4 and was drawn up after his first year of trading:

EXHIBIT 8.4

B Swift
Trial Balance as on 31 December 2005

	Dr	Cr
	£	£
Sales		3,850
Purchases	2,900	
Rent	240	
Lighting	150	
General expenses	60	
Fixtures and fittings	500	
Debtors	680	
Creditors		910
Bank	1,510	
Cash	20	
Drawings	700	
Capital		2,000
	6,760	6,760

Note: On 31 December 2005, at the close of trading, B Swift had goods costing £300 that were unsold.

The cost of goods sold figure will be:

	£
Purchases	2,900
Less Closing stock	300
Cost of goods sold	2,600

The gross profit will be:

	£
Sales	3,850
Less Cost of goods sold	2,600
Gross profit	1,250

The net profit will be:

	£	£
Gross profit		1,250
Less Expenses		
Rent	240	
Lighting	150	
General expenses	60	
		450
Net profit		800

We will now see this shown in double entry form:

Sales Account

Dr					*Cr*
2005		£	2005		£
Dec 31	Trading a/c	3,850	Dec 31	Balance b/d	3,850

Purchases Account

Dr					*Cr*
2005		£	2005		£
Dec 31	Balance b/d	2,900	Dec 31	Trading a/c	2,900

Rent Account

Dr					*Cr*
2005		£	2005		£
Dec 31	Balance b/d	240	Dec 31	Profit and loss a/c	240

Lighting Account

Dr					*Cr*
2005		£	2005		£
Dec 31	Balance b/d	150	Dec 31	Profit and loss a/c	150

General Expenses Account

Dr					*Cr*
2005		£	2005		£
Dec 31	Balance b/d	60	Dec 31	Profit and loss a/c	60

To record the stock we have entered the following:

Debit: stock account
Credit: trading account.

This yields the accounts shown in Exhibit 8.5.

Exhibit 8.5

Stock Account

Dr			*Cr*
2005	£		
Dec 31 Trading a/c	300		

B Swift
Trading and Profit and Loss Account for the year ended 31 December 2005

2005	£	2005	£
Purchases	2,900	Sales	3,850
Gross profit c/d	1,250	Closing stock	300
	4,150		4,150
Rent	240	Gross profit b/d	1,250
Lighting	150		
General expenses	60		
Net profit	800		
	1,250		1,250

The figures shown in Exhibit 8.5 mean that there is now a balance on the stock account. We had to record it there because at 31 December 2005 we had an asset, namely £300 of stock, but there was no record of that fact in our books. We have now brought our records up to date by showing the stock in our accounts.

8.7 The capital account

The capital account for B Swift can now be completed, thus:

Capital Account

Dr			*Cr*
2005	£	2005	£
Dec 31 Drawings	700	Jan 1 Cash	2,000
Dec 31 Balance c/d	2,100	Dec 31 Net profit from profit and loss a/c	800
	2,800		2,800
		2006	
		Jan 1 Balance b/d	2,100

Drawings Account

Dr			*Cr*
2005	£	2005	£
Dec 31 Balance b/d	700	Dec 31 Capital	700

8.8 The vertical style for trading and profit and loss accounts

The trading and profit and loss account shown above is written in the *horizontal* format to demonstrate how the double entry system works. However, the trading and profit and loss account is more often shown in the *vertical* format, and it is this format that we will use in future in this book. You may none the less wish to carry on preparing the horizontal format trading and profit and loss account before drawing up the vertical format, until you are sure you understand how to double enter directly into the vertical format.

The trading and profit and loss account of B Swift, in the vertical format, is shown below:

B Swift
Trading and Profit and Loss Account for the year ended 31 December 2005

	£	£
Sales		3,850
Less Cost of goods sold		
Purchases	2,900	
less Closing stock	300	
		2,600
Gross profit		1,250
Less Expenses		
Rent	240	
Lighting	150	
General expenses	60	
		450
Net profit		800

8.9 The balances still in our books

Taking Exhibit 8.4, but including the adjustment for closing stock of £300, we can now see which balances still exist. We can do this by drawing up a trial balance as it would appear once the trading and profit and loss account has been completed. We will show it as Exhibit 8.6.

The following accounts have been closed in this process:

Sales Purchases	transferred to trading account
Rent Lighting General expenses	transferred to profit and loss account
Drawings	transferred to capital account

The balances still in our books

Exhibit 8.6

B Swift **Trial Balance as on 31 December 2005** (after Trading and Profit and Loss Accounts completed)		
	Dr	*Cr*
	£	£
Fixtures and fittings	500	
Debtors	680	
Creditors		910
Stock	300	
Bank	1,510	
Cash	20	
Capital		2,100
	3,010	3,010

The one account that was not in the original trial balance was the stock account. It was not brought into our books until the trading account was prepared. These balances will be used by us when we look at the balance sheets.

New terms

Cost of goods sold (p. 73): Calculated as follows: Opening stock plus Purchases during the period less the value of the stock at the end of the period (closing stock).

Gross loss (p. 74): When the cost of goods sold exceeds sales, then the business has incurred a gross loss.

Gross profit (p. 73): Found by deducting cost of goods sold from sales.

Net profit (p. 73): Gross profit less expenses.

Profit and loss account (p. 73): Account in which net profit is calculated.

Trading account (p. 73): Account in which gross profit is calculated.

Trading and profit and loss account (p. 72): Combined account in which both gross and net profits are calculated.

EXERCISES

***Note**: All answers should show the vertical layout of the trading and profit and loss accounts.*

8.1 From the following details of I Simpson, draw up her trading and profit and loss account using the vertical style for the year ended 31 December 2008, this being her first year of trading:

Year to 31 December 2008	£
Purchases	24,190
Sales	38,220
Rent	4,170
Wages and salaries	5,390
Postage and stationery	840
Electricity expenses	710
General expenses	370

Note: At 31 December 2008, the stock was valued (at cost) at £4,310.

8.2X From the following details of C Newman, draw up his trading and profit and loss account using the vertical style for his first year of trading for the year ended 31 December 2009.

Year to 31 December 2009:	£
Rent	4,990
Motor expenses	2,370
Sundry expenses	410
Travel expenses	600
Office expenses	720
Sales	57,090
Purchases	42,910

Note: Stock at 31 December 2009 amounted in value to £8,220.

8.3 From the following trial balance of C Worth, who has been trading for one year, you are required to draw up a trading and profit and loss account for the year ended 30 June 2004. A balance sheet is not required.

Trial Balance as at 30 June 2004		
	Dr	*Cr*
	£	£
Sales		28,794
Purchases	23,803	
Rent and rates	854	
Lighting expenses	422	
Salaries and wages	3,164	
Insurance	105	
Shop buildings	50,000	
Shop fixtures	1,000	
Debtors	3,166	
Trade expenses	506	
Creditors		1,206
Cash at bank	3,847	
Drawings	2,400	
Motor vans	5,500	
Motor running expenses	1,133	
Capital		65,900
	95,900	95,900

Stock at 30 June 2004 was £4,166.
(Keep your answer – it will be used later in Exercise 9.1.)

8.4X From the following trial balance of F Chaplin, draw up a trading and profit and loss account for the year ended 31 December 2008. A balance sheet is not required. She has been in business for one year only.

Trial Balance as at 31 December 2008		
	Dr	*Cr*
	£	£
General expenses	210	
Rent and rates	400	
Motor expenses	735	
Salaries	3,560	
Insurance	392	
Purchases	18,385	
Sales		26,815
Motor vehicle	2,800	
Creditors		5,160
Debtors	4,090	
Premises	20,000	
Cash at bank	1,375	
Cash in hand	25	
Capital		24,347
Drawings	4,350	
	56,322	56,322

Stock at 31 December 2008 was £4,960.
(Keep your answer – it will be used later in Exercise 9.2X.)

8.5 Mrs P Stewart commenced trading as a card and gift shop with a capital of £6,855 on 1 April 2007. At the end of her first year's trading on 31 March 2008, she was able to identify from her accounting records that she had received £24,765 sales in the year. These sales had cost her £13,545 to purchase, and she had £2,345 cards and gifts, at cost, in stock on 31 March 2008. In the year she had also spent £2,100 on staff wages, and drawn personal cash of £5,500. Other overhead costs incurred were:

	£
Rent and rates	1,580
Electricity	565
Motor expenses	845
Insurance	345
General expenses	245

On 31 March 2008, Mrs P Stewart had cash in hand of £135, a bank balance of £2,675, and owed £3,285 to creditors. Mrs Stewart's business owned a car, which had a value of £5,875 at 31 March 2008. She had also bought shelving and fixtures and fittings in the year to the value of £1,495.

You are required to draw up the trading and profit and loss account for the first year's trading.

(*Exam hint*: Before you attempt to draw up the trading and profit and loss account, it would be a good idea to extract the trial balance at 31 March 2008 from the information given.) The closing stock figure should be shown as a note at the foot of the trial balance.
(Keep your answer – it will be used later in Exercise 9.3.)

8.6X Miss R Burgess has just completed her first year of trading for the year ended 30 April 2008, as a manufacturer of model railway accessories. Her initial capital was £9,025. At 30 April 2008, she was owed £5,600 by customers, and owed £4,825 to suppliers. She calculated that she had stock in hand, at cost, at the year end of £7,670, and her bank account was overdrawn by £2,560. The petty cash float held £25 at 30 April 2008.

From her records, she calculated her income and expenditure for the year ended 30 April 2008 as:

	£
Sales	56,540
Purchases	34,315
Rent of factory	6,000
Drawings	10,000
Motor expenses	1,735
Insurance	345
General expenses	780
Salaries	7,550

Miss R Burgess had plant and equipment to the value of £3,750 and a van worth £2,850 at 30 April 2008.

You are required to draw up the trading and profit and loss account for the first year's trading.
(Keep your answer – it will be used later in Exercise 9.5X.)

8.7X A business has been trading for one year. Extract a trading and profit and loss account for the year ended 30 June 2004 for M Kent. The trial balance as at 30 June 2004 is as follows:

M Kent
Trial Balance as at 30 June 2004

	Dr	*Cr*
	£	£
Rent and rates	1,560	
Insurance	305	
Lighting expenses	516	
Motor expenses	1,960	
Salaries and wages	4,850	
Sales		35,600
Purchases	30,970	
Trade expense	806	
Motor van	3,500	
Creditors		3,250
Debtors	6,810	
Shop fixtures	3,960	
Shop buildings	28,000	
Cash at bank	1,134	
Drawings	6,278	
Capital		51,799
	90,649	90,649

Stock at 30 June 2004 was £9,960.
(Keep your answer – it will be used later in Exercise 9.6X.)

CHAPTER 9

The balance sheet

Learning objectives

After you have studied this chapter you should be able to:

- **draw up a balance sheet from information given in a trial balance**
- **understand that balance sheets are not part of the double entry system**
- **appreciate the need for showing balances under the headings 'fixed assets', 'current assets', 'current liabilities' and 'capital'.**

9.1 Contents of the balance sheet

You saw in Chapter 2 that a balance sheet contains details of assets, capital and liabilities. These details have to be found in our records and then written out as a balance sheet.

It is easy to find these details. They consist of all the balances remaining in our records once the trading and profit and loss account for the period has been completed. All balances remaining have to be assets, capital or liabilities. All the other balances should have been closed off when the trading and profit and loss account was completed.

9.2 Drawing up a balance sheet

Let us look at Exhibit 9.1, the trial balance of B Swift (from Exhibit 8.6) as on 31 December 2005 after the trading and profit and loss account had been prepared.

EXHIBIT 9.1

B Swift **Trial Balance as on 31 December 2005** (after Trading and Profit and Loss Accounts completed)		
	Dr	*Cr*
	£	£
Fixtures and fittings	500	
Debtors	680	
Creditors		910
Stock	300	
Bank	1,510	
Cash	20	
Capital		2,100
	3,010	3,010

We can now draw up a balance sheet as at 31 December 2005, and this is shown in Exhibit 9.2. The layout is discussed further in Section 9.4.

EXHIBIT 9.2

B Swift
Balance Sheet as at 31 December 2005

	£	£	£
Fixed assets			
Fixtures and fittings			500
Current assets			
Stock	300		
Debtors	680		
Cash at bank	1,510		
Cash in hand	20		
		2,510	
less Current liabilities			
Creditors		910	
Net current assets			1,600
Long-term liabilities			
Long-term loan			–
Net assets			2,100
Financed by:			
Capital account			
Cash introduced			2,000
Add net profit for the year			*800*
			2,800
Less Drawings			700
			2,100

9.3 No double entry in balance sheets

It might seem very strange to you to learn that balance sheets are *not* part of the double entry system.

When we draw up accounts such as the cash account, rent account, sales account, trading and profit and loss account, and so on, we are writing up part of the double entry system. We make entries on the debit and credit sides of these accounts.

In drawing up a balance sheet, we do not enter anything in the various accounts. We do not actually transfer the fixtures balance or the stock balance, or any of the others, to the balance sheet. All that we do is to list the balances for assets, capital and liabilities so as to form a balance sheet. This means that none of these accounts have been closed off. *Nothing is entered in the accounts.*

When the next accounting period starts, these accounts are still open containing balances. As a result of business transactions, entries are then made in these accounts to add to, or deduct from, the amounts shown in the accounts using normal double entry.

If you see the word 'account' you will know that it is part of the double entry system, and it will include debit and credit entries. If the word 'account' cannot be used, it is not part of double entry. For instance:

Trial balance:	A list of balances to see whether the records are correct.
Balance sheet:	A list of balances arranged according to whether they are assets, capital or liabilities.

9.4 Balance sheet layout

You would not expect to go into a department store and see goods for sale all mixed up and not laid out properly; you would expect that the goods would be displayed so that you could easily find them. Similarly, in balance sheets we do not want the items shown in a random order; we want them displayed so that useful information can easily be seen.

For users of the accounts, such as bank managers, accountants and investors, conformity of layout is needed in order to make a comparison of balance sheets easier. The standard layout is shown in Exhibit 9.2 and examined in more detail below.

Assets

The first section is Assets: Assets are shown under two headings, namely fixed assets and current assets.

Assets are called **fixed assets** when they:

- are of long life
- are to be used in the business, and
- were not bought only for the purposes of resale.

Examples are buildings, machinery, motor vehicles, fixtures and fittings. Fixed assets are listed starting with those with the longest life expectancy down to those with the shortest life expectancy. For instance:

Fixed Assets	
(i)	Land and buildings
(ii)	Fixtures and fittings
(iii)	Machinery
(iv)	Motor vehicles

Current assets are cash in hand, cash at bank, items held for resale at a profit, or items that have a short life. These are listed starting with the asset furthest away from being turned into cash, finishing with cash itself. For instance:

Current Assets	
(i)	Stock
(ii)	Debtors
(iii)	Cash at bank
(iv)	Cash in hand

Liabilities

Liabilities are categorised under two headings:

1 **Current liabilities**. Current liabilities are liabilities due for repayment in the short term. Examples of current liabilities are bank overdrafts, trade creditors and sundry creditors. Current liabilities are deducted from current assets, as shown in Exhibit 9.2, to give **net current assets** (or net current liabilities, also known as working capital).

2 **Long-term liabilities**. Long-term liabilities are liabilities not due for repayment in the short term. Examples of long-term liabilities are loans and mortgages. Long-term liabilities are deducted after the net current assets/ liabilities figure in the balance sheet, also shown in Exhibit 9.2.

Capital account

This is the proprietor's or partner's account with the business. It will start with the balance brought forward from the previous accounting period, to which is added any personal cash introduced into the business and the net profit made by the business in this accounting period. Deducted from the capital account will be amounts drawn from the business and any loss made by the business. The final balance on the capital account should equal the net assets or net liabilities figure – and hence the balance sheet balances. Exhibit 9.3 gives the standard format.

Exhibit 9.3

Capital Account

		£	£
Balance b/d			X
Add	Cash introduced		X
	Net profit for the period		X
			X
Less	Drawings	X	
	Net loss for the period	X	
			X
			X

It is important to note that the balance sheet shows the position of the business at one point in time: the balance sheet date. It is like taking a snapshot of the business at one moment in time. The trading and profit and loss account shows the profit/loss of that business for a period of time (normally a year).

New terms

Current assets (p. 89): Assets consisting of cash, goods for resale, or items having a short life.

Current liabilities (p. 90): Liabilities to be paid for in the near future.

Fixed assets (p. 89): Assets bought which have a long life and are to be used in the business.

Long-term liabilities (p. 90): Liabilities not having to be paid for in the near future.

Net current assets (p. 90): The value of current assets less that of current liabilities. Also known as 'working capital'.

EXERCISES

9.1 Complete exercise 8.3 by drawing up a balance sheet as at 30 June 2004 for C Worth.

9.2X Complete exercise 8.4X by drawing up a balance sheet as at 31 December 2008 for F Chaplin.

9.3 Complete exercise 8.5 by drawing up a balance sheet as at 31 March 2008 for Mrs P Stewart.

9.4 Miss V Holland had been trading for a number of years as a cheese retailer, making up accounts each year to 30 June. As at 30 June 2008 she was able to extract the following information from her accounting records and has asked you as her accountant to draw up the balance sheet at that date:

(*a*) She owed amounts to businesses that had supplied her with cheese, totalling £4,565
(*b*) She was owed £2,375 by a customer who bought goods on credit
(*c*) She had cash in hand of £150
(*d*) Her bank account was overdrawn by £1,785
(*e*) She had stock of cheese unsold totalling £1,465
(*f*) She had a van that was used for deliveries and that was valued at £3,400 on 30 June 2008
(*g*) She had equipment valued at £2,885 at the year end
(*h*) She had introduced £2,000 of her own money in the year, when she was nearing her overdraft limit
(*i*) The business made a net profit of £2,525 in the year to 30 June 2008
(*j*) Miss V Holland drew £50 each week, for the whole year, and had no other drawings from the business
(*k*) The business had a loan from V Holland's mother for £2,000. This was not due to be repaid until the year 2012.

9.5X Complete exercise 8.6X by drawing up a balance sheet as at 30 April 2008 for Miss R Burgess.

9.6X Complete exercise 8.7X by drawing up a balance sheet as at 30 June 2004 for M Kent.

CHAPTER 10

Further considerations regarding final accounts

Learning objectives

After you have studied this chapter you should be able to:

- record returns inwards and returns outwards in the final accounts
- understand that carriage inwards on goods is treated as being part of the cost of the goods
- realise that carriage outwards is an expense to be entered in the profit and loss account
- adjust the final accounts properly for both the opening and closing stocks of the period
- appreciate that costs of putting goods into a saleable condition should be charged to the trading account in a merchandising firm
- see the accountant's job as being that of a communicator of information.

10.1 Vertical format of trading and profit and loss account

In Chapter 8 we introduced the vertical format of the trading and profit and loss account. From now on, you should get used to the vertical format as this is the format we will use from this point on, and you will also come across it in your exams. Exhibit 10.1 shows the standard vertical format with some sample figures.

EXHIBIT 10.1

C Raines
Trading and Profit and Loss Account
for the year ended 31 December 2006

	£	£
Sales		6,000
Less Cost of goods sold		
Opening stock	–	
Purchases	4,000	
Carriage inwards	350	
	4,350	
Less Closing stock	650	
		3,700
Gross Profit		2,300
Less Expenses		
Carriage outwards	280	
Other expenses	220	
		500
Net profit		1,800

Three new concepts, shown in Exhibit 10.1, now need further consideration:

- Carriage inwards
- Carriage outwards
- Opening stock.

10.2 Carriage inwards

Carriage (the cost of transport of goods) into a firm is called **carriage inwards.**

When you buy goods, the cost of carriage inwards may either be included as part of the price, or else the firm may have to pay separately for it. Suppose you were buying two sets of exactly the same goods. One supplier might sell them to you for £100, and he would deliver the goods and not send you a bill for carriage. Another supplier might sell the goods to you for £95, but you would have to pay £5 to a haulage firm for carriage inwards, i.e. a total cost of £100.

To keep the cost of buying goods shown on the same basis, carriage inwards is always added to the purchases cost in the trading account.

10.3 Carriage outwards

Carriage from a firm out to its customers is called **carriage outwards**. This is always treated as an expense to be transferred to the debit of the profit and loss account.

Exhibit 10.2 shows extracts from the trial balance from which the trading and profit and loss account for the year ended 31 December 2006 in Exhibit 10.1 has been drawn up. The closing stock on 31 December 2006 was £650.

EXHIBIT 10.2

C Raines Trial Balance as at 31 December 2006 (extracts)		
	Dr	*Cr*
	£	£
Sales		6,000
Purchases	4,000	
Carriage inwards	350	
Carriage outwards	280	
Other expenses	220	

10.4 The second year of a business

Following on from Exhibit 9.2 in the last chapter, we assume that B Swift carries on his business for another year. He then extracts a trial balance as on 31 December 2006 as shown as Exhibit 10.3. Closing stock as at that date was valued at £550.

EXHIBIT 10.3

B Swift Trial Balance as at 31 December 2006		
	Dr	*Cr*
	£	£
Sales		6,700
Purchases	4,260	
Lighting	190	
Rent	240	
Wages: store assistant	520	
General expenses	70	
Carriage outwards	110	
Shop premises	2,000	
Fixtures and fittings	750	
Debtors	1,200	
Creditors		900
Bank	120	
Cash	40	
Loan from J Marsh		1,000
Drawings	900	
Capital		2,100
Stock (at 1 January 2005)	300	
	10,700	10,700

Adjustments needed for stock

Previously we have prepared the accounts for new businesses only. They started without stock and therefore had closing stock only. When we prepare the trading and profit and loss account for the second year, we can now see the difference.

Looking at Exhibits 9.1 and 10.3 for B Swift, we can see the stock figures needed for the trading accounts:

Trading Account for period →	Year to 31 December 2005	Year to 31 December 2006
Opening stock 1.1.2005	None	
Closing stock 31.12.2005	£300	
Opening stock 1.1.2006		£300
Closing stock 31.12.2006		£550

This means that calculations for the first year of trading, to 31 December 2005, had only one stock figure included in them. This was the closing stock. For the second year of trading, to 31 December 2006, both opening and closing stock figures will be in the calculations.

The stock shown in the trial balance given in Exhibit 10.3 is that brought forward from the previous year on 31 December 2005; it is, therefore, the opening stock of 2006. The closing stock at 31 December 2006 can only be found by stocktaking. Assume it amounts at cost to be £550.

Let us first of all calculate the cost of goods sold for 2006, thus:

	£
Stock of goods at start of year	300
Add Purchases	4,260
Total goods available for sale	4,560
Less What remains at the end of the year:	
i.e. stock of goods at end of year	550
Therefore cost of goods that have been sold =	4,010

The gross profit can now be found, taking into consideration the effect the closing stock has on the gross profit. As stated previously:

Gross profit = Sales – Cost of goods sold
= 6,700 – 4,010
Gross Profit = £2,690

Now the trading and profit and loss accounts can be drawn up using double entry (*see* Exhibit 10.4.). For purposes of illustration, the stock account will be shown.

Exhibit 10.4

Stock Account

Dr					*Cr*
2005		£	2006		£
Dec 31	Balance b/d	300	Dec 31	Trading a/c	300
2006					
Dec 31	Trading a/c	550			

B Swift

Trading and Profit and Loss Account for the year ended 31 December 2006

	£		£
Opening stock	300	Sales	6,700
Purchases	4,260	Closing stock	550
Gross profit c/d	2,690		
	7,250		7,250
Wages	520	Gross profit b/d	2,690
Carriage outwards	110		
Lighting expenses	190		
Rent	240		
General expenses	70		
Net profit	1,560		
	2,690		2,690

The stock at 31 December 2006 is £550 and had not been previously shown in the accounts. It has now been entered using double entry:

Debit: stock account £550
Credit: trading account £550.

Display of cost of goods sold in the trading account

Accountants like to see a figure for cost of goods sold actually shown in the trading account. This is because they use it for various calculations to be described later in your course.

Exhibit 10.4 shows a trading account where the normal double entry is shown. However, although the stock account would stay exactly as in Exhibit 10.4, accountants would prefer to show the trading account part as in Exhibit 10.5. The figure of gross profit stays the same; the only difference is in display.

Exhibit 10.5

B Swift Trading and Profit and Loss Account for the Year Ended 31 December 2006		
	£	£
Sales		6,700
Less Cost of goods sold		
Opening stock	300	
Add Purchases	4,260	
	4,560	
Less Closing stock	550	
		4,010
Gross profit		2,690
Less Expenses		
Wages	520	
Carriage outwards	110	
Lighting expenses	190	
Rent	240	
General expenses	70	
		1,130
Net profit		1,560

The balances remaining in the books, including the new balance on the stock account, are now drawn up in the form of a balance sheet (*see* Exhibit 10.6).

EXHIBIT 10.6

B Swift Balance Sheet as at 31 December 2006			
	£	£	£
Fixed assets			
Shop premises			2,000
Fixtures and fittings			750
			2,750
Current assets			
Stock	550		
Debtors	1,200		
Cash at bank	120		
Cash in hand	40		
		1,910	
Current liabilities			
Creditors		900	
Net current assets			1,010
			3,760
Long-term liabilities			
Loan from J Marsh			1,000
Net assets			2,760
Financed by			
Capital account			
Balance at 1 January 2006			2,100
Add Net profit for the year			1,210
			3,310
Less Drawings			550
			2,760

10.5 Final accounts

The term **final accounts** is used to describe the final figures of a period of account, and they comprise the trading and profit and loss account (*see* Exhibit 10.5), the balance sheet (*see* Exhibit 10.6).

10.6 Other expenses in the trading account

The cost of putting goods into a saleable condition should be charged in the trading account. In the case of a trader, these are relatively few. An example of this type of expense is a trader who sells clocks packed in boxes. To do this he:

(i) buys clocks from one supplier
(ii) buys boxes from a different supplier
(iii) pays wages to a person to pack the clocks into the boxes.

Expenses (i) (ii) and (iii) will be transferred to the trading account when calculating gross profit.

Note that the wages of a person selling the clocks will *not* be transferred to the trading account. Instead, these wages will be transferred to the profit and loss account.

10.7 Treatment of returns inwards and returns outwards in final accounts

When a business buys and sells goods, it is very probable that some of the goods will turn out to be either faulty or unsuitable. A large number of firms will return such goods to their suppliers (returns outwards), and will have goods returned to them by their customers (returns inwards). When the gross profit is calculated, these returns will have to come into the calculations.

Treatment of returns

In the trading account:

- returns inwards should be deducted from 'Sales'
- returns outwards should be deducted from 'Purchases'.

In Exhibit 10.5, if sales had been £7,200, returns inwards £500, purchases £4,460 and returns outwards £200, then the trading account would have appeared as shown in Exhibit 10.7 (using the vertical style of presentation).

EXHIBIT 10.7

B Swift Trading Account for the year ended 31 December 2006			
	£	£	£
Sales		7,200	
Less Returns inwards		500	6,700
Less Cost of goods sold:			
Opening stock		300	
Add Purchases	4,460		
Less Returns outwards	200	4,260	
		4,560	
Less Closing stock		550	4,010
Gross profit			2,690

10.8 Losses

So far, we have looked at the situation in which both a gross profit and a net profit have been made by a business. This will not always be the case in every business. For all kinds of reasons, such as poor trading conditions, bad management, or unexpected increases in expenses, the business may trade at a loss for a given period.

We will look at two cases, A Barnes, who made a gross profit but a net loss for the year, and K Jackson, who made both a gross loss and a net loss. The details for the trading and profit and loss accounts for the year ended 31 December 2005 for Barnes and Jackson are as follows:

	A Barnes	*K Jackson*
	£	£
Opening stock 1 January 2005	3,500	9,200
Sales	21,000	33,000
Purchases	15,000	29,800
Closing stock 31 December 2005	2,200	4,800
Other expenses	6,300	3,900

We can now draw up the trading and profit and loss accounts for each business. In Exhibits 10.8 and 10.9 we will show the trading and profit and loss account for A Barnes using both the horizontal and vertical styles respectively, whilst the same is shown for K Jackson in Exhibits 10.10 and 10.11.

Exhibit 10.8

A Barnes
Trading and Profit and Loss Account
for the year ended 31 December 2005 (horizontal style)

	£		£
Opening stock	3,500	Sales	21,000
Add Purchases	15,000		
	18,500		
Less Closing stock	2,200		
Cost of goods sold	16,300		
Gross profit c/d	4,700		
	21,000		21,000
Other expenses	6,300	Gross profit b/d	4,700
		Net loss	1,600
	6,300		6,300

For A Barnes, you can see that there was a gross profit of £4,700 but expenses of £6,300 were greater than that, and so the final result is a net loss.

Exhibit 10.9

A Barnes
Trading and Profit and Loss Account
for the year ended 31 December 2005 (vertical style)

	£	£
Sales		21,000
Less Cost of goods sold		
Opening stock	3,500	
Add Purchases	15,000	
	18,500	
Less Closing stock	2,200	16,300
Gross profit		4,700
Less Other expenses		6,300
Net loss		1,600

EXHIBIT 10.10

K Jackson
Trading and Profit and Loss Account
for the year ended 31 December 2005 (horizontal style)

	£		£
Opening stock	9,200	Sales	33,000
Add Purchases	29,800	Gross loss c/d	1,200
	39,000		
Less Closing stock	4,800		
Cost of goods sold	34,200		34,200
Gross loss b/d	1,200	Net loss	5,100
Other expenses	3,900		
	5,100		5,100

EXHIBIT 10.11

K Jackson
Trading and Profit and Loss Account
for the year ended 31 December 2005 (vertical style)

	£	£
Sales		33,000
Less Cost of goods sold		
Opening stock	9,200	
Add Purchases	29,800	
	39,000	
Less Closing stock	4,800	34,200
Gross loss		1,200
Add Other expenses		3,900
Net loss		5,100

The double entry for the gross loss has already been shown because it has been shown as a credit in the trading account and a debit in the profit and loss account. Double entry for the net loss (for both Barnes and Jackson) is:

Debit: capital account
Credit: profit and loss account.

10.9 The accountant as a communicator

Quite often the impression is given that all that the accountant does is to produce figures arranged in various ways. Naturally, such forms of computation take up a great deal of an accountant's time, but what then takes up the rest of his or her time relates to communication of these figures to other people.

The figures produced could be given to several people, all of whom are very knowledgeable about accounting. The accountant could, in such an instance, present the figures in a normal accounting way, knowing full well that the recipients of the information will understand it.

On the other hand, the accounting figures may well be needed by people who have little or no knowledge of accounting. In such a case, a normal accounting statement would be of no use to them; they would not understand it. Accordingly, the accountant might set out the figures in a completely different way to try to make it easy for them to grasp. For instance, instead of preparing a normal trading and profit and loss account he or she might show the information in a more descriptive report, as follows:

	£	£
In the year ended 31 December 2005 you sold goods for		50,000
Now how much had those goods cost you to buy?		
At the start of the year you had stock costing	6,000	
+ You bought some more goods in the year costing	28,000	
So altogether you had goods available to sell of	34,000	
– At the end of the year you had stock of goods unsold of	3,000	
So the goods you sold in the year had cost you	31,000	
Let us deduct this from what you had sold the goods for		31,000
This means that you had made a profit on buying and selling goods, before any other expenses had been paid, amounting to (We call this sort of profit the Gross Profit)		19,000
But you suffered other expenses such as wages, rent, lighting and so on, and during the year the amount of these expenses, not including anything taken for yourself, amounted to		9,000
So for this year your sales value exceeded all the costs involved in running the business by (We call this sort of profit Net Profit)		10,000

If an accountant cannot arrange the figures to make them meaningful to the recipient, then he or she is failing in the task. The accountant's job is not just to produce figures for likeminded colleagues to look at, but it is also to communicate these results to other people. Very often, an accountant will have to talk to people to explain the figures, or send a letter or write a report concerning them. Exactly what sort of accounting information is required will also have to be determined. This means that if accounting examinations consist simply of computational-type questions, then they will not test the ability of the candidate to communicate in any other way than by writing down accounting figures. In recent years, more attention has been paid by examining boards to these other aspects of an accountant's work.

Note: Treatment of discounts allowed and discounts received in final accounts will be dealt with in Chapter 29. Accruals, prepayments and other adjustments will be dealt with after we have covered the double entry of these items in Part 3 of the book.

New terms

Carriage inwards (p. 94): Cost of transport of goods into a business.

Carriage outwards (p. 94): Cost of transport of goods to the customers of a business.

Final accounts (p. 99): At the end of the accounting period, a business usually prepares its final accounts, which includes the trading and profit and loss account and balance sheet.

EXERCISES

10.1 From the following details, draw up in vertical format the trading account for the year ended 31 December 2007.

		£
Carriage inwards		670
Sales		38,742
Purchases		26,409
Stocks of goods:	1 January 2007	6,924
	31 December 2007	7,489

10.2X The following details for the year ended 31 March 2008 are available. Draw up the trading account for that year, in vertical format.

		£
Stocks:	31 March 2007	16,492
	31 March 2008	18,504
Purchases		36,905
Carriage inwards		1,122
Sales		54,600

10.3 Draw up the trading and profit and loss account for the year ended 31 December 2006, in respect of T Mann, from the following details:

		£
Returns inwards		490
Returns outwards		560
Purchases		31,000
Sales		52,790
Stocks of goods:	1 January 2006	5,690
	31 December 2006	4,230
Carriage inwards		1,700
Salaries and wages		5,010
Rent		1,460
Motor expenses		3,120
General expenses		420
Carriage outwards		790

10.4X A trading and profit and loss account for the year ended 31 December 2008 is to be drawn up for K Lake from the following:

		£
Carriage outwards		490
Carriage inwards		210
Returns inwards		1,500
Returns outwards		1,580
Salaries and wages		6,250
Rent		1,750
Sundry expenses		360
Sales		99,500
Purchases		64,570
Stocks of goods:	1 January 2008	18,280
	31 December 2008	17,360

10.5 From the following trial balance of S Makin, draw up a trading and profit and loss account for the year ended 30 September 2006, and balance sheet as at that date.

	Dr	*Cr*
	£	£
Stock 1 October 2005	2,368	
Carriage outwards	200	
Carriage inwards	310	
Returns inwards	205	
Returns outwards		322
Purchases	11,874	
Sales		18,600
Salaries and wages	3,862	
Rent and rates	304	
Insurance	78	
Motor expenses	664	
Office expenses	216	
Lighting and heating expenses	166	
General expenses	314	
Premises	15,000	
Motor vehicles	1,800	
Fixtures and fittings	350	
Debtors	3,896	
Creditors		1,731
Cash at bank	482	
Drawings	1,200	
Capital		22,636
	43,289	43,289

Stock at 30 September 2006 was £2,946.

10.6X The following trial balance was extracted from the books of B Jackson on 30 April 2008. From it, and the note, prepare Jackson's trading and profit and loss account for the year ended 30 April 2008, and a balance sheet as at that date, in vertical format.

	Dr	*Cr*
	£	£
Sales		18,600
Purchases	11,556	
Stock 1 May 2007	3,776	
Carriage outwards	326	
Carriage inwards	234	
Salaries and wages	2,447	
Motor expenses	664	
Rent	456	
Rates	120	
Sundry expenses	1,202	
Motor vehicles	2,400	
Fixtures and fittings	600	
Debtors	4,577	
Creditors		3,045
Cash at bank	3,876	
Cash in hand	120	
Drawings	2,135	
Capital		12,844
	34,489	34,489

Stock at 30 April 2008 was £4,998.

10.7X G Bowyer manufactures sportswear, and for the year ended 31 October 2008 his sales were £76,540. He also paid carriage outwards of £4,275 to transport the sportswear to customers.

The materials purchased in the year amounted to £33,325, with an additional amount paid for carriage inwards of £2,715. Bowyer had stock of £8,255 on 1 November 2007, and of £7,985 on 31 October 2008. He was owed £6,285 by customers, and owed £4,825 to suppliers on 31 October 2008. His bank balance was overdrawn by £3,335, and he had equipment valued at £11,125 and a van valued at £2,225 on that date.

His overheads for the year ended 31 October 2008 were:

	£
Rent and rates	6,000
Motor expenses	3,110
Salaries	7,450
Telephone	495
Insurance	500
General expenses	750

He drew £3,675 in the year to 31 October 2008 and had a balance brought forward on his capital account on 1 November 2007 of £5,485.

You are required to draw up, in the vertical format, the trading and profit and loss account for the year ended 31 October 2008, and a balance sheet for G Bowyer at that date.

10.8 The following is the trial balance of J Smailes as at 31 March 2007. Draw up a set of final accounts for the year ended 31 March 2007 in vertical format.

	Dr	*Cr*
	£	£
Stock 1 April 2006	18,160	
Sales		92,340
Purchases	69,185	
Carriage inwards	420	
Carriage outwards	1,570	
Returns outwards		640
Wages and salaries	10,240	
Rent and rates	3,015	
Communication expenses	624	
Commissions payable	216	
Insurance	405	
Sundry expenses	318	
Buildings	20,000	
Debtors	14,320	
Creditors		8,160
Fixtures	2,850	
Cash at bank	2,970	
Cash in hand	115	
Loan from K Ball		10,000
Drawings	7,620	
Capital		40,888
	152,028	152,028

Stock at 31 March 2007 was £22,390.

10.9X L Stokes drew up the following trial balance as at 30 September 2008. You are required to draft trading and profit and loss accounts for the year to 30 September 2008 and a balance sheet as at that date in vertical format.

	Dr	*Cr*
	£	£
Loan from P Owens		5,000
Capital		25,955
Drawings	8,420	
Cash at bank	3,115	
Cash in hand	295	
Debtors	12,300	
Creditors		9,370
Stock 30 September 2007	23,910	
Motor van	4,100	
Office equipment	6,250	
Sales		130,900
Purchases	92,100	
Returns inwards	550	
Carriage inwards	215	
Returns outwards		307
Carriage outwards	309	
Motor expenses	1,630	
Rent	2,970	
Telephone charges	405	
Wages and salaries	12,810	
Insurance	492	
Office expenses	1,377	
Sundry expenses	284	
	171,532	171,532

Stock at 30 September 2008 was £27,475.

CHAPTER 11

Accounting principles, concepts and conventions

Learning objectives

After you have studied this chapter you should be able to:

- appreciate the assumptions that are made when recording accounting data
- realise that one set of accounts is used for several different purposes
- understand what is meant by objectivity and subjectivity
- know the basic concepts of accounting
- see that the further overriding conventions of materiality, prudence, consistency and substance over form affect the recording and adjustment of data.

11.1 Introduction

So far, we have been concerned with recording transactions in the books. While we have been making such records, we have been following certain rules. These rules are known as accounting 'concepts' and 'conventions'.

An owner of a business may not be the only person to see the final accounts. He or she may have to show them to the bank manager if they want to borrow money, or to a potential buyer if they are looking at selling the business. Under the United Kingdom's self-assessment process, accounts are used as a basis for completing the annual self-assessment tax return, and may be required by the Inland Revenue if enquiries are made into the business's affairs.

11.2 One set of final accounts for all purposes

If it had always been the custom to draft different kinds of final accounts for different purposes, so that one type was given to a banker, another type to someone wishing to buy the business, etc., then Accounting would be different from what it is today. However, copies of the same set of final accounts are given to all the different people.

This means that a banker, a prospective buyer of the business, an owner and all the other people with an interest see the same trading and profit and loss account and balance sheet. Interests of each party are different and different kinds of information are needed from that wanted by the others. For instance, a bank manager would really like to know how much the assets would sell for if the firm ceased trading, he could then see what the possibility would be of the bank obtaining repayment of its loan. Other people would also like to see the information in the way that is most useful to them. Yet, normally, only one sort of final accounts is available for these different people. So trading and profit and loss accounts and balance sheets have to be used for different needs; and to be of any use, the different parties have to agree to the way in which they are drawn up.

Assume that you are in a class of students and that you have the problem of valuing your assets, which consist of ten textbooks. The first value you decide is that of how much you could sell them for. Your own guess is £30, but the other members of the class may give figures from £15 to £50.

Suppose that you now decide to put a value on their use to you. You may well think that the use of these books will enable you to pass your examinations and so you will get a good job. Another person may have the opposite idea concerning the use of the books, and the use-value placed on the books by others in the class is likely to be quite different.

Finally, you decide to value them by reference to cost. You take out of your pocket the bills for the books, which show that you paid a total of £60 for the books. If the rest of the class do not think that you have altered the bills, then they also can all agree that the value expressed as cost is £60. As this is the only value that you can all agree to, then each of you decides to use the idea of showing the value of his asset of books at the cost price.

11.3 Objectivity and subjectivity

The use of a method that all can agree to, instead of everyone using their own method, is said to be **objective**. To use cost for the value of an asset is, therefore, a way to be objective. When you are **subjective**, this means that you want to use your own method, even though no one else may agree to it.

Objectivity – using methods that all people can agree to – is what financial accounting ensures. The rules that state how the transactions are recorded are usually known as accounting 'concepts'.

11.4 Basic accounting concepts

Over the years, accounting systems have developed more for practical reasons than for theoretical ones. Consequently, several basic procedures have evolved that form the basic rules of accounting. As mentioned above, these are often referred to as accounting concepts.

A concept may be defined as an idea. Thus, an accounting concept is an assumption that underlies the preparation of the financial statements of the organisation. There are several accounting concepts that are followed when preparing the financial accounts of a business – and all of which you may be required to know when taking an examination. These are as set out next.

The cost concept

The need for this has already been described. It means that assets are normally shown at cost price and this is the basis for valuation of the asset.

The money measurement concept

Accounting is concerned only where:

- facts can be measured in money, and
- most people will agree to the money value of the transaction.

This means that accounting can never tell you everything about a business. For example, accounting does not show the following:

(i) whether the firm has good or bad managers
(ii) that there are serious problems with the workforce
(iii) that a rival product is about to take away many of its best customers
(iv) that the government is about to pass a law that will cost the business extra expense in future.

The reason that (i) to (iv) above, or similar items, are not recorded is that it would be impossible to work out a money value for them that most people would agree to. Thus, accounting can only provide *financial* information about a business.

The going concern concept

Normally, we assume that a business will continue for a long time. Only if the business was going to be sold would we show how much the assets would sell for. This is because we use the cost concept. If businesses were not assumed to be **going concerns**, the cost concept could not be used. Should firms be expected to be sold immediately, then the saleable value of assets would be used instead of cost.

The business entity concept

The items recorded in a firm's books are limited to the transactions that affect the firm as a **business entity**. Suppose that the proprietor of a firm buys a diamond necklace for his wife by using his personal monies. As the money spent was not out of the firm's bank account or cash box, then this item will not be entered in the firm's books.

The only time that personal resources of a proprietor affect the firm's accounting records is when that proprietor brings new capital into the firm or takes drawings out of the firm.

The realisation concept

Normally, profit is said to be earned at the time when:

(i) goods or services are passed to the customer, and
(ii) he then incurs liability for them.

This concept of profit is known as the **realisation concept**. Notice that it is:

(i) *not* when the order is received, and
(ii) *not* when the customer pays for the goods.

The dual aspect concept

This states that there are two aspects of Accounting, one represented by the assets of a business and the other by the claims against them. The concept states that these two aspects are always equal to each other. In other words:

Assets = Capital + Liabilities

Double entry is the name given to the method of recording the transactions for the **dual aspect concept**.

The accrual concept

The **accrual concept** says that net profit is the difference between revenues and expenses, i.e.

Revenues – Expenses = Net Profit

Determining the expenses used up to obtain the revenues is referred to as 'matching' expenses against revenues.

Many people who have not studied Accounting do not understand this concept. They think that receipts of a period, less payments of the period, equal net profit.

You know that expenses consist of the assets used up in a period. You also know that cash paid in a period and expenses of a period are usually different figures. You know further, however, that we have to make adjustments for items such as expenses owing, payments in advance, depreciation and provisions for bad debts etc. Only then can we calculate net profit.

11.5 The assumption of the stability of monetary measures

As we have seen, Accounting uses the cost concept, which states that each asset is normally shown at its cost price. This means that accounting statements can be misleading, because assets will be bought at different times at the prices then ruling, and the figures will be totalled up to show the value of the assets in cost terms.

For instance, suppose that you bought a building 20 years ago for £20,000. You now decide to buy an identical additional building, but the price has risen to £40,000. You buy it, and the buildings account now shows buildings at a figure of £60,000. One building is in the currency of 20 years ago, while the other is at today's currency value. The figure of £60,000 spent out in total is historically correct but cannot be used for much else.

When we look at final accounts, we must understand such problems. There are ways of adjusting accounts to make the figures more useful, but these are not in your syllabus. You will have to study them if you take accounting examinations at an advanced level.

11.6 The conventions of accounting

The concepts of Accounting have become accepted in the business world. The concepts, however, could have been looked at in many ways if nothing had been done to bring about standard methods. Accounting has therefore tried to make certain that similar items are dealt with in similar ways. As a result we have Accounting 'conventions'.

The main conventions may be said to be: **materiality**, **prudence**, and **consistency**. These are described further next.

Materiality

This convention is applied to try to stop you wasting time and effort doing completely unnecessary work. Accounting does not serve a useful purpose if the effort of recording a transaction in a certain way is not worthwhile. As an example, if a box of paperclips was bought, it would be used over a period of time and this cost is gradually used up every time someone uses a paperclip. It is possible to record this as an expense every time it happens, but obviously the price of a box of paperclips is so little that it is not worth recording it in this way. You should not waste your time in the unnecessary recording of trivial items.

The box of paperclips is not a 'material' item, and it would therefore be charged as an expense in the period in which it was bought even though it could last for more than one accounting period. Similarly, the purchase of a cheap metal waste-bin would also be charged as an expense in the period it was bought because it is not a material item, even though it may last 20 years. It would not be worth calculating depreciation on it. A lorry, on the other hand, would be deemed to be a material item. We then calculate the depreciation to be charged in each period, with the cost consumed in each period of its use. Depreciation is dealt with in Chapters 26 and 27.

You can see that small amounts are not material, while larger amounts are material. The question is, at what figure does an item become material? There is no fixed rule for this; firms make all sorts of rules to say what is material and what is not, and there is no law that says what these should be.

What is material and what is not depends upon judgement. A firm may decide that all items under £100 should be treated as expenses in the period in which they were bought, even though they may be in use in the firm for the following ten years. Another firm – especially a large one – may put the limit at £1,000. Different limits may even be set for different types of items. The size and type of firm will also affect the decisions as to what is material, and what is not.

Prudence

Very often, accountants have to use their judgement to decide which figure they will take for an item. Suppose a debt has been owing for quite a long time and no one knows whether it will be paid. Should the accountant be an optimist in thinking that it will be paid, or be more pessimistic?

It is the accountant's duty to see that people get the proper facts about a business. They should make certain that assets are not valued too highly. Similarly, liabilities should not be shown at values too low. Otherwise, people might inadvisedly lend money to a firm, which they would not do so had the proper facts been known.

The accountant should always be on the side of caution, and this is known as 'prudence'. The prudence convention means that, normally, accountants will take the figure that will understate rather than overstate the profit. Thus, they should choose the figure that will cause the capital of the firm to be shown at a lower amount rather than at a higher one. They will also normally make sure that all losses are recorded in the books, but profits should not be anticipated by recording them before they are realised.

Consistency

Even if we do everything already listed under concepts and conventions, there will still be quite a few different ways in which items could be recorded. Each firm should try to choose the methods that give the most reliable picture of the business.

This cannot be done if one method is used in one year and another method in the next year, and so on. Constantly changing the methods would lead to misleading profits being calculated from the accounting records. Therefore the convention of 'consistency' is used. This convention says that when a firm has fixed a method for the accounting treatment of an item, it will enter all similar items in exactly the same way in following years.

However, it does not mean that the firm has to follow the method until the firm closes down. A firm can change the method used, but such a change is not taken without due consideration. When such a change occurs and the profits calculated in that year are affected by a material amount, then either in the profit and loss account itself or in one of the reports with it, the effect of the change should be stated.

11.7 Accounting terminology

Unfortunately, many of the terms used in the description of Accounting theory mean quite different things to different people. Things described as 'concepts' and 'conventions' in this book may well be called 'principles' by someone else. They might be called 'concepts' without any attempt to distinguish between 'concepts' and 'conventions'. Provided that the reader realises this, there is no problem.

Probably, the most recent attempt to change a term is the use of the word prudence instead of **conservatism**. As most accounting books now use the word 'prudence', this is the one used in this book. Both of these words can be taken to mean the same.

Quantifiability means the ability to make a proper measure of a transaction. This must take place if the transaction is to be measured in money.

New terms

Accrual concept (p. 113): Where net profit is the difference between revenues and expenses.

Business entity concept (p. 112): Concerning only transactions which affect the firm, and ignoring the owner's private transactions.

Conservatism: See Prudence.

Consistency (p. 115): To keep to the same method, except in special cases.

Dual aspect concept (p. 113): Dealing with both aspects of a transaction.

Going concern concept (p. 112): Where a business is assumed to continue for a long time.

Materiality (p. 114): To record something in a special way only if the amount is not a small one.

Objectivity (p. 111): Using a method that everyone can agree to.

Prudence, or **conservatism** (p. 114): To ensure that profit is not shown as being too high, or assets shown at too high a value.

Quantifiability (p. 115): The ability to make a proper measure of a transaction, where it needs to be measured in money terms.

Realisation concept (p. 112): The point at which profit is treated as being earned.

Subjectivity (p. 111): Using a method that other people may not agree to.

EXERCISES

11.1 Which accounting concept is used in each of the following accounting treatments? Explain.

(*a*) The cost of a tape dispenser has been charged to an expense account, although in fact it could still be in use in ten years' time.

(*b*) A sole proprietor has sold his private house, but has not recorded anything about it in the business records.

(*c*) A debt has been written off as a bad debt even though there is still a chance that the debtor eventually may be able to pay it.

(*d*) A machine has been bought for an exceedingly low figure, and it has been entered in the asset account at that figure even though it is worth more.

(*e*) An expert says that the value of the management team to the company is worth well over a million pounds, yet nothing is entered for it in the books.

(*f*) A motor van broke down in December 2007. The repair bill for it was not paid until 2008 yet it has been treated as a 2007 expense.

(*g*) A customer saw a carpet in 2007 and said he might well buy it. He phoned in 2008 to ask us to deliver the carpet. The item was not treated as a sale in 2007 but was treated instead as within 2008 sales.

(*h*) The final day of the financial year saw the passing of a law that would render trading in our sort of goods illegal, and the business will have to close. The accountant says that our stock figure cannot be shown at cost in the balance sheet.

(*i*) We have been told that we cannot show our asset of motor cars at cost in one year and at cost plus the price increase the next year when the manufacturer increases prices of all cars, which also includes our unsold stock.

(*j*) We have shown all items of machinery costing less than £100 as machinery operating expenses.

11.2X When preparing the final accounts of your company, name the accounting concepts you should follow to deal with each of the following:

(*a*) Electricity consumed during the accounting period is still unpaid at the year end.

(*b*) The owner of the company has invested her private assets in the company.

(*c*) A debtor who owes the company a large amount has been declared bankrupt, and the outstanding amount due to the company is now considered to be irrecoverable.

(*d*) The company has suffered substantial losses in the past few years, and it is extremely uncertain whether the company can continue to operate next year.

11.3X Accounting concepts and conventions are used in preparing financial accounts of a business.

(*a*) Briefly explain any three of the following concepts:
- (i) Going concern concept
- (ii) Accrual concept
- (iii) Consistency convention
- (iv) Prudence convention.

(*b*) Objectivity is important in analysing and preparing accounting information. Explain the term 'objectivity', giving an example as to how it might be applied.

11.4 Explain briefly what you understand by the 'cost concept'. Give an advantage in using the cost method of valuation.

PART 3

Books of original entry

12 Division of the ledger: books of original entry

13 The analytical petty cash book and the imprest system

14 The banking system

15 Two-column cash books

16 Three-column and analytical cash books, and cash discounts

17 Bank reconciliation statements

18 Capital and revenue expenditures

19 The sales day book, sales ledger, related documentation, and other considerations

20 The purchases day book, purchases ledger and related documentation

21 The returns day books and documentation

22 Value added tax

23 Analytical sales and purchases day books

24 Control accounts

25 The journal

This part is concerned with the books and journals into which transactions are first entered, together with chapters on the banking system, capital and revenue expenditure, and VAT.

CHAPTER 12

Division of the ledger: books of original entry

Learning objectives

After you have studied this chapter you should be able to:

- know the need for books of original entry
- understand what each book is used for
- appreciate how the books of original entry are used alongside the ledgers
- list accounts as either personal or impersonal
- enter up a private or nominal ledger.

12.1 Introduction

While a business is very small, all of the double entry accounts can be kept in one book, which we call the **ledger**. In a larger business, it would be impossible to use one book because the large number of pages needed for the numerous transactions would mean that the book would be too big to handle. Also, if there were several book-keepers, they could not all do their work properly if there was only one ledger.

The answer to this problem is to use different books, in which we put similar types of transactions together (but see also Section 12.9).

12.2 Books of original entry

Books of original entry are books in which we record transactions first of all. We have a separate book for each different kind of transaction. The nature of the transaction affects which book it is entered into. Sales will be entered in one book, purchases in another book, cash in another book, and so on. We enter the transactions in these books as follows:

Date	*Customer/Supplier detail*	*Invoice no*	*Folio no*	*Total (£)*

The layouts for each of the types of books of original entry are described in the appropriate chapters that follow in this Part of the book.

12.3 Types of books of original entry

These are:

- **sales day book** – for credit sales (Chapter 19)
- **purchases day book** – for credit purchases (Chapter 20)
- **returns inwards day book** – for returns inwards (Chapter 21)
- **returns outwards day book** – for returns outwards (Chapter 21)
- **cash book** – for receipts and payments of cash (Chapters 15 and 16)
- **general journal** – for other items (Chapter 25).

12.4 The ledgers

The books of original entry list the transactions but do not show the effects of the transaction on the accounts. We must therefore enter the transactions in an appropriate ledger.

A separate ledger will be kept for different types of transactions, as listed in Section 12.5.

12.5 Types of ledgers

The different types of ledgers are:

- **sales ledger** – contains the record of customers' personal accounts
- **purchases ledger** – contains the record of suppliers' personal accounts
- **general ledger** – contains the remaining double entry accounts such as expenses, fixed assets, capital, etc. (also known as **nominal ledger**).

12.6 Diagram of books used

The books used in Accounting are shown in linked diagram form in Exhibit 12.1.

Exhibit 12.1

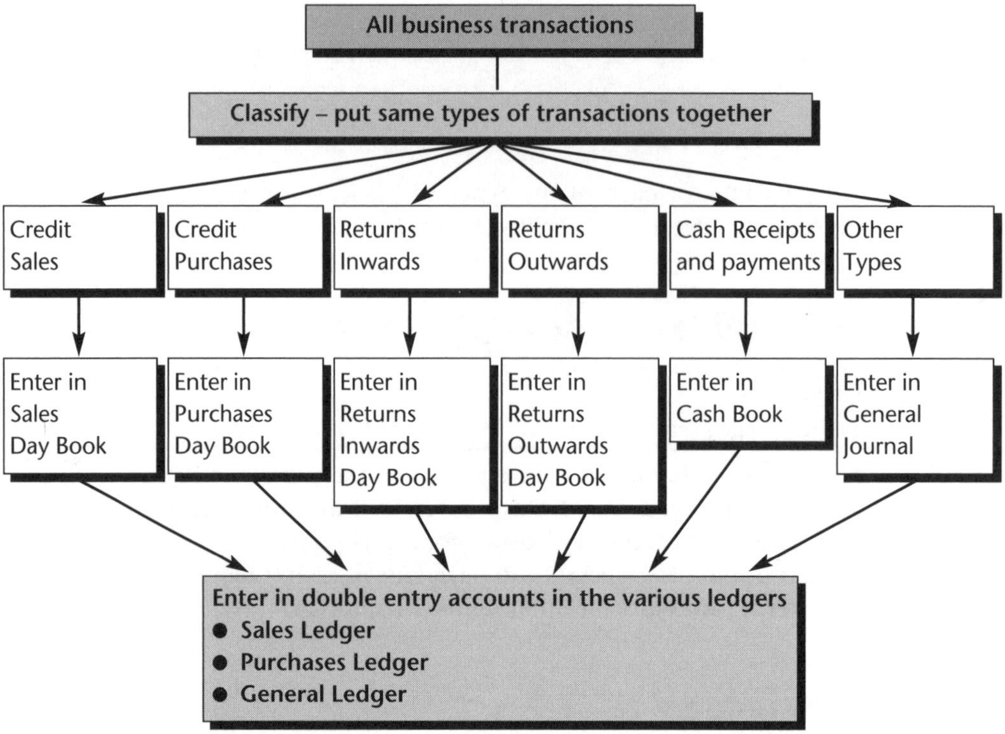

12.7 Types of account

Some people describe all accounts as **personal accounts** or as **impersonal accounts**. There are, in fact, four distinct types of account:

- **personal accounts** – for debtors and creditors.
- **impersonal accounts** – all other accounts, divided between real accounts and nominal accounts.
- **real accounts** – accounts in which property is recorded, examples being buildings, machinery, fixtures and stock.
- **nominal accounts** – accounts in which expenses, income and capital are recorded.

The diagram shown in Exhibit 12.2 might enable you to understand it better:

EXHIBIT 12.2

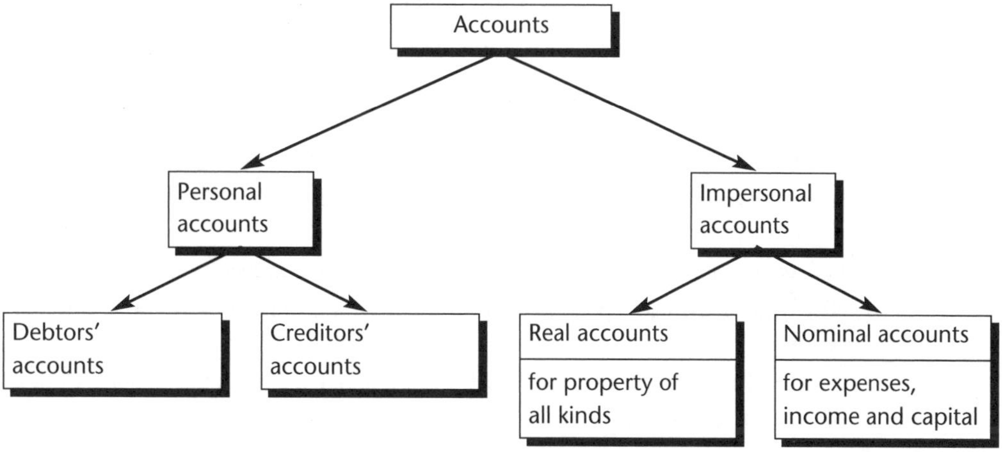

12.8 Nominal and private ledgers

The ledger in which the impersonal accounts are kept is known as the **nominal (or general) ledger**. Very often, to ensure privacy for the proprietor(s), the capital and drawing accounts and similar accounts are kept in a **private ledger**. By doing this, the proprietors ensure that office staff cannot see details of items that the proprietors want to keep confidential.

12.9 The use of computers in accounting

So far, it has been assumed that all book-keeping procedures are carried out using manual systems. But nowadays many businesses use computer systems, especially when dealing with large numbers of transactions. Computers are used for recording information in the same way as manual systems; thus, throughout the book the accounting terms of 'book' or 'journal' will be referred to for their use in either system.

New terms

Books of original entry (p. 120): Books where the first entry of a transaction is made.

Cash book (p. 121): Book of original entry for cash and bank receipts and payments.

General journal (p. 121): Book of original entry for all items other than those for cash or goods.

General ledger (p. 121): All accounts other than those for customers and suppliers.

Impersonal accounts (p. 122): All accounts other than debtors' and creditors' accounts.

Ledger (p. 121): A book for recording accounting transactions.

Nominal accounts (p. 122): Accounts in which expenses, revenue and capital are recorded.

Nominal ledger (p. 121): Ledger for impersonal accounts (also called General Ledger).

Personal accounts (p. 122): Accounts for both creditors and debtors.

Private ledger (p. 123): Ledger for capital and drawings accounts.

Purchases day book (p. 121): Book of original entry for credit purchases.

Purchases ledger (p. 121): A ledger for suppliers' personal accounts.

Real accounts (p. 122): Accounts in which property of all kinds is recorded.

Returns inwards day book (p. 121): Book of original entry for goods returned by customers.

Returns outwards day book (p. 121): Book of original entry for goods returned to suppliers.

Sales day book (p. 121): Book of original entry for credit sales.

Sales ledger (p. 121): A ledger for customers' personal accounts.

EXERCISES

12.1 For each of the following types of transactions, state the book of original entry, and the ledger and type of account, in which you would enter the transaction:

(*a*) Sales invoice
(*b*) Bank receipt
(*c*) Purchase invoice
(*d*) Bank payment
(*e*) Sales credit note
(*f*) Returns inwards
(*g*) Purchases credit note
(*h*) Closing stock.

12.2X (*a*) State which document(s) would be entered into the following books of original entry:
(i) Purchases day book
(ii) Returns inwards day book
(iii) Cash book
(iv) Sales day book
(v) Returns outwards day book.

(*b*) Distinguish between personal and impersonal accounts.

12.3 Show, by placing **one** tick in the appropriate column, whether each of the following accounts is personal, nominal or real. Account (a) has been completed as an example.

Name of Account	Personal	Nominal	Real
(a) Stock			✓
(b) Wages			
(c) Bank			
(d) Debtor			
(e) Office equipment			
(f) Purchases			
(g) Rent received			

NEAB (GCSE)

CHAPTER 13

The analytical petty cash book and the imprest system

Learning objectives

After you have studied this chapter you should be able to:

- **write up a petty cash book**
- **post the petty cash items to ledger accounts**
- **understand the imprest system.**

13.1 Division of the cash book

With the growth of the firm, it has been seen that it becomes necessary to have several books instead of just one ledger. These ideas can be extended to the cash book.

It is obvious that in almost any firm there will be many small cash payments to be made. It would be an advantage if the records of these payments could be kept separate from the main cash book. Where a separate book is kept, it is known as a **petty cash book**.

The advantages of such an action can be summarised thus:

- The task of handling and recording small cash payments could be given by the cashier to a junior member of staff. That person would then be known as the petty cashier. The cashier, who is a higher paid member of staff, would be saved from routine work.
- If small cash payments were entered into the main cash book, these items would then need posting one-by-one to the ledgers. If travelling expenses were paid to staff on a daily basis, this could mean more than 250 postings to the staff travelling expenses account during the year, i.e. 5 days per week x 50 working weeks per year. However, if a special form of petty cash book is kept, it would only be the monthly totals for each period that would need posting to the general ledger. If this was done, only 12 entries would be needed in posting to the staff travelling expenses account instead of around 250.

When the petty cashier makes a payment to someone, then that person will have to fill in a voucher showing exactly what the payment was for. He or she may have to attach bills - e.g. receipts for petrol - to the **petty cash voucher**. The person would sign the voucher to certify that the expenses had been reimbursed by the petty cashier.

To illustrate the petty cash vouchers, we show two examples in Exhibit 13.1, namely Petty Cash Vouchers numbers 9 and 16.

Exhibit 13.1

No *9*

Petty Cash Voucher

Date *15/9/2004*

For what required	Amount £	p
Refund of overpayment: L. Waites Sales Ledger 121	*50*	*00*
	50	*00*

Signature *L. Waites*

Passed by *E. Charles*

No *16*

Petty Cash Voucher

Date *29/9/2004*

For what required	Amount £	p
Parcel to Miami	*22*	*00*
	22	*00*

Signature *K. Young*

Passed by *E. Charles*

13.2 The imprest system

The **imprest system** is where the cashier gives the petty cashier enough cash to meet the needs of the following period. At the end of the period, the cashier finds out the amounts spent by the petty cashier, and tops up the petty cashier's cash by an amount equal to that spent. The petty cash in hand should then be equal to the original amount with which the period was started. Exhibit 13.2 shows an example of this method.

Exhibit 13.2

		£
Period 1	The cashier gives the petty cashier	100
	The petty cashier pays out in the period	78
	Petty cash now in hand	22
	The cashier now gives the petty cashier the amount spent	78
	Petty cash in hand at the end of period 1	100
Period 2	The petty cashier pays out in the period	84
	Petty cash now in hand	16
	The cashier now gives the petty cashier the amount spent	84
	Petty cash in hand end of period 2	100

It may be necessary to increase the fixed sum, often called the **cash float,** to be held at the start of each period. In the above case, if we had wanted to increase the float at the end of the second period to £120, then the cashier would have given the petty cashier an extra £20, i.e. £84 + 20 = 104.

13.3 Illustration of an analytical petty cash book

An *analytical* petty cash book is often used. One of these is shown as Exhibit 13.3.

Exhibit 13.3

2004			£
Sept	1	The cashier gave £600 as float to the petty cashier	
		Payments out of petty cash during September:	
Sept	2	Petrol	63
Sept	3	K Long – travelling expenses	32
Sept	3	Postage	24
Sept	4	D Campbell – travelling expenses	21
Sept	7	Cleaning expenses	15
Sept	9	Petrol	19
Sept	12	K Lee – travelling expenses	30
Sept	14	Petrol	35
Sept	15	L Waites – refund: sales ledger account overpaid (*see* Exhibit 13.1 voucher 9)	50
Sept	16	Cleaning expenses	15
Sept	18	Petrol	24
Sept	20	Postage	28
Sept	22	Cleaning expenses	19
Sept	24	H Wood – travelling expenses	75
Sept	27	Settlement of K Young's account in the purchase ledger	33
Sept	29	Postage (*see* Exhibit 13.1 voucher 16)	22
Oct	1	The cashier reimbursed the petty cashier the amount spent in the month.	

EXHIBIT 13.3 (*continued*)

Petty Cash Book *(p. 31)*

Receipts	*Folio*	*Date*	*Details*	*Voucher no.*	*Total*	*Motor expenses*	*Staff travelling expenses*	*Postages*	*Cleaning*	*Ledger folio*	*Ledger accounts*
£		2004			£	£	£	£	£		£
600	CB 19	Sept 1	Cash								
		Sept 2	Petrol	1	63	63					
		Sept 3	K Long	2	32		32				
		Sept 3	Postage	3	24			24			
		Sept 4	D Campbell	4	21		21				
		Sept 7	Cleaning	5	15				15		
		Sept 9	Petrol	6	19	19					
		Sept 12	K Lee	7	30		30				
		Sept 14	Petrol	8	35	35					
		Sept 15	L Waites	9	50					SL 121	50
		Sept 16	Cleaning	10	15				15		
		Sept 18	Petrol	11	24	24					
		Sept 20	Postage	12	28			28			
		Sept 22	Cleaning	13	19				19		
		Sept 24	H Wood	14	75		75				
		Sept 27	K Young	15	33					PL 18	33
		Sept 29	Postage	16	22			22			
					505	141	158	74	49		83
						GL 17	GL 29	GL 44	GL 64		
		Sept 30	Balance c/d		95						
600					600						
95		Oct 1	Balance b/d								
505	CB 22	Oct 1	Cash								

Reimbursement equals the total amount spent in September 2004

Total amount spent in September 2004

The receipts column is the debit side of the petty cash book. On giving £600 to the petty cashier on 1 September, the credit entry is made in the cash book while the debit entry is made in the petty cash book. A similar entry is made on 1 October for the £505 paid by the chief cashier, to the petty cashier, which amount covers all expenses paid by the petty cashier during September.

On the credit side of the petty cash book, the following needs to happen:

1 Enter the date and details of each payment. Put the amount in the total column.
2 Also put the amount in the column for the type of expense.
3 At the end of each period, add up the totals column.
4 Now add up each of the expense columns. The total from step 3 should equal the total of all the expense columns. In Exhibit 13.3 this is £505.
5 Balance off the petty cash book, carrying down the balance of petty cash in hand to the next period.

To complete double entry for petty cash expenses paid:

6 The total of each expense column is debited to the expense account in the general ledger.
7 Enter the folio number of each general ledger page under each of the expense columns in the petty cash book. This enables cross-reference to be made easily.
8 The last column in the petty cash book is a ledger column. In this column, items paid out of petty cash that need posting to the sales ledger and purchase ledger are shown.

The circumstances described in item 8 would happen if a purchases ledger account was settled out of petty cash, or if a refund was made out of the petty cash to a customer who had overpaid his account.

The double entry for all the items in Exhibit 13.3 appears as Exhibit 13.4.

Exhibit 13.4

Cash Book (Bank column only) *Page 19*

Dr				*Cr*		
				2004		£
				Sept 1 Petty cash	PCB 31	600
				Oct 1 Petty cash	PCB 31	505

General Ledger

Motor Expenses Account *Page 17*

Dr			*Cr*
2004		£	
Sept 30 Petty cash	PCB 31	141	

Staff Travelling Expenses Account *Page 29*

Dr			*Cr*
2004		£	
Sept 30 Petty cash	PCB 31	158	

Postages Account *Page 44*

Dr			*Cr*
2004		£	
Sept 30 Petty cash	PCB 31	74	

Cleaning Account *Page 64*

Dr			*Cr*
2004		£	
Sept 30 Petty cash	PCB 31	49	

Purchases Ledger

K Young Account *Page 18*

Dr			*Cr*	
2004		£	2004	£
Sept 27 Petty cash	PCB 31	33	Sept 1 Balance b/d	33

Sales Ledger

L Waites *Page 121*

Dr					*Cr*
2004		£	2004		£
Sept 15 Petty cash	PCB 31	50	Sept 1 Balance b/d		50

In a firm with both a cash book and a petty cash book, the cash book is often known as a **bank cash book.** This means that *all* cash payments are entered in the petty cash book, and the bank cash book will contain *only* bank columns and discount columns. When this arrangement is in operation, any cash sales will be paid directly into the bank.

New terms

Bank cash book (p. 131): The cash book for other than petty cash.

Cash float (p. 127): The sum held as petty cash.

Imprest system (p. 127): A system used for controlling expenditure of small cash items which are recorded in the petty cash book. A cash 'float' of a fixed amount is provided initially to the person responsible for operating the petty cash system. Any cash paid out during a particular period, i.e. a week, is reimbursed to the petty cashier so restoring the 'float' to its original sum.

Petty cash book (p. 126): A cash book used for making small (petty) payments. Payments are usually analysed and the totals of each column later posted to the various accounts in the general ledger. The source document used for entry into the petty cash book is a petty cash voucher.

Petty cash voucher (p. 126): The form used by anyone requesting payment for a small item of expenditure incurred on behalf of the business. The form gives details of the expense and should be signed and duly authorised.

EXERCISES

13.1 Enter the following transactions in a petty cash book that has analysis columns for motor expenses, postage and stationery, cleaning, sundry expenses, and a ledger column. This is to be kept on the imprest system, the amount spent to be reimbursed on the last day of each month. The opening petty cash float is £1,000.

2006			£
May	1	Cleaning	36
May	3	Speedy Garage - petrol	24
May	4	Postage stamps	55
May	5	Envelopes	17
May	6	Poison licence	18
May	8	Unique Garage - petrol	57
May	9	Corner Garage - petrol	64
May	11	Postage stamps	58
May	12	F Lee - ledger account (PL 121)	99
May	13	H Norman - ledger account (PL 168)	44
May	15	Sweeping brush (cleaning)	23
May	16	Bends Garage - petrol	77
May	17	K King - stationery	65
May	19	Driving licences	11
May	21	C Hope - ledger account (PL 15)	72
May	25	Cleaning	68
May	27	Licence for guard dog	12
May	28	Guard dog - food	29
May	31	Corner Garage - petrol	54

13.2 Write up a petty cash book with analysis columns for office expenses, motor expenses, cleaning expenses and casual labour. The cash float brought down is £500 and the amount spent is reimbursed on 30 June. Show the balance carried down to 1 July.

2007			£
June	1	H Sangster - casual labour	13
June	2	Letterheadings	22
June	2	Unique Motors - motor repairs	30
June	3	Cleaning materials	16
June	6	Envelopes	14
June	8	Petrol	28
June	11	J Hogan - casual labour	15
June	12	Paper-clips	12
June	12	Mrs Bell - cleaner	27
June	14	Petrol	11
June	16	Computer disks	31
June	16	Petrol	29
June	21	Motor vehicle repair	50
June	22	T Cooke - casual labour	21
June	23	Mrs Bell - cleaner	10
June	24	P King - causal labour	19
June	25	Stationery	27
June	26	Flat Cars - motor repairs	21
June	29	Petrol	12
June	30	J Young - casual labour	16

Also show how the items for motor expenses and office expenses would appear in the firm's general ledger.

13.3X From the following details you are required to:

(*a*) record a petty cash book, with headings for school bus expenses, staff travelling expenses, postage, cleaning and ledger accounts;

(*b*) balance down to 1 October 2004, replenishing the amount spent to restore the imprest;

(*c*) show how the items would be entered in the general ledger.

2004			£
Sept	1	The headteacher gave £300 as float to the petty cashier	
		Payments out of petty cash during September:	
Sept	2	Petrol: school bus	16
Sept	3	T Keats - travelling expenses of staff	23
Sept	3	Postage	12
Sept	4	D Twist - travelling expenses of staff	32
Sept	7	Cleaning expenses	11
Sept	9	Petrol: school bus	21
Sept	12	K Woods - travelling expenses of staff	13
Sept	14	Petrol: school bus	23
Sept	15	L Blake - travelling expenses of staff	5
Sept	16	Cleaning expenses	11
Sept	18	Petrol: school bus	22
Sept	20	Postage	12
Sept	22	Cleaning expenses	11
Sept	24	H Williams - travelling expenses of staff	7
Sept	27	Settlement of T Clarke's account in the purchases ledger (PL 18)	13
Sept	29	Postage	12
Sept	30	The headteacher reimbursed the petty cashier the amount spent in the month	

13.4 You work for S Dickinson (Estate Agents) as a receptionist, although some of your duties include administration tasks and dealing with the firm's petty cash, which is operated using the imprest system. A float of £120 is used by the firm for petty cash and this is given to you on 1 March.

Required:

(*a*) From the following petty cash vouchers (Exhibit 13.5), you are required to enter them in the petty cash book using analysis columns as you think appropriate. Balance off at the end of the month and obtain cash to restore the imprest from Ms Dickinson.

(*b*) Post the petty cash expense columns to the accounts in the general ledger and enter the cash obtained to restore the imprest in the cash book.

(*c*) What are the advantages to using the imprest system? Draft a short memo outlining these to Ms Dickinson.

(NVQ Level 2)

EXHIBIT 13.5

No 1

Petty Cash Voucher

Date 2/3/2009

For what required	Amount £	p
Postage Stamps	6	50
	6	50

Signature A. Bond

Passed by SMD

No 2

Petty Cash Voucher

Date 3rd March 2009

For what required	Amount £	p
Second-class rail fare to Stourbridge	23	—
	23	—

Signature G. Jones

Passed by SMD

No 3

Petty Cash Voucher

Date 7th March 2009

For what required	Amount £	p
Parcel Post to London	4	—
	4	—

Signature A. Bond

Passed by SMD

No 4

Petty Cash Voucher

Date 9th March 2009

For what required	Amount £	p
Window cleaning	8	—
	8	—

Signature C. Cotton

Passed by SMD

No 5

Petty Cash Voucher

Date 12th March 2009

For what required	Amount £	p
Envelopes	2	64
VAT		46
	3	10

Signature A. Bond

Passed by SMD

No 6

Petty Cash Voucher

Date 14th March 2009

For what required	Amount £	p
Tea etc (Hospitality)	6	40
	6	40

Signature A. Bond

Passed by SMD

EXHIBIT 13.5 *(continued)*

No 7

Petty Cash Voucher

Date 16th March 2009

For what required	Amount £	p
Petrol (including VAT)	10	—
	10	—

Signature G. Jones
Passed by SMD

No 8

Petty Cash Voucher

Date 19th March 2009

For what required	Amount £	p
Computer Discs	11	06
VAT @ 17.5%	1	94
	13	—

Signature S. Dickinson
Passed by SMD

No 9

Petty Cash Voucher

Date 20 March 2009

For what required	Amount £	p
Dusters & Polish	1	47
17.5% VAT		26
	1	73

Signature J. Pratt
Passed by SMD

No 10

Petty Cash Voucher

Date 23 March 2009

For what required	Amount £	p
Postage Stamps	2	40
	2	40

Signature A. Bond
Passed by SMD

No 11

Petty Cash Voucher

Date 27th March 2009

For what required	Amount £	p
Payment of creditors:-		
J. Cheetham (A/c No C44)	7	30
	7	30

Signature S. Dickinson
Passed by SMD

No 12

Petty Cash Voucher

Date 31st March 2009

For what required	Amount £	p
Magazines, Newspapers etc. (for reception)	6	40
	6	40

Signature A. Bond
Passed by SMD

13.5X You are employed as junior accountant's assistant of Morridge Products Ltd and one of your main tasks is that of petty cashier. The company uses an analytical petty cash book with columns for travelling expenses, postage, stationery, cleaning, sundry expenses and VAT, and they operate the imprest system.

Required:

(*a*) On 1 January 2004 the company's accountant, Mr Brammer, restores the petty cash float to £100 and gives you the petty cash vouchers shown in Exhibit 13.6. You are required to enter them in the petty cash book, balance off the book at the end of January, and obtain reimbursement from Mr Brammer to restore the imprest.

(*b*) Mr Brammer is anxious for you to become involved with all the financial aspects of the business and would like you to complete the book-keeping entries by posting the totals of the 'petty cash analysis columns' to the relevant accounts in the general ledger.

(*c*) Unfortunately, you have to go in hospital for a few days and will probably be absent from work for a couple of weeks. Mr Brammer asks you to write out a set of instructions in note form on the operation of the petty cash book as Jenny Cadwaller, his secretary, will be taking over in your absence. Ensure the instructions are clear, concise and easy to follow.

(NVQ Level 2)

Exhibit 13.6

No 1

Petty Cash Voucher

Date 1st Jan 2004

For what required	Amount £	p
Travelling Expenses to Crewe	5	36
	5	36

Signature Jim Steadman

Passed by G Brammer

No 2

Petty Cash Voucher

Date 5 Jan 2004

For what required	Amount £	p
Office Cleaning	10	—
	10	—

Signature A. Duffy

Passed by G. Brammer

No 3

Petty Cash Voucher

Date 9 Jan 2004

For what required	Amount £	p
Parcel to Northampton	1	98
	1	98

Signature Tom Finikin

Passed by G Brammer

No 4

Petty Cash Voucher

Date 10 Jan 2004

For what required	Amount £	p
Milk & Coffee for Office	6	50
	6	50

Signature J. Cadwaller

Passed by G. Brammer

No 5

Petty Cash Voucher

Date 12 Jan 2004

For what required	Amount £	p
Air-mail Stationery	7	15
VAT	1	25
	8	40

Signature J. Cadwaller

Passed by G. Brammer

No 6

Petty Cash Voucher

Date 15 Jan 2004

For what required	Amount £	p
Light Bulbs & 3 plugs.	3	64
VAT		64
	4	28

Signature Tom Finikin

Passed by G Brammer

Exhibit 13.6 *(continued)*

No 7

Petty Cash Voucher

Date 21 Jan 2004

For what required	Amount £	p
Office cleaning (2 weeks)	20	—
	20	—

Signature A. Duffy
Passed by G Brammer

No 8

Petty Cash Voucher

Date 22 Jan 2004

For what required	Amount £	p
1 Ream Copier Paper	4	30
+ VAT		75
	5	05

Signature J. Cadwaller
Passed by G. Brammer

No 9

Petty Cash Voucher

Date 24 Jan 2004

For what required	Amount £	p
Car Allowance: Manchester – Visiting Customer 60 miles x 25p	15	—
	15	—

Signature J. Steadman
Passed by G. Brammer

No 10

Petty Cash Voucher

Date 24 Jan 2004

For what required	Amount £	p
Financial Times & Economist for Reception	2	10
	2	10

Signature J. Cadwaller
Passed by G Brammer

No 11

Petty Cash Voucher

Date 30 Jan 2004

For what required	Amount £	p
Milk	1	50
	1	50

Signature P. Fisher
Passed by G. Brammer

No 12

Petty Cash Voucher

Date 31 Jan 2004

For what required	Amount £	p
First Class Stamps	4	80
	4	80

Signature J. Cadwaller
Passed by G. Brammer

13.6X (*a*) Why do some businesses keep a petty cash book as well as a cash book?

(*b*) List *three* items of information that must appear on a petty cash voucher.

(*c*) Give *one* reason why many businesses use the imprest system for recording petty cash.

(*d*) Jenny Clare keeps her petty cash book on the imprest system, the imprest being £50. For the month of February 2004, her petty cash transactions were as follows:

			£
Feb	1	Petty cash balance	10.50
	2	Petty cashier presented vouchers to cashier and obtained cash to restore the imprest	39.50
	5	Bought petrol	10.00
	8	Bought envelopes	2.50
	12	Paid to Mary Kenny, a creditor	3.16
	15	Paid bus fares	0.85
	20	Bought book of ten first class stamps at 26p each	2.60
	24	Received cash for personal telephone call	0.90
	27	Bought petrol	15.00

(i) Enter the above transactions in a petty cash book with analysis columns for Travelling Expenses, Postage and Stationery, and Ledger Accounts. Then balance the petty cash book at 28 February, bringing down the balance on 1 March.

(ii) On 1 March Jenny Clare received an amount of cash from the cashier to restore the imprest. Enter this transaction in the petty cash book.

(*e*) Open the ledger accounts to complete the double entry for the following:

(i) the petty cash analysis columns headed *Postage and Stationery* and *Travelling Expenses*;

(ii) the transactions dated 12 and 24 February 2004.

NEAB (GCSE)

CHAPTER 14

The banking system

Learning objectives

After you have studied this chapter you should be able to:

- know the difference between current accounts and deposit accounts
- make out cheques
- understand the effect of various kinds of crossing on cheques
- fill in bank paying-in slips
- understand other forms of making payments, i.e. bank giro credits, credit transfers and BACS
- understand the difference between making payments by standing order and by direct debit
- realise the timing differences between entries in a cash book and those on a bank statement.

14.1 Introduction

We will be looking at payments into and out of bank accounts in Chapters 15 and 16. You therefore need to know some details about bank accounts.

14.2 Types of account

There are two main types of bank account:

- **Current account** This is used for everyday payments into and out of a bank account. A **cheque book** will be given by the bank to the holder of the account. The cheque book will be used to make payments to people to whom the account holder owes money. So that account holders can pay money into their current account, they are given a **paying-in book**. Current accounts do not usually earn interest.
- **Deposit account** Such a bank account is used for holding money that is not needed for making payments in the foreseeable future. Interest is given by the bank on money kept in such accounts.

14.3 Cheques

When a bank has agreed to let you open a current account, it will ask you for a specimen signature. This allows the bank to prove that your cheques are in fact signed by you and have not been forged. You will then be issued with a cheque book.

You can use the cheques in the cheque book to make payments out of the account. Normally, you must make sure that you have more money in the account than the amount paid out. If you wish to pay out more money than you have banked, you will need to discuss the reasons for this with your bank and, if they find these acceptable, they will give their permission for you to 'overdraw' your account. This is known as a **bank overdraft**.

The person writing a cheque and using it for payment is known as the **drawer**. The person to whom the cheque is paid is known as the **payee**.

We can now look at Exhibit 14.1, which shows a blank cheque before it has been filled in.

EXHIBIT 14.1

On the face of the cheque are various sets of numbers. These are:

914234 Every cheque printed for the Cheshire Bank will be given a different number so that individual items can be traced.

09-07-99 Each branch of each bank in the United Kingdom has a different number given to it. Thus, this branch has a 'sort code' number of 09-07-99.

058899 Each account with the bank is given a different number. This particular number is kept only for the account of J Woodstock at the Stockport branch.

When we fill in a cheque, we should copy the details onto the counterfoil, which we can keep for our own records once the cheque has been detached.

We can now look at the completion of a cheque. Let us assume that we are paying seventy-two pounds and eighty-five pence to K Marsh on 22 May 2004. Exhibit 14.2 shows the completed cheque.

EXHIBIT 14.2

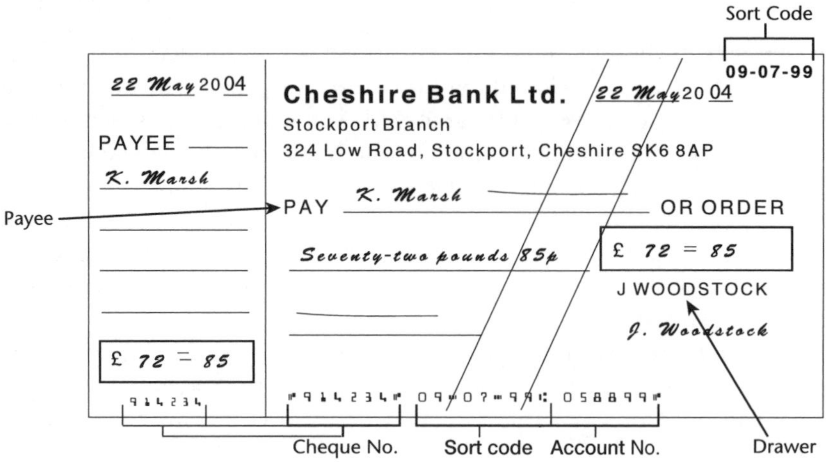

In Exhibit 14.2, the drawer is J Woodstock and the payee is K Marsh.

The two parallel lines across the face of the cheque are drawn (usually preprinted nowadays) as a safeguard. If we had not had this, the cheque would have been an 'uncrossed' cheque. If someone had stolen a signed uncrossed cheque he could have gone to the Stockport branch of the Cheshire Bank and obtained cash in exchange for the cheque. When the cheque is crossed, it means it *must* be paid into a bank account, Building Society account, Post Office Giro bank or Savings Bank. Virtually all cheques today are pre-printed and crossed as 'Account payee'.

14.4 Cheque crossing

Cheques can be further safeguarded by using specific crossing, i.e. writing a form of instruction within the crossing on the cheques, as shown in Exhibit 14.3.

EXHIBIT 14.3

The styles shown are specific instructions to the banks about the use of the cheque. The use of 'A/c Payee only' means the cheques should be paid only into the account of the payee named. If cheques are lost or stolen, the drawer must advise his bank immediately, and normally confirm by letter. These cheques will be 'stopped', i.e. payment will not be made on these cheques, provided that the drawer acts swiftly.

The safest crossing is that of 'A/c Payee only, Not negotiable'. If the cheque is lost or stolen it will be of no use to the thief or finder. This is because it is impossible for this cheque to be paid into any bank account other than that of the named payee.

14.5 Paying-in slips

When we want to pay money into our current account – either cash or cheques or both – we use a **paying-in slip**. One of these is shown as Exhibit 14.4.

J Woodstock has banked the following items, which can be seen set out in the paying-in slip: four £5 notes, three £1 coins, one 50p coin, other silver to the value of 30p, bronze coins amounting to 12p and cheques received from E Kane & Son (£184.15, code number 02-58-76) and J Gale (£65.44 code number 05-77-85).

Exhibit 14.4

Face of paying-in slip

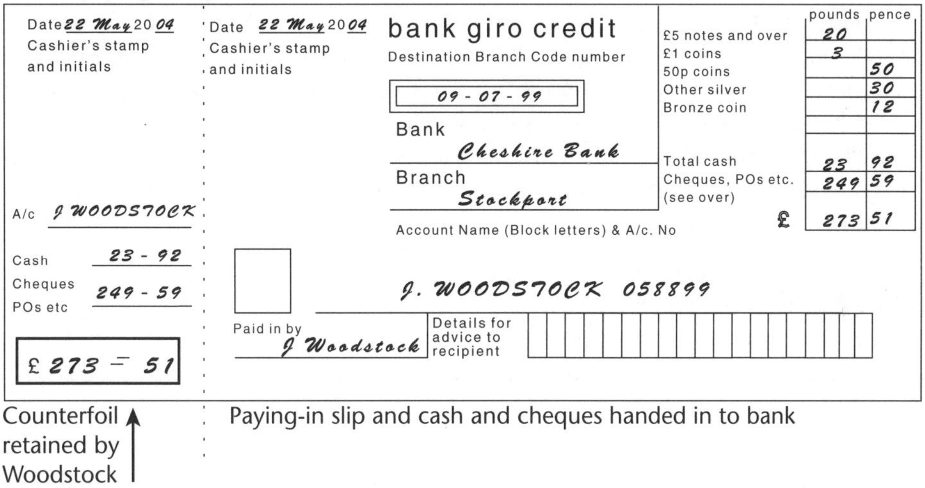

Reverse side of paying-in slip

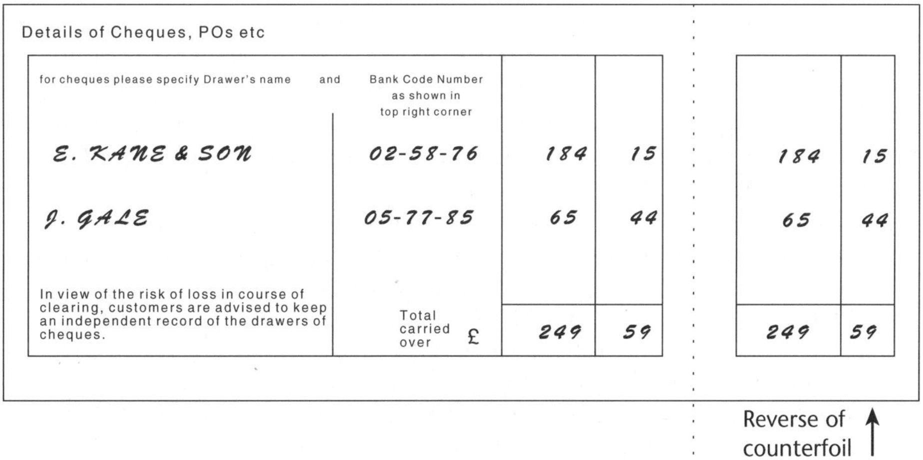

14.6 Bank giro credits/credit transfers

Another way of paying creditors, wages and salaries, etc. is by **bank giro credits,** also known as credit transfers. Here, a business prepares payments in the usual way but in addition prepares a list and a set of bank giro credit slips detailing each payee's name, account number, bank code number, bank name and branch title, and the amount of the payment. The list and slips are then sent to the bank with one cheque to cover all the payments and the payments are automatically credited to the various bank accounts via a centralised banking system.

One distinct advantage is that only one cheque has to be made out by the drawer and signed. The disadvantage is the preparation of the bank giro credit list and slips. This method is now very outdated and very few organisations nowadays use this method of payment.

14.7 Payment by BACS

Many businesses nowadays make their payments via **Bankers' Automated Clearing Services (BACS)**. BACS is a company owned by the Bank of England, the high-street banks and some building societies. It offers a computerised payment-transfer system that organisations may use to pay not only employee wages and salaries but also other creditors, dividends, grants, pensions, etc.

If an employer decides to use this method for paying creditors, wages and/or salaries, then the employer needs to send to BACS a disk cassette or magnetic tape giving the following details of each employee or organisation to be paid:

- person's or organisation's name
- bank name and branch title
- bank sort code number
- person's or organisation's bank account number.

The information is sent prior to the payment and held permanently on computer file by BACS's Processing Computer Centre.

As payments are prepared periodically on the business's own computer, a magnetic tape or disk containing details of the total payments to be made is prepared at the same time and the data is then sent by courier or telephone link to BACS. BACS then automatically processes the data, crediting each person's or organisation's bank or building society account and debiting the business's account. Processing the transfers is a three-day cycle: the information is received on the first day, processed on the second day and then sent for checking by the employers prior to the transfers being made on the third day.

Sometimes a business may not have the computer facilities to enable payment to be made in this way. In these circumstances the managers of the business may wish to use the services of a computer bureau or bank, who, on receipt of a list of payments, will process – for a fee – the data to BACS via magnetic tape or disk.

14.8 Standing orders and direct debits

A person may make a regular payment from a current account, or receive a regular amount into an account, by **standing order** or **direct debit**.

Standing order

This method is a straightforward one for making regular fixed payments over which the payer has full control. The steps necessary to make payments by standing order are as follows:

1. Payer instructs the bank in writing to pay a certain amount, on a particular day (each month, each quarter, etc.), to a specific organisation.
2. Bank makes payment via the computerised banking system.

A payer can instruct the bank to cease or amend the payment at any time by giving written notification.

Direct debit

This payment method is becoming more common for paying both fixed and variable amounts of money. The system of operation is as follows:

1. The proposed receiver (the payee) of the money sends a mandate to the payer.
2. The payer completes the mandate and returns it to the payee.
3. The payee sends the mandate to the payer's bank who will arrange to send the money to the payee's bank via the computerised banking system.

The amounts that the payer has authorised to be withdrawn from an account can vary as the payee makes changes. Typical examples of variations are usually increases in insurance premiums, business rates and loan repayments. It is normal for the payee to advise the payer of such increase.

Payees prefer this method of regular payments since they have control over them and, should the payer wish to cancel a direct debit, the payer should instruct the bank to cease payments and advise the payee of the cancellation. While this method of payment is convenient for both parties, the payer should exercise great care in giving permission for the setting-up of direct debits.

14.9 Cheque clearings

We now look at how cheques paid from one person's bank account pass into another person's bank account.

Let us look at the progress of the cheque in Exhibit 14.2. We will assume that the Post Office is being very efficient and delivering all letters the following day after being posted. With regard to the details in Exhibit 14.2:

2004

May 22 J Woodstock, in Stockport, sends the cheque to K Marsh, who lives in Leeds. Woodstock enters the payment in his cash book.

May 23 Cheque received by Marsh. He banks it the same day in his .bank account at Barclays Bank in Leeds. Marsh shows the cheque in his cash book as being received and banked on 23 May.

May 24 Barclays in London receive the cheque. They exchange it with the head office of the Cheshire Bank in London. The Cheshire Bank send the cheque to their Stockport branch.

May 25 The Stockport branch of the Cheshire Bank examine the cheque. If there is nothing wrong with it, the cheque can now be debited by the bank to J Woodstock's account.

In Chapter 17 we will be examining bank reconciliation statements. What we have looked at in relation to May 22 (the day on which Woodstock has made the entry in his cash book) and May 25 (the day when the bank makes an entry in Woodstock's account in respect of the cheque) will become an important part of your understanding of such statements.

New terms

Bank giro credits (p. 144): Method used by businesses to pay creditors, wages and/or salaries. A bank giro credit list and slips containing information about each person or organisation to be paid and the amount payable are sent to the bank, together with one cheque to cover all the payments. The bank then automatically transfers the funds from the business's account to the account of each of the respective people or organisations.

Bank overdraft (p. 141): When we have paid more out of our bank account than we have paid into it.

Bankers' Automated Clearing Service (BACS) (p. 144): Computerised payment transfer system that is a very popular way of paying creditors, wages and salaries.

Cheque book (p. 141): Book containing forms (cheques) used to pay money out of a current account.

Current account (p. 140): Bank account used for regular payments in and out of the bank.

Deposit account (p. 140): Bank account for money to be kept in for a long time. Interest is given on money deposited.

Direct debit (p. 145): Payment made out of a payer's bank, direct to the payee's bank, on the *payee's* instructions.

Drawer (p. 141): The person making out a cheque and using it for payment.

Payee (p. 141): The person to whom a cheque is paid.

Paying-in book (p. 140): A book of suitably preprinted paying-in slips and counterfoils.

Paying-in slip (p. 143): Form used for paying money into a bank account.

Standing order (p. 145): Payment made out of a payer's bank, direct to the payee's bank, on the *payer's* instructions.

EXERCISES

14.1 Explain the difference between a current account and a deposit account. Which account would be most suitable for making regular savings?

14.2 Describe the difference, when making out a cheque, between the drawer and the payee.

14.3X Organisations today pay many of their creditors and staff salaries using BACS. Explain fully how the system operates and its main advantage.

14.4 Morridge Products Ltd receives a cheque which has a special crossing.

(*a*) Explain briefly what is meant by a special crossing.
(*b*) Explain briefly the effect of a special crossing.

14.5 Many payments are made by either standing order or direct debit. Explain these methods of payment and state the advantages of using each method.

CHAPTER 15

Two-column cash books

Learning objectives

After you have studied this chapter you should be able to:

- **enter data into cash books and balance off**
- **use folio columns for cross-referencing purposes**
- **enter 'contra' items in the cash book.**

15.1 Introduction

The cash book consists of the cash account and the bank account put together in one book. Initially, we showed these two accounts on different pages of the ledger; now it is easier to put the two sets of account columns together. This means that we can record all money received and paid out on a particular date on the same page.

In the cash book, the debit column for cash is put next to the debit column for bank. The credit column for cash is put next to the credit column for bank.

15.2 Drawing up a cash book

We can now look at a cash account and a bank account (in Exhibit 15.1) as they would appear if they had been kept separately. Then, in Exhibit 15.2, they are shown as if the transactions had, instead, been kept in a cash book.

The bank column contains details of the payments made by cheque and of the money received and paid into the bank account. The bank will have a copy of the account in its own books.

The bank will send a copy of the account in its books to the firm, this copy usually being known as the **bank statement**. When the firm receives the bank statement, it will check it against the bank column in its own cash book to ensure that there are no errors.

Exhibit 15.1

Cash Account

Dr			*Cr*
2004	£	2004	£
Aug 2 T Moore	33	Aug 8 Rent	20
Aug 5 K Charles	25	Aug 12 C Potts	19
Aug 15 F Hughes	37	Aug 28 Wages	25
Aug 30 H Howe	18	Aug 31 Balance c/d	49
	113		113
Sept 1 Balance b/d	49		

Bank Account

Dr			*Cr*
2004	£	2004	£
Aug 1 Capital	1,000	Aug 7 Rates	105
Aug 3 W P Ltd	244	Aug 12 F Small Ltd	95
Aug 16 K Noone	408	Aug 26 K French	268
Aug 30 H Sanders	20	Aug 31 Balance c/d	1,204
	1,672		1,672
Sept 1 Balance b/d	1,204		

Exhibit 15.2

Cash Book

Dr	*Cash*	*Bank*		*Cash*	*Bank* *Cr*
2004	£	£	2004	£	£
Aug 1 Capital		1,000	Aug 7 Rates		105
" 2 T Moore	33		" 8 Rent	20	
" 3 W P Ltd		244	" 12 C Potts	19	
" 5 K Charles	25		" 12 F Small Ltd		95
" 15 F Hughes	37		" 26 K French		268
" 16 K Noone		408	" 28 Wages	25	
" 30 H Sanders		20	" 31 Balance c/d	49	1,204
" 30 H Howe	18				
	113	1,672		113	1,672
Sept 1 Balances b/d	49	1,204			

15.3 Cash paid into the bank

In Exhibit 15.2 the payments into the bank have been cheques received by the firm, which have been banked immediately. We must now consider cash being paid into the bank.

(i) Let us look at the position when a customer pays his account in cash, and later a part of this cash is paid into the bank. The receipt of the cash is debited to the cash column on the date received, the credit entry being in the customer's personal account. The cash banked has the following effect, needing action as shown:

Effect	Action
(a) Asset of cash is decreased	Credit the asset account, i.e. the cash account that is represented by the cash column in the cash book.
(b) Asset of bank is increased	Debit the asset account, i.e. the bank account that is represented by the bank column in the cash book.

Now let us look at an example:

Example 1: A cash receipt of £100 from M Davies on 1 August 2004, later followed by the banking on 3 August of £80 of this amount, would appear in the cash book as follows:

Dr	Cash Book			*Cr*	
	Cash	*Bank*		*Cash*	*Bank*
2004	£	£	2004	£	£
Aug 1 M Davies	100		Aug 3 Bank	80	
Aug 3 Cash		80			

The details column shows entries against each item stating the name of the account in which the completion of double entry has taken place. Against the cash payment of £80 appears the word 'bank', meaning that the debit £80 is to be found in the bank column, and the opposite applies.

(ii) Where the whole of the cash received is banked immediately, the receipt can be treated in exactly the same manner as a cheque received, i.e. it can be entered directly in the bank column.

(iii) If the firm requires cash, it may withdraw cash from the bank. This is done by making out a cheque to pay itself a certain amount in cash. The bank will give cash in exchange for the cheque.

The twofold effect and the action required may be shown:

Effect	Action
(a) Asset of bank is decreased	Credit the asset account, i.e. the bank column in the cash book.
(b) Asset of cash is increased	Debit the asset account, i.e. the cash column in the cash book.

This can be shown in the following example:

Example 2: A withdrawal of £75 cash on 1 June 2004 from the bank would appear in the cash book thus:

Cash Book					
Dr					*Cr*
	Cash	*Bank*		*Cash*	*Bank*
2004	£	£	2004	£	£
June 1 Bank	75		June 1 Cash		75

Both the debit and credit entries for this item are in the same book. When this happens it is known as a **contra** item.

15.4 The use of folio columns

As you have already seen, the details column in an account contains the name of the other account in which double entry has been completed. Anyone looking through the books would, therefore, be able to find where the other half of the double entry had been entered. However, when many books are being used, just to mention the name of the other account would not be enough information to find the other account quickly. More information is needed, and this is given by using **folio columns.**

In each account and in each book being used, a folio column is added, always shown on the left of the money columns. In this column the name of the other book, in abbreviated form, and the number of the page in the other book where double entry is completed are stated against each and every entry in the books. For instance, an entry of receipt of cash from C Kelly whose account was on page 45 of the sales ledger, and the cash recorded on page 37 of the cash book, would use the folio column thus:

In the cash book, in the folio column would appear 'SL 45'.
In the sales ledger, in the folio column would appear 'CB 37'.

By using this method, full cross references can be given. Each of the contra items being shown on the same page of a cash book would use the letter 'C' in the folio column.

The act of using one book as a means of entering the transaction to the other account, in order to complete the double entry, is known as **posting** the items.

15.5 Advantages of folio columns

Advantages are as follows:

- As described in Section 15.4, the system speeds up reference to the other book where double entry for the item is completed.
- The folio column is filled in when double entry has been completed. If it has not been filled in, double entry will not have been made.

Looking through the folio columns to ensure they have all been filled in will help us to detect errors.

15.6 Example of a cash book with folio columns

The following transactions are written up in the form of a cash book. The folio columns are filled in as though double entry had been completed to other accounts.

2005			£
Sept	1	Proprietor puts capital into a bank account for the business	940
Sept	2	Received cheque from M Boon	115
Sept	4	Cash sales	102
Sept	6	Paid rent by cash	35
Sept	7	Banked £50 of the cash held by the firm	50
Sept	15	Cash sales paid direct into the bank	40
Sept	23	Paid cheque to S Wills	277
Sept	29	Withdrew cash from bank for business use	120
Sept	30	Paid wages in cash	118

Cash Book

Dr	*Folio*	*Cash*	*Bank*		*Folio*	*Cash*	*Bank* *Cr*
2005		£	£	2005		£	£
Sept 1 Capital	GL1		940	Sept 6 Rent	GL65	35	
" 2 M Boon	SL98		115	" 7 Bank	C	50	
" 4 Sales	GL87	102		" 23 S Wills	PL23		277
" 7 Cash	C		50	" 29 Cash	C		120
" 15 Sales	GL87		40	" 30 Wages	GL39	118	
" 29 Bank	C	120		" 30 Balances	c/d	19	748
		222	1,145			222	1,145
Oct 1 Balances	b/d	19	748				

The abbreviations used in the folio column are as follows: GL = General Ledger; SL = Sales Ledger; C = Contra; PL = Purchases Ledger.

15.7 Receipts

A **receipt,** is a form stating how much cash has been received and the date of payment. When a cash sale is made, it is not necessary for a receipt to be given. This is because the goods are handed over immediately and there is, therefore, no need to keep a check on the identity of the payer. However, quite a lot of businesses, for example retail stores, give receipts in such cases even though it is not legally necessary. However, payment by cash for payments in respect of goods sold on credit would need the evidence of a receipt for, in the event of a problem arising with the goods, a receipt would provide the payer with proof of purchase.

A receipt might look as set out in Exhibit 15.3.

Exhibit 15.3

Date 15 May 2005

Received from A Reader

the sum of Fifty pounds 40p

in respect of Settlement of account

Signed J Hall

on behalf of Johnson and Longden Ltd

When payment is made by cheque, a receipt is not necessary, as the paid cheque will act as evidence of payment. Similarly, payments by standing order and direct debit will mean that receipts are not needed.

New terms

Bank statement (p. 148): Copy of a current account given by a bank.

Contra (p. 151): One of a pair of entries where both the debit and credit entries are shown in the cash book.

Folio columns (p. 151): Columns used in books of account for entering reference numbers.

Posting (p. 151): Entering a transaction in a book of account.

Receipt (p. 152): A form acknowledging receipt of money for goods or services rendered.

EXERCISES

15.1 Write up a two-column cash book from the following details, and balance off as at the end of the month:

2005		
May	1	Started business with capital in cash £100
May	2	Paid rent by cash £10
May	3	F Lake lent us £500, paying by cheque
May	4	We paid B McKenzie by cheque £65
May	5	Cash sales £98
May	7	N Miller paid us by cheque £62
May	9	We paid B Burton in cash £22
May	11	Cash sales paid direct into the bank £53
May	15	G Moores paid us in cash £65
May	16	We took £50 out of the cash till and paid it into the bank account
May	19	We repaid F Lake £100 by cheque
May	22	Cash sales paid direct into the bank £66
May	26	Paid motor expenses by cheque £12
May	30	Withdrew £100 cash from the bank for business use
May	31	Paid wages in cash £97.

15.2X A two-column cash book is to be written up from the following, carrying the balances down to the following month:

2004		
Jan	1	Started business with £4,000 in the bank
Jan	2	Paid for fixtures by cheque £660
Jan	4	Cash sales £225: Paid rent by cash £140
Jan	6	T Thomas paid us by cheque £188
Jan	8	Cash sales paid direct into the bank £308
Jan	10	J King paid us in cash £300
Jan	12	Paid wages in cash £275
Jan	14	J Walters lent us £500 paying by cheque
Jan	15	Withdrew £200 from the bank for business use
Jan	20	Bought stationery paying by cash £60
Jan	22	We paid J French by cheque £166
Jan	28	Cash drawings £100
Jan	30	J Scott paid us by cheque £277
Jan	31	Cash sales £66.

15.3X Write up a two-column cash book from the following:

2006		
Nov	1	Balance brought forward from last month: Cash £105; Bank £2,164
Nov	2	Cash sales £605
Nov	3	Took £500 out of the cash till and paid it into the bank
Nov	4	J Matthews paid us by cheque £217
Nov	5	We paid for postage stamps in cash £60
Nov	6	Bought office equipment by cheque £189
Nov	7	We paid J Lucas by cheque £50
Nov	9	Received rates refund by cheque £72
Nov	11	Withdrew £250 from the bank for business use
Nov	12	Paid wages in cash £239
Nov	14	Paid motor expenses by cheque £57
Nov	16	L Levy lent us £200 in cash
Nov	20	R Norman paid us by cheque £112
Nov	28	We paid general expenses in cash £22
Nov	30	Paid insurance by cheque £74.

15.4 You work for Stott & Co, a medium-sized clothes manufacturer, whose offices and works are situated in Derby. As book-keeper to the firm, one of your main duties is to enter up the cash book on a regular basis.

Required:
From the information given below, enter up the transactions for May 2005, balance off at the end of the month, and bring the balances down.

		£
May 1	Balances b/d	
	Cash in hand	14.72
	Bank (overdrawn)	820.54
May 2	Bought stationery by cash	10.00
May 3	Banked cheques received from:	
	P Wrench	432.36
	R Whitworth	634.34
	J Summers	341.00
May 6	South West Rail Ltd, cheque for travel expenses of company secretary to London	37.50
May 9	Paid the following accounts by cheque,	
	Fabulous Fabrics Ltd	450.80
	Mellors Manufacturing Co	348.32
May 12	Received from cash sale	76.00
May 14	Paid employees PAYE and NI to the Inland Revenue, by cheque	221.30
May 17	Received cheque from Trentam Traders	32.81
May 20	Foreign currency drawn from bank for director's visit to Italy	250.00
	Bank charges re currency	3.20
May 24	Received cash from sale of goods	350.00
May 26	Cash to bank	300.00
May 27	Salaries by cheque	5,720.00
May 31	Received cheques from the following:	
	J Summers	1,231.00
	Bradnop Manufacturing Co	725.00
	Taylors	2,330.50

(NVQ Level 2)

15.5X As a trainee accounts clerk at Jepsons & Co you have as one of your tasks the job of entering-up the firm's cash book at the end of each month.

Required:

From the details listed below, enter up the cash book for February 2006, balance off at the end of the month, and bring the balances down.

2006			£
Feb	1	Balances brought down from January	
		Cash in hand	76.32
		Cash at bank	2,376.50
Feb	2	Paid electricity bill by cheque	156.00
Feb	4	Paid motor expenses by cash	15.00
Feb	6	Received cheques from the following debtors:	
		D Hill	300.00
		A Jackson	275.00
		H Wardle	93.20
Feb	7	Paid for stationery by cash	3.70
Feb	10	Sold goods for cash	57.10
Feb	12	Paid for purchases from Palmer & Sons by cheque	723.50
Feb	14	Received loan by cheque from D Whitman	500.00
Feb	16	Paid Wright Brothers for repairs to office machinery by cheque	86.20
Feb	17	The proprietor, Stan Jepson, took cash for his own use.	50.00
		He asks you to pay his personal telephone bill by cheque to the post office	140.60
Feb	22	J Smith paid his account by cheque	217.00
Feb	23	Petrol bill paid by cash	21.00
Feb	26	Received cheque for sale of goods	53.00
Feb	27	Bought new photocopier from Bronsons of Manchester and paid by cheque	899.00
Feb	28	Paid monthly salaries by cheque	2,400.00

CHAPTER 16

Three-column and analytical cash books, and cash discounts

Learning objectives

After you have studied this chapter you should be able to:

- **understand and complete entries for discounts allowed and discounts received**
- **understand and be able to enter transactions into an analytical cash book.**

16.1 Cash discounts

It is better if customers pay their accounts quickly. A firm may accept a smaller sum in full settlement if payment is made within a certain period of time. The amount of the reduction of the sum to be paid is known as a **cash discount.** The term 'cash discount' thus refers to the allowance given for quick payment. It is still called a cash discount even if the account is paid by cheque.

The rate of cash discount is usually stated as a percentage. Full details of the percentage allowed, and the period within which payment is to be made, are quoted on all sales documents by the selling company. A typical period during which a discount may be allowed is one month from the date of the original transaction.

16.2 Discounts allowed and discounts received

A firm may have two types of cash discounts in its books. These are:

- **Discounts allowed** – cash discounts allowed by a firm to its customers when they pay their accounts quickly.
- **Discounts received** – cash discounts received by a firm from its suppliers when it pays their accounts quickly.

We can now see the effect of discounts by looking at two examples.

Example 1: W Clarke owed us £100. He pays on 2 September 2005 by cash within the time limit laid down, and the firm allows him 5 per cent cash discount. So he will pay £100 – £5 = £95 in full settlement of his account.

Effect	Action
1 Of cash: Cash is increased by £95. Asset of debtors is decreased by £95.	 Debit: Cash Account, i.e. enter £95 in debit column of cash book. Credit: W Clarke £95.
2 Of discounts: Asset of debtors is decreased by £5. (After the cash was paid the balance of £5 still appeared. As the account has been paid this asset must now be cancelled.) Expenses of discounts allowed increased by £5.	 Credit: W Clarke £5. Debit: Discounts allowed account £5.

This means that W. Clarke's debt of £100 has now been shown as fully settled, and exactly how the settlement took place has also been shown.

Example 2: The firm owed S Small £400. It pays him on 3 September 2005 by cheque within the time limit laid down by him and he allows $2^1/_2$ per cent cash discount. Thus the firm will pay £400 - £10 = £390 in full settlement of the account.

Effect	Action
1 Of cheque: Asset of bank is reduced by £390. Liability of creditors is reduced by £390.	 Credit: Bank, i.e. enter in credit bank column, £390. Debit: S Small's account £390.
2 Of discounts: Liability of creditors is reduced by £10. (After the cheque was paid, the balance of £10 remained. As the account has been paid, the liability must now be cancelled.) Revenue of discounts received increased by £10.	 Debit: S Small's account £10. Credit: Discounts received account £10.

The accounts in the firm's books would appear thus:

Cash Book *(page 32)*

Dr *Cr*

	Cash	*Bank*		*Cash*	*Bank*
2005	£	£	2005	£	£
Sept 2 W Clarke SL12	95		Sept 3 S Small PL75		390

Discounts Received Account (General Ledger *page 18*)

Dr				*Cr*		
			2005			£
			Sept 2	S Small	PL75	10

Discounts Allowed Account (General Ledger *page 17*)

Dr						*Cr*
2005			£			
Sept 2	W Clarke	SL12	5			

W Clarke Account (Sales Ledger *page 12*)

Dr							*Cr*
2005			£	2005			£
Sept 1	Balance b/d		100	Sept 2	Cash	CB32	95
				Sept 2	Discount	GL17	5
			100				100

S Small Account (Purchases Ledger *page 75*)

Dr							*Cr*
2005			£	2005			£
Sept 3	Bank	CB32	390	Sept 1	Balance b/d		400
Sept 3	Discounts	GL18	10				
			400				400

It is accounting custom to enter the word 'Discount' in the personal accounts, not stating whether it is a discount received or a discount allowed.

16.3 Discount columns in the cash book

The discounts allowed account and the discounts received account are in the general ledger, along with all the other revenue and expense accounts. It has already been stated that every effort should be made to avoid too much reference to the general ledger.

In the case of discounts, this is done by adding an extra column on each side of the cash book in which the amounts of discounts are entered. Discounts received are entered in the discounts column on the credit side of the cash book, and discounts allowed in the discounts column on the debit side of the cash book.

The cash book, if completed for the two examples so far dealt with, would appear thus:

Cash Book (*page 32*)

	Folio	*Discount*	*Cash*	*Bank*		*Folio*	*Discount*	*Cash*	*Bank*
2005		£	£	£	2005		£	£	£
Sept 2 W Clarke	SL12	5	95		Sept 3 S Small	PL75	10		390

There is no alteration to the method of showing discounts in the personal accounts.

To make entries in the discount accounts

Total of discounts column on receipts side of cash book	Enter on debit side of Discounts Allowed Account
Total of discounts column on payments side of cash book	Enter on credit side of Discounts Received Account

16.4 A worked example

The following is an example of a three-column cash book for the whole of a month, showing the ultimate transfer of the totals of the discounts columns to the discount accounts.

2005			£
May	1	Balances brought down from April:	
		Cash Balance	29
		Bank Balance	654
		Debtors accounts:	
		B King	120
		N Campbell	280
		D Shand	40
		Creditors accounts:	
		U Barrow	60
		A Allen	440
		R Long	100
May	2	B King pays us by cheque, having deducted $2^1/_2$ per cent cash discount £3	117
May	8	We pay R Long his account by cheque, deducting 5 per cent cash discount £5	95
May	11	We withdrew £100 cash from the bank for business use	100
May	16	N Campbell pays us his account by cheque, deducting $2^1/_2$ per cent discount £7	273
May	25	We paid wages in cash	92
May	28	D Shand pays us in cash after having deducted $2^1/_2$ per cent cash discount	38
May	29	We pay U Barrow by cheque less 5 per cent cash discount £3	57
May	30	We pay A Allen by cheque less $2^1/_2$ per cent cash discount £11	429

Cash Book *(page 64)*

Dr	Folio	Discount	Cash	Bank	*Cr*	Folio	Discount	Cash	Bank
2005		£	£	£	2005		£	£	£
May 1 Balances	b/d		29	654	May 8 R Long	PL58	5		95
May 2 B King	SL13	3		117	May 11 Cash	C			100
May 11 Bank	C		100		May 25 Wages	GL77		92	
May 16 N Campbell	SL84	7		273	May 29 U Barrow	PL15	3		57
May 28 D Shand	SL91	2	38		May 30 A Allen	PL98	11		429
					May 31 Balances	c/d		75	363
		12	167	1,044			19	167	1,044
Jun 1 Balances	b/d		75	363					

Sales Ledger

B King Account *Page 13*

Dr		£	*Cr*		£
2005			2005		
May 1 Balance b/d		120	May 2 Bank	CB 64	117
			May 2 Discount	CB 64	3
		120			120

N Campbell Account *Page 84*

Dr		£	*Cr*		£
2005			2005		
May 1 Balance b/d		280	May 16 Bank	CB 64	273
			May 16 Discount	CB 64	7
		280			280

D Shand Account *Page 91*

Dr		£	*Cr*		£
2005			2005		
May 1 Balance b/d		40	May 28 Cash	CB 64	38
			May 28 Discount	CB 64	2
		40			40

Purchases Ledger

U Barrow Account *Page 15*

Dr				Cr	
2005		£	2005		£
May 29 Bank	CB 64	57	May 1 Balance b/d		60
May 29 Discount	CB 64	3			
		60			60

R Long Account *Page 58*

Dr				Cr	
2005		£	2005		£
May 8 Bank	CB 64	95	May 1 Balance b/d		100
May 8 Discount	CB 64	5			
		100			100

A Allen Account *Page 98*

Dr				Cr	
2005		£	2005		£
May 30 Bank	CB 64	429	May 1 Balance b/d		440
May 30 Discount	CB 64	11			
		440			440

General Ledger

Wages Account *Page 77*

Dr				Cr
2005		£		
May 25 Cash	CB 64	92		

Discounts Received Account *Page 88*

Dr			Cr
		2005	£
		May 31 Cash book CB 64	19

Discounts Allowed Account

Dr				Cr
2005		£		
May 31 Cash book	CB 64	12		

Is the above method of entering discounts correct? You can easily check. See the following:

Discounts in Ledger Accounts	Debits		Credits	
		£		
Discounts received	U Barrow	3	Discounts	
	R Long	5	Received	
	A Allen	11	Account	£19
		19		
				£
Discounts allowed	Discounts		B King	3
	Allowed		N Campbell	7
	Account	£12	D Shand	2
				12

You can see that proper double entry has been carried out. Equal amounts, in total, have been entered on each side of the accounts.

16.5 Bank overdrafts and the cash book

A firm may borrow money from a bank by means of a bank overdraft. This means that the firm is allowed to pay more out of the bank account, by paying out cheques, than the total amount placed in the account.

Up to this point the bank balances have all been money at the bank, and so they have all been assets, i.e. debit balances. When the account is overdrawn, the firm owes money to the bank and so the account is a liability and the balance becomes a credit one.

Taking the cash book shown in Section 16.3, suppose that the amount payable to A Allen was £1,429 instead of £429. Thus the amount in the bank account, £1,044, is exceeded by the amount withdrawn. The cash book would appear as follows:

Cash Book

Dr	*Discount*	*Cash*	*Bank*		*Discount*	*Cash*	*Bank* *Cr*
2005	£	£	£	2005	£	£	£
May 1 Balances b/d		29	654	May 8 R Long	5		95
" 2 B King	3		117	" 11 Cash			100
" 11 Bank		100		" 25 Wages		92	
" 16 N Campbell	7		273	" 29 U Barrow	3		57
" 28 D Shand	2	38		" 30 A Allen	11		1,429
" 31 Balance c/d			637	" 31 Balance c/d		75	
	12	167	1,681		19	167	1,681
Jun 1 Balance b/d		75		Jun 1 Balance b/d			637

On a balance sheet, a bank overdraft will be shown as an item included under the heading Current Liabilities.

16.6 Analytical cash book

Many businesses use an analytical cash book in a similar way to the analytical petty cash book. This has several advantages.

One advantage is that it enables the business to have the use of a VAT (Value Added Tax) column to record payments/receipts of VAT. At the end of each month, the VAT columns are added up and the totals transferred to the VAT account in the general ledger. This VAT column is especially useful if the business buys and sells goods and/or services for immediate payment. The topic of value added tax will be dealt with more fully in Chapter 22.

Another advantage is that it allows for analysis of, say sales or purchases. In the example below, Whitehead's Electrical Co wants to monitor the sales and profit margins of its various lines. The owner of Whitehead's uses four analysis columns:

- Electrical goods
- 'White' goods (e.g. washing machines, which are usually white)
- Sundry sales
- VAT.

Payments from the cash book are analysed in a similar way.

Some businesses have a separate sales ledger and purchase ledger, which are self-balancing by the use of control accounts. Analysis columns are used in an analytical cash book to record monies received from debtors or paid to creditors. At the end of each month, the columns are added up and the totals are posted to the respective sales and purchase ledger control accounts.

There is no set format for the number and names of the columns used in an analytical cash book; it is up to the organisation to adapt the cash book to meet its own requirements.

A worked example

Whitehead's Electrical Co is an independent electrical shop that sells television sets, radios and videos, as well as washing machines, dryers, fridges, etc. In order to monitor sales and profit margins, Mr Whitehead operates a columnar cash book, as follows.

Receipts
These are split between four main headings, namely:

- Electrical goods
- 'White' goods
- Sundry sales
- VAT.

Payments

The payments side of the cash book has headings as follows:

- VAT
- Electrical purchases
- White goods purchases
- Wages and salaries
- General overheads.

During October 2006, the following transactions took place:

2006				
Oct	1	Balance of cash in hand £64.92 Balance at bank £416.17		
	2	Bought radios from Shaws (Wholesalers) Ltd, £187.36 plus VAT of £32.78 paid by cheque.		
	4	Sold goods as follows: – Washing machine £360.00 plus VAT of £63 to K Walters who paid by cheque – Video to S Worrall who paid by cheque £330.00 plus VAT of £57.75 Both cheques were paid into the bank. – Sundry cash sales, plugs, etc., £27.50 including VAT of £4.10		
	7	Paid postage £76.30 by cheque.		
	7	Paid wages £245. Drew cash from bank for this purpose.		
	10	Sold goods as follows:		
		Mrs J White – Colour TV	£550	(including VAT £81.92)
		Dr V Ford – Fridge	£180	(including VAT £26.81)
		Mr J Summers – Dryer	£225.50	(including VAT £33.59)
		Cheques were received in respect of the above and duly banked.		
	12	Cash sales: radio, £80.00 (including VAT £11.91).		
	14	Purchased the following goods from Allan's Electrical Ltd, and paid by cheque. This totalled £2,056.25.		
		Fridges	£450.00 plus VAT £78.75	
		Televisions	£1,300.00 plus VAT £227.50	
	14	Paid wages £245.00. Drew cash from bank.		
	18	Cash sale, one fridge £163.50 (including VAT £24.35).		
	20	Paid cash for petrol £20.00 (including VAT £2.98).		
	23	Paid wages £252.00. Drew cash from bank.		
	24	Sold TV and video to J Pratt £964.67 (including VAT £143.67). He paid by cheque.		
	26	Bought electrical clocks and radios from B McDonald and Son for £327.50 (including VAT £48.78). Paid by cheque.		
	30	Sundry cash sales paid direct into the bank £367.00 (including VAT £54.66).		
	31	Paid rent £200.00 in cash.		

Cash Book (debit side only)

Dr CB1

Date	Details	Folio	VAT	Electrical sales	White goods sales	Sundry sales	Cash	Bank
2006			£	£	£	£	£	£
Oct 1	Balance b/d						64.92	416.17
4	K Walters		63.00		360.00			423.00
"	S Worrall		57.75	330.00				387.75
	Cash sales		4.10			23.40	27.50	
10	Mrs J White		81.92	468.08				550.00
"	Dr V Ford		26.81		153.19			180.00
"	Mr J Summers		33.59		191.91			225.50
12	Cash sales		11.91	68.09			80.00	
18	"		24.35		139.15		163.50	
24	J Pratt		143.67	821.00				964.67
30	Cash sales		54.66			312.34		367.00
			501.76	1,687.17	844.25	335.74	335.92	3,514.09
Nov 1	Balance b/d						115.92	91.90
			GL1	GL2	GL3	GL4		

Cash Book (credit side only)

Cr CB1

Date	Details	Folio	VAT	Electrical purchases	White goods purchases	Wages and salaries	General overheads	Cash	Bank
2006			£	£	£	£	£	£	£
Oct 2	Shaws (Wholesalers) Ltd		32.78	187.36					220.14
7	Postage						76.30		76.30
7	Wages					245.00			245.00
14	Allan's Electrical Ltd		306.25	1,300.00	450.00				2,056.25
"	Wages					245.00			245.00
20	Petrol		2.98				17.02	20.00	
23	Wages					252.00			252.00
26	B McDonald & Son		48.78	278.72					327.50
31	Rent						200.00	200.00	
31	Balance c/d							115.92	91.90
			390.79	1,766.08	450.00	742.00	293.32	335.92	3,514.09
			GL1						

Full coverage of the treatment of discounts allowed and discounts received in final accounts is shown in Chapter 29.

New terms

Cash discount (p. 157): An allowance given for quick payment of an amount owing.

Discounts allowed (p. 157): A reduction given to customers who pay their accounts within the time allowed.

Discounts received (p. 157): A reduction given to us by a supplier when we pay their account before the time allowed has elapsed.

EXERCISES

16.1 Enter up a three-column cash book from the details following. Balance off at the end of the month, and show the relevant discount accounts as they would appear in the general ledger.

2004

May	1	Started business with £6,000 in the bank
May	1	Bought fixtures paying by cheque £950
May	2	Bought goods paying by cheque £1,240
May	3	Cash sales £407
May	4	Paid rent in cash £200
May	5	N Morgan paid us his account of £220 by a cheque for £210, we allowed him £10 discount
May	7	Paid S Thompson & Co £80 owing to them by means of a cheque £76, they allowed us £4 discount
May	9	We received a cheque for £380 from S Cooper, discount having been allowed £20
May	12	Paid rates by cheque £410
May	14	L Curtis pays us a cheque for £115
May	16	Paid M Monroe his account of £120 by cash £114, having deducted £6 cash discount
May	20	P Exeter pays us a cheque for £78, having deducted £2 cash discount
May	31	Cash sales paid direct into the bank £88.

16.2 From the following details, write up a three-column cash book, balance off at the end of the month, and show the relevant discount accounts as they would appear in the general ledger.

2003

Mar	1	Balances brought forward: Cash in hand £211 Cash at bank £3,984
Mar	2	We paid each of the following accounts by cheque, in each case we deducted a 5 per cent discount: T Adams £80; C Bibby £260; D Clarke £440
Mar	4	C Potts pays us a cheque for £98
Mar	6	Cash sales paid direct into the bank £49
Mar	7	Paid insurance by cash £65
Mar	9	The following persons pay us their accounts by cheque, in each case they deducted a discount of 2½ per cent: R Smiley £160; J Turner £640; R Pimlott £520
Mar	12	Paid motor expenses by cash £100
Mar	18	Cash sales £98
Mar	21	Paid salaries by cheque £120
Mar	23	Paid rent by cash £60
Mar	28	Received a cheque for £500 being a loan from R Godfrey
Mar	31	Paid for stationery by cheque £27.

16.3X Enter the following in a three-column cash book. Balance off the cash book at the end of the month and show the discount accounts in the general ledger.

2008		
June	1	Balances brought forward: Cash £97; Bank £2,186
June	2	The following paid us by cheque, in each case deducting a 5 per cent cash discount: R Harris £1,000; C White £280; P Peers £180; O Hardy £600
June	3	Cash sales paid direct into the bank £134
June	5	Paid rent by cash £88
June	6	We paid the following accounts by cheque, in each case deducting 2½ per cent cash discount: J Charlton £400; H Sobers £640; D Shallcross £200
June	8	Withdrew cash from the bank for business use £250
June	10	Cash sales £206
June	12	D Deeds paid us their account of £89 by cheque less £2 cash discount
June	14	Paid wages by cash £250
June	16	We paid the following accounts by cheque: L Lucas £117 less cash discount £6; D Fisher £206 less cash discount £8
June	20	Bought fixtures by cheque £8,000
June	24	Bought motor lorry paying by cheque £7,166
June	29	Received £169 cheque from D Steel
June	30	Cash sales £116
June	30	Bought stationery paying by cash £60.

16.4X You are to write up a three-column cash book for M Pinero from the details that follow. Then balance off at the end of the month and show the discount accounts in the general ledger.

2006		
May	1	Balances brought forward: Cash in hand £58 Bank overdraft £1,470
May	2	M Pinero pays further capital into the bank £1,000
May	3	Bought office fixtures by cheque £780
May	4	Cash sales £220
May	5	Banked cash £200
May	6	We paid the following by cheque, in each case deducting 2½ per cent cash discount: B Barnes £80; T Horton £240; T Jacklin £400
May	8	Cash sales £500
May	12	Paid motor expenses in cash £77
May	15	Cash withdrawn from the bank £400
May	16	Cash drawings £120
May	18	The following firms paid us their accounts by cheque, in each case deducting a 5 per cent discount: L Graham £80; B Crenshaw £140; H Green £220
May	20	Salaries paid in cash £210
May	22	T Weiskopf paid us his account in cash £204
May	26	Paid insurance by cheque £150
May	28	We banked all the cash in our possession except for £20 in the cash till
May	31	Bought motor van, paying by cheque £4,920.

CHAPTER 17

Bank reconciliation statements

Learning objectives

After you have studied this chapter you should be able to:

- reconcile cash book balances with bank statement balances
- understand how bank overdrafts affect the reconciliation process
- be able to make necessary entries for dishonoured cheques
- be able to reconcile ledger accounts to suppliers' statements.

17.1 The need for bank reconciliation statements

At the end of each chosen period we will balance off our cash book. At the same time we should ensure that our bank supplies us with a copy of our bank statement. When we look at the closing balance in our cash book, and then compare it with the balance on that date on the bank statement, we will usually find that the two balances are different.

We should then draw up a **bank reconciliation statement**, and the methods for doing this are shown in this chapter. This will either mean:

- that the reasons for the difference in balances are valid ones, showing that it has not been as a result of errors made by us or the bank, or
- that there is not a good reason for the difference between the balances.

In the second case we will have to find out exactly what the errors are. They can then be corrected.

We can now look at a sample of a bank statement:

Date	Details	Withdrawals	Deposits	Balance £
2005				
1 Jun	Balance b/f			11,238.48
6 Jun	Cheque 8564	1,260.00		9,978.48
7 Jun	Cheque 8565	2,899.90		7,078.58
11 Jun	Cheque Deposit		699.20	7,777.78
13 Jun	Cheque 8563	500.00		7,277.78
15 Jun	Cheque Deposit		4,597.00	11,874.78
19 Jun	Cheque Deposit		5,000.00	16,874.78
23 Jun	Cheque 8566	389.50		16,485.28
24 Jun	Cheque 8567	9,344.20		7,141.08
28 Jun	Cheque Deposit		11,119.00	18,260.08
30 Jun	Balance c/f			18,260.08

On the bank statement you can see:

- the balance brought forward from the previous period
- details of all cheques paid out (withdrawn), showing numbers of the cheques used
- details of all bankings (deposits)
- the balance carried forward to the next period.

17.2 An example of a bank reconciliation statement

Let us assume that we have just written up our cash book on 30 June 2005. By the next day's mail we receive a copy of our bank statement from the bank, made up to 30 June 2005. We then tick off the items in our cash book and on the bank statement which match each other. Copies of our cash book (bank columns only) and of our bank statement are shown as Exhibit 17.1.

Exhibit 17.1

Cash Book (bank columns only)

Dr			*Cr*		
2005		£	2005		£
June 1	Balance b/f	80	June 27	I Gordon	35
June 28	D Jones	100	June 29	B Tyrell	40
			June 30	Balance c/d	105
		180			180
July 1	Balance b/d	105			

Bank Statement

			Dr	*Cr*	*Balance*
2005			£	£	£
June 26	Balance b/f	✓			80 Cr
June 28	Banking	✓		100	180 Cr
June 30	I Gordon	✓	35		145 Cr

By comparing the cash book and the bank statement, it can be seen that the only item that was not in both of these was the cheque payment to B Tyrell for £40 in the cash book. The reason why this was entered in the cash book but does not appear on the bank statement is simply one of timing. The cheque had been posted to B Tyrell on 29 June, but there had not been time for it to be banked by Tyrell and passed through the banking system. Such a cheque is called an **unpresented cheque** because it has not yet been presented at the drawer's bank.

To prove that the balances are not different because of errors, even though they show different figures, a bank reconciliation statement is drawn up. This is given in Exhibit 17.2.

EXHIBIT 17.2

Bank Reconciliation Statement as at 30 June 2005

	£
Balance in hand as per cash book	105
Add unpresented cheque: Tyrell	40
Balance in hand as per bank statement	145

It would have been possible for the bank reconciliation statement to have started with the bank statement balance:

Bank Reconciliation Statement as at 30 June 2005

	£
Balance in hand as per bank statement	145
Less unpresented cheque: Tyrell	40
Balance in hand as per cash book	105

You should notice that the bank account is shown as a debit balance in the firm's cash book because, to the firm, it is an asset. In the bank's books the bank account is shown as a credit balance because this is a liability of the bank to the firm.

17.3 Some reasons for differences in balances

We can now look at a more complicated example in Exhibit 17.3. Similar items in both cash book and bank statement are shown ticked.

Exhibit 17.3

Cash Book

Dr						*Cr*
2005		£	2005			£
Dec 27	Total b/f	2,000	Dec 27	Total b/f		1,600
Dec 29	J Potter ✓	60	Dec 28	J Jacobs	✓	105
Dec 31	M Johnson (B)	220	Dec 30	M Chatwood (A)		15
			Dec 31	Balance c/d		560
		2,280				2,280
2006						
Jan 1	Balance b/d	560				

Bank Statement

2005	*Dr* £	*Cr* £	*Balance* £
Dec 27 Balance b/f			400 Cr
Dec 29 Cheque ✓		60	460 Cr
Dec 30 J Jacobs ✓	105		355 Cr
Dec 30 Credit transfers: L Shaw (C)		70	425 Cr
Dec 30 Bank charges (D)	20		405 Cr

The balance brought forward in the bank statement (£400) is the same figure as that in the cash book, i.e. totals b/f £2,000 – £1,600 = £400. However, items (A) and (B) are in the cash book only, and (C) and (D) are on the bank statement only. We can now examine these in detail:

(A) This is a cheque recently sent by us to Mr Chatwood. It has neither yet passed through the banking system nor been presented to our bank, and it is therefore an unpresented cheque.

(B) This is a cheque banked by us on our visit to the bank when we collected the copy of our bank statement. As we handed this banking item over the counter at the same time as the bank clerk gave us our bank statement, naturally it has not yet been entered on the statement.

(C) A customer, L Shaw, has paid his account by instructing his bank to pay us direct through the banking system, instead of paying by cheque. Such a transaction is usually called a **credit transfer**.

(D) The bank has charged us for the services given in keeping a bank account for us. It did not send us a bill; it simply takes the money from our account by debiting it and reducing the amount of our balance.

We can show these differences in the form of a table. This is followed by bank reconciliation statements drawn up both ways. This arrangement is for illustration only; we do not have to draw up a table or prepare two bank reconciliation statements. All we need in practice is one bank reconciliation statement, drawn up whichever way we prefer.

			Adjustment required to one balance to reconcile it with the other	
Items not in both sets of books	*Effect on Cash Book balance*	*Effect on Bank Statement*	*To Cash Book balance*	*To Bank Statement balance*
A Payment M Chatwood £15	reduced by £15	none – not yet entered	add £15	deduct £15
B Banking M Johnson £220	increased by £220	none – not yet entered	deduct £220	add £220
C Credit Transfers £70	none – not yet entered	increased by £70	add £70	deduct £70
D Bank Charges £20	none – not yet entered	reduced by £20	deduct £20	add £20

Bank Reconciliation Statement as on 31 December 2005

	£	£
Balance in hand as per cash book		560
Add Unpresented cheque – M Chatwood	15	
Credit transfers	70	
		85
		645
Less Bank charges	20	
Bank lodgement not yet entered on bank statement	220	
		240
Balance in hand as per bank statement		405

A bank reconciliation statement starting with the bank statement balance appears thus:

Bank Reconciliation Statement as on 31 December 2005

	£	£
Balance in hand as per bank statement		405
Add Bank charges	20	
Bank lodgement not yet entered on bank statement	220	
		240
		645
Less Unpresented cheque – M Chatwood	15	
Traders credit transfers	70	
		85
Balance in hand as per bank statement		560

17.4 Writing up the cash book before attempting a reconciliation

It is better if the cash book is written up-to-date before the bank reconciliation statement is attempted. This means that the bank statement will be checked against the cash book. All items on the bank statement, but that have not yet been put in the cash book, are then entered in the cash book. At the same time, any errors found in the cash book by such a check will be corrected. This means that the only differences will be items that are in the cash book but that have not yet appeared on the bank statement.

Although this would be the normal way to proceed before actually drawing up a bank reconciliation statement, it is possible that an examiner will ask you not to do it this way. If, in Exhibit 17.3 the cash book had been written up before the bank reconciliation statement was drawn up, then the cash book and the reconciliation statement would have appeared as follows in Exhibit 17.4.

Exhibit 17.4

Cash Book

Dr				*Cr*	
2005		£	2005		£
Dec 27	Total b/fwd	2,000	Dec 27	Total b/fwd	1,600
Dec 29	J Potter	60	Dec 28	J Jacobs	105
Dec 31	M Johnson	220	Dec 30	M Chatwood	15
Dec 31	Credit transfers:		Dec 31	Bank charges*	20
	L Shaw*	70	Dec 31	Balance c/d	610
		2,350			2,350
2006					
Jan 1	Balance b/d	610			

*Adding items that appear in the bank statement but not in the cashbook.

Bank Reconciliation Statement as on 31 December 2005

	£
Balance in hand as per cash book	610
Add Unpresented cheque – M Chatwood	15
	625
Less Bank lodgement not yet entered on bank statement	220
Balance in hand as per bank statement	405

17.5 Bank overdrafts

When there is a bank overdraft (shown by a credit balance in the cash book), the adjustments needed for reconciliation work are opposite to those needed for a debit balance.

Exhibit 17.5 shows a cash book, and a bank statement, showing an overdraft. Only the cheque for G Cumberbatch (A) £106 and the cheque paid to J Kelly (B) £63 need adjusting. Work through the reconciliation statement and then see the note after it.

Exhibit 17.5

Cash Book (Bank columns only)

Dr			*Cr*		
2004		£	2004		£
Dec 5	I Howe	308	Dec 1	Balance b/f	709
Dec 24	L Mason	120	Dec 9	P Davies	140
Dec 29	K King	124	Dec 27	J Kelly (B)	63
Dec 31	G Cumberbatch (A)	106	Dec 29	United Trust	77
Dec 31	Balance c/f	380	Dec 31	Bank charges	49
		1,038			1,038
			2005		
			Jan 1	Balance b/f	380

Bank Statement

2004		*Dr* £	*Cr* £	*Balance* £
Dec 1	Balance b/f			709 O/D
Dec 5	Cheque		308	401 O/D
Dec 14	P Davies	140		541 O/D
Dec 24	Cheque		120	421 O/D
Dec 29	K King: Credit transfer		124	297 O/D
Dec 29	United Trust: Standing order	77		374 O/D
Dec 31	Bank charges	49		423 O/D

Note: On a bank statement an overdraft is often shown with the letters O/D following the amount; or else it is shown as a debit balance, indicated by the letters DR after the amount.

Bank Reconciliation Statement as on 31 December 2004

	£
Overdraft as per cash book	380
Add Bank lodgements not on bank statement	106
	486
Less Unpresented cheque	63
Overdraft per bank statement	423

Now compare the reconciliation statements in Exhibits 17.4 and 17.5. This comparison reveals the following:

	Exhibit 17.4	***Exhibit 17.5***
	Balances	*Overdrafts*
Balance/Overdraft per cash book	XXXX	XXXX
Adjustments		
Unpresented cheque	PLUS	LESS
Banking not entered	LESS	PLUS
Balance/Overdraft per bank statement	XXXX	XXXX

Adjustments are, therefore, made in the opposite way when there is an overdraft.

17.6 Dishonoured cheques

When a cheque is received from a customer and paid into the bank, it is recorded on the debit side of the cash book. It is also shown on the bank statement as a deposit to the bank. However, at a later date, it may be found that the customer's bank will not pay us the amount due on the cheque. The cheque is therefore worthless. It is known as a **dishonoured cheque**.

There are several possible reasons for this. As an example, let us suppose that K King gave us a cheque for £5,000 on 20 May 2002. We banked it, but on 25 May 2002 our bank returned the cheque to us. Typical reasons are:

- King had put £5,000 in figures on the cheque, but had written it in words as five thousand five hundred pounds. You will have to give the cheque back to King for amendment or reissue.
- King had put the year 2001 on the cheque instead of 2002. Normally, cheques are considered 'stale' six months after the date on the cheque; in other words, the banks will not pay cheques over six months' old.
- King simply did not have sufficient funds in his bank account. Suppose he had previously only got a £2,000 balance and yet he has given us a cheque for £5,000. His bank has not allowed him to have an overdraft. In such a case the cheque would be dishonoured. The bank would write on the cheque 'refer to drawer', and we would have to get in touch with King to see what he was going to do to settle his bill.

In all of these cases the bank would show the original banking as being cancelled, by showing the cheque paid out of our bank account. As soon as this happens, they will notify us. We will then also show the cheque being cancelled by a credit in the cash book. We will then debit that amount to this account.

When King originally paid his account, our records would appear as:

K King Account

Dr			*Cr*		
2002		£	2002		£
May 1	Balance b/d	5,000	May 20	Bank	5,000

Bank Account

Dr			*Cr*		
2002		£			
May 20	K King	5,000			

After our recording the dishonoured cheque, the records will appear as:

K King Account

Dr			*Cr*		
2002		£	2002		£
May 1	Balance b/d	5,000	May 20	Bank	5,000
May 25	Bank: cheque dishonoured	5,000			

Bank Account

Dr				*Cr*
2002	£		2002	£
May 20 K King	5,000		May 25 K King: cheque dishonoured	5,000

In other words, King is once again shown as owing us £5,000.

17.7 Some other reasons for differences in balances

As you will recall from Chapter 14, both standing orders and direct debits can be set up to move money regularly out of one bank account and into another. As far as bank reconciliation statements are concerned, both of these types of payments will have passed through the bank account but will have not been entered in the cash book.

17.8 Reconciliation of our ledger accounts with suppliers' statements

Because of differences in timing, the balance on a supplier's statement on a certain date can differ from the balance on that supplier's account in our purchases ledger. This is similar to the fact that a bank statement balance may differ from the cash book balance. In similar fashion, a reconciliation statement may also be necessary. This can now be shown through the example given as Exhibit 17.6.

Exhibit 17.6

(a) Our Purchases Ledger

C Young Ltd Account

Dr				*Cr*
2006	£		2006	£
Jan 10 Bank	1,550		Jan 1 Balance b/d	1,550
Jan 29 Returns (i)	116		Jan 6 Purchases	885
Jan 31 Balance c/d	1,679		Jan 18 Purchases	910
	3,345			3,345
			Feb 1 Balance b/d	1,679

(b) Supplier's statement

C Young Ltd
Market Place, Leeds

STATEMENT

Account Name: A Hall Ltd
Account Number: H93 Date: 31 January 2006

	Debit	*Credit*	*Balance*
2006	£	£	£
Jan 1 Balance			1,550 Dr
Jan 4 Invoice No 3250	885		2,435 Dr
Jan 13 Payment received		1,550	885 Dr
Jan 18 Invoice No 3731	910		1,795 Dr
Jan 31 Invoice No 3894	425		2,220 Dr

Comparing our purchases ledger account with the supplier's statement, two differences can be seen:

(i) We sent returns £116 to C Young Ltd, but they had not received them and recorded them in their books by the end of January.
(ii) Our supplier sent goods to A Hall Ltd (our company), but we had not received them and had not entered the £425 in our books by the end of January.

A reconciliation statement can be drawn up by us, A Hall Ltd, as on 31 January 2006.

Reconciliation of Supplier's Statement
C Young Ltd as on 31 January 2006

		£	£
Balance per our purchases ledger			1,679
Add Purchases not received by us	(ii)	425	
Returns not received by supplier	(i)	116	
			541
Balance per supplier's statement			2,220

New terms

Bank reconciliation statement (p. 169): A calculation comparing the cash book balance with the bank statement balance.

Credit transfer (p. 172): An amount paid by someone direct into our bank account.

Dishonoured cheque (p. 176): A cheque that is found to be worth nothing.

Unpresented cheque (p. 171): A cheque that has been sent but has not yet gone through the bank account of the receiver.

EXERCISES

17.1 The following are extracts from the cash book and the bank statement of J Roche. You are required to:

(*a*) write the cash book up to date, and state the new balance as on 31 December 2005

(*b*) draw up a bank reconciliation statement as on 31 December 2005.

Cash Book

Dr			*Cr*		
2005		£	2005		£
Dec 1	Balance b/d	1,740	Dec 8	A Dailey	349
Dec 7	T J Masters	88	Dec 15	R Mason	33
Dec 22	J Ellis	73	Dec 28	G Small	115
Dec 31	K Wood	249	Dec 31	Balance c/d	1,831
Dec 31	M Barrett	178			
		2,328			2,328

Bank Statement

2005		*Dr* £	*Cr* £	*Balance* £
Dec 1	Balance b/d			1,740
Dec 7	Cheque		88	1,828
Dec 11	A Dailey	349		1,479
Dec 20	R Mason	33		1,446
Dec 22	Cheque		73	1,519
Dec 31	Credit transfer: J Walters		54	1,573
Dec 31	Bank charges	22		1,551

17.2X The following are extracts from the cash book and bank statement of Preston & Co

Cash Book

Dr			*Cr*		
2009		£	2009		£
Dec 1	Balance b/d	8,700	Dec 6	S Little	1,745
Dec 7	T J Blake	440	Dec 14	L Jones	165
Dec 20	P Dyson	365	Dec 21	E Fraser	575
Dec 30	A Veale	945	Dec 31	Balance c/d	9,155
Dec 31	K Woodburn	300			
Dec 31	N May	890			
		11,640			11,640

Bank Statement

	Dr	Cr	Balance
2009	£	£	£
Dec 1 Balance b/d			8,700
Dec 9 Cheque		440	9,140
Dec 10 S Little	1,745		7,395
Dec 19 L Jones	165		7,230
Dec 20 Cheque		365	7,595
Dec 26 Credit transfer: P Todd		270	7,865
Dec 31 Bank Charges	110		7,755

You are required to:

(*a*) write up the cash book and state the new balance on 31 December 2009

(*b*) prepare a bank reconciliation statement as on 31 December 2009.

17.3 The bank statement for James Baxter for the month of March 2006 is as follows:

Bank Statement

2006	Dr £	Cr £	Balance £
Mar 1 Balance b/d			2,598 O/D
8 L Young	61		2,659 O/D
16 Cheque		122	2,537 O/D
20 A Duffy	104		2,641 O/D
21 Cheque		167	2,474 O/D
31 Credit Transfer: A May		929	1,545 O/D
31 Standing Order: Oak plc	100		1,645 O/D
31 Bank Charges	28		1,673 O/D

The Cash Book for March 2006 is shown below:

Cash Book

Dr		Cr	
2006	£	2006	£
Mar 16 N Morris	122	Mar 1 Balance b/d	2,598
" 21 P Fraser	167	" 6 L Young	61
" 31 Southern Elect. Co	160	" 30 A Duffy	104
" 31 Balance c/d	2,804	" 30 C Clark	490
	3,253		3,253

You are required to:

(*a*) write the cash book up to date

(*b*) draw up a bank reconciliation statement as at 31 March 2006.

17.4X Following is the cash book (bank columns) of E Flynn for December 2007:

Cash Book

Dr			*Cr*		
2007		£	2007		£
Dec 6	J Hall	155	Dec 1	Balance b/d	3,872
Dec 20	C Walters	189	Dec 10	P Wood	206
Dec 31	P Miller	211	Dec 19	M Roberts	315
Dec 31	Balance c/d	3,922	Dec 29	P Phillips	84
		4,477			4,477

The bank statement for the month is:

2007	*Dr* £	*Cr* £	*Balance* £
Dec 1 Balance			3,872 O/D
Dec 6 Cheque		155	3,717 O/D
Dec 13 P Wood	206		3,923 O/D
Dec 20 Cheque		189	3,734 O/D
Dec 22 M Roberts	315		4,049 O/D
Dec 30 Mercantile: Standing order	200		4,249 O/D
Dec 31 K Saunders: Trader's credit		180	4,069 O/D
Dec 31 Bank charges	65		4,134 O/D

You are required to:
(*a*) write the cash book up to date to take the necessary items into account
(*b*) draw up a bank reconciliation statement as on 31 December 2007.

17.5 On 31 December 2006 the bank columns of K Talbot's cash book showed a balance of £4,500. The bank statement as at 31 December 2006 showed a credit balance of £8,850 on the account. You checked the bank statement with the cash book and found that the following had not been entered in the cash book:

(i) A standing order to RB Insurance for £600 had been paid by the bank.
(ii) Bank interest receivable of £720 had not been entered into the account.
(iii) Bank charges of £90 had been made.
(iv) A credit transfer of £780 from KB Ltd had been paid direct into the account.
(v) Talbot's deposit account balance of £4,200 had been transferred into her bank current account.
(vi) A returned cheque of £210, dishonoured by C Hill, had been entered on the bank statement.

You also found that two cheques, payable to L Young £750 and K Clark £870, had been entered in the cash book but had not been presented for payment. In addition, a cheque for £2,070 had been paid into the bank on 31 December 2006 but had not been credited on the bank statement until 2 January 2007.

Required:
(*a*) Starting with the cash book debit balance of £4,500, write the cash book up to date.
(*b*) Draw up a bank reconciliation statement as on 31 December 2006.

17.6X Alex Hunt is a sole trader dealing in photographic equipment. He received his bank statement for the month of June 2004 and discovered the balance shown did not agree with the credit balance in the bank column of the cash book, which was £4,005. On investigation the following items were discovered:

(i) A cheque for £750 in payment of rent had not been entered in the cash book.
(ii) A credit transfer had been received from Pennington's Co amounting to £8,250 on 20 June but had not been entered in the cash book.
(iii) Mr Hunt had withdrawn cash of £885 from the bank for private use. This has not been entered in the cash book.
(iv) Cheques made out to suppliers amounting to £5,700 had not been presented to the bank.
(v) A cheque received from S Ward amounting to £2,250 had been banked on 24 June, only to be returned on 29 June by the bank marked 'Refer to drawer'. This had not been entered in the cash book.
(vi) Mr Hunt paid £300 by cheque to Beech Hospital as a donation, but this had not been entered in the cash book.
(vii) Cheques totalling £3,075 had been received from customers and entered in the cash book, but they did not appear on the bank statement until 4 July 2004.

You are required to:
(*a*) write the cash book up to date.
(*b*) prepare a bank reconciliation statement as at 30 June 2004.

17.7X Cunningham & Co is an old-established firm of accountants in Huddersfield. You have been employed as book-keeper to the company to assist the senior partner, Mr Cunningham, with the accounting records and day-to-day routine duties. The company's policies when dealing with both payments and receipts is extremely strict. All cash and cheques received are to be banked immediately. Any payments over £10 must be made by cheque. Small cash payments are all paid by the petty cash system.

One of your tasks is to enter the company's cash book and reconcile this with the bank statement. This task must be carried out on a weekly basis.

Required:
(*a*) Having obtained the company's cheque book and paying-in book (Exhibits 17.7 and 17.8), enter up the cash book (bank columns only) for the week commencing 3 November 2006. Unfortunately, on that date the company was overdrawn by £2,356.00.
(*b*) Balance up the cash book at the end of the week and bring the balance down.
(*c*) From the bank statement (Exhibit 17.9) you are required to prepare:
   (i) The corrected cash book balance as at 10 November 2006
   (ii) A bank reconciliation statement as at 10 November 2006.

(NVQ Level 2)

EXHIBIT 17.7 • Details of cheque book stubs – Cunningham & Co

Date	3 Nov 2006
Payee	Post Office
	Stamps

Amount £ 146.50

001763

Date	3 Nov 2006
Payee	The Law
	Society

Amount £ 121.80

001764

Date	4 Nov 2006
Payee	Bayleys
	Office Supplies

Amount £ 94.10

001765

Date	5 Nov 2006
Payee	Lower Bents
	Garage
	(Petrol A/c – Sept)

Amount £ 450.15

001766

Date	6 Nov 2006
Payee	Wages

Amount £ 489.20

001767

Date	10 Nov 2006
Payee	Petty Cashier
	(Restoring
	Imprest)

Amount £ 46.00

Exhibit 17.8 • Details from paying-in book – Cunningham & Co

Date	A/c	Cash	Cheques	£
3 Nov 2006	Cunningham & Co		Mrs Stoddard £540.00	540.00
5 Nov 2006	Cunningham & Co	Bent Garage £221.00	P Ralphs £53.00; Gardeners £1500.00	1774.00
6 Nov 2006	Cunningham & Co	Mr Prince £130.50	Stephens & Smith £523.10	653.60
7 Nov 2006	Cunningham & Co		Rileys (Printers) & Co £759.00	759.00
7 Nov 2006	Cunningham & Co	Brindle Bros £165.50	Robert Andrews Ltd £325.00	490.50

Exhibit 17.9 • Bank Statement – Cunningham & Co

TUDOR BANK **CONFIDENTIAL**

High Street
Huddersfield

Account: Cunningham & Co
Chestergate
Huddersfield

Account:No: 0012770123

Sheet No: 67
Date: 8 November 2006

2006				*Dr*	*Cr*	*Balance*
Nov	3	Balance b/d				2,356.00 O/D
	4	Cheque	001763	146.50		2,502.50 O/D
	3	Deposit			540.00	1,962.50 O/D
	5	Deposit			1,774.00	188.50 O/D
	6	S/O Noble Insurance		62.00		250.50 O/D
	6	Cheque	001767	489.20		739.70 O/D
	6	Deposit			653.60	86.10 O/D
	7	Deposit			759.00	672.90
	7	Bank charges		22.45		650.45
	7	Cheque	001765	94.10		556.35

17.8X The following are extracts from the cash book and bank statement of Noshin Choudhary for the month of February 2002.

Cash Book (Bank columns only) – N Choudhary

Dr				*Cr*	
2002		£	2002		£
Feb 1	Balance b/d	2200	Feb 10	J Fairhurst	157
8	P Burlace	98	16	B Shaw	243
18	P Burlace	140	28	T Rungren	130
28	J Garcia	124	28	Balance c/d	2,032
		2,562			2,562

N Choudhary Bank Statement as at 28 February 2002

		Debit £	*Credit* £	*Balance* £
2002				
Feb 1	Balance b/d			2,200
8	Cheque		98	2,298
13	J Fairhurst	157		2,141
18	Cheque		140	2,281
20	B Shaw	243		2,038
26	Standing order	42		1,996
28	Bank charges	26		1,970
28	Credit transfer		91	2,061

Using the above information:

(*a*) bring the cash book up to date to show a corrected bank balance

(*b*) prepare a statement reconciling the *corrected* cash book balance with the bank statement.

NEAB (GCSE)

17.9X Vantage Products is one of your suppliers. Its account in your ledger is as follows:

Vantage Products

2004		£	2004		£
12 Oct	Purchase returns	75	1 Oct	Balance b/d	1,625
28	Bank	1,570	8	Purchases	1,050
28	Discount	55	19	Purchases	1,675
30	Purchase returns	105			
31	Balance c/d	2,545			
		4,350			4,350
			1 Nov	Balance b/d	2,545

On 2 November, the following statement of account is received from Vantage Products:

Vantage Products: Statement

	Debit £	*Credit* £	*Balance* £
2004			
Oct 1 Balance			3,175
3 Bank		1,500	1,675
3 Discount		50	1,625
8 Sales	1,050		2,675
15 Returns inwards		75	2,600
19 Sales	1,675		4,275
28 Sales	1,550		5,825

You are required to do the following:

(*a*) Prepare a reconciliation statement, ***starting with the balance in your books of £2,545,*** to explain the difference between the balance in your ledger and the closing balance on the statement of account.

(*b*) If the outstanding balance in your ledger on 1 November was settled less a 2½% discount:

(i) state the amount of discount

(ii) state the amount of the cheque.

OCR

CHAPTER 18

Capital and revenue expenditures

Learning objectives

After you have studied this chapter you should be able to:

- **distinguish between expenditure that is capital in nature and that which is revenue**
- **understand that some expenditure is part capital expenditure and part revenue expenditure**
- **realise the effect on the final accounts, and the profits shown there, if revenue expenditure is wrongly treated as being capital expenditure, and vice versa.**

18.1 Introduction

This chapter will deal with the distinction between capital and revenue expenditure and show the importance of careful classification, which can ultimately affect the recorded profits and the balance sheet valuations of a business.

18.2 Capital expenditure

Capital expenditure is expenditure on the purchase of fixed assets or of additions to existing fixed assets. Fixed assets, you will remember from Chapter 9 are those assets that have an expected life of greater than one year and are used in the business to enable it to generate income and, ultimately, profit. Examples include:

- premises, land and buildings
- machinery, plant and equipment
- office and computer equipment
- furniture and fittings.

Additions to existing fixed assets should also be classified as capital expenditure, and examples include:

- purchasing a scanner for the computer
- adding extra storage capacity to a mainframe computer
- expenses incurred in updating machinery to increase production
- additional shelving and fittings in a retail store.

It is important to include the following items of expenditure when fixed assets are purchased:

- the cost of acquiring the fixed assets
- the cost of delivery of the assets to the firm
- legal costs of buying premises, land and buildings
- installation costs
- architects' fees for building plans and for supervising the construction of buildings
- demolition costs to remove obsolete buildings before new work can begin.

18.3 Revenue expenditure

Revenue expenditure is expenditure that does not increase the value of fixed assets but is incurred in the day-to-day running expenses of the business.

The difference from capital expenditure can be seen when considering the cost of running a motor vehicle for a business. The expenditure incurred in acquiring the motor vehicle is classed as capital expenditure, while the cost of the petrol used to run the vehicle is revenue expenditure. This is because the revenue expenditure is used up in a few days and does not add to the value of the fixed asset.

18.4 Difference between capital and revenue expenditure

The difference between capital and revenue expenditure can be seen more generally in the following table (Exhibit 18.1). Revenue expenditure is the day-to-day running expense of the business and, as such, is chargeable to the trading and profit and loss account. Capital expenditure, in contrast, results in an increase in the fixed assets shown in the balance sheet.

EXHIBIT 18.1

Capital	Revenue
Premises purchased	Rent of premises
Legal charges for conveyancing	Legal charges for debt collection
New machinery	Repairs to machinery
Installations of machinery	Electricity costs of using machinery
Additions to assets	Maintenance of assets
Motor vehicles	Current Road Fund Tax
Delivery charges on new assets	Carriage on purchases and sales
Extension costs of new offices	Redecorating existing offices
Cost of adding air-conditioning to room	Interest on loan to purchase air-conditioning

18.5 Joint expenditure

In certain cases, an item of expenditure will need dividing between capital and revenue expenditure. Suppose a builder was engaged to carry out some work on your premises, the total bill being £30,000. If one-third of this was for repair work and two-thirds for improvements, then £10,000 should be charged to the profit and loss account as revenue expenditure, and £20,000 should be identified as capital expenditure and added to the value of the firm's premises and shown as such in the balance sheet.

18.6 Incorrect treatment of expenditure

If one of the following occurs:

- capital expenditure is incorrectly treated as revenue expenditure, or
- revenue expenditure is incorrectly treated as capital expenditure,

then both the balance sheet figures and the trading and profit and loss account figures will be incorrect. This means that the net profit figure will also be incorrect.

If the expenditure affects items in the trading account, then the gross profit figure will also be incorrect (e.g. if a motor vehicle was posted to the motor expenses account instead of the motor vehicle account), then net profit would be understated *and* the balance sheet values would not include the value of the asset.

18.7 Treatment of loan interest

If money is borrowed to finance the purchase of a fixed asset, then interest will have to be paid on the loan. The loan interest, however, is *not* a cost of acquiring the asset but is simply a cost of financing it. This means that loan interest is revenue expenditure and *not* capital expenditure.

18.8 Capital and revenue receipts

When an item of capital expenditure is sold, the receipt is called a capital receipt. Suppose a motor van is bought for £10,000, and sold five years later for £2,000. The £10,000 was treated as capital expenditure; the £2,000 received is treated as a capital receipt.

Revenue receipts are sales or other revenue items, such as rent receivable or commissions receivable.

New terms

Capital expenditure (p. 187): When a firm spends money to buy or add value to a fixed asset.

Revenue expenditure (p. 188): Expenses needed for the day-to-day running of the business.

EXERCISES

18.1 For the business of K Thorne, wholesale chemist, classify the following between 'capital' and 'revenue' expenditure:

(*a*) Purchase of an extra motor van.
(*b*) Cost of rebuilding a warehouse wall which had fallen down.
(*c*) Building extension to the warehouse.
(*d*) Painting extension to warehouse when it is first built.
(*e*) Repainting extension to warehouse three years later than that done in (*d*).
(*f*) Carriage costs on bricks for new warehouse extension.
(*g*) Carriage costs on purchases.
(*h*) Carriage costs on sales.
(*i*) Legal costs of collecting debts.
(*j*) Legal charges on acquiring new premises for office.
(*k*) Fire insurance premium.
(*l*) Costs of erecting new machine.

18.2X For the business of H Ward, a food store, classify the following between 'capital' and 'revenue' expenditure:

(*a*) Repairs to meat slicer.
(*b*) New tyre for van.
(*c*) Additional shop counter.
(*d*) Renewing signwriting on store.
(*e*) Fitting partitions in store.
(*f*) Roof repairs.
(*g*) Installing thief detection equipment.
(*h*) Wages of store assistant.
(*i*) Carriage on returns outwards.
(*j*) New cash register.
(*k*) Repairs to office safe.
(*l*) Installing extra toilet.

18.3X (*a*) Star Fashions Ltd, which manufactures children's clothing, is planning to purchase a new cutting machine costing £20,000. Would the following items of expenditure be classed as capital or revenue expenditure?
(i) The purchase price of the cutting machine.
(ii) The cost of installing the machine.
(iii) The significant cost of initial training for the staff to operate the new machine.
(iv) The cost of future repairs and maintenance of the machine.

(*b*) If capital expenditure is treated as revenue expenditure, then:
(i) How would the total expenses and the net profit for the period be affected?
(ii) What effect would the error have on the value of the fixed assets in the balance sheet?

18.4 T Taylor has drawn up his final accounts for the year ended 31 December 2008. On examining them, you find that:
(*a*) Taylor has debited the cost of office equipment £311 to the purchases account.
(*b*) Taylor has debited the cost of repairing office equipment £290 to the motor repairs account.
(*c*) Sale of a building for £10,000 has been credited to the sales account.
(*d*) Repayment of a loan £500 has been debited to the loan interest account.

From his figures he had calculated gross profit as £95,620 and net profit as £28,910.

Ignoring any adjustments for depreciation, calculate revised figures of gross and net profits after taking (*a*) to (*d*) into account.

18.5X S Simpson has calculated her gross profit for the year to 30 June 2006 as £129,450 and her net profit as £77,270. You find that Simpson's books show:

(*a*) Sale of a motor vehicle for £4,100 has been credited to the sales account.
(*b*) Fixtures, bought for £750, have been debited to the repairs account.
(*c*) Receipt of a loan for £6,000 has been credited to the sales account.
(*d*) Repairs to motor vehicles £379 have been debited to the general expenses account.

Ignoring any adjustments for depreciation, calculate the revised figures of gross and net profits.

18.6X A business has incorrectly charged some of its expenditure in its final accounts. The incorrect figures shown were as follows:

(*a*) Gross profit £216,290
(*b*) Net profit £110,160
(*c*) Fixed assets £190,000
(*d*) Current assets £77,600.

Required:
You are to show, for each of the following, the effects on the calculations of (*a*) gross profit, (*b*) net profit, (*c*) fixed assets in the balance sheet and (*d*) current assets in the balance sheet. (Ignore depreciation.)
(i) Motor van costing £5,500 debited to motor expenses account.
(ii) Carriage outwards £77 debited to fixtures account.
(iii) Rent £2,000 debited to buildings account.
(iv) Machinery £6,000 debited to fixtures account.
(v) Office equipment £790 debited to purchases account.
(vi) Discounts allowed £2,380 debited to machinery account.

18.7X (*a*) For each of the following transactions place *one* tick (✓) in the appropriate column to indicate whether the item is an example of capital expenditure, revenue expenditure, revenue receipt or capital receipt.
Transaction (i) is done as an example for you.

Transaction	Capital expenditure	Capital receipt	Revenue expenditure	Revenue receipt
(i) Purchase of goods for resale			✓	
(ii) Rent received for office sub-let				
(iii) Purchase of stationery for office use				
(iv) Sale of old equipment no longer required				
(v) Cost of building an extension to premises				
(vi) Sale of stock				
(vii) Repairs to existing premises				

(*b*) How should items of capital expenditure be treated when preparing final accounts?

NEAB (GCSE)

CHAPTER 19

The sales day book, sales ledger, related documentation, and other considerations

Learning objectives

After you have studied this chapter you should be able to:

- **draw up a sales invoice**
- **enter items in a sales day book and post to the sales ledger**
- **understand how trade discounts differ from cash discounts**
- **appreciate documentation used in the sale of goods**
- **understand the importance of internal control**
- **understand terms and abbreviations used in trading activity**
- **appreciate the need for credit control.**

19.1 Introduction

In Chapter 12 we saw that the ledger had been split up into a set of day books, journals and ledgers. This chapter explains about sales day books and sales ledgers.

19.2 Cash sales

When goods are paid for immediately by cash, there is no need to enter these sales in the sales day book. In such cases we do not need to know the names and addresses of customers and what has been sold to them, because we don't need to keep a record of money owing to us.

19.3 Credit sales

In many businesses, most of the sales will be made on credit rather than for cash. In fact, the sales of some businesses will consist entirely of credit sales.

For each credit sale the selling firm will send a document to the buyer showing full details of the goods sold and the prices of the goods. This document is known as an **invoice**, and to the seller it is known as a **sales invoice**. The seller will keep one or more copies of each sales invoice for internal use. Exhibit 19.1 is an example of an invoice.

EXHIBIT 19.1

Your Purchase Order 10/A/980		J Blake 7 Over Warehouse Leicester LE1 2AP
Invoice No: 16554 To: D Poole & Co Deansgate Restaurant 45 Charles Street Manchester M1 5ZN	**INVOICE**	1 September 2005
Quantity and description	*Per unit*	*Total*
	£	£
21 cases Cape Glory Pears	20	420
5 cartons Kay's Flour	4	20
6 cases Joy's Sauce	20	120
		560
Terms: 1¼% cash discount if paid within one month		

You must not think that all invoices will look exactly like the one chosen as Exhibit 19.1. Each business will have its own design. But all invoices will be numbered, and they will contain the names and addresses both of the supplier and of the customer. In this case the supplier is J Blake and the customer is D Poole.

19.4 Copies of sales invoices

As soon as a sales invoice for goods being sent has been made out, the top copy is sent to the customer. The selling firm will keep copies of all these sales invoices for future reference.

19.5 Entering credit sales into the sales day book

From the retained copy of the sales invoice, the seller enters up the sales day book. This book is merely a list, showing the following:

- date of sale
- name of customer to whom the goods have been sold
- invoice number
- final amount of invoice.

There is no need to show details of the goods sold in the sales day book. This can be found by looking at copy invoices.

Since the sales invoice represents the *source* from which the sales day book is written up, it is often known as a 'source document'. We will see other source documents in later chapters.

We can now look at Exhibit 19.2, which is a sales day book, starting with the record of the sales invoice already shown in Exhibit 19.1. Let us assume that the entries are on page 26 of the day book.

EXHIBIT 19.2

Sales Day Book				*(page 26)*
			Invoice No	*Amount*
2005				£
Sept	1	D Poole & Co	16554	560
	8	T Cockburn	16555	1,640
	28	C Carter	16556	220
	30	D Stevens & Co	16557	1,100
				3,520

19.6 Posting credit sales to the sales ledger

Instead of having one ledger for all accounts, we now have a sales ledger that is used for recording credit sale transactions.

The credit sales are now posted, one by one, to the debit side of each customer's account in the sales ledger. At the end of each period, the total of the credit sales is posted to the credit of the sales account in the general ledger. You may find it easier to use 'IN' and 'OUT', as we did in Chapter 3, to post these transactions; i.e. the goods sold go 'into' each individual customer's account and they come 'out' of the sales account. This is now illustrated in Exhibit 19.3.

EXHIBIT 19.3 • Posting Credit Sales

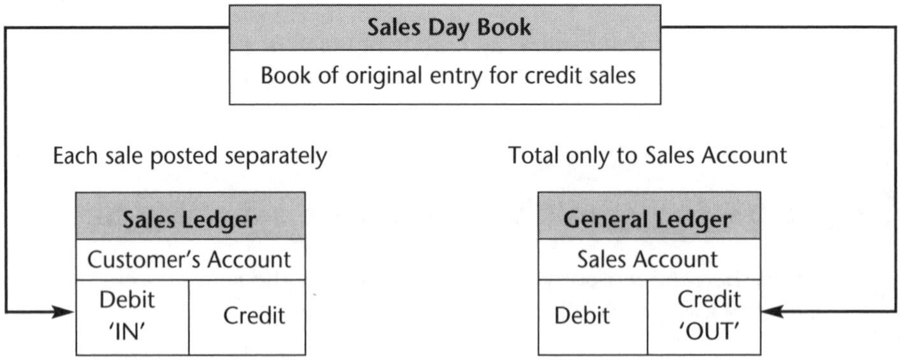

19.7 An example of posting credit sales

The sales day book in Exhibit 19.2 is now shown again. This time, posting is made to the sales ledger and the general ledger. Notice the completion of the folio columns with the reference numbers.

Sales Day Book *(page 26)*

		Invoice No	*Folio*	*Amount*
2005				£
Sept 1	D Poole & Co	16554	SL 12	560
8	T Cockburn	16555	SL 39	1,640
28	C Carter	16556	SL125	220
30	D Stevens & Co	16557	SL249	1,100
	Transferred to Sales Account		GL 44	3,520

Sales Ledger

D Poole & Co Account *(page 12)*

Dr				*Cr*
2005			£	
Sept 1	Sales	SJ 26	560	

T Cockburn Account *(page 39)*

Dr				*Cr*
2005			£	
Sept 8	Sales	SJ 26	1,640	

C Carter Account *(page 125)*

Dr				*Cr*
2005			£	
Sept 28	Sales	SJ 26	220	

D Stevens & Co Account *(page 249)*

Dr				*Cr*
2005			£	
Sept 30	Sales	SJ 26	1,100	

General Ledger

Sales Account *(page 44)*

Dr				*Cr*
	2005			£
	Sept 30	Credit Sales for the month	SJ 26	3,520

Alternative names for the sales day book are the sales book and the sales journal. Before you continue, you should attempt Exercise 19.1.

19.8 Trade discounts

Suppose you are the proprietor of a business. You are selling to three different kinds of customers:

(i) traders who buy many goods from you.
(ii) traders who buy only a few items from you.
(iii) the general public.

The traders themselves in categories (i) and (ii) have to sell goods to the general public in their own areas. They have to make a profit, so they will want to pay you less than the retail price. The traders in category (i) who buy in large quantities will not want to pay as much as traders in category (ii), who buy in small quantities. You want to attract large customers, and so you are happy to sell to them at a lower price.

This means that your selling prices are at three levels: (i) to traders buying large quantities; (ii) to traders buying small quantities; and (iii) to the general public. All goods are shown at the same price so that your staff do not need three different price lists; however, a reduction (discount), called a **trade discount** is given to traders in categories (i) and (ii).

As an example, assume that you are selling food-mixing machines, and that the retail price per item is £200. Traders in category (i) are given 25 per cent trade discount, traders in (ii), 20 per cent, and the general public (iii) pay the full retail price. The prices paid by each type of customer would then be:

		Trader (i)		Trader (ii)	General Public (iii)
		£		£	£
Retail price		200		200	200
Less Trade discount	(25%)	50	(20%)	40	nil
Price to be paid by customer		150		160	200

Exhibit 19.4 is an invoice for goods sold to D Poole. It is for the same items as were shown in Exhibit 19.1, but this time the seller is R Grant and he uses trade discounts to get the price down to that paid by his customers. By comparing Exhibits 19.1 and 19.5 you can see that the prices paid by D Poole were the same. It is simply the method of calculating the price that is different.

Exhibit 19.4

INVOICE

R GRANT (CATERING SUPPLIES)
HIGHER SIDE PRESTON PR1 2NL

Telephone: (01703) 33122
Fax: (01703) 22331

D Poole & Co
Deansgate Restaurant
45 Charles Street
Manchester M1 5ZN

Invoice No 30756
Account No P/4298
Date: 1 September 2005

Your Purchase Order 11/A/G80

Quanity	***Per unit***	***Total***
	£	£
21 cases Cape Glory Pears	25	525
5 cartons Kay's Flour	5	25
6 cases Joy's Sauce	25	150
		700
Less 20% Trade Discount		140
		560

19.9 Trade discounts and cash discounts compared

As the trade discount is simply a way of calculating sales prices, no entry for a trade discount should be made in the double entry records nor in the sales day book. Cash discounts are given for prompt payment, and do not affect the amounts of balances on the personal accounts. They are, therefore, part of double entry accounting (see Chapter 16).

The recording of Exhibit 19.4 in R Grant's sales day book and D Poole's personal account will appear thus:

Sales Day Book *(page 87)*

	Invoice No	Folio	Amount
			£
2005			
Sept 2 D Poole & Co	30756	SL 32	560

Sales Ledger *(page 32)*

D Poole & Co Account

Dr			*Cr*
2005		£	
Sept 2 Sales	SJ 87	560	

To compare with cash discounts:

- trade discounts are not shown in double entry accounts
- cash discounts *are* shown in double entry accounts.

19.10 Other documentation

Each firm will have its own system of making out documents. All but the very smallest organisations will have their documents prepared via computer.

The sales invoice is the document from which the book-keeping records are prepared. There will usually be several other documents prepared at the same time, so that the firm may properly organise the sending of the goods and ensuring that they are safely received. These extra documents may be as set out next.

Advice note

Advice notes will be sent to the customer before the goods are dispatched. This means that the customer will know that the goods are on the way and when they should arrive. If the goods do not arrive within a reasonable time, the customer will notify the seller so that enquiries may be made with the carrier to establish what has happened to the goods.

The document will look something like that shown in Exhibit 19.5. Compare it with the invoice sent out as Exhibit 19.4.

Exhibit 19.5

ADVICE NOTE | **R GRANT (CATERING SUPPLIES)** | No 178554
Higher Side
Preston | Tel (01703) 33122
30 August 2005 | **PR1 2NL** | Fax (01703) 22331

J. Jones, Head Buyer
D Poole & Co
Deansgate Restaurant
45 Charles Street
Manchester M1 5ZN

Your order No 11/A/G80
Despatch details: 27 cases and 5 cartons

Quantity	*Cat No*	*Description*	*Price*
21 cases	M566	Cape Glory Pears	£25 each
5 cartons	K776	Kay's Flour	£5 each
6 cases	J865	Joy's Sauce	£25 each
			All less 20%

Delivery to:
D Poole & Co, Warehouse 2,
Longmills Trading Estate, Manchester M14 2TT

Delivery note

When goods are sent out, they usually have a delivery note to accompany them. This means that the customer can check immediately, and easily, what goods are being received. Very often, a copy will be retained by the carrier, with the customer having to sign to say that the goods have been received as stated on the note.

In connection with the goods shown on the advice note in Exhibit 19.5 a delivery note may appear as in Exhibit 19.6.

Exhibit 19.6

DELIVERY NOTE **R GRANT (CATERING SUPPLIES)** No 194431
Higher Side
Preston Tel (01703) 33122
11 September 2005 **PR1 2NL** Fax (01703) 22331

J. Jones, Head Buyer
D Poole & Co
Deansgate Restaurant
45 Charles Street
Manchester M1 5ZN

Order No 11/A/G80
Despatch details: 27 cases, 5 cartons by road

Quantity	*Cat No*	*Details*
21 cases	M566	Cape Glory Pears
5 cartons	K776	Kay's Flour
6 cases	J865	Joy's Sauce

Delivery to: Warehouse 2, Longmills Trading Estate,
Manchester M14 2TT

Received 27 cases and 5 cartons

Signed ....

On behalf of ....

Other documents

Each firm may vary in the type and number of documents used. Some of these other documents may be:

- *Despatch notes* These will resemble delivery notes, and are used by the despatch department.
- *Acknowledgement letters* These may be sent to customers to show that their orders have been received, and whether delivery will be made as per the order.

19.11 Manufacturer's recommended retail price

Looking at an item displayed in a shop window, you will frequently see something like the following:

Automatic Washer:	Manufacturer's Recommended Retail Price	£500
	Less discount of 20 per cent	£100
	You pay only	£400

Very often the manufacturer's recommended retail price is a figure above what the manufacturer would expect the public to pay for its product. Probably, in the case shown, the manufacturer would have expected the public to pay around £400 for its product.

The inflated figure used for the 'manufacturer's recommended retail price' is simply a sales gimmick. Most people like to feel they are getting a bargain. The salesmen know that someone usually would prefer to get '20 per cent off' and pay £400, rather than for the price simply be shown as £400 with no mention of a discount.

19.12 Credit control

Any organisation that sells goods on credit should keep a close check to ensure that debtors pay their accounts on time. If this is not done properly, the amount of debtors can grow to an amount that will cripple the business.

The following four procedures should be carried out:

1 For each debtor, a limit should be set and the debtor should not be allowed to owe more than this limit. The amount of the limit will depend on the circumstances. Such things as the size of the customer's firm and the amount of business done with it, as well as its past record of payments, will help in choosing the limit figure.
2 As soon as the payment date has been reached, check to see whether payment has been made or not. Failure to pay on time may mean you refuse to supply any more goods unless payment is made quickly.
3 Where payment is not forthcoming, after investigation it may be necessary to take legal action to sue the customer for the debt. This will depend on the circumstances.
4 It is important that customers are made aware of what will happen if they do not pay their account by the due date.

19.13 Internal checks

When sales invoices are being made out, they should be scrutinised very carefully. A system is usually set up so that each stage of the preparation of the invoice is checked by someone other than the person whose job it is to send out the invoice. If this was not done, it would be possible for someone inside a firm to send out an invoice, as an instance, at a price less than the true price. Any difference could then be split between that person and someone outside the firm. If an invoice should have been sent to Ivor Twister & Co for £2,000, but the invoice clerk deliberately made it out for £200, then, if there was no cross-check, the difference of £1,800 could be split between the invoice clerk and Ivor Twister & Co.

Similarly, outside firms could send invoices for goods that were never received by the firm. This might be in collaboration with an employee within the firm, but there are firms sending false invoices that rely on the firms receiving them being inefficient and paying for items never received. There have certainly been firms sending invoices for such items as advertisements that have never been published. The cashier of the firm receiving the invoice, if the firm is an inefficient one, might possibly think that someone in the firm had authorised the advertisements and would pay the bill. Besides these cases, there are, of course, genuine errors, and these should also be detected.

A system therefore needs to be set up whereby the invoices have to be subject to scrutiny, at each stage, by someone other than the person who sends out the invoices or is responsible for paying them. Naturally, in a small firm – simply because the number of office staff might be few – this cross-check may be in the hands of only one person other than the person who will pay it.

A similar sort of check will be made in respect of sales invoices being sent out.

19.14 Factoring

One of the problems that face many businesses is the time taken by debtors to pay their accounts. Few businesses have so much cash available to them that they do not mind how long the debtor takes to pay. It is a fact that many businesses that become bankrupt do so, not because the business is not making profits, but because the business has run out of cash funds. Once that happens, the confidence factor in business evaporates, and the business then finds that very few people will supply it with goods, and it also cannot pay its employees. Closure of the firm then generally happens fairly quickly.

In the case of debtors, the cash problem may be alleviated by using the services of a financial intermediary called a 'factor'. **Factoring** is a financial service designed to improve the cash flow of healthy, growing companies, enabling them to make better use of management time and the money tied up in trade credit to customers. In essence, factors provide their clients with three closely integrated services, covering sales accounting and collection, credit management (which can include protection against bad debts), and the availability of finance against sales invoices.

19.15 Slip system

Some organisations avoid using day books by using the **slip system.** This involves putting information such as lists of invoices in 'slip' form, which can then be entered directly into the ledger accounts. The entry into the appropriate day book is thus eliminated.

For instance, banks use the slip system, whereby a customer makes out a paying-in slip to pay money into his or her account, and the slip is then used to enter the details of the transaction and become the documentary evidence.

Nowadays, with most organisations using computerised accounting systems, invoices tend to be collated into batches prior to entry. The invoices are then entered directly onto the system and the total checked, with the slip, prior to processing the invoices by computer.

The advantages of the slip system are that:

- it is easy to operate
- it is quicker than using day books
- it minimizes the risk of error, i.e. batch totals should be verified before processing when using a computerised system of accounting.

The disadvantages are:

- if invoices are lost, this can cause problems
- fraud is made easier to get away with
- it is not easy to analyse items, e.g. sales of different kinds of goods.

19.16 Abbreviations

Business documents frequently contain abbreviations and terms of trade, the most common of which are as follows:

- **Carriage paid** Another word for carriage is transport costs. Thus 'carriage paid' indicates that the cost of transport has been included in the cost of the goods.
- **COD** This abbreviation stands for 'cash on delivery' and means that the goods must be paid for on delivery.
- **E & OE** On some invoices and other documents you will see the initials 'E & OE' printed at the bottom of the invoice. This abbreviation stands for 'errors and omissions excepted'. Basically, this is a warning that there may possibly be errors or omissions, which could mean that the figures shown are incorrect, and that the recipient should check the figures carefully before taking any action concerning them.
- **Ex works** An indication that the price of the goods does not include delivery costs.
- **Net monthly** This phrase frequently appears at the foot of an invoice and means that the full amount of the invoice is due for payment within one month of the date of the invoice.

New terms

Advice note (p. 198): A note sent to a customer by the supplier prior to goods being despatched, advising them of the goods to be despatched and the estimated date of delivery.

Carriage paid (p. 202): See Section 19.16.

COD (p. 202): See Section 19.16.

Delivery note (p. 199): A note that accompanies goods being despatched, enabling the customer to check what goods have been received. The carrier often retains a copy and asks the customer to sign this to verify that the customer has received the goods.

E & OE (p. 202): See Section 19.16.

Ex works (p. 202): See Section 19.16.

Factoring (p. 201): A system used by a business to improve its cash flow. This involves 'selling' its debtors to a factoring company, which is then responsible for collecting debts as they become due and which keeps a percentage of the money collected (usually around 10 per cent).

Invoice (p. 192): A sales invoice (see below, p. 193).

Net monthly (p. 202): See Section 19.16.

Sales invoice (p. 192): A document showing details of goods sold and the prices of those goods.

Slip system (p. 201): See section 19.15.

Trade discount (p. 196): A reduction given to a customer when calculating the selling prices of goods.

EXERCISES

19.1 You are to enter up the sales day book from the following details. Post the items to the relevant accounts in the sales ledger and then show the transfer to the sales account in the general ledger.

2006			
Mar	1	Credit sales to J Gordon	£187
Mar	3	Credit sales to G Abrahams	£166
Mar	6	Credit sales to V White	£12
Mar	10	Credit sales to J Gordon	£55
Mar	17	Credit sales to F Williams	£289
Mar	19	Credit sales to C Richards	£66
Mar	27	Credit sales to V Wood	£28
Mar	31	Credit sales to L Simes	£78

19.2X Enter up the sales day book from the following, then post the items to the relevant accounts in the sales ledger. Show the transfer to the sales account in the general ledger.

2006			
May	1	Credit sales to J Johnson	£305
May	3	Credit sales to T Royes	£164
May	5	Credit sales to B Howe	£45
May	7	Credit sales to M Lee	£100
May	16	Credit sales to J Jakes	£308
May	23	Credit sales to A Vinden	£212
May	30	Credit sales to J Samuels	£1,296

19.3 F Benjamin of 10 Lower Street, Plymouth, is selling the following items, with the recommended retail prices as shown: white tape at £10 per roll; green baize at £4 per metre; blue cotton at £6 per sheet; and black silk at £20 per dress length. He makes the following sales:

2007

May 1 To F Gray, 3 Keswick Road, Portsmouth: 3 rolls white tape, 5 sheets blue cotton, 1 dress length black silk. Less 25 per cent trade discount.

May 4 To A Gray, 1 Shilton Road, Preston: 6 rolls white tape, 30 metres green baize. Less $33^1/_3$ per cent trade discount.

May 8 To E Hines, 1 High Road, Malton: 1 dress length black silk. No trade discount.

May 20 To M Allen, 1 Knott Road, Southport: 10 rolls white tape, 6 sheets blue cotton, 3 dress lengths black silk, 11 metres green baize. Less 25 per cent trade discount.

May 31 To B Cooper, 1 Tops Lane, St Andrews: 12 rolls white tape, 14 sheets blue cotton, 9 metres green baize. Less $33^1/_3$ per cent trade discount.

You are required to:

(*a*) draw up a sales invoice for each of the above sales,
(*b*) enter them up in the sales day book, posting to the personal accounts, and
(*c*) transfer the total to the sales account in the general ledger.

19.4X J Fisher, White House, Bolton, is selling the following items, with the retail prices as shown: plastic tubing at £1 per metre; polythene sheeting at £2 per length; vinyl padding at £5 per box; and foam rubber at £3 per sheet. He makes the following sales:

2005

June 1 To A Portsmouth, 5 Rockley Road, Worthing: 22 metres plastic tubing, 6 sheets foam rubber, 4 boxes vinyl padding. Less 25 per cent trade discount.

″ 5 To B Butler, 1 Wembley Road, Colwyn Bay: 50 lengths polythene sheeting, 8 boxes vinyl padding, 20 sheets foam rubber. Less 20 per cent trade discount.

″ 11 To A Gate, 1 Bristol Road, Hastings: 4 metres plastic tubing, 33 lengths of polythene sheeting, 30 sheets foam rubber. Less 25 per cent trade discount.

″ 21 To L Mackeson, 5 Maine Road, Bath: 29 metres plastic tubing. No trade discount is given.

″ 30 To M Alison, Daley Road, Box Hill: 32 metres plastic tubing, 24 lengths polythene sheeting, 20 boxes vinyl padding. Less $33\frac{1}{3}$ per cent trade discount.

Required:

(*a*) Draw up a sales invoice for each of the above sales.
(*b*) Then enter up in the sales day book and post to the personal accounts.
(*c*) Transfer the total to the sales account in the general ledger.

19.5X Morridge Products Ltd is a small manufacturing company that makes parts for tractors, farm equipment and general machine parts. In addition to manufacturing, the company also carries out repairs.

As accounts assistant, you have as one of your tasks the duty to prepare sales invoices and enter the details into the books of account. This involves entering them initially in the sales day book, then posting each individual item to the respective debtors accounts in the sales ledger; finally, at the end of the month, you have to post the totals in the day book to the respective accounts in the general ledger.

Required:

(*a*) From the following details, prepare invoices using the blank form provided (Exhibit 19.7, you may photo-copy extra copies to enable you to carry out this task) and date them 3 December 2004. VAT is to be calculated at $17^{1}/_{2}$ per cent and applies to all invoices except item 6 (which already includes VAT). The next Invoice No is 0932.

Invoice Details

	Name/Address	*Details of Order*	*Price* £	*Order No*
1	Price, Barlow & Co	1 Fork for	240.00	PB 323
	Hulme End	Fordson tractor		
	Derbyshire			
2	Rowley Farmers	Repairs to		Via
	Dove End Farm	muckspreader		telephone
	Bakewell	Parts	73.50	
	Derbyshire	Labour	38.00	
3	Stoke Engineering Co Ltd	Machine parts		
	Blythe End Works	to your specification		64394
	Stoke-on-Trent	as per quotation	347.30	
4	Peak Manufacturing Co	6 Tractor Back Boxes		K 2314
	Town End	as per your drawing		
	Buxton	Price as quoted (each)	234.70	
	Derbyshire			
5	Robinson (Plant Hire)	Repair to JCB arm		
	Leek	Parts	125.70	R 945
	Staffs	Labour	210.00	
6	Bennetts Farm Machinery	Baler modified		Per
	c/o Holly Bank Farm	as per our telephone		telephone
	Monyash	conversation		
	Derbyshire	As agreed	220.00	
			(inclusive)	

(*b*) Enter the sales invoices in the day book and post to the various customer accounts in the sales ledger.

EXHIBIT 19.7

MORRIDGE PRODUCTS LTD **Moor Top Lane** **Leek** Telephone: 01538 703101 Fax: 01538 703203 VAT Reg No 761 9849 16	**INVOICE**		**Invoice No:** **Account No:** Date/Tax point:	
Product code	*Description*	*Quantity*	*Unit price £ p*	*Total amount £ p*
Comments:		Net total VAT @ 17.5%		
		Total		
Registered office:16 Brook Lane, Manchester			Registered No: 384 1758	

(*c*) Finally, post the day book totals to the accounts in the general ledger.

NVQ (Level 2)

19.6 Why is it important to ensure that sales invoices are thoroughly checked before being sent out to customers?

19.7 What is meant by the term 'factoring'?

CHAPTER 20

The purchases day book, purchases ledger and related documentation

Learning objectives

After you have studied this chapter you should be able to:

- **draw up a purchase order**
- **authorise and code invoices for payment**
- **enter purchase invoices into the purchases day book**
- **post the purchases day book to the purchases ledger.**

20.1 Purchase orders

When a business or organisation decides to buy goods or engage the services of another company, it usually issues a **purchase order.** Such a document contains the following information:

- name and address of supplier
- purchase order number
- date of order
- details of the goods or services ordered, including part numbers or catalogue references
- quantity required
- delivery date
- authorised signature of a senior member of the company such as the buyer.

Each purchase order is normally raised by the customer's purchasing office and then sent to the supplier. Once it has been accepted by the supplier a formal contract will exist between the two parties. An example of a purchase order is shown in Exhibit 20.1.

Exhibit 20.1 • Purchase order

PURCHASE ORDER

Stoke Engineering Co Ltd
Blythe End Works
Stoke-on-Trent

Telephone:	01782 923116	Order No:	ST 6032
Fax:	01782 923431	Date:	12 March 2004
VAT Reg No:	964 7688 21		

Morridge Products Ltd
Moor Top Lane
Leek

Please supply the following:

120 off	Suspension arm	Part No B402	£38.50 each
60 off	Axle Shaft	Part No B424	£27.65 each
120 off	Backplate	Part No B432	£43.20 each

Delivery required: by end April 2004 to our works.
If there are any queries regarding this order please contact the undersigned immediately.

Signed *A Barton*
Buyer

20.2 Purchase invoices

An invoice is a **purchase invoice** when it is entered in the books of the firm purchasing the goods. The same invoice, in the books of the seller, would be a sales invoice.

For example, look again at Exhibit 19.1 in Chapter 19: in the books of D Poole it is a purchase invoice; in the books of J Blake it is a sales invoice.

20.3 Entering into the purchases day book

From the purchase invoices for goods bought on credit, the purchaser enters the details in his purchases day book. This book is merely a list, showing the following:

- date of purchase
- name of supplier from whom the goods were purchased
- reference number of the invoice
- final amount of invoice.

There is no need to show details of the goods bought in the purchases day book; this can be found by looking at the invoices themselves. Exhibit 20.2 is an example of a purchases day book.

EXHIBIT 20.2

Purchases Day Book				*(page 49)*
		Invoice No	*Folio*	*Amount*
2005				£
Sept 2	R Simpson	9/101		670
8	B Hamilton	9/102		1,380
19	C Brown	9/103		120
30	K Gabriel	9/104		510
				2,680

The purchases day book is often known also as the purchases book or the purchases journal.

20.4 Posting credit purchases to the purchases ledger

We now have a separate purchases ledger. The double entry is as follows:

- The credit purchases are posted one by one, to the credit of each supplier's account in the purchases ledger.
- At the end of each period, the total of the credit purchases is posted to the debit of the purchases account in the general ledger. Again, you may find it easier to use 'IN' and 'OUT', as discussed in Chapters 3 and 19; i.e. the goods purchased come from each supplier and therefore their accounts are entered on the 'OUT' side. The total purchases for the period are then entered on the 'IN' side of the purchases account since the goods are coming 'IN' to us. This is illustrated in Exhibit 20.3.

EXHIBIT 20.3 • Posting Credit Purchases

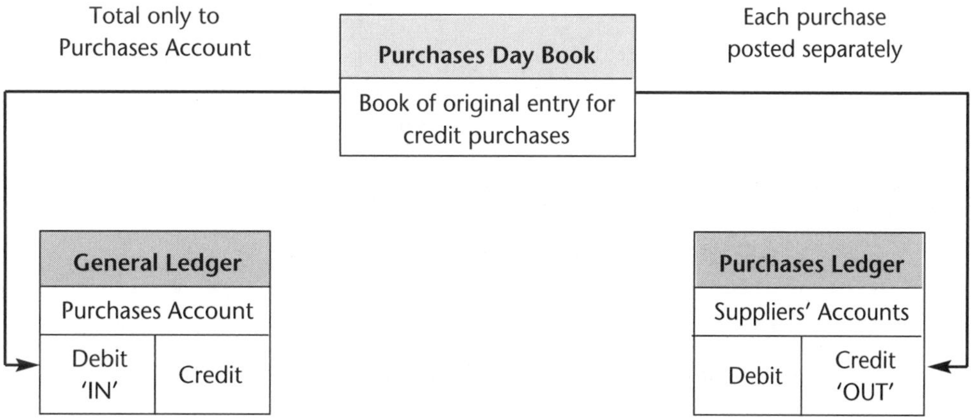

20.5 A worked example of posting credit purchases

The purchases day book in Exhibit 20.2 is shown again below. This time, posting is made to the purchases ledger and the general ledger. Notice the completion of the folio columns.

Purchases Day Book *(page 49)*

	Invoice No	*Folio*	*Amount*
2005			£
Sept 2 R Simpson	9/101	PL16	670
8 B Hamilton	9/102	PL29	1,380
19 C Brown	9/103	PL55	120
30 K Gabriel	9/104	PL89	510
Transferred to purchases account		GL63	2,680

Purchases Ledger

R Simpson Account *(page 16)*

Dr					*Cr*
		2005			£
		Sept 2	Purchases	PJ 49	670

B Hamilton Account *(page 29)*

Dr					*Cr*
		2005			£
		Sept 8	Purchases	PJ 49	1,380

C Brown Account *(page 55)*

Dr					*Cr*
		2005			£
		Sept 19	Purchases	PJ 49	120

K Gabriel Account *(page 89)*

Dr					*Cr*
		2005			£
		Sept 30	Purchases	PJ 49	510

General Ledger

Purchases Account *(page 63)*

Dr					*Cr*
2005			£		
Sept 30	Credit purchases for the month	PJ 49	2,680		

20.6 Authorisation and coding of invoices

Authorisation of purchase invoices

When purchase invoices are received from various suppliers of goods or services, it is important to check the invoices for accuracy in the calculations and to ensure that the goods invoiced have been received and agree with the relevant purchase order and specifications.

On receipt, each purchase invoice should be numbered, recorded and stamped with an appropriate rubber stamp (*see* Exhibit 20.4), to enable the invoice to be checked and coded.

Exhibit 20.4

Invoice no	
Purchase order no	
Goods received	
Extensions	
Passed for payment	
Code	

Coding of invoices

After stamping, it is necessary to perform the **coding of invoices**. Each invoice should be sent to the department responsible for ordering the goods, the invoice should be checked and, if everything is satisfactory, it is coded, passed for payment by a department head and returned to the accounts department for entry into the books of account and, ultimately, payment.

Organisations using computer accounting systems need to give unique numbers to all their various accounts that the computer can recognise instantly:

- *Purchases Ledger* Suppliers are given account numbers – for example:

	Account number
Blackshaws	0207
Harvey Construction Ltd	0243
Morridge Products	0275
Travis and Humphreys	0284

- *Sales Ledger* Customers' account numbers may be thus:

	Account number
Heath Manufacturing Ltd	1084
Office Supplies Ltd	1095
Seddon & Sons	1098
Yeoman's Supplies	1099

- *General Ledger* Examples of account codes are as follows:

	Account number
Capital account	4003
Motor expenses account	4022
Printing and stationery account	4074
Sales account	4098

A register of code numbers allocated to specific accounts must be maintained and updated as necessary. This register may be a manual one or held on the computer system.

New terms

Coding of invoices (p. 211): A process used, particularly in computerised accounting, to code the invoice to the supplier or purchaser, and also to the relevant account in the general ledger.

Purchase invoice (p. 208): A document received by purchaser showing details of goods bought and their prices.

Purchase order (p. 207): This is a document prepared by the purchaser and it contains details of the goods or services required by the purchaser.

EXERCISES

20.1 B Mann has the following purchases for the month of May 2004:

2004
May 1 From K King: 4 radios at £30 each, 3 music centres at £160 each. Less 25 per cent trade discount.
May 3 From A Bell: 2 washing machines at £200 each, 5 vacuum cleaners at £60 each, 2 dish dryers at £150 each. Less 20 per cent trade discount.
May 15 From J Kelly: 1 music centre at £300 each, 2 washing machines at £250 each. Less 25 per cent trade discount.
May 20 From B Powell: 6 radios at £70 each, less $33^1/_3$ per cent trade discount.
May 30 From B Lewis: 4 dish dryers at £200 each, less 20 per cent trade discount.

Required:
(*a*) Enter up the purchases day book for the month.
(*b*) Post the transactions to the suppliers' accounts.
(*c*) Transfer the total to the purchases account.

20.2X A Rowland has the following purchases for the month of June 2009:

2009
June 2 From C Lee: 2 sets golf clubs at £250 each, 5 footballs at £20 each. Less 25 per cent trade discount.
June 11 From M Elliott: 6 cricket bats at £20 each, 6 ice skates at £30 each, 4 rugby balls at £25 each. Less 25 per cent trade discount.
June 18 From B Wood: 6 sets golf trophies at £100 each, 4 sets golf clubs at £300 each. Less $33^1/_3$ per cent trade discount.
June 25 From B Parkinson: 5 cricket bats at £40 each. Less 25 per cent trade discount.
June 30 From N Francis: 8 goal posts at £70 each. Less 25 per cent trade discount.

Required:
(*a*) Enter up the purchases day book for the month.
(*b*) Post the items to the suppliers' accounts.
(*c*) Transfer the total to the purchases account.

20.3 C Phillips, a sole trader, has the following purchases and sales for March 2005:

2005
Mar 1 Bought from Smith Stores: silk £40, cotton £80, all less 25 per cent trade discount.
Mar 8 Sold to A Grantley: linen goods £28, woollen items £44. No trade discount.
Mar 15 Sold to A Henry: silk £36, linen £144, cotton goods £120. All less 20 per cent trade discount.
Mar 23 Bought from C Kelly: cotton £88, linen £52. All less 25 per cent trade discount.
Mar 24 Sold to D Sangster: linen goods £42, cotton £48. Less 10 per cent trade discount.
Mar 31 Bought from J Hamilton: linen goods £270 less $33^1/_3$ per cent trade discount.

Required:
(*a*) Prepare the purchases and sales day books of C Phillips from the above.
(*b*) Post the items to the personal accounts.
(*c*) Post the totals of the day books to the sales and purchases accounts.

20.4X A Hogg had the following purchases and sales for May 2006:

2006
May 1 Sold to MM Ltd: brass goods £24, bronze items £36. Less 25 per cent trade discount.
" 7 Sold to R Finn: tin goods £70, lead items £230. Less $33^1/_3$ per cent trade discount.
" 9 Bought from C Chandler: tin goods £400. Less 40 per cent trade discount.
" 16 Bought from A Fraser: copper goods £320. Less 50 per cent trade discount.
" 23 Sold to T Young: tin goods £50, brass items £70, lead figures £80. All less 20 per cent trade discount.
" 31 Bought from RR Ltd: brass figures £100. Less 50 per cent trade discount.

Required:
In A Hogg's books:
(*a*) Write up sales and purchases day books.
(*b*) Post the items to the personal accounts.
(*c*) Post the totals of the day books to the sales and purchases accounts.

20.5X You are employed as a sales assistant for a small company, Wilshaws Ltd, who sell farm supplies. As the company employs the minimum administrative staff, one of your duties is to look after the purchases ledger. This task involves entering the invoices received from suppliers into the day book and posting to the relevant creditors' accounts in the ledger.

Wilshaw's purchase invoices received for November 2004 are as follows:

Date	*Supplier*	*Our Inv No*	*Total*
2004			£
Nov 1	Bould & Co	SR2103	104.26
Nov 3	Hambleton's	SR2104	140.57
Nov 7	Farm Supplies Co	SR2105	448.12
Nov 10	Worthington's Ltd	SR2106	169.91
Nov 12	Sigley Bros	SR2107	47.00
Nov 15	Hambleton's	SR2108	259.09
Nov 20	Harlow's Mfr	SR2109	84.96
Nov 20	Bould & Co	SR2110	29.14
Nov 25	Clark & Robinson	SR2111	61.63
Nov 30	T Adams Ltd	SR2112	233.83

Required:

(*a*) Draw up a purchase day book, enter the invoices, and total up at the end of the month.

(*b*) Open accounts for each of the suppliers, using your own folio numbers, and post the invoices to the suppliers' accounts in the purchases ledger.

(*c*) Post the totals to the purchases account in the general ledger.

CHAPTER 21

The returns day books and documentation

Learning objectives

After you have studied this chapter you should be able to:

- **enter credit notes in the returns inwards day book**
- **enter debit notes in the returns outwards day book**
- **post the day book entries to the sales and purchases ledgers**
- **make out statements**
- **understand the use of statements.**

21.1 Returns inwards and credit notes

Customers may return goods to the supplier if they are faulty, damaged or not suitable for their requirements, where the consignment is incomplete when compared with the delivery note, or where an overcharge has been made. When this happens, the supplier will make an allowance to correct the situation. Occasionally, a customer may decide to keep the goods but will expect a reduction in price as compensation.

Since customers will have been sent an invoice at the same time as the goods were delivered, they will be in debt to the supplier for the value of the goods. When a supplier makes an allowance for goods that have been returned, or a reduction in price has been agreed, the supplier will issue a **credit note** to the customer. It is called a credit note since the customer's account will be credited with the amount of the allowance, thereby showing a reduction in the amount owed by the customer. This procedure involving credit notes is necessary so that the various books of account that are maintained by the supplier and customer do, in fact, reflect the correct amount owed.

Exhibit 21.1 shows an example of a credit note – and note that credit notes are usually printed in red to distinguish them from invoices.

Exhibit 21.1

CREDIT NOTE

R GRANT (CATERING SUPPLIES)
HIGHER SIDE PRESTON PR1 2NL

Telephone:	(01703) 33122
Fax:	(01703) 22331

D Poole & Co
Deansgate Restaurant
45 Charles Street
Manchester M1 5ZN

Credit Note No	0/37
Account No	P/4298
Date:	8 September 2005

Quantity	***Per unit***	***Total***
	£	£
2 cases Cape Glory Pears	25	50
Less 20% Trade Discount		10
		40

21.2 Returns inwards day book

Credit notes are listed in a returns inwards day book. This is then used for posting the items, as follows:

- *Sales ledger* Credit the amount of credit notes, one by one, to the accounts of the customers in the sales ledger.
- *General ledger* At the end of the period, the total of the returns inwards day book is posted to the debit of the returns inwards account.

Again, you may find it easier to use 'IN' and 'OUT' as discussed previously; i.e. goods returned to us are entered on the 'IN' side of the returns inwards account since the goods are coming 'IN' to us, and on the 'OUT' side of the individual customers' accounts.

Alternative names in use for the returns inwards day book are the returns inwards journal or the sales returns book.

21.3 Example of a returns inwards day book

An example of a returns inwards day book showing the items posted to the sales ledger and the general ledger is now shown:

Returns Inwards Day Book	Note No	Folio	*(page 10)* Amount
2005			£
Sept 8 D Poole & Co	9/37	SL 12	40
17 A Brewster	9/38	SL 58	120
19 C Vickers	9/39	SL 99	290
29 M Nelson	9/40	SL 112	160
Transferred to returns inwards account		GL 114	610

Sales Ledger

D Poole & Co Account *(page 12)*

Dr				*Cr*			
				2005			£
				Sept 8	Returns inwards	RI 10	40

A Brewster Account *(page 58)*

Dr				*Cr*			
				2005			£
				Sept 17	Returns inwards	RI 10	120

C Vickers Account *(page 99)*

Dr				*Cr*			
				2005			£
				Sept 19	Returns inwards	RI 10	290

M Nelson Account *(page 112)*

Dr				*Cr*			
				2005			£
				Sept 29	Returns inwards	RI 10	160

General Ledger

Returns Inwards Account *(page 114)*

Dr				*Cr*			
2005			£				
Sept 30	Returns for the month	RI 10	610				

21.4 Returns outwards and debit notes

If the supplier agrees, goods bought previously may be returned. When this happens, a **debit note** is sent to the supplier giving details of the goods and the reason for their return.

Also, an allowance might be given by the supplier for any faults in the goods. Here also, a debit note should be sent to the supplier.

Exhibit 21.2 shows an example of a debit note.

EXHIBIT 21.2

DEBIT NOTE

R GRANT (CATERING SUPPLIES)
HIGHER SIDE PRESTON PR1 2NL

Telephone: (01703) 33122
Fax: (01703) 22331

B Hamilton Food Supplies
20 Fourth Street
Kidderminster
KD2 4PP

Debit Note No 9/34
Account No H/3752
Date: 11 September 2005

Quantity	*Per unit*	*Total*
	£	£
4 cases Canadian Salmon	60	240
Less 25% Trade Discount		60
		180
Returned damaged in transit		

21.5 Returns outwards day book

Debit notes are listed in a returns outwards day book. This is then used for posting the items, as follows:

- *Purchases ledger* Debit the amounts of debit notes, one by one, to the accounts of the suppliers in the purchases ledger.
- *General ledger* At the end of the period, the total of the returns outwards day book is posted to the credit of the returns outwards account.

Using 'IN' and 'OUT', the entries would be as follows: the goods returned by us to the supplier go 'IN' to the suppliers' accounts and come 'OUT' of the returns outwards account.

Other names in use for the returns outwards day book are the returns outwards journal or the purchases returns book.

21.6 A worked example of a returns outwards day book

An example of a returns outwards day book, showing the items posted to the purchases ledger and the general ledger, is now shown.

Returns Outwards Day Book					*(page 7)*
			Note No	*Folio*	*Amount*
2005					£
Sept	11	B Hamilton	9/34	PL 29	180
	16	B Rose	9/35	PL 46	100
	28	C Blake	9/36	PL 55	30
	30	S Saunders	9/37	PL 87	360
Transferred to returns outwards account				GL 116	670

Purchases Ledger

B Hamilton Account *(page 29)*

Dr				*Cr*
2005			£	
Sept 11	Returns outwards	RO 7	180	

B Rose Account *(page 46)*

Dr				*Cr*
2005			£	
Sept 16	Returns outwards	RO 7	100	

C Blake Account *(page 55)*

Dr				*Cr*
2005			£	
Sept 28	Returns outwards	RO 7	30	

S Saunders Account *(page 87)*

Dr				*Cr*
2005			£	
Sept 30	Returns outwards	RO 7	360	

General Ledger

Returns Outwards Account *(page 116)*

Dr				*Cr*
	2005			£
	Sept 30	Returns for the month	RO 7	670

21.7 Double entry and returns

Exhibit 21.3 shows how double entry is made for both returns inwards and returns outwards.

Exhibit 21.3 • Posting returns inwards and returns outwards

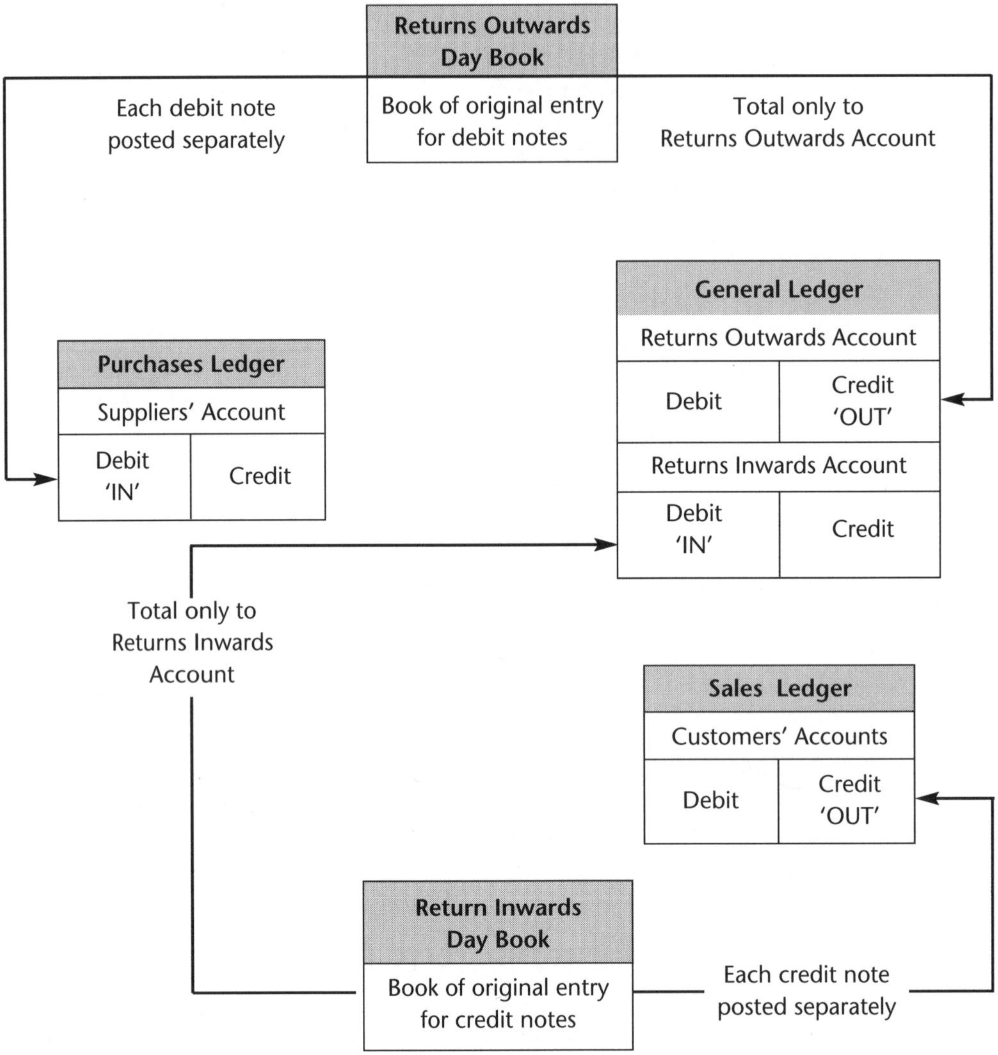

Note that full coverage of the treatment of returns inwards and returns outwards in the final accounts has already been shown in Chapter 10 (Section 10.7).

21.8 Reasons for keeping separate returns accounts

It might be thought that the returns inwards could have been debited to the sales account rather than to a separate returns inwards account. This, however, would have meant that it would only be the net figure of sales that appeared in the trading account.

It is important for the owners of a business to check on how much in sales is being returned. This may show that too many faulty goods are being sold, thus needing to be returned. This would involve the business in a lot of unnecessary costs, such as carriage outwards, packing expenses and so on. Showing the figures separately will highlight an excessive amount of returns.

Similar considerations will apply with returns outwards, and therefore a separate returns outwards account will be kept.

21.9 Statements

At the end of each month a **statement of account** should be sent to each debtor that owes money on the last day of that month. It is really a copy of the debtor's account in our books. It should show:

- amount owing at start of month
- amount of each sales invoice sent to them during the month
- any credit notes sent to them during the month
- cash and cheques received from them during the month
- the amount due from the debtor at the end of the month.

Debtors will use these statements to see whether the accounts in their own accounting records agrees with their account in our records. If in our books a debtor is shown as owing £798 then, depending on items in transit between us, the debtors books should show us as a creditor for £798.

The statements also act as a reminder to debtors that money is owed, and will show the date by which payment should be made.

An example of a statement is shown in Exhibit 21.4.

Exhibit 21.4

STATEMENT OF ACCOUNT

R GRANT (CATERING SUPPLIES)
HIGHER SIDE PRESTON PR1 2NL

Telephone: (01703) 33122
Fax: (01703) 22331

Accounts Department
D Poole & Co
Deansgate Restaurant
45 Charles Street
Manchester M1 5ZN

Date: 30 September 2005

Date	*Details*	*Debit*	*Credit*	*Balance*
2005		£	£	£
Sept 1	Balance b/f			880
Sept 2	Invoice 30956	560		1,440
Sept 3	Returns 9/37		40	1,400
Sept 25	Bank		880	520
Sept 30	Balance owing c/f			520

All accounts due and payable within one month

21.10 Sales and purchases via credit cards

Various banks, building societies and other financial organisations issue credit cards to their customers. Examples are Visa, Mastercard and American Express.

The holder of a credit card purchases items or services without giving cash or cheques, but simply signs a special voucher used by the store or selling organisation. Later on - usually several weeks later - the credit card holder pays the organisation for which they hold the card (e.g. Visa) for all or part of their previous month's expenditure. The sellers of the goods or services then present the vouchers to the credit card company, and the total of the vouchers less commission is paid to them by that credit card company.

In effect, the sales are 'cash sales' for as far as the purchasers are concerned: they have seen goods (or obtained services) and have received them, and in their eyes they have paid for them by using their credit card. Such sales are very rarely sales to anyone other than the general public, as compared with sales to professionals in a specific trade.

Once a customer has received the goods or services from the seller, he or she does not need to be entered in the sales ledger as a debtor. All the selling company is then interested in, from a recording point of view, is collecting the money from the credit card company.

The double entry needed is:

• Sale of items via credit cards:	Dr: Credit card company Cr: Cash sales
• Receipt of money from credit card company:	Dr: Bank Cr: Credit card company
• Commission charged by credit card company:	Dr: Selling expenses Cr: Credit card company

New terms

Credit note (p. 215): A document sent to a customer showing the allowance given by the supplier in respect of unsatisfactory goods.

Debit note (p. 218): A document sent to a supplier showing the allowance given for unsatisfactory goods.

Statement of account (p. 221): This is normally sent to purchasers at the end of each month and it states the amount owing to the supplier at the end of that particular month.

EXERCISES

21.1 You are to enter up the purchases day book and the returns outwards day book from the following details, then post the items to the relevant accounts in the purchases ledger, and then show the transfers to the general ledger at the end of the month.

2007
May 1 Credit purchase from H Lloyd £119
May 4 Credit purchases from the following: D Scott £98; A Simpson £114; A Williams £25; S Wood £56
May 7 Goods returned by us to the following: H Lloyd £16; D Scott £14
May 10 Credit purchase from A Simpson £59
May 18 Credit purchases from the following: M White £89; J Wong £67; H Miller £196; H Lewis £119
May 25 Goods returned by us to the following: J Wong £5; A Simpson £11
May 31 Credit purchases from: A Williams £56; C Cooper £98.

21.2X Enter up the sales day book and the returns inwards day book from the following details. Then post to the customer's accounts and show the transfers to the general ledger.

2004
June 1 Credit sales to: A Simes £188; P Tulloch £60; J Flynn £77; B Lopez £88
June 6 Credit sales to: M Howells £114; S Thompson £118; J Flynn £66
June 10 Goods returned to us by: A Simes £12; B Lopez £17
June 20 Credit sales to M Barrow £970
June 24 Goods returned to us by S Thompson £5
June 30 Credit sales to M Parkin £91.

21.3 On 30 April 2008, the balances in the sales and purchases ledgers of a particular company were as follows: Debtors – C Cook £240; K King £560; AB Ltd £40; Creditors – S Todd £120; W Mears £520; K Fisher £280.

The following are transactions for May 2008:

2008
May 2 Sold goods on credit to K King £119.
" 4 Bought goods on credit from S Todd £200.
" 6 C Cook paid us the balance on his account by cheque less cash discount of 5 per cent.
" 8 We returned goods £40 to W Mears.
" 11 Sold goods on credit to AB Ltd £99.
" 14 Sold goods on credit to K King £720.
" 15 AB Ltd returned goods to us £19.
" 17 Bought goods on credit from T Jay £142.
" 19 We paid W Mears the balance on his account by cheque, less 5 per cent cash discount.
" 20 Bought goods on credit from K Fisher £180.
" 22 We returned goods £49 to K Fisher.
" 24 K King returned goods to us £39.
" 27 K King paid his account in full, less 5 per cent discount, by cheque.
" 28 We paid S Todd's account by cash less 5 per cent cash discount.

Write up the following for May 2008:
(*a*) Sales day book.
(*b*) Purchases day book.
(*c*) Returns inwards day book.
(*d*) Returns outwards day book.
(*e*) Cash book extracts.
(*f*) Sales ledger.
(*g*) Purchases ledger.
(*h*) All the necessary accounts in the general ledger.

21.4X On 30 June 2009, the balances in the purchases and sales ledgers accounts were as follows: Creditors – D Kay £188; K Webb £380; N New £1,600; Debtors – W Cox £300; T King £20; BE Ltd £189.

The following are transactions for July 2009:

2009
July 1 Sold goods on credit to W Cox £540.
" 3 T King paid us £20 in cash.
" 6 BE Ltd returned goods to us £29.
" 8 We paid D Kay's account less £17 cash discount by cheque.
" 11 Bought goods on credit from N New £375.
" 12 Sold goods on credit to T Salt £399.
" 13 We returned £40 goods to N New.
" 15 Bought goods on credit from K Webb £220.
" 18 We returned £39 goods to D Kay.
" 22 Sold goods on credit to BE Ltd £400.
" 24 Bought goods on credit from C Cope £510.
" 25 BE Ltd returned £29 goods to us.
" 26 We paid a cheque for £200 to K Webb.
" 28 T Salt returned goods to us £20.
" 29 We received a cheque for £360 from T Salt in full settlement of his account.
" 31 We paid C Cope a cheque for £497 in full settlement of his account.

Write up the following books for July 2009:

(*a*) Sales journal.
(*b*) Purchases journal.
(*c*) Returns inwards journal.
(*d*) Returns outwards journal
(*e*) Cash book extracts.
(*f*) Sales ledger. Accounts to be balanced off.
(*g*) Purchases ledger. Accounts to be balanced off.
(*h*) The necessary accounts in the general ledger.

21.5X You are employed as an accounts clerk for Elder's Printing Co, 36 High Street, Shrewsbury SH4 8JK. One of your tasks is to prepare statements of account which are sent out to customers at the end of each month. Two of the customers' accounts are shown below.

Sales Ledger

Dr *D Hammond Ltd Account* *Cr*

2002	£		2002	£
Jan 1 Balance b/d	1,403		Jan 7 Bank	1,380
Jan 3 Sales	177		Jan 12 Credit note	23
Jan 10 Sales	527			
Jan 25 Sales	200			

Dr *Alex Richards Ltd Account* *Cr*

2002	£		2002	£
Jan 1 Balance b/d	346		Jan 7 Bank	292
Jan 7 Sales	27		Jan 7 Discount	8
Jan 9 Sales	521		Jan 12 Credit note	46
Jan 27 Sales	400			
Jan 31 Sales	53			

The addresses of the above customers are as follows:

D Hammond Ltd Bay House Heath Road Shrewsbury SH7 3KL	Alex Richards Ltd Unit 12 Greenways Industrial Estate Chester CE21 9HU

Required:

(*a*) Balance each of the above accounts off, and state the amount owing by each of the customers.
(*b*) Draft a statement of account to be sent to each customer.

CHAPTER 22

Value added tax

Learning objectives

After you have studied this chapter you should be able to:

- **enter value added tax (VAT) in the necessary books of account**
- **distinguish between taxable businesses and other businesses where special regulations apply**
- **prepare sales invoices including charges for VAT**
- **fill in a value added tax return form.**

22.1 Introduction

This chapter looks at the accounting requirements when a tax is levied on sales by the government. The system in operation in the United Kingdom is called value added tax (VAT). Student studying in the UK will be examined on their knowledge and understanding of this system. For students studying in other countries, it is important to be familiar with the appropriate sales tax in operation and also advisable to seek the advice of a teacher or lecturer.

Value added tax (VAT) is a tax on turnover, not on profits. It is described as an 'indirect' tax, and ultimately the tax is paid by the final consumer of the goods or services. VAT is administered in the United Kingdom by HM Customs and Excise.

22.2 The scope of VAT

VAT is charged on the supply of most goods or services by a VAT registered trader. A VAT-registered trader may be a sole proprietor, a partnership or a limited company.

Not all goods and services are subject to VAT. Some goods and services are **zero-rated**. This means that VAT is charged at the rate of zero per cent. Examples of zero-rated supplies are:

- human and animal food
- water and sewerage charges
- books and periodicals
- clothing and footwear for young children.

Some goods and services are **exempt** from VAT. This means that such supplies are outside the scope of VAT, and VAT cannot be charged. Examples of exempt supplies are:

- financial services
- postal services provided by the Post Office
- education.

It is very important to differentiate between zero-rated and exempt supplies, as we will see later.

22.3 The rate of VAT

The rate of VAT is decided by Parliament through the Finance Acts, which are passed each year after the budget(s). The rates at the publication of this book were:

• all zero-rated goods and services	0%
• fuel and power for domestic or charity use only	5%
• all other standard rated supplies	17.5%

The VAT charged *by* a business on its supplies (**outputs**) is called **output VAT**, and is payable by the business to HM Customs and Excise. The VAT charged *to* a business on its purchases and expenses (**inputs**), is called **input VAT** and is reclaimable by the business from HM Customs and Excise (HM C&E).

22.4 Example: how the VAT system works

A toymaker manufactures toys from scraps of material and sells them to a wholesaler for £200 plus VAT. The wholesaler sells these toys to a chain of retailers for £300 plus VAT, who in turn retail the toys in their shops for £400 plus VAT. VAT accounting per unit is as follows:

(i) The toymaker accounts for VAT as follows:

	Net (£)	*VAT (£) @ 17.5%*
Sale of toys	200.00	35.00
Cost	–	–
VAT payable to HM C&E		35.00

(ii) The wholesaler accounts for VAT as follows:

	Net (£)	*VAT (£) @ 17.5%*
Sale of toys	300.00	52.50
Cost of toys	200.00	35.00
VAT payable to HM C&E		17.50

(iii) The retailer accounts for VAT as follows:

	Net (£)	*VAT (£) @ 17.5%*
Sale of toys	400.00	70.00
Cost of toys	300.00	52.50
VAT payable to HM C&E		17.50

It will be seen that the total output VAT paid to HM Customs and Excise is £70.00, as charged by the retailer to its customers. The VAT, however, has been paid to HM Customs and Excise at various stages in the distribution of the toys, as follows:

	£
Toymaker	35.00
Wholesaler	17.50
Retailer	17.50
	70.00

22.5 Zero-rated supplies

In Section 22.2, we introduced the concept of zero-rated supplies. The important matter to note is that items are charged to VAT at 0 per cent, which is a rate of VAT. In some EU countries, supplies that are zero-rated in the UK are charged to VAT at that country's VAT rate.

As the supplies are sold at a rate of VAT, (albeit 0 per cent), any input VAT incurred, relating to the business, can all be reclaimed.

Example 1: A book dealer sells £100,000 worth of books in a year and, during that year, purchases book shelving for £10,000 plus VAT.

The VAT reclaimable is therefore:

	Net (£)	*VAT (£) @ 17.5%*
Sales	100,000	Nil
Purchases	10,000	1,750
VAT reclaimable		1,750

22.6 Exempt supplies

In Section 22.2 we introduced the concept of exempt supplies. There are two types of exempt supplies:

- supplies of specifically exempted items, such as those stated in Section 22.2
- all supplies of goods and services by non-VAT-registered businesses, for example exempt businesses such as banks and insurance companies, and businesses that do not need to register because their annual turnover is below the VAT registration limit.

The important matter to note is that input VAT directly attributable to exempt supplies or to non-VAT registered businesses cannot be reclaimed from HM Customs and Excise.

Example 2: An insurance company sells £100,000 worth of insurance, and purchases furniture for its office for £10,000 plus VAT.

This business cannot reclaim the £1,750 input VAT on the furniture as it does not have any vatable supplies. The total amount paid for the furniture, £11,750, will be the cost to the business. Contrast this situation with the zero-rated supplier in Example 1 above, which was able to reclaim £1,750.

22.7 Partly exempt traders

Some VAT-registered traders will sell some goods that are exempt from VAT and some that are either standard-rated or zero-rated. These businesses may reclaim part of the input VAT paid by them, but not all of it. The rules are complicated, but in essence the input VAT reclaimable will be proportionate to the standard- and zero-rated percentage of the business's total annual turnover.

22.8 Firms that can recover VAT paid

Two types of firms need to be avoided under this heading namely taxable firms and zero-rated firms. Each is dealt with below.

Taxable firms

Value Added Tax and sales invoices

A taxable firm will have to add VAT to the value of its sales invoices. It must be pointed out that this is based on the amount of the invoice *after* any trade discount has been deducted.

Exhibit 22.1 is an invoice drawn up from the following details. On 2 March 2004, W Frank & Co, Hayburn Road, Stockport, sold goods to R Bainbridge Ltd, 267 Star Road, Colchester: Bainbridge's Order No was A/4/559, for the following items:

- 220 Rolls T56 Black Tape at £6 per 10 rolls
- 600 Sheets R64 Polythene at £10 per 100 sheets
- 7,000 Blank Perspex B49 Markers at £20 per 1,000.

All of these goods are subject to VAT at the rate of 17.5 per cent. A trade discount of 25 per cent is given by Frank & Co. The sales invoice is numbered 8851.

Exhibit 22.1

<table>
<tr><td colspan="2" align="center">W Frank & Co
Hayburn Road
Stockport SK2 5DB

INVOICE No 8851</td></tr>
<tr><td colspan="2" align="right">Date/tax point: 2 March 2004</td></tr>
<tr><td colspan="2">To: R Bainbridge
267 Star Road
Colchester CO1 1BT
 Your order no: A/4/559
Account no: F/1896 </td></tr>
<tr><td></td><td>£</td></tr>
<tr><td>200 Rolls T56 Black Tape @ £6 per 10 rolls</td><td>120</td></tr>
<tr><td>600 Sheets R64 Polythene @ £10 per 100 sheets</td><td>60</td></tr>
<tr><td>7,000 Blank Perspex B49 Markers @ £20 per 1,000</td><td>140</td></tr>
<tr><td></td><td>320</td></tr>
<tr><td>Less Trade Discount 25%</td><td>80</td></tr>
<tr><td></td><td>240</td></tr>
<tr><td>Add VAT 17.5%</td><td>42</td></tr>
<tr><td></td><td>282</td></tr>
<tr><td>VAT Registration No: 469 2154 42</td><td></td></tr>
</table>

The sales day book will normally have an extra column for the VAT contents of the sales invoice (*see* Chapter 23). This is needed to make it easier to account for VAT. The entry of several sales invoices in the sales day book and in the ledger accounts can now be examined for our sample case.

W Frank & Co sold the following goods during the month of March 2004:

		Total of invoice, after trade discount deducted but before VAT added	*VAT 17.5%*
2004		£	£
March 2	R Bainbridge Ltd (*see* Exhibit 22.1)	240	42
March 10	S Lange & Son	200	35
March 17	K Bishop	160	28
March 31	R Andrews & Associates	80	14

Sales Day Book					Page 58
	Invoice No	*Folio*	*Total*	*Net*	*VAT*
2004			£	£	£
March 2 R Bainbridge Ltd	8851	SL 77	282	240	42
March 10 S Lange & Son	8852	SL 119	235	200	35
March 17 K Bishop	8853	SL 185	188	160	28
March 31 R Andrews & Associates	8854	SL 221	94	80	14
Transferred to General Ledger			799	680	119
				GL 76	GL 90

Now that the sales day book has been written up, the next task is to enter the amounts of the invoices in the individual customer's accounts in the sales ledger. These are simply charged with the full amounts of the invoices, including VAT.

As an instance of this, K Bishop will be shown as owing £188. When she pays her account she will pay £188. It will then be the responsibility of W Frank & Co to ensure that the figure of £28 VAT in respect of this item is included in the total cheque payable to HM Customs and Excise.

Sales Ledger

R Bainbridge Ltd — *Page 77*

Dr			*Cr*
2004	£		
March 2 Sales SB 58	282		

S Lange & Son — *Page 119*

Dr			*Cr*
2004	£		
March 10 Sales SB 58	235		

K Bishop — *Page 185*

Dr			*Cr*
2004	£		
March 17 Sales SB 58	188		

R Andrews & Associates — *Page 221*

Dr			*Cr*
2004	£		
March 31 Sales SB 58	94		

In total, therefore, the personal accounts have been debited with £799, this being the total of the amounts that the customers will have to pay. The actual sales of the firm are not £799; the amount that is actually sales is £680, the other £119 being simply the VAT that W Frank & Co are collecting on behalf of the Government.

The double entry is made in the general ledger thus:

- credit the sales account with the sales content only, i.e. £680
- credit the VAT account with the VAT content only, i.e. £119.

These are shown as:

General Ledger

Sales — *Page 76*

Dr					Cr
	2004				£
	March 31	Credit Sales for the month	SB 58		680

Value Added Tax — *Page 90*

Dr					Cr
	2004				£
	March 31	Sales Book: VAT content	SB58		119

Value Added Tax and purchases

In the case of a taxable firm, the firm will have to add VAT to its sales invoices, but it will *also* be able to get a refund of the VAT it pays on its purchases.

Instead of paying VAT to HM Customs and Excise and then claiming a refund of the VAT on purchases, the firm can offset the amount paid as VAT on purchases against the amount payable as VAT on sales. This means that only the difference has to be paid to HM Customs and Excise. It is shown as:

	£
(a) Output VAT collected on sales invoices	xxx
(b) Less Input VAT already paid on purchases	xxx
(c) Net amount to be paid to HM Customs and Excise	xxx

In certain fairly rare circumstances (a) may be less than (b). If that were to be the case, then it would be HM Customs and Excise that would refund the difference (c) to the firm. Such a settlement between the firm and HM Customs and Excise will take place at least every three months.

The recording of purchases in the purchases day book and purchases ledger follows a similar method to that of sales, but with the personal accounts being credited instead of debited. We can now look at the records of purchases for W. Frank & Co., whose sales have been dealt with in Exhibit 22.1. The firm made the following purchases for March 2004:

		Total invoice, after trade discount deducted but before VAT added	*VAT 17.5%*
2004		£	£
March 1	E Lyal Ltd (*see* Exhibit 22.2)	200	35
March 11	P Portsmouth & Co	280	49
March 24	J Davidson	40	7
March 29	B Cofie & Son Ltd	80	14

Before looking at the recording of these in the purchases records, compare the first entry for E Lyal Ltd with Exhibit 22.2 to ensure that the correct amounts have been shown.

Exhibit 22.2

E Lyal Ltd
College Avenue
St Albans
Hertfordshire ST2 4JA

INVOICE No K 453/A

Date/tax point: 1/3/2004
Your order no BB/667

To: W Frank & Co
Hayburn Road
Stockport

Terms: Strictly net 30 days
VAT Reg. No: 236 4054 56

	£
50 metres of BYC plastic 1 metre wide x £3.60 per metre	180
1,200 metal tags 500mm x 10p each	120
	300
Less Trade Discount at 33 1/3%	100
	200
Add VAT 17.5%	35
	235

The purchases day book can now be entered up.

Purchases Day Book *Page 38*

	Folio	*Total*	*Net*	*VAT*
2004		£	£	£
March 1 E Lyal Ltd	PL 15	235	200	35
March 11 P Portsmouth & Co	PL 70	329	280	49
March 24 J Davidson	PL114	47	40	7
March 29 B Cofie & Son Ltd	PL166	94	80	14
Transferred to General Ledger		705	GL54 600	GL90 105

These transactions are entered in the purchases ledger. Once again, there is no need for the VAT to be shown as separate amounts in the accounts of the suppliers.

Purchases Ledger

E Lyal Ltd *Page 15*

Dr				*Cr*
	2004			£
	March 1	Purchases	PB 38	235

P Portsmouth & Co — *Page 70*

Dr						Cr
			2004			£
			March 11	Purchases	PB 38	329

J Davidson — *Page 114*

Dr						Cr
			2004			£
			March 24	Purchases	PB 38	47

B Cofie & Son Ltd — *Page 166*

Dr						Cr
			2004			£
			March 29	Purchases	PB 38	94

The personal accounts have been credited with a total of £705, this being the total of the amounts which W Frank & Co will have to pay to them. The actual cost of purchases is not, however, £705. You can see that the correct amount is £600. The other £105 is the VAT that the various firms are collecting for HM Customs and Excise. This amount is also the figure for VAT that is reclaimable from HM Customs and Excise by W Frank & Co.

The debit entry in the purchases account is, therefore, £600, as this is the actual cost of the goods to the firm. The other £105 is entered on the debit side of the VAT account. Notice that there is already a credit of £119 in the VAT account in respect of the VAT added to sales.

General Ledger

Purchases — *Page 54*

Dr					Cr
2004		£			
March 31	Credit Purchases for the month	600			

Value Added Tax — *Page 90*

Dr					Cr
2004		£	2004		£
March 31	Purchases Day Book: VAT content PB 38	105	March 31	Sales Day Book: VAT content SB 58	119
March 31	Balance c/d	14			
		119			119
			April 1	Balance b/d	14

In the final accounts of W Frank & Co, the following entries would be made:

(*a*) trading account for the month ended 31 March 2004:

- debited with £600 as a transfer from the purchases account
- credited with £680 as a transfer from the sales account.

(*b*) balance sheet as at 31 March 2004:
- balance of £14 (credit) on the VAT account would be shown as a current liability, as it represents the amount owing to HM Customs and Excise for VAT.

Zero-rated firms

Zero-rated firms:

(*a*) do not have to add VAT onto their sales invoices, as their rate of VAT is zero or nil, but
(*b*) can, however, reclaim from HM Customs and Excise any VAT paid on goods or services bought.

Accordingly, because of (*a*) no VAT is entered in the sales day book; VAT on sales does not exist. Because of (*b*) the purchases day book and purchases ledger will appear exactly in the same manner as for taxable firms, as already shown in the case of W Frank & Co. The VAT account will only have debits in it, being the VAT on purchases. Any balance on this account will be shown in the balance sheet as a debtor.

22.9 VAT and cash discounts

Where a cash discount is offered for speedy payment, VAT is calculated on an amount represented by the value of the invoice less such a discount. Even if the cash discount is lost because of late payment, the VAT will not change.

Exhibit 22.3 shows an example of such a sales invoice, assuming a cash discount offered of 2.5 per cent and a VAT rate at 17.5 per cent.

Exhibit 22.3

ATC Ltd
18 High Street
London WC2E 9AN

INVOICE No ZT 48910

VAT Reg No: 313 5924 71
Date/tax point: 11 May 2002
Your order no: TS/778

To: R Noble
Belsize Road
Edgeley
Stockport

	£
500 paper dispensers @ £20 each	10,000
Less Trade Discount @ 20%	2,000
	8,000
Add VAT 17.5%	1,365 *
	9,365

*The VAT has been calculated on the net price of £8,000 *less* the cash discount 2.5 per cent, i.e. £7,800. Then the VAT at 17.5% on £7,800 is calculated as £1,365.

22.10 Firms that cannot get refunds of VAT paid

As some firms do not add VAT on to the value of their sales invoices, there is obviously no entry for VAT in the sales day book or the sales ledger. Such firms do not get a refund of VAT on purchases. This means that there will not be a VAT account; all that will happen is that VAT paid is included as part of the cost of the goods bought.

In the purchases day book, goods bought for £80 (+ VAT £14) will simply appear as purchases £94. The double entry will show a credit of £94 in the supplier's account.

Both the sales and purchases records will, therefore, not show anything separately for VAT. For comparison, let us look at the accounting records of two firms for an item that costs £120 (+ VAT £21), the item being bought from D Oswald Ltd. The records for the month of May 2004 would appear as follows:

(i) Firm that cannot recover VAT (e.g. exempted firms):

Purchases Day Book

2004		£
May 16	D Oswald Ltd	141

Purchases Ledger

D Oswald Ltd

Dr					*Cr*
			2004		£
			May 16	D Oswald Ltd	141

General Ledger

Purchases

Dr					*Cr*
2004		£	2004		£
May 31	Credit Purchases for the month	141	May 31	Transfer to Trading Account	141

Trading Account for the month ended 31 May 2004 (extract)

	£	
Purchases	141	

(ii) Firm that can recover VAT (e.g. zero-rated firm):

Purchases Day Book

		Net	*VAT*
2004		£	£
May 16	D Oswald Ltd	120	21

Purchases Ledger

D Oswald Ltd

Dr					*Cr*
			2004		£
			May 16	Purchases	141

General Ledger

Purchases

Dr					*Cr*
2004		£	2004		£
May 31	Credit Purchases for the month	120	May 31	Transfer to Trading Account	120

Value Added Tax

Dr			*Cr*
2004		£	
May 31	Purchases Book	21	

Trading Account for the month ended 31 May 2004 (extract)

	£	
Purchases	120	

Balance sheet as at 31 May 2004 (extract)

	£	
Debtor	21	

22.11 VAT included in gross amount

You will often know only the gross amount of an item, and this figure will be made up of the net amount plus VAT. To find the amount of VAT that has been added to the net amount, a formula capable of being used with any rate of VAT is:

$$\frac{\%\text{ rate of VAT}}{100 + \%\text{ Rate of VAT}} \times \text{Gross Amount} = \text{VAT in £}$$

Suppose that the gross amount of sales was £940 and the rate of VAT was 17.5 per cent. Finding the amount of VAT and the net amount before VAT was added using the formula yields:

$$\text{VAT} = \frac{17.5}{100 + 17.5} \times £940 = \frac{17.5}{117.5} \times £940 = 140.$$

Therefore, the net amount was £800, which, with VAT £140 added, becomes £940 gross.

22.12 VAT on items other than sales and purchases

VAT is not just paid on purchases. It is also payable on many items of expense and on the purchase of fixed assets.

Firms that *can* get refunds of VAT paid will not include VAT as part of the cost of the expense or fixed asset. Firms that *cannot* get refunds of VAT paid will include the VAT cost as part of the expense or fixed asset. For example, two firms buying similar items would treat the following items as shown:

	Firm that can reclaim VAT		*Firm that cannot reclaim VAT*	
Buys Machinery	Debit Machinery	£200	Debit Machinery	£235
£200 + VAT £35	Debit VAT Account	£35		
Buys Stationery	Debit Stationery	£160	Debit Stationery	£188
£160 + VAT £28	Debit VAT Account	£28		

22.13 VAT owing

VAT owing by or to a firm can be included with debtors or creditors, as the case may be. There is no need to show the amount(s) owing as separate items.

22.14 Relief from VAT on bad debts

It is possible to claim relief on any debt that is more than six months old and has been written off in the accounts. Should the debt later be paid, the VAT refunded will then have to be paid back to HM Customs and Excise.

22.15 Purchase of cars

Normally, the VAT paid on a car bought for a business is not reclaimable.

22.16 VAT records

All VAT records must be retained by a business for a period of six years.

22.17 Columnar day books and VAT

The use of columns for VAT in both sales and purchases analysis books is demonstrated in Chapter 23.

22.18 VAT return forms

At the end of each VAT accounting period, a form VAT 100 has to be filled in and sent to HM Customs and Excise. The most important part of the form is concerned with columns 1–9, which are shown in Exhibit 22.4. For illustration, we have assumed a VAT rate of 10 per cent.

Exhibit 22.4

		£	
VAT due in this period on **sales** and other outputs	1	8,750	–
VAT due in this period on **acquisitions** from other **EC Member States**	2	–	–
Total VAT due **(the sum of boxes 1** and **2)**	3	8,750	–
VAT reclaimed in this period on **purchases** and other inputs (including acquisitions from the EC)	4	6,250	–
Net VAT to be paid to Customs or reclaimed by you (difference between boxes 3 and 4)	5	2,500	–
Total value of **sales** and all other outputs excluding any VAT, **Include your box 8 figure**	6	97,500	–
Total value of **purchases** and all other inputs excluding any VAT. **Include your box 9 figure**	7	71,900	–
Total value of all supplies of goods and related services, excluding any VAT, to other **EC Member States**	8	10,000	–
Total value of all **acquisitions** of goods and related services, excluding any VAT, from other **EC Member States**	9	1,450	–

The contents of the columns on form VAT 100 are now explained:

1 We have added £8,750 VAT on to our sales invoices for the period.

2 This column would show the VAT due (but not paid) on all goods and related services acquired in this period from other EC member states. In this case there were no such transactions.

3 Total of columns 1 and 2.

4 We have made purchases and incurred expenses during the period, on which we have been charged £6,250 VAT.

5 As we have collected £8,750 VAT from our customers, but only suffered £6,250 on all purchases and expenses, we therefore owe HM Customs and Excise £2,500, i.e. £8,750 - £6,250.

6 Our total value of sales for the period was £97,500.

7 Our total value of purchases and expenses was £71,900, but some of these expenses were not subject to a charge for VAT.

8 Of the sales included under item 6, £10,000 of it was to other countries within the European Community. VAT was not charged on these sales.
9 Of the total purchases under item 7 £1,450 was from other countries within the European Community.

Only columns 1, 3, 4 and 5 actually refer to accounting for VAT. The other columns are for statistical purposes so that the UK government can assess the performance of the economy and similar matters.

22.19 VAT on goods taken for private use

If a trader takes some goods out of his own business stock for his own private use, the trader should be charged with any VAT due on these goods.

For instance, suppose that Smith, a furniture dealer, takes a table and chairs out of stock for permanent use in his own home. The cost to the business has been (cost price + value added tax). Therefore the proprietor's drawing should be charged with both the cost price of goods plus the VAT.

The double entry needed, assuming goods taken of £1,000 + VAT at 10 per cent, would therefore be:

Drawings:	Debit	£1,100
Purchases:	Credit	£1,000
VAT account:	Credit	£100

There can be complicating circumstances, outside the scope of this book, that might influence the amount of VAT to be charged on such drawings.

New terms

Exempt supplies (p. 227): Supplies which are outside the scope of VAT and therefore VAT cannot be charged.

Exempted firms (p. 236): Firms that do not have to add VAT to the price of goods and services supplied by them, and that cannot obtain a refund of VAT paid on goods and services purchased by them.

Inputs (p. 227): The value of goods and services purchased by a business.

Input tax (p. 227): The VAT charged to a business on its purchases and expenses (inputs).

Outputs (p. 227): The value of goods and services sold to a business.

Output tax (p. 227): The VAT charged *by* a business on its supplies (outputs).

Value added tax (VAT) (p. 226): A tax charged on the supply of most goods and services. The tax is borne by the final consumer of the goods or services, not by the business selling them to the consumer. VAT is administered by HM Customs and Excise.

Zero-rated firms (p. 235): Firms that do not have to add VAT to goods and services supplied by them to others, and that receive a refund of VAT paid on goods and services purchased by them.

Zero-rated goods or services: (p. 226): Goods or services where VAT is charged at the rate of 0%.

EXERCISES

22.1 On 1 May 2005, D Wilson Ltd, 1 Hawk Green Road, Stockport, sold the following goods on credit to G Christie & Son, The Golf Shop, Hole-in-One Lane, Marple, Cheshire:

Order No A/496
3 sets of 'Boy Michael' golf clubs at £240 per set.
150 Watson golf balls at £8 per 10 balls.
4 Faldo golf bags at £30 per bag.
Trade discount is given at the rate of $33^1/_3$%.
All goods are subject to VAT at 17.5%.

Required:

(*a*) Prepare the sales invoice to be sent to G Christie & Son. The invoice number will be 10586.

(*b*) Show the entries in the personal ledgers of D Wilson Ltd and G Christie & Son.

22.2 The following sales have been made by S Thompson Ltd during the month of June 2006. All the figures are shown 'net' after deducting trade discount, but before adding VAT at the rate of 17.5 per cent.

2006			
August	1	to M Sinclair & Co	£160
"	8	to M Brown & Associates	£240
"	19	to A Axton Ltd	£80
"	31	to T Christie	£40

You are required to enter up the sales day book, sales ledger and general ledger in respect of the above items for the month.

22.3 The following sales and purchases were made by R Colman Ltd during the month of May 2004:

			Net	*VAT added*
2004			£	£
May	1	Sold goods on credit to B Davies & Co	160	28
"	4	Sold goods on credit to C Grant Ltd	200	35
"	10	Bought goods on credit from:		
		- G Cooper & Son	400	70
		- J Wayne Ltd	240	42
"	14	Bought goods on credit from B Lugosi	40	7
"	16	Sold goods on credit to C Grant Ltd	120	21
"	23	Bought goods on credit from S Hayward	40	7
"	31	Sold goods on credit to B Karloff	80	14

Enter up the sales and purchases day books, sales and purchases ledgers, and the general ledger for the month of May 2004. Carry the balance down on the VAT account.

22.4X On 1 March 2005, C Black, Curzon Road, Stockport, sold the following goods on credit to J Booth, 89 Andrew Lane, Stockport, under Order No 1697:

20,000 coils sealing tape @ £4.70 per 1,000 coils
40,000 sheets A5 paper @ £4.50 per 1,000 sheets
30,000 sheets A4 paper @ £4.20 per 1,000 sheets
All goods are subject to VAT at 17.5%.

Required:
(*a*) Prepare the sales invoice to be sent to J Booth.
(*b*) Show the entries in the personal ledgers of J Booth and C Black.

22.5 Comart Supplies Ltd recently purchased from Ace Import Ltd 10 printers originally priced at £200 each. A 10-per-cent trade discount was negotiated, together with a 5 per cent cash discount if payment was made within 14 days. Calculate the following:

(*a*) the total of the trade discount
(*b*) the total of the cash discount
(*c*) the total of the VAT.

AAT (part of Central Assessment)

22.6 A manufacturer sells a product to a wholesaler for £200 plus VAT of £35. The wholesaler sells the same product to a retailer for £280 plus VAT of £49. The retailer then sells the product to a customer for £320 plus VAT of £56. What is the amount of VAT collectable by HM Customs and Excise?

AAT (part of Central Assessment)

22.7

(*a*) Should the total of the VAT column in the petty cash book be debited or credited to the VAT account in the general ledger?
(*b*) For what period of time must VAT records be retained?
(*c*) MMS Textiles Ltd is a VAT-registered firm. Should it charge VAT on goods supplied to a customer that is not VAT-registered?
(*d*) What book-keeping entries would be necessary to record a cash refund of £94 (inclusive of VAT) to a customer?

AAT (part of Central Assessment)

22.8X

Bloomers Ltd purchases 40 glass crystal vases for £7.50 each plus VAT. The vases are then all sold to a hotel gift shop for £517 inclusive of VAT. How much is owed by Bloomers to HM Customs and Excise in respect of the vases?

AAT (part of Central Assessment)

CHAPTER 23

Analytical sales and purchases day books

Learning objectives

After you have studied this chapter you should be able to:

- **enter invoices into analytical sales and purchases day books**
- **post transactions from analytical sales and purchases day books to the personal accounts in the sales and purchases ledgers**
- **post totals from the analytical day books to the general ledger.**

23.1 Introduction

In Chapters 19 and 20, the sales and purchases day books were shown using only one total column for the value of the goods sold or purchased. Sometimes goods are subject to VAT, as discussed in Chapter 22. In that chapter you will have noticed that additional columns were used to take account of the VAT, as shown in the sales day book in Exhibit 22.1 and the Purchases Day Book in Exhibit 22.2.

In addition to accounting for VAT, many businesses find it useful to analyse their sales and purchases between different types of goods bought and sold, or perhaps between different departments. For example, a coffee shop may sell refreshments and gifts and wish to ascertain the profit on the two different sales areas. In this example it would be advantageous to analyse both sales and purchases to reflect the goods/services bought or sold in each area. The purchases day book could be ruled as follows:

Purchases Day Book						
Date	*Details*	*Folio*	*Total*	*Gifts*	*Food*	*VAT*
			£	£	£	£

23.2 Entering sales invoices into an analytical sales day book

When a business requires additional information from its records, the books can easily be adapted to meet particular needs.

Let us consider a retail computer shop that sells hardware and software to the public, local businesses and schools. The proprietor, Mr Harlow, wishes to monitor the sales of each of these lines separately. Exhibit 23.1 shows an example of Mr Harlow's **analytical sales day book**.

EXHIBIT 23.1

Sales Day Book						
Date	*Details*	*Folio*	*Total*	*Software*	*Hardware*	*VAT*
			£	£	£	£
April 1	Mount Hey School	SL1	705		600	105
3	Ashby Marketing	SL2	564	480		84
15	Davenport Manufacturing	SL3	4,700		4,000	700
20	St James College	SL4	23,500		20,000	3,500
			29,469	480	24,600	4,389
				GL1	GL2	GL3

23.3 Posting credit sales

Each sale now has to be posted to the individual debtors accounts in the sales ledger, as follows:

(i) The total of each sales invoice (i.e. the net price of the goods plus VAT) is posted to each individual debtors account on the debit side, since the goods are going 'into' their account.

(ii) At the end of the period, the sales day book is added up and the totals posted on the credit, or 'OUT', side of the following accounts:
- sales of software account
- sales of hardware account
- VAT account.

The results are shown below:

Sales Ledger

Mount Hey School *SL 1*

Dr					*Cr*
		£			
April 1	Sales	705			

Ashby Marketing Co *SL 2*

Dr					*Cr*
		£			
April 3	Sales	564			

Davenport Manufacturing Co — *SL 3*

Dr			*Cr*
	£		
April 15 Sales	4,700		

St James College — *SL 4*

Dr			*Cr*
	£		
April 22 Sales	23,500		

General Ledger

Sale of Software — *GL 1*

Dr			*Cr*
			£
		April 30 Credit sales for April	480

Sale of Hardware — *GL 2*

Dr			*Cr*
			£
		April 30 Credit sales for April	24,600

VAT — *GL 3*

Dr			*Cr*
			£
		April 30 VAT on credit sales for April	4,389

23.4 Entering purchase invoices into an analytical purchases day book

Another business might wish to monitor its purchases that might include goods for resale and business expenses such as electricity, motor expenses, etc. The example shown in Exhibit 23.2 illustrates how a business could analyse its purchase invoices using an **analytical purchases day book.**

Exhibit 23.2

Purchases Day Book							
Date	*Details*	*Folio*	*Total*	*Goods*	*Motor Exp*	*Stationery*	*VAT*
			£	£	£	£	£
Nov 1	Bould & Co	PL1	4,230	3,600			630
10	Sigley's (Stat)	PL2	47			40	7
17	T Adams Ltd	PL3	940	800			140
30	Robinson's Garage	PL4	188		160		28
			5,405	4,400	160	40	805
				GL 1	GL 2	GL 3	GL 3

23.5 Posting credit purchases

Each purchase now has to be posted to the individual creditors' accounts in the purchase ledger, as follows:

(i) The *total* of each purchase invoice (i.e. the net price of the goods, plus VAT) is posted to each individual creditor's account on the *credit* side, since the goods are coming 'OUT' of their accounts.

(ii) At the end of the period, the purchases day book is added up and the totals are posted on the *debit*, or 'IN', side of the following accounts:

- purchases account
- motor expenses account
- stationery account
- VAT account.

Purchases Ledger

Bould & Co — *PL 1*

Dr				*Cr*
				£
		Nov 1	Purchases	4,230

Sigley's Stationers — *PL 2*

Dr				*Cr*
				£
		Nov 10	Purchases	47

T Adams Ltd — *PL 3*

Dr				*Cr*
				£
		Nov 17	Purchases	940

Robinson's Garage — *PL 4*

Dr				*Cr*
				£
		Nov 30	Purchases	188

General Ledger

Purchases — *GL 1*

Dr				*Cr*
		£		
Nov 30	Credit purchases for November	4,400		

Motor Expenses — *GL 2*

Dr				*Cr*
		£		
Nov 30	Purchases day book	160		

Stationery GL 3

Dr			Cr
		£	
Nov 30	Purchases day book	40	

VAT GL 4

Dr			Cr
		£	
Nov 30	Purchases day book	805	

23.6 Advantages of analysis books

The advantages of analysis books are that businesses can be provided with exactly the information that they need, at the time when they want it. Different firms have different needs, and they therefore analyse their books in different ways.

Analysis books enable firms to do such things as:

- calculate the profit or loss made by each part of a business
- draw up control accounts for the sales and purchases ledgers (*see* Chapter 24)
- keep a check on the sales of each type of goods
- keep a check on goods sold in the United Kingdom and those sold overseas
- find the purchases of each type of goods.

23.7 Books as collection points

We can see that the various sales and purchases day books, and the ones for returns, are simply collection points for data to be entered in the accounts of the double entry system. There is nothing in law that says that, for instance, a sales day book has to be written up.

It would be possible to use a firm's sales invoices to enter the debits in the customer's personal accounts. The sales invoices would then be held in a file until the end of the month, when they would then be added up. The total would be entered to the credit of the sales account in the general ledger.

New term

Analytical day book (pp. 244–5): Book of original entry in which sales or purchase invoices are entered. The book has various analysis columns, which are totalled at the end of the month and posted to the general ledger and control accounts.

EXERCISES

23.1 The Curtain Design Company sells both ready-made and custom-made curtains to local hotels, nursing homes and the public. It operates an analytical sales day book, where it analyses the sales into sales of ready-made curtains and custom-made curtains.

The following invoices were sent during November 2006. All goods are subject to VAT at 17.5 per cent.

Date	*Customer*	*Ready-made* £	*Custom-made* £
Nov 1	Jarvis Arms Hotel		2,300
Nov 8	Springs Nursing Home	1,000	
Nov 15	J P Morten	220	
Nov 17	Queen's Hotel		1,500
Nov 30	W Blackshaw	90	

You are required to:

(*a*) record the above transactions in an analytical sales day book

(*b*) post the invoices to the personal accounts in the sales ledger

(*c*) post the totals to the appropriate accounts in the general ledger.

23.2 The Hall Engineering Company manufactures small engineering components for the motor-car industry. It operates an analytical purchases day book, in which the purchases invoices are recorded.

During May 2004, the following invoices were received. All goods are subject to VAT at 17.5 per cent.

			£
May 1	Black's Engineering Co	Engineering goods	520
May 3	Ace Printing Co	Printing catalogues	145
May 24	Morgan's Garage	Petrol Account	120
May 26	Martin's Foundry	Engineering parts	700
May 28	Office Supplies	Stationery	126
May 29	Black's Engineering Co	Engineering parts	220

Required:

(*a*) Enter the purchase invoices in an analytical purchases day book using the following analysis columns:
- Engineering parts
- Printing and stationery
- Motor expenses
- VAT.

(*b*) Post the transactions to the personal accounts in the purchases ledger.

(*c*) Post the totals to the appropriate accounts in the general ledger.

23.3 Smart Campers supplies an extensive range of camping equipment and accessories. It has three branches, situated at Horsforth, Moortown and Otley. Sales day books are kept at Head Office and are compiled from information received from branches.

During the month of May 2002, credit sales were as follows. All sales are subject to VAT at 10 per cent.

2 May Outdoor Centre
Moortown branch
12 Flair cools boxes at £15.90 each
6 Camping stoves at £29.95 each
All less trade discount 20%

8 May Premier Leisure
Hosforth branch
10 Explorer rucksacks at £34.99 each
Less trade discount 20%
12 Trekker ridge tents at £59.95 each
Less trade discount 15%

16 May Airedale Sport
Otley branch
8 Palma cool bags at £7.85 each
15 Flair cool boxes at £15.90
All less trade discount 20%

28 May Empire Products
Moortown branch
14 Dome tents at £47.90 each
8 trekker ridge tents at £59.95 each
All less trade discount 15%

You are required to draw up a sales day book with analysis columns as follows: Total, Horsforth, Moortown, Otley, and VAT. Once that has been done, enter the above transactions for May 2002.

OCR

23.4X Adel Garden Centre divides its purchases of stock into two main departments: Outdoor Furniture and Garden Tools. Credit purchases during the month of October 2003 were as set out below, with VAT at 10 per cent to be included on all transactions.

2 October Oakland Supplies
6 steel spades at £18.75 each
8 garden forks at £10.50 each
Less trade discount 20%

14 October Airedale Products
4 patio furniture sets at £49.60 each
Less trade discount 15%

22 October Oakland Supplies
6 garden tool sets at £34.90 each
4 garden forks at £10.50 each
Less trade discount 20%
8 sun loungers at £39.95 each
Less trade discount 25%

20 October Airedale Products
1 patio furniture set invoiced on 14 October was returned because it was damaged. A credit note was issued.

28 October Oakland Supplies
2 garden tool sets were returned because they were faulty. A credit note was issued.

You are required to do the following:

(*a*) Draw up a purchases day book and purchases returns day book with analysis columns for Total, Outdoor Furniture, Garden Tools and VAT. Enter the date, name of supplier and the amounts of money into the appropriate columns. (Details of invoices are NOT required in the day books.)

(*b*) Total the day books.

(*c*) Write up the purchases ledger accounts from the day books, and balance the accounts at the end of the month.

OCR

CHAPTER 24

Control accounts

Learning objectives

After you have studied this chapter you should be able to:

- **draw up sales ledger control accounts**
- **draw up purchases ledger control accounts**
- **know the sources of information for control accounts**
- **understand the double entry aspect of control accounts.**

24.1 Need for control accounts

When all accounts were kept in one ledger, a trial balance could be drawn up as a test of the arithmetical accuracy of the accounts. It must be remembered that certain errors were not revealed by such a trial balance. If the trial balance totals disagreed, the books of a small business could easily and quickly be checked so as to find the errors.

However, when the firm has grown and the accounting work has been so divided up that there are several or many ledgers, any errors could be very difficult to find. We could have to check every item in every ledger. What is required is a type of trial balance for each ledger, and this requirement is met by the **control account**. Then it is only the ledgers whose control accounts do not balance that need detailed checking to find errors.

24.2 Principle of control accounts

The principle on which the control account is based is simple, and is as follows. If the opening balance of an account is known, together with the information of the additions and deductions entered in the account, the closing balance can be calculated.

This idea can be applied to a complete ledger. Suppose that there were only four accounts in the sales ledger, and for the month of May 2002, the accounts were as laid out below.

Sales Ledger

T Sangster

2002		£	2002		£
May 1	Balance b/d	850	May 7	Bank	820
" 4	Sales	900	" 7	Discounts allowed	30
" 30	Sales	350	" 31	Balance c/d	1,250
		2,100			2,100
Jun 1	Balance b/d	1,250			

P May

2002		£	2002		£
May 1	Balance b/d	1,500	May 9	Returns inwards	200
" 28	Sales	400	" 14	Bank	900
			" 14	Discounts allowed	20
			" 31	Balance c/d	780
		1,900			1,900
Jun 1	Balance b/d	780			

K White

2002		£	2002		£
May 1	Balance b/d	750	May 20	Returns inwards	110
" 15	Sales	600	" 31	Balance c/d	1,240
		1,350			1,350
Jun 1	Balance b/d	1,240			

C Shenton

2002		£	2002		£
May 1	Balance b/d	450	May 28	Bad debts	450

A control account, in this case a *sales ledger* control account, would consist only of the totals of each of the items in the sales ledger. Let us therefore first list the totals for each type of item.

May 1 Balances b/d:	£850 + £1,500 + £750 + £450 = £3,550
Sales in May:	£900 + £350 + £400 + £600 = £2,250
Cheques received in May:	£820 + £900 = £1,720
Discounts allowed in May:	£30 + £20 = £50
Returns inwards in May:	£200 + £110 = £310
Bad debts written off in May:	£450

Now, looking at the totals only, it is possible to draw up a sales ledger control account. Debits are shown as usual on the left-hand side, and credits on the right-hand side. Thus:

Sales Ledger Control Account

2002			£	2002			£
May	1	Balance b/d	3,550	May	31	Bank	1,720
"	31	Sales for the month	2,250	"	31	Discounts allowed	50
				"	31	Returns inwards	310
				"	31	Bad debts	450
				"	31	Balances c/d (A)	?
			5,800				5,800
Jun	1	Balances b/d (B)	?				

From your studies so far of double entry, you should be able to see that the Balance c/d (A) is the figure needed to balance the account, i.e. the difference between the two sides. It works out to be £3,270.

We can now look at the ledger and see if that is correct. The balances are £1,250 + £780 + £1,240 = £3,270. As this has now proved to be correct, the figure of £3,270 can be shown in the sales ledger control account as the balances carried down (A) and the balances brought down (B).

In the above very simple example, there were only four ledger accounts. Suppose instead that there were 400 – or 4,000 or 40,000 – ledger accounts. In these cases, the information concerning the totals of each type of item cannot be obtained so easily.

Remember that the main purpose of a control account is to act as a check on the accuracy of the entries in the ledgers. The total of a list of all the balances extracted from the ledger should equal the balance on the control account. If not, a mistake – or even many mistakes – may have been made and will have to be found.

24.3 Information for control accounts

The following tables show where information is obtained from in order to draw up control accounts.

Sales Ledger Control	Source
1 Opening debtors	List of debtors' balances drawn up at the end of the previous period.
2 Credit sales	Total from sales journal.
3 Returns inwards	Total of returns inwards journal.
4 Cheques received	Cash book: Bank column on received side. All transactions of credit sales extracted.
5 Cash received	Cash book: Cash column on received side. All transactions of cash sales extracted.
6 Discounts allowed	Total of discounts allowed column in the cash book.
7 Closing debtors	List of debtors' balances drawn up at the end of the period.

Purchases Ledger Control	Source
1 Opening creditors	List of creditors' balances drawn up at the end of the previous period.
2 Credit purchases	Total from purchases journal.
3 Returns outwards	Total of returns outwards journal.
4 Cheques paid	Cash book: Bank column on payments side. All transactions of credit purchases extracted.
5 Cash paid	Cash book: Cash column on payments side. All transactions of cash purchases extracted.
6 Discounts received	Total of discounts received column in the cash book.
7 Closing creditors	List of creditors' balances drawn up at the end of the period.

24.4 Form of control accounts

It is usual to find control accounts in the same format as an account with the totals of the debit entries in the sales and purchases ledgers on the left-hand side of the control account, and the totals of the various credit entries in the ledgers on the right-hand side of the control account.

This can also be shown in the form of two diagrams. Exhibit 24.1 shows how information is used to construct a sales ledger control account for the month of May 2006, and Exhibit 24.2 illustrates the construction of a purchases ledger control account for May 2006. The letters A, B, C and so on refer to the information used in the control accounts.

Exhibit 24.1 • Sales ledger control account – source of data

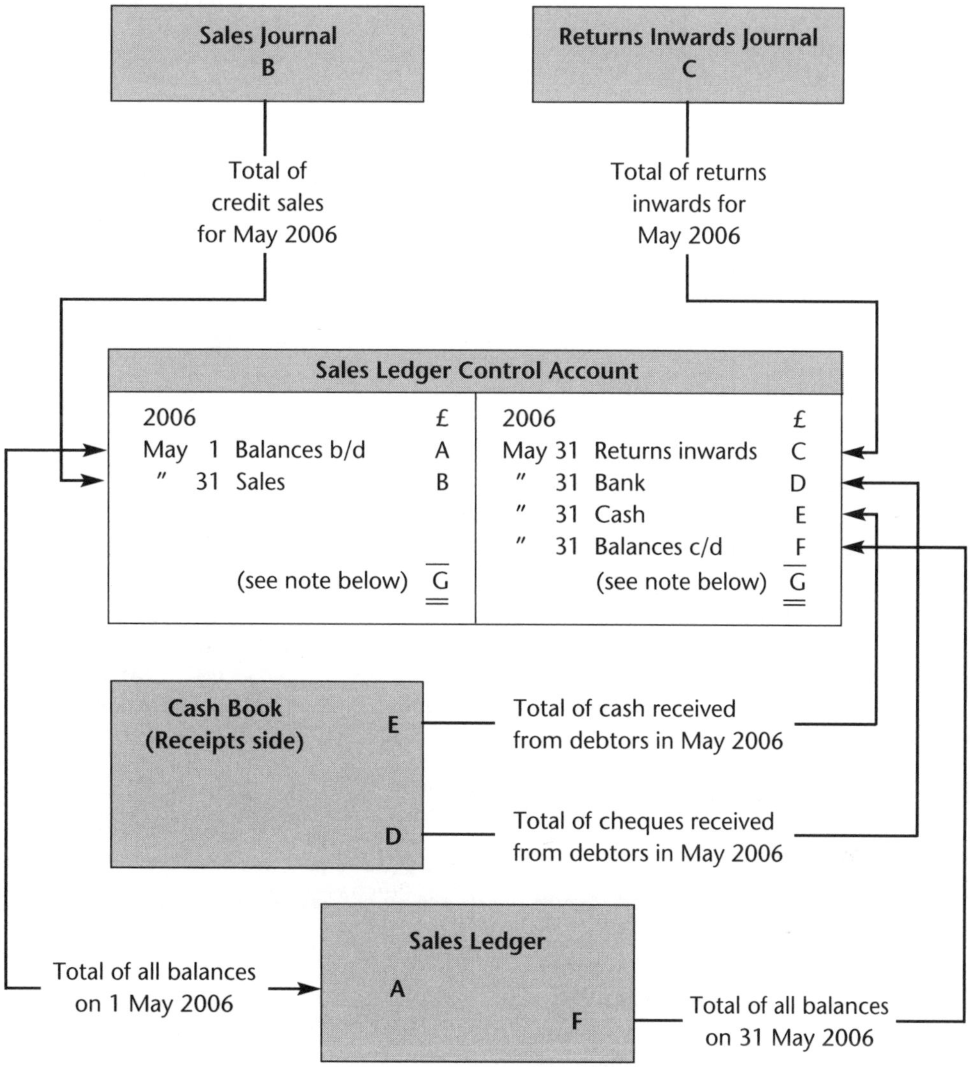

Note for the letter G: If the two totals labelled G are not equal to each other, then there is an error somewhere in the books.

Exhibit 24.2 • Purchases ledger control account – source of data

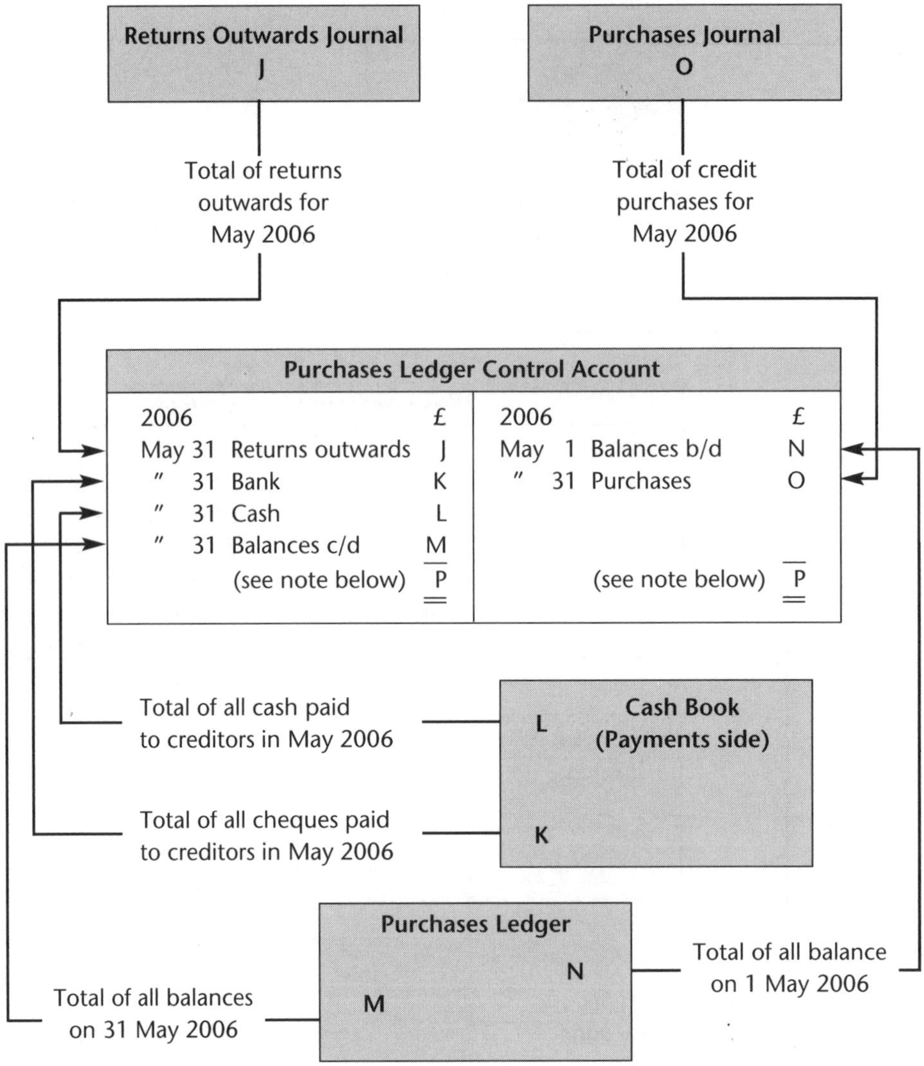

Note for the letter P: If the two totals labelled P are not equal to each other, then there is an error somewhere in the books.

Exhibit 24.3 shows an example of a sales ledger control account for a sales ledger in which all the entries are arithmetically correct.

EXHIBIT 24.3

Sales ledger	£
Debit balances on 1 January 2006	1,894
Total credit sales for the month	10,290
Cheques received from customers in the month	7,284
Cash received from customers in the month	1,236
Returns inwards from customers during the month	296
Debit balances on 31 January 2006 as extracted from the sales ledger	3,368

Sales Ledger Control Account

Dr					*Cr*
2006		£	2006		£
Jan 1	Balances b/d	1,894	Jan 31	Bank	7,284
Jan 31	Sales	10,290		Cash	1,236
				Returns inwards	296
				Balances c/d	3,368
		12,184			12,184

We have proved the ledger to be arithmetically correct, because the totals of the control account equal each other. If the totals were not equal, then this would prove that there is an error somewhere.

Exhibit 24.4 shows an example where an error is found to exist in a purchases ledger. The ledger will have to be checked in detail, the error found, and the control account then corrected.

EXHIBIT 24.4

Purchases ledger	£
Credit balances on 1 January 2006	3,890
Cheques paid to suppliers during the month	3,620
Returns outwards to suppliers in the month	95
Bought from suppliers in the month	4,936
Credit balances on 31 January as extracted from the purchases ledger	5,151

Purchases Ledger Control Account

Dr					*Cr*
2006		£	2006		£
Jan 31	Bank	3,620	Jan 1	Balances b/d	3,890
Jan 31	Returns outwards	95	Jan 31	Purchases	4,936
Jan 31	Balances c/d	5,151			
		8,866*			8,826*

* As can be seen from the totals at the bottom of the control account, there is a £40 (£8,866 - £8,826) error in the purchases ledger. We will have to check that ledger in detail to find the error. Notice that a double line does not appear under the totals figures. We will not finalise the account (and double-rule it) until the error is traced and corrected.

24.5 Other transfers

Transfers to bad debt accounts will have to be recorded in the sales ledger control account because they involve entries in the sales ledgers.

Similarly, a contra account, whereby the same firm is both a supplier and a customer and inter-indebtedness is set off, will also need entering in the control accounts. An example of this follows:

(i) The firm has sold A Hughes £600 goods on 1 May 2005.
(ii) Hughes has supplied the firm with £880 goods on 12 May 2005.
(iii) The £600 owing by Hughes is set off against £880 owing to him on 30 May 2005.
(iv) This leaves £280 owing to Hughes on 31 May 2005.

Sales Ledger

A Hughes

Dr				*Cr*		
2005		£				
May 1 Sales	(i)	600				

Purchases Ledger

A Hughes

Dr				*Cr*		
			2005			£
			May 12	Purchases	(ii)	880

The set-off now takes place:

Sales Ledger

A Hughes

Dr				*Cr*		
2005		£	2005			£
May 1 Sales	(i)	600	May 30	Set-off Purchases ledger	(iii)	600

Purchases Ledger

A Hughes

Dr				Cr		
2005		£	2005			£
May 30 Set-off: Sales ledger	(iii)	600	May 12	Purchases	(ii)	880
May 31 Balance c/d	(iv)	280				
		880				880
			2005			
			Jun 1	Balance b/d	(iv)	280

The transfer of the £600 will appear on the credit side of the sales ledger control account and on the debit side of the purchases ledger control account.

Students often find it difficult to work out which side of each control account contra items (set-offs) are shown. Think of it as cash received and cash paid, for the entries go on the same sides of the control accounts as these items. Thus a contra item will appear on the credit side of the sales ledger control account (the same side as cash received from debtors) and will appear on the debit side of the purchases ledger control account (the same side as cash paid to creditors would appear). Remember this and you won't get it wrong.

24.6 A more complicated example

Exhibit 24.5 shows a worked example of a more complicated control account. You will see that there are sometimes credit balances in the sales ledger as well as debit balances. Suppose, for instance, that we sold £500 goods to W Young, she then paid in full for them, and then afterwards she returned £40 goods to us. This would leave a credit balance of £40 on the account, whereas usually the balances in the sales ledger are debit balances.

There may also be reason to write off a debt as bad where a business finds it impossible to collect the debt. If this happens, the double entry would be as follows:

- debit: bad debts account
- credit: individual debtors' accounts.

Ultimately, the bad debts account would be credited and the profit and loss account would be debited (see Chapter 28). If the business uses control accounts, then the sales ledger control account would also be credited, as shown in Exhibit 24.5.

Exhibit 24.5

2006		£
Aug 1	Sales ledger – debit balances	3,816
Aug 1	Sales ledger – credit balances	22
Aug 31	Transactions for the month:	
	Cash received	104
	Cheques received	6,239
	Sales	7,090
	Bad debts written off	306
	Discounts allowed	298
	Returns inwards	664
	Cash refunded to a customer who had overpaid his account	37
	Dishonoured cheques	29
	Interest charged by us on overdue debt	50
	At the end of the month:	
	Sales ledger – debit balances	3,429
	Sales ledger – credit balances	40

Sales Ledger Control Account

Dr						Cr
2006		£	2006			£
Aug 1	Balances b/d	3,816	Aug 1	Balances b/d		22
Aug 31	Sales	7,090	Aug 31	Cash		104
	Cash refunded	37		Bank		6,239
	Bank: dishonoured			Bad debts		306
	cheques	29		Discounts allowed		298
	Interest on debt	50		Returns inwards		664
	Balances c/d	40		Balances c/d		3,429
		11,062				11,062

24.7 Control accounts and double entry

When a business operates control accounts, it has to decide where the control accounts should be kept within the book-keeping system. There are two options:

- the control accounts within the double entry system
- control accounts as memorandum accounts.

These two options are discussed next.

Control accounts within the double entry system

In order to maintain the control accounts within the general ledger, the control account becomes part of the double entry system and the individual debtors and creditors accounts become memorandum accounts (*see* Exhibit 24.6).

EXHIBIT 24.6 • Control Account as Part of a Double Entry System

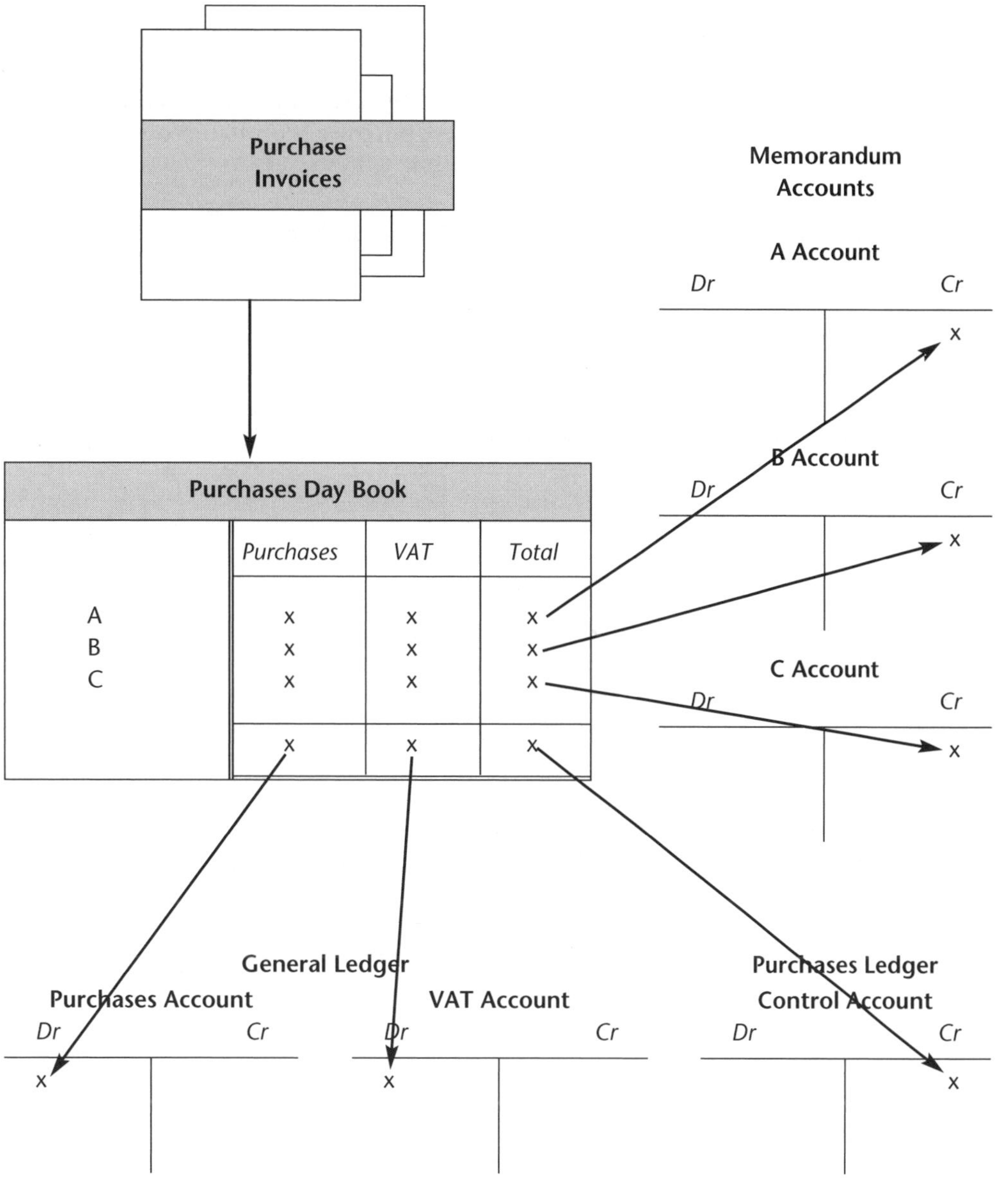

In Exhibit 24.6, the balance of outstanding debtors and creditors is taken from the control accounts and included in the trial balance at the end of the month or year end, as required. In this case, the personal accounts of the debtors and creditors (i.e. A Account, B Account, C Account, etc.) are not part of the double entry and are referred to as **memorandum accounts**. It is, however, important to balance the memorandum accounts periodically with the sales and purchases ledger control accounts so that errors can be located and corrected.

Control accounts as memorandum accounts

In order to maintain the control accounts in the sales and purchases ledgers, the control accounts become memorandum accounts. Using this method, the debtors' and creditors' personal accounts are included in the double entry system via the sales and purchases ledgers, while the control account becomes the memorandum account (*see* Exhibit 24.7).

Exhibit 24.7 • Control Account as a Memorandum Account

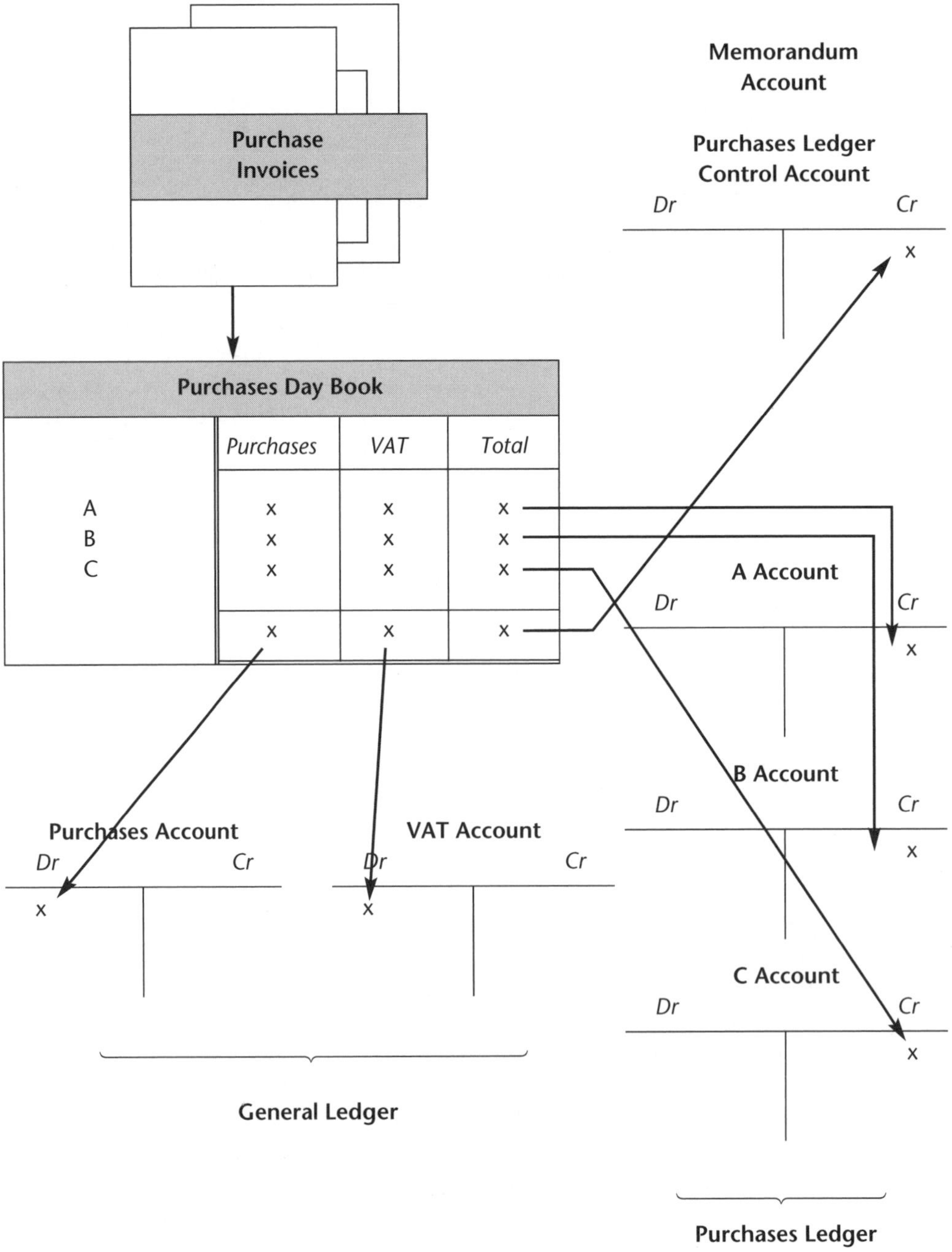

Note that many students become confused when making postings to control accounts, and you might find it useful to remember that when posting entries to control accounts the entry goes on the same side as it would in the personal account. Another useful hint can also be applied when entering 'contra' or 'set-off' items: here, think of the contra or set-off as *cash* and enter the item where you would normally enter cash on the respective control account (as mentioned previously in Section 24.5).

New terms

Control account (p. 252): An account that checks the arithmetical accuracy of a ledger.

Memorandum account (p. 261): An account which is not part of the double entry system.

EXERCISES

24.1 You are required to prepare a sales ledger control account from the following:

2004		£
May 1	Sales ledger balances	4,560
	Total of entries for May:	
	Sales day book	10,870
	Returns inwards day book	460
	Cheques and cash received from customers	9,615
	Discounts allowed	305
May 31	Sales ledger balances	5,050

24.2 You are to prepare a sales ledger control account from the following. Deduce the closing figure for the sales ledger balance as at 31 March 2008.

2008		£
Mar 1	Sales ledger balances	6,708
	Totals for March:	
	Discounts allowed	300
	Cash and cheques received from debtors	8,970
	Sales day book	11,500
	Bad debts written off	115
	Returns inwards day book	210
Mar 31	Sales ledger balances	?

24.3X Draw up a purchases ledger control account from the following:

2002		£
June 1	Purchases ledger balances	3,890
	Totals for June:	
	Purchases day book	5,640
	Returns outwards day book	315
	Cash and cheques paid to creditors	5,230
	Discounts received	110
June 30	Purchases ledger balances	?

24.4 Prepare a sales ledger control account from the following.

2005		£
May 1	Debit balances	6,420
	Totals for May:	
	Sales journal	12,800
	Cash and cheques received from debtors	10,370
	Discounts allowed	395
	Debit balances in the sales ledger set off against credit balances in the purchases ledger	145
May 31	Debit balances	?
	Credit balances	50

24.5X Draw up a sales ledger control account from the following.

2006		£
Apr 1	Debit balances	4,960
	Credit balances	120
	Totals for April:	
	Sales journal	8,470
	Cash and cheques received from debtors	7,695
	Discounts allowed	245
	Debit balances in the sales ledger set off against credit balances in the purchases ledger	77
Apr 30	Debit balances	?
	Credit balances	46

24.6 On 1 January 2004, the balances on Shery Tatupu's sales ledger were as follows:

	£
L Barker	62 Cr
D Blackhurst	1,466 Dr
H Brackenbridge	58 Cr

During the three months ended 31 March 2004, the following transactions took place:

	Credit sales	Cash sales	Sales returns	Payments received on account by cheque	Discount allowed by cheque
	£	£	£	£	£
L Barker	18,642	946	–	15,023	142
D Blackhurst	16,428	–	88	16,009	–
H Brackenbridge	19,886	887	–	17,332	227

You are required to:

(*a*) write up the sales ledger accounts for the quarter ended 31 March 2004

(*b*) prepare the sales ledger control account for the quarter ended 31 March 2004

(*c*) reconcile the control account balance with the ledger account balances.

Pitman Qualifications

24.7X On 1 September 2005, the balances on Neil Weeke's Purchase Ledger were as follows:

	£
D Betts	3,240 Cr
S Haughton	2,228 Cr
M Cassidy	44 Dr

During the month of September 2005, the following transactions took place:

	Cash purchases £	Credit purchases £	Purchase returns £	Payments by cheque £	Discount received £
D Betts	340	6,430	860	9,650	255
S Haughton	180	4,667	328	5,108	187
M Cassidy	-	4,387	-	3,600	-

You are required to:

(*a*) write up the purchase ledger accounts for the month ended 30 September 2005

(*b*) prepare the purchase ledger control account for the month ended 30 September 2005

(*c*) reconcile the control account balance with the ledger account balances.

Pitman Qualifications

CHAPTER 25

The journal

Learning objectives

After you have studied this chapter you should be able to:

- **enter up the journal**
- **post from the journal to the ledgers**
- **complete opening entries for a set of books**
- **understand the accounting cycle.**

25.1 Main books of original entry

It has already been shown in earlier chapters that most transactions are entered in one of the following books of original entry:

- cash book
- sales day book
- purchases day book
- returns inwards day book
- returns outwards day book.

These books have grouped together similar things, e.g. all credit sales are in the sales day book. To trace any of them would be relatively easy, as we know exactly which book would contain the item.

25.2 The journal: the other book of original entry

The other items that do not pass through the above books are much less common, and sometimes much more complicated. It would be easy for a book-keeper to forget the details of these transactions; or perhaps the book-keeper may leave the company, making it impossible at a later date to understand such book-keeping entries.

It is therefore important to record such transactions in a form of a diary prior to entries being made in the double entry accounts. The book used to record these transactions is called the **journal** and contains the following details for each transaction:

- date
- name of account(s) to be debited, and the amount(s)
- name of the account(s) to be credited and the amount(s)
- description of the transaction (this is called a **narrative**)
- reference number allotted to the documents that give proof of the transaction.

The use of the journal makes errors or fraud by book-keepers more difficult. It also reduces the risk of entering the item once only, instead of having a complete double entry. Despite these advantages, there are many firms that do not use a journal.

25.3 Typical uses of the journal

Some of the main uses of the journal are listed next. It must not be thought that this list is a full one.

- the purchase and sale of fixed assets on credit
- writing off bad debts
- the correction of errors
- **opening entries**, which are the entries needed to open a new set of books
- other items.

The layout of the journal can be shown as follows:

The Journal

Date	*Folio*	*Dr*	*Cr*
The name of the account to be debited. The name of the account to be credited. The narrative.			

It can be seen that on the first line the name of the account to be *debited* is entered while the second line gives the account to be *credited*. The name of the account to be credited is indented slightly and not shown directly under the name of the account to be debited, because this makes it easier to distinguish between the debit and credit items.

It should be remembered that the journal is not a double entry account; it is a form of diary, and entering an item in the journal is not the same as recording an item in an account. Once the journal entry has been made, the entry into the double entry accounts can be made.

Examples of the uses of the journal are given more fully in Sections 25.5 to 25.8.

25.4 Journal entries and examination questions

If you were to ask examiners about what types of book-keeping and accounting questions are most often answered badly, they would certainly include 'Questions involving journal entries'. This is not because questions about journal entries are actually more difficult than other types, but rather because many students seem to get some sort of a mental block when dealing with them.

The author, who has been an examiner for a large number of accounting bodies around the world, believes that this difficulty arises because students often think in terms of the debits and credits in accounts. Instead, they should think of the journal simply as a form of written instruction stating which account is to be debited and which account is to be credited, with a description of the transaction involved.

To try to help you avoid this sort of problem with journal entries, we will first show what the entries are in the accounts, and then write up the journal for those entries. We will now look at a few examples, which include folio numbers.

25.5 Purchase and sale on credit of fixed assets

Example 1: A machine was bought on credit from Toolmakers for £550 on 1 July 2005. From what you have learned in earlier chapters, you will know that the double entry accounts would be as follows:

Machinery *(Folio GL 1)*

2005			£				
Jul 1	Toolmakers	PL 55	550				

Toolmakers *(Folio PL 55)*

				2005			£
				Jul 1	Machinery	GL 1	550

Now we have to record these entries in the journal. Remember, the journal is simply a kind of diary, not in account form but in ordinary written form. It says which account has been debited, which account has been credited, and then gives a narrative that simply describes the nature of the transaction.

For the transaction above, the journal entry will appear as follows:

The Journal

Date	*Details*	*Folio*	*Dr*	*Cr*
2005			£	£
Jul 1	Machinery	GL 1	550	
	Toolmakers	PL 55		550
	Purchase of milling machine on credit, purchases invoice no 7/159			

Example 2: Sale of stationery but not now needed, for £300 on credit to K King on 2 July 2005. Here again, it is not difficult to work out what entries are needed in the double entry accounts. They are as follows:

K King *(Folio SL 79)*

2005			£	
Jul 2	Stationery	GL 51	300	

Stationery *(Folio GL 51)*

				2005			£
				Jul 2	K King	SL 79	300

These are shown in journal form as follows:

The Journal

Date	*Details*	*Folio*	*Dr*	*Cr*
2005			£	£
Jul 2	K King	SL 79	300	
	Stationery	GL 51		300
	Sale of some stationery not now needed – see letter 1/55/68			

25.6 Writing off bad debts

Example 3: A debt of £78 owing to us from H Mander is written off as a bad debt on 31 August 2005. As the debt is now of no value, we have to stop showing it as an asset. This means that we will need to credit H Mander's account to cancel the amount out of his account. A bad debt is an expense, and so we will debit the amount to the bad debts account.

In double entry form this is shown as:

Bad debts *(Folio GL 16)*

2005			£				
Aug 31	H Mander	SL 99	78				

H Mander *(Folio SL 99)*

2005			£	2005			£
Aug 1	Balance b/d		78	Aug 31	Bad debts	GL 16	78

The journal entry showing the same transaction would be as follows:

The Journal

Date	*Details*	*Folio*	*Dr*	*Cr*
2005			£	£
Aug 31	Bad debts	GL 16	78	
	H Mander	SL 99		78
	Debt writen off as bad. See letter in file 7/8906			

25.7 Opening entries

Example 4: J Brew, after being in business for some years without keeping proper records, now decides to keep a double entry set of books. On 1 July 2006, he establishes that his assets and liabilities are as follows:

- *Assets*: Motor van £840, Fixtures £700, Stock £390, Debtors – B Young £95, D Blake £45, Bank £80, Cash £20.
- *Liabilities*: Creditors – M Quinn £129, C Walters £41.

The assets therefore total (£840 + £700 + £390 + £95 + £45 + £80 + £20) = £2,170; and the liabilities total (£129 + £41) = £170. The capital in the business consists of assets minus liabilities, which in Brew's case is (£2,170 – £170) = £2,000.

We must start the writing up of the books on 1 July 2006. To do this:

1 Open asset accounts, one for each asset. Each opening asset is shown as a debit balance.
2 Open liability accounts, one for each liability. Each opening liability is shown as a credit balance.
3 Open an account for the capital. Show it as a credit balance.
4 Record steps 1–3 in the journal.

Exhibit 25.1 shows the journal and the opening entries in the double entry accounts.

Exhibit 25.1

The Journal *Page 5*

Date	*Details*	*Folio*	*Dr*	*Cr*
2006			£	£
July 1	Motor van	GL 1	840	
	Fixtures	GL 2	700	
	Stock	GL 3	390	
	Debtors – B Young	SL 1	95	
	D Blake	SL 2	45	
	Bank	CB 1	80	
	Cash	CB 1	20	
	Creditors – M Quinn	PL 1		129
	C Walters	PL 2		41
	Capital	GL 4		2,000
	Assets and liabilities at the date entered to open the books		2,170	2,170

General Ledger

Motor Van Account *Page 1*

Dr				*Cr*
2006			£	
July 1	Balance	J 5	840	

Fixtures Account *Page 2*

Dr				*Cr*
2006			£	
July 1	Balance	J 5	700	

Stock Account *Page 3*

Dr							*Cr*
2006			£				
July 1	Balance	J 5	390				

Capital Account *Page 4*

Dr							*Cr*
				2006			£
				July 1	Balance	J 5	2,000

Sales Ledger

B Young Account *Page 1*

Dr							*Cr*
2006			£				
July 1	Balance	J 5	95				

D Blake *Page 2*

Dr							*Cr*
2006			£				
July 1	Balance	J 5	45				

Purchases Ledger

M Quinn Account *Page 1*

Dr							*Cr*
				2006			£
				July 1	Balance	J 5	129

C Walters Account *Page 2*

Dr							*Cr*
				2006			£
				July 1	Balance	J 5	41

Cash Book

Cash Bank *Page 1*

Dr					*Cr*
2006			£	£	
July 1	Balances	J 5	20	80	

The books are now open. After this day, daily entries are to be entered. The opening entries are needed only *once* in the life of the business.

25.8 Other items

Items other than those already described in Sections 25.5 to 25.7 can be of many kinds and it is impossible to write out a complete list. Correction of errors is explained in Chapters 31 and 32. Several other examples are now shown:

Example 5: K Young, a debtor, owes £2,000 on 1 July 2006. He is unable to pay his account in cash, but offers a motor car in full settlement of the debt. The offer is accepted on 5 July 2006.

The personal account is now no longer owed and therefore needs to be credited. On the other hand, the firm now has an extra asset, a motor car, and therefore the motor car account needs to be debited.

The double entry records are therefore thus:

K Young *(SL 333)*

2006		£	2006			£
July 1	Balance b/d	2,000	July 5	Motor car	GL 171	2,000

Motor Car *(GL 171)*

2006			£			
July 5	K Young	SL 333	2,000			

This is shown in the journal as follows:

The Journal

		Folio	*Dr*	*Cr*
2006			£	£
July 5	Motor car	GL 171	2,000	
	K Young	SL 333		2,000
	Accepted motor car in full settlement of debt per letter dated 5/7/2006			

Example 6: T Jones is a creditor. On 10 July 2006 his business is taken over by A Lee, to whom the debt of £150 is to be paid. Here, one creditor is being exchanged for another. The action needed is to cancel the amount owing to T Jones by debiting his account, and to show it owing to A Lee by opening an account for A Lee and crediting it.

The double entry records are therefore thus:

T Jones *(SL 92*

2006			£	2006		£
July 10	A Lee	SL 244	150	July 1	Balance b/d	150

A Lee *(SL 244)*

		2006			£
		July 10	T Fung	SL 92	150

The journal entries are thus:

The Journal

	Folio	Dr	Cr
2006		£	£
July 10 T Jones	SL 92	150	
A Lee	SL 244		150
Transfer of indebtedness as per letter ref G/1335			

Example 7: We had previously bought an office photocopier for £1,310. It has been found to be faulty, and on 12 July 2006 we return it to the supplier, RS Ltd. An allowance of £1,310 is agreed, so that we will not have to pay for it.

The double entry records are therefore thus:

RS Ltd *(PL 124)*

2006		£	2006		£
July 12	Office machinery GL 288	1,310	July 1	Balance b/d	1,310

Office machinery *(GL 288)*

2006		£	2006		£
July 1	Balance b/d	1,310	Jul 12	RS Ltd PL 124	1,310

The journal entries are thus:

The Journal

	Folio	Dr	Cr
2006		£	£
July 12 RS Ltd	PL 124	1,310	
Office machinery	GL 288		1,310
Faulty photocopier returned to supplier.			
Full allowance given. See letter 10/7/2006			

25.9 Examination guidance

Later on in your studies, you may find that some of the journal entries become rather more complicated than those you have seen so far. The best plan for nearly all students would be to follow this advice during examinations:

- On your examination answer paper, write a heading entitled 'Workings'. Then under that show the double entry accounts.
- Now put a heading entitled 'Answer', and show the answer in the form of the journal, as shown in this chapter.

If you are already confident about dealing with these questions and you feel that you can manage them without showing your workings, then you may wish to leave out your workings from your answer.

If the question asks for 'journal entries' you must *not* fall into the trap of just showing the double entry accounts, as you could get no marks at all even though your double entry records are correct. The examiner wants to see the *journal* entries, and you must show them as your answer.

25.10 The accounting cycle

Each accounting period sees a cycle of recording transactions, being completed when the trading and profit and loss account and the balance sheet are prepared. The **accounting cycle** through which all accounting transactions pass can be shown in the form of a diagram, Exhibit 25.2 shows the accounting cycle for a profit-making organisation.

Exhibit 25.2 • The accounting cycle for a profit-making organisation

Source documents

Where original information is to be found

- Sales and purchases invoices
- Debit and credit notes for returns
- Bank paying-in slips and cheque counterfoils
- Receipts for cash paid out and received
- Correspondence containing other financial information

↓

Original entry

What happens to it

Classified and then entered in books of prime entry:

- Sales and purchases journals
- Returns inwards and outwards journals
- Cash books*
- The journal

↓

Double entry

How the dual aspect of each transaction is recorded

Double entry accounts

General ledger	*Sales ledger*	*Purchases ledger*	*Cash books**
Real and nominal accounts	Debtors' accounts	Creditors' accounts	Cash book and petty cash book

(**Note*: Cash books fulfil both the roles of books of prime entry and double entry accounts)

↓

Check arithmetic

Checking the arithmetical accuracy of double entry accounts

Trial balance

↓

Profit or loss

Calculation of profit or loss for the accounting period

Trading and profit and loss account

↓

Closing financial position

Financial statement showing liabilities, assets and capital at the end of the accounting period

Balance sheet

Each accounting period will see the same cycle performed. The connection between one period and the next are the balances remaining on the balance sheet, each of which is carried forward to start the next period's recording.

25.11 Multiple-choice questions

Now attempt Set No. 2 of the multiple-choice questions in Appendix C. This set contains 35 questions.

New terms

Accounting cycle (p. 274): The period in which a business operates – its financial year. It involves recording all trading activities from source documents to the preparation of the final accounts.

Journal (p. 266): A book used to record rare or exceptional transactions that should not appear in the other books of original entry in use.

Narrative (p. 267): A description and explanation of a transaction recorded in a journal.

Opening entry (p. 269): An entry needed to open a new set of books of account.

EXERCISES

25.1 You are to show the journal entries necessary to record the following items:

2005

(*a*) May 1 Bought a motor vehicle on credit from Kingston Garage for £6,790

(*b*) May 3 A debt of £34 owing from H Newman was written off as a bad debt

(*c*) May 8 Office furniture bought by us for £490 was returned to the supplier, Unique Offices, as it was unsuitable. Full allowance will be given to us

(*d*) May 12 We are owed £150 by W Charles. He is declared bankrupt and we receive £39 in full settlement of the debt

(*e*) May 14 We take £45 goods out of the business stock without paying for them

(*f*) May 28 Some time ago we paid an insurance bill thinking that it was all in respect of the business. We now discover that £76 of the amount paid was in fact insurance of our private house

(*g*) May 29 Bought machinery £980 on credit from Systems Accelerated.

25.2X Show the journal entries for April 2007 necessary to record the following items:

(*a*)	Apr	1	Bought fixtures on credit from J Harper £1,809
(*b*)	Apr	4	We take £500 goods out of the business stock without paying for them
(*c*)	Apr	9	£28 worth of the goods taken by us on 4 April are returned back into stock by us. We do not take any money for the return of the goods
(*d*)	Apr	12	K Lamb owes us £500. He is unable to pay his debt. We agree to take some office equipment from him at the value and so cancel the debt
(*e*)	Apr	18	Some of the fixtures bought from J Harper, £65 worth, are found to be unsuitable and are returned to him for full allowance
(*f*)	Apr	24	A debt owing to us by J Brown of £68 is written off as a bad debt
(*g*)	Apr	30	Office equipment bought on credit from Super Offices for £2,190.

25.3 (*a*) J Green's financial position at 1 May 2008 is as follows:

		£
Bank		2,910
Cash		160
Equipment		5,900
Premises		25,000
Creditors:	R Smith	890
	T Thomas	610
Debtors:	J Carnegie	540
Loan from:	J Higgins	4,000

You are required to show the opening entries needed to open a double entry set of books for Green as at 1 May 2008. Then open up the necessary accounts in J Green's ledger to record the above, as well as the succeeding transactions.

(*b*) During May 2008, Green's transactions were as follows:

2008		
May	2	Bought goods from T Thomas on credit, £2,100.
May	5	Paid R Smith on account by cheque, £500.
May	12	Repaid J Higgins by cheque, £1,000.
May	24	Sold goods to J Carnegie on credit, £2,220.
May	31	Total cash sales for the month £8,560, of which £8,000 banked on 31 May.
May	31	J Carnegie returned goods to us, £400.
May	31	Paid loan interest to Higgins by cheque, £200.

You are required to post all accounts and to extract a trial balance as at 31 May 2008, but only the cash book needs balancing down. Note that the sales, purchases and returns journals are *not* needed.

25.4X M Maxwell is in business as a trader. During February 2003, the following transactions took place:

February
3 Purchased a motor vehicle from J Saunders costing £5,000 paying 50% of the total cost by cheque with the remainder due in 6 months.
8 Purchased fixtures and fittings on credit from J McNulty. List price £200 less trade discount of 15%.
9 M Maxwell put a further £10,000 into the business, 25% went into cash and the remainder into the firm's bank account.
10 A Robinson, a debtor owing £250 was declared bankrupt. M Maxwell received 10% of the amount outstanding by cheque. The remainder to be written off to bad debts.
16 It was found that the £5,000 paid for the motor vehicle purchased on 3 February included Road Fund Licence valued at £150.
22 An account of £50 for petrol for M Maxwell's private car had been posted to the firm's Motor Expenses Account.
24 Rent received of £125 had been posted to the Commissions Received Account.
24 Purchased a piece of machinery on credit from C Mattey. The list price was £6,000 but a trade discount of 20% was allowed.
26 The machine, purchased on 24 February, had chipped paintwork. Maxwell kept it but Mattey agreed to a credit of £100.

You are required to enter these transactions (including cash) into the journal, giving suitable brief narratives.

OCR

PART 4

Adjustments before preparing final accounts

26 Methods of depreciation

27 Double entry records for depreciation and the disposal of assets

28 Bad debts and provision for bad debts

29 Other adjustments for final accounts

30 Stock valuation

31 Accounting errors and their effect on accounting records

32 Suspense accounts and errors

This part is concerned with all the adjustments that have to be made before final accounts can be prepared.

CHAPTER 26

Methods of depreciation

Learning objectives

After you have studied this chapter you should be able to:

- **explain the need for a charge for depreciation expense**
- **understand the causes of depreciation**
- **calculate depreciation using both the straight line and the reducing balance methods.**

26.1 Introduction

In Chapter 18 we considered the distinction between capital and revenue expenditure. From there, you will remember that capital expenditure involves the purchase of fixed assets. This present chapter covers the causes of depreciation and the need for charging depreciation on assets. The manner of calculating depreciation usually involves either the straight line method or the reducing balance method (*see* later in chapter).

The double entry aspect of recording the transactions of purchase, disposal and charges for depreciation will be shown in the following Chapter 27.

26.2 Depreciation of fixed assets

Fixed assets are those assets of material value that are:

- of long life, and
- to be used in the business, and
- not bought with the intention of being resold.

However, fixed assets such as machinery, motor vehicles, fixtures and even buildings do not last for ever. If the amount received (if any) on disposal is deducted from the cost of buying them, the difference is called **depreciation**.

The only time that depreciation can be calculated accurately is when the fixed asset is disposed of, and the difference between the cost to its owner and the amount received on disposal is then calculated. If a motor vehicle were to be bought for

£10,000 and sold five years later for £2,000, then the amount of depreciation is £10,000 - £2,000 = £8,000.

26.3 Depreciation as an expense

Depreciation then, is the part of the original cost of a fixed asset consumed during its period of use by a firm. It is an expense for services consumed, in the same way as expenses for items such as wages, rent or electricity. Since depreciation is an expense, it will have to be charged to the profit and loss account and will, therefore, reduce net profit.

You can see that the only real difference between the cost of depreciation for a motor vehicle and the cost of petrol for the motor vehicle is that the petrol cost is used up in a day or two, whereas the cost of depreciation for the motor vehicle is spread over several years. Both costs are costs to the business.

26.4 Causes of depreciation

The principal causes of depreciation are:

- physical deterioration
- economic factors
- the time factor
- depletion.

These are described in greater detail below.

Physical depreciation

Physical depreciation can come in two basic forms:

- *Wear and tear* When a motor vehicle, or machinery, or fixtures and fittings are used, they eventually wear out. Some last many years, but others last only a few. This is even true of buildings, although some may last for a very long time.
- *Erosion, rust, rot and decay* Land may be eroded or wasted away by the action of wind, rain, sun or the other elements of nature. Similarly, the metals in motor vehicles or machinery will rust away. Wood will rot eventually. Decay is a process, which will be present due to the elements of nature and the a lack of proper attention.

Economic factors

Economic factors may be said to be the reasons for an asset being put out of use even though it is in good physical condition. The two main factors are usually **obsolescence** and **inadequacy**, described further thus:

- *Obsolescence* This is the process of becoming out of date. For instance, over the years there has been great progress in the development of synthesisers and electronic devices used by leading commercial musicians. The old equipment will therefore have become obsolete, and much of it will have been taken out of use by such musicians. This does not mean that the equipment is worn out. Other people may well buy the old equipment and use it, possibly because they cannot afford to buy new up-to-date equipment.

- *Inadequacy* This arises when an asset is no longer used because of the growth and change in the size of the firm. For instance, a small ferryboat that is operated by a firm at a coastal resort will become entirely inadequate when the resort becomes more popular. Then it will be found that it would be more efficient and economical to operate a larger ferryboat, and so the smaller boat will be taken out of use by the firm. In this case, it does not mean that he ferryboat is no longer in good working order; it may be sold to a firm at a smaller resort.

Both obsolescence and inadequacy do not necessarily mean that the asset is destroyed. It is merely put out of use by the firm, and another firm will often buy it. For example, many of the aeroplanes no longer used by the large airlines are bought by smaller airlines.

The time factor

Obviously, time has to elapse for wear and tear, erosion, obsolescence and inadequacy to occur. However, there are fixed assets to which the time factor is connected in a different way. These are assets that have a legal life fixed in terms of years.

For instance, you may agree to rent some buildings for ten years. Such an agreement is normally called a **lease**. When a lease expires, it is worth nothing to you as it has finished; whatever you paid for the lease is now of no value.

A similar asset is where you buy a patent with complete rights, so that only you are able to produce something using that patent. When the patent's time has expired, it then has no value. The usual length of life of a patent is 16 years.

Instead of using the term depreciation, the term **amortisation** is often used for these assets.

Depletion

Other assets are of a 'wasting' character, perhaps due to the extraction of raw materials from them. The materials are then either used by the firm to make something else, or are sold in their raw state to other firms. Natural resources such as mines, quarries and oil wells come under this heading.

To provide for the consumption of an asset of a wasting character is called provision for **depletion**.

26.5 Land and buildings

Prior to the accounting regulation known as SSAP 12, which applied after 1977, freehold and long leasehold properties were very rarely subject to a charge for depreciation. It was contended that, as property values tended to rise instead of fall, it was inappropriate to charge depreciation.

However, SSAP 12 requires that depreciation be charged over the property's useful life, with the exception that freehold land will not normally require a provision for depreciation. This is because land does not normally depreciate. Buildings do, however, eventually fall into disrepair or become obsolete and must be subject to a charge for depreciation each year. When a revaluation of property takes place, the depreciation charge must be on the revalued figure.

An exception to all this is **investment properties**. These are properties owned not for use but simply for investment. In this case, investment properties will be shown in the balance sheet at their open-market value.

26.6 Appreciation

At this stage, readers may well begin to ask themselves about the assets that increase (appreciate) in value. The answer to this is that normal accounting procedure would be to ignore any such **appreciation**, as to bring appreciation into account would be to contravene both the cost concept and the prudence concept (as discussed in Chapter 11). Nevertheless, in certain circumstances, appreciation is taken into account in partnership and limited company accounts, but this topic is left until partnerships and limited companies are considered.

26.7 Provision for depreciation as an allocation of cost

Depreciation in total over the life of an asset can be calculated quite simply as cost less amount receivable when the asset is put out of use by the firm. If the item is bought and sold within one accounting period, then the depreciation for that period is charged as a revenue expense in arriving at that period's net profit. The difficulties start when the asset is used for more than one accounting period, and an attempt has to be made to charge each period with the depreciation for that period.

Even though depreciation provisions are now regarded as allocating cost to each accounting period (except for accounting for inflation), it does not follow that there is any 'true' method of performing even this task. All that can be said is that the cost should be allocated over the life of the asset in such a way as to charge it as equitably as possible to the periods in which the asset is used.

The difficulties involved are considerable, and some of them are now listed.

- Apart from a few assets, such as a lease, how accurately can a firm assess an asset's useful life? Even a lease may be put out of use if the premises leased have become inadequate.
- How does one measure 'use'? A car owned by a firm for two years may have been driven one year by a very careful driver and another year by a reckless driver. The standard of driving will affect the motor car and also the amount of cash receivable on its disposal. How should such a firm apportion the car's depreciation costs?
- There are other expenses beside depreciation, such as repairs and maintenance of the fixed asset. As both of these affect the rate and amount of depreciation, should they not also affect the depreciation provision calculations?
- How can a firm possibly know the amount receivable in a number of years' time when the asset is put out of use?

These are only some of the difficulties. Therefore, the methods of calculating provisions for depreciation are mainly accounting customs.

26.8 Methods of calculating depreciation charges

The two main methods in use for calculating depreciation charges are the **straight line method** and the **reducing balance method**. Most accountants think that, although other methods may be needed in certain cases, the straight line method is the one that is generally most suitable. Both are described next.

Straight line method

By this method, sometimes also called the 'fixed instalment' method, the number of years of use is estimated. The cost is then divided by the number of years, to give the depreciation charge each year.

For instance, if a lorry was bought for £22,000 and we thought we would keep it for four years and then sell it for £2,000, the depreciation to be charged would be:

$$\frac{\text{Cost (£22,000) – Disposal value (£2,000)}}{\text{Number of years use (4)}} = \frac{\text{£20,000}}{4}$$

= £5,000 depreciation each year for four years.

If, after four years, the lorry would have had no disposal value, the charge for depreciation would have been:

$$\frac{\text{Cost (£22,000)}}{\text{Number of years use (4)}} = \frac{\text{£22,000}}{4}$$

= £5,500 depreciation each year for four years.

Reducing balance method

By this method a fixed percentage for depreciation is deducted from the cost in the first year. In the second or later years the same percentage is taken of the reduced balance (i.e. cost *less* depreciation already charged). This method is also known as the 'diminishing balance' method.

For instance, if a machine is bought for £10,000 and depreciation is to be charged at 20 per cent, the calculations for the first three years would be as follows:

	£
Cost	10,000
First year: depreciation (20% of £10,000)	2,000
	8,000
Second year: depreciation (20% of £8,000)	1,600
	6,400
Third year: depreciation (20% of £6,400)	1,280
Net book value at the end of the third year	5,120

Note that **net book value** means the cost of a fixed asset with depreciation deducted. It is sometimes simply known as 'book value'.

Using this method means that much larger amounts are charged in the earlier years of use as compared with the latter years of use. It is often said that repairs and upkeep in the early years will not cost as much as when the asset becomes old. This means that:

In the early years		In the later years
A higher charge for depreciation + A lower charge for repairs and upkeep	will tend to be fairly equal to	A lower charge for depreciation + A higher charge for repairs and upkeep

The worked example in Section 26.9 gives a comparison of the calculations using the two methods, if the same cost applies for the two methods.

26.9 A worked example

A firm has just bought a machine for £8,000. It will be kept in use for four years, and then it will be disposed of for an estimated amount of £500. The firm's management asks for a comparison of the amounts charged as depreciation using both methods.

For the straight line method, a figure of (£8,000 – £500) ÷ 4 = £7,500 ÷ 4 = £1,875 per annum is to be used. For the reducing balance method a percentage figure of 50 per cent will be used.

	Method 1 Straight Line		Method 2 Reducing Balance
	£		£
Cost	8,000		8,000
Depreciation: year 1	1,875	(50% of £8,000)	4,000
	6,125		4,000
Depreciation: year 2	1,875	(50% of £4,000)	2,000
	4,250		2,000
Depreciation: year 3	1,875	(50% of £2,000)	1,000
	2,375		1,000
Depreciation: year 4	1,875	(50% of £1,000)	500
Disposal value	500		500

This illustrates the fact that using the reducing balance method there is a much higher charge for depreciation in the early years, and lower charges in the later years.

Other methods

There are many more methods of calculating depreciation but they are outside the scope of this volume. Special methods are often used in particular industries, where there are circumstances which are peculiar to that industry.

New terms

Amortisation (p. 282): A term used instead of depreciation when assets are used up simply because of the time factor.

Appreciation (p. 283): The increase in value over the cost of an asset, usually land and buildings.

Depletion (p. 282): The wasting-away of an asset as it is used up.

Depreciation (p. 280): The part of the cost of the fixed asset consumed during its period of use by the firm.

Inadequacy (p. 282): When an asset is no longer used because of changes within an organisation due to growth, competition or product range changes.

Investment property (p. 283): Property purchased with the intent of making a profit, usually by leasing it.

Lease (p. 282): An agreement to rent property for a period.

Net book value (p. 284): The cost of fixed asset with depreciation deducted; also known as 'book value'.

Obsolescence (p. 281): Becoming out of date.

Reducing balance method (p. 284): Depreciation calculation that is at a lesser amount every following period.

Straight line method (p. 284): Depreciation calculation that remains at an equal amount each year.

EXERCISES

26.1 D Sankey, a manufacturer, purchases a lathe for the sum of £4,000. It has an estimated life of five years and a scrap value of £500. Sankey is not certain whether he should use the 'straight line' or the 'reducing balance' basis for the purpose of calculating depreciation on the machine.

You are required to calculate the depreciation on the lathe using both methods, showing clearly the balance remaining in the lathe account at the end of each of the five years for each method. (Assume that 40 per cent per annum is to be used for the reducing balance method, and make your calculations to the nearest £.)

26.2 A machine costs £12,500. It will be kept for four years and then sold for an estimated figure of £5,120. Show the calculations of the figures for depreciation for each of the four years using (*a*) the straight line method, and (*b*) the reducing balance method. For the latter method, use a depreciation rate of 20 per cent.

26.3 A motor vehicle costs £6,400. It will be kept for five years and then sold for scrap for £200. Calculate the depreciation for each year using (*a*) the reducing balance method, using a depreciation rate of 50 per cent, and (*b*) the straight line method.

26.4X A machine costs £5,120. It will be kept for five years and then sold at an estimated figure of £1,215. Show the calculations of the figures for depreciation each year using (*a*) the straight line method, and (*b*) the reducing balance method using a depreciation rate of 25 per cent.

26.5X A bulldozer costs £12,150. It will be kept in use for five years. At the end of that time, agreement has already been reached that it will be sold for £1,600. Show your calculation of the amount of depreciation each year if (*a*) the reducing balance method at a rate of $33\frac{1}{3}$ per cent is used, and (*b*) the straight line method is used.

26.6X A tractor is bought for £6,000. It will be used for three years and then sold back to the supplier for £3,072. Show the depreciation calculations for each year using (*a*) the reducing balance method with a rate of 20 per cent, and (*b*) the straight line method.

26.7X From the following information, which shows the depreciation for the first two years of use for two assets, you are required to answer the questions set out below.

	Machinery	*Fixtures*
	£	£
Cost Year 1	8,000	3,600
Year 1 Depreciation	1,600	900
	6,400	2,700
Year 2 Depreciation	1,600	675
	4,800	2,025

(*a*) Which type of depreciation method is used for each asset?
(*b*) What will be the book value of each of the assets after four years of use?
(*c*) If, instead of the method used, the machinery had been depreciated by the alternative method but using the same percentage rate, what would have been the book value after four years? (Calculate your answer to the nearest £.)

CHAPTER 27

Double entry records for depreciation and the disposal of assets

Learning objectives

After you have studied this chapter you should be able to:

- **incorporate depreciation calculations into the accounting records**
- **record the disposal of fixed assets and the adjustments needed to the provision for depreciation accounts.**

27.1 Recording depreciation

Looking back a number of years, the charge for depreciation always used to be shown in the fixed asset accounts themselves. However, this method has now fallen into disuse. The method now used is where the fixed assets accounts show the assets at cost price, the depreciation being shown separately and accumulating in a **provision for depreciation account**.

The following example illustrates the accounting records.

Example 1: A machine is bought for £2,000 on 1 January 2005. It has been depreciated at the rate of 20 per cent using the reducing balance method. The asset account, depreciation account, profit and loss account and balance sheet in respect of the first three years are shown in Exhibit 27.1. Notice that no entry is made in the asset account for depreciation. This means that the fixed asset accounts will normally be shown at cost price.

The double entry for depreciation is:

- debit the profit and loss account
- credit the provision for depreciation account.

Exhibit 27.1

Machinery

Dr					Cr
2005		£	2005		£
Jan 1	Cash	2,000	Dec 31	Balance c/d	2,000
2006			2006		
Jan 1	Balance b/d	2,000	Dec 31	Balance c/d	2,000
2007			2007		
Jan 1	Balance b/d	2,000	Dec 31	Balance c/d	2,000
2008					
Jan 1	Balance b/d	2,000			

Provision for Depreciation – Machinery Account

Dr					Cr
2005		£	2005		£
Dec 31	Balance c/d	400	Dec 31	Profit and loss a/c	400
2006			2006		
Dec 31	Balance c/d	720	Jan 1	Balance b/d	400
			Dec 31	Profit and loss a/c	320
		720			720
2007			2007		
Dec 31	Balance c/d	976	Jan 1	Balance b/d	720
			Dec 31	Profit and loss a/c	256
		976			976
			2008		
			Jan 1	Balance b/d	976

Profit and Loss account for the year ended 31 December

Dr			Cr
		£	
2005	Depreciation	400	
2006	Depreciation	320	
2007	Depreciation	256	

Now, the balance on the Machinery Account is shown on the balance sheet at the end of each year, less the balance on the Provision for Depreciation Account.

Balance Sheets as at 31 December

	Cost	Total depreciation	Net book value
2005	£	£	£
Machinery	2,000	400	1,600
2006			
Machinery	2,000	720	1,280
2007			
Machinery	2,000	976	1,024

Another example can now be given in Exhibit 27.2. This is of a business with financial years ending 30 June. A motor car is bought on 1 July 2001 for £8,000. Another car is bought on 1 July 2002 for £11,000. Each car is expected to be in use for five years, and the disposal value of the first car is expected to be £500 and of the second car £1,000. The method of depreciation to be used is the straight line method. The first two years' accounts are shown in the Exhibit.

Exhibit 27.2

Motor Cars Account

Dr					*Cr*
2001		£	2002		£
Jul 1	Bank	8,000	Jun 30	Balance c/d	8,000
2002			2003		
Jul 1	Balance b/d	8,000	Jun 30	Balance c/d	19,000
Jul 1	Bank	11,000			
		19,000			19,000
2003					
Jul 1	Balance b/d	19,000			

Provision for Depreciation – Motor Cars Account

Dr					*Cr*
2002		£	2002		£
Jun 30	Balance c/d	1,500	Jun 30	Profit and loss a/c	1,500
			Jul 1	Balance b/d	1,500
2003			2003		
Jun 30	Balance c/d	5,000	Jun 30	Profit and loss a/c	3,500
		5,000			5,000
			Jul 1	Balance b/d	5,000

Profit and Loss Account for the year ended 30 June (extracts)

		£	
2002	Depreciation	1,500	
2003	Depreciation	3,500	

Balance Sheet as at 30 June 2002

	Cost	*Total depreciation*	*Net book value*
	£	£	£
Motor car	8,000	1,500	6,500

Balance Sheet as at 30 June 2003

	Cost	*Total depreciation*	*Net book value*
	£	£	£
Motor cars	19,000	5,000	14,000

27.2 The sale of an asset

Reason for accounting entries

Upon the sale of an asset, we will want to delete it from our accounts. This means that the cost of that asset needs to be taken out of the asset account. In addition, the depreciation of the asset that has been sold will have to be taken out of the depreciation provision. Finally, the profit or loss on sale, if any, will have to be calculated.

When we charge depreciation on a fixed asset, we are having to make estimates. We cannot be absolutely certain how long we will keep an asset in use, nor can we be certain at the date of purchase how much the asset will be sold for on disposal. Nor will we always estimate correctly. This means that when the asset is disposed of, the cash received for it is usually different from our original estimate.

Accounting entries needed

On the sale of a fixed asset, the following entries are needed (for instance, let us assume the sale of machinery):

(A) Transfer the cost price of the asset sold to an Assets Disposal Account (in this case a Machinery Disposals Account).	Debit Machinery Disposals Account. Credit Machinery Account.
(B) Transfer the depreciation already charged to the Assets Disposal Account.	Debit Provision for Depreciation – Machinery Account. Credit Machinery Disposals Account.
(C) For remittance received on disposal.	Debit Cash Book. Credit Machinery Disposals Account.
(D) Transfer balance (difference) on Machinery Disposals Account to the Profit and Loss Account.	
(i) If the difference is on the debit side of the Disposals Account, it is a *profit* on sale.	Debit Machinery Disposals Account. Credit Profit and Loss Account.
(ii) If the difference is on the credit side of the Disposal Account, it is a *loss* on sale.	Debit Profit and Loss Account. Credit Machinery Disposals Account.

These entries can be illustrated by looking at those needed if the machinery already shown in Exhibit 27.1 was sold. The records to 31 December 2007 show that the cost of the machine was £2,000 and a total of £976 has been written off as depreciation, leaving a net book value of (£2,000 - £976) = £1,024. If, therefore, the machine is sold on 2 January 2008 for *more than* £1,024, a profit on sale will be made; if, on the other hand, the machine is sold for *less than* £1,024, then a loss on disposal will be incurred.

Exhibit 27.3 shows the entries needed when the machine has been sold for £1,070 and a small profit on sale has been made. Exhibit 27.4 shows the entries where the machine has been sold for £950, thus incurring a loss on sale. In both cases the sale is on 2 January 2008 and no depreciation is charged for the two days' ownership in 2008. And the letters (A) to (D) in Exhibits 27.3 and 27.4 are references to the table of instructions shown above.

EXHIBIT 27.3

Machinery Account

Dr			*Cr*
2005	£	2008	£
Jan 1 Cash	2,000	Jan 2 Machinery disposals (A)	2,000

Provision for Depreciation: Machinery Account

Dr			*Cr*
2008	£	2008	£
Jan 2 Machinery disposals (B)	976	Jan 1 Balance b/d	976

Machinery Disposals Account

Dr					Cr
2008		£	2008		£
Jan 2 Machinery	(A)	2,000	Jan 2 Cash	(C)	1,070
Dec 31 Profit and loss a/c	(D)	46	2 Provision for depreciation	(B)	976
		2,046			2,046

Profit and Loss Account for the year ended 31 December 2008

		£
Gross Profit		xxx
Add Profit on sale of machinery	(D)	46

Exhibit 27.4

Machinery Account

Dr					Cr
2005		£	2008		£
Jan 1 Cash		2,000	Jan 2 Machinery disposals	(A)	2,000

Provision for Depreciation: Machinery Account

Dr				Cr
2008		£	2008	£
Jan 2 Machinery disposals	(B)	976	Jan 1 Balance b/d	976

Machinery Disposals Account

Dr					Cr
2008		£	2008		£
Jan 2 Machinery	(A)	2,000	Jan 2 Cash	(C)	950
			2 Provision for depreciation	(B)	976
			Dec 31 Profit and loss	(D)	74
		2,000			2,000

Profit and Loss Account for the year ended 31 December 2008

		£
Gross Profit		xxx
Less Loss on sale of machinery	(D)	74

In this chapter, all unnecessary difficulties have been avoided. For instance, all assets have been bought, or sold, on the first day of a financial year. Exactly what happens when assets are sold or bought part way through the year is dealt with in Frank Wood's *Business Accounting 1*.

Note: A step-by-step guide to dealing with depreciation in final accounts is shown in Appendix B Step-by-step guides, at the end of this book.

New term

Provision for depreciation account (p. 288): The account where depreciation is accumulated for balance sheet purposes. In the balance sheet the cost price of the asset is shown less the depreciation to date to give the net book value.

EXERCISES

27.1 A White, an exporter, bought a new car for his business on 1 January 2002 for £12,500. He decided to write off depreciation at the rate of 20 per cent, using the reducing balance method.

Show the following for each of the financial years ended 31 December 2002, 2003 and 2004.

(*a*) motor cars account
(*b*) provision for depreciation account
(*c*) extracts from the profit and loss accounts
(*d*) extracts from the balance sheets.

27.2X H Slater, a jewellery manufacturer, purchased a new machine for £18,000 on 1 November 2007. Her business year end is 31 October, but she cannot decide which method of depreciation she should use in respect of the machine – the straight line method or the reducing balance method.

Required:
In order to assist her in making a decision, draw up the machinery account and the provision for depreciation account for the three years from 1 November 2007 using:

(*a*) the straight line method.
(*b*) the reducing balance method.

Each account must indicate which method is being used, and each account should be balanced at the end of each of the three years. In both cases the rate of depreciation is to be 10 per cent, and calculations should be made to the nearest £.

(*c*) Also show the extracts from the profit and loss accounts and balance sheets for each of the three years.

27.3 On 1 January 2002, which was the first day of a financial year, T Young bought networked computer hardware for £9,500. It is to be depreciated by the straight line method at the rate of 20 per cent, ignoring salvage value. On 1 January 2005 the system was sold for £4,250.

Show the following for the complete period of ownership.

(*a*) The computer account.
(*b*) The provision for depreciation.
(*c*) The computer disposal account.
(*d*) The extracts from profit and loss accounts for four years.
(*e*) The extracts from three years' balance sheets – 2002, 2003 and 2004.

27.4 Show the relevant disposal account for each of the following cases, including the transfers to the profit and loss account.

(*a*) Motor vehicle: cost £12,000; depreciated £9,700 to date of sale; sold for £1,850.
(*b*) Machinery: cost £27,900; depreciated £19,400 to date of sale; sold for £11,270.
(*c*) Fixtures: cost £8,420; depreciated £7,135 to date of sale; sold for £50.
(*d*) Buildings: cost £200,000; depreciated straight line 5 per cent on cost for 11 years to date of sale; sold for £149,000.

27.5X On 1 January 2004, K Lee, an engineer, bought three machines for his factory. They cost £54,000 each. He estimated that the machines would be efficient for use for 6 years and could then be sold for scrap for £3,000 each. One of the machines was damaged in use so that one function was unusable. This machine was sold on 1 January 2006 for £24,600.

Using the straight line method of depreciation and allowing for financial year to end 31 December, show for the years 2004, 2005 and 2006 the following:

(*a*) machinery account
(*b*) machinery disposals account
(*c*) provision for depreciation of machinery account
(*d*) extracts from the profit and loss account for each of the years ended 31 December 2004, 2005 and 2006
(*e*) extracts from the balance sheets as at 31 December 2004, 2005 and 2006.

27.6X (*a*) What is meant by the term depreciation?
(*b*) Which accounting concept is being ignored if a business changes the method of charging depreciation each year?
(*c*) Name *two* methods of charging depreciation provision.
(*d*) The accountant for a business recommends that, because of the size of the organisation, all items of machinery less than £500 should be treated as revenue expenditure. What accounting concept or convention is being applied in this example?
(*e*) A business whose financial year ends on 31 December each year purchased a delivery van by cheque for £20,000 on 1 January 2006. Depreciation is to be charged on delivery vans at 20% p.a. on cost. The delivery van was sold on 30 June 2008 for a cheque of £13,000. Depreciation is not charged in the year of disposal. Show the *relevant entries* in *each* of the following accounts for the years ended 31 December 2006, 2007 and 2008:
(i) delivery van account
(ii) provision for depreciation account
(iii) delivery van disposal account
(iv) profit and loss account.

NEAB (GCSE)

CHAPTER 28

Bad debts and provisions for bad debts

Learning objectives

After you have studied this chapter you should be able to:

- **understand how bad debts can be written off**
- **make provisions for possible bad debts**
- **understand the accounting entries for bad debts recovered**
- **show an aged debtors schedule.**

28.1 Bad debts

If a firm finds that it is impossible to collect a debt, then that debt should be written off as a **bad debt**. This could happen if the debtor is suffering a loss in the business, or may even have gone bankrupt and is thus unable to pay the debt. A bad debt is, therefore, an expense on the firm that is owed the money.

An example of debts being written off as bad is shown next.

Example 1: We sold £50 goods to K Leeming on 5 January 2005, but that firm became bankrupt. On 16 February 2005 we sold £240 goods to T Young. Young managed to pay £200 on 17 May 2005, but it became obvious that he would never be able to pay the final £40.

When drawing up our final accounts to 31 December 2005, we decided to write these off as bad debts. The accounting entries are shown in the table below.

Accounting entries	Explanation
Debit: Bad debts account Credit: Debtor's account	To transfer the amount of unpaid debt to the bad debts account To reduce the liability of the debtor who is unable to settle the debt
Debit: Profit and loss account Credit: Bad debts account	To record the amount of bad debts of the period concerned To transfer the amount of bad debts to profit and loss account

The accounts would appear as follows:

Dr			**K Leeming Account**		*Cr*
2005		£	2005		£
Jan 5	Sales	50	Dec 31	Bad debts	50

Dr			**T Young Account**		*Cr*
2005		£	2005		£
Feb 16	Sales	240	May 17	Cash	200
			Dec 31	Bad debts	40
		240			240

Dr			**Bad Debts Account**		*Cr*
2005		£	2005		£
Dec 31	K Lee	50	Dec 31	Profit and loss a/c	90
Dec 31	T Young	40			
		90			90

Profit and Loss Account for the year ended 31 December 2005 (extract)

		£
Gross profit		xxx
Less Expenses:		
Bad debts	90	90

28.2 Provisions for bad debts

Let us look, as an example, at the accounts of K Clark, who started in business on 1 January 2000 and has just completed his first year of trading on 31 December 2000.

He has sold goods for £50,000 and they cost him £36,000, so his gross profit was (£50,000 – £36,000) = £14,000. However, included in the £50,000 sales was a credit sale to C Yates for £250. C Yates has died, leaving no money, and he had not paid his account. The £250 debt is therefore a bad debt and should be charged in the profit and loss account as an expense.

Beside that debt, a credit sale of £550 on 1 December 2000 to L Hall is unlikely to get paid. Clark cannot yet be certain about this, but he has been told by others that Hall had not paid his debts to other businesses. As Clark had given three months' credit to Hall, the debt is not repayable until 28 February 2001. However, the final accounts for the year 2000 are to be drawn up in January 2001 because the bank wants to see them. Clark cannot wait until after 28 February 2001 to see whether the debt of £550 owing by Hall will be a bad debt.

What, therefore, can Clark do? When he shows the bank his final accounts, he wants to achieve the following objectives:

(*a*) to charge as expenses in the profit and loss account for the year 2000 an amount representing sales of that year for which he will never be paid (*b*) to show in the balance sheet as correct a figure as possible for the true value of debtors at the balance sheet date.

He can carry out (*a*) above by writing off Yates's debt of £250 and then charging it as an expense in his profit and loss account. For (*b*) he cannot yet write off Hall's debt of £550 as a bad debt because he is not certain about it being a bad debt. If he does nothing about it, the debtors shown on the balance sheet will include a debt that is probably of no value. The debtors on 31 December 2000, after deducting Yates' £250 bad debt, amount to £10,000.

The answer to Clark's dilemma is demonstrated through Exhibit 28.1.

EXHIBIT 28.1

K Clark
Trading and Profit and Loss Account
for the year ended 31 December 2000

	£	£
Sales		50,000
Less Cost of goods sold:		36,000
Gross profit		14,000
Less Expenses:		
Other expenses	5,000	
Bad debts	250	
Provision for bad debts	550	
		5,800
Net profit		8,200

K Clark
Balance Sheet as at 31 December 2000 (extracts)

	£	£
Debtors	10,000	
Less Provision for bad debts	550	
		9,450

Exactly how we will do the double entry for this is explained in Section 28.4 following. What we have achieved so far is to show bad debts and **provision for bad debts** as an expense in the year when the sales were made. The debtors are also shown at probably what is their true value.

28.3 Provisions for bad debts: estimating provisions

The estimates of provisions for bad debts can be made thus:

- by looking into each debt, and estimating which ones will be bad debts
- by estimating, on the basis of experience, what percentage of the debts will result in bad debts.

It is well known that the longer a debt is owing, the more likely it will become a bad debt. Some firms draw up an ageing debtors schedule, showing how long debts have been owing. Older debtors need higher percentage estimates of bad debts than newer debtors. Exhibit 28.2 gives an example of such an ageing schedule.

Exhibit 28.2 • Ageing Debtors Schedule

Period debt owing	*Amount*	*Estimated percentage doubtful*	*Provision for bad debts*
	£		£
Less than one month	5,000	1	50
1 month to 2 months	3,000	3	90
2 months to 3 months	800	5	40
3 months to 6 months	200	20	40
Over 6 months	160	50	80
	9,160		300

A provision may be a specific one – for example, a £5,000 provision to cover the specified debts of W Cooper £3,000 and T Smith £2,000. On the other hand, it may be a general provision not linked to any specified debts and usually calculated in a percentage fashion.

28.4 Accounting entries for provisions for bad debts

When a decision has been taken as to the amount of provision to be made, then the accounting entries needed for the provision relate to the year in which provision is *first* made, as follows:

- debit: profit and loss account with the amount of provision
- credit: provision for bad debts account.

Let us look at an example that shows the entries needed for a provision for bad debts.

Example 2: As at 31 December 2003, the debtors' figure for a firm amounted to £10,000 after writing off £422 of definite bad debts. It is estimated that 2 per cent of debts (i.e. £10,000 × 2% = £200) will prove to be bad debts, and it is decided to make a provision for these. The accounts would appear as follows:

Profit and Loss Account for the year ended 31 December 2003 (extracts)

	£	£
Gross profit		xxx
Less Expenses:		
Bad debts	422	
Provision for bad debts	200	
		622

Provision for Bad Debts Account

Dr			Cr		
2003		£	2003		£
Dec 31	Balance c/d	200	Dec 31	Profit and loss a/c	200
			2004		
			Jan 1	Balance b/d	200

In the balance sheet, the balance on the provision for bad debts will be deducted from the total of debtors, thus:

Balance Sheet (extracts) 31 December 2003

	£	£
Current assets		
Debtors	10,000	
Less Provision for bad debts	200	9,800

28.5 Increasing the provision

Taking the same example as shown in Example 2 above, let us suppose that at the end of the following year, on 31 December 2004, the bad debts provision needed to be increased because the provision could be kept at 2 per cent but the debtors had risen to £12,000. Not included in the figure of £12,000 debtors is £884 in respect of debts that had already been written off as bad debts during the year. A provision of £200 had been brought forward from the *previous* year, but we now want a total provision of £240 (i.e. 2 per cent of £12,000). All that is needed is a provision for an extra £40.

The double entry will be:

- debit: profit and loss account
- credit: provision for bad debts account,

and the relevant accounts will look as set out below.

Profit and Loss Account for the year ended 31 December 2004

	£	£
Gross profit		xxx
Less Expenses:		
Bad debts	884	
Provision for bad debts	40	

Provision for Bad Debts Account

Dr			Cr		
2004		£	2004		£
Dec 31	Balance c/d	240	Jan 1	Balance b/d	200
			Dec 31	Profit and loss a/c	40
		240			240
			2005		
			Jan 1	Balance b/d	240

Balance Sheet as at 31 December 2004 (extracts)

Current Assets	£	£
Debtors	12,000	
Less Provision for bad debts	240	11,760

28.6 Reducing the provision

The provision is shown as a credit balance. To reduce it, we would need a debit entry in the provision account. The credit would be in the profit and loss account. Again, using Example 2 above, let us assume that on 31 December 2005 the debtors figure had fallen to £10,500 but the provision remained at 2 per cent, i.e. £210 (£10,500 × 2%). As the provision had previously been £240, it now needs a reduction of £30. Bad debts of £616 had already been written off during the year and are not included in the debtors figure of £10,500.

The double entry is:

- debit: provision for bad debts account
- credit: profit and loss account,

and the relevant accounts look thus:

Profit and Loss Account for the year ended 31 December 2005

	£	£
Gross profit		xxx
Add Reduction in provision for bad debts		30
		xxx
Less Expenses:		
Bad debts	616	616

Provision for Bad Debts Account

Dr					*Cr*
2005		£	2005		£
Dec 31	Profit and loss a/c	30	Jan 1	Balance b/d	240
Dec 31	Balance c/d	210			
		240			240
			2006		
			Jan 1	Balance b/d	210

Balance Sheet as at 31 December 2005 (extracts)

Current Assets	£	£
Debtors	10,500	
Less Provision for bad debts	210	10,290

The main points that you have to remember about provisions for bad debts are:

- *Year 1 – provision first made:* (*a*) debit profit and loss account with full provision
  (*b*) show in balance sheet as a deduction from debtors.

- *Later years:*
  (*a*) only the increase, or decrease, in the provision is shown in the profit and loss account, as follows:
  - *to increase*: debit the profit and loss account, and credit the provision for bad debts account.
  - *to decrease*: credit the profit and loss account, and debit the provision for bad debts account.

  (*b*) the balance sheet will show the amended figure of the provision as a deduction from debtors.

28.7 A worked example

Let us now look at a comprehensive example.

Example 3: A business started on 1 January 2002 and its financial year end is 31 December. A table of debtors, the bad debts written off and the estimated bad debts at the rate of 2 per cent of debtors at the end of each year, as well as the double entry accounts and the extracts from the final accounts, follow as Exhibit 28.3.

Exhibit 28.3

Year to 31 December	*Debtors at end of year (after bad debts written off)*	*Bad debts written off during year*	*Debts thought at end of year to be impossible to collect: 2% of debtors*
	£	£	£
2002	6,000	423	120 (2% of £6,000)
2003	7,000	510	140 (2% of £7,000)
2004	7,750	604	155 (2% of £7,750)
2005	6,500	610	130 (2% of £6,500)

Provision for Bad Debts Account

Dr			*Cr*		
2002		£	2002		£
Dec 31	Balance c/d	120	Dec 31	Profit and loss a/c	120
2003			2003		
Dec 31	Balance c/d	140	Jan 1	Balance b/d	120
			Dec 31	Profit and loss a/c	20
		140			140
2004			2004		
Dec 31	Balance c/d	155	Jan 1	Balance b/d	140
			Dec 31	Profit and loss a/c	15
		155			155
2005			2005		
Dec 31	Profit and loss a/c	25	Jan 1	Balance b/d	155
Dec 31	Balance c/d	130			
		155			155
			2006		
			Jan 1	Balance b/d	130

Bad Debts Account

Dr			*Cr*		
2002		£	2002		£
Dec 31	Debtors	423	Dec 31	Profit and loss a/c	423
2003			2003		
Dec 31	Debtors	510	Dec 31	Profit and loss a/c	510
2004			2004		
Dec 31	Debtors	604	Dec 31	Profit and loss a/c	604
2005			2005		
Dec 31	Debtors	610	Dec 31	Profit and loss a/c	610

Profit and Loss Account(s) (extracts) for the year ended

		£	£
Gross profit for 2002, 2003, 2004			xxx
2002	*Less* Expenses:		
	Bad debts	423	
	Provision for bad debts (increase)	120	543
2003	*Less* Expenses:		
	Bad debts	510	
	Provision for bad debts (increase)	20	530
2004	*Less* Expenses:		
	Bad debts	604	
	Provision for bad debts (increase)	15	619
2005	Gross profit for 2005		xxx
	Add Reduction in provision for bad debts		25
			xxx
	Less Bad debts		610
			xxx

Balance Sheet (extracts) as at 31 December

		£	£
2002	Debtors	6,000	
	Less Provision for bad debts	120	5,880
2003	Debtors	7,000	
	Less Provision for bad debts	140	6,860
2004	Debtors	7,750	
	Less Provision for bad debts	155	7,595
2005	Debtors	6,500	
	Less Provision for bad debts	130	6,370

You may see the term 'provision for doubtful debts'. This means exactly the same as 'provision for bad debts'. It is simply that some accountants prefer the other wording.

28.8 Bad debts recovered

It is not uncommon for a *debt written off* in previous years to be *recovered* in later years. When this occurs, the book-keeping procedures are such that, first, you should reinstate the debt by making the following entries:

- debit: debtor's account
- credit: bad debts recovered account.

The reason for reinstating the debt in the ledger account of the debtor is to have a detailed history of the account as a guide for granting credit in the future. By the time a debt is written off as bad, it will be recorded in the debtors' ledger account. Thus, when such a debt is recovered, it must also be shown in the debtors' ledger account.

When cash or a cheque is later received from the debtor in settlement of the account or part thereof, other book-keeping entries are necessary:

- debit: cash/bank with the amount received
- credit: debtor's account with the amount received.

At the end of the financial year, the credit balance on the bad debts recovered account will be transferred to either the bad debts account or direct to the credit side of the profit and loss account. The net effect of either of these entries is the same, since the bad debts account will be transferred to the profit and loss account at the end of the financial year. In other words, the net profit will be the same no matter which method is used.

Note: A step-by-step guide to dealing with bad debts and provision for and debts in final accounts is shown in Appendix B Step-by-step guides, at the end of this book.

New terms

Bad debts (p. 296): A debt owing to a business, which is unlikely to be paid.

Bad debt recovered (p. 304): A debt that has previously been written off and that is subsequently paid by the debtor.

Provision for bad debts (p. 297): An account showing the expected amounts of debtors who, at the balance sheet date, may not be able to pay their outstanding accounts.

EXERCISES

28.1 Data Computer Services commences in business on 1 January 2004, and during its first year of trading the following debts are found to be bad and the firm decided to write them off as bad:

2004		
April 30	H Gordon	£1,110
August 31	D Bellamy Ltd	£640
October 31	J Alderton	£120

On 31 December 2004, the schedule of remaining debtors, amounting in total to £68,500, is examined, and it is decided to make a provision for bad debts of £2,200.

You are required to show:

(*a*) the bad debts account and the provision for bad debts account
(*b*) the charge to the profit and loss account
(*c*) the relevant extracts from the balance sheet as at 31 December 2004.

28.2 A business has always made a provision for bad debts at the rate of 5% of debtors. On 1 January 2003 the provision for this, brought forward from the previous year, amounted to £2,600. During the year to 31 December 2003 the bad debts written off amounted to £540. On 31 December 2003 the remaining debtors totalled £62,000 and the usual provision for bad debts is to be made.

You are to show:

(*a*) the bad debts account for the year ended 31 December 2003
(*b*) the provision for bad debts account for the year
(*c*) an extract from the profit and loss account for the year
(*d*) the relevant extract from the balance sheet as at 31 December 2003.

28.3 A business started trading on 1 January 2006. During the two years ended 31 December 2006 and 2007, the following debts were written off to the bad debts account on the dates stated:

31 August 2006	W Best	£85
30 September 2006	S Avon	£140
28 February 2007	L J Friend	£180
31 August 2007	N Kelly	£60
30 November 2007	A Oliver	£250

On 31 December 2006 there had been a total of debtors remaining of £40,500, and it was decided to make a provision for doubtful debts of £550. On 31 December 2007 there had been a total of debtors remaining of £47,300, and it was decided to make a provision for doubtful debts of £600.

You are required to show:
(*a*) the bad debts account and the provision for bad debts account for each of the two years
(*b*) the relevant extracts from the balance sheets as at 31 December 2006 and 2007.

28.4X A business that started trading on 1 January 2005 adjusted its bad debt provisions at the end of each year on a percentage basis, but each year the percentage rate is adjusted in accordance with the current 'economic climate'. The following details are available for the three years ended 31 December 2005, 2006, and 2007:

Bad debts written off year to 31 December		*Debtors at 31 December*	*Per cent provision for bad debts*
	£	£	
2005	656	22,000	5
2006	1,805	40,000	7
2007	3,847	60,000	6

You are required to show:
(*a*) the bad debts accounts for each of the three years
(*b*) the provision for bad debts accounts for each of the three years
(*c*) the balance sheet extracts as at 31 December 2005, 2006 and 2007.

28.5X From the details below, write up the accounts shown in the ledger of C Bedford Ltd, a wholesaler, for the year ended 31 December 2008. You should show clearly the amounts transferred to the profit and loss account. Information of relevance is as follows:

- At 1 January 2008, T Strange owed C Bedford Ltd £2,000. On 30 November 2008, C Bedford Ltd is notified that T Strange has been declared bankrupt and Bedford receives a cheque for 25p for each £1 owed. The balance owing by T Strange is written off as a bad debt.
- C Bedford Ltd also maintains a provision for doubtful debts equivalent to 1% of outstanding debts at the end of the year. On 1 January 2008 the balance on this account is £500. At 31 December 2008 C Bedford is owed £52,000 by debtors.

NEAB (GCSE)

28.6X (*a*) On 1 January 2004, there was a balance of £2,500 in the provision for bad debts account and it was decided to maintain the provision at 5% of the debtors at the end of each year. The debtors on 31 December each year were as follows:

	£
2004	60,000
2005	40,000
2006	40,000

You are required to show the accounting entries for the three years ended 31 December 2004, 2005 and 2006 as follows:
(i) the provision for bad debts account
(ii) the profit and loss account
(iii) the balance sheet extract.

(*b*) Explain the difference between bad debts and a provision for bad debts.

(*c*) As more and more businesses are experiencing difficulty collecting debts they find it important to create a provision for bad debts to provide for such a contingency. What is the purpose of creating such a provision, and which accounting concept covers this area.

CHAPTER 29

Other adjustments for final accounts

Learning objectives

After you have studied this chapter you should be able to:

- adjust expense accounts for accruals and prepayments
- adjust revenue accounts for amounts owing
- ascertain the amounts of expense and revenue items to be shown in the profit and loss account
- show accruals, prepayments and revenue debtors in the balance sheet
- enter up the necessary accounts for goods taken for own use
- know how to prepare final accounts for service sector organisations.

29.1 The final accounts so far

The trading and profit and loss account that has been considered up to now has taken sales for a period and deducted *all* the expenses for that period, resulting in either a net profit or net loss.

So far, it has been assumed that the expenses incurred have belonged exactly to the period of the trading and profit and loss account. If, for example, the trading and profit and loss account for the year ended 31 December 2005 was being drawn up, then the rent paid as shown in the trial balance was exactly that due for 2005 - There being no rent owing at the beginning of 2005 nor any owing at the end of 2005, nor had any rent been paid in advance. It is easier to consider a simple example at first to understand the principles of final accounts.

29.2 Adjustments needed for expenses owing or paid in advance

Not all businesses pay their rent exactly on time and, indeed, some businesses prefer to pay for their rent in advance. The following examples will illustrate the adjustments necessary if expenses are either owing, or paid in advance, at the end of a financial period.

As our first example, let us consider two firms that rent their premises for £1,200 per year. Firm A pays £1,000 during the year and owes £200 rent at the end of the year. So:

- rent expense used up during the year = £1,200
- rent actually paid in the year = £1,000.

Firm B pays £1,300 during the year, including £100 in advance for the following year. So:

- rent expense used up during the year = £1,200
- rent actually paid for in the year = £1,300.

A profit and loss account for the 12 months needs 12 months' rent as an expense (= £1,200). This means that in the above two examples the double entry accounts will have to be adjusted.

In all the examples following in this chapter, the trading and profit and loss accounts are for the period ended 31 December 2005.

29.3 Accrued expenses (i.e. expenses owing)

Assume that rent of £1,000 per year is payable at the end of every three months but that the rent is not always paid on time. Details are given in the table below.

Amount	Rent due	Rent paid
£250	31 March 2005	31 March 2005
£250	30 June 2005	2 July 2005
£250	30 September 2005	4 October 2005
£250	31 December 2005	5 January 2006

The rent account appears thus:

Dr			**Rent Account**	*Cr*
2005			*£*	
Mar	31	Cash	250	
Jul	2	"	250	
Oct	4	"	250	

The rent paid on 5 January 2006 will appear in the books of the year 2006 as part of the double entry.

The expense for 2005 is obviously £1,000 as that is the year's rent, and this is the amount needed to be transferred to the profit and loss account. But if £1,000 was put on the credit side of the rent account (the debit being in the profit and loss account), the account would not balance. We would have £1,000 on the credit side of the account and only £750 on the debit side.

To make the account balance, the £250 rent owing for 2005 but paid in 2006 must be carried down to 2006 as a credit balance because it is a liability on 31 December

2005. Instead of rent owing, it could be called rent accrued (or just simply an **accrual**). The completed account can now be shown, thus:

Dr			**Rent Account**				*Cr*
2005			£	2005			£
Mar	31	Cash	250	Dec	31	Profit and loss	1,000
Jul	2	"	250				
Oct	4	"	250				
Dec	31	Accrued c/d	250				
			1,000				1,000
				2006			
				Jan	1	Accrued b/d	250

The balance c/d has been described as 'accrued c/d', rather than as a balance. This is to explain what the balance is for; it is for an **accrued expense.**

29.4 Prepaid expenses

Insurance for a firm is at the rate of £840 a year, starting from 1 January 2005. The firm has agreed to pay this at the rate of £210 every three months. However, payments were not made at the correct times. Details were as given in the table below:

Amount	Insurance due	Insurance paid
£210	31 March 2005	£210 28 February 2005
£210	30 June 2005	£420 31 August 2005
£210	30 September 2005	
£210	31 December 2005	£420 18 November 2005

The insurance account for the year ended 31 December 2005 will be shown in the books thus:

Dr			**Insurance Account**	*Cr*
2005			£	
Feb	28	Bank	210	
Aug	31	"	420	
Nov	18	"	420	

The last payment shown of £420 is not just for 2005; it can be split as £210 for the three months to 31 December 2005 and £210 for the three months ended 31 March 2006. For a period of 12 months the cost of insurance is £840 and this therefore is the figure needing to be transferred to the profit and loss account.

If this figure of £840 is entered, then the amount needed to balance the account will be £210 and at 31 December 2005 there is a benefit of a further £210 paid for but not used up – an asset that needs carrying forward as such to 2006, i.e. as a debit balance. It is a **prepaid expense.** The account can now be completed as follows:

Dr			Insurance Account				*Cr*
2005			£	2005			£
Feb	28	Bank	210	Dec	31	Profit and loss	840
Aug	31	"	420				
Nov	18	"	420	"	31	Prepaid c/d	210
			1,050				1,050
2006							
Jan	1	Prepaid b/d	210				

Prepayment will also happen when items other than purchases are bought for use in the business and they are not fully used up in the period. For instance, packing materials and stationery items are normally not entirely used up over the period in which they are bought, there being a stock in hand at the end of the accounting period. This stock is, therefore, a form of prepayment and needs carrying down to the following period in which it will be used. This can be seen in the following example for the year ended 31 December 2005:

packing materials bought in the year £2,200
stock of packing materials in hand as at 31 December 2005 £400.

Looking at the example, it can be seen that in 2005 the packing materials used up will have been (£2,200 - £400) = £1,800. We will still have a stock of £400 packing materials at 31 December 2005, to be carried forward to 2006 as an asset balance (debit balance). Thus:

Dr			Packing Materials Account				*Cr*
2005			£	2005			£
Dec	31	Bank	2,200	Dec	31	Profit and loss	1,800
				Dec	31	Stock c/d	400
			2,200				2,200
2006							
Jan	1	Stock b/d	400				

The stock of packing materials is not added to the stock of unsold goods in hand in the balance sheet, but it is added to the other prepayments of expenses.

29.5 Revenue owing at the end of period

The revenue owing for sales is already shown in the books. These are the debit balances on our customers' accounts, i.e. debtors. There may be other kinds of revenue, all of which have not been received by the end of the period - e.g. rent receivable. An example now follows.

A firm's warehouse is larger than it needs to be. The firm rents part of it to another firm for £800 per annum. Details for the year ended 31 December are as shown in the table below.

Amount	Rent due	Rent received
£200	31 March 2005	4 April 2005
£200	30 June 2005	6 July 2005
£200	30 September 2005	9 October 2005
£200	31 December 2005	7 January 2006

The account for 2005 will appear as follows:

Rent Receivable Account

Dr				*Cr*			
				2005			£
				Apr	4	Bank	200
				Jul	6	Bank	200
				Oct	9	Bank	200

The rent received of £200 on 7 January 2006 will be entered in the books in 2006 (not shown).

Any rent paid by the firm would be charged as a debit to the profit and loss account. Any rent received, being the opposite, is transferred to the credit of the profit and loss account because it is a revenue.

The amount to be transferred for 2005 is that earned for the 12 months, i.e. £800. The rent received account is completed by carrying down the balance owing as a debit balance to 2006. The £200 owing is an asset on 31 December 2005.

The rent receivable account can now be completed:

Rent Receivable Account

Dr				*Cr*			
2005			£	2005			£
Dec	31	Profit and loss	800	Apr	4	Bank	200
				Jul	6	Bank	200
				Oct	9	Bank	200
				Dec	31	Accrued c/d	200
			800				800
2006							
Jan	1	Accrued b/d	200				

29.6 Expenses and revenue account balances and the balance sheet

In all the cases listed dealing with adjustments in the final accounts, there will still be a balance on each account after the preparation of the trading and profit and loss account. All such balances remaining should appear in the balance sheet. The only question left is where and how they should be shown.

The amounts owing for expenses are usually added together and shown as one figure. These could be called 'expense creditors', 'expenses owing' or 'accrued expenses'. The item would appear under current liabilities because it is for expenses that have to be discharged in the near future.

Items prepaid are also added together and called 'prepayments', 'prepaid expenses' or 'payments in advance'. They are shown next under the debtors. Amounts owing for rents receivable or other revenue owing are usually added to debtors.

The balance sheet in respect of the accounts so far seen in this chapter would appear thus:

Balance Sheet as at 31 December 2005

	£	£	£
Current assets			
Stock		xxx	
Debtors		200	
Prepayments (210 + 400)		610	
Bank		xxx	
Cash		xxx	
		x,xxx	
Less Current liabilities			
Trade creditors	xxx		
Accrued expenses	250	xxx	
Net current assets		xxx	

29.7 Expenses and revenue accounts covering more than one period

Students are often asked to draw up an expense or revenue account for a full year, and there are amounts owing or prepaid at both the beginning and end of a year. We can now see how this is done.

Example 1: The following details are available:

(A) On 31 December 2004, three months' rent of £3,000 is owing.
(B) The rent chargeable per year is £12,000.
(C) The following payments are made in the year 2005: 6 January £3,000; 4 April £3,000; 7 July £3,000; 18 October £3,000.
(D) The final three months rent for 2005 is still owing.

Now we can look at the completed rent account. The letters (A) to (D) give reference to the details above.

Dr **Rent Account** *Cr*

2005				£	2005				£
Jan	6	Bank	(C)	3,000	Jan	5	Owing b/d	(A)	3,000
Apr	4	Bank	(C)	3,000	Dec	31	Profit and loss	(B)	2,000
Jul	7	Bank	(C)	3,000					
Oct	18	Bank	(C)	3,000					
Dec	31	Accrued c/d	(D)	3,000					
				15,000					15,000
					2006				
					Jan	1	Accrued b/d		3,000

Example 2: The following details are available:

(A) On 31 December 2004, packing materials in hand amount in value to £1,850.
(B) During the year to 31 December 2005, £27,480 is paid for packing materials.
(C) There are no stocks of packing materials on 31 December 2005.
(D) On 31 December 2005, we still owed £2,750 for packing materials already received and used.

The packing materials account will appear thus:

Packing Materials Account

Dr				*Cr*			
2005			£	2005			£
Jan	1	Stocks b/d (A)	1,850	Dec	31	Profit and loss	32,080
Dec	31	Bank (B)	27,480				
Dec	31	Owing c/d (D)	2,750				
			32,080				32,080
				2006			
				Jan	1	Owing b/d	2,750

The figure of £32,080 is the difference on the account, and is transferred to the profit and loss account. We can prove it is correct through the following:

	£	£
Stock at start of year		1,850
Add Bought and used:		
Paid for	27,480	
Still owed for	2,750	30,230
Cost of packing materials used in the year		32,080

Example 3: Where different expenses are put together in one account, it can get even more confusing. Let us look at where rent and rates are joined together. Here are the details for the year ended 31 December 2005:

(A) Rent is payable of £6,000 per annum.
(B) Rates of £4,000 per annum are payable by instalments.
(C) At 1 January 2005, rent £1,000 has been prepaid in 2004.
(D) On 1 January 2005 rates are owed of £400.
(E) During 2005, rent of £4,500 is paid.
(F) During 2005, rates of £5,000 were paid.
(G) On 31 December 2005, rent £500 is owing.
(H) On 31 December 2005, rates of £600 have been prepaid.

A combined rent and rates account is to be drawn up for the year 2005 showing the transfer to the profit and loss account, and balances are to be carried down to 2006. Thus:

Dr		Rent and Rates Account					*Cr*
2005			£	2005			£
Jan 1	Rent prepaid b/d	(C)	1,000	Jan 1	Rates owing b/d	(D)	400
Dec 31	Bank: rent	(E)	4,500	Dec 31	Profit & loss a/c	(A)+(B)	10,000
Dec 31	Bank: rates	(F)	5,000				
Dec 31	Rent owing c/d	(G)	500	Dec 31	Rates prepaid c/d	(H)	600
			11,000				11,000
2006				2006			
Jan 1	Rates prepaid b/d	(H)	600	Jan 1	Rent owing b/d	(G)	500

29.8 Goods for own use

Traders will often take items out of their business stocks for their own use, without paying for them. There is nothing wrong about this, but an entry should be made to record the event. This is done thus:

- credit the purchases account, to reduce cost of goods available for sale
- debit the drawings account, to show that the proprietor has taken the goods for private use.

In the United Kingdom, an adjustment may be needed for value added tax. If goods supplied to a trader's customers have VAT added to their price, then any such goods taken for own use will need such an adjustment. This is because the VAT regulations state that VAT should be added to the cost of goods taken. The double entry for the VAT content would be:

- debit the drawings account
- credit VAT account.

Adjustments may also be needed for other private items. For instance, if a trader's private insurance had been incorrectly charged to the insurance account, then the correction would be:

- credit the insurance account
- debit the drawings account.

29.9 Goodwill

When starting in business, we could start from nothing. At that time we would have no customers at all. Over the years we might work hard, and then have a lot of customers who would buy or trade with us year after year.

As an alternative way of starting up, we might buy an existing business. We would need to look at it carefully and put a value on the items in the business. These are (say):

	£
Premises	50,000
Equipment	20,000
Stock	12,000
	82,000

But the owner wants £100,000 for the business, an extra £18,000. He says it is worth £18,000 extra because he has made the business into a very good one, with many customers. Most of the customers trade continually with him.

We agree to pay the extra £18,000. This extra amount is known as **goodwill.** And we do this because we will get many customers immediately - it might take us many years to do this if we start from nothing.

In the balance sheet, we will show goodwill as an **intangible fixed asset** - that is, an asset that cannot be physically seen or touched.

29.10 Distinctions between various kinds of capital

The capital account represents the claim of the proprietor against the assets of a business at a point in time. The word 'capital' is, however, often used in a specific sense. The main uses are listed below.

Capital invested

Capital invested means the actual amount of money, or money's worth, brought into a business by its proprietor from his or her outside interests. The amount of capital invested is not disturbed by the amounts of profits made by the business or any losses incurred.

Capital employed

The term **capital employed** has many meanings but basically it means the amount of money that is being used (or 'employed') in the business. If, therefore, all the assets were added up in value and the liabilities of the business deducted, the answer would be that the difference is the amount of money employed in the business (i.e. the net assets).

Another way of looking at the calculation of capital employed is to take the balance of the capital account and add this to any long-term loan. The result will be the same as the net assets, i.e. the capital employed.

Working capital (net current assets)

The difference between the current assets and current liabilities is often referred to as **working capital** or 'net current assets'. This amount represents the money that is available to pay the running expenses of the business and, ideally, the current assets should exceed the current liabilities twice over, i.e. in the ratio 2 : 1. In simple terms it means that, for every £1 owed, the business should be able to raise £2.

29.11 Final accounts in the services sector

All the accounts considered so far have been accounts for businesses that trade in some sort of goods. To enable the business to ascertain the amount of gross profit made on selling the goods, a trading account has been drawn up. There are, however, many organisations that do not deal in goods but instead supply customers with a 'service'. These will include professional firms such as accountants, solicitors, doctors, estate agents and the like, as well as firms with services such as those that repair and provide maintenance for washing machines, etc, window-cleaning, gardening, hairdressing and so on. Since 'goods' are not dealt in, there is no need for trading accounts to be drawn up. Instead, a profit and loss account together with a balance sheet is prepared.

The first item in the profit and loss account will be the revenue, which might be called 'fees', 'charges', 'accounts rendered', etc., depending on the nature of the organisation. Any other item of income will also be added (e.g. rent receivable), and following this the expenses incurred in running the business will be deducted so as to arrive at the business's net profit or loss.

An example of the profit and loss account of a solicitor is illustrated below in Exhibit 29.1.

Exhibit 29.1

E B Brown, Solicitor
Profit and Loss Account for the year ended 31 December 2003

	£	£
Revenue:		
Fees charged		87,500
Insurance commissions		1,300
		88,800
Less Expenses:		
Wages and salaries	29,470	
Rent and rates	11,290	
Office expenses	3,140	
Motor expenses	2,115	
General expenses	1,975	
Depreciation	2,720	50,710
Net profit		38,090

29.12 Treatment of discounts allowed and discounts received in final accounts

In Chapter 16 we dealt with recording cash discounts in the cash book and ledgers and you will recall that such a discount could be either 'discounts allowed', which represents a reduction given to our customers for prompt payment of their account or 'discounts received' when the reduction is given by a supplier to us when we pay their account within a specified period.

Using the example below of D Marston (Exhibit 29.2) let us assume that the discount allowed amounted to £310 and the discount received totalled £510. These items would appear in the trading and profit and loss account as follows:

Exhibit 29.2

Trading and Profit and Loss Account of D Marston for the year ended 31 December 2006

	£	£
Gross profit		30,500
Less Expenses		
Discounts allowed	310	
Other expenses	10,000	10,310
		20,190
Add Income		
Discounts received		510
Net profit		20,700

29.13 Preparation of final accounts

A full step-by-step guide to the preparation of final accounts, including a step-by-step guide to dealing with adjustments, is given in Appendix B. The Appendix also provides a model layout of the final accounts of a sole trader.

New terms

Accrual (p. 310): An accrued expense. An amount owing.

Accrued expenses (p. 309): Expenses that have been incurred and the benefit received but which have not been paid for at the end of the accounting period.

Capital employed (p. 316): This term has many meanings but basically it means the amount of money that is being used up (or 'employed') in the business. It is the balance of the capital account plus any long-term loan or, alternatively, the total net assets of the business.

Capital invested (p. 316): The amount of money, or money's worth, brought into a business by its proprietor from outside.

Goodwill (p. 315): The extra amount paid for an existing firm above the value of its other assets.

Intangible fixed asset (p. 316): A fixed asset that cannot be physically seen or touched.

Prepaid expense (p. 310): An expense – usually a service – that has been paid for in one accounting period, the benefit of which will not be received until a subsequent period. It is a payment for an expense that has been paid for in advance.

Working capital (p. 316): The amount by which the current assets exceed the current liabilities. Also known as 'net current assets'.

EXERCISES

29.1 The financial year of H Saunders ended on 31 December 2008. Show the ledger accounts for the following items, including the balance transferred to the necessary part of the final accounts, and the balances carried down to 2009.

(*a*) Motor expenses: paid in 2008 £744; owing at 31 December 2008 £28.
(*b*) Insurance: paid in 2008 £420; prepaid as at 31 December 2008 £35.
(*c*) Stationery: paid during 2008: £1,800; owing as at 31 December 2007 £250; owing as at 31 December 2008 £490.
(*d*) Rent: paid during 2008 £950; prepaid as at 31 December 2007 £220; prepaid as at 31 December 2008 £290.
(*e*) Saunders sub-lets part of the premises. Receives £550 during the year ended 31 December 2008. The tenant owed Saunders £180 on 31 December 2007 and £210 on 31 December 2008.

29.2 The following is the trial balance of J Smailes as at 31 March 2007. Draw up a set of final accounts for the year ended 31 March 2007 in vertical format.

	Dr	*Cr*
	£	£
Stock 1 April 2006	18,160	
Sales		92,340
Purchases	69,185	
Carriage inwards	420	
Carriage outwards	1,570	
Returns outwards		640
Wages and salaries	10,240	
Rent and rates	3,015	
Communication expenses	624	
Commissions payable	216	
Insurance	405	
Sundry expenses	318	
Buildings	20,000	
Debtors	14,320	
Creditors		8,160
Fixtures	2,850	
Cash at bank	2,970	
Cash in hand	115	
Loan from K Ball		10,000
Drawings	7,620	
Capital		40,888
	152,028	152,028

Stock at 31 March 2007 was £22,390.

29.3X L Stokes drew up the following trial balance as at 30 September 2008. You are to draft trading and profit and loss accounts for the year to 30 September 2008 and a balance sheet as at that date in vertical format.

	Dr	*Cr*
	£	£
Loan from P Owens		5,000
Capital		25,955
Drawings	8,420	
Cash at bank	3,115	
Cash in hand	295	
Debtors	12,300	
Creditors		9,370
Stock 30 September 2007	23,910	
Motor van	4,100	
Office equipment	6,250	
Sales		130,900
Purchases	92,100	
Returns inwards	550	
Carriage inwards	215	
Returns outwards		307
Carriage outwards	309	
Motor expenses	1,630	
Rent	2,970	
Telephone charges	405	
Wages and salaries	12,810	
Insurance	492	
Office expenses	1,377	
Sundry expenses	284	
	171,532	171,532

Stock at 30 September 2008 was £27,475.

29.4 The following balances were part of the trial balance of C Cainen on 31 December 2008:

	Dr	*Cr*
	£	£
Stock at 1 January 2008	2,050	
Sales		18,590
Purchases	11,170	
Rent	640	
Wages and salaries	2,140	
Insurance	590	
Bad debts	270	
Telephone	300	
General expenses	180	

On 31 December 2008 you ascertain that:

(*a*) the rent for four months of 2009, £160, has been paid in 2008
(*b*) £290 is owing for wages and salaries
(*c*) insurance has been prepaid £190
(*d*) a telephone bill of £110 is owed
(*e*) stock is valued at £3,910.

Draw up Cainen's trading and profit and loss account for the year ended 31 December 2008.

29.5X The following were part of the trial balance of K Tyler on 31 December 2007:

	Dr	*Cr*
	£	£
Stock at 1 January 2007	8,620	
Sales		54,190
Purchases	30,560	
Returns inwards	200	
Wages and salaries	4,960	
Motor expenses	2,120	
Rent and rates	1,200	
Discounts allowed	290	
Lighting expenses	580	
Computer running expenses	1,210	
General expenses	360	

Given the information that follows, you are to draw up a trading and profit and loss account for the year ended 31 December 2007.

(*a*) stock on 31 December 2007 is £12,120
(*b*) items prepaid: rates £160; computer running expenses £140
(*c*) items owing: wages £510; lighting expenses £170
(*d*) £700 is to be charged as depreciation of motor vehicles.

29.6 From the following trial balance of J Sears, a store owner, prepare a trading and profit and loss account for the year ended 31 December 2007 and a balance sheet as at that date, taking into consideration the adjustments shown below:

Trial Balance as at 31 December 2007

	Dr	*Cr*
	£	£
Sales		80,000
Purchases	70,000	
Returns inwards	1,000	
Returns outwards		1,240
Stock at 1 January 2007	20,000	
Provision for bad debts		160
Wages and salaries	7,200	
Telephone	200	
Store fittings	8,000	
Motor van	6,000	
Debtors and creditors*	1,960	1,400
Bad debts	40	
Capital		35,800
Bank balance	600	
Drawings	3,600	
	118,600	118,600

Adjustments:

(*a*) closing stock at 31 December 2007 is £24,000
(*b*) accrued wages £450
(*c*) telephone prepaid £20
(*d*) provision for bad debts to be increased to 10 per cent of debtors
(*e*) depreciation on store fittings £800, and motor van £1,200.

**Note by authors*:
Sometimes, in examinations, two items will be shown on the same line. The examiner is testing to see whether the student knows which of the figures relate to the account titles. In Exercises 29.6 and 29.7X the item 'Debtors and creditors' is shown on the same line.

29.7X The following trial balance was extracted from the records of L Robinson, a trader, as at 31 December 2006:

	Dr	*Cr*
	£	£
Discounts allowed	410	
Discounts received		506
Carriage inwards	309	
Carriage outwards	218	
Returns inwards	1,384	
Returns outwards		810
Sales		120,320
Purchases	84,290	
Stock at 31 December 2000	30,816	
Motor expenses	4,917	
Repairs to premises	1,383	
Salaries and wages	16,184	
Sundry expenses	807	
Rates and insurance	2,896	
Premises at cost	40,000	
Motor vehicles at cost	11,160	
Provision for depreciation – motors as at 31 December 2006		3,860
Debtors and creditors*	31,640	24,320
Cash at bank	4,956	
Cash in hand	48	
Drawings	8,736	
Capital		50,994
Loan from P Hall (repayable 2008)		40,000
Bad debts	1,314	
Provision for bad debts as at 31 December 2006		658
	241,468	241,468

**Note*: See footnote to exercise 29.6 for an explanation of why two figures are on one line.

The following matters are to be taken into account at 31 December 2006:

(*a*) stock £36,420
(*b*) expenses owing: sundry expenses £62; motor expenses £33
(*c*) prepayment: rates £166
(*d*) provision for bad debts to be reduced to £580
(*e*) depreciation for motor vehicles to be £2,100 for the year
(*f*) part of the premises were let to a tenant, who owed £250 at 31 December 2006
(*g*) loan interest owing to P Hall £4,000.

Draw up a trading and profit and loss account for the year ended 31 December 2006 and a balance sheet as at that date.

CHAPTER 30

Stock valuation

Learning objectives

After you have studied this chapter you should be able to:

- **understand that there can be more than one way of valuing stocks**
- **calculate the value of stock using the different methods**
- **adjust stock valuations, where necessary, by a reduction to net realisable values**
- **understand the factors affecting the choice of method taken.**

30.1 Different valuations of stock

Most people would assume that there can only be one figure for the valuation of stock. This is, however, untrue. This chapter will examine how the valuation of stock can be calculated using different figures.

Assume that a firm has just completed its first financial year and is about to value stock on hand at cost price. The firm has only dealt with one type of goods. A record of the transactions is now shown below in Exhibit 30.1.

Exhibit 30.1

Bought				Sold			
2005			£	2005			£
January	10	at £30 each	300	May	8	for £50 each	400
April	10	at £34 each	340	November	24	for £60 each	1,440
October	20	at £40 each	800				
	40		1,440		32		1,840

The balance of stock on hand at 31 December 2005 is 8 units. The total figure of purchases is £1,440 and that of sales is £1,840. The trading account for the first year of trading can now be completed if the closing stock is brought into the calculations.

But what value do we put on each of the 8 units left in stock at the end of the year? If all of the units bought during the year had cost £30 each, then the closing stock would be 8 × £30 = £240. However, we have bought goods at different prices. This means that the valuation depends on which goods are taken for this calculation: the units at £30, or those at £34, or yet others at £40.

Many firms do not know exactly whether they have sold all the oldest units before they sell new units. For instance, a firm selling spanners may not know whether the oldest spanners had been sold before the newest spanners.

With this in mind, stock valuation will be based on an accounting custom, and not on the facts of exactly which units were still in stock at the year end. The three main methods of doing this are described next.

30.2 First in, first out method

This is usually known as **FIFO**, the first letters of each word. The method says that, as far as the accounts are concerned, the first goods to be received are the first to be issued. Using the figures in Exhibit 30.1, we can now calculate the closing figure of stock as follows:

2005	Received	Issued	Stock	£	£
Jan	10 × £30 each		10 × £30		300
April	10 × £34 each		10 × £30 10 × £34	300 340	640
May		8 × £30 each	2 × £30 10 × £34	60 340	400
Oct	20 × £40 each		2 × £30 10 × £34 20 × £40	60 340 800	1,200
Nov		2 × £30 each 10 × £34 each 12 × £40 each	8 × £40		320

The closing stock at 31 December 2005 is therefore valued at £320.

30.3 Last in, first out method

This is usually known as **LIFO**. As each issue of goods is made, the goods are said to be from the last batch received before that date. Where there is not enough left of the last batch, then the balance of goods needed is said to come from the previous batch still unsold.

From the information shown in Exhibit 30.1, the calculation under this basis can now be shown.

2005	Received	Issued	Stock	£	£
Jan	10 × £30 each		10 × £30		300
April	10 × £34 each		10 × £30 10 × £34	300 340	640
May		8 × £34 each	10 × £30 2 × £34	300 68	368
Oct	20 × £40 each		10 × £30 2 × £34 20 × £40	300 68 800	1,168
Nov		20 × £40 each 2 × £34 each 2 × £30 each	8 × £30		240

The closing stock at 31 December 2005 is therefore valued at £240.

30.4 Average cost method (AVCO)

Using the **AVCO** method, with each receipt of goods the average cost for each item of stock is recalculated. Further issues of goods are then at that figure, until another receipt of goods means that another recalculation is needed.

From the information in Exhibit 30.1, the calculation can be shown thus:

Received		Issued	Average cost per unit of stock held	Number of units in stock	Total value of stock
			£		£
January	10 × £30		30	10	300
April	10 × £34		32*	20	640
May		8 × £32	32	12	384
October	20 × £40		37*	32	1,184
November		24 × £37	37	8	296

**Note*: In April, the average cost is calculated as follows:
stock 10 × £30 = £300 + stock received (10 × £34) £340 = total £640.
20 units in stock, so the average is £640 ÷ 20 = £32.

In October, the average is calculated as follows:
stock 12 × £32 = £384 + stock received (20 × £40) £800 = £1,184.
32 units in stock, so the average is £1,184 ÷ 32 = £37.

The closing stock at 31 December 2005 is therefore valued at £296.

30.5 Stock valuation and the calculation of profits

Using the figures from Exhibit 30.1, with stock valuations shown by the three methods of FIFO, LIFO, and AVCO, the trading accounts would appear as set out in the table.

Trading Account for the year ended 31 December 2005

	FIFO		LIFO		AVCO	
	£	£	£	£	£	£
Sales		1,840		1,840		1,840
Less Cost of sales						
Purchases	1,440		1,440		1,440	
Less Closing stock	320	1,120	240	1,200	296	1,444
Gross Profit		720		640		696

As can be seen from the table above, different methods of stock valuation will mean that different profits are shown.

30.6 Reduction to net realisable value

The **net realisable value** of stock is calculated as the saleable value *less* any expenses needed to complete the item or get it in a condition to be sold.

The concept of prudence is used when stock is valued. Stock should not be overvalued; otherwise, profits shown will be too high. Therefore, if the net realisable value of stock is less than the cost of the stock, prudence dictates that the figure to be taken for the final accounts is that of net realisable value.

Example 1: An item of stock was purchased at cost price £300. Unfortunately, the item was damaged in the warehouse and the cost of repair and repainting amounted to £50 after which it was estimated it could be sold for £200. The item would be valued as follows:

Saleable value £200 less cost of repair and repainting £50 = Net realisable value of £150.

30.7 Goods on sale or return

Goods received on sale or return

Sometimes we might receive goods from one of our suppliers on a **sale or return** basis. What this means is that we do not have to pay for the goods until we sell them. If we do not sell them, we have to return them to our supplier.

This means in turn that the goods do not belong to us. If we have some goods on sale or return at the stocktaking date, they should not be included in our stock valuation.

Goods sent to our customers on sale or return

We may send goods on a sale or return basis to our customers. The stock will belong to us until it is sold. At our stocktaking date, any goods held by our customers on sale or return should be included in our stock valuation.

30.8 Stocktaking and the balance sheet date

Students often think that all the counting and valuing of stock is done on the last day of the accounting period. This might be true in a small business, but it is often impossible in larger businesses. There may be too many items of stock to do it so quickly.

This means that stocktaking may take place over a period of days. To get the figure of the stock valuation as on the last day of the accounting period, we will have to make adjustments. Exhibit 30.2 gives an example of such calculations.

EXHIBIT 30.2

Lee Ltd has a financial year that ends on 31 December 2007. The stocktaking is not in fact done until 8 January 2008. When the items in stock on that date are priced out, it is found that the stock value amounts to £28,850. The following information is available about transactions between 31 December 2007 and 8 January 2008.

(*a*) Purchases since 31 December 2007 amounted to £2,370 at cost.
(*b*) Returns inwards since 31 December 2007 were £350 at selling price.
(*c*) Sales since 31 December 2007 amounted to £3,800 at selling price.
(*d*) The selling price is always cost price + 25 per cent.

Lee Ltd
Computation of stock as on 31 December 2007

			£
Stock (at cost)			28,850
Add Items which were in stock on 31 December 2007 (at cost)			
		£	
Sales		3,800	
Less Profit content (20 per cent of selling price)*		760	3,040
			31,890
Less Items which were not in stock on 31 December 2007 (at cost)			
	£	£	
Returns inwards	350		
Less Profit content (20 per cent of selling price)*	70	280	
Purchases (at cost)		2,370	2,650
Stock in hand as on 31 December 2007			29,240

**Note*: Stock is at cost (or net realisable value) and not at selling price. As this calculation has a sales figure in it, which includes profit, we must deduct the profit part to get to the cost price. This is true also for returns inwards.

At one time it was very rare for auditors to attend at stocktaking time as observers. The professional accounting bodies now encourage auditors to be present if at all possible.

30.9 Stock records: quantities only

Quite often a firm will keep records of quantities only so as to check whether items are being stolen, broken, wasted or lost. Exhibit 30.3 shows the stock quantity records for two items of stock, namely components FG and JK.

EXHIBIT 30.3

Component FG			*No of items*	Component JK			*No of items*
2009				2009			
Jan	1	Stock b/fwd	86	Jan	1	Stock b/fwd	28
"	2	Received (invoice 5543)	20	"	2	Received (invoice 5549)	300
"	4	Issue P67	16	"	3	Issue R323	44
"	6	Issue P68	29	"	5	Issue R324	23
"	10	Issue P132	19	"	9	Issue R129	107
"	21	Received (invoice 5874)	70	"	11	Issue R325	79
"	25	Issue P69	33	"	13	Return in RA229	18
"	31	Issue P243	18	"	19	Received (invoice 5799)	200
				"	22	Issue R354	96
				"	29	Issue R130	64
				"	31	Return in RA230	5

From these stock records we should be able to work out exactly how many of component FG and of component JK are in store on 31 January 2009. We also do a physical stockcheck (i.e. we actually look at and count the items in the store) and find that we have 61 of FG and 134 of JK on that date.

We can now draft up a stock record card for each of these components. As each item is issued or received we alter the balance of stock in hand, as shown in Exhibit 30.4 for components FG and JK respectively.

Exhibit 30.4

Component FG					
Date		*Ref*	*In*	*Out*	*Balance*
2009					
Jan	1	Opening balance			86
"	2	5543	20		106
"	4	P67		16	90
"	6	P68		29	61
"	10	P132		19	42
"	21	5874	70		112
"	25	P69		33	79
"	31	P243		18	61

With component FG the actual stock equals the stock per the stock card, verifying that there has been no stock losses. With component JK we can see that the stock card record discloses a stock loss of four items.

Component JK					
Date		*Ref*	*In*	*Out*	*Balance*
2009					
Jan	1	Opening balance			28
"	2	5549	300		328
"	3	R323		44	284
"	5	R324		23	261
"	9	R129		107	154
"	11	R325		79	75
"	13	RA229	18		93
"	19	5799	200		293
"	22	R354		96	197
"	29	R130		64	133
"	31	RA230	5		138
"	31	Stock loss		4	134

The stock loss for four items of component JK will have to be investigated. There may be a satisfactory explanation, or it might even be a case of theft, with the police being called in to investigate. It is up to the individual firm to decide what course of action is to be taken, but the stock loss should be looked into in order to establish the reason for the deficiency.

New terms

AVCO (p. 326): A method by which the goods used are priced out at average cost.

FIFO (p. 325): A method by which the first goods to be received are said in the accounts to be the first to be sold.

LIFO (p. 325): A method by which the goods sold are said in the accounts to have come from the last batch of goods to be received.

Net realisable value (p. 327): The value of goods, calculated as the selling price less expenses before sale.

Sale or return (p. 327): Goods that do not belong to the person holding them.

EXERCISES

30.1 (*a*) From the following figures, calculate the closing stock in trade that would be shown using (i) FIFO, (ii) LIFO, (iii) AVCO methods.

2007	*Bought*	*2007*	*Sold*
January	24 at £10 each	June	30 at £16 each
April	16 at £12.50 each	November	34 at £18 each
October	30 at £13 each		

(*b*) Draw up trading accounts for 2007 using each of the three methods for stock valuation.

30.2X (*a*) From the following figures, calculate the closing stock-in-trade that would be shown using (i) FIFO, (ii) LIFO, (iii) AVCO methods.

2009	*Bought*	*2009*	*Sold*
January	30 at £12 each	July	24 at £15.50 each
May	30 at £14 each	November	16 at £18 each

(*b*) Draw up trading accounts for 2009 using each of the three methods for stock valuation.

30.3 Rule up a card suitable for the recording of the quantity of an item in stock. The card should show receipts, issues and balance. The names of suppliers should be shown against receipts, and the requisition number against issues.

Item number 24			*Quantity*
1 May 2009	Balance in stock		500
Receipts			
2 May 2009	Starlight Co Ltd		300
8 May 2009	Moonbeam & Sons		200
24 May 2009	Starlight Co Ltd		350
Issues			
8 May 2009	Requisition number	740	173
10 May 2009		810	294
14 May 2009		976	104
28 May 2009		981	206

30.4X C Jones, a builder's merchant, has no reliable method of recording his stock receipts and issues. At the present time he has no means of obtaining a valuation for his stock-in-trade (without undertaking a lengthy and costly stocktaking). Jones has produced the following data from the month ended 30 September 2009.

Marble chippings stock	1 Sept	2 tonnes
Purchased from J. Brown	4 Sept	8 tonnes
Sold to T. Williams	10 Sept	6 tonnes
Purchased from B. Green	14 Sept	9 tonnes
Sold to W. Thomas	20 Sept	2 tonnes
Sold to B. Dunstan	25 Sept	7 tonnes

All stock and purchases are priced at £50 per tonne. All issues of stock are priced at £65 per tonne.

You are required to show Jones's trading account for the month ended 30 September 2009.

30.5 DC Ltd, for which the financial year end was 31 December 2008, does not take a stock check until 8 January 2009, when it is shown to be £50,850 at cost. It is then established that:

(*a*) a calculation of 1,000 items at £1.60 was shown as £160
(*b*) during the period from the year end to 8 January 2009, no purchases were made but sales of £500 were made. The profit margin is 20 per cent
(*c*) some goods costing £560 had a net realisable value of £425
(*d*) one stock sheet has been added up to be £2,499. The total should have been £4,299.

Calculate the correct figure of stock on 31 December 2008.

30.6 Chung Ltd makes up its accounts to 31 December each year. The valuation of the stock, at cost, as at 31 December 2008 is not attempted until 11 January 2009, when a physical stock-check revealed a total per the stock sheets of £198,444 at cost.

Further investigation reveals that:

(*a*) all goods are sold at a uniform profit of 50 per cent on cost
(*b*) sales for the period 1 January 2009 to 11 January 2009 for which goods had been despatched amounted to £6,960
(*c*) one stock sheet is undercast by £50 and another one overcast by £1,000
(*d*) an extension of 660 articles at £0.80 each is shown as £560
(*e*) the stock figure includes goods held on approval £3,000 and for which no invoices has been received, nor are the goods to be kept by Chung Ltd
(*f*) a total at the bottom of one page, £105,680, has been carried forward to the next page as £106,850.

Calculate the figure of stock for the final accounts as at 31 December 2008.

30.7X You are valuing stock at your business as it was at 31 December 2007. The actual date on which the stock was counted was 7 January 2008. The stock sheets show a total of £85,980 at cost as on that date. You are to adjust this figure to find out the stock as at 31 December 2007. The rate of gross profit is 25% on selling price.

On further scrutiny you find:

(*a*) goods received after 1 January and for which invoices bear the date of January amount to £3,987
(*b*) one of the stock sheets has been added up to give a total of £4,897 instead of £4,798
(*c*) goods selling at £480 have been sent to a customer on 'sale or return' during December – these had not been sold by the customer but they had been omitted from the stock figures

(*d*) an item of 360 units priced at £1.60 each has been extended on the stock sheets as £420
(*e*) goods amounting to £98 have been returned to suppliers during the first week of January.

30.8X (*a*) If the closing stock of a business had been mistakenly overvalued by £5,000 and the error has gone unnoticed, what would be the effect of the error on:

(i) this year's profit?
(ii) next year's profit?

(*b*) A company that sells videos and electrical goods values its closing stock at £72,050 (cost price) at 30 June 2003. However, it has found that this figure includes the following:

(i) Five videos that had cost £300 each have now been replaced by an improved model. In order to sell these obsolete models, it is thought that they will have to be sold at £250 each.
(ii) A hi-fi system that cost £500 has been damaged and it is estimated that repairs will cost £100 before it can be sold.

Calculate the value of the closing stock after taking into the account the above adjustments.

CHAPTER 31

Accounting errors and their effect on accounting records

Learning objectives

After you have studied this chapter you should be able to:

- **correct all errors that do not affect trial balance totals being equal**
- **distinguish between the different kinds of errors.**

31.1 Trial balance agreement and errors

There are two main classifications of errors: those that do not affect the trial balance agreement and those that do.

Errors not affecting trial balance agreement

These errors result in the same amount of debits being entered as there are credits, or no entry being made either on the debit or the credit side. This means that the trial balance will still balance even though errors have been made in the accounts.

Examples of the different types of errors that come under this heading are described in Sections 31.3–31.8 that follow. You are also shown in these sections how to correct this type of error.

Errors affecting trial balance agreement

These errors result in the total of the debit columns in the trial balance *not* being the same as the total of the credit columns. For instance, suppose we have made only one error in our books, where we received cash £103 on 1 May 2005 from H Lee, our debtor, but we entered it as shown below.

Cash Book (debit side only)

	Cash	Bank	
2005	£	£	
May 1 H Lee	103		

Sales Ledger **H Lee**

	2005	£
	May 1 Cash	13

We have put £103 on the debit side of our books, and £13 on the credit side. When we draw up a trial balance, its totals will be different by (£103 – £13) = £90.

This effect will arise in every case where a debit entry does not equal a credit entry for an item. Correction of such errors is described fully in Chapter 32 following.

31.2 Method for correction of errors

Most errors are found at a date later than the one on which they were first made. When we correct them, we should not do so by crossing out items, tearing out accounts or throwing them away, or using chemicals to make the writing disappear. If we allowed people to alter the books in this way, we would be making it easier for people to commit frauds.

We have to do corrections in double entry accounts by writing in the corrections in a double entry fashion. We should:

- show the corrections by means of journal entries, and then
- show the corrections in the double entry set of accounts, by posting these journal entries to the ledger accounts affected.

31.3 Errors of commission (not affecting trial balance agreement)

An **error of commission** arises when a correct amount is entered in the books, but in the wrong person's account.

Example 1: D Long paid us £50 by cheque on 18 May 2005. The transaction is correctly entered in the cash book, but it was entered by mistake in the account for D Longman. This means that there had been both a debit of £50 and a credit of £50. It has appeared in the personal account as:

D Longman Account

Dr		*Cr*
	2005	£
	May 18 Bank	50

The error was found on 31 May 2005. This will now have to be corrected and needs two entries:

Accounting entries	Explanation
Debit D Longman's account	To cancel out the error on the credit side of that account
Credit D Long's account	To enter the amount in the correct account

The accounts will now appear thus:

D Longman Account

Dr		£		Cr	£
2005		£	2005		£
May 31	D Long: Error corrected	50	May 18	Bank	50

D Long Account

Dr		£		Cr	£
2005		£	2005		£
May 1	Balance b/d	50	May 31	Cash entered in error in D Longman's account	50

The journal

The ways by which errors have been corrected should all be entered in the journal. The correction has already been shown above in double entry. In fact, the journal entries should be made before completing the double entry accounts for the transaction. For teaching purposes only in this chapter, the journal entries are shown last.

The journal entry will be thus:

The journal	Dr	Cr
2005	£	£
May 31 D Longman	50	
D Long		50
Cheque received ... entered in wrong personal account, now corrected.		

31.4 Errors of principle (not affecting trial balance agreement)

An **error of principle** is where a transaction is entered in the wrong type of account. For instance, the purchase of a fixed asset should be debited to a fixed asset account. If in error it is debited to an expense account, then it has been entered in the wrong type of account.

Example 2: The purchase of a motor car for £5,500 by cheque on 14 May 2005 has been debited in error to a motor expenses account. In the cash book it is shown correctly. This means that there has been both a debit of £5,500 and a credit of £5,500.

It will have appeared in the expense account as:

Motor Expenses Account

Dr					*Cr*
2005		£			
May 14	Bank	5,500			

The error is detected on 31 May 2005 and is corrected. To do so, two entries are needed:

Accounting entry	Explanation
Debit Motor Car account Credit Motor Expenses account	To put the amount in the correct account To cancel the error previously made in the Motor Expenses account

The accounts then are corrected thus:

Motor Expenses Account

Dr					*Cr*
2005		£	2005		£
May 14	Bank	5,500	May 31	Motor car error corrected	5,500
		=====			=====

Motor Car Account

Dr					*Cr*
2005		£			
May 31	Bank: entered originally in Motor expenses	5,500			

The journal

The journal entries to correct the error will be shown as:

The Journal			Dr	Cr
2005			£	£
May	31	Motor car	5,500	
		Motor expenses		5,500
		Correction of error whereby purchase of motor car was debited to motor expenses account.		

31.5 Errors of original entry (not affecting trial balance agreement)

An **error of original entry** occurs where an original amount is incorrect and is then entered in double entry.

Example 3: Sales of £150 to T Higgins on 13 May 2005 have been entered as both a debit and a credit of £130. The accounts would appear thus:

T Higgins Account

Dr			*Cr*
2005	£		
May 13 Sales	130		

Sales Account

Dr			*Cr*
		2005	£
		May 31 Sales journal (part of total)	130

The error is found on 31 May 2005. The entries to correct it are now shown:

T Higgins Account

Dr			*Cr*
2005	£		
May 13 Sales	130		
May 31 Sales: error	20		

Sales Account

Dr			*Cr*
		2005	£
		May 31 Sales journal	130
		May 31 T Higgins: error corrected	20

The journal

To correct the error, the journal entries will be:

The Journal	Dr	Cr
2005	£	£
May 31 T Higgins	20	
Sales account		20
Correction of error. Sales of £150 had been incorrectly entered as £130.		

31.6 Errors of omission (not affecting trial balance agreement)

Errors of omission are where transactions are not entered into the books at all.

Example 4: We purchased goods from T Hope for £250 on 13 May 2005 but did not enter the transaction in the accounts. So there were nil debits and nil credits. We found the error on 31 May 2005. The entries to correct it will be thus:

Purchases Account

Dr			*Cr*
2005	£		
May 13 T Hope: error corrected	250		

T Hope Account

Dr			*Cr*
		2005	£
		May 31 Purchases: error corrected	250

The journal

The journal entries to correct the error will be:

The Journal	Dr	Cr
2005	£	£
May 31 Purchases	250	
T Hope		250
Correction of error. Purchase omitted from books.		

31.7 Compensating errors (not affecting trial balance agreement)

These errors are where they cancel each other out.

Example 5: Let us take a case where incorrect totals had purchases of £7,900 and sales of £9,900. The purchases journal adds up to be £100 too much. In the same period, the sales journal also adds up to be £100 too much.

If these were the only errors in our books, the trial balance totals would equal each other. Both totals would be wrong – they would both be £100 too much – but they would be equal. In this case, the accounts would have appeared as follows:

Purchases Account

Dr					*Cr*
2005		£			
May 13	Purchases	7,900			

Sales Account

Dr					*Cr*
			2005		£
			May 31	Sales	9,900

When corrected, the accounts will appear as:

Purchases Account

Dr					*Cr*
2005		£	2005		£
May 13	Purchases	7,900	May 31	The Journal: error corrected	100

Sales Account

Dr					*Cr*
2005		£	2005		£
May 31	The Journal: error corrected	100	May 31	Sales	9,900

The journal

Journal entries to correct these two errors will be thus:

The Journal			*Dr*	*Cr*
2005			£	£
May	31	Sales account	100	
		Purchases account		100
		Correction of compensating errors. Totals of both purchases and sales day books incorrectly added up to £100 too much.		

31.8 Complete reversal of entries (not affecting trial balance agreement)

This error is where the correct amounts are entered in the correct accounts, but each item is shown on the wrong side of each account.

Example 6: We pay a cheque for £200 on 28 May 2005 to D Charles. We have entered it as follows in accounts with the letter (A). There has therefore been both a debit and a credit of £200.

Cash Book (A)

Dr	*Cash*	*Bank*		*Cash*	*Cr* *Bank*
2005	£	£		£	£
May 28 D Charles		200			

D Charles (A)

Dr			*Cr*
		2005	£
		May 28 Bank	200

The transaction is incorrectly recorded. Both items have been entered in the correct accounts, but each is on the wrong side of its account. The recording should have been thus:

Dr:	D Charles	£200	
Cr:	Bank		£200

The way to correct this is more difficult to understand than with other errors. Let us look at how the items would have appeared if we had done it correctly in the first place. We will show the letter (B) behind the account names.

Cash Book (B)

Dr	*Cash*	*Bank*		*Cash*	*Cr* *Bank*
	£	£	2005	£	£
			May 28 D Charles		200

D Charles (B)

Dr			*Cr*
2005	£		
May 28 Bank	200		

We found the error on May 31. By using double entry we have to make the amounts shown to cancel the error by twice the amount of the error. This is because, first, we have to cancel the error. This would mean entering these amounts:

Dr:	D Charles	£200	
Cr:	Bank		£200

Then we have to enter up the transaction:

Dr:	D Charles	£200	
Cr:	Bank		£200

Altogether then, the entries to correct the error are twice the amounts first entered. When corrected, the accounts appear as follows, marked (C).

Cash Book (C)

Dr	*Cash*	*Bank*		*Cash*	*Bank* *Cr*
2005	£	£	2005	£	£
May 8 D Charles		200	May 31 D Charles: error corrected		400

D Charles (C)

Dr			*Cr*
2005	£	2005	£
May 28 Bank: error corrected	400	May 28 Bank	200

You can see that accounts (C) give the same final answer as accounts (B).

			£	£
(B)	*Dr:*	D Charles	200	
	Cr:	Bank		200
(C)	*Dr:*	D Charles (£400 – £200)	200	
	Cr:	Bank (£400 – £200)		200

The journal

Journal entries. These would be shown as follows:

The Journal

	Dr	*Cr*
2005	£	£
May 31 D Charles	400	
Bank		400
Payment of £200 on 28 May 2005 to D Charles incorrectly credited to his account, and debited to bank. Error now corrected.		

31.9 Casting

You will often notice the use of the expression **casting**, which means adding up. **Overcasting** means incorrectly adding up a column of figures to give an answer that is *greater* than it should be. **Undercasting** means incorrectly adding up a column of figures to give an answer that is *less* than it should be.

New terms

Casting (p. 343): Adding up figures.

Compensating error (p. 340): Where two errors of equal amounts but on opposite sides of the accounts, cancel out each other.

Error of commission (p. 335): Where a correct amount is entered, but in the wrong person's account.

Error of omission (p. 339): Where a transaction is completely omitted from the books.

Error of original entry (p. 338): Where an item is entered, but both debit and credit entries are of the same incorrect amount.

Error of principle (p. 337): Where an item is entered in the wrong type of account, e.g. a fixed asset entered in an expense account.

Overcasting (p. 343): Incorrectly adding up a column of figures to give an answer that exceeds the correct total.

Undercasting (p. 343): Incorrectly adding up a column of figures to give an answer that is less than the correct total.

EXERCISES

31.1 Show the journal entries necessary to correct the following errors:

(*a*) A sale of goods £678 to J Harkness had been entered in J Harker's account.
(*b*) The purchase of a machine on credit from L Pearson for £4,390 had been completely omitted from our books.
(*c*) The purchase of a motor vehicle for £3,800 had been entered in error in the motor expenses account.
(*d*) A sale of £221 to E Fletcher had been entered in the books – both debit and credit – as £212.
(*e*) Commission received £257 had been entered in error in the sales account.

31.2X Show the journal entries needed to correct the following errors:

(*a*) Purchases £699 on credit from K Webb had been entered in H Weld's account.
(*b*) A cheque of £189 paid for advertisements had been entered in the cash column of the cash book instead of in the bank column.
(*c*) Sale of goods £443 on credit to B Maxim had been entered in error in B Gunn's account.
(*d*) Purchase of goods on credit from K Innes £89 entered in two places in error as £99.
(*e*) Cash paid to H Mersey £89 has been entered on the debit side of the cash book and the credit side of H Mersey's account.

31.3 At the close of business on 30 April 2009, your new book-keeper gave you the following ledger account balances:

	£
Capital	15,000
Drawings	1,500
Sales	27,250
Purchases	13,225
Motor Expenses	790
Rent received	285
General expenses	2,190
Wages	6,320
Motor Vehicles	6,000
Premises	27,000
Bank (overdrawn)	13,164

You are required to:

(*a*) prepare a trial balance from the figures which you have been given

(*b*) briefly outline ONE procedure that you would take upon finding that the trial balance did not agree.

OCR

31.4 Elaine Rowe extracted the following balances from her books on 31 May 2008:

	£
Equipment	9,750
General expenses	1,394
Sales	15,863
Purchases	7,590
Sales returns	426
Purchases return	674
Creditors	2,095
Drawings	1,420
Debtors	3,738
Bank overdraft	372
Capital	5,314

A short time later the following errors and omissions were discovered.

(*a*) A sales invoice for £392 has not been entered in the sales day book.

(*b*) A cheque of £545, received from a customer, has not been recorded in the books.

(*c*) An invoice for £196, received from a supplier, has been entered in the accounts twice.

(*d*) Elaine Rowe has taken £150 by cheque for her own use, but no entries have been made in the accounts.

You are required to prepare a trial balance as at 31 May 2008 after considering the above information.

OCR

31.5X On 31 October 2008, the following trial balance was extracted from the books of Whinfield Enterprises.

Trial Balance as at 31 October 2008

	£	£
Premises	37,900	
Salaries	8,350	
Purchases	12,309	
Sales		19,024
Wages	1,675	
General expenses	2,916	
Discount allowed	282	
Discount received		230
Debtors	6,237	
Creditors		3,906
Bank loan		9,650
Cash	148	
Bank overdraft		826
Equipment	1,819	
Capital		39,204
Drawings	1,568	
	73,204	72,840

A short time later, the following information was discovered.

(*a*) A repayment of £350 of the loan has been made by direct debit, but no entry has been made in the accounts.
(*b*) A sales invoice of £308 has been entered in the accounts as £380.
(*c*) A balance of £274 on a supplier's account has been omitted from the trial balance.
(*d*) the owner of the business has taken £75 in cash for his own use, but no entry has been made in the books.
(*e*) Goods costing £250, bought on credit from M Nichols, have been posted to M Nicholson's account.
(*f*) New equipment costing £695 less 20% trade discount has been bought on credit. The invoice had been entered in the purchase day book and included in the total purchases for the month.
(*g*) the discount received balance is £320 not £230.
(*h*) A payment of £95 for wages has been incorrectly entered in general expenses.

You are required to prepare a corrected trial balance after considering the above information and making the necessary adjustments.

OCR

31.6X D Singh, a retail trader, has a lot still to learn about accounting but has managed to draw up the following trial balance from his business records.

	£	£
Stock 1 April 2007		21,400
Stock 31 March 2008	15,600	
Discounts allowed		620
Discounts received	900	
Purchases	188,000	
Returns outwards	2,800	
Sales		264,200
Returns inwards	2,200	
Buildings at cost	140,000	
Provision for depreciation of buildings	7,000	
Motor vehicles at cost	30,000	
Provision for depreciation of motor vehicles	9,000	
Capital: D Singh		169,200
Bank	14,200	
Debtors		22,600
Provision for bad debts	1,920	
Creditors	15,200	
General expenses	33,200	
Drawings	18,000	
	478,020	478,020

Required:

(*a*) Prepare a corrected trial balance as at 31 March 2008.

(*b*) After the preparation of the corrected trial balance, but before drawing up the final accounts, the following items were discovered:

(i) A credit note for £148 had been received from FH Ltd. This was in respect of goods returned by Singh in December 2007. No entry was made in the books.

(ii) No entry has been made in the books in respect of £333 goods taken for own use.

(iii) a payment by a debtor, T Hall, of £168 has been credited in error to T Hallworth's account.

(iv) Free samples sent to a customer, L Shah, have been charged to him as though they were sales for £88.

(v) A discount allowed to K Young of £64 was found to be incorrect. It should have been £94.

Show the journal entries needed for items (i) to (v) above.

CHAPTER 32

Suspense accounts and errors

Learning objectives

After you have studied this chapter you should be able to:

- **correct errors using a suspense account**
- **recalculate profits after errors have been corrected.**

32.1 Errors and the trial balance

In the previous chapter we largely looked at errors that still left equal totals in the trial balance. However, many errors will mean that trial balance totals will not be equal. Let us now look at some of these:

- incorrect additions in any account
- making an entry on only one side of the accounts – e.g. a debit but no credit, or a credit but no debit
- entering a different amount on the debit side from the amount on the credit side.

32.2 Suspense accounts

We should try very hard to find errors immediately when the trial balance totals are not equal. When they cannot be found, the trial balance totals should be made to agree with each other by inserting the amount of the difference between the two sides in a **suspense account**. This occurs in Exhibit 32.1, where there is a £40 difference.

EXHIBIT 32.1

Trial Balance as on 31 December 2005

	Dr	*Cr*
	£	£
Totals after all the accounts have been listed	100,000	99,960
Suspense account		40
	100,000	100,000

To make the two totals the same, a figure of £40 for the suspense account has been shown on the credit side. A suspense account is opened and the £40 difference is also shown there on the credit side.

Suspense Account

Dr				*Cr*
		2005		£
		Dec 31	Difference per trial balance	40

32.3 Suspense account and the balance sheet

If the errors are not found before the final accounts are prepared, the suspense account balance will be included in the balance sheet. Where the balance is a credit balance, it should be included under current liabilities on the balance sheet. When the balance is a debit balance, it should be shown under current assets on the balance sheet. Large errors should always be found before the final accounts are drawn up.

32.4 Correction of errors

When errors are found, they must be corrected using double entry. Each correction must be described by an entry in the journal. Reparatory action depends on how complex the error is.

One error only

We will look at two examples:

Example 1: Assume that the error of £40 as shown in Exhibit 32.1 is found in the following year on 31 March 2006, the error being that the sales account was undercast by £40. The action taken to correct this is:

- Debit the suspense account to close it: £40.
- Credit the sales account to show item where it should have been: £40.

The accounts now appear as Exhibit 32.2.

Exhibit 32.2

Suspense Account

Dr					*Cr*
2006		£	2005		£
			Dec 31	Difference per	
Mar 31	Sales	40		trial balance	40

Sales Account

Dr			Cr		
			2006		£
			Mar 31	Suspense	40

This can be shown in journal form as follows:

The Journal

			Dr	Cr
2006			£	£
Mar	31	Suspense	40	
		Sales		40
		Correction of undercasting of sales by £40 in last year's accounts.		

Example 2: The trial balance on 31 December 2006 shows a difference of £168, being a shortage on the debit side of the trial balance. A suspense account is opened, the difference of £168 is entered on the debit side.

On 31 May 2007 the error is found. We had made a payment of £168 to D Miguel to close his account. It was correctly entered in the cash book, but it was not entered in Miguel's account.

To correct the error, the account of D Miguel is debited with £168, as it should have been in 2006, and the suspense account is credited with £168 so that the account can be closed. The accounts and journal entry now appear as in Exhibit 32.3

Exhibit 32.3

D Miguel Account

Dr			Cr		
2007		£	2007		£
May 31	Bank	168	Jan 1	Balance b/d	168

Suspense Account

Dr			Cr		
2007		£	2007		£
May 31	Difference per trial balance	168	May 31	D Miguel	168

The Journal

			Dr	Cr
2007			£	£
May	31	D Miguel	168	
		Suspense		168
		Correction of non-entry of payment last year in D Miguel's account.		

More than one error

We can now look at an example where the suspense account difference has been caused by more than one error.

Example 3: A trial balance at 31 December 2007 shows a difference of £77, being a shortage on the debit side. A suspense account is opened, and the difference of £77 is entered on the debit side of the account.

On 28 February 2008 all the errors from the previous year were found:

(*a*) A cheque of £150 paid to L Kent had been correctly entered in the cash book, but had not been entered in Kent's account.
(*b*) The purchases account has been undercast by £20.
(*c*) A cheque of £93 received from K Sand has been correctly entered in the cash book but has not been entered in Sand's account.

These three errors have resulted in a net error of £77, shown by a debit of £77 on the debit side of the suspense account.

These are corrected by:

- making correcting entries in the accounts for (*a*), (*b*) and (*c*)
- recording the double entry for these items in the suspense account.

L Kent Account

Dr					*Cr*
2008		£			
Feb 28	Suspense (*a*)	150			

Purchases Account

Dr					*Cr*
2008		£			
Feb 28	Suspense (*b*)	20			

K Sand Account

Dr					*Cr*
			2008		£
			Feb 28	Suspense (*c*)	93

Suspense Account

Dr					*Cr*
2008		£	2008		£
Jan 1	Balance b/d	77	Feb 28	L Kent (*a*)	150
Feb 28	K Sand (*c*)	93	Feb 28	Purchases (*b*)	20
		170			170

The Journal

			Dr	Cr
2008			£	£
Feb	28	L Kent	150	
		Suspense		150
		Cheque paid omitted from Kent's account		
Feb	28	Purchases	20	
		Suspense		20
		Undercasting of purchases by £20 in last year's accounts		
Feb	28	Suspense	93	
		K Sand		93
		Cheque received omitted from Sand's account		

Only those errors that make the trial balance totals different from each other have to be corrected via the suspense account.

32.5 The effect of errors on profits

Some of the errors will have meant that original profits calculated will be wrong. Other errors will have no effect upon profits. We will use Exhibit 32.4 to illustrate the different kinds of errors.

Exhibit 32.4

K Davis
Trading and Profit and Loss Account for the year ended 31 December 2005

		£	£
Sales	(A)		8,250
Less Cost of goods sold			
Opening stock		500	
Purchases	(B)	6,100	
		6,600	
Less Closing stock		700	
			5,900
Gross profit			2,350
Less Expenses			
Rent	(C)	200	
Insurance	(D)	120	
Lighting			180
Depreciation		250	
			750
Net profit			1,600

K Davis
Balance Sheet as at 31 December 2005

		£	£	£
Fixed assets		*Cost*	*Depreciation*	
Fixtures and fittings		2,200	800	1,400
Current assets				
Stock		700		
Debtors	(E)	600		
Cash at bank		340		
Suspense	(G)	60	1,700	
Current liabilities				
Creditors	(F)	600	600	
Net current assets				1,100
Net assets				2,500
Financed by				
Capital Account				
Balance as at 1 January 2005				1,800
Add Net profit for the year				1,600
				3,400
Less Drawings				(900)
				2,500

Errors that *do not* affect profit calculations

If an error affects items only in the balance sheet, then the original calculated profit will not need altering. The example below shows this:

Example 4: Assume that in Exhibit 32.4 the £60 debit balance on the suspense account shown in the balance sheet was because, on 1 November 2005, we paid £60 to a creditor T Monk and it was correctly entered in the cash book, but it was not entered anywhere else. The error was found on 1 June 2006.

We can see that when this error is corrected, only two items in the final accounts will have to be altered. These are (F) Creditors, which will have to be reduced by £60, and (G) Suspense account, which will now be cancelled and not shown in the balance sheet. This means that neither the trading account nor the profit and loss account have been affected. The profit as shown for 2005 is correct; what is incorrect is the balance sheet.

The double entry records needed are as follows:

T Monk

2006		£	2006		£
June 1	Suspense (Correction)	60	Jan 1	Balance b/d	60

Suspense Account

2006		£	2006		£
Jan 1	Balance b/d (Difference in last year's trial balance)	60	June 1	T Monk	60

The journal entries to correct it will be thus:

The Journal

		Dr	*Cr*
2006		£	£
June 1	T Monk	60	
	Suspense account		60
	Payment to T Monk on 1 November 2005 not entered in his account. Correction now made.		

Errors that *do* affect profit calculations

If the error is in one of the numbers labelled (A), (B), (C) or (D) shown in the trading and profit and loss account, then the original profit will need altering. Example 5 shows this:

Example 5: Assume that in Exhibit 32.4 the £60 debit balance was because the rent account (C) was added up incorrectly: it should be shown as £260 instead of £200. The error was found on 1 June 2006. The journal entries to correct it are:

The Journal

		Dr	*Cr*
2006		£	£
June 1	Rent	60	
	Suspense		60
	Correction of rent undercast last year.		

Rent last year should have been increased by £60. This would have reduced net profit by £60. A statement of corrected profit for the year is now shown.

K Davis
Statement of Corrected Net Profit for the year ended 31 December 2005

	£
Net profit per the accounts	1,600
Less Rent understated	60
	1,540

Where there have been several errors

Example 6: If in Exhibit 32.4 there had been four errors found in the accounts of K Davis on 31 March 2006, their correction can now be seen. Assume that the net difference had also been £60, with the four errors as:

		£
(A)	Sales overcast by	70
(B)	A credit purchase from C Hall of £59 that has not yet been paid was entered in the books, debit and credit entries, as	95
(D)	Insurance undercast by	40
(E)	Cash received from a debtor, L Young entered in the cash book only	50

Error (A) affected the profits: both gross and net profit were shown £70 too much because of this error. It also affected the Suspense account (G).

Error (B) showed purchases too high by (£95 − £59) = £36. This means that gross and net profits were shown £36 too little. The other item affected is (F) Creditors, which is shown as being £36 too much. This error does not affect (G) Suspense account.

Error (D) needs insurance increasing by £40. This will reduce the net profit by £40. It also affects the Suspense account (G).

Error (E) does not affect the profits at all. It affects only items in the balance sheet, namely (E) Debtors and (G) Suspense.

The entries in the ledger accounts are as follows:

General Ledger **Sales**

		£			£
2006					
Mar 31	Suspense (Correction) (A)	70			

General Ledger **Purchases**

		£			£
			2006		
			Mar 31	C Hall (Correction) (B)	36

Purchases Ledger **C Hall**

		£			£
2006					
Mar 31	Purchases (Correction) (B)	36			

General Ledger **Insurance**

		£			£
2006					
Mar 31	Suspense (Correction) (D)	40			

Sales Ledger **L Young**

		£			£
			2006		
			Mar 31	Suspense (Correction) (E)	50

The entries in the suspense account and the journal entries will be as follows:

General Ledger **Suspense Account**

			£				£
2006				2006			
Jan 1	Balance b/d		60	Mar 31	Sales	(A)	70
Mar 31	L Young	(E)	50	" 31	Insurance	(D)	40
			110				110

The Journal

			Dr	Cr
2006				
			£	£
(A) Mar 31	Sales		70	
	Suspense			70
	Sales overcast of £70 in 2005.			
(B) Mar 31	C Hall		36	
	Purchases*			36
	Credit purchase of £59 entered both as debit and credit as £95 in 2005.			
(D) Mar 31	Insurance		40	
	Suspense			40
	Insurance expense undercast by £40 in 2005.			
(E) Mar 31	Suspense		50	
	L Young			50
	Cash received omitted from L Young's account in 2005.			

**Note*: In (B), the correction of the understatement of purchases does not pass through the Suspense account.

Now we can calculate the corrected net profit for the year 2005. Only items (A), (B) and (D) affect figures in the trading and profit and loss account. These are the only adjustments to be made to profit.

K Davis
Statement of corrected Net Profit for the year ended 31 December 2006

		£	£
Net profit per the accounts			1,600
Add Purchases overstated	(B)		36
			1,636
Less Sales overcast	(A)	70	
Insurance undercast	(D)	40	110
Corrected net profit for the year			1,526

32.6 Limitations of trial balances

In this and the previous chapter, you have seen various kinds of errors. Those in Chapter 31 were not revealed by trial balance totals being unequal, which shows a serious limitation to depending completely on the trial balance as an absolute check on the accuracy of the entries in the books of account. To refresh your memory, the kinds of errors not disclosed by a trial balance are:

- errors of commission
- errors of principle
- errors of original entry
- errors of omission
- compensating errors
- complete reversal of entries.

Even when the balances in a trial balance agree, there can be very large errors of various kinds, which may mean that profits have been wrongly calculated and that the balance sheet is incorrect. This current chapter has demonstrated these kinds of errors, where they have resulted in a difference being put into a suspense account until the error(s) have been found.

A very small amount in a suspense account could hide very large errors. For instance, a £50 credit in a suspense account could eventually be found to be either of the following:

- Sales overcast £10,000, debtors total overcast £10,050. If the errors are not found, then both the gross and net profits will be overstated by £10,000 and the figure of debtors in the balance sheet overstated by £10,050.
- Rent expense undercast by £2,000, total of creditors undercast by £1,950. In this case the net profit will be shown at £2,000 more than it should be, while creditors in the balance sheet will be understated by £1,950.

This shows that there is always a possibility of serious errors occurring without it being obvious at first sight.

Every attempt should be made to find errors. Opening a suspense account should be done only if all other efforts have failed.

32.7 Suspense accounts: examinations

Unless it is part of a question, do not make your balance sheet totals agree by using a suspense account. The same applies to trial balances. If you do, you will lose marks.

New term

Suspense account (p. 347): Account showing its balance equal to difference in trial balance.

EXERCISES

32.1 On 31 March 2005 the following items are to be corrected via the journal. Show the corrections. Narratives are not required.

(*a*) T Thomas, a customer, had paid us a cheque for £900 to settle his debt. The cheque has now been returned to us marked 'Dishonoured'.
(*b*) We had allowed C Charles, a debtor, a cash discount of £35. Because of a dispute with her, we have now disallowed the cash discount.
(*c*) Office equipment bought for £6,000 has been debited to motor vehicles account.
(*d*) the copy sales invoice of sales to J Graham £715 was lost, and therefore was completely omitted from our books.
(*e*) Cash drawings of £210 have been correctly entered in the cash book, but have been credited to the wages account.

32.2 On 31 December 2004 your book-keeper extracted a trial balance that failed to agree by £330, being a shortage on the credit side of the trial balance. A suspense account was opened for the difference.

In January 2005 the following errors made in 2004 were found:

(i) Sales day book had been undercast by £100.
(ii) Sales of £250 to K Hart had been debited in error to K Hartley's account.
(iii) Rent account had been undercast by £70.
(iv) Discounts received account had been undercast by £300.
(v) the sale of a motor vehicle at net book value had been credited in error to sales account £360.

Required:
(*a*) Show the journal entries necessary to correct the errors.
(*b*) Draw up the suspense account after the errors described have been corrected.
(*c*) If the net profit had previously been calculated at £7,900 for the year ended 31 December 2004, show the calculation of the corrected net profit.

32.3X You have extracted a trial balance and drawn up accounts for the year ended 31 December 2006. There was a shortage of £292 on the credit side of the trial balance, a suspense account being opened for that amount.

During 2007 the following errors made in 2006 were located:

(i) £55 received from sales of old office equipment had been entered in the sales account.
(ii) Purchases day book had been overcast by £60.
(iii) A private purchase of £115 had been included in the business purchases.
(iv) Bank charges £38 entered in the cash book had not been posted to the bank charges account.
(v) A sale of goods to C Clay for £690 was correctly entered in the sales book but entered in the personal account as £960.

Required:
(*a*) Show the journal entries to correct the errors.
(*b*) Write up the suspense account showing the correction of the errors.
(*c*) the net profit originally calculated for 2006 was £11,370. Show your calculation of the correct figure.

32.4X The following is a trial balance which has been incorrectly drawn up:

Trial Balance as at 31 January 2009

	£	£
Capital 1 February 2008	5,500	
Drawings	2,800	
Stock 1 February 2008		2,597
Trade debtors		2,130
Furniture and fittings	1,750	
Cash in hand	1,020	
Trade creditors		2,735
Sales		7,430
Returns inwards		85
Discount received	46	
Business expenses	950	
Purchases	4,380	
	16,446	14,977

In addition to the mistakes evident above, the following errors were also discovered:

(i) A payment of £75 made to a creditor had not been posted from the cash book into the purchases ledger.
(ii) A cheque for £56 received from a customer had been correctly entered in the cash book but posted to the customer's account as £50.
(iii) A purchase of fittings £120 had been included in the purchases account.
(iv) The total of the discounts allowed column in the cash book of £38 had not been posted into the general ledger.
(v) A page of the sales day book was correctly totalled as £564 but carried forward as £456.

Show the trial balance as it would appear after all the errors had been corrected. You are required to show all workings.

32.5 The following trial balance was extracted by K Woodburn from her books as at 30 June 2008. She is unable to get the totals to agree.

Trial Balance as at 30 June 2008

	Dr £	*Cr* £
Sales		87,050
Purchases	62,400	
Discounts allowed and received	305	410
Salaries and wages	3,168	
General expenses	595	
Fixtures	10,000	
Stock 1 July 2007	12,490	
Debtors and creditors	8,120	5,045
Bank	6,790	
Drawings	4,520	
Capital		17,017
Suspense	1,134	
	109,522	109,522

The following errors are found:

(i) Sales journal overcast by £350.
(ii) Discounts allowed undercast by £100.
(iii) Fixtures, bought for £850, have been entered in the cash book but not in the fixtures account.
(iv) Credit purchase of £166 was entered in the purchases journal only, but not in the creditor's account.
(v) Cheque payment to a creditor of £490 had been debited to the drawings account in error.

You are required to:
(*a*) draw up the suspense account to record the corrections
(*b*) redraft the trial balance after all corrections have been made.

32.6X T Sawyer extracted the following trial balance from his books. He could not get the totals to agree with each other.

Trial Balance as at 31 December 2007

	Dr	*Cr*
	£	£
Capital		25,621
Drawings	13,690	
Sales		94,630
Purchases	60,375	
Returns inwards and outwards	1,210	1,109
Wages and salaries	14,371	
Sundry expenses	598	
Stock 1.1.2007	8,792	
Debtors and creditors	11,370	4,290
Loan from J Chandler		5,000
Equipment	16,000	
Bank	5,790	
Suspense		1,546
	132,196	132,196

The following errors are discovered:

(i) Purchases journal was overcast by £258.
(ii) A repayment of loan £2,000 was debited in error to the wages account.
(iii) A cheque payment for equipment £1,500 has been entered in the equipment account but not in the cash book.
(iv) Returns outwards £168 have been entered in the returns journal but not in the creditor's account.
(v) Sundry expenses £44 have been entered in the cash book but not in the sundry expenses account.

You are required to:
(*a*) draw up the suspense account, showing corrections
(*b*) redraft the trial balance after all corrections have been made.

32.7 The trial balance of Philip Hogan as at 31 December 2003 does not balance. The difference of £5,400 has been credited to a suspense account. The following errors were subsequently discovered:

(*a*) The sales day book is undercast by £3,000.
(*b*) Purchases received from Dawson & Co, amounting to £1,147, had been received on 31 December 2003, and included in the closing stock at that date. Unfortunately, the invoice had not been entered in the purchases day book.
(*c*) Motor repairs of £585 have been charged to the motor vehicles account.
(*d*) Credit sales of £675 made to J Greenway have been debited to the account of J Green.
(*e*) A payment of £425 in respect of electricity has been debited to the electricity account as £575.
(*f*) A cheque for £2,250 received from Teape Ltd, a debtor, has been correctly entered in the cash book but no entry has been made in Teape's account.

Required:
Show the journal entries, including narratives, to correct the above errors, and write up the suspense account after the corrections have been made.

32.8X A trial balance does not balance and a suspense account has been opened with a credit balance of £510. The following errors are then discovered.

(i) Cash purchases of £450 were recorded in both the cash book and ledger as £540.
(ii) The total of the motor expenses account was undercast by £70.
(iii) Cash received from a debtor £150 is entered in the cash book only.
(iv) The sales account was undercast by £350.
(v) The insurance account was overcast by £80.

Required:
(*a*) Show the journal entries to correct the errors.
(*b*) Write up the suspense account showing correction of the errors.
(*c*) The net profit figure originally calculated for the year ended 31 December 2008 was £12,250. Calculate the corrected net profit figure.

NEAB (AQA) (GCSE)

PART 5

Final accounts of other organisations

33 Single entry and incomplete records

34 Club and society accounts

35 Manufacturing accounts

36 Partnership accounts

37 Limited company accounts

38 Analysis and interpretation of accounts

This part is concerned with the accounting procedures that have to be followed with different forms of organisations. It also includes a chapter outlining the basic ratios that are used for analysis and interpretation of accounts.

CHAPTER 33

Single entry and incomplete records

Learning objectives

After you have studied this chapter you should be able to:

- **deduce the figure of profits where only the increase in capital and details of drawings are known**
- **draw up a trading and profit and loss account and balance sheet from records not kept on a double entry system**
- **deduce the figures of sales and purchases from incomplete records.**

33.1 Why double entry is sometimes not used

For every small shopkeeper, market stall or other small business to keep its books using a full double entry system would not be practical. First of all, a large number of the owners of such firms would not know how to write up double entry records, even if they wanted to.

It is more likely that they would enter details of a transaction once only, using a **single entry** system. Also many of them would fail to record every transaction, resulting in **incomplete records.**

Somehow, however, the profits will have to be calculated. This could be for the purpose of calculating income tax payable. How can profits be calculated if the book-keeping records are inadequate or incomplete?

33.2 Profit as an increase in capital

Probably the way to start is to recall that, unless there has been an introduction of extra cash or resources into the firm, the only way that capital can be increased is by making profits. Therefore, profits can be found by comparing capital at the end of the last period with that at the end of this period.

Let us look at a firm where capital at the end of 2004 is £2,000. During 2005 there have been no drawings, and no extra capital has been brought in by the owner. At the end of 2005 the capital is £3,000. Then:

	This year's capital		Last year's capital	
Net profit =	£3,000	–	£2,000	= £1,000

If on the other hand the drawings had been £700, the profits must have been £1,700, calculated thus:

Last year's Capital	+	Profits	–	Drawings	=	This year's Capital
£2,000	+	?	–	£700	=	£3,000

We can see that £1,700 profits was the figure needed to complete the formula, filling in the missing figure by normal arithmetical deduction:

$$£2,000 + £1,700 - £700 = £3,000$$

Example 1 shows the calculation of profit where insufficient information is available to draft a trading and profit and loss account, only information of assets and liabilities being known.

Example 1: H Taylor has not kept proper book-keeping records, but he has kept notes in diary form of the transactions of his business. He is able to give details of his assets and liabilities as at 31 December 2005 and at 31 December 2006 as follows:

- At 31 December 2005: *Assets*: Motor van £1,000; Fixtures £700; Stock £850; Debtors £950; Bank £1,100; Cash £100. *Liabilities*: Creditors £200.
- At 31 December 2006: *Assets*: Motor van (after depreciation) £800; Fixtures (after depreciation) £630; Stock £990; Debtors £1,240; Bank £1,700; Cash £200. *Liabilities*: Creditors £300; Loan from J Ogden £400. Drawings were £900.

First of all a statement of affairs is drawn up as at 31 December 2005, now shown:

H Taylor
Statement of Affairs as at 31 December 2005

	£	£
Fixed Assets		
Motor van		1,000
Fixtures		1,700
		1,700
Current Assets		
Stock	850	
Debtors	950	
Bank	1,100	
Cash	100	
	3,000	
Less Current Liabilities		
Creditors	200	
Net current assets		2,800
		4,500
Financed by		
Capital (difference)		4,500

We can see that the **statement of affairs** is the same as a balance sheet. We do not call it a balance sheet since it has not been drawn up from a properly kept set of books. Instead, it is a list of all the same items as would appear in a balance sheet but with figures supplied by the proprietor from whatever information he possesses.

As with a balance sheet, the totals of the statement of affairs should equal each other. The top part we know shows a total figure of £4,500, so that the bottom part, which is only capital, should also show a figure of £4,500.

Another statement of affairs is now drawn up as at 31 December 2006. With this one, as we know the opening capital for the year and can find the closing capital at the end of the year, we should be able to work out the net profit. This is shown as (C) below. We will have to work out first of all what (A) is, and then what (B) is. Then we will be able to work out (C), the figure for net profit.

H Taylor
Statement of Affairs as at 31 December 2006

		£		£
Fixed Assets				
Motor van				800
Fixtures				630
				1,430
Current Assets				
Stock		990		
Debtors		1,240		
Bank		1,700		
Cash		200		
		4,130		
Less Current Liabilities				
Creditors		300		
Net current assets				3,830
				5,260
Financed by				
Capital				
Balance at 1.1.2006		4,500		
Add Net profit	(C)	?		
	(B)	?		
Less Drawings		900	(A)	?
				5,260

The closing capital (A) must be £5,260 to equal the total of the top part.

We know that:

Opening Capital	+ Net Profit	– Drawings	= Closing Capital
£4,500	+ (C)?	– £900	= £5,260

Therefore net profit is £1,660. To put the same equation another way:

	£
Capital at 1.1.2006	4,500
Add Net profit	1,660
	6,160
Less Drawings	900
Capital at 31.12.2006	5,260

Clearly, this method of calculating profit is very unsatisfactory as it is much more informative when a trading and profit and loss account can be drawn up. Therefore, whenever possible, the 'comparison of capital' method of ascertaining profit should be avoided and a full set of final accounts drawn up from the available records.

It is important to realise that a business would have exactly the same trading and profit and loss account and balance sheet whether the managers kept their books by single entry or double entry. However, as you will see, whereas the double entry system uses the trial balance in preparing the final accounts, the single entry system will have to arrive at the same answer by different means.

33.3 Drawing up the final accounts

The following example shows the various stages of drawing up final accounts from a single entry set of records.

Example 2: The accountant for J Frank's retail store discerns the following details of transactions for the year ended 31 December 2005:

(a) The sales are mostly on a credit basis. No record of sales has been made, but £10,000 has been received, £9,500 by cheque and £500 by cash, from persons to whom goods have been sold.

(b) The amount paid by cheque to suppliers during the year = £7,200.

(c) Expenses paid during the year: by cheque, rent £200, general expenses £180; by cash, rent £50.

(d) J Frank took £10 cash per week (for 52 weeks) as drawings.

(e) Other information is available:

	At 31.12.2004	At 31.12.2005
	£	£
Debtors	1,100	1,320
Creditors for goods	400	650
Rent owing	–	50
Bank balance	1,130	3,050
Cash balance	80	10
Stock	1,590	1,700

(f) The only fixed asset consists of fixtures that were valued at 31 December 2004 at £800. These are to be depreciated at 10 per cent per annum.

Final accounts: Stage 1

First, draw up a statement of affairs on the closing day of the last accounting period. This is shown thus:

J Frank
Statement of Affairs as at 31 December 2004

	£	£
Fiixed Assets		
Fixtures		800
Current Assets		
Stock	1,590	
Debtors	1,100	
Bank	1,130	
Cash	80	
	3,900	
Less Current Liabilities		
Creditors	400	
Net current assets		3,500
		4,300
Financed by		
Capital (difference)		4,300
		4,300

All of these opening figures are then taken into account when drawing up the final accounts for 2005.

Stage 2

Next, a cash and bank summary, showing the totals of each separate item plus opening and closing balances, is drawn up. Thus:

Dr	*Cash*	*Bank*		*Cash*	*Bank* *Cr*
	£	£		£	£
Balances 31.12.2004	80	1,130	Suppliers		7,200
Receipts from debtors	500	9,500	Rent	50	200
			General expenses		180
			Drawings	520	
			Balances 31.12.2005	10	3,050
	580	10,630		580	10,630

Stage 3

Calculate the figures for purchases and sales to be shown in the trading account. Remember that the figures needed are the same as those which would have been found if double entry records had been kept.

Purchases

In double entry, purchases means the goods that have been bought in the period, irrespective of whether or not they have been paid for during the period. The figure of payments to suppliers must therefore be adjusted to find the figure for purchases. In our example we have:

	£
Paid during the year	7,200
Less Payments made, but which were for goods which were purchased in a previous year (creditors 31.12.2004)	400
	6,800
Add Purchases made in this year, but for which payment has not yet been made (creditors 31.12.2005)	650
Goods bought in this year, i.e. purchases	7,450

The same answer could have been obtained if the information had been shown in the form of a total creditors account, the figure for purchases being the amount required to make the account totals agree:

Total Creditors' Account

Dr			*Cr*
	£		£
Cash paid to suppliers	7,200	Balances b/f	400
Balances c/d	650	Purchases (missing figure)	7,450
	7,850		7,850

Sales

The sales figure will only equal receipts where all the sales are for cash. Therefore, the receipts figures need adjusting to find sales. This can only be done by constructing a total debtors' account, the sales figure being the one needed to make the totals agree.

Total Debtors' Account

Dr			*Cr*
	£		£
Balances b/f	1,100	Receipts: Cash	500
		Cheque	9,500
Sales (missing figure)	10,220	Balances c/d	1,320
	11,320		11,320

The above accounts are exactly the same as the creditors and debtors control accounts, described in Chapter 24.

Stage 4

Expenses

Where there are no accruals or prepayments either at the beginning or end of the accounting period, the expenses paid will equal the expenses used up during the period. These figures will be charged to the trading and profit and loss account.

In contrast, where such prepayments or accruals exist, then an expense account should be drawn up for that particular item. When all known items have been entered, the missing figure will be the expenses to be charged for the accounting period.

In our example, only the rent account needs to be drawn up:

Rent Account

Dr			*Cr*
	£		£
Cheques	200	Rent (missing figure)	300
Cash	50		
Accrued c/d	50		
	300		300

Stage 5

Now draw up the final accounts:

J Frank
Trading and Profit and Loss Account for the year ended 31 December 2005

	£	£
Sales (Stage 3)		10,220
Less Cost of goods sold		
Stock at 1.1.2005	1,590	
Add Purchases (Stage 3)	7,450	
	9,040	
Less Stock at 31.12.2005	1,700	7,340
Gross profit		2,880
Less Expenses		
Rent (Stage 4)	300	
General expenses	180	
Depreciation: Fixtures	80	560
Net profit		2,320

Balance Sheet as at 31 December 2005

	£	£	£
Fixed Assets			
Fixtures at 1.1.2005		800	
Less Depreciation		80	720
Current Assets			
Stock		1,700	
Debtors		1,320	
Bank		3,050	
Cash		10	
		6,080	
Less Current Liabilities			
Creditors	650		
Rent owing	50	700	
Net current assets			5,380
			6,100
Financed by			
Capital			
Balance 1.1.2005 (per opening statement of affairs)			4,300
Add Net profit			2,320
			6,620
Less Drawings			520
			6,100

33.4 Incomplete records and missing figures

In practice, part of the information relating to cash receipts or payments is often missing. If the missing information is in respect of one type of payment, then it is normal to assume that the missing figure is the amount required to make both totals agree in the cash column of the cash and bank summary. This does not happen with bank items since another copy of the bank statement can always be obtained from the bank.

Exhibit 33.1 shows an example when the drawings figure is unknown; Exhibit 33.2 is an example where the receipts from debtors had not been recorded.

Exhibit 33.1

The following information on cash and bank receipts and payments is available:

	Cash	*Bank*
	£	£
Cash paid into the bank during the year	5,500	
Receipts from debtors	7,250	800
Paid to suppliers	320	4,930
Drawings during the year	?	–
Expenses paid	150	900
Balances at 1.1.2005	35	1,200
Balances at 31.12.2005	50	1,670

Dr	Cash	Bank			Cash	Bank Cr
	£	£			£	£
Balances 1.1.2005	35	1,200	Bankings	C	5,500	
Received from debtors	7,250	800	Suppliers		320	4,930
Bankings C		5,500	Expenses		150	900
			Drawings		?	
			Balances 31.12.2005		50	1,670
	7,285	7,500			7,285	7,500

The amount needed to make the two sides of the cash columns agree is £1,265. Therefore, this is taken as the figure of drawings.

Exhibit 33.2

Information of cash and bank transactions is available as follows:

	Cash	Bank
	£	£
Receipts from debtors	?	6,080
Cash withdrawn from the bank for business use (this is the amount which is used besides cash receipts from debtors to pay drawings and expenses)		920
Paid to suppliers		5,800
Expenses paid	640	230
Drawings	1,180	315
Balances at 1.1.2005	40	1,560
Balances at 31.12.2005	70	375

Dr	Cash	Bank		Cash	Bank Cr
	£	£		£	£
Balances 1.1.2005	40	1,560	Suppliers		5,800
Received from debtors	?	6,080	Expenses	640	230
Withdrawn from Bank C	920		Withdrawn from Bank C		920
			Drawings	1,180	315
			Balances 31.12.2005	70	375
	1,890	7,640		1,890	7,640

Receipts from debtors is, therefore, the amount needed to make each side of the cash column agree, namely £930.

It must be emphasised that balancing figures are acceptable only when all the other figures have been verified. Should, for instance, a cash expense be omitted when cash received from debtors is being calculated, then this would result in an understatement not only of expenses but also ultimately of sales.

Note: A step-by-step guide to incomplete records is shown in Appendix B Step-by-step guides at the end of this book.

New terms

Incomplete records (p. 362): Where only some transactions are recorded in the books of account, the missing information has to be obtained by other means.

Single entry (p. 362): Where transactions are only recorded once in the books of account.

Statement of affairs (p. 364): A statement from which the capital of the owner is deduced by estimating assets and liabilities. Then: Capital = Assets *less* Liabilities.

EXERCISES

33.1 The following figures have been extracted from the records of K Rogers, who does not keep a full record of his transactions on the double entry system:

			£
1 November	2005	Debtors	2,760
1 November	2005	Creditors	1,080
1 November	2005	Stock	2,010
31 October	2006	Debtors	3,090
31 October	2006	Creditors	1,320
31 October	2006	Stock	2,160

All goods were sold on credit and all purchases were made on credit. During the year ended 31 October 2006, cash received from debtors amounted to £14,610, whereas cash paid to creditors amounted to £9,390.

Required:

(*a*) Calculate the amount of sales and purchases for the year ended 31 October 2006.
(*b*) Draw up the trading account for the year ended 31 October 2006.

33.2X The following figures for a business are available:

			£
1 June	2007	Stock	11,590
1 June	2007	Creditors	3,410
1 June	2007	Debtors	5,670
31 May	2008	Stock	13,425
31 May	2008	Creditors	4,126
31 May	2008	Debtors	6,108
Year to 31 May 2008:			
Received from debtors			45,112
Paid to creditors			29,375

All goods were bought or sold on credit.

Required:

Draw up the trading account for the year 31 May 2008, deducing any figures that might be needed.

33.3 On 1 July 2005, D Lewinski commenced business with £6,000 in his bank account. After trading for a full year, he ascertained that his position on 30 June 2006 was as follows:

	£		£
Plant	3,600	Fixtures	360
Creditors	720	Bank balance	600
Debtors	930	Stock-in-trade	1,350
Cash in hand	135	Drawings	1,600

You are required to:
(*a*) calculate D Lewinski's capital at 30 June 2006
(*b*) prepare D Lewinski's balance sheet at 30 June 2006 (assuming a profit of £1,855), set out in such a manner as to show clearly the totals normally shown in a balance sheet.

33.4 J Marcano is a dealer who has not kept proper books of account. At 31 August 2006 her state of affairs was as follows.

	£
Cash	115
Bank balance	2,209
Fixtures	3,500
Stock	16,740
Debtors	11,890
Creditors	9,952
Motor van (at valuation)	3,500

During the year to 31 August 2007, her drawings amounted to £7,560. Winnings from the national lottery of £12,800 were put into the business. Extra fixtures were bought for £2,000. At 31 August 2007 Marcano's assets and liabilities were: cash £84; bank overdraft, £165; stock, £24,891; creditors for goods £6,002; creditors for expenses £236; fixtures to be depreciated by £300; motor van to be valued at £2,800; debtors, £15,821; prepaid expenses, £72.

You are required to draw up a statement showing the profit or loss made by Marcano for the year ended 31 August 2007.

33.5X A Hanson is a sole trader who, although keeping very good records, does not operate a full double entry system. The following figures have been taken from his records:

	31 March 2008	*31 March 2009*
	£	£
Cash at bank	1,460	1.740
Office furniture	600	500
Stock	2,320	2,620
Cash in hand	60	80

Debtors on 31 March 2008 amounted to £2,980 and sales for the year ended 31 March 2009 to £11,520. During the year ended 31 March 2009, cash received from debtors amounted to £10,820.

Creditors on 31 March 2008 amounted to £1,880 and purchases for the year ended 31 March 2009 to £8,120. During the year ended 31 March 2009, cash paid to creditors amounted to £7,780.

During the year to 31 March 2009 no bad debts were incurred. Also during the same period, there was neither discounts allowed nor discounts received.

Required (with all calculations shown):

(*a*) Calculate debtors and creditors as at 31 March 2009.

(*b*) Calculate Hanson's capital as at 31 March 2008 and 31 March 2009.

(*c*) Calculate his net profit for the year ended 31 March 2009, allowing for the fact that during the year Hanson's drawings amounted to £2,540.

33.6 Following is a summary of P Kelly's bank account for the year ended 31 December 2007:

P Kelly Bank Account

	£		£
Balance 1.1.2007	405	Payments to creditors	
Receipts from debtors	37,936	for goods	29,487
Balance 31.12.2007	602	Rent	1,650
		Rates	890
		Sundry expenses	375
		Drawings	6,541
	38,943		38,943

All of the business takings have been paid into the bank, with the exception of £9,630. Out of this, Kelly has paid wages of £5,472, drawings of £1,164 and purchase of goods £2,994.

The following additional information is available:

	31.12.2006	*31.12.2007*
	£	£
Stock	13,862	15,144
Creditors for goods	5,624	7,389
Debtors for goods	9,031	8,624
Rates prepaid	210	225
Rent owing	150	-
Fixtures at valuation	2,500	2,250

You are required to draw up a set of final accounts for the year ended 31 December 2007. Show all of your workings.

33.7X An accountant has prepared quarterly accounts for Linda Goodheart, who runs a small newsagent's shop. After he had prepared the accounts for the third quarter of the year to 31 July 2008, the trial balance was as follows:

	£	£
Fixtures and fittings, at cost	7,800	
Provision for depreciation of fixtures and fittings		1,600
Balance at bank	1,572	
Prepayment for shop expenses	250	
Trade creditors		11,980
Sundry debtors	11,156	
Capital account		20,632
Stock	13,434	
	34,212	34,212

Due to illness of her accountant, she has asked you to prepare the accounts for the final quarter of her financial year. Looking through the bank statements you have elicited this information:

	Quarter to 31/10/08
Paid into bank:	
Cash sales	16,216
Receipts from debtors	22,860
Bank interest	47
Cheque from creditor, who had been overpaid	381
Amounts withdrawn –	
Purchases	34,886
Shop expenses	5,401
For personal use	3,000
Wages	440

You have also discovered that:

(i) all receipts and payments for the business go through the bank account
(ii) the business is owed £11,340 by customers at 31 October 2008
(iii) shop expenses are paid for at the time of purchase
(iv) sales produce a gross profit of 35 per cent
(v) fixtures and fittings are depreciated at the rate of 10 per cent p.a. on cost
(vi) the stock at 31 October 2008 is valued at £16,111.

You are required (showing all workings) to:

(*a*) produce a summary bank account for the quarter to 31 October 2008
(*b*) prepare the business profit and loss account for the period from 1 August to 31 October 2008
(*c*) prepare the balance sheet as at 31 October 2008.

OCR (Accounting Stage II)

33.8X S Allen has lost his records of sales, and you will have to deduce the sales figure. The summary of his bank account for the year ended 31 December 2006 is as follows:

S Allen Bank Account

	£		£
Receipts from debtors	67,595	Balance 1 Jan 2006	2,059
Extra capital introduced	3,000	Suppliers for goods	49,382
		Motor expenses	4,624
		Rent and rates	3,728
		General expenses	846
		Fixtures bought	3,500
		Drawings	1,364
		Balance 31 Dec 2006	5,092
	70,595		70,595

A cash loan of £500 was received on 1 July 2006. Interest is to be paid on this at the rate of 16% per annum. Cash payments were as follows:

	£
Drawings	6,070
Suppliers	406
General expenses	707

Cash received from debtors was £6,630.

Motor vehicles owned by the firm had cost £8,000 in January 2004, and depreciation should be written off at 25% using the reducing balance method. Fixtures costing £2,000 were bought in January 2003, and depreciation is being written off at the rate of 10%, using the straight-line method.

The following information is also given:

	31.12.2005	*31.12.2006*
	£	£
Stock	10,500	11,370
Cash in hand	165	112
Creditors for goods	6,238	4,187
Debtors	16,840	19,385
Motor expenses owing	123	238
Rent paid in advance	115	-
Rent owing	-	230

You are required to:

(*a*) Draw up a total debtors' and total creditors' accounts.
(*b*) Draw up a cash account summary for the year.
(*c*) Calculate the opening capital as on 1 January 2006.
(*d*) Prepare the trading and profit and loss account for the year ended 31 December 2006.

CHAPTER 34

Club and society accounts

Learning objectives

After you have studied this chapter you should be able to:

- draw up income and expenditure accounts and balance sheets for non-trading organisations
- calculate profits and losses from special activities, and to incorporate them into the final accounts
- understand that various forms of revenue may need special treatment
- be aware of treasurers' responsibilities.

34.1 Non-trading organisations

Clubs, associations and other **non-profit-making organisations** do not have trading and profit and loss accounts drawn up for them, as their purpose is not trading or profit making. They are operated so that their members can do things such as play football or chess. The kind of final accounts prepared by these organisations are either **receipts and payments accounts** or **income and expenditure accounts** - both described below.

34.2 Receipts and payments accounts

Receipts and payments accounts are a summary of the cash book for the period. Exhibit 34.1 is an example.

EXHIBIT 34.1

The Homers Running Club
Receipts and Payments Account for the year ended 31 December 2005

Receipts	£	*Payments*	£
Bank balance 1.1.2005	236	Groundsman's wages	728
Subscriptions received for 2005	1,148	Sports stadium expenses	296
Rent received	116	Committee expenses	58
		Printing and stationery	33
		Bank balance 31.12.2005	385
	1,500		1,500

34.3 Income and expenditure accounts

When assets are owned, and there are liabilities, the receipts and payments account is not a good way of drawing up final accounts. Other than the cash received and paid out, it shows only the cash balances; the other assets and liabilities are not shown at all.

What is required is:

- a balance sheet, and
- an account showing whether the association's capital has increased.

The second of these two requirements is provided via an income and expenditure account. Such an account follows the same rules as trading and profit and loss accounts, the only differences being the terms used.

A comparison of terms used now follows:

Profit-making firm	Non-profit organisation
1 Trading and profit and loss account	1 Income and expenditure account
2 Net profit	2 Surplus of income over expenditure
3 Net loss	3 Excess of expenditure over income

34.4 Profit or loss for a special purpose

Sometimes there are reasons why a non-profit-making organisation would want a profit and loss account. This is where something is done to make a profit. The profit is not to be kept, but used to pay for the main purpose of the organisation.

For instance, a football club may have discos or dances that people pay to attend. Any profit from these events helps to pay football expenses. For these discos and dances a trading and profit and loss account would be drawn up. Any profit (or loss) would be transferred to the income and expenditure account.

34.5 Accumulated fund

A sole trader or a partnership would have capital accounts. A non-profit-making organisation would instead have an **accumulated fund**. It is in effect the same as a capital account, for it is the difference between assets and liabilities.

For a sole trader or partnership:

Capital + Liabilities = Assets

In a non-profit-making organisation:

Accumulated Fund + Liabilities = Assets

34.6 Drawing up income and expenditure accounts

We can now look at the preparation of an income and expenditure account and a balance sheet of a club. A separate trading account is to be prepared for a bar, where food and alcohol are sold to make a profit.

Long Lane Football Club
Trial Balance as at 31 December 2008

	Dr	*Cr*
	£	£
Sports equipment	8,500	
Club premises	29,600	
Subscriptions received		6,490
Wages of staff	4,750	
Furniture and fittings	5,260	
Rates and insurance	1,910	
General expenses	605	
Accumulated fund 1 January 2008		42,016
Donations received		360
Telephone and postage	448	
Bank	2,040	
Bar purchases	9,572	
Creditors for bar supplies		1,040
Bar sales		14,825
Bar stocks 1 January 2008	2,046	
	64,731	64,731

The following information is also available:

(i) Bar stocks at 31 December 2008 amount in value to £2,362.

(ii) There is a need to provide for depreciation: sports equipment £1,700; furniture and fittings £1,315.

The club's trading account will look thus:

Long Lane Football Club Bar
Trading Account for the year ended 31 December 2008

	£	£
Sales		14,825
Less Cost of goods sold		
Opening stock	2,046	
Purchases	9,572	
	11,618	
Closing stock	2,362	
		9,256
Gross profit		5,569

The result of the club bar operation is calculated separately. The gross profit/loss will then be incorporated into the club's income and expenditure account for calculation of the overall result, as shown below:

Income and Expenditure Account
for the year ended 31 December 2008

	£	£
Income		
Gross profit from bar		5,569
Subscriptions		6,490
Donations received		360
		12,419
Less Expenditure		
Wages to staff	4,750	
Rates and insurance	1,910	
Telephone and postage	448	
General expenses	605	
Depreciation: Furniture	1,315	
Sports equipment	1,700	
		10,728
Surplus of income over expenditure		1,691

Balance Sheet at 31 December 2008

	£	£	£
Fixed assets	*Cost*	*Depreciation*	*Net book value*
Club premises	29,600	–	29,600
Furniture and fittings	5,260	1,315	3,945
Sports equipment	8,500	1,700	6,800
	43,360	3,015	40,345
Current assets			
Bar stocks		2,362	
Cash at bank		2,040	
		4,402	
Current liabilities			
Creditors for bar supplies		1,040	
Net current assets			3,362
Net assets			43,707
Accumulated fund			
Balance at 1 January 2008			42,016
Add Surplus of income over expenditure			1,691
			43,707

34.7 Subscriptions

No subscriptions owing

Where there are no **subscriptions** owing, and none paid in advance, at the beginning and the end of a financial year, then the amount shown on the credit side of the subscriptions account can be transferred to the credit side of the income and expenditure account, as follows:

Dr	Subscriptions			*Cr*
2003		£	*2003*	£
Dec 31	Income & expenditure a/c	3,598	Dec 31 Bank (total received)	3,598

Income and Expenditure Account
for the year ended 31 December 2003 (extract)

	£
Income:	
Subscriptions	3,598

Subscriptions owing

On the other hand, there may be subscriptions owing at both the start and the end of the financial year. In a case where £325 was owing at the start of the year, a total of £5,668 was received during the year, and £554 was owing at he end of the year, the transactions would appear as follows:

Dr			Subscriptions				Cr
2005			£	*2005*			£
Jan	1	Owing b/d	325	Dec	31	Bank (total received)	5,668
Dec	31	Income & expenditure a/c (difference)	5,897	Dec	31	Balance c/d	554
			6,222				6,222

Income and Expenditure Account
for the year ended 31 December 2005 (extract)

Income:	£
Subscriptions	5,897

In the balance sheet, the subscription owing at the end of December 2005 would be shown under the heading of 'Current assets' as a debtor, as shown below:

Balance Sheet as at 31 December 2005 (extract)

Current assets	£
Stock	x,xxx
Debtors (xxx + 554)	xxx

Subscriptions owing and paid in advance

In a third case, at the start of the year there could be both subscriptions owing from the previous year and also subscriptions paid in advance. In addition, there could also be subscriptions paid in the current year for the next year (in advance) and subscriptions unpaid (owing) at the end of the current year. The example below concerns an amateur theatre organisation.

An amateur theatre organisation charges its members an annual subscription of £20 per member. It accrues for subscriptions owing at the end of each year and also adjusts for subscriptions received in advance. The following applies:

(A) On 1 January 2002, 18 members owed a total of £360 for the year 2001.
(B) In December 2001, 4 members paid a total of £80 for the year 2002.
(C) During the year 2002, the organisation received cash subscriptions of £7,420, made up as follows:

For 2001	£360
For 2002	£6,920
For 2003	£140
	£7,420

(D) At the close of 31 December 2002, 11 members had not paid their 2002 subscriptions.

These facts are translated into the accounts as set out below:

Subscriptions

Dr					*Cr*				
2002				£	*2002*				£
Jan	1	Owing b/d	(A)	360	Jan	1	Prepaid b/d	(B)	80
Dec	31	Income and expenditure a/c		*7,220	Dec	31	Bank	(C)	7,420
Dec	31	Prepaid c/d	(C)	140	Dec	31	Owing c/d	(D)	220
				7,720					7,720
2003					*2003*				
Jan	1	Owing b/d	(D)	220	Jan	1	Prepaid b/d	(C)	140

*The difference between the two sides of the account.

Income and Expenditure Account
for the year ended 31 December 2002 (extract)

Income:	£
Subscriptions	7,220

As shown in the balance sheet as at 31 December 2002, the amounts owing for subscriptions (D), £220, will be shown under current assets as a debtor. The subscriptions (C) paid in advance for 2003 will appear as an item under current liabilities as subscriptions received in advance, £140.

34.8 Donations

Any **donations** received are shown as income in the year that they are received.

34.9 Entrance fees

New members often have to pay an entrance fee in the year that they join, in addition to the membership fee for that year. Entrance fees are normally included as income in the year that they are received.

34.10 Life membership

Sometimes members can pay one amount for **life membership**, and they will never have to pay any more money. This membership will last for their lifetime. In this case, all of the money received from life membership should not be credited to the income and expenditure account of the year in which it is received.

In a club where members joined at age 20 and would probably be members for 40 years, then one-fortieth (2½ per cent) of the life membership fee should be credited in the income and expenditure account each year. The balance not transferred to the income and expenditure account would appear in the balance sheet as a long-term liability. This is because it is the liability of the club to allow the members to use the club for the rest of their lives without paying any more for membership.

On the other hand, a club especially for old men over the age of 60 would transfer a much bigger share of the life membership fee paid to the income and expenditure account. This is because the number of years of future use of the club will be far less because people are already old when they join. It may be, in those circumstances, that 10 per cent of the life membership fee per year would be transferred to the credit of the income and expenditure account.

34.11 Treasurers' responsibilities

Treasurers of clubs or societies have a responsibility for maintaining proper accounting records in the same way as an accountant has when looking after the financial affairs of a business. It is important to ensure that any monies paid out by the treasurer have been properly authorised, especially when purchasing an item of capital expenditure (such as new sound equipment for a dramatic society). In such cases, the authorisation for purchase will more than likely have been approved at a committee meeting and noted in the minutes of the meeting. For smaller items of expenditure such as postages, telephone calls etc., the club or society's rules will provide the treasurer with the authority to make payments against receipted bills.

It is also important for the treasurer to keep all invoices, receipted accounts and any other documents as evidence against payments. Treasurers should also provide receipts for any monies received. All documents should be filed and available at the year end for the club's auditor to carry out an audit and for preparation of the club's year-end financial statements.

New terms

Accumulated fund (p. 378): A form of capital account for a non-profit-making organisation.

Donation (p. 382): A monetary gift donated to a club or society. Monies received should be shown as income in the year that they are received.

Income and expenditure account (p. 376): An account for a non-profit making organisation to find the surplus or loss made during an accounting period.

Life membership (p. 382): Where members pay one amount for membership to last them their lifetime.

Non-profit-making organisations (p. 376): Clubs, associations and societies operated to provide a service or activity for members since their main purpose is not trading or profit making.

Receipts and payments account (p. 376): A summary of the cash book of a non-profit-making organisation.

Subscriptions (p. 380): Amounts paid by members of a club or society, usually on an annual basis, to enable them to participate in the activities of the organisation.

EXERCISES

34.1 You are given the following details of the Horton Hockey Club for its year to 30 June 2008:

	£
Payments:	
Teams' travel expenses	1,598
Groundsman's wages	3,891
Postage and stationery	392
Rent of pitches and clubhouse	4,800
General expenses	419
Cost of prizes for raffles	624
Receipts:	
Subscriptions	8,570
Donations	1,500
Receipts from raffles	3,816

Cash and bank balances:	£
1 July 2007	2,715
30 June 2008	4,877

You also find out that members owe £160 subscriptions on 30 June 2008. On that date, the club owed £400 for rent and £75 for wages.

You are required to draw up:

(*a*) a receipts and payments account for the year ended 30 June 2008.
(*b*) an income and expenditure account for the year ended 30 June 2008.

34.2X These are the financial details of the Superball Football Club for the year to 31 May 2006:

	£
Payments:	
Hire of transport	3,710
Ground maintenance costs	1,156
Groundsman's wages	5,214
Committee expenses	906
Costs of disco	1,112
Rent of ground	2,450
General expenses	814
Receipts:	
Members' subscriptions	8,124
Prize money for winning cup	1,000
Receipts from disco	3,149
Collections at matches	5,090

Cash and bank balances:	£
1 June 2005	905
31 May 2006	2,906

Members' subscriptions owing on 31 May 2005 amount to £160 and on 31 May 2006 to £94. On 31 May 2006 the rent had been prepaid £200, and owing were transport hire £90 and committee expenses £170.

You are required to draw up:

(*a*) a receipts and payments account for the year ended 31 May 2006.

(*b*) an income and expenditure account for the year ended 31 May 2006.

34.3 The following receipts and payments account for the year ending 31 May 2008 was prepared by the treasurer of the Down Town Sports and Social Club.

Receipts	£	*Payments*	£
Balance at bank 1 June 2007	286	Purchases of new equipment	166
Subscriptions	135	Bar stocks purchased	397
Net proceeds of jumble sale	91	Hire of rooms	64
Net proceeds of dance	122	Wages of part-time staff	198
Sale of equipment	80	Balance at bank 31 May 2008	352
Bar takings	463		
	1,177		1,177

Notes:

(i) On 1 June 2007, the club's equipment was valued at £340. Included in this total, valued at £92, was the equipment sold during the year for £80.

(ii) Bar stocks were valued as follows: 31 May 2007, £88; 31 May 2008, £101. There were no creditors for bar supplies on either of these dates.

(iii) Allow £30 for depreciation of equipment during the year ending 31 May 2008. This is additional to the loss on equipment sold during the year.

(iv) No subscriptions were outstanding at 31 May 2007, but on 31 May 2008 subscriptions due but unpaid amounted to £14.

Required (with calculations shown):

(*a*) Calculate the accumulated fund of the club as at 1 June 2007.

(*b*) Draw up the income and expenditure account of the club for the year ending 31 May 2008.

34.4X The following trial balance was extracted from the books of the Upper Harbour Sports Club at the close of business on 31 March 2008:

	Dr £	*Cr* £
Club premises	13,500	
Sports equipment	5,100	
Bar purchases and sales	9,540	15,270
Bar stocks 1 April 2007	2,190	
Balance at bank	2,790	
Subscriptions received		8,640
Accumulated fund 1 April 2007		22,290
Salary of secretary	3,600	
Wages of staff	5,280	
Postage and telephone	870	
Office furniture	1,200	
Rates and insurance	1,230	
Cash in hand	60	
Sundry expenses	840	
	46,200	46,200

Notes:
(i) All bar purchases and sales are on a cash basis. Bar stocks at 31 March 2008 were £2,460.
(ii) No subscriptions have been paid in advance but subscriptions in arrears at 31 March 2008 amounted to £90.
(iii) Rates pre-paid at 31 March 2008: £60.
(iv) Provision for depreciation as follows: sports equipment £600; office furniture £120.

Required:
Prepare the bar trading account and the income and expenditure account of the club for the year ended 31 March 2008, together with a balance sheet as on that date. For this purpose, the wages of staff £5,280 should be shown in the income and expenditure account and not the bar trading account.

34.5X On 1 June 2002 the assets and liabilities of the Hartdale Social Club, which meets during the evenings in the local village hall, were as follows:

	£
Cash at bank	1,640
Snack bar stocks	360
Equipment (cost £1,800)	1,440

During the year to 31 May 2003, the club received and paid the following amounts that are shown in the cash book summary shown below:

Cash Book Summary

Receipts	£	*Payments*	£
Subscriptions	4,230	Rent and rates	1,600
Snack bar income	4,500	Snack bar purchases	2,500
Jumble sale proceeds	823	Postage and stationery	115
Donation	50	Prizes for competitions	225
		Secretarial expenses	128
		Hi-fi equipment	2,230
		Snack bar expense	570

Notes:
(i) The snack bar stock at 31 May 2003 was valued at £420.
(ii) The equipment should be depreciated at 20% per annum using the straight line method.
(iii) Subscriptions owing at 31 May 2003 amounted to £45.

You are required to:
(*a*) calculate the accumulated fund on 1 June 2002
(*b*) calculate the amount of cash at bank on 31 May 2003
(*c*) prepare a trading account to ascertain the amount of profit made on the snack bar
(*d*) prepare an income and expenditure account for the year ended 31 May 2003 and a balance sheet as at that date.

34.6 The treasurer of a local amateur dramatic society is trying to ascertain the amount of subscriptions to transfer to the society's income and expenditure account for the year ended 31 December 2002 and asks for your help.

The following information is made available to you:

	2001	*2002*
	£	£
Subscriptions in arrears	235	185
Subscriptions in advance	220	140

In addition, you are told that the amount received from members during the year 2002 amounted to £2,600, all of which was banked immediately.

You are required to draw up the society's subscriptions account for the year ended 31 December 2002, showing clearly the amount of subscriptions to be transferred to the income and expenditure account.

34.7X Pat Hall is the treasurer of a local tennis club that has 420 members. The subscription details for the club are as follows:

Subscriptions for year to 31 December 2007 – £220 per member
Subscriptions for year to 31 December 2008 – £240 per member
Subscriptions for year to 31 December 2009 – £250 per member

On 31 December 2007, 6 members had prepaid their subscriptions for 2008. By 31 December 2008, 8 members will have prepaid their subscriptions for 2009. All other members have paid, and will continue to pay their subscriptions during the relevant year.

You are required (showing all your workings) to:

(*a*) calculate the subscriptions figure to be entered in the income and expenditure account for the year ended 31 December 2008

(*b*) calculate the total amount of money received for subscriptions during the year ended 31 December 2008.

AAT (Central Assessment)

34.8X The following items represented the assets and liabilities of the Torrevieja Club at 1 January 2006:

	£
Rent paid in advance	400
Cash at bank	800
Subscriptions in advance	1,200
Equipment	40,000
Lawn mower	600
Subscriptions in arrears	200
Insurance in arrears	100
Heating in advance	200

The Receipts and Payments Account for the year to 31 December 2006 reveals the following:

	£		£
Subscriptions	26,000	Purchase of lawn mower	1,100
Dinner and dance ticket sales	4,650	Soft drink purchases	3,600
Sale of existing lawn mower	700	Insurance	1,050
Soft drink sales	7,200	Rent	4,420
		Heating	1,450
		Dinner dance expenses	3,200

The following additional information is also available:

(i) The club depreciates its lawn mowers by 15% on those in existence at 31 December 2006.

(ii) Subscriptions in arrears at 31 December 2006 amounted to £750, whilst those in advance amounted to £590.

(iii) Unsold soft drinks at 31 December 2006 amounted to £1,400.

(iv) Dinner dance expenses in arrears at 31 December amounted to £160.

(v) Insurance paid in advance at 31 December 2006 amounted to £180.

You are required to:

(*a*) calculate the club's accumulated fund at 1 January 2006

(*b*) prepare the club's income and expenditure account for the year ended 31 December 2006.

(*c*) prepare the club's balance sheet as at 31 December 2006.

Pitman Qualifications

CHAPTER 35

Manufacturing accounts

Learning objectives

After you have studied this chapter you should be able to:

- **calculate prime cost and production costs of goods manufactured**
- **distinguish between stock of raw materials, work in progress and finished goods**
- **draw up manufacturing accounts**
- **adjust accounts in respect of work in progress.**

35.1 Manufacturing: not retailing

The accounts dealt with so far have related to retailing businesses. Now we will consider firms that are manufacturers. For these firms a **manufacturing account** is prepared in addition to the trading and profit and loss accounts.

35.2 Divisions of costs

In a manufacturing firm the costs are divided into different types. These may be summarised in chart form as shown in Exhibit 35.1.

EXHIBIT 35.1

Direct materials Direct labour Direct expenses	**Prime cost**	**Production cost**	**Total cost**
Plus			
Factory or Work overhead expenses			
Plus			
Administrative expenses Selling and distribution expenses			

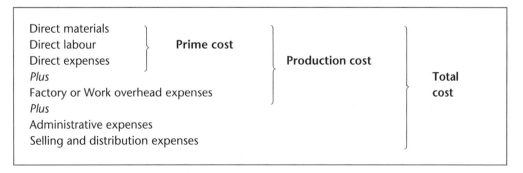

35.3 Direct and indirect costs

When you see the words **direct costs** you know that it has been possible to trace the costs of making an item being manufactured. If it cannot easily be traced to the item being manufactured, then it is an indirect expense, and will be included under factory overhead expenses (see below).

For example, the wages of a machine operator making a particular item will be direct labour. But the wages of a foreman in charge of many men on different jobs will be indirect labour and will be part of factory overhead expenses. Other instances of costs being direct costs are the cost of direct materials (which will include carriage inwards on raw materials) and the hire of special machinery for a job.

35.4 Factory overhead expenses

Factory overhead costs are all those costs that occur in the factory where production is being done but that cannot easily be traced to the items being manufactured. Examples are:

- wages of cleaners
- wages of crane drivers
- rent and rates for the factory
- depreciation of plant and machinery
- costs of operating fork-lift trucks
- factory power
- factory lighting.

35.5 Administration expenses

Administration expenses consist of such items as managers' salaries, legal and accountancy charges, the depreciation of office equipment, and secretarial salaries.

35.6 Selling and distribution expenses

Selling and distribution expenses are items such as sales staff salaries and commission, carriage outwards, depreciation of delivery vehicles, advertising, and display expenses.

35.7 Format of final accounts

Manufacturing account section

This section is debited with the production cost of goods completed during the accounting period. It contains the costs of:

- direct materials
- direct labour
- direct expenses
- factory overhead expenses.

When completed, this account will show the total of production cost. This figure will then be transferred down to the trading account.

Trading account section

This account includes:

- production cost brought down from the manufacturing account
- opening and closing stocks of finished goods
- sales.

When completed, this account will disclose the gross profit. This figure will then be carried down to the profit and loss account section of the final accounts.

The Manufacturing Account and the Trading Account can be shown in the form of a diagram - *see* Exhibit 35.2.

EXHIBIT 35.2

Manufacturing Account

	£
Production costs for the period:	
Direct materials	xxx
Direct labour	xxx
Direct expenses	xxx
Factory overhead expenses	xxx
Production cost of goods completed c/d to trading account	xxx

Trading Account

		£	£
Sales			xxx
Less Production cost of goods sold:			
Opening stock of finished goods	(A)	xxx	
Add Production costs of goods completed b/d		xxx	
		xxx	
Less Closing stock of finished goods	(B)	xxx	xxx
Gross profit			xxx

(A) is production costs of goods unsold in previous period.
(B) is production costs of goods unsold at end of the period.

Profit and loss account section

This section includes:

- gross profit brought down from the trading account
- all administration expenses
- all selling and distribution expenses.

When completed, this section of the accounts will show the net profit.

35.8 A worked example of a manufacturing account

Exhibit 35.3 shows the necessary details for a manufacturing account. It has been assumed that there were no partly completed units (known as **work in progress**) either at the beginning or end of the period.

Exhibit 35.3

Details of production cost for the year ended 31 December 2007:

	£
1 January 2007, stock of raw materials	500
31 December 2007, stock of raw materials	700
Raw materials purchased	8,000
Manufacturing (direct) wages	21,000
Royalties	150
Indirect wages	9,000
Rent of factory – excluding administration and selling and distribution blocks	440
Depreciation of plant and machinery in factory	400
General indirect expenses	310

Manufacturing Account for the year ended 31 December 2007

	£	£
Stock of raw materials 1.1.2007		500
Add Purchases		8,000
		8,500
Less Stock of raw materials 31.12.2007		700
Cost of raw materials consumed		7,800
Manufacturing wages		21,000
Royalties		150
Prime cost		28,950
Factory Overhead Expenses		
Rent	440	
Indirect wages	9,000	
General expenses	310	
Depreciation of plant and machinery	400	10,150
Production cost of goods completed c/d		39,100

Sometimes, if a firm has produced less than its customers have demanded, the firm may well have bought an outside supply of finished goods. In this case, the trading account will have both a figure for purchases and for the production cost of goods completed.

35.9 Work in progress

The production cost to be carried down to the trading account is that of production cost of goods completed during the period. If items have not been completed, they cannot be sold. Then they should not appear in the trading account.

For instance, if we have the following information, we can calculate the transfer to the trading account:

	£
Total production costs expended during the year	5,000
Production costs last year on goods not completed last year, but completed in this year (work in progress)	300
Production costs this year on goods which were not completed by the year end (work in progress)	440

The calculation is:	
Total production costs expended this year	5,000
Add Costs from last year, in respect of goods completed in this year (work in progress)	300
	5,300
Less Costs in this year, for goods to be completed next year (work in progress)	440
Production costs expended on goods completed this year	4,860

35.10 A worked example for a manufacturing account

Consider the case whose details are given in Exhibit 35.4.

EXHIBIT 35.4

	£
1 January 2007, Stock of raw materials	800
31 December 2007, Stock of raw materials	1,050
1 January 2007, Work in progress	350
31 December 2007, Work in progress	420
Year to 31 December 2007.	
Wages: Direct	3,960
Indirect	2,550
Purchase of raw materials	8,700
Fuel and power	990
Direct expenses	140
Lubricants	300
Carriage inwards on raw materials	200
Rent of factory	720
Depreciation of factory plant and machinery	420
Internal transport expenses	180
Insurance of factory buildings and plant	150
General factory expenses	330

Manufacturing Account for the year ended 31 December 2007

	£	£
Stock of raw materials 1.1.2007		800
Add Purchases		8,700
Carriage inwards		200
		9,700
Less Stock of raw materials 31.12.2007		1,050
Cost of raw materials consumed		8,650
Direct wages		3,960
Direct expenses		140
Prime cost		12,750
Factory Overhead Expenses		
Fuel and power	990	
Indirect wages	2,550	
Lubricants	300	
Rent	720	
Depreciation of plant	420	
Internal transport expenses	180	
Insurance	150	
General factory expenses	330	5,640
		18,390
Add Work in progress 1.1.2007		350
		18,740
Less Work in progress 31.12.2007		420
Production cost of goods completed c/d		18,320

The trading account is concerned with finished goods. If in Exhibit 35.4 there had been £3,500 stock of finished goods at 1 January 2007 and £4,400 at 31 December 2007, and the sales of finished goods amounted to £25,000, then the trading account would appear thus:

Trading Account for the year 31 December 2007

	£	£
Sales		25,000
Less Cost of goods sold		
Stock of finished goods 1.1.2007	3,500	
Add Production cost of goods completed b/d	18,320	
	21,820	
Less Stock of finished goods 31.12.2007	4,400	17,420
Gross profit c/d		7,580

The profit and loss account is then constructed in the normal way.

35.11 Apportionment of expenses

Quite often, expenses will have to be split between:

- Factory overhead expenses: to be charged in the manufacturing account section
- Administration expenses: }
- Selling and distribution expenses: } to be charged in the profit and loss account section

An instance of this could be the rent expense. If the rent is paid separately for each part of the organisation, then it is easy to charge the rent to each sort of expense. However, only one figure of rent might be paid, without any indication as to how much is for the factory part, how much is for the selling and distribution part and that for the administration buildings.

How the rent expense will be apportioned in the latter case will depend on circumstances, using the most equitable way of doing it. For instance, one of the following methods may be used:

- by floor area
- by property valuations of each part of the buildings and land.

35.12 Full set of final accounts: worked example

A complete worked example is now given in Exhibit 35.5. Note that in the profit and loss account the expenses have been separated so as to show whether they are administration expenses, selling and distribution expenses, or financial charges.

The trial balance in Exhibit 35.5 has been extracted from the books of J Jarvis, Toy Manufacturer, as on 31 December 2007.

EXHIBIT 35.5

J Jarvis
Trial Balance as on 31 December 2007

	Dr	*Cr*
	£	£
Stock of raw materials 1.1.2007	2,100	
Stock of finished goods 1.1.2007	3,890	
Work in progress 1.1.2007	1,350	
Wages (direct £18,000); factory indirect £14,500)	32,500	
Royalties	700	
Carriage inwards (on raw materials)	350	
Purchases of raw materials	37,000	
Productive machinery (cost £28,000)	23,000	
Accounting machinery (cost £2,000)	1,200	
General factory expenses	3,100	
Lighting	750	
Factory power	1,370	
Administrative salaries	4,400	
Salesmen's salaries	3,000	
Commission on sales	1,150	
Rent	1,200	
Insurance	420	
General administration expenses	1,340	
Bank charges	230	
Discounts allowed	480	
Carriage outwards	590	
Sales		100,000
Debtors and creditors	14,230	12,500
Bank	5,680	
Cash	150	
Drawings	2,000	
Capital as at 1.1.2007		29,680
	142,180	142,180

Notes at 31.12.2007:

(i) Stock of raw materials £2,400; stock of finished goods £4,000; work in progress £1,500.
(ii) Lighting, rent and insurance are to be apportioned: factory five-sixths, administration one-sixth.
(iii) Depreciation on productive and accounting machinery is at 10 per cent per annum on cost.

J Jarvis
Manufacturing, Trading and Profit and Loss Account
for the year ended 31 December 2007

	£	£	£
Stock of raw materials 1.1.2007			2,100
Add Purchases			37,000
Carriage inwards			350
			39,450
Less Stock raw materials 31.12.2007			2,400
Cost of raw materials consumed			37,050
Direct labour			18,000
Royalties			700
Prime cost			55,750
Factory Overhead Expenses			
General factory expenses		3,100	
Lighting ⅚ths		625	
Power		1,370	
Rent ⅚ths		1,000	
Insurance ⅚ths		350	
Depreciation of plant		2,800	
Indirect labour		14,500	23,745
			79,495
Add Work in progress 1.1.2007			1,350
			80,845
Less Work in progress 31.12.2007			1,500
Production cost of goods completed c/d			79,345
Sales			100,000
Less Cost of goods sold			
Stock of finished goods 1.1.2007		3,890	
Add Production cost of goods completed		79,345	
		83,235	
Less Stock of finished goods 31.12.2007		4,000	79,235
Gross profit			20,765
Administration Expenses			
Administrative salaries	4,400		
Rent ⅙th	200		
Insurance ⅙th	70		
General expenses	1,340		
Lighting ⅙th	125		
Depreciation of accounting machinery	200	6,335	
Selling and Distribution Expenses			
Sales representatives' salaries	3,000		
Commission on sales	1,150		
Carriage outwards	590	4,740	
Financial Charges			
Bank charges	230		
Discounts allowed	480	710	11,785
Net profit			8,980

J Jarvis
Balance Sheet as at 31 December 2007

	Cost	Total Depreciation	Net Book Value
	£	£	£
Fixed Assets			
Productive machinery	28,000	7,800	20,200
Accounting machinery	2,000	1,000	1,000
	30,000	8,800	21,200
Current Assets			
Stock:			
Raw materials	2,400		
Finished goods	4,000		
Work in progress	1,500		
Debtors	14,230		
Bank	5,680		
Cash	150	27,960	
Less Current Liabilities			
Creditors	12,500	12,500	
Net current assets			15,460
			36,660
Financed by			
Capital			
Balance as at 1.1.2007			29,680
Add Net profit			8,980
			38,660
Less Drawings			2,000
			36,660

Note: A Step-by-step guide to manufacturing accounts is shown in Appendix B Step-by-step guides, at the end of this book.

New terms

Direct costs (p. 390): Costs that can be traced to the item being manufactured.

Factory overhead costs (p. 390): Costs in the factory for production, but not traced to the item being manufactured.

Manufacturing account (p. 389): An account in which production cost is calculated.

Prime cost (p. 389): Direct materials plus direct labour plus direct expenses.

Production cost (p. 389): Prime cost plus factory overhead costs.

Total cost (p. 389): Production cost plus administration, selling and distribution expenses.

Work in progress (p. 393): Items not completed at the end of a period.

EXERCISES

35.1 From the following information, prepare the manufacturing and trading account of E Smith for the year ended 31 March 2008.

	£
Stocks at 1 April 2007:	
Finished goods	6,724
Raw materials	2,400
Work in progress	955
Carriage on purchases (raw materials)	321
Sales	69,830
Purchases of raw materials	21,340
Manufacturing wages	13,280
Factory power	6,220
Other manufacturing expenses	1,430
Factory rent and rates	2,300
Stocks at 31 March 2008	
Raw materials	2,620
Work in progress	870
Finished goods	7,230

35.2X From the following details, you are to draw up a manufacturing, trading and profit and loss account of P Lucas for the year ended 30 September 2004.

	30.9.2003	30.9.2004
	£	£
Stocks of raw materials, at cost	8,460	10,970
Work in progress	3,070	2,460
Finished goods stock	12,380	14,570

For the year:	£
Raw materials purchased	38,720
Manufacturing wages	20,970
Factory expenses	12,650
Depreciation:	
Plant and machinery	7,560
Delivery vans	3,040
Office equipment	807
Factory power	6,120
Advertising	5,080
Office and administration expenses	5,910
Sales representatives' salaries and expenses	6,420
Delivery van expenses	5,890
Sales	134,610
Carriage inwards	2,720

35.3X CCC Ltd makes ornaments, which it sells in wooden cases. The following information is made available to you in respect of the year ended 31 December 2003:

	1 Jan 2003	31 Dec 2003
	£	£
Raw materials	4,500	5,800
Wooden cases	2,250	1,920
Work-in-progress	1,250	1,900

The activities for the year ended 31 December 2003 were:	
Raw materials purchased	8,800
Purchases of wooden cases	2,250
Carriage outwards	210
Carriage inwards on raw materials	390
Wages	22,500
Salary of factory manager	1,650
Factory power	1,820
Factory rates	910
Lighting	600
Administration expenses	2,400
Salesmen's salaries	5,950

The firm completely finished the manufacture of 1,000 ornaments. All ornaments were sold immediately on completion for £80 each. In addition:

- Factory plant was valued at £100,000 on 1 January 2003. It depreciates by 20% for 2003.
- 80% of the wages are for productive workers, and 20% for factory overheads.
- 50% of the lighting is for the factory.

Required:

(*a*) Draw up a manufacturing account to disclose:
  (i) cost of raw materials used
  (ii) cost of wooden cases used
  (iii) prime cost
  (iv) factory overheads
  (v) cost of production.

(*b*) Draft the trading and profit and loss account for the year ended 31 December 2003.

(*c*) Ascertain the production cost of each boxed ornament.

(*d*) Calculate the gross profit on each boxed ornament sold.

35.4X The following balances have been extracted from the books of Tan Guat Hoon as at 31 August 2007:

	£
Stock at 1 September 2006	
Raw materials	16,300
Work in progress	21,200
Finished goods	43,100
Provision for doubtful debts at 1 September 2006	1,460
Purchases of raw materials	71,200
Returns of raw materials	700
Sales	187,300
Discounts allowed	640
Discounts received	700
Production wages	21,300
Office salaries	11,300
Production equipment (cost £60,000)	29,400
Office equipment (at cost)	5,400
Carriage on raw materials	930
Rent and rates	8,000
Heat and light	1,100
Insurance	500

The following information is also relevant at 31 August 2007:

(i) Closing stocks are:

- Raw materials £15,800
- Work in progress £20,100
- Finished goods £36,400.

(ii) The following amounts remain outstanding:

- Rent and rates £500
- Heat and light £220
- Production wages £2,600.

(iii) £100 insurance has been prepaid.

(iv) Three-quarters of insurance relates to the factory and the remainder to the office.

(v) Two-thirds of heat and light relates to the factory and the remainder to the office.

(vi) Eighty per cent of rent and rates relates to the factory and the remainder to the office.

(vii) The provision for doubtful debts is to be reduced to £1,010.

(viii) Depreciation is to be provided:

- on production equipment at 30% reducing (diminishing) balance basis
- on office equipment at 40% on cost.

You are required to:

(*a*) prepare a Manufacturing Account for the year ended 31 August 2007

(*b*) prepare a Trading, Profit and Loss Account for the year ended 31 August 2007.

Pitman Qualifications

CHAPTER 36

Partnership accounts

Learning objectives

After you have studied this chapter you should be able to:

- **understand exactly what a partnership is**
- **distinguish between limited partners and those with unlimited liability**
- **know what the main features of a partnership agreement should be**
- **realise what will happen if no agreement has been made to share profits and losses**
- **draw up capital and current accounts for the partnership**
- **draw up the final accounts of a partnership.**

36.1 The need for partnerships

So far, we have mainly considered businesses owned by only one person. Businesses set up to make a profit can often have more than one owner. There are various reasons for multiple ownership:

- The capital required is more than one person can provide.
- The experience or ability required to manage the business cannot be found in one person alone.
- Many people want to share management instead of doing everything on their own.
- Very often, members of the same family want to work together.

There are two types of multiple ownership; partnerships and limited companies. This chapter deals only with partnerships, limited companies are dealt with in Chapter 37.

36.2 Nature of a partnership

A partnership has the following characteristics:

(i) It is formed to make profits.

(ii) It must obey the law as given in the Partnership Act 1890. If there is a limited partner, as described in Section 36.3, there is the Limited Partnerships Act 1907 to comply with as well.

(iii) Normally, there can be a minimum of two and a maximum of twenty partners. Exceptions are banks, where there cannot be more than ten partners; also, there is no maximum limit for firms of accountants, solicitors, stock exchange members or other professional bodies receiving the approval of the relevant government body for this purpose.

(iv) Each partner (except for limited partners, described below) must pay his or her share of any debts that the partnership is unable to pay; they are personally liable. If necessary, partners could be forced to sell their private possessions to pay their share of any debts. This can be said to be 'unlimited' liability.

36.3 Limited partners

Limited partners are not liable for the debts in the manner described in Section 36.2 (iv) above. They have the following characteristics:

(i) Their liability for the debts of the partnership is limited to the capital they have put in. They can lose that capital, but they cannot be asked for any more money to pay the debts.

(ii) They are not allowed to take part in the management of the partnership business.

(iii) All the partners cannot be limited partners, so that there must be at least one partner with unlimited liability.

36.4 Partnership agreements

Agreements in writing are not necessary for partnerships. However, it is better if a proper written **partnership agreement** is drawn up by a lawyer or accountant, for where there is such a written agreement there will be fewer problems between partners. A written agreement means less confusion about what has been agreed.

36.5 Contents of partnership agreements

A written agreement can contain as much – or as little – as the partners want; the law does not stipulate what it must contain. Nevertheless, the usual accounting contents are:

(i) The capital to be contributed by each partner.
(ii) The ratio in which profits (or losses) are to be shared.
(iii) The rate of interest, if any, to be paid on capital before the profits are shared.
(iv) The rate of interest, if any, to be charged on partners' drawings.
(v) Salaries paid to partners.
(vi) Performance-related payments to partners.

Points (i) to (vi) in the list above are now examined in detail.

Capital contributions

Partners need not contribute equal amounts of capital. What matters is how much capital each partner *agrees* to contribute.

Profit (or loss) sharing ratios

Partners can agree to share profits/losses in any ratio or any way that they may wish. Even so, it is often thought by students that profits should be shared in the same ratio as that in which capital is contributed. For example, suppose the initial capital injections were Allen £2,000 and Beet £1,000; many people would share the profits in the ratio of two-thirds to one-third, even though the work to be done by each partner is similar. A look at the division of the first few years' profits on such a basis would be:

Years	*1*	*2*	*3*	*4*	*5*	*Total*
	£	£	£	£	£	£
Net profits	1,800	2,400	3,000	3,000	3,600	
Shared:						
Allen 2/3	1,200	1,600	2,000	2,000	2,400	9,200
Beet 1/3	600	800	1,000	1,000	1,200	4,600

It can be seen from the above table that Allen would receive £9,200, or £4,600 more than Beet. To treat each partner fairly, the difference between the two shares of profit (in this case), as the duties of the partners are the same, should be adequate to compensate Allen for putting extra capital into the firm. It is clear that £4,600 extra profits is far more than adequate for this purpose, as Allen only put in an extra £1,000 as capital.

Consider, too, the position of capital-ratio sharing of profits if one partner put in £99,000 and the other put in £1,000 as capital.

To overcome the difficulty of compensating for the investment of extra capital, the concept of interest on capital was devised.

Interest on capital

If the work to be done by each partner is of equal value but the capital contributed is unequal, it is reasonable to grant **interest on the partners' capital** input. This interest is treated as a deduction prior to the calculation of profits and the latter's distribution according to the profit-sharing ratio. The rate of interest is a matter of agreement between the partners, but it should equal the return that they would have received if they had invested the capital elsewhere.

Taking Allen and Beet's firm again, but sharing the profits equally after charging 5 per cent per annum interest on capital, the division of profits would become:

Years	*1*	*2*	*3*	*4*	*5*		*Total*
	£	*£*	*£*	*£*	*£*		*£*
Net profits	1,800	2,400	3,000	3,000	3,600		
Interest on capital							
Allen	100	100	100	100	100	=	500
Beet	50	50	50	50	50	=	250
Remainder shared:							
Allen 1/2	825	1,125	1,425	1,425	1,725	=	6,525
Beet 1/2	825	1,125	1,425	1,425	1,725	=	6,525

Summary	*Allen*	*Beet*
	£	*£*
Interest on capital	500	250
Balance of profits	6,525	6,525
	7,025	6,775

Interest on drawings

It is clearly in the best interests of the firm if cash is withdrawn from the firm by the partners in accordance with the two basic principles of: (*a*) as little as possible, and (*b*) as late as possible. The more cash that is left in the firm, the more expansion can be financed, the greater the economies of having ample cash to take advantage of bargains and of not missing cash discounts because cash is not available, and so on.

To deter the partners from taking out cash unnecessarily, the concept can be used of charging the partners **interest on each withdrawal**, calculated from the date of withdrawal to the end of the financial year. The amount charged to them helps to swell the profits divisible between the partners. The rate of interest should be sufficient to achieve this without being too harsh.

Suppose that Allen and Beet have decided to charge interest on drawings at 5 per cent per annum, that their year end is 31 December, and that the following drawings are made:

Allen

Drawings		*Interest*		*£*
1 January	£100	5% of £100 for 1 year	=	5
1 March	£240	5% of £240 for 10 months	=	10
1 May	£120	5% of £120 for 8 months	=	4
1 July	£240	5% of £240 for 6 months	=	6
1 October	£ 80	5% of £80 for 3 months	=	1
		Interest charged to Allen	=	26

Beet

Drawings		*Interest*		£
1 January	£ 60	5% of £60 for 1 year	=	3
1 August	£480	5% of £480 for 5 months	=	10
1 December	£240	5% of £240 for 1 month	=	1
		Interest charged to Beet	=	14

The interest charged to each partner would vary depending on when and how much money was taken out as drawings.

Salaries to partners

One partner may have more responsibility or tasks than others. As a reward for this, rather than change the profit and loss sharing ratio, that **partner may have a salary**, which is deducted before sharing the balance of profits.

Performance-related payments to partners

Partners may agree that commission or performance-related bonuses should be payable to some or all the partners in a way that is linked to their individual performance. As with salaries, these would be deducted before sharing the balance of profits.

36.6 An example of the distribution of profits

Taylor and Clarke have been in partnership for one year, sharing profits and losses in the ratio of Taylor three-fifths and Clarke two-fifths. They are entitled to 5 per cent per annum interest on capital, Taylor having put in £2,000 and Clarke £6,000. Clarke is to have a salary of £500. They charge interest on drawings, Taylor being charged £50 and Clarke £100. The net profit, before any distributions to the partners, amounts to £5,000 for the year ended 31 December 2004.

The results are shown in Exhibit 36.1.

EXHIBIT 36.1

	£	£	£
Net profit			5,000
Add Charged-for interest on drawings:			
Taylor		50	
Clarke		100	
			150
			5,150
Less Salary: Clarke		500	
Interest on capital (@5%)			
Taylor	100		
Clarke	300		
		400	
			900
			4,250
Balance of profits shared:			
Taylor (three-fifths)		2,550	
Clarke (two-fifths)		1,700	
			4,250

The £5,000 net profits have therefore been shared as follows:

	Taylor	*Clarke*
	£	£
Balance of profits	2,550	1,700
Interest on capital	100	300
Salary	–	500
	2,650	2,500
Less Interest on drawings	50	100
	2,600	2,400
	£5,000	

36.7 The final accounts

If the sales, stock and expenses of a partnership were exactly the same as that of a sole trader, then the trading and profit and loss account would be identical with that as prepared for the sole trader. However, a partnership would have an extra section shown under the profit and loss account. This section is called the profit and loss **appropriation account**, and it is in this account that the distribution of profits is shown. The heading to the trading and profit and loss account does not include the words 'appropriation account', and it is purely an accounting custom not to include it in the heading.

The trading and profit and loss account of Taylor and Clarke from the details given would appear as shown in Exhibit 36.2.

EXHIBIT 36.2

Taylor and Clarke
Trading and Profit and Loss Account
for the year ended 31 December 2001

(Trading Account – same as for sole trader)

			£
Profit and Loss Account – same as for sole trader)			
	£	£	£
Net profit			5,000
Interest on drawings:			
Taylor		50	
Clarke		100	150
			5,150
Less:			
Interest on capital:			
Taylor	100		
Clarke	300	400	
Salary		500	900
			4,250
Balance of profits shared:			
Taylor (three-fifths)		2,550	
Clarke (two-fifths)		1,700	4,250

36.8 Fixed and fluctuating capital accounts

There is a choice available in partnership accounts. Partnerships can operate either fixed capital accounts plus current accounts, or fluctuating capital accounts. Each option is described below, with a final comment on which is generally preferable.

Fixed capital accounts plus current accounts

With **fixed capital accounts,** the capital account for each partner remains year by year at the figure of capital put into the firm by the partners. The profits, interest on capital, and the salaries to which the partner may be entitled are then credited to a separate current account for the partner, and the drawings and the interest on drawings are debited to it. The balance of the current account at the end of each financial year will then represent the amount of undrawn (or withdrawn) profits. A credit balance will be undrawn profits, while a debit balance will be drawings in excess of the profits to which the partner is entitled.

For Taylor and Clarke, capital and current accounts, assuming drawings of £2,000 each, will appear thus:

Taylor
Capital Account

Dr						*Cr*
			2001			£
			Jan 1	Bank		2,000

Clarke
Capital Account

Dr						*Cr*
			2001			£
			Jan 1	Bank		6,000

Taylor
Current Account

Dr					*Cr*
2001		£	2001		£
Dec 31	Cash: Drawings	2,000	Dec 31	Profit and loss	
Dec 31	Profit and loss			appropriation account:	
	appropriation account:			Interest on capital	100
	Interest on drawings	50		Share of profits	2,550
Dec 31	Balance c/d	600			
		2,650			2,650
			2002		
			Jan 1	Balance b/d	600

Clarke
Current Account

Dr					*Cr*
2001		£	2001		£
Dec 31	Cash: Drawings	2,000	Dec 31	Profit and loss	
Dec 31	Profit and loss			appropriation account:	
	appropriation account:			Interest on capital	300
	Interest on drawings	100		Share of profits	1,700
Dec 31	Balance c/d	400		Salary	500
		2,500			2,500
			2002		
			Jan 1	Balance b/d	400

Notice that the salary of Clarke was not paid to him but was merely credited to his account. If in fact it was paid in addition to his drawings, the £500 cash paid would have been debited to the current account, changing the £400 credit balance into a £100 debit balance.

Examiners often ask for the capital accounts and current accounts to be shown in columnar form. For the previous accounts of Taylor and Clarke, these would appear as follows:

Capital Accounts

	Taylor	*Clarke*			*Taylor*	*Clarke*
	£	£	2001		£	£
			Jan 1	Bank	2,000	6,000

Current Accounts

		Taylor	Clarke			Taylor	Clarke
2001		£	£	2001		£	£
Dec 31	Cash: Drawings	2,000	2,000	Dec 31	Interest on capital	100	300
Dec 31	Interest on drawings	50	100	Dec 31	Share of profits	2,550	1,700
				Dec 31	Salary		500
Dec 31	Balances c/d	600	400				
		2,650	2,500			2,650	2,500
				2002			
				Jan 1	Balances b/d	600	400

Fluctuating capital accounts

In this arrangement of **fluctuating capital accounts** the distribution of profits would be credited to the capital account, and the drawings and interest on drawings is debited. Therefore, the balance on the capital account will change each year, i.e. it will fluctuate.

If fluctuating capital accounts had been kept for Taylor and Clarke, they would have appeared:

Taylor
Capital Account

Dr					*Cr*
2001		£	2001		£
Dec 31	Cash: Drawings	2,000	Jan 1	Bank	2,000
Dec 31	Profit and loss appropriation account: Interest on drawings	50	Dec 31	Profit and loss appropriation account: Interest on capital	100
Dec 31	Balance c/d	2,600		Share of profits	2,550
		4,650			4,650
			2002		
			Jan 1	Balance b/d	2,600

Clarke
Capital Account

Dr					*Cr*
2001		£	2001		£
Dec 31	Cash: Drawings	2,000	Jan 1	Bank	6,000
Dec 31	Profit and loss appropriation account: Interest on drawings	100	Dec 31	Profit and loss appropriation account: Interest on capital	300
Dec 31	Balance c/d	6,400		Salary	500
				Share of profits	1,700
		8,500			8,500
			2002		
			Jan 1	Balance b/d	6,400

Fixed capital accounts preferred

The keeping of fixed capital accounts plus current accounts is considered preferable to operating fluctuating capital accounts. When partners are taking out greater amounts than the share of the profits that they are entitled to, this is shown up by a debit balance on the current account and so acts as a warning.

36.9 Where no partnership agreement exists

Where no formal partnership agreement exists - either express or implied - section 24 of the Partnership Act 1890 governs the situation. The accounting content of this section states:

- Profits and losses are to be shared equally.
- There is to be no interest allowed on capital.
- No interest is to be charged on drawings.
- Salaries are not allowed.
- If a partner puts a sum of money into a firm in excess of the capital he or she has agreed to subscribe, that partner is entitled to interest at the rate of 5 per cent per annum on such an advance.

This section applies where there is no agreement. There may be an agreement not by a partnership deed but in a letter, or it may be implied by conduct - for instance, when a partner signs a balance sheet that shows profits shared in some ratio other than equally. Where a dispute arises as to whether agreement exists or not, and this cannot be resolved by the partners, only the courts will be competent to decide.

36.10 The balance sheet

The capital side of the balance sheet will appear as follows for our example. Note that figures in brackets, e.g. '(2,000)', is an accounting convention indicating a negative amount.

Balance Sheet as at 31 December 2001

			£	£
Capital accounts	Taylor		2,000	
	Clarke		6,000	
				8,000
Current accounts	*Taylor*	*Clarke*		
	£	£		
Interest on capital	100	300		
Share of profits	2,550	1,700		
Salary	–	500		
	2,650	2,500		
Less Drawings	(2,000)	(2,000)		
Interest on drawings	(50)	(100)		
	(2,050)	(2,100)		
	600	400		
				1,000

If one of the current accounts had finished in debit – for instance, if the current account of Clarke had finished up as £400 debit – the figure of £400 would appear in brackets and the balances would appear net in the totals column:

	Taylor	*Clarke*	
	£	£	£
Closing balance	600	(400)	200

If the net figure, e.g. the £200 just shown, turned out to be a debit figure, then this would be deducted from the total of the fixed capital accounts.

36.11 A fully worked exercise

We can now look at a fully worked exercise covering nearly all the main points shown in this chapter.

Luty and Minchin are in partnership. They share profits in the ratio: Luty three-fifths to Minchin two-fifths. The following trial balance was extracted as at 31 March 2004:

Trial balance as on 31 March 2004

	Dr	Cr
	£	£
Office equipment at cost	6,500	
Motor vehicles at cost	9,200	
Provision for depreciation at 31.3.2003:		
Motor vehicles		3,680
Office equipment		1,950
Stock at 31 March 2003	24,970	
Debtors and creditors	20,960	16,275
Cash at bank	615	
Cash in hand	140	
Sales		90,370
Purchases	71,630	
Salaries	8,417	
Office expenses	1,370	
Discounts allowed	563	
Current accounts at 31.3.2003:		
Luty		1,379
Minchin		1,211
Capital accounts:		
Luty		27,000
Minchin		12,000
Drawings:		
Luty	5,500	
Minchin	4,000	
	153,865	153,865

A set of final accounts for the year ended 31 March 2004 for the partnership are to be drawn up. The following notes are applicable at 31 March 2004:

(i) Stock at 31 March 2004 was valued at £27,340.
(ii) Office expenses owing £110.
(iii) Provision for depreciation: motor vehicles 20 per cent of cost, office equipment 10 per cent of cost.
(iv) Charge interest on capital at 10 per cent.
(v) Charge interest on drawings: Luty £180; Minchin £210.
(vi) Charge £500 for salary for Minchin.

The final accounts then look as set out in Exhibit 36.3.

EXHIBIT 36.3

Luty and Minchin
Trading and Profit and Loss Account
for the year ended 31 March 2004

	£	£	£
Sales			90,370
Less Cost of goods sold:			
Opening stock		24,970	
Add Purchases		71,630	
		96,600	
Less Closing stock		27,340	69,260
Gross profit			21,110
Less Expenses:			
Salaries*		8,417	
Office expenses (1,370 + 110)		1,480	
Discounts allowed		563	
Depreciation: Motor vehicles	1,840		
Office equipment	650	2,490	12,950
Net profit			8,160
Add Interest on drawings: Luty		180	
Minchin		210	390
			8,550
Less Interest on capital: Luty	2,700		
Minchin	1,200	3,900	
Less Salary: Minchin		500	4,400
			4,150
Balance of profits shared: Luty (three-fifths)		2,490	
Minchin (two-fifths)		1,660	4,150

**Does not include partner's salary.*

Luty and Minchin
Balance Sheet as at 31 March 2004

		Cost		*Depreciation*	*NBV*
Fixed Assets		£		£	£
Office equipment		6,500		2,600	3,900
Motor vehicles		9,200		5,520	3,680
		15,700		8,120	7,580
Current assets					
Stock				27,340	
Debtors				20,960	
Bank				615	
Cash				140	
				49,055	
Less Current Liabilities					
Creditors		16,275			
Expenses owing		110		16,385	
Net Current assets					32,670
					40,250
Capital					
Luty				27,000	
Minchin				12,000	39,000
Current accounts		*Luty*		*Minchin*	
Balances 1.4.2003		1,379		1,211	
Add Interest on capital		2,700		1,200	
Add Salary				500	
Add Share of profits		2,490		1,660	
		6,569		4,571	
Less Drawings	5,500		4,000		
Less Interest on drawings	180	5,680	210	4,210	
Balances 31.3.2004		889		361	1,250
					40,250

New terms

Appropriation Account (p. 408): An addition to the profit and loss account of a partnership or company. The appropriation account shows how profit earned is divided. In a partnership it is divided in accordance with the partnership deed or agreement. With a company it is apportioned to reserve accounts or provisions for taxation, and distributed as a dividend to the shareholders.

Fixed capital accounts (p. 409): Capital accounts that consist only of the original capital invested in the business.

Fluctuating capital accounts (p. 409): Capital accounts whose balances change from one period to the next.

Interest on capital (p. 405): An amount, based on an agreed rate, that is credited to a partner based on the amount of capital contributed by him or her.

Interest on drawings (p. 406): An amount, based on an agreed rate of interest, that is based on the drawings taken out, and is debited to the partners.

Limited partner (p. 404): A partner whose liability is limited to the capital invested in the firm.

Partnership agreement (p. 404): The contractual relationship - either written or verbal - between partners, which usually covers details such as how profits or losses should be shared and the relevant responsibilities of the partners.

Partnership salaries (p. 407): Agreed amounts payable to partners in respect of duties undertaken by them.

EXERCISES

36.1 Stead and Jackson are partners in a retail business in which they share profits and losses equally. The balance on the partners' capital and current accounts at the year end 31 December 2002 were as follows:

	Capital Account	*Current Account*
	£	£
Stead	24,000	2,300 Cr
Jackson	16,000	3,500 Cr

During the year, Stead had drawings amounting to £15,000 and Jackson £19,000. Jackson was to receive a partnership salary of £5,000 for extra duties undertaken. The net profit of the partnership, before taking any of the above into account, was £45,000.

You are required to:

(*a*) draw up the appropriation account for the partnership for the year ended 31 December 2002

(*b*) show the partners' capital and current accounts.

36.2X Wain, Brown and Cairns own a garage, and the partners share profits and losses in the ratio of Wain 50 per cent, Brown 30 per cent and Cairns 20 per cent. Their financial year end is 31 March 2004 and the following details were extracted from their books on that date:

	Wain £	*Brown* £	*Cairns* £
Capital account balances	30,000	50,000	70,000
Current account balances	2,400 Cr	3,100 Cr	5,700 Cr
Partnership salaries	10,000	8,000	–
Drawings	12,000	15,050	14,980

The net profit for the year ended 31 March 2004 amounted to £60,000 before taking any of the above into account.

You are required to:
(*a*) prepare an appropriation account for the year ended 31 March 2004
(*b*) draw up the partners' capital and current accounts in columnar form for the year ended 31 March 2004.

36.3X The following balances were extracted from the books of Bradford and Taylor as at 31 December 2007:

	£
Capital accounts	
Bradford	40,000
Taylor	30,000
Current accounts	
Bradford	3,450 Cr
Taylor	2,680 Dr
Drawings	
Bradford	8,000
Taylor	12,000
Net profit for the year	44,775

The following information is also available from their partnership agreement:
(i) The partners are entitled to receive 5% interest on capital.
(ii) Taylor is to receive a partnership salary of £6,000.
(iii) Interest is to be charged on drawings as follows: Bradford £200; Taylor £125.
(iv) Bradford and Taylor are to share profits and losses in the ratio 3:2.

Required:
(*a*) Show the profit and loss appropriation account for the year ended 31 December 2007.
(*b*) Show the partners' capital and current accounts for the year ended 31 December 2007.
(*c*) Show how the profits and losses would be distributed and how much each partner would receive if there was no partnership agreement.

36.4 Simpson and Young are in partnership, sharing profits and losses in the ratio 3:2. At the close of business on 30 June 2003 the following trial balance was extracted from their books:

		Dr £	*Cr* £
Premises at cost		28,000	
Motor vans (cost £16,000)		11,000	
Office equipment (cost £8,400)		5,600	
Stock 1 July 2002		18,000	
Purchases		184,980	
Sales			254,520
Wages and salaries		32,700	
Rent, rates and insurance		3,550	
Electricity		980	
Stationery and printing		420	
Motor expenses		3,480	
General office expenses		1,700	
Debtors and creditors		28,000	15,200
Capital accounts:	Simpson		50,000
	Young		20,000
Drawings:	Simpson	10,000	
	Young	5,000	
Current accounts:	Simpson		640
	Young		300
Cash at bank		7,250	
		340,660	340,660

Notes:

(i) Interest is to be allowed on capital accounts at the rate of 10% per annum, and no interest is to be charged on drawings.

(ii) Rates prepaid at 30 June 2003 amount to £250.

(iii) Wages due at 30 June 2003 are £500.

(iv) Provision for depreciation is as follows: motor van at 20% per annum on cost; office equipment at 10% using the reducing balance method.

(v) Stock 30 June 2003 was valued at £19,000.

Required:

Prepare the trading and profit and loss appropriation account for the year ended 30 June 2003, and a balance sheet as at that date.

36.5X Kirkham and Keeling are in partnership, sharing profits and losses in the ratio of 3:2. Their partnership agreement also provides for interest on capital to be given to the partners at 10% per annum, but no interest may be charged on drawings. The following trial balance was drawn up at the end of the financial year:

Trial Balance of Kirkham and Keeling as at 30 June 2005

		£	£
Premises		59,200	
Motor vehicles (cost £30,000)		24,000	
Computer equipment (cost £12,000 at 1.7.2003)		8,000	
Cash at bank		12,500	
Debtors		56,000	
Creditors			30,400
Sales			509,040
Purchases		369,960	
Stock 1 July 2004		36,000	
Salaries		65,400	
Electricity		1,960	
Telephone		840	
Motor expenses		3,960	
Printing, stationery and advertising		3,000	
Rates and insurance		7,100	
General expenses		3,400	
Capital accounts:	Kirkham		100,000
	Keeling		40,000
Current accounts:	Kirkham		1,280
	Keeling		600
Drawings:	Kirkham	20,000	
	Keeling	10,000	
		681,320	681,320

Notes:

(i) The closing stock has been valued at £38,000.

(ii) Insurance paid in advance at 30 June 2005 amounted to £1,000.

(iii) Motor expenses owing at 30 June 2005 amounted to £400.

(iv) You are to provide for depreciation on the motor vehicles at 20% on cost. The computer equipment is expected to last three years from the date of purchase.

You are required to prepare the trading and profit and loss appropriation account for the year ended 30 June 2005 and a balance sheet as at that date.

36.6X Bhayani and Donnell are in partnership, sharing profits and losses in the ratio 2:1. The following trial balance was extracted after the preparation of their trading account for the year ended 31 December:

		Dr £	*Cr* £
Provision for depreciation: Vehicles			3,000
Provision for depreciation: Fittings			2,000
Bank balance			950
Drawings:	Bhayani	2,000	
	Donnell	600	
Vehicles (at cost)		35,000	
Fittings (at cost)		12,000	
Premises (at cost)		20,000	
Rent received			500
Debtors and creditors		25,700	15,600
Current accounts:	Bhayani	600	
	Donnell	nil	nil
Provision for doubtful debts			950
Gross profit			32,000
Heating and lighting		1,400	
Wages and salaries		4,100	
Cash		600	
Capital accounts:	Bhayani		35,000
	Donnell		12,000
		102,000	102,000

At 31 December the following information needs to be taken into consideration:

(i) The provision for doubtful debts is to be maintained at 3% of debtors.
(ii) Rent received of £100 has been paid in advance.
(iii) A heating invoice of £100 has yet to be paid.
(iv) £200 of wages have been prepaid.
(v) Depreciation needs to be provided for on the following basis:
- vehicles at 10% straight line method
- fittings at 15% reducing (diminishing) balance method.

(vi) The partnership agreement provides for the following:
- interest on drawings is charged at 6% per annum
- interest on capital is allowed at 8% per annum
- Donnell is to receive a salary of £3,263.

You are required to:

(*a*) prepare the partnership profit and loss account for the year ended 31 December
(*b*) prepare the partnership appropriation account for the year ended 31 December
(*c*) prepare each partner's current account at 31 December
(*d*) prepare the partnership balance sheet as at 31 December.

Pitman Qualifications

CHAPTER 37

Limited company accounts

Learning objectives

After you have studied this chapter you should be able to:

- understand how limited companies differ from other organisations
- calculate how distributable profits available for dividends are divided between the different classes of shares
- realise the differences between shares and debentures
- draw up the trading and profit and loss accounts for a limited company
- draw up a balance sheet for a limited company.

37.1 Introduction

This chapter looks at further ways of owning a business other than the arrangements of sole traders and partnerships. When a business needs to expand, additional capital will probably be needed, and forming a limited company makes it possible to raise more funds for the expansion.

37.2 Limited companies

Limited companies are formed because of the advantages they provide over the status of partnerships.

The previous chapter has stated the terms under which a partnership operates. Briefly, a partnership can have no more than 20 owners, not counting limited partners. In addition, if a partnership fails, a partner is responsible for the business assets and could lose all or part of privately owned assets. In contrast, a public limited company can have as many owners as it wants and each owner cannot lose more than the amount invested in the company. No private assets can be lost.

The law governing the preparation and publication of the final accounts of limited companies in the United Kingdom is contained in two Acts of Parliament. These are the Companies Acts of 1985 and 1989. Both Acts are in force for this purpose, the 1989 Act adding to and amending the 1985 Act.

37.3 Limited liability

The capital of a limited company is divided into **shares**. These can be shares of £1 each, £5 each, £10 each or any other amount per share. To become a member of a limited company – a **shareholder** – a person must buy one or more of the shares.

If a shareholder has paid in full for the shares, his liability is limited to those shares. If a company loses all its assets, all the shareholder can lose is his shares. He cannot be forced to pay anything out of his private money in respect of the company's losses. If a shareholder has only partly paid for the shares, he can be forced to pay the balance owing on the shares. Apart from that, he cannot be forced to pay out of his private money for the company's losses.

This is known as **limited liability** and the company is known as a **limited company**. You can see that these fit the need for organisations needing limited liability for their owners where it is also possible to have a large amount of capital.

37.4 Public and private companies

There are two classes of company, the public company and the private company. In the United Kingdom, private companies far outnumber public companies.

In the Companies Acts, a public company is defined as one that fulfils the following conditions:

- Its Memorandum of Association (*see* Section 37.5 below) states that it is a public company, and has registered as such.
- It has an authorised share capital of at least £50,000.
- Minimum membership is two; there is no maximum.
- Its name must end with the words 'public limited company', or its abbreviation 'plc'.

A private company is usually – but not always – a smaller business, and may be formed by one or more persons. It is defined by the Companies Act as a company that is not a public company. The main differences between a private company and a public company are that a private company:

- can have an authorised capital of less than £50,000
- cannot offer its shares for subscription to the public at large (whereas public companies can).

37.5 Legal status of a limited company

The most important feature of a limited company is its status in law as a 'separate legal entity'. This means that no matter how many individuals have bought its shares, it is treated in its dealings with the outside world as if it were a 'person' in its own right.

When a limited company is formed, it is required by law to raise two documents known as the Memorandum of Association and the Articles of Association. The first document sets down the details of the company and its objectives, while the Articles of Association state the regulations concerning the powers of the directors. These regulations are of the utmost importance when it is realised that the legal owners of the business, namely the shareholders, have entrusted the running of the company to the directors.

37.6 Company directors

A shareholder normally has the right to attend the general meetings of a company, and can vote at such meetings. Shareholders use their votes to appoint **directors** who manage the business on behalf of the shareholders.

At each **Annual General Meeting**, the final accounts for the year are given to the shareholders. The directors at the meeting have to give a report about the performance made by the company.

37.7 Share capital and dividends

The term 'share capital' refers to:

(*a*) **Authorised share capital** - the total of the share capital that the company would be allowed to issue (as stated in the Memorandum of Association); also called 'nominal capital'.

(*b*) **Issued share capital** - the amount of share capital actually issued to shareholders.

(*c*) **Called-up capital** - where only part of the amounts payable on each share has been asked for; the total amount requested on all the shares is known as the 'called-up capital'.

(*d*) **Uncalled capital** - the amount that is to be received in future, but which has not yet been requested.

(*e*) **Calls in arrear** - the amount for which payment has been requested (i.e. called for), but has not yet been paid by shareholders.

(*f*) **Paid-up capital** - the total of the amount of share capital that has been paid for by shareholders.

If all of the authorised share capital has been issued, then items (*a*) and (*b*) above are the same.

Example 1 below illustrates these different meanings.

Example 1: Better Enterprises Ltd was formed with the legal right to be able to issue 100,000 shares of £1 each. The company has actually issued 75,000 shares. None of the shares has yet been fully paid-up; so far the company has made calls of 80p (£0.80) per share. All of the calls have been paid by shareholders, except for £200 owing from one particular shareholder. On this basis, therefore:

(*a*) Authorised (or nominal) share capital is £100,000.
(*b*) Issued share capital is £75,000.
(*c*) Called-up capital is (75,000 × £0.80) = £60,000.
(*d*) Calls in arrear amounted to £200.
(*e*) Paid-up capital is £60,000 less (*d*) £200 = £59,800.

When a company makes a profit, the directors will have to decide how this is to be used. They will probably retain part of the profit as reserves, which will be used to grow the business. The remaining part is likely to be used to reward the shareholders for investing in the company. This share of the profits is known as the **dividend.**

The dividend is usually shown as a percentage. A dividend of 10 per cent in Firm A on 500,000 ordinary shares of £1 each will amount to £50,000. A dividend of 6 per cent in Firm B on 200,000 ordinary shares of £2 each will amount to £24,000. A shareholder having 100 shares in each firm would receive £10 from Firm A and £12 from Firm B.

There are two main types of shares:

- **Preference shares** Preference shareholders get an agreed percentage rate of dividend before the ordinary shareholders receive anything.
- **Ordinary shares** Ordinary shareholders receive the remainder of the total profits available for dividends. There is no upper limit to the amounts of dividends they can receive.

For example, if a company had 10,000 5-per-cent preference shares of £1 each and 20,000 ordinary shares of £1 each, then the dividends would be payable as in Exhibit 37.1.

EXHIBIT 37.1

Year	*1*	*2*	*3*	*4*	*5*
	£	£	£	£	£
Profits appropriated for dividends	900	1,300	1,600	3,100	2,000
Preference dividends	(5%) 500	500	500	500	500
Ordinary dividends	(2%) 400	(4%) 800	(5½%) 1,100	(13%) 2,600	(7½%) 1,500

It can be seen that preference shareholders receive a fixed amount of dividend each year, whilst the ordinary shareholders receive a variable amount depending on the performance of the company. The profit level in Year 4 was very good and the ordinary shareholders received a substantial 13% dividend.

There are two main types of preference shares:

- Non-cumulative shares.
- Cumulative shares.

The description of the shares refers to their differing rights for the payment of dividends, but you do not require further knowledge of these at this stage.

37.8 Debentures

The term **debenture** is used when a limited company receives money on loan, and certificates called 'debenture certificates' are issued to the lender. Interest will be paid to the holder of the debenture, the rate of interest being shown on the certificate. **Debenture interest** has to be paid irrespective of whether the company makes a profit. Debentures are, therefore, different from shares, where dividends depend on profits being made.

37.9 Trading and profit and loss accounts

The trading and profit and loss accounts are drawn up in exactly the same way for both private and public companies.

The trading account of a limited company is no different from that of a sole trader or a partnership. However, some differences may be found in the profit and loss account. The two main expenses that would be found only in company accounts are directors' remuneration and any debenture interest.

Directors' remuneration

As directors exist only in companies, this type of expense is found only in company accounts.

Directors are, in legal terms, employees of the company, appointed by the shareholders. **Directors' remuneration** is charged to the main profit and loss account.

Debenture interest

The interest payable for the use of the money is an expense of the company and is payable whether profits are made or not. This means that debenture interest is charged as an expense in the profit and loss account itself. Contrast this with dividends, which are dependent on profits having been made (see above Sections 37.7 and 37.8).

37.10 The appropriation account

There is a section under the profit and loss account called the profit and loss appropriation account (*see* Section 36.7). The appropriation account shows how the net profits are to be appropriated, i.e. how the profits are to be used.

We may find any of the following in the appropriation account:

Credit side

(*a*) *Net profit for the year* This is the net profit brought down from the main profit and loss account.

(*b*) *Balance brought forward from last year* As you will see, all the profits may not be appropriated during a period. This will be the balance on the appropriation account, as brought forward from the previous year. They are usually called **retained profits.**

Debit side

(*c*) *Transfers to reserves* The directors may decide that some of the profits should not be included in the calculation of how much should be paid out as dividends. These profits are transferred to **reserve accounts.** There may be a specific reason for the transfer, such as a need to replace fixed assets; in this case an amount would be transferred to a fixed assets replacement reserve account. Alternatively, the reason may not be specific, and in this case an amount would be transferred to a general reserve account.

(*d*) *Amounts of goodwill written off* Any amounts written off as goodwill should be shown in the appropriation account and not in the main profit and loss account.

(*e*) *Amounts of* ***preliminary expenses*** *written off* When a company is formed, there are many kinds of expenses concerned with its formation. These include, for example, legal expenses and various government taxes. The amount of preliminary expenses can be written off and charged in the appropriation account.

(*f*) *Taxation payable on profits* As taxation is not in your syllabus, we will not examine it here.

(*g*) *Dividends* Out of the remainder of the profits, the directors propose what dividends should be paid.

(*h*) *Balance carried forward to next year* After the dividends have been proposed, there will probably be some profits that have not been appropriated. These retained profits will be carried forward to the following year.

Exhibit 37.2 shows the profit and loss appropriation account of a new business for its first three years of trading.

EXHIBIT 37.2

IDO Ltd has a share capital of 40,000 ordinary shares of £1 each and 20,000 5-per-cent preference shares of £1 each.

- The net profits for the first three years of business ended 31 December are: 2004 £5,967; 2005 £7,864; 2006 £8,822.
- Transfers to reserves are made as follows: 2004 nil; 2005 general reserve £1,000; 2006, fixed assets replacement reserve £1,500.
- Dividends were proposed for each year on the preference shares and on the ordinary shares at: 2004 10 per cent; 2005 12.5 per cent; 2006 15 per cent.
- In 2006, £750 was written off as goodwill.

Thus we have:

IDO Ltd
Profit and Loss Appropriation Accounts
(1) For the year ended 31 December 2004

		£	£
Net profit b/d			5,967
Less:	Appropriations:		
	Proposed dividends:		
	5% Preference dividend (£20,000 x 5%)	1,000	
	Ordinary dividend (£40,000 x 10%)	4,000	5,000
Retained profits carried forward to next year			967

(2) For the year ended 31 December 2005

		£	£
Net profit b/d			7,864
Add	Retained profits brought forward from last year		967
			8,831
Less	Appropriations:		
	Transfer to general reserve	1,000	
	Proposed dividends:		
	5% Preference dividend (£20,000 x 5%)	1,000	
	Ordinary dividend (£40,000 x 12.5%)	5,000	7,000
Retained profits carried forward to next year			1,831

(3) For the year ended 31 December 2006

		£	£
Net profit b/d			8,822
Add	Retained profits brought forward from last year		1,831
			10,653
Less	Appropriations:		
	Transfer to fixed assets replacement reserve	1,500	
	Goodwill written off	750	
	Proposed dividends:		
	5% Preference dividend (£20,000 x 5%)	1,000	
	Ordinary dividend (£40,000 x 15%)	6,000	9,250
Retained profits carried forward to next year			1,403

The reserves mentioned in this chapter are all classed as **revenue reserves**, there are, however, other reserves, such as the 'share premium account', that are classed as a '**capital reserve**'. These topics fall outside the scope of this book, and students are advised to refer to *Business Accounting 1* for further details.

37.11 The balance sheet

Prior to the Companies Act 1981 in the United Kingdom, a company could, provided it disclosed the necessary information, draw up its balance sheet and profit and loss account for publication in any way that it wished. The 1981 Act, however, stopped such freedom of display, and laid down the precise details to be shown. These have been repeated in the Companies Acts of 1985 and 1989.

As many of the readers of this book will not be sitting UK examinations, they will not have to comply with the UK Companies Acts. We are, therefore, showing two specimen balance sheets containing the same facts:

- Exhibit 37.3 is for students sitting examinations based on UK laws. The specimen shown does not contain all the possible items that could be shown, as this chapter is an introduction to the topic only. Students are advised to refer to *Business Accounting 1* and *2* for greater insight.

- Exhibit 37.4 is for students sitting local overseas examinations not based on UK legislation.

EXHIBIT 37.3

Balance Sheet as at 31 December 2007

Letters in brackets (A) to (F) refer to the notes following the balance sheet

		£	£	£
Fixed assets				
Intangible assets	(A)			
Goodwill			10,000	
Tangible assets	(B)			
Buildings		9,000		
Machinery		5,600		
Motor vehicles		2,400	17,000	27,000
Current assets				
Stock		6,000		
Debtors		3,000		
Bank		4,000	13,000	
Creditors: Amounts falling due within one year	(C)			
Proposed dividend		1,000		
Creditors		5,000	6,000	
Net current assets	(D)			7,000
Total assets less current liabilities				34,000
Creditors: amounts falling due after more than one year	(E)			
Debenture loans				8,000
				26,000
Capital and reserves				
Called-up share capital	(F)			20,000
Other reserves				
General reserve				5,000
Profit and loss account				1,000
				26,000

Notes:

(A) Intangible assets are those not having a 'physical' existence; for instance, you can see and touch tangible assets under (B), i.e. buildings, machinery etc., but you cannot see and touch goodwill.

(B) Tangible fixed assets under a separate heading. Notice that figures are shown net of depreciation. In a note accompanying the accounts, the cost and depreciation on these assets would be given.

(C) Only items payable within one year go under this heading.

(D) The term 'net current assets' replaces the more familiar term of 'working capital'.

(E) These particular debentures are repayable several years hence. If they had been payable within one year, they would have been shown under (C).

(F) An analysis of share capital will be given in supplementary notes to the balance sheet.

Exhibit 37.4

Balance Sheet as at 31 December 2007

		Cost	Depreciation to date (b)	Net
Fixed assets	(*a*)	£	£	£
Goodwill		15,000	5,000	10,000
Buildings		15,000	6,000	9,000
Machinery		8,000	2,400	5,600
Motor vehicles		4,000	1,600	2,400
		42,000	15,000	27,000
Current assets				
Stock			6,000	
Debtors			3,000	
Bank			4,000	
			13,000	
Less Current liabilities				
Proposed dividend		1,000		
Creditors		5,000	6,000	
Working capital				7,000
				34,000
Financed by:				
Share capital				
Authorised 30,000 shares of £1 each	(*c*)			30,000
Issued 20,000 ordinary shares of £1 each, fully paid	(*d*)			20,000
Reserves	(*e*)			
General reserve			5,000	
Profit and loss account			1,000	
				6,000
	(*f*)			26,000
Debentures				
Six per cent debentures: repayable 2010				8,000
				34,000

Notes:

(*a*) Fixed assets should normally be shown either at cost or, alternatively, at some other valuation. In either case, the method chosen should be clearly stated.

(*b*) The total depreciation from date of purchase to the date of the balance sheet should be shown.

(*c*) The authorised share capital, where it is different from the issued share capital, is shown as a note.

(*d*) Where shares are only partly called up, then it is the amount actually called up that appears in the balance sheet and not the full amount.

(*e*) Reserves consist either of those unused profits remaining in the appropriation account, or those transferred to a reserve account appropriately title e.g. general reserve, fixed assets replacement reserve. At this point, all that needs to be said is that any account labelled as a reserve has originated by being charged as a debit in the appropriation account and credited to a reserve account with an appropriate title. These reserves are shown in the balance sheet after share capital under the heading of 'Reserves'.

(*f*) The share capital and reserves should be totalled so as to show the book value of all the shares in the company. Either the term 'shareholders' funds' or 'members' equity' is often given to the total of share capital plus reserves.

37.12 Investments

Where a company buys shares in another company as an investment, the investment is shown as an asset in the balance sheet. It is shown as a separate item in the accounts between the fixed assets and the current assets.

The market value of such investments is shown in the balance sheet as a note in brackets, e.g.

Balance Sheet (Extracts)

	£
Investments at cost (market value £10,000)	7,500

In the above case, the market value is above cost. If the market value falls below cost, then the difference is written off to the debit of the profit and loss appropriation account, so that the balance sheet will then show the investment at the written-down figure.

37.13 Revaluation of land and buildings

When there is a surplus on revaluation, the value of land and buildings in the balance sheet is shown at the higher figure. The amount of surplus cannot be used for the payment of cash dividends and is therefore shown as an addition to reserves in the balance sheet. It must be described as, for example, 'surplus on revaluation of land and buildings'.

37.14 Loan capital

The term **loan capital** includes money owing on debentures, and loans from banks and other sources not repayable in the near future.

37.15 A full example of the final accounts

Two examples of a limited company's final accounts are now shown as Exhibits 37.5 and 37.6. They contain most types of accounts that will be found in a company final accounts. Exhibit 37.6 contains a more complicated example including preference shares and debentures.

EXHIBIT 37.5

The following trial balance is extracted from the books of an imaginary company called Ashford Ltd as at 31 December 2006:

Ashford Ltd
Trial Balance as at 31 December 2006

	Dr	Cr
	£	£
Ordinary share capital		150,000
Premises at cost	97,500	
Equipment at cost	82,500	
Provision for depreciation on equipment as at 31.12.05		23,700
Purchases	302,547	
Sales		475,215
Wages and salaries	61,310	
Directors' remuneration	20,000	
General expenses	48,252	
Rates and insurance	6,450	
Electricity	2,324	
Bad debts	1,122	
Provision for bad debts 31.12.05		1,291
Debtors	32,676	
Creditors		26,240
Stock as at 1.1.06	38,534	
Bank	34,651	
Profit and loss account unappropriated profits as at 31.12.05		51,420
	727,866	727,866

The following adjustments are needed:

(i) The authorised and issued share capital is divided into 150,000 shares of £1 each.
(ii) Stock in trade at 31 December 2006 is valued at £43,713.
(iii) Wages and salaries due at 31 December 2006 amount to £872.
(iv) Rates and insurance paid in advance at 31 December 2006 amount to £450.
(v) A dividend of 10% is proposed for 2006 on the ordinary shares.
(vi) The provision for doubtful debts is to be increased to £1,407.
(vii) A depreciation charge is to be made on equipment at the rate of 10 per cent per annum on cost.
(viii) Transfer £10,000 to a general reserve account.

The final accounts will now be shown using a vertical form. The profit and loss account will be suitable for both those sitting UK examinations, and those sitting local overseas examinations; the balance sheets will be shown separately for both kinds of students.

Ashford Ltd
Trading and Profit and Loss and Appropriation Account
for the year ended 31 December 2006
(suitable for both UK and overseas examinations)

		£	£
Sales			475,215
Less	*Cost of goods sold*:		
	Opening stock	38,534	
	Add Purchases	302,547	
		341,081	
	Less Closing stock	43,713	297,368
Gross profit			177,847
Less	*Expenses*:		
	Salaries and wages (61,310 + 872)	62,182	
	Directors' remuneration	(A) 20,000	
	General expenses	48,252	
	Rates and insurance (6,450 - 450)	6,000	
	Electricity	2,324	
	Bad debts	1,122	
	Increase in provision for bad debts (1,407 - 1,291)	116	
	Depreciation: Equipment	8,250	148,246
Net profit			29,601
Add	Unappropriated profits brought forward from last year		51,420
			81,021
Less	*Appropriations*:		
	Transfer to general reserve	10,000	
	Ordinary share dividends (10% of 150,000)	(B) 15,000	25,000
Unappropriated profits carried forward to next year			56,021

Notes:
(A) Directors' remuneration is shown as an expense in the profit and loss account.
(B) The dividend of 10 per cent is based on the issued ordinary share capital.

Ashford Ltd
Balance Sheet as at 31 December 2006
(based on UK legislation)

		Cost	Depreciation to date (b)	Net Book Value
Fixed assets		£	£	£
Tangible assets	(A)			
Premises			97,500	
Equipment			50,550	148,050
Current assets				
Stock		43,713		
Debtors		31,719		
Bank		34,651	110,083	
Creditors: Amounts falling due within one year				
Creditors		27,112		
Proposed dividend		15,000	42,112	
Net current assets				67,971
				216,021
Capital and reserves	(B)			
Called-up share capital				150,000
Reserves:				
General reserve			10,000	
Profit and loss account			56,021	66,021
				216,021

Notes:

(A) Notes to be given in an appendix as to cost, acquisitions and sales in the year and depreciation.

(B) 'Reserves' consist either of those unused profits remaining in the appropriation account, or those transferred to a reserve account appropriately titled (e.g. general reserve, fixed assets replacement reserve).

Ashford Ltd
Balance Sheet as at 31 December 2006
(for students sitting local overseas examinations)

	Cost	Depreciation to date	Net Book Value
Fixed assets	£	£	£
Premises	97,500		97,500
Equipment	82,500	31,950	50,550
	180,000	31,950	148,050
Current assets			
Stock	43,713		
Debtors	31,719		
Bank	34,651	110,083	
Less Current Liabilities			
Creditors	27,112		
Dividends owing	15,000	42,112	
Working capital			67,971
			216,021
Financed by:			
Share Capital	*Authorised*	*Issued*	
	£	£	£
Ordinary shares	150,000	150,000	150,000
Reserves			
General Reserve		10,000	
Profit and Loss		56,021	66,021
			216,021

A more complicated worked example including preference shares and debentures follows in Exhibit 37.6.

Exhibit 37.6

The following trial balance was extracted from the books of an imaginary company called Dyson Ltd as on 31 December 2005:

Dyson Ltd
Trial Balance as at 31 December 2005

	Dr	*Cr*
	£	£
8% Preference share capital		35,000
Ordinary share capital		125,000
10% Debentures (repayable 2010)		20,000
General reserve		21,000
Profit and loss account 31.12.04		13,874
Equipment at cost	122,500	
Motor vehicles at cost	99,750	
Provision for depreciation: Equipment 1.1.05		29,400
Provision for depreciation: Motor vehicles 1.1.05		36,225
Stock 1.1.05	136,132	
Sales		418,250
Purchases	232,225	
Returns inwards	4,025	
General expenses	1,240	
Salaries and wages	46,260	
Directors' remuneration	18,750	
Rent, rates and insurance	18,095	
Motor expenses	4,361	
Debenture interest	1,000	
Bank	12,751	
Cash	630	
Debtors	94,115	
Creditors		93,085
	791,834	791,834

The following adjustments are needed:

(i) Stock at 31.12.05 was £122,000.
(ii) Accrue rent £2,000.
(iii) Accrue debenture interest £1,000.
(iv) Depreciate the equipment at 10% on cost and motor vehicles at 20% on cost.
(v) Transfer to general reserve £5,000.
(vi) It is proposed to pay the 8% preference dividend and a 10% dividend on the ordinary shares.
(vii) Authorised share capital is £35,000 in preference shares and £200,000 in £1 ordinary shares.

Dyson Ltd
Trading and Profit and Loss and Appropriation Account
for the year ended 31 December 2005
(suitable for both UK and overseas examinations)

		£	£
Sales			418,250
Less Returns inwards			4,025
			414,225
Less Cost of goods sold:			
Opening stock		136,132	
Add Purchases		232,225	
		368,357	
Less Closing stock		122,000	246,357
Gross profit			167,868
Less Expenses:			
Salaries and wages		46,260	
Rent, rates and insurance (18,095 + 2,000)		20,095	
Motor expenses		4,361	
General expenses		1,240	
Directors' remuneration	(A)	18,750	
Debenture interest (1,000 + 1,000)	(B)	2,000	
Depreciation:			
Equipment (10% × 122,500)		12,250	
Motor vehicles (20% × 99,750)		19,950	124,906
Net profit			42,962
Add Unappropriated profit brought forward from last year			13,874
			56,836
Less Appropriations			
Transfer to general reserve		5,000	
Preference share dividend (8% × 35,000)		2,800	
Ordinary share dividend (10% × 125,000)	(C)	12,500	20,300
Unappropriated profits carried forward to next year			36,536

Notes:

(A) Directors' remuneration is shown as an expense in the profit and loss account.
(B) Debenture interest is an expense to be shown in the profit and loss account.
(C) The final dividend of 10 per cent is based on the issued ordinary share capital and *not* on the authorised ordinary share capital.

Dyson Ltd
Balance Sheet as at 31 December 2005
(based on UK legislation)

	£	£	£
Fixed assets			
Tangible assets (A)			
Equipment		80,850	
Motor vehicles		43,575	124,425
Current assets			
Stock	122,000		
Debtors	94,115		
Bank	12,751		
Cash	630	229,496	
Creditors: Amounts falling due within one year			
Creditors (93,085 + 2,000)	95,085		
Proposed dividends: Preference shares	2,800		
Ordinary shares	12,500		
Debenture interest due	1,000	111,385	
Net current assets			118,111
			242,536
Creditors: Amounts falling due after more than one year			
10% Debentures			20,000
			222,536
Capital and reserves			
Called-up share capital (B)			160,000
Reserves			
General reserve (21,000 + 5,000)		26,000	
Profit and loss account		36,536	62,536
			222,536

Notes:

(A) Notes to be given in an appendix as to cost, acquisitions and sales in the year and depreciation.

(B) 'Reserves' consist either of those unused profits remaining in the appropriation account, or those transferred to a reserve account appropriately titled (e.g. general reserve, fixed assets replacement reserve).

Dyson Ltd
Balance Sheet as at 31 December 2005
(for students sitting local overseas examinations)

	Cost	*Dep'n to date*	*Net Book Value*
Fixed assets	£	£	£
Equipment	122,500	41,650	80,850
Motor vehicles	99,750	56,175	43,575
	222,250	97,825	124,425
Current assets			
Stock	122,000		
Debtors	94,115		
Bank	12,751		
Cash	630	229,496	
Less Current liabilities			
Creditors (93,085 + 2,000)	95,085		
Dividends owing	15,300		
Debenture interest owing	1,000	111,385	
Working capital			118,111
			242,536
Financed by:			
Share capital	*Authorised*	*Issued*	
	£	£	£
Preference shares	35,000	35,000	
Ordinary shares	200,000	125,000	160,000
	235,000		
Reserves			
General reserve		26,000	
Profit and loss		36,536	62,536
			222,536
Loan capital			
10% Debentures			20,000
			242,536

New terms

Annual General Meeting (AGM) (p. 424): A meeting held every year that all shareholders in a company are invited to attend. At the meeting, the latest set of final accounts is considered, together with the appointment or removal of directors and/or auditors.

Authorised share capital (p. 424): The total amount of share capital, or number of shares, that a company can have in issue at any given time.

Called-up capital (p. 424): Where only part of the amounts payable on each share have been asked for, the total amount requested on all the shares is known as the 'called-up capital'.

Calls in arrear (p. 424): The amount for which payment has been requested (i.e. called for) but has not yet been paid by shareholders.

Capital reserve (p. 428): A type of reserve account.

Debenture (p. 425): Loan to a company.

Debenture interest (p. 425): An agreed percentage of interest paid to a debenture holder for lending money to a company.

Directors (p. 424): Officials appointed by shareholders to manage the company for them.

Directors' remuneration (p. 426): Directors are legally employees of the company, and any pay they receive is called directors' remuneration.

Dividends (p. 425): The amount given to shareholders as their share of the profits of the company.

Issued share capital (p. 424): The amount of a company's authorised share capital that has been issued to shareholders.

Limited company (p. 423): An organisation owned by its shareholders, whose liability is limited to their share capital.

Limited liability (p. 423): The liability of shareholders in a company is limited to any amount they have agreed to invest.

Loan capital (p. 431): Money owing by a company for debentures and for loans from banks and other sources that are not repayable in the near future.

Ordinary shares (p. 425): Shares entitled to dividends (after the preference shareholders have been paid their dividends).

Paid-up capital (p. 424): The total of the amount of share capital that has been paid for by shareholders.

Preference shares (p. 425): Shares that are entitled to an agreed rate of dividend before the ordinary shareholders receive anything.

Preliminary expenses (p. 427): All the costs that are incurred when a company is formed.

Reserve accounts (p. 427): The transfer of apportioned profits to accounts for use in future years.

Retained profits (p. 426): Profits earned in a year but not paid out in dividends or debenture interest.

Revenue reserve (p. 428): A type of reserve account.

Shareholder (p. 423): An owner of shares in a company.

Shares (p. 423): The division of the capital of a limited company into parts.

Uncalled capital (p. 424): The amount that is to be received in future, but which has not yet been requested.

EXERCISES

37.1 Draw up a balance sheet for LMT Ltd from the following as at 31 December 2004:

	£
Premises at cost	45,000
Machinery at cost	24,000
Fixtures at cost	12,000
Stock	18,000
Bank	6,000
Debtors	9,000
Depreciation to date:	
Premises	18,000
Machinery	7,200
Fixtures	4,800
Authorised share capital: Ordinary shares £1	60,000
Issued share capital: Fully paid	36,000
Debentures: 10%	18,000
Proposed dividend owing	3,000
Creditors	9,000
General reserve	15,000
Profit and loss account (balancing figure, for you to ascertain)	?

37.2X C Blake Ltd has an authorised share capital of 90,000 ordinary shares of £1 each and 10,000 10% preference shares of £1 each. The company's trial balance, extracted after one year of trading, was as follows on 31 December 2004:

	£
Net profit for the year to 31 December 2004	11,340
Debentures	30,000
Issued ordinary share capital, fully paid	60,000
Issued preference share capital, fully paid	10,000
Creditors	3,550
Debtors	4,120
Cash	2,160
Stock	8,800
Provision for bad debts	350
Provision for depreciation: Equipment	4,500
Equipment at cost	45,000
Premises at cost	50,000
Bank (use the balancing figure)	?

The directors decide to transfer £1,500 to the general reserve and to recommend a dividend of 12½% on the ordinary shares. The preference dividend was not paid until after January 2005.

You are required to:
(*a*) draw up the appropriation account for the year ended 31 December 2004
(*b*) draft a balance sheet as at 31 December 2004.

37.3 CA Company Ltd, manufacturing agricultural implements, made a net profit of £210,000 for the year to 31 December 2002. Retained profits at 31 December 2001 amounted to £17,000. At the directors' meeting, the following appropriations were agreed:

	£
• to be transferred to general reserve:	30,000
• to be transferred to foreign exchange reserve:	16,000

It had also been agreed that a dividend of 10% be proposed on the ordinary share capital. This amounted to 500,000 shares of £2 each. Preference share dividends of 10% have been paid during the year on 250,000 preference shares of £1 each.

You are required to draw up the company's profit and loss appropriation account for the year ended 31 December 2002.

37.4 The trial balance extracted from the books of Chang Ltd at 31 December 2004 was as follows:

	£	£
Share capital		100,000
Unappropriated profits brought forward from last year		34,280
Freehold premises at cost	65,000	
Machinery at cost	55,000	
Provision for depreciation on machinery account as at 31 December 2003		15,800
Purchases	201,698	
Sales		316,810
General expenses	32,168	
Wages and salaries	54,207	
Rent	4,300	
Lighting expenses	1,549	
Bad debts	748	
Provision for doubtful debts as at 31 December 2003		861
Debtors	21,784	
Creditors		17,493
Stock in trade as at 31 December 2003	25,689	
Bank balance	23,101	
	485,244	485,244

You are given the following additional information:

(i) The authorised and issued share capital is divided into 100,000 shares of £1 each.
(ii) Stock in trade as at 31 December 2004 was £29,142.
(iii) Wages and salaries due at 31 December 2004 amounted to £581.
(iv) Rent paid in advance at 31 December 2004 amounted to £300.

(v) A dividend of £10,000 is proposed for 2004.
(vi) The provision for doubtful debts is to be increased to £938.
(vii) A depreciation charge is to be made on machinery at the rate of 10 per cent per annum at cost.

Required:
Draw up a trading and profit and loss account for the year ended 31 December 2004 and a balance sheet as at 31 December 2004.

37.5X On 30 September 2007, Reynolds Ltd had an authorised capital of £250,000, divided into 200,000 ordinary shares of £1 each and 50,000 7% preference shares of £1 each. All the preference shares were issued and fully paid, while 150,000 of the ordinary shares were issued and fully paid. The company also had a balance on the general reserve account of £45,000 and a balance brought forward on the profit and loss account of £30,000.

During the year ended 30 September 2008, the company made a net profit of £70,000, out of which a transfer of £8,000 was made to the general reserve account. The directors had paid an interim dividend of 6p per share on the ordinary share capital and now propose to pay the preference dividend and a final dividend of 14p per share on the ordinary share capital.

From the information given above you are required to prepare for Reynolds Ltd:

(*a*) a profit and loss appropriation account for the year ended 30 September 2008
(*b*) the capital and reserves section of the balance sheet as at 30 September 2008.

37.6 Jaspa West Ltd has an authorised share capital of £300,000, divided into 200,000 ordinary shares of £1 each and 100,000 8% preference shares of £1 each. The following balances remained in the accounts of the company after the preparation of the trading and profit and loss account for the year ended 31 December 2006:

	Dr	*Cr*
	£	£
Premises at cost	270,600	
Bank balance		21,400
Heating and lighting	3,800	
Provision for depreciation on machinery		18,400
Machinery at cost	72,600	
Preference share capital: fully paid		80,000
Ordinary share capital: fully paid		150,000
Profit and loss account balance: 1 January 2006		92,000
Debtors and creditors	80,000	37,000
Stock	56,000	
Wages and salaries		4,200
Net profit (for the year ended 31 December 2006)		80,000
	483,000	483,000

The directors have recommended:

- the creation of a general reserve, amounting to 40% of the year's net profit
- an ordinary dividend of 4%
- payment of the year's preference dividend.

You are required to:

(*a*) prepare the profit and loss appropriation account for the year ended 31 December 2006

(*b*) prepare the balance sheet as at 31 December 2006.

Pitman Qualifications

37.7X Cityjag plc has an authorised capital of 500,000 £1 ordinary shares and 250,000 £1 (9%) preference shares. The following balances remained in the books after the profit and loss account has been prepared for the year ended 31 December 2008:

	Dr £	*Cr* £
140,000 £1 ordinary shares		140,000
90,000 £1 (9%) Preference shares		90,000
Profit and loss account balance 1 January 2008		10,000
Premises at cost	180,000	
Motor vehicles at cost	90,200	
Fixtures and fittings at cost	45,000	
Provision for depreciation on motor vehicles		30,200
Provision for depreciation on fixtures and fittings		25,000
Trade debtors and trade creditors	7,700	9,000
Bank	8,500	
Expenses prepaid and owing	2,000	1,000
Stock at 31 December 2008	21,800	
General reserve		10,000
Net trading profit for the year ended 31 December 2008		40,000
	355,200	355,200

The directors of Cityjag plc have decided to transfer £20,000 to the general reserve; to recommend payment of the preference share dividend; and to recommend a dividend of 11% on ordinary shares.

From the information given, you are required to prepare for Cityjag plc

(*a*) a profit and loss appropriation account for the year ended 31 December 2008

(*b*) a balance sheet as at 31 December 2008.

NEAB (GCSE)

CHAPTER 38

Analysis and interpretation of accounts

Learning objectives

After you have studied this chapter you should be able to:

- **understand the difference between margin and mark-up**
- **use that understanding to draw up accounts from incomplete records**
- **know how accounting ratios can be used to assess the performance of a business**
- **calculate various accounting ratios.**

38.1 Introduction

It has been noted in Chapter 33 that sole traders and small businesses may not use a full double entry system. It is more likely that they would enter details of a transaction only once, using a single entry system; they may also fail to record every transaction, resulting in incomplete records. The ratios, margin and mark-up can be used to calculate missing figures from incomplete records and to show the relationship between profit and selling price, and profit and cost price, respectively.

38.2 Mark-up and margin

The purchase and sale of goods may be shown as

Cost price + Profit = Selling Price

The profit, when shown as a fraction (or percentage) of the cost price is known as the **mark-up**. The profit when shown as a fraction (or percentage) of the selling price is known as the **margin**.

We can now calculate these values in an example where

Cost Price	+ Profit	= Selling Price.
£4	+ £1	= £5.

Mark-up = Profit/Cost Price (and if required as a percentage, multiply by 100), so that in our example:

$$\text{Mark-up} = \frac{£1}{£4} = \tfrac{1}{4}\text{, or 25 per cent.}$$

Margin = Profit/Selling Price (and if required as a percentage, multiply by 100), so that:

$$\text{Margin} = \frac{£1}{£5} = \tfrac{1}{5}\text{, or 20 per cent.}$$

Author's hint

Students often confuse the relationship between the selling price and profit (margin) and cost price and profit (mark-up). This can easily be remembered using the mnemonic 'Mrs Muc', as shown in Exhibit 38.1.

EXHIBIT 38.1

38.3 Calculating missing figures

We can use the ratios given in Section 38.2 to complete trading accounts where some of the figures are missing. For ease of illustrating this fact, all examples in this chapter:

- assume that all the goods in a firm have the same rate of mark-up
- ignore wastages and theft of goods.

Example 1: The following figures apply for the year 2009:

	£
Stock 1.1.2009	400
Stock 31.12.2009	600
Purchases	5,200

A uniform rate of mark-up of 20 per cent is applied. We need to find the gross profit and the sales figure within the following account:

Trading Account for the year ended 31 December 2009

	£	£
Sales		?
Less Cost of goods sold		
Stock 1.1.2009	400	
Add Purchases	5,200	
	5,600	
Less Stock 31.12.2009	600	
		5,000
Gross profit		?

It is known that Cost of goods sold + Profit = Sales, and also that Cost of goods sold + mark-up = Sales. In our example, with a mark-up of 20 per cent of cost price (£5,000), we can deduce sales as

$$£5{,}000 + (20\% \times £5{,}000) = £6{,}000$$

The trading account can be completed by inserting £6,000 for sales and £1,000 for gross profit.

Example 2: Another firm has the following figures for 2008:

	£
Stock 1.1.2008	500
Stock 31.12.2008	800
Sales	6,400

A uniform rate of margin of 25 per cent is in use. Find the gross profit and the figure of purchases.

Trading Account for the year ended 31 December 2008

	£	£
Sales		6,400
Less Cost of goods sold		
Stock 1.1.2008	500	
Add Purchases	?	
	?	
Less Stock 31.12.2008	800	?
Gross profit		?

Again, Cost of goods sold + Gross profit = Sales. Therefore Sales – Gross profit = Cost of goods sold, which in this case, means £6,400 – £1,600 (25% margin) = £4,800.

Now the following figures are known:

		£	£
Cost of goods sold:			
Stock 1.1.2008		500	
Add Purchases	(A)	?	
	(B)	?	
Less Stock 31.12.2008		800	
			4,800

The two missing figures are found by normal arithmetical deduction:

(B) *less* £800	= £4,800
Therefore (B)	= £5,600

Then

£500 opening stock + (A)	= £5,600
(A)	= £5,100

The completed trading account can now be shown:

Trading Account for the year ended 31 December 2008

	£	£
Sales		6,400
Less Cost of goods sold		
Stock 1.1.2008	500	
Add Purchases	5,100	
	5,600	
Less Stock 31.12.2008	800	4,800
Gross profit		1,600

This technique is found very useful by retail stores when estimating the amount to be bought if a certain sales target is to be achieved. Alternatively, stock levels or sales figures can be estimated given information as to purchases and opening stock figures.

38.4 The relationship between mark-up and margin

As both of these figures refer to the same profit but are expressed as a fraction or a percentage of different figures, there is a relationship between them. If one is known as a fraction, the other can soon be found.

If the mark-up is known, in order to find the margin you need to take the same numerator to be the numerator of the margin. Then, for the denominator of the margin, take the total of the mark-up's denominator *plus* the numerator. An example can now be shown:

Mark-up	Margin
$\frac{1}{4}$	$\frac{1}{4+1} = \frac{1}{5}$
$\frac{2}{11}$	$\frac{2}{11+2} = \frac{2}{13}$

If the margin is known, to find the mark-up take the same numerator to be the numerator of the mark-up. Then, for the denominator of the mark-up, take the figure of the margin's denominator *less* the numerator:

Margin	Mark-up		
$\frac{1}{6}$	$\frac{1}{6-1}$	=	$\frac{1}{5}$
$\frac{3}{13}$	$\frac{3}{13-3}$	=	$\frac{3}{10}$

38.5 Interpretation of accounts

The whole purpose of recording and classifying financial information about a firm, and communicating this to the owners and managers in the form of final accounts, is to assess the performance of the business. The information contained in the final accounts can be used to evaluate various aspects of the company by the use of accounting ratios.

For the ratios to be a reliable guide to performance, two criteria need to be applied:

- The final accounts used for calculating the current ratios must be *up to date.*
- Each ratio must be *compared* with the same ratio from the previous year's accounts or with those from a competitor's accounts.

The concept of comparison is crucial, since this identifies trends in the business and allows action to be taken.

The analysis of a business using accounting ratios is widely practised by both internal and external parties and the main ones are listed in Exhibit 38.2.

Exhibit 38.2

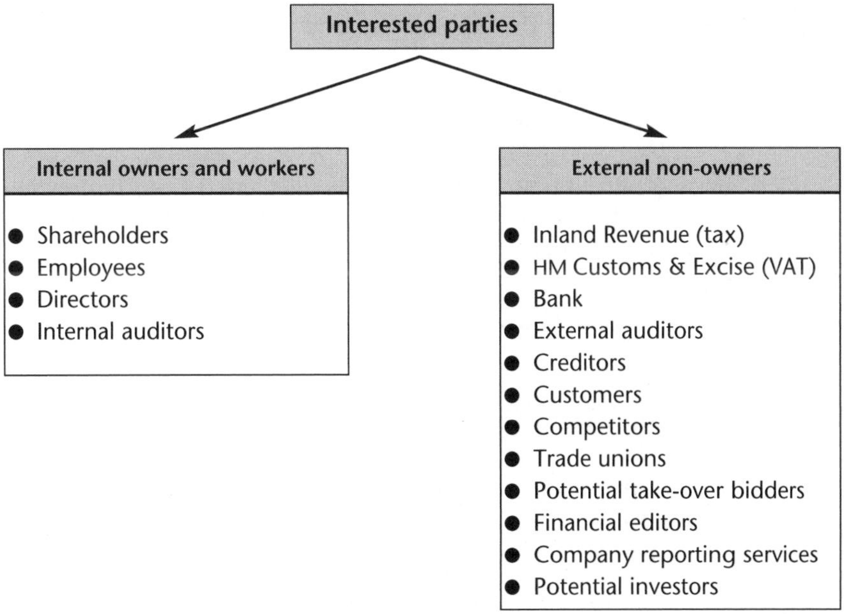

38.6 Profitability and liquidity

The two most important factors in the running of a business are, first, to see that it operates at a profit and, second, to organise it so that it can pay its creditors and expenses at the correct times. If either of these points is not covered effectively, it could mean that the business might have to be closed down.

The ability to pay one's debts as they fall due is known as having **liquidity**. The ability to make a profit is known as **profitability**, and the ratios commonly used to give valuable information on a business's performance are known as **profitability ratios**.

38.7 Profitability ratios

The main ratios used to examine profitability are:

- **Gross profit : sales ratio**
- **Net profit : sales ratio**
- **Expenses : sales ratio**
- **Return on capital employed (ROCE) ratio**
- **Stock turnover ratio**

Each is examined in turn in the sections following.

38.8 Gross profit to sales ratio

The basic formula for the gross profit ratio (as it is also called) is:

$$\frac{\text{Gross profit}}{\text{Sales}} \times 100\% = \text{Gross profit as a percentage of sales}$$

The gross profit ratio as a percentage is calculated from figures found in the trading account and shows the gross profit for every £100 of sales. For example, if the answer turned out to be 20%, this would mean that for every £100 of sales, £20 gross profit was made.

The ratio measures how effectively a company has controlled its cost of goods.

38.9 Net profit to sales ratio

The net profit ratio is calculated from the profit and loss account and brings the expenses into the calculation, as opposed to the gross profit percentage (which ignores expenses). The ratio is:

$$\frac{\text{Net profit}}{\text{Sales}} \times 100\% = \text{Net profit as a percentage of sales}$$

Changes in the ratio will be due either to:

- the gross profit ratio changing, and/or
- the expenses per £100 of sales changing.

When changes are due to the second effect (expenses), they ought to be examined to see whether anything could be done in future to control expenses better.

38.10 Expenses to sales ratio

The expenses ratio (as it is also called) uses figures from the trading and profit and loss account and is calculated as follows:

$$\frac{\text{Expenses}}{\text{Sales}} \times 100\% = \text{Expenses as a percentage of sales}$$

An increase in the percentage over the previous period would indicate either an increase in spending on expenses or, if the expenses had remained stable, a decrease in sales. Either cause would require management action.

38.11 Return on capital employed (ROCE) ratio

The formula for this ratio is:

$$\frac{\text{Net profit}}{\text{Capital employed}} \times 100\% = \text{Return on capital employed}$$

It shows (as a percentage) the net profit made for each £100 of capital employed. The higher the ratio, the more profitable the firm. This is the most important ratio of all.

There has never been an agreed definition of the term 'capital employed'. Very often it has been taken to mean the average capital. For this, the opening capital for the period is added to the closing capital and then the total is divided by two. In an examination, use the method stated by the examiner. If you are given only the closing capital, use the closing capital figure.

In the following example, two businesses of sole traders (A) and (B) have made the same profits, but the capital employed in each case is different. From the balance sheets that follow, the return on capital employed is calculated using the average of the capital account as capital employed.

Balance Sheets	(A)	(B)
	£	£
Fixed Assets + Current Assets – Current Liabilities	10,000	16,000
Capital Accounts:		
Opening balance	8,000	14,000
Add Net profits	3,600	3,600
	11,600	17,600
Less Drawings	1,600	1,600
	10,000	16,000

Return on capital employed is calculated thus for the two firms:

(A)
$$\frac{£3{,}600}{£8{,}000 + £10{,}000 \div 2} \times 100\% = 40\%$$

(B)
$$\frac{£3{,}600}{£14{,}000 + £16{,}000 \div 2} \times 100\% = 24\%$$

The ratio illustrates that what is important is not simply how much profit has been made but how well the capital has been employed. Business (A) has made far better use of its capital, achieving a return of £40 net profit for every £100 invested, whereas (B) has received a net profit of only £24 per £100.

In this case, only the accounts of sole traders have been dealt with, so that a straightforward example could be used. In Section 38.18 other meanings of 'capital employed' will be considered, when dealing with:

- sole traders who have received loans to help finance their businesses
- partnerships
- limited companies.

38.12 Stock turnover ratio

Every business should operate both to keep its stock to as low a figure as possible without losing profitability, and to sell its goods as quickly as possible. The stock turnover ratio measures how well the firm is managing to do these things. Any increase in stocks or slowdown in sales will show a lower ratio.

The ratio is calculated as follows:

$$\frac{\text{Cost of goods sold}}{\text{Average stock}} = \text{Stock turnover ratio}$$

If only the opening and closing stocks are known, the average stock is found by adding these two figures and dividing them by two (i.e. averaging them). That is the usual situation in examinations.

The higher this ratio, the more profitable the firm. Take the example of a product on which £5 gross profit is made on sales per unit. With stock turnover of 6 for this item, the firm would make a gross profit of 6 × £5 = £30. If the stock turnover ratio for it increased to 9, then 9 × £5 = £45 gross profit would be made.

38.13 Liquidity ratios

A business that has satisfactory liquidity (*see* Section 38.6 above) will have sufficient funds, normally referred to as 'working capital', to pay creditors at the required time. The ability to pay creditors on time is vital to ensure that good business relationships are maintained.

The ratios used to examine liquidity i.e. the **liquidity ratios** are:

- **Current ratio (working capital ratio)**
- **Acid test ratio (quick ratio)**
- **Debtors : sales ratio**
- **Creditors : purchases ratio.**

Each of the liquidity ratios stated can be compared period by period to see whether that particular aspect of liquidity is getting better or worse. In the case of the current ratio, it was often thought in the past that the ideal ratio should be around 2:1 and that, ideally, the acid test ratio should be in the region of 1:1 to 1.5:1. However, in recent years it has become recognised that such a fixed figure cannot possibly apply to every business, as the types and circumstances of businesses vary so widely.

38.14 Current ratio (or working capital ratio)

The current ratio measures current assets against current liabilities. It will compare assets that will be turned into cash within the next 12 months with any liabilities that will have to be paid within the same period. The current ratio is thus stated as:

$$\frac{\text{Current assets}}{\text{Current liabilities}}$$

If, therefore, the current assets are £125,000 and the current liabilities are £50,000, the current ratio will be:

$$\frac{£125{,}000}{£50{,}000} = 2.5 : 1\text{, or 2.5 times}$$

If the ratio increases by a large amount, the firm may have more current assets than it needs. If the ratio falls by a large amount, then perhaps too little is being kept as current assets.

38.15 Acid test ratio (or quick ratio)

To determine a further aspect of liquidity, the acid test ratio takes into account only those current assets that are cash or can be changed very quickly into cash. This will normally mean Cash + Bank + Debtors. You can see that this means exactly the same as current assets less stock. The acid test ratio may, therefore, be stated as:

$$\frac{\text{Current assets } \textit{less} \text{ stock}}{\text{Current liabilities}}$$

For instance, if the total of current assets is £40,000 and stock is £10,000, and the total of current liabilities is £20,000, then the ratio will be:

$$\frac{£40,000 - £10,000}{£20,000} = 1.5:1, \text{ or } 1.5 \text{ times}$$

This ratio shows whether there are enough liquid assets to be able to pay current liabilities quickly. It is dangerous if this ratio is allowed to fall to a very low figure. If suppliers and others cannot be paid on time, supplies to the firm may be reduced or even stopped completely. Eventually, the firm may not have enough stock to be able to sell properly. In that case, it may have to cease business.

38.16 Debtors to sales ratio

This ratio assesses how long it takes for debtors to pay what they owe. The calculation is made as follows:

$$\frac{\text{Debtors}}{\text{Sales for the year}} \times 12 = \text{number of months that debtors (on average) take to pay up}$$

For example:

	(C)	(D)
Sales for the year	£240,000	£180,000
Debtors as per balance sheet	£60,000	£30,000

In firm (C), debtors therefore take three months on average to pay their accounts, calculated from:

$$\frac{£60,000}{£240,000} \times 12 = 3 \text{ months}$$

In firm (D), debtors therefore take two months on average to pay their accounts, given from:

$$\frac{£30,000}{£180,000} \times 12 = 2 \text{ months}$$

If the ratio is required to be shown in days instead of months, the formula should be multiplied by 365 instead of 12. The higher the ratio, the worse a firm is at getting its debtors to pay on time. The lower the ratio, the better it is at managing its debtors.

Firms should make certain that debtors pay their accounts on time. There are two main reasons for this. First, the longer a debt is owed, the more likely it will become a bad debt. Second, any payment of money can be used in the firm as soon as it is received, and so this increases profitability; it can help reduce expenses. For example, it would reduce a bank overdraft and therefore reduce the bank overdraft interest.

38.17 Creditors to purchases ratio

This ratio shows how long it takes a firm (on average) to pay its suppliers. The calculation is made as follows:

$$\frac{\text{Creditors}}{\text{Purchases for the year}} \times 12 = \text{Number of months it takes (on average) to pay suppliers}$$

For example:

	(E)	(F)
Purchases for the year	£120,000	£90,000
Creditors as per balance sheet	£40,000	£22,500

Firm (E) therefore takes four months' credit on average from its suppliers, i.e.

$$\frac{£40,000}{£120,000} \times 12 = 4 \text{ months}$$

Firm (F) takes on average three months to pay its suppliers, i.e.

$$\frac{£22,500}{£90,000} \times 12 = 3 \text{ months}$$

Taking longer to pay suppliers could be a good thing or a bad thing, depending upon circumstances. If so long is taken to pay that possible discounts are lost, or that suppliers refuse to supply again, then it would be undesirable. On the other hand, paying before it is necessary simply takes money out of the firm early without gaining any benefit.

38.18 Definition of capital employed in various circumstances

In Section 38.11, it was pointed out that there is not one single agreed definition of the term 'capital employed'. In answering an exam question in this area, you must follow the examiner's instructions, if any are given; otherwise, state what basis you have used.

Sole proprietorships

'Capital employed' could mean any of the following:

- closing balance on capital account at the end of a financial period
- average of opening and closing balances on the capital account for the accounting period
- capital balances plus any long-term loans.

Partnerships

'Capital employed' could mean any of the following:

- closing balance on the fluctuating capital accounts at the end of a financial period
- average of opening and closing balances on the fluctuating capital accounts for an accounting period
- total of fixed capital accounts plus total of partners' current accounts at the end of a financial period
- average of opening and closing balances on the partners' capital and current accounts for an accounting period
- any of the above, plus long-term loans to the partnership.

Limited companies

Given the following details, different figures for capital employed may be used.

		£
(*a*)	Ordinary share capital	100,000
(*b*)	Preference share capital	40,000
(*c*)	Total of different types of reserves including balance in profit and loss account	35,000
(*d*)	Debentures	60,000

- To calculate return on ordinary shareholders' funds, it would be (*a*) £100,000 + (*c*) £35,000 = £135,000.
- To calculate return on total shareholders' fund, it would be (*a*) £100,000 + (*b*) £40,000 + (*c*) £35,000 = £175,000.
- To calculate return on total capital employed, i.e. including borrowed funds, it would be (*a*) £100,000 + (*b*) £40,000 + (*c*) £35,000 + (*d*) £60,000 = £235,000.

Any question involving return of capital employed for limited companies should be read very carefully indeed. Use the method suggested by the examiner. If no indication is given, use that of (*a*) + (*c*) above, but you must state what method you have used.

38.19 Definition of working capital

Working capital is the amount by which current assets exceed current liabilities. It is also known as 'net current assets'. (*See* Chapter 9.)

It is vital for businesses to have sufficient working capital to enable them to have funds available to pay everyday running expenses. Working capital tends to circulate through a business, as shown in the diagram in Exhibit 38.3. As it flows, profits are made as stock is sold to debtors; the quicker it is sold, the quicker the business makes profits.

EXHIBIT 38.3

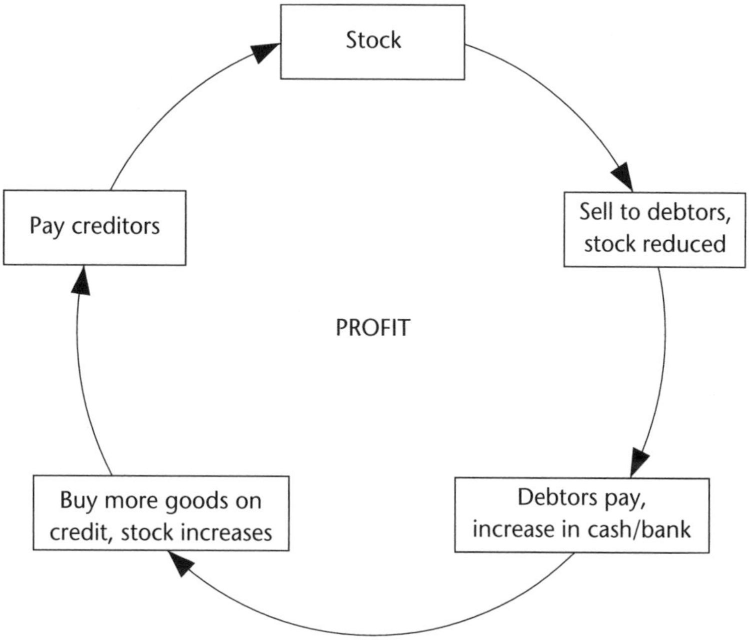

38.20 A fully worked example of calculating ratios

A fully worked example of calculating ratios and interpreting accounts is shown in Exhibit 38.4. Check all the calculations yourself and see whether your conclusions about the changes in the ratios agree with the author's.

EXHIBIT 38.4

The following are the final accounts for two similar types of retail stores:

Trading and Profit and Loss Accounts

	J		K	
	£	£	£	£
Sales		80,000		120,000
Less Cost of goods sold:				
Opening stock	25,000		22,500	
Add Purchases	50,000		91,000	
	75,000		113,500	
Less Closing stock	15,000	60,000	17,500	96,000
Gross profit		20,000		24,000
Less Depreciation	1,000		3,000	
Other expenses	9,000	10,000	6,000	9,000
Net profit		10,000		15,000

Balance Sheets

	J		K	
Fixed Assets	£	£	£	£
Equipment at cost	10,000		20,000	
Less Depreciation to date	8,000	2,000	6,000	14,000
Current Assets				
Stock	15,000		17,500	
Debtors	25,000		20,000	
Bank	5,000		2,500	
	45,000		40,000	
Less Current Liabilities				
Creditors	5,000		10,000	
Net current assets		40,000		30,000
		42,000		44,000
Financed by:				
Capital				
Balance at start of year		38,000		36,000
Add Net profit		10,000		15,000
		48,000		51,000
Less Drawings		6,000		7,000
		42,000		44,000

We will now calculate the following ratios (with all calculations shown correct to one decimal place):

(*a*) Gross profit as a percentage of sales
(*b*) Net profit as a percentage of sales
(*c*) Expenses as a percentage of sales
(*d*) Stock turnover ratio
(*e*) Rate of return of net profit on capital employed (use the average of the capital account for this purpose)
(*f*) Current ratio
(*g*) Quick ratio
(*h*) Debtors : Sales ratio
(*i*) Creditors : Purchases ratio

	J	K
(*a*) Gross profit as a % of sales	$\frac{£20,000}{£80,000} \times 100\% = 25\%$	$\frac{£24,000}{£120,000} \times 100\% = 20\%$
(*b*) Net profit as a % of sales	$\frac{£10,000}{£80,000} \times 100\% = 12.5\%$	$\frac{£15,000}{£120,000} \times 100\% = 12.5\%$
(*c*) Expenses as a % of sales	$\frac{£10,000}{£80,000} \times 100\% = 12.5\%$	$\frac{£9,000}{£120,000} \times 100\% = 7.5\%$
(*d*) Stockturn	$\frac{£60,000}{(£25,000 + £15,000) \div 2} = 3$ times	$\frac{£96,000}{(£22,500 + £17,500) \div 2} = 4.8$ times
(*e*) Rate of return on capital employed	$\frac{£10,000}{(£38,000 + £42,000) \div 2} \times 100\% = 25\%$	$\frac{£15,000}{(£36,000 + £44,000) \div 2} \times 100\% = 37.5\%$
(*f*) Current ratio	$\frac{£45,000}{£5,000} = 9 : 1$	$\frac{£40,000}{£10,000} = 4 : 1$
(*g*) Quick ratio	$\frac{£45,000 - £15,000}{£5,000} = 6 : 1$	$\frac{£40,000 - £17,500}{£10,000} = 2.25 : 1$
(*h*) Debtors : Sales ratio	$\frac{£25,000}{£80,000} \times 12 = 3.75$ months	$\frac{£20,000}{£120,000} \times 12 = 2$ months
(*i*) Creditors : Purchases ratio	$\frac{£5,000}{£50,000} \times 12 = 1.2$ months	$\frac{£10,000}{£91,000} \times 12 = 1.3$ months

Having calculated the ratios, we will now attempt briefly to see what we have learned from studying the accounts and the ratios. At this stage in your studies, we would not expect a very long analysis. Instead, you should know what your examiner would expect of you in the examination.

You should not just say that the ratios differ. You should try to see why the ratios are different. Show the examiner that you are looking at the ratios as though they belong to a business for which the ratios mean something. He will not give you any marks for this part of the question if you talk only about the arithmetic of the ratios.

Business K is more profitable, both in terms of actual net profits (£15,000 compared with £10,000), but also in terms of capital employed. K has managed to achieve a return of £37.50 for every £100 invested, i.e. 37.5%. J has managed a lower return of 25%.

The conclusions are only possible reasons because you must know more about the business before you can give a definite answer.

- Possibly K managed to sell far more merchandise because of lower prices, i.e. it took only 20% margin as compared with J's 25% margin.
- Maybe K made more efficient use of mechanised means in the business. Note that it has more equipment, and perhaps as a consequence it kept other expenses down to £6,000 as compared with J's £9,000.

- K did not have as much stock lying idle. K turned over stock 4.8 times in the year, as compared with 3 times for J.
- J's current ratio of 9 : 1 was far greater than normally needed. K kept it down to 4 : 1. J therefore had too much money lying idle.
- The acid test ratio for J was higher than necessary and followed a similar trend to that shown by the current ratio.
- One reason for the better current and acid test ratios for K was that debts were collected on a 2 months' average.
- J also paid creditors more quickly than K – but only slightly faster.

When all thİese factors are considered, it is clear that business K is being run much more efficiently and, consequently, more profitably.

38.21 Summary of the formulae appearing in this chapter

The formulae for this chapter are summarised in Exhibit 38.5.

Exhibit 38.5

Mark-up $= \dfrac{\text{Profit}}{\text{Cost price}}$ (or if required as a percentage, multiply by 100%)

Margin $= \dfrac{\text{Profit}}{\text{Selling price}}$ (or if required as a percentage, multiply by 100%)

Gross profit as a percentage of sales $= \dfrac{\text{Gross profit}}{\text{Sales}} \times 100\%$

Net profit as a percentage of sales $= \dfrac{\text{Net profit}}{\text{Sales}} \times 100\%$

Expenses as a percentage of sales $= \dfrac{\text{Expenses}}{\text{Sales}} \times 100\%$

Return on capital employed (ROCE) $= \dfrac{\text{Net profit}}{\text{Capital employed}} \times 100\%$

Stock turnover $= \dfrac{\text{Cost of goods sold}}{\text{Average stock}}$,

where average stock $= \dfrac{\text{Opening stock + closing stock}}{2}$

Current ratio (working captial ratio) $= \dfrac{\text{Current assets}}{\text{Current liabilities}}$

Acid test ratio (quick ratio) $= \dfrac{\text{Current assets - stock}}{\text{Current liabilities}}$

Debtors : Sales ratio = Number of months debtors (on average) take to pay

$$= \frac{\text{Debtors}}{\text{Sales for the year}} \times 12$$

(If days instead of months are required, the formula should be multiplied by 365 instead of 12.)

Creditors : Sales ratio = Number of months it takes (on average) to pay suppliers

$$= \frac{\text{Creditors}}{\text{Purchases for the year}} \times 12$$

(If days instead of months are required, the formula should be multiplied by 365 instead of 12.)

38.22 Multiple choice questions

Now attempt Set No 3 of the multiple-choice questions in Appendix C, which contains 27 questions.

New terms

Acid test ratio (p. 453): A ratio comparing current assets less stock with current liabilities.

Creditor : purchases ratio (p. 453): A ratio assessing how long it takes a business to pay its creditors.

Current ratio (p. 453): A ratio comparing current assets with current liabilities.

Debtors : sales ratio (p. 453): A ratio assessing how long it takes debtors to pay a business.

Expenses : sales ratio: (p. 450) A ratio that indicates whether costs are rising against sales or whether sales are falling against expenses.

Gross profit : sales ratio (p. 450): A ratio that states gross profit as a percentage of sales, and which can also indicate how effectively a business has controlled the cost of its goods.

Liquidity (p. 450): The ability of a business to pay its debts as they fall due and to meet unexpected expenses within a reasonable settlement period.

Liquidity ratios (p. 453): Ratios that attempt to indicate the ability of a business to meet its debts as they become due (including both the current ratio and acid test ratio).

Margin (p. 445): Profit shown as a percentage or fraction of the selling price.

Mark-up (p. 445): Profit shown as a percentage or fraction of the cost price.

Net profit : sales ratio (p. 450): A ratio that states net profit as a percentage of sales and brings expenses into the calculation.

Profitability (p. 450): The effective operation of a business to make ongoing profits, so as to ensure its long-term viability.

Profitability ratios (p. 450): Ratios that attempt to indicate the trend in a business's ability to make a profit. These include gross profit and net profit to sales, and the return on capital employed.

Quick ratio (p. 453–4): Same as the acid test ratio.

Return on capital employed (ROCE) ratio (p. 450): A ratio that shows the net profit made for each unit of capital employed.

Stock turnover (or stockturn) ratio (p. 450): A ratio comparing the cost of goods sold to the average stock. It shows the number of times stock is sold in an accounting period.

Working capital ratio (p. 453): Same as the current ratio.

EXERCISES

38.1
(*a*) If an item costs £20 and is sold for £25, what are the mark-up and margin, expressed as percentages?
(*b*) If the mark-up on a unit is 33⅓ per cent, what is the margin?
(*c*) If the margin is 16⅔ per cent, what is the mark-up?

38.2X
(*a*) If an item costs £60 and is sold for £90, what are the mark-up and margin, expressed as percentages?
(*b*) If the margin on a unit is 50 per cent, what is the mark-up?
(*c*) If the mark-up is 50 per cent, what is the margin?

38.3 K Young is a trader who marks up the selling price of his goods to 25 per cent above cost. His books give the following information at 31 July 2003:

	£
Stock as at 1 August 2002	4,936
Stock as at 31 July 2003	6,310
Sales for the year	30,000

You are required to create a trading account for Young showing:
(*a*) the cost of goods sold
(*b*) the value of purchases during the year
(*c*) the profit that Young made.

38.4 T Rigby produced from his trial balance as at 31 August 2009 the following information:

	£
Stock as at 1 September 2008	2,000
Purchases for the year	18,000

Rigby has a 'mark-up' of 50 per cent on 'cost of sales'.
His average stock during the year was valued at £4,000.

You are required to:
(*a*) calculate the closing stock for Rigby as at 31 August 2009
(*b*) prepare his trading account for the year ended 31 August 2009
(*c*) ascertain the total amount of expenses that Rigby *must not exceed* if he is to maintain a net profit on sales of 10 per cent.

38.5 The following accounts are of two companies that each sell sports goods:

Trading and Profit and Loss Accounts

	M Ltd		*N Ltd*	
	£	£	£	£
Sales		360,000		250,000
Less Cost of goods sold:				
Opening stock	120,000		60,000	
Add Purchases	268,000		191,500	
	388,000		251,500	
Less Closing stock	100,000	288,000	64,000	187,500
Gross profit		72,000		62,500
Less Expenses:				
Wages	8,000		11,300	
Directors' remuneration	12,000		13,000	
Other expenses	8,800	28,800	3,200	27,500
Net profit		43,200		35,000
Add Retained profits from last year		16,800		2,000
		60,000		37,000
Less Appropriations:				
General reserve	8,000		2,000	
Dividends	40,000	48,000	30,000	32,000
Retained profits carried to next year		12,000		5,000

Balance Sheets

	M Ltd		*N Ltd*	
	£	£	£	£
Fixed Assets:				
Fixtures at cost	200,000		180,000	
Less Depreciation to date	50,000	150,000	70,000	110,000
Motor vans at cost	80,000		120,000	
Less Depreciation to date	30,000	50,000	40,000	80,000
		200,000		190,000
Current Assets:				
Stock	100,000		64,000	
Debtors	60,000		62,500	
Bank	40,000		3,500	
	200,000		130,000	
Less Current Liabilities				
Creditors	50,000		65,000	
Net current assets		150,000		65,000
		350,000		255,000
Financed by:				
Issued share capital		300,000		200,000
General reserve		38,000		50,000
Profit and loss		12,000		5,000
		350,000		255,000

Required:

(*a*) Calculate the following ratios to one decimal place:
- (i) current ratio
- (ii) acid test ratio
- (iii) stockturn
- (iv) debtors : sales ratio
- (v) creditors : purchases ratio
- (vi) gross profit as a percentage of sales
- (vii) net profit as a percentage of sales
- (viii) rate of return on shareholders' funds.

(*b*) Compare the results of the two companies, giving possible reasons for the different results.

38.6X The owners of Hailstone company and Taylor company are having a friendly argument over the relative performance of their two similar businesses. The following information is available:

	Hailstone company	Taylor company
	£	£
Cash	4,000	100
Sales	200,000	200,000
Operating expenses	8,000	80,000
Closing stock	8,000	30,000
Debtors	3,000	33,000
Bank overdraft	nil	5,000
Opening stock	10,000	40,000
Capital employed	320,000	320,000
Creditors	7,500	50,000
Purchases	140,000	60,000

Required:

(*a*) For each company, calculate to one decimal place:

- (i) gross profit margin
- (ii) stock turnover (use cost of goods sold divided by average stock)
- (iii) net profit margin
- (iv) return on capital employed
- (v) debtors collection period
- (vi) current ratio.

(*b*) Comment on the performance of each of the companies, using the ratios you have calculated.

Pitman Qualifications

38.7X The following figures are extracted from the final accounts of a company for the year ended 31 December 2008:

	£
Opening stock	5,000
Purchases	32,000
Closing stock	7,000
Sales	60,000
Debtors	7,500

For the year ended 31 December 2008, calculate:

(*a*) cost of goods sold
(*b*) average stock
(*c*) rate of stockturnover
(*d*) debtors collection period.

For the year ended 31 December 2007, the following had been calculated.

- Rate of stockturnover (stockturn) = 6 times p.a.
- Debtors collection period = 31 days (1 month)

(*e*) With that additional information in mind, state which you think was the better year out of 2007 and 2008. Give *two* reasons to support your answer.

NEAB (GCSE)

PART 6

Wage books and records

39 Wage books and records

This section of the book deals with the various methods of calculating wages, payroll procedures and records.

CHAPTER 39

Wage books and records

Learning objectives

After you have studied this chapter you should be able to:

- **understand the functions of the payroll**
- **calculate employees' pay using various methods**
- **distinguish between statutory deductions and voluntary deductions**
- **calculate the net pay of an employee, given details of the employee's gross pay and PAYE income tax and other deductions, and be able to complete a wages book and cash analysis.**

39.1 Introduction

To enable the payment of **wages** and **salaries** to be carried out efficiently and accurately, all organisations, whether large or small, need to keep records of their **employees.** The need for this is essential, not only for recording the payment of wages and income tax etc. but also for recording basic personal details. Such personal records are usually kept in the **personnel department** of an organisation.

39.2 Functions of the payroll

The payroll is a list of employees that specifies the wage or salary that each employee receives. The procedures and calculations that are necessary to produce this list need to be fully understood and applied to ensure that all employees are paid promptly and correctly.

The responsibility for producing the payroll will depend on the size of the organisation. A large organisation will probably have a wages department, whereas a small one will rely on a wages clerk. Irrespective of who carries out the function, that person must ensure that the payments are:

(*a*) *Accurate*:

- correct basic payment for work done
- additional entitlements such as **bonus**, overtime, expenses, etc. included correctly

- correct deduction of taxes, National Insurance contributions due to the government
- correct deduction of contributions to pension and medical schemes
- reliable wage-cost information for the **employer**.

(*b*) *Regular and on time*:

- enables the employees to meet his or her own financial commitments and plan future expenditure
- in contrast, late or irregular payment would harm the morale of employees and cause them to doubt the financial stability of the organisation.

(*c*) *Confidential*:

- staff involved in preparing the payroll must not divulge any of its contents except to authorised people, e.g. company executives, Inland Revenue
- staff must only discuss with an employee that particular employee's wage/salary details.

(*d*) *Secure*:

- the handling of cash and cheques must be done in a secure environment to prevent loss, theft or loss of confidentiality
- checks must be built into the procedures to guard against the possibility of fraud by wages staff
- the distribution of wages must be organised so that each employee receives his or her own wage, and not someone else's
- all employee records must be kept securely. If a manual system is used, records should be held in a locked cabinet with access limited to staff from the personnel/wages department; if a computerised system is used, a password should be given only to authorised personnel so that the information may be accessed only by them.

39.3 Payments to employees

Payments to employees may be made by wage or salary. Wages are usually paid weekly, often in cash, and often to manual workers. Salaries are paid monthly by cheque, credit transfer (i.e. paid direct into the employee's bank account) or direct into a building society account.

Pay may also be referred to as **remuneration**, which simply means to reward or pay for work carried out. This term 'remuneration' is often attached to pay given to the directors of a company, where their pay is recorded in the accounts as 'directors' remuneration'.

39.4 Gross pay and net pay

All employees are subject to Income Tax (PAYE: Pay As You Earn) and National Insurance contributions (NIC). These and other deductions *have* to be made by the employer from the **gross pay**, and so it is important to distinguish between the gross pay figure and **net pay**. Gross pay is the amount of wage or salary due to the employee before deductions are made. Net pay is the amount of wage or salary received by the employee after all deductions have been made. Many employees talk about 'take-home pay'; this is in fact the net pay.

39.5 Methods of calculating pay

The methods for calculating pay vary across employers, and maybe also across employees within an organisation. The main methods are as follows:

- fixed amount of salary or wage
- time rates
- basic rate plus bonus
- piece rate
- commission.

Each is described further below.

Fixed amount of salary or wage

These represent an agreed annual or weekly wage.

Example 1: For an annual salary of £11,604 the monthly salary would be:

$$\frac{£11,604}{12} = £967 \text{ per month}$$

whereas an equivalent weekly wage would be the set figure of £223.15 per week (£11,604 ÷ 52).

Time rates

Here, a fixed basic rate per hour is paid, multiplied by the number of hours worked.

Example 2: A bricklayer receives £8.20 per hour. If he works for 40 hours during a particular week, his gross pay will come to

$$40 \text{ hours} \times £8.20 = £328 \text{ per week}$$

If additional hours are worked, it is usual to pay overtime to each worker on this pay scheme, and this payment is normally at a higher rate. Extra hours worked during the week are often paid at 'time-and-a-half', and 'double time' is frequently paid for weekend work.

Example 3: Richard Kerr worked the following hours during the week ended 31 March 2003:

	Hours
Monday	9
Tuesday	8
Wednesday	8.5
Thursday	10
Friday	8
Saturday	4

His basic rate of pay is £8.60 per hour and he works a standard week of 40 hours (i.e. 8 hours a day for 5 days). Overtime is paid at time-and-a-half during the week and double time on Saturday and Sunday.

Richard Kerr's gross wage for week ending 31 March 2003 is calculated as follows:

	£
Basic pay 40 hours at £8.60	344.00
Overtime:	
Week 3.5 hours at (£8.60 × 1.5)	
= £12.90 per hour	45.15
Saturday 4 hours at (£8.60 × 2)	
= £17.20 per hour	68.80
Gross wage	£457.95

Basic rate plus bonus

Many organisations offer bonus payments as an incentive to workers to reach and exceed set targets. Sometimes the bonus is referred to as a 'productivity bonus' and can be either a set sum of money or a percentage of the basic wage.

Example 4: Electronic Supreme Ltd manufactures television sets for both the home and overseas markets. It pays its workers a basic wage of £268 per week, plus a productivity bonus of £40 per worker if 1,500 televisions are produced in the factory per week; the bonus increases to £60 per week if production exceeds 2,000 televisions.

During the first week of November the company produces 1,600 televisions. Thus, the workers will receive:

	£
Basic wage	268.00
Bonus	40.00
	£308.00

Piece rate

Here, payment is based on the number of units produced or operations completed. The employee is paid only for work *completed* although most employers agree a minimum wage regardless of work completed. **Piece rate** payment is an incentive to encourage workers to work faster - although it is important to ensure that quality does not suffer as a result of faster production.

Example 5: Lowe Production Co manufactures parts for the motor-car industry. It pays its workers piecework rates as follows:

- Part PCD 27 = £2.10 per unit
- Part JB 103 = £7.45 per unit

The company also has a minimum wage agreement of £175.00 per week.

During the first week of January, one of the workers, Jack Murphy, produces 60 Part PCD 27s and 12 Part JB 103s. His wage for the week would be:

		£
$60 \times £2.10$	=	126.00
$12 \times £7.45$	=	89.40
		215.40

Another worker, Thomas Hobson, produces 50 Part PCD 27s and 8 Part JB 103s; his wage is calculated by the piece rates as:

		£
$50 \times £2.10$	=	105.00
$8 \times £7.45$	=	59.60
		164.60

but, because there is a minimum wage agreement, Thomas Hobson receives £175.00.

Commission

Commission is a percentage based on the amount of sales made by an employee. Commission may be paid in addition to a basic salary or instead of a salary.

Example 6: Carol Chapman and Dianne Dawson work for a computer software company. Their salaries were £12,000 and £10,800 a year respectively, plus commission of 1 per cent of total sales made each month.

During July, Carol's sales totalled £30,000 and Dianne's £17,000. Their July salaries would be as follows:

Carol	$\frac{£12,000}{12}$	= £1,000 per month
	plus 1% of £30,000	= 300
	Month's salary	= £1,300
Dianne	$\frac{£10,800}{12}$	= £900
	plus 1% of £17,000	= 170
	Month's salary	= £1,070

39.6 Clock cards

Some organisations require their workers to 'clock in' and 'clock out' at work in order to enable accurate payment to be made in respect of time spent at work.

Under this arrangement, on arrival at work each employee removes his or her personal **clock card** from a rack and slots it into a time-recorder clock, which records the time of arrival. The same procedure is carried out on leaving work.

At the end of the week, the card is passed to the wages department to enable it to calculate the actual hours worked by each employee.

A clock card after completion by the wages department is shown in Exhibit 39.1.

With regard to Exhibit 39.1, the firm works a 39 hour week, Monday to Thursday 8 hours per day and Friday 7 hours, all at £7.60 per hour. Overtime is paid at time-and-a-half during the week and at double time on Saturday and Sunday. These parameters yield the figures shown in Exhibit 39.2.

Exhibit 39.1

CLOCK CARD

Name: B. Sullivan **No:** 98

Week ending: 11 April 2003

Day	In	Out	In	Out	Total hours
Mon	8.00	12.01	1.00	5.03	8
Tue	8.00	12.00	1.00	5.00	8
Wed	8.01	12.02	12.57	5.01	8
Thu	8.03	12.00	12.59	5.30	8½
Fri	8.00	12.01	1.01	4.00	7
Sat	7.30	12.00			4½
Total					44

Ordinary time	39 hrs x £7.60	296.40
Overtime	1/2 hr x £11.40 plus 4 1/2 hrs x £15.20	74.10
Bonus		
	Gross pay	£370.50

39.7 Time sheets

Time sheets are usually used by employees who work away from the main business premises, e.g. in a decorating company where workers are employed at various locations according to the requirements of the individual jobs.

See Exhibit 39.2, showing time sheets completed by an employee called Gary Lester in such a firm. You will notice that Gary is required to complete details of work carried out and the hours worked on the job, together with the time spent on travelling to the job. At the end of the week the time sheet will be checked by the supervisor or foreman before being passed to the wages department for completion.

In respect of this example, the firm works a basic 40-hour week, Lester's time is paid at £8.00 per hour, and travelling time is paid at £6.00 per hour. Overtime is paid at time-and-a-half during the week and at double time on Saturday and Sunday. These costing figures yield the results shown in Exhibit 39.2.

EXHIBIT 39.2

A time sheet showing calculations of hours worked and gross pay.

TIME SHEET

Name: *Gary Lester* **Week ending:** *20 March 2003*

Day	Job description	Hours worked	Travel time	Total
Mon	*Decorating Casino*	8	½	8½
Tue	,,	8½	½	9
Wed	,,	8	½	8½
Thu	*External work at Stanton offices*	9	1	10
Fri	,,	8½	1	9½
Sat	*Decorating office – Black's Estate Agents*	6	1	7
Sun	,,	4	1	5
	Totals	52	5½	57½

Basic:	40 hrs ×	£8.00	**Total**	320.00
O/T – Week:	2 hrs ×	£12.00		24.00
– Weekend	10 hrs ×	£16.00		160.00
Travel:	5½ hrs ×	£6.00		33.00
Foreman:	*R Derbyshire*		**Gross pay**	537.00

Time sheets can also be used by workers based at the main office of a firm but involved in work for various clients or customers. A typical example here would be a firm of solicitors or accountants, where employees carry out specific duties for clients and need to record the time spent on each particular job to enable correct costings to be carried out prior to invoicing each client.

One of the main advantages of using this method of recording time spent on each job is that employees are more conscious of their time and therefore (in theory) deploy time more effectively. Also, clients are charged more fairly, according to the time spent on a particular job. However, one of the disadvantages is that clients could be overcharged if an employee records job time inaccurately or charges time to a particular client's job when that time was spent in other areas of work or in inactivity.

Many organisations also require payroll information and data to be fed into the costing system so as to enable management information to be available for budgeting, costing and profitability analysis.

39.8 Computer cards

Many organisations nowadays use **computerised card** systems, whereby employees carry computer cards that they insert into a computerised time clock on arrival and departure. In the same way as clock cards, the computerised card automatically records their hours of work.

This method of recording hours worked is often used by employers using a **flexitime system** (*see* Section 39.9).

39.9 Flexitime system

Flexitime is a system permitting flexibility of working hours at the beginning or end of the day provided that an agreed period of time, called **core time**, is spent at work.

Staff are usually free to choose their starting and finishing times but must work the normal number of hours per week. However, it is possible to carry forward time worked in excess of the normal time, or owed, to another period and then take time off in lieu, although the time allowed to be carried forward is usually limited (say to only one day per fortnight).

Flexitime is widely used in large organisations and local authorities while not so popular in smaller private companies.

39.10 Deductions from pay

There are two types of deductions which are made from wages and salaries:

- **statutory deductions**
- **voluntary deductions.**

Each is analysed further below.

Statutory deductions

Deductions that an employer has to make by law (i.e. by statute) from employees' gross pay are known as statutory deductions. The most common are:

- income tax
- National Insurance contributions.

Income tax

In the United Kingdom, the wages and salaries of all employees are liable to income tax deductions. This does not mean, however, that everyone will pay income tax; it depends upon the amount of earnings and the tax allowances that can be offset against that **income**. If income tax is found to be payable, then the employer will deduct the tax from the employee's wage or salary. This is then paid to the Inland Revenue, the government department responsible for collection of income tax.

National Insurance contributions (NIC)

National Insurance contributions (NIC) are also deducted by the employer from the employee in a similar way to income tax deductions, but the employer also has to contribute a certain amount of money, again depending upon the amount of gross pay.

All contributions are sent to the Inland Revenue, which collects them on behalf of the government's Department of Social Security.

Voluntary deductions

As the name suggests, these are deductions made from pay at the employee's request. They include payments to:

- occupational **pension funds** or **superannuation schemes**
- charitable organisations
- savings schemes
- trade unions and/or social clubs.

39.11 A fully worked example

The following example shows the preparation of a wages book, cash analysis and finally the cheque for withdrawing the money from the bank.

Example 7: Spencers (Exhibition Suppliers) Co of Nottingham is a small company specialising in the supply of exhibition display units and materials to industrial and commercial organisations. It employs a small workforce of four people, details of which are as follows:

Employee's name	*Gross weekly wage*	*Income tax due*	*NIC employee*	*NIC employer*
Julie L Gibbons	£185.00	£25.17	£13.91	£12.98
David R Hall	£265.00	£40.17	£21.91	£27.08
Andrew M Turner	£250.00	£35.92	£20.41	£25.55
Amanda Whitehouse	£220.00	£33.42	£17.41	£22.49

Each of the above employees also contributes £1.00 per week each to the company's social club.

The completed wages book for Spencers (Exhibition Suppliers) Co is now shown in Exhibit 39.3.

EXHIBIT 39.3

WAGES BOOK - Spencers

Week ending: 6 April 2003

Number	Name	Earnings				Deductions					
		Basic £	Over-time £	Bonus £	Total gross pay £	PAYE (Income Tax) £	National Insurance £	Other deductions £	Total deductions £	Net pay £	Employer's NI contributions £
	J.L. Gibbons	185-			185-	25.17	13.91	1.00	40.08	144.92	12.98
	D.R.Hall	265-			265-	40.17	21.91	1.00	63.08	201.92	27.08
	A.M. Turner	250-			250-	35.92	20.41	1.00	57.33	192.67	25.55
	A. Whitehouse	220-			220-	33.42	17.41	1.00	51.83	168.17	22.49
	Totals	920-			920-	134.68	73.64	4.00	212.32	707.68	88.10

The wages clerk would then prepare a cash analysis to ensure that the notes and coins obtained from the bank will enable the wage packets to be filled with the correct amount of money. To carry out the calculation, it is necessary to make a list of the note and coin values across the top and list the employees down the side. After working out what is needed for each single employee, the quantities required for all the employees are added up; this is shown in Exhibit 39.4. (In this particular example, the company pays the first £100 in £20 notes and any amount thereafter in £10 and £5 notes or £1 coins, as appropriate.)

Exhibit 39.4

CASH ANALYSIS – Spencers

Week ending: *6 April 2003*

Name	£20	£10	£5	£1	50p	20p	10p	5p	2p	1p	Amount £ p
J.L. Gibbons	5	4		4	1	2			1		144.92
D.R. Hall	5	10		1	1	2			1		201.92
A.M. Turner	5	9		2	1		1	1	1		192.67
A Whitehouse	5	6	1	3			1	1	1		168.17
Number of notes and coins required	20	29	1	10	3	4	2	2	4		
Totals Cross-check	400	290	5	10	1.50	.80p	.20p	.10p	.8p		707.68

Now we need to check that we have carried out the cash analysis correctly by adding up the notes and coins required as follows:

Notes and coins required

				£
20	×	£20	=	400.00
29	×	£10	=	290.00
1	×	£5	=	5.00
10	×	£1	=	10.00
3	×	50p	=	1.50
4	×	20p	=	0.80
2	×	10p	=	0.20
2	×	5p	=	0.10
4	×	2p	=	0.08
				707.68

The total of the coin analysis agrees with the net pay figure as shown in the wages book (Exhibit 39.3) and so we can assume that the analysis has been carried out correctly.

Finally, a cheque is made out to enable the cash to be withdrawn from the bank (*see* Exhibit 39.5) in order to pay the employees. The cash will be taken in the manner required by the cash analysis.

Exhibit 39.5

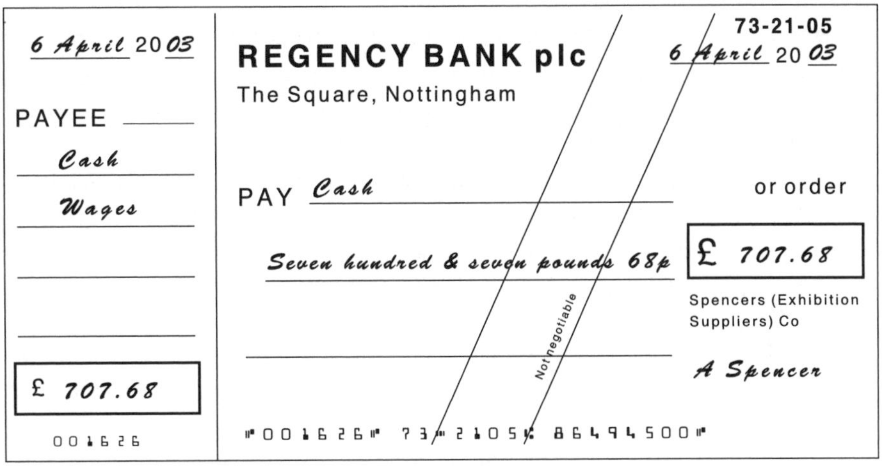

6 April 2003

PAYEE
Cash
Wages

£ 707.68

001626

REGENCY BANK plc
The Square, Nottingham

73-21-05
6 April 2003

PAY Cash or order

Seven hundred & seven pounds 68p

£ 707.68

Not negotiable

Spencers (Exhibition Suppliers) Co

A Spencer

⑈001626⑈ 73⑆21050⑆ 86494500⑈

New terms

Bonus (p. 468): An additional amount paid to an employee if a set target is achieved.

Clock card (p. 472): Card issued to employees to enable them to 'clock in' and 'clock out' at work. The card is then used to calculate the employees' wages according to the number of hours spent at work.

Commission (p. 472): A percentage, based on the amount of sales made by an employee, that may be paid in addition to a basic salary or instead of a salary.

Computerised card (p. 475): Card used by staff to record the time spent on the business premises by inserting the card into a computerised time clock on arrival and departure.

Core time (p. 475): The time that an employee is required to be at work under a flexitime system, unless that employee is on leave, sick, or otherwise has permission to be absent.

Employee (p. 468): A person who is hired to work for an organisation in return for payment.

Employer (p. 469): A person or organisation that employs workers and pays them wages or salaries in return for services rendered.

Flexitime system (p. 475): System of permitting flexibility of working hours at the beginning and end of the day, provided that an agreed 'core time' is spent on the premises.

Gross pay (p. 469): The amount of wage or salary before deductions are made.

Income (p. 476): Pay that is subject to income tax.

Net pay (p. 469): The amount of wage or salary after deductions are made (the net wage is often referred to as 'take-home pay').

Pension fund/superannuation scheme (p. 476): Scheme set up by employers to provide their employees with a pension.

Personnel department (p. 468): An organisation's department that deals with interviewing and appointing staff, together with the keeping of accurate employee records.

Piece rate (p. 471): Pay based on the number of units produced or operations completed.

Remuneration (p. 469): Reward for work carried out.

Salary (p. 468): Fixed payment, usually monthly, to an employee for professional or office work.

Statutory deductions (p. 475): Deductions that an employer has to make by law (statute) from workers' gross pay.

Time sheet (p. 473): A form used by employees, who often work away from the main business premises, to record the time spent on various jobs and the overall weekly attendance.

Voluntary deductions (p. 475): Deductions made from pay at an employee's request.

Wage (p. 468): Payment made to a worker in return for services rendered, and usually paid weekly.

EXERCISES

39.1 Kevin Chandler is employed by a firm of joiners and is paid at the rate of £7.50 per hour. During the week to 18 May 2004 he works a basic week of 40 hours. The income tax due on his wages is £55, and he is also liable to pay National Insurance contributions of 6 per cent of his gross wage. Calculate Kevin's net wages.

39.2 Michael Ford works as an electrician and is paid a basic rate of £7.20 per hour for a 40-hour week; overtime is paid at a rate of 1½ times the basic pay. During the week ending 28 April 2003, Michael works 50 hours. He pays National Insurance at 6 per cent of his gross pay, pension contributions at 8 per cent of the basic pay, and income tax at 22 per cent on all earnings after deducting £80 tax-free pay. Michael also pays £2 per week for his union subscriptions.

You are required to:
(*a*) calculate Michael Ford's gross pay
(*b*) calculate each of the deductions
(*c*) show the amount Michael Ford will take home.

39.3 You are employed as a wages clerk for Whittaker and Co. The basic working week is 37 hours, overtime is paid at time-and-a-half for the first six hours and any further hours are paid at double time.

During the week ended 8 May 2004, Andrew Hill works 47 hours. His basic rate is £7.90 per hour, National Insurance is calculated at 8 per cent of gross pay, and the weekly contribution to the pension fund is reckoned on 5 per cent of basic pay. Income tax is £95.50. Andrew also makes a weekly payment of £3.00 to the firm's social club. The company's National Insurance contribution on behalf of Andrew Hill is £27.60.

You are required to complete the pay slip shown in Exhibit 39.6.

39.4X Belfield Manufacturing Co employs assembly-line workers who are paid piece rates of £9.00 for every 50 items manufactured.

During week 16, ending 5 August 2005, one of the employees, Marlene Ross, whose clock number is 22, made 1,800 items. Deductions from her pay are to be calculated as follows:

- income tax £52.00
- National Insurance contributions 8% of gross pay
- contributions to pension fund 5% of gross pay
- union fees £4.10.

You are required to complete the payslip given in Exhibit 39.7.

39.5X Diane Burton manages a small firm employing six staff. Burton herself is on a monthly salary, but the net wages of the other six employees for the week ending 5 July 2004 are shown below:

	£
D Ball	93.86
P Crofts	154.16
J Henshaw	158.26
H Stevens	151.01
K Webster	181.66
D Martin	132.56
	871.51

You are required to:

(*a*) rule up and complete a note and coin analysis in table form using columns as follows: £20, £10, £5, £1, 50p, 20p, 10p, 5p, 2p and 1p

(*b*) reconcile the value of the total notes and coins with the total wages.

39.6X You have been given the task of making up the wage packets for four employees for the week ending 2 May 2008. The wages to be paid to the employees are:

	£
S Goldberg	190.65
J Lander	143.80
V Turner	155.85
L Thrussell	137.55

You pay the wages in cash at the end of each week, using notes and coins of denominations £20, £10, £5, £1, 50p, 20p, 10p and 5p. It is the company's policy to give each employee at least one £1 coin.

Required:

(*a*) Rule up and prepare a note/coin analysis in table form using columns as follows: £20, £10, £5, £1, 50p, 20p, 10p, 5p 2p and 1p. You should use the least number of notes and coins permissible.

(*b*) Reconcile the total value of the notes and coins with the total pay bill.

OCR

39.7X A firm operates a normal working week of 40 hours, and the basic rate of pay is £4.28 per hour. Overtime is paid as follows:

- Weekdays Time and a quarter
- Saturdays Time and a half
- Sundays Double time

Exhibit 39.6

Week ending				Deductions						
Name	Hours	Rate	Gross Pay	Income Tax	National Insurance	Pension	Others	Total deductions	Net	Employer's National Insurance contribution

Exhibit 39.7

Clock No			Week No			Week ending				
			Deductions							
Name	Numbers produced	Rate	Gross pay	Tax	National Insurance	Pensions	Others	Total deductions	Net pay	Employer's National Insurance contribution

In a particular week, the hours worked by a group of employees is thus:

Employee	*Hours Worked*			
	Normal	*Weekday*	*Sat*	*Sun*
R Giles	40	4	4	-
R Paskes	40	6	-	4
I Hargreaves	40	-	-	4
S Worrall	40	3	4	4

Calculate the gross wages for each of the employees.

39.8 A firm operates such that its normal hours worked are 40 hours, paid at £5.20 per hour plus an incentive bonus scheme of 75 pence for each unit of output. In a particular week, the following employee output is recorded:

Employee	*Hours Worked*	*Output*
A Taylor	35	30
S McKenzie	42	40
R Brindley	40	36
W Baseley	44	36
W Warburton	45	52

Calculate the gross pay that each of the workers would receive.

APPENDICES

A Glossary of accounting terms

B Step-by-step guides

C Multiple-choice questions

D Answers to multiple-choice questions

E Answers to exercises

F Specimen examination papers

The Appendices provide ancillary information to aid understanding of the main narrative of the book. Test questions are also included.

APPENDIX A

Glossary of accounting terms

The chapter where the term first appears is shown at the end of each definition.

Account	The place in a ledger where all the transactions relating to a particular asset, liability or capital, expenses or revenue item are recorded. Accounts are part of the double entry book-keeping system. They are sometimes referred to as 'T accounts' or ledger accounts. (**3**)
Accounting	A skill or practice of maintaining accounts and preparing reports to aid the financial control and management of a business. (**1**)
Accounting cycle	The period in which a business operates its financial year. It involves recording all trading activities from source documents to the preparation of final accounts. (**25**)
Accrual	An accrued expense. An amount owing. (**29**)
Accrual concept	Where net profit is the difference between revenues and expenses. (**11**)
Accrued expense	An expense that has been incurred and the benefit received but that has not been paid for at the end of the accounting period. Also referred to as an accrual. (**29**)
Accumulated fund	A form of capital account for a non-profit making organisation. (**34**)
Acid test ratio	A ratio comparing current assets less stock with current liabilities. Also known as the 'quick ratio'. (**38**)
Advice note	A note sent to a customer by the supplier prior to goods being despatched, advising of the goods to be despatched and the estimated date of delivery. (**19**)
Amortisation	A term used instead of depreciation when assets are used up simply because of the time factor. (**26**)
Analytical day book	Book of original entry in which sales and/or purchase invoices are entered. The book has various analysis columns, which are totalled at the end of the month and posted to the general ledger and control accounts. (**23**)
Annual General Meeting (AGM)	A meeting held every year to which all shareholders in a company are invited to attend. At the meeting, the latest set of final accounts is considered, together with the appointment or removal of directors and/or auditors. (**37**)

Appreciation The increase in value over the cost of an asset, usually land and buildings. (**26**)

Appropriation Account An addition to the Profit and Loss Account of partnerships and companies. The appropriation account shows how profit earned is divided. In a partnership it is divided in accordance with the partnership deed or agreement. With a company it is apportioned to reserve accounts, provision for taxation and distributed as a dividend to the shareholders. (**36**)

Assets Resources owned by the business. (**2**)

Authorised share capital The total amount of share capital or number of shares which a company can have in issue at any given time. (**37**)

AVCO A method by which the goods used are priced out at average cost. (**30**)

Bad debt A debt owing to a business which is unlikely to be paid. (**28**)

Bad debt recovered A debt, previously written off, that is subsequently paid by the debtor. (**28**)

Balance sheet A statement showing the assets, capital and liabilities of a business. (**2**)

Balancing the account Finding and entering the difference between the two sides of an account. (**6**)

Bank giro credits Method used by businesses to pay creditors, wages and/or salaries. A bank giro credit list and slips containing information about each person or organisation to be paid and the amount payable are sent to the bank, together with one cheque to cover all the payments. The bank then automatically transfers the funds from the business's account to the account of each of the respective people or organisations. (**14**)

Bank overdraft What results when we have paid more out of our bank account than we have paid into it. (**14**)

Bank reconciliation statement A calculation comparing the cash book balance with the bank statement balance. (**17**)

Bank statement Copy of our current account given to us by our bank. (**15**)

Bankers' Automated Clearing Service (BACS) Computerised payment transfer system that is a very popular way of paying creditors, wages and salaries. (**14**)

Bonus An additional amount paid to an employee once a set target is achieved. (**39**)

Book-keeping The recording of accounting data. (**1**)

Books of original entry Books where the first entry of a transaction is made. (**12**)

Business entity concept Concerning only transactions that affect the firm, and ignoring the owner's private transactions. (**11**)

Called-up capital Where only part of the amounts payable on each share have been asked for. The total amount requested on all the shares is known as the 'called-up capital'. (**37**)

Calls in arrear The amount for which payment has been requested (i.e. called for), but has not yet been paid by shareholders. (**37**)

Capital The total of resources supplied to a business by its owner. (**2**)

Capital employed This term has many meanings, but basically it means the amount of money that is being used up (or 'employed') in the business. It is the balance of the capital account plus any long-term loan or, alternatively, the total net assets of the business. (**29**)

Capital expenditure When a firm spends money to buy or add value to a fixed asset. (**18**)

Capital invested The amount of money, or money's worth, brought into a business by its proprietor from outside. (**29**)

Capital reserve Reserves which cannot be used for the payment of dividends. The two most common types of capital reserve are the Share Premium Account and Revaluation Reserve Account (Capital reserves are outside the scope of this book.) (**37**)

Carriage inwards Cost of transport of goods into a business. (**10**)

Carriage outwards Cost of transport of goods to the customers of a business. (**10**)

Carriage paid See Section 19.16. (**19**)

Cash book Book of original entry for cash and bank receipts and payments. (**12**)

Cash discount An allowance given for quick payment of an account owing. (**16**)

Cash float The sum held as petty cash. (**13**)

Casting Adding up figures. (**31**)

Cheque book Book containing forms (cheques) used to pay money out of a current account. (**14**)

Clock card Card issued to employees to enable them to 'clock in and out' of work. The card is then used to calculate the employees' wages according to the number of hours spent at work. (**39**)

COD Literally 'Cash on delivery'. (**19**)

Coding of invoices A process used, particularly in computerised accounting, to code the invoice to the supplier or purchaser, and also to the relevant account in the general ledger. (**20**)

Commission A percentage, based on the amount of sales made by an employee, may be paid in addition to a basic salary or instead of a salary. (**39**)

Compensating error Where two errors of equal amounts but on opposite sides of the accounts, cancel out each other. (**31**)

Computerised card Card used by staff to record the time spent on the business premises by inserting the card into a computerised time clock on arrival and departure. (**39**)

Conservatism An older term for 'prudence'. (**11**)

Consistency To keep the same method, except in special cases. (**11**)

Contra A contra is where both the debit and credit entries are shown in the cash book. (**15**)

Control account An account which checks the arithmetical accuracy of a ledger. (**24**)

Core time The time that an employee is required to be at work under a

	flexitime system, unless that employee is on leave, sick, or otherwise has permission to be absent. (**39**)
Cost of goods sold	This is calculated as follows: Opening stock plus purchases during the period less the value of the stock at the end of the period (closing stock). (**8**)
Credit	The right-hand side of the accounts in double entry. (**3**)
Credit note	A document sent to a customer showing allowance given by supplier in respect of unsatisfactory goods. (**21**)
Credit transfer	An amount paid by someone direct into our bank account. (**17**)
Creditor	A person to whom money is owed for goods or services. (**2**)
Creditors : Purchases ratio	A ratio assessing how long it takes a business to pay its creditors. (**38**)
Current account	Bank account used for regular payments in and out of the bank. (**14**)
Current assets	Assets consisting of cash, goods for resale, or items having a shorter life. (**9**)
Current liabilities	Liabilities to be paid for in the near future. (**9**)
Current ratio	A ratio comparing current assets with current liabilities. Also known as the 'working capital' ratio. (**38**)
Debenture	Loan to a company. (**37**)
Debenture interest	An agreed percentage of interest paid to a debenture holder for lending a company money. (**37**)
Debit	The left-hand side of the accounts in double entry. (**3**)
Debit note	A document sent to a supplier showing allowance given for unsatisfactory goods. (**21**)
Debtor	A person who owes money to the business for goods or services supplied. (**2**)
Debtors : Sales ratio	A ratio assessing how long it takes debtors to pay a business. (**38**)
Delivery note	A note which accompanies goods being despatched, enabling the customer to check what goods have been received. The carrier often retains a copy and asks the customer to sign this to verify that the customer has received the goods. (**19**)
Depletion	The wasting away of an asset as it is used up. (**26**)
Deposit account	Bank account for money to be kept in for a long time. Interest is given on money deposited. (**14**)
Depreciation	The part of the cost of the fixed asset consumed during its period of use by a firm. (**26**)
Direct costs	Costs which can be traced to the item being manufactured. (**35**)
Direct debit	Payment made out of payer's bank, direct to payee's bank, on *payee's* instructions. (**14**)
Directors	Officials appointed by shareholders to manage the company for them. (**37**)
Directors' remuneration	Directors are legally employees of the company and any pay they receive is call directors' remuneration. (**37**)

Discounts allowed A reduction given to customers who pay their accounts within the time allowed. **(16)**

Discounts received A reduction given to us by a supplier when we pay their account before the time allowed has elapsed. **(16)**

Dishonoured cheque A cheque that is found to be worth nothing. **(17)**

Dividends The amount given to shareholders as their share of the profits of the company. **(37)**

Donation A monetary gift donated to the club or society, monies received should be shown as income in the year that they are received. **(34)**

Double entry book-keeping A system where each transaction is entered twice, once on the debit side and once on the credit side. **(3)**

Drawer The person making out a cheque and using it for payment. **(14)**

Drawings Cash or goods taken out of a business by the owner for private use. **(5)**

Dual aspect concept Dealing with both aspects of a transaction. **(11)**

E & OE See Section 19.16. **(19)**

Employee A person who is hired to work for an organisation in return for payment. **(39)**

Employer A person or organisation that employs workers and pays them wages or salaries in return for services rendered. **(39)**

Equity Another name for the capital of the owner. Also described as 'net worth'. **(2)**

Error of commission Where a correct amount is entered, but in the wrong person's account. **(31)**

Error of omission Where a transaction is completely omitted from the books. **(31)**

Error of original entry Where an item is entered, but both debit and credit entries are of the same incorrect amount. **(31)**

Error of principle Where an item is entered in the wrong type of account, e.g. a fixed asset entered in an expense account. **(31)**

Ex works An indication that the price of certain goods does not include delivery costs. **(19)**

Exempted firms Firms that do not have to add VAT to the price of goods and services supplied by them, and that cannot obtain a refund of VAT paid on goods and services purchased by them. **(22)**

Expenses Costs of operating the business. **(5)**

Expenses : Sales ratio A ratio which indicates whether costs are rising against sales or whether sales are falling against expenses. **(38)**

Factoring A system used by a business to improve its cash flow. This involves 'selling' its debtors to a factoring company, which is then responsible for collecting debts as they become due and which keeps a percentage of the money collected, usually around 10 per cent. **(19)**

Factory overhead costs Costs in the factory for production, but not traced to the item being manufactured. (**35**)

FIFO A method by which the first goods to be received are said to be the first to be sold. (**30**)

Final accounts At the end of the accounting period or year a business usually prepares its final accounts, which includes the trading and profit and loss account and balance sheet. (**10**)

Financial statements Formal documents produced by an organisation to show the financial status of the business at a particular time. These include the trading and profit and loss account and the balance sheet. (**1**)

Fixed assets Assets bought which have a long life and are to be used in the business. (**9**)

Fixed capital accounts Capital accounts which consist only of the original capital invested in the business. (**36**)

Flexitime system System of permitting flexibility of working hours at the beginning and end of the day provided an agreed 'core time' is spent on the premises. (**39**)

Fluctuating capital accounts Capital accounts whose balances change from one period to the next. (**36**)

Folio columns Columns used for entering reference numbers. (**15**)

General journal Book of original entry for all items other than those for cash or goods. (**12**)

General ledger All accounts other than those for customers and suppliers. (**12**)

Going concern concept Where a business is assumed to continue for a long time. (**11**)

Goodwill The extra amount paid for an existing firm above the value of its other assets. (**29**)

Gross loss When the 'cost of goods sold' exceeds 'sales', then the business has incurred a gross loss. (**8**)

Gross pay This is the amount of wages or salary before deductions are made. (**39**)

Gross profit Found by deducting cost of goods sold from sales. (**8**)

Gross profit : Sales ratio A ratio which states gross profit as a percentage of sales; can indicate how effectively a business has controlled their cost of goods. (**38**)

Impersonal accounts All accounts other than debtors' and creditors' accounts. (**12**)

Imprest system A system used for controlling expenditure of small cash items which are recorded in the petty cash book. A cash 'float' of a fixed amount is provided initially to the person responsible for operating the petty cash system. Any cash paid out during a particular period, i.e. a week, is reimbursed to the petty cashier so restoring the 'float' to its original sum. (**13**)

Inadequacy When an asset is no longer used because of changes within an organisation due to growth, competition or product range changes. (**26**)

Income	Pay that is subject to income tax. (39)
Income and expenditure account	An account for a non-profit making organisation to find the surplus or loss made during a period. (34)
Incomplete records	Where only some transactions are recorded in the books of account, the missing information has to be obtained by other means. (33)
Input tax	The VAT charged to a business on its purchases and expenses (inputs). (22)
Inputs	The value of goods and services purchased by a business. (22)
Intangible fixed asset	A fixed asset that cannot be physically seen or touched. (29)
Interest on capital	An amount, at an agreed rate of interest, that is credited to a partner based on the amount of capital contributed by him/her. (36)
Interest on drawings	An amount, at an agreed rate of interest, that is based on the drawings taken out and is debited to the partners. (36)
Investment property	Property purchased with the intent of making profit, usually by leasing it. (26)
Invoice	A document prepared by the seller and sent to the purchaser whenever a business buys goods or services on credit. It gives details of the supplier and the customer, the goods purchased and their price. (19)
Issued share capital	The amount of the authorised share capital of a company that has been issued to shareholders. (37)
Journal	A book of account used to record rare or exceptional transactions that should not appear in the other books of original entry in use. (25)
Lease	An agreement to rent property for a period of time. (26)
Liabilities	Total of money owed for assets supplied to the business. (2)
Life membership	Where members pay one amount for membership to last them their lifetime. (34)
LIFO	A method by which the goods sold are said to have come from the last lot of goods to be received. (30)
Limited company	An organisation owned by its shareholders, whose liability is limited to their share capital. (37)
Limited liability	The liability of shareholders, in a company, is limited to any amount they have agreed to invest. (37)
Limited partner	A partner whose liability is limited to the capital invested in the firm. (36)
Liquidity	The ability of a business to pay its debts as they fall due and to meet unexpected expenses within a reasonable settlement period. (38)
Liquidity ratios	Ratios that attempt to indicate the ability of a business to meet its debts as they become due and include current ratio and acid test ratio. (38)

Loan capital	Money owing by a company for debentures and for loans from banks and other sources that are not repayable in the near future. **(37)**
Long-term liabilities	Liabilities not having to be paid for in the near future. **(9)**
Loss	Result of selling goods for less than they have cost the business. **(5)**
Manufacturing account	An account in which production cost is calculated. **(35)**
Margin	Profit shown as a percentage or fraction of the selling price. **(38)**
Mark-up	Profit shown as a percentage or fraction of the cost price. **(38)**
Materiality	To record something in a special way only if the amount is not a small one. **(11)**
Memorandum account	An account which is not pat of the double-entry system. These may be the personal accounts of debtors or creditors where the control account is part of the double entry and the personal accounts are classified as 'memorandum accounts'. Alternatively, the sales and purchases ledgers may be part of the double entry and the control accounts classified as 'memorandum accounts'. **(24)**
Narrative	A description and explanation of the transaction recorded in the journal. **(25)**
Net book value	The cost of a fixed asset with depreciation deducted, also known as 'book value'. **(26)**
Net current assets	The value of current assets less that of current liabilities. Also known as 'working capital'. **(9)**
Net monthly	See Section 19.13. **(19)**
Net pay	This is the amount of wages or salary after deductions are made (the net wage is often referred to as 'take-home pay'). **(39)**
Net profit	Gross profit less expenses. **(8)**
Net profit : Sales ratio	A ratio that states net profit as a percentage of sales and brings expenses into the calculation. **(38)**
Net realisable value	The value of goods calculated as the selling price less expenses before sale. **(30)**
Net worth	See 'equity'. **(2)**
Nominal accounts	Accounts in which expenses, revenue and capital are recorded. **(12)**
Nominal ledger	Ledger for impersonal accounts (also called general ledger). **(12)**
Non-profit making organisations	Clubs, associations and societies operated to provide a service or activity for members since their main purpose is not trading or profit making. **(34)**
Non-trading organisations	These include clubs, associations and other non-profit-making organisations that are normally run for the benefit of their members to engage in a particular activity. **(1)**
Objectivity	Using a method that everyone can agree to. **(11)**
Obsolescence	Becoming out of date. **(26)**
Opening entry	An entry needed to open a new set of books of account. **(25)**

Ordinary shares	Shares entitled to dividends after the preference shareholders have been paid their dividends. (**37**)
Output tax	The VAT charged by a business on its supplies (outputs). (**22**)
Outputs	The value of goods and services sold to a business. (**22**)
Overcasting	Incorrectly adding up a column of figures to give an answer which exceeds the correct total. (**31**)
Paid-up capital	The total of the amount of share capital that has been paid for by shareholders. (**37**)
Partnership	A group of more than two people and a maximum of twenty, who together are carrying on a particular business with a view to making profit. (**1**)
Partnership agreement	The contractual relationship, either written or verbal, between partners, which usually covers details such as how profits or losses should be shared and the relevant responsibilities of the partners. (**36**)
Partnership salaries	Agreed amounts payable to partners in respect of duties undertaken by them. (**36**)
Payee	The person to whom a cheque is paid. (**14**)
Paying-in book	A book of suitability preprinted paying-in slips and counterfoils used to pay cash and cheques into a bank account. (**14**)
Paying-in slip	Form used for paying money into a bank account. (**14**)
Pension fund/ Superannuation Scheme	Schemes set up by employers to provide their employees with a pension. (**39**)
Personal accounts	Accounts for both creditors and debtors. (**12**)
Personnel department	An organisation's department that deals with interviewing and appointing staff, together with the keeping of accurate employee records. (**39**)
Petty cash book	A cash book used for making small (petty) payments. Payments are usually analysed and the totals of each column later posted to the various accounts in the general ledger. The source document used for entry into the petty cash book is a petty cash voucher. (**13**)
Petty cash voucher	The form used by anyone requesting payment for a small item of expenditure incurred on behalf of the business. The form gives details of the expense and should be signed and duly authorised. (**13**)
Piece rate	Pay based on the number of units produced or operations completed. (**39**)
Posting	The act of using one book as a means of entering the transactions to another account. (**15**)
Preference shares	Shares that are entitled to an agreed rate of dividend before the ordinary shareholders receive anything. (**37**)
Preliminary expenses	All the costs that are incurred when a company is formed. (**37**)
Prepaid expense	An expense – usually a service – that has been paid for in one accounting period, the benefit of which will not be received until a

	subsequent period. It is a payment for an expense that has been paid for in advance. (**29**)
Prime cost	Direct materials plus labour plus direct expenses. (**35**)
Private ledger	Ledger for capital and drawings accounts. (**12**)
Private limited company	A legal entity with at least two shareholders, where the liability of the shareholders is limited to the amount of their investment. The public cannot subscribe for its shares. (**1**)
Production cost	Prime cost plus factory overhead costs. (**35**)
Profit	The result when goods are sold for more than they cost. (If they are sold for less than they cost, then a *loss* is incurred.) (**5**)
Profit and loss account	Account in which net profit is calculated. (**8**)
Profitability	The effective operation of a business to make ongoing profits to ensure its long-term viability. (**38**)
Profitability ratios	Ratios that attempt to indicate the trend in a business's ability to make profit. These include gross profit and net profit to sales and return on capital employed. (**38**)
Provision for bad debts	An account showing the expected amounts of debtors, who at the balance sheet date, may not be able to pay their outstanding accounts. (**28**)
Provision for depreciation account	The account where depreciation is accumulated for balance sheet purposes. In the balance sheet the cost price of the asset is shown, less the depreciation to date, to give the net book value. (**27**)
Prudence or **conservatism**	To ensure that profit is not shown as being too high, or assets shown at too high a value. (**11**)
Public limited company	A legal entity with many shareholders since the public can subscribe for its shares. Shareholder liability is limited to the amount of their investment. (**1**)
Purchase invoice	A document received by purchaser showing details of goods bought and their prices. (**20**)
Purchase order	This is a document prepared by the purchaser and it contains details of the goods or services required by the purchaser. (**20**)
Purchases	Goods bought by the business for the purpose of selling them again. (**4**)
Purchases day book	Book of original entry for credit purchases. (**12**)
Purchases ledger	A ledger for suppliers' personal accounts. (**12**)
Quick ratio	Same as the acid test ratio. (**38**)
Real accounts	Accounts in which property of all kinds is recorded. (**12**)
Realisation concept	The point at which profit is treated as being earned. (**11**)
Receipt	A form acknowledging receipt of money for goods or services rendered. (**15**)
Receipts and payments account	A summary of the cash book of a non-profit making organisation. (**34**)

Reducing balance method Depreciation calculation which is at a lesser amount every following period. (**26**)

Remuneration Reward for work carried out. (**39**)

Reserve accounts The transfer of apportioned profits to accounts for use in future years. (**37**)

Retained profits Profits earned in a year but not paid out in dividends. (**37**)

Return on capital employed (ROCE) ratio A ratio that shows the net profit made for each £100 of capital employed. (**38**)

Returns inwards Goods returned to the business by its customers. (**4**)

Returns inwards day book Book of original entry for goods returned by customers. (**12**)

Returns outwards Goods returned by the business to its suppliers. (**4**)

Returns outwards day book Book of original entry for goods returned to suppliers. (**12**)

Revenue expenditure Expenses needed for the day-to-day running of the business. (**18**)

Revenue reserve Reserves of a company which are available for distribution as a dividend. (**37**)

Revenues Monetary value of goods and services supplied to the customers. (**5**)

Salary Fixed payment, usually monthly, to an employee for professional or office work. (**39**)

Sale or return Goods that do not belong to the person holding them. (**30**)

Sales Goods sold by the business. (**4**)

Sales day book Book of original entry for credit sales. (**12**)

Sales invoice A document showing the details of goods sold and the prices of those goods. (**19**)

Sales ledger A ledger for customers' personal accounts. (**12**)

Shareholder An owner of shares in a company. (**37**)

Shares The division of the capital of a limited company into parts. (**37**)

Single entry Where transactions are only recorded once in the books of account. (**33**)

Slip system This involves putting information, such as lists of invoices, in slip form which can then be entered directly into the ledger accounts, eliminating the need to enter them in the day books. Also used by banks whereby a customer makes out a paying-in slip to pay money into their account, the slip is used to enter details of the transaction. The slip is used as documentary evidence. (**19**)

Sole trader A business owned by one person only. (**1**)

Standing order Payment made out of payer's bank, direct to payee's bank, on the *payer's* instructions. (**14**)

Statement of account This is normally sent to purchasers at the end of each month and it states the amount owing to the supplier at the end of that particular month. (**21**)

Statement of affairs A statement from which the capital of the owner is deduced by

	estimating assets and liabilities. Then Capital = Assets *less* Liabilities. **(33)**
Statutory deductions	Deductions that an employer has to make by law (statute) from workers' gross pay. **(39)**
Stock	Unsold goods. **(2)**
Stock turnover (or stockturn) ratio	A ratio comparing the cost of goods sold to the average stock. It shows the number of times stock is sold in an accounting period. **(38)**
Straight line method	Depreciation calculation which remains at an equal amount each year. **(26)**
Subjectivity	Using a method which other people may not agree to. **(11)**
Subscriptions	Amounts paid by members of a club or society, usually on an annual basis, to enable them to participate in the activities of the organisation. **(34)**
Suspense account	Account showing balance equal to difference in trial balance. **(32)**
Time sheet	A form used by employees, who often work away from the main business premises, to record the time spent on various jobs and their overall weekly attendance. **(39)**
Total cost	Production cost plus administration, selling and distribution expenses. **(35)**
Trade discount	A reduction given to a customer when calculating the selling prices of goods. **(19)**
Trading account	Account in which gross profit is calculated. **(8)**
Trading and profit and loss account	Combined account in which both gross and net profits are calculated. **(8)**
Trial balance	A list of all the balances in the books at a particular point in time. The balances are shown in debit and credit columns. These columns should balance provided no errors have occurred. **(7)**
Uncalled capital	The amount that is to be received in future, but which has not yet been requested. **(37)**
Undercasting	Incorrectly adding up a column of figures to give an answer which is less than the correct total. **(31)**
Unpresented cheque	A cheque which has been sent but has not yet gone through the bank account of the receiver of it. **(17)**
Value Added Tax (VAT)	A tax charged on the supply of most goods and services. The tax is borne by the final consumer of the goods or services, not by the business selling them to the consumer. VAT is administered by HM Customs and Excise. **(22)**
Voluntary deductions	Deductions made from pay at an employee's request. **(39)**
Wage	Payment made to a worker in return for services rendered, and usually paid weekly. **(39)**

Work in progress Items not completed at the end of a period. (**35**)

Working capital The amount by which the current assets exceed the current liabilities. Also known as 'net current assets'. (**29**)

Working capital ratio Same as the current ratio. (**38**)

Zero-rated firm Firms that do not have to add VAT to goods and services supplied by them, to others, and that receive a refund of VAT paid on goods and services purchased by them. (**22**)

APPENDIX B

Step-by-step guides

Many students have difficulty in the preparation of final accounts and in remembering the layout. The following step-by-step guides should help to ensure speed and accuracy in their preparation and to ensure that confidence and competence is achieved.

Three step-by-step guides now follow:

- Preparation of final accounts
- Dealing with adjustments in final accounts
- Preparation of final accounts from incomplete records.

There is also a model layout of the trading and profit and loss accounts, and the balance sheet.

Preparation of final accounts

1 Before starting the exercise, rule lines connecting each item. This avoids picking up a wrong figure - easily done under the stress of an examination.

2 Decide where each item is going *before* you start to prepare the final accounts.

3 An *almost* inviolable rule:

- Each item displayed in the trial balance must only be entered *once* in the final accounts.
- Any item noted below a trial balance exercise should be dealt with *twice*, (i.e. when an item is prepaid at the date of the final accounts).
- *Exception to the rule!* In the case of limited companies showing information on their authorised and issued capital,
  - enter issued capital once in the balance sheet
  - enter authorised capital once at the foot of the balance sheet.

Dealing with adjustments in final accounts

1 Returns inwards and returns outwards:

(*a*) Returns inwards - deduct from sales in the trading account.
(*b*) Returns outwards - deduct from purchases in the trading account.

2 Carriage inwards and carriage outwards:

(*a*) Carriage inwards - add to purchases in the trading account.
(*b*) Carriage outwards - charge as an expense in profit and loss account.

3 Prepayments (amounts paid in advance):

(*a*) Deduct the amount from expenses in the trial balance.
(*b*) Add the amount to debtors in the trial balance.

4 Accruals (amounts owing):

(*a*) Add the amount to expenses in the trial balance.
(*b*) Add the amount to creditors in the trial balance.

5 Depreciation:

Straight line or on-cost:

(*a*)	Find cost price of asset (say)		£24,000
(*b*)	Using percentage given (say)		20%
	calculate 20% of £24,000	=	£4,800

then

(*c*) Charge £4,800 as an expense in the profit and loss account.
(*d*) In the balance sheet, deduct *total* depreciation (i.e. £4,800) from this year plus any depreciation deducted in previous years, (see figure on credit side in trial balance) from cost price of asset (£24,000) to arrive at net book value (NBV)

Reducing balance or written-down value

(*a*)	Find cost price of asset (say)		£10,000
(*b*)	Find total amount of depreciation deducted to date (see credit side of trial balance) – say		£4,000
(*c*)	Find the difference		£6,000
(*d*)	Using percentage given (say)		10%
	calculate 10 per cent of £6,000	=	£600

then

(*e*) Charge £600 as an expense in the profit and loss account.
(*f*) In the balance sheet deduct *total* depreciation (i.e. £600) from this year plus any depreciation deducted in previous years (£4,000, *see* figure on credit side in the trial balance) from cost price.

6 **Bad debts provision:**

Creation

(*a*) Decide on the amount of provision to be created (say 1 per cent of debtors of £5,000 = £50).

then

(*b*) Charge the provision £50 to the profit and loss account as an expense.

(*c*) In the balance sheet, deduct provision £50 from debtors.

Increase in provision

(*a*) Calculate the new provision (i.e. this year's).

(*b*) Find out the old provision (i.e. last year's - look in the trial balance - credit side).

(*c*) Find the difference.

then

(*d*) Charge just the difference to the profit and loss account.

(*e*) Deduct the new provision from debtors in the balance sheet.

Reduction in provision

(*a*) Calculate the new provision (i.e. this year's)

(*b*) Find out the old provision (i.e. last year's - look in the trial balance - credit side).

(*c*) Find the difference.

then

(*d*) Add back the difference as income in the profit and loss account.

(*e*) Deduct the new provision from debtors in the balance sheet.

7 **Bad debts:**

Simply write them off as an expense in the profit and loss account.

Preparation of final accounts from incomplete records

1 Prepare a statement of affairs on the closing day of the last accounting period to ascertain the initial capital. Remember to include the cash and bank balances.

2 *Either* draw up and balance a cash and bank summary *or*, if a cash and bank summary is shown, it may only be necessary to balance the account off. Remember to include the final cash and bank balances in the final balance sheet.

3 Calculate the figures for purchases and sales to be shown in the trading account. There are two ways that this may be achieved: either as a calculation or by using double entry in a 'T account'. Refer to Section 33.3.

4 Calculate the figures for expenses. If there were no accruals or prepayments either at the beginning or end of the accounting period, the expenses paid will equal the expenses used up during the period. If, however, there *are* accruals

and prepayments, then it will be necessary to make adjustments; again, this may be carried out as a calculation or by using 'T accounts'. An example of using the calculation method is shown below and the T-account method is shown in Section 33.3 (Rent account):

Accrual – Rent

	£
Paid - Bank	1,650
Less Owing 1.1.2006	150
	1,500
Add Owing 31.12.2006	Nil
Rent for the year	1,500

The above figures are taken from Exercise 33.6 at the end of the chapter (P Kelly). All expenses for the year must be charged to the trading and profit and loss account.

5 Take account of any depreciation before preparing the final accounts. You may know the amount of depreciation to be allowed for or, alternatively, you may have to compare the value of each asset at the beginning of the period with that at the end of the period - the difference being the depreciation. Remember to check to see whether there are any additions to assets and, if so, to ensure that you include them on the balance sheet and depreciate them as required.

6 Finally, prepare the final accounts: the trading and profit and loss account, and the balance sheet.

Model layout of final accounts for sole trader

Trading and Profit and Loss Account of ... for the year ended ...

	£	£
Sales		xxx
Less Returns inwards		xx
		xxx
Less Cost of goods sold		
Opening stock	x	
Add Purchases	x	
Add Carriage inwards	x	
	xx	
Less Returns outwards	x	
	xx	
Less Closing stock	x	xxx
Gross profit		xxx
Less Expenses		
Bad debts (written off)	x	
Wages and salaries	x	
Rates	x	
Insurance	x	
Rent	x	
General expenses	x	
Postages	x	
Stationery	x	
Carriage outwards	x	
Discounts allowed	x	
Heating	x	
Electricity	x	
Depreciation	x	
Increase in provision for bad debts	x	xxx
		xxx
Add income		
Discounts + interest received	x	
Reductions in provision for bad debts	x	xx
Net profit		£xxx

Note: Alternatively, the Income can be added to Gross Profit before deducting expenses.

Model layout for balance sheet

Balance Sheet of ... as at ...			
	Cost	*Total depreciation*	*Net book value*
Fixed assets	£	£	£
Premises	x	x	x
Motor vehicle	x	x	x
Office furniture	x	x	x
Office equipment	x	x	x
Machinery	x	x	x
	xx	xx	x
Current assets			
Stock (closing)	x		
Debtors (*Less* Provision for bad debts)	x		
Prepayment	x		
Cash at bank	x		
Cash in hand	x	xx	
Less Current liabilities			
Creditors	x		
Expenses owing	x		
Bank overdraft	x	xx	
Net current assets			xx
			xxx
Less Long-term liabilities			
Long-term loan			x
			£xxx
Financed by			
Capital			xxx
Add Profit			x
			xxx
Less Drawings			x
			£xxx

Manufacturing accounts

Manufacturers need to draw up manufacturing accounts in which the production costs of the goods are shown. Set out below are some guidelines for doing this:

1 Model layout of manufacturing account:

Manufacturing Account

	£
Opening stock of raw materials	xx
Add Purchases of raw materials	xx
Carriage inwards	xx
	xxx
Less Closing stock of raw materials	xx
Cost of raw materials consumed	xxx
Direct labour	xx
Direct expenses	xx
Prime cost	xxx
Add Factory overhead expenses	xx
	xxx
Add Opening work-in-progress	xx
	xxx
Less Closing work-in-progress	xx
Production cost of goods completed c/d	xxx
(to be transferred to the trading account)	

2 The trading account is used for calculating the gross profit made by selling the goods manufactured.

3 The profit and loss account shows the net profit or net loss after deducting all administration, selling and distribution costs from the gross profit or gross loss.

4 Work in progress both at the start and at the close of a period must be adjusted in order to ascertain the production costs of goods completed in the period.

5 In the balance sheet, closing stocks should be included of:
- raw materials
- work in progress
- finished goods.

APPENDIX C

Multiple-choice questions

Each multiple-choice question has four suggested answers, either letter (A), (B), (C) or (D). You should read each question and then decide which choice is best, either (A) or (B) or (C) or (D). On a separate piece of paper you should then write down your choice. Unless the textbook you are reading belongs to you, you should not make a mark against your choice in the textbook.

When you have completed a set of questions, check your answers against those given in Appendix D.

Set No 1: Questions MC1–MC20

MC1 Which of the following statements is *in*correct?

(A) Assets – Liabilities = Capital
(B) Capital – Liabilities = Assets
(C) Assets = Capital + Liabilities
(D) Assets – Capital = Liabilities.

MC2 Which of the following is not an asset?

(A) Debtor
(B) Motor Vehicle
(C) Creditor
(D) Stock of Goods.

MC3 Which of the following is a liability?

(A) Cash balance
(B) Loan from J Owens
(C) Debtor
(D) Buildings.

MC4 Which of the following is *in*correct?

	Assets	*Liabilities*	*Capital*
	£	£	£
(A)	9,460	2,680	6,780
(B)	7,390	1,140	6,250
(C)	6,120	2,490	4,630
(D)	8,970	3,580	5,390

MC5 Which of the following statements is *in*correct?

		Effect upon	
		Assets	*Liabilities*
(A)	Paid creditor by cheque	– Bank	+ Creditors
(B)	Bought goods on credit	+ Stock	+ Creditors
(C)	Received cash from debtor	+ Cash – Debtor	
(D)	Sold goods for Cash	+ Cash – Stock	

MC6 Which of the following are correct?

	Accounts	*To record*	*Entry in the account*
(i)	Assets	a decrease	Debit
		an increase	Credit
(ii)	Capital	a decrease	Debit
		an increase	Credit
(iii)	Liabilities	a decrease	Debit
		an increase	Credit

(A) (i) and (ii)
(B) (i) and (iii)
(C) (ii) and (iii)
(D) None of them.

MC7 Which of the following are correct?

		Account to be debited	*Account to be credited*
(i)	Bought motor van by cheque	Motor van	Bank
(ii)	Paid a creditor, T Allen, by cheque	Cash	T Allen
(iii)	Loan repaid to C Kirk by cheque	Loan from Kirk	Bank
(iv)	Sold goods for cash	Sales	Cash

(A) (i) and (ii) only
(B) (ii) and (iii) only
(C) (iii) and (iv) only
(D) (i) and (iii) only.

MC8 Which of the following are *in*correct?

		Account to be debited	*Account to be credited*
(i)	Sold goods on credit to P Moore	P Moore	Sales
(ii)	Bought Fixtures on credit from Furnishers Ltd	Fixtures	Furnishers Ltd
(iii)	Introduce more capital in cash	Capital	Cash
(iv)	A debtor, L Sellars, pays by cheque	Cash	L Sellars

(A) (iii) and (iv) only
(B) (ii) and (iii) only
(C) (i) and (iv) only
(D) (i) and (iii) only.

MC9 Which of the following should not be called 'sales'?

(A) Goods sold, to be paid for in one month's time
(B) Goods sold, cash being received immediately
(C) Item previously included in purchases, now sold on credit
(D) Sale of a motor lorry not now required.

MC10 Which of the following should not be called 'purchases'?

(A) Items bought for the prime purpose of resale
(B) Goods bought on credit
(C) Office stationery purchased
(D) Goods bought for cash.

MC11 Which of the following are *in*correct?

		Account to be debited	*Account to be credited*
(i)	B Ash returns goods to us	Returns Inwards	B Ash
(ii)	Goods bought on credit from L Thomas	L Thomas	Purchases
(iii)	Motor van bought on Credit from X L Garages	Purchases	X L Garages
(iv)	Goods sold for cash	Cash	Sales

(A) (i) and (ii) only
(B) (i) and (iii) only
(C) (ii) and (iii) only
(D) (iii) and (iv) only.

MC12 Of the following, which are correct?

		Account to be debited	*Account to be credited*
(i)	Surplus office furniture sold for cash	Cash	Sales
(ii)	We returned goods to F Ward	F Ward	Returns Inwards
(iii)	Goods bought for cash	Purchases	Cash
(iv)	Goods sold on credit to F Clarke	F Clarke	Sales

(A) (i) and (ii) only
(B) (iii) and (iv) only
(C) (ii) and (iii) only
(D) (ii) only.

MC13 What is the amount of capital, given the following information? Buildings £30,000, Stock £5,600, Bank £750, Creditors £2,200, Loan from K Noone £7,000:

(A) £29,150
(B) £36,350
(C) £41,150
(D) None of the above.

MC14 Which of these statements is *in*correct?

(A) Profit is another word for capital
(B) A loss decreases capital
(C) Profit increases capital
(D) Drawings decreases capital.

MC15 Which of the following are *in*correct?

		Account to be debited	*Account to be credited*
(i)	Paid insurance by cheque	Insurance	Bank
(ii)	Paid telephone bill by cash	Telephone	Cash
(iii)	Received refund of part of motor expenses by cheque	Cash	Motor Expenses
(iv)	Took cash out of business for personal use	Drawings	Capital

(A) (i) and (iii) only
(B) (ii) and (iv) only
(C) (iii) and (iv) only
(D) (iv) only.

MC16 Of the following, which are correct?

		Account to be debited	*Account to be credited*
(i)	Paid rent by cheque	Rent	Cash
(ii)	Received commission in cash	Commissions	Cash
(iii)	Introduced extra capital in cash	Cash	Capital
(iv)	Sold surplus stationery for cash	Cash	Stationery

(A) None of them
(B) (i) and (iv) only
(C) (ii) and (iii) only
(D) (iii) and (iv) only.

MC17 What is the balance on the following account on 30 June 2005?

Dr *N Garth* *Cr*

2005	£	2005	£
June 18 Bank	400	June 1 Purchases	870
June 22 Returns	44	June 15 Purchases	245
		June 29 Purchases	178

(A) A debit balance of £849
(B) A credit balance of £829
(C) A credit balance of £849
(D) There is a nil balance on the account.

MC18 What was the balance on the account of N Garth, in MC17, on 20 June 2005?
(A) A credit balance of £671
(B) A debit balance of £715
(C) A credit balance of £715
(D) A debit balance of £671.

MC19 Of the following, which *best* describes a trial balance?
(A) Is the final account in the books
(B) Shows all the asset balances
(C) Is a list of balances on the books
(D) Discloses the financial position of a business.

MC20 When should the trial balance totals differ?

(A) Only when it is drawn up by the accountant
(B) When drawn up before the profit and loss account is prepared
(C) If drawn up half-way through the financial year
(D) Never.

Set No 2: Questions MC21–MC55

MC21 Gross profit is:

(A) Excess of cost of goods sold over sales
(B) Purchases + Sales
(C) Net profit less expenses
(D) Excess of sales over cost of goods sold.

MC22 Net profit is calculated in the:

(A) Trial balance
(B) Trading account
(C) Profit and loss account
(D) Balance sheet.

MC23 The credit entry for net profit is shown in the:

(A) Capital account
(B) Profit and loss account
(C) Balance sheet
(D) Trading account.

MC24 The value of closing stock is found by:

(A) Adding opening stock to purchases
(B) Deducting purchases from sales
(C) Looking in the stock account
(D) Doing a stock-taking.

MC25 Which of the following are *not* part of the double entry system?

(i) Trading account
(ii) Balance sheet
(iii) Trial balance
(iv) Profit and loss account.

(A) (i) and (ii)
(B) (i) and (iii)
(C) (ii) and (iii)
(D) (ii) and (iv).

MC26 Which is the *best* definition of a balance sheet?

(A) A list of balances after calculating net profit
(B) A statement of all liabilities
(C) A trial balance at a different date
(D) A list of balances before calculating net profit.

MC27 The descending order in which current assets should be shown in the balance sheet are:

(A) Debtors, Bank, Stock, Cash
(B) Stock, Debtors, Bank, Cash
(C) Stock, Debtors, Cash, Bank
(D) Cash, Bank, Debtors, Stock.

MC28 Carriage inwards is charged to the trading account because:

(A) It is not a balance sheet item
(B) It is not part of motor expenses
(C) Returns inwards also goes in the trading account
(D) It is basically part of the cost of buying goods.

MC29 Given figures showing Sales £28,500, Opening stock £4,690, Closing stock £7,240, Carriage inwards £570 and Purchases £21,360, the cost of goods sold figure is:

(A) £19,830
(B) £19,380
(C) £18,810
(D) Another figure.

MC30 If someone owns a grocery store, which of the following are *not* capital expenditure?

(i) Rent
(ii) Motor van
(iii) Fixtures
(iv) Fire insurance

(A) (ii) and (iii)
(B) (i) and (ii)
(C) (i) and (iii)
(D) (i) and (iv).

MC31 The purchases day book is *best* described as:

(A) A list of purchases bought on credit
(B) Containing suppliers' accounts
(C) A list of purchases bought for cash
(D) Part of the double entry system.

MC32 Customers' personal accounts are found in:

(A) The private ledger
(B) General ledger
(C) Purchases ledger
(D) Sales ledger.

MC33 Which of the following are *not* personal accounts?

(i) Debtors
(ii) Drawings
(iii) Rent
(iv) Creditors.

(A) (iii) only
(B) (i) and (ii) only
(C) (i) and (iv) only
(D) (ii) and (iii) only.

MC34 A debit balance of £500 in the cash columns of the cash book would mean:
(A) The book-keeper has made a mistake
(B) We have £500 cash in hand
(C) We have spent £500 cash more than we have received
(D) Someone has stolen £500 cash.

MC35 A sum of £200 withdrawn from the bank and placed in the cash till is entered:
(A) Debit bank column £200: Credit bank column £200
(B) Debit cash column £200: Credit bank column £200
(C) Debit bank column £200: Credit cash column £200
(D) Debit cash column £400: Credit cash column £400.

MC36 A contra item is where:
(A) Cash is banked before it has been paid out
(B) Where double entry is completed within the cash book
(C) Where the proprietor has repaid his capital in cash
(D) Where sales have been paid by cash.

MC37 An invoice shows a total of £3,200 less a $2^1/_2$-per-cent cash discount. If this was paid in time, the amount of the cheque paid would be for:
(A) £2,960
(B) £3,040
(C) £3,120
(D) £2,800.

MC38 The total of the discounts received column in the cash book is posted to:
(A) The credit of the discounts received account
(B) The credit of the discounts allowed account
(C) The debit of the discounts allowed account
(D) The debit of the discounts received account.

MC39 A bank overdraft is *best* described as:
(A) A firm wasting its money
(B) Having more receipts than payments
(C) A firm having bought too many goods
(D) A firm having paid more out of its bank account than it has put in it.

MC40 A cash discount is *best* described as a reduction in the sum to be paid:
(A) If goods are bought on credit and not for cash
(B) If either cheque or cash payment is made within an agreed period
(C) If cash is paid instead of cheques
(D) If trade discount is also deducted.

MC41 If a sales invoice shows 12 items of £250 each, less trade discount of 20 per cent and cash discount of 5 per cent, then the amount to be paid, if the payment is made within the credit period, will be for:

(A) £2,440
(B) £2,360
(C) £2,280
(D) £2,500.

MC42 The total of the sales day book is entered on:

(A) The debit side of the sales day book
(B) The credit side of the sales account in the general ledger
(C) The debit side of the sales account in the general ledger
(D) The debit side of the sales day book.

MC43 A trade discount is *best* described as:

(A) A discount given if the invoice is paid
(B) A discount given for cash payment
(C) A discount given to suppliers
(D) A discount given to traders.

MC44 The sales day book does *not* contain:

(A) Credit sales made without deduction of trade discount
(B) Credit sales made to overseas customers
(C) Cash sales
(D) Credit sales which eventually turn out to be bad debts.

MC45 The purchases day book consists of:

(A) Cash purchases
(B) Suppliers' ledger accounts
(C) A list of purchases invoices
(D) Payments for goods.

MC46 The total of the purchases day book is transferred to the:

(A) Debit side of the purchases account
(B) Credit side of the purchases day book
(C) Debit side of the purchases day book
(D) Debit side of the purchases ledger.

MC47 The balances in the purchases ledger are usually:

(A) Credit balances
(B) Contras
(C) Nominal account balances
(D) Debit balances.

MC48 Debit notes are entered in the:

(A) Returns outwards day book
(B) Returns inwards day book
(C) Purchases account
(D) Returns outwards account.

MC49 A statement of account:
(A) Is used instead of an invoice
(B) Means that customers need not keep accounts
(C) Saves sending out invoices
(D) Acts as a reminder to the purchaser of the amount owed.

MC50 Originally we bought 80 items at £60 each, less trade discount of 25 per cent. We now return 5 items, so we will issue a debit note amounting to:
(A) £270
(B) £240
(C) £225
(D) £220.

MC51 A cheque given to you by a customer and banked by you, but for which he has proved not to have enough funds to meet it, is known as:
(A) A dishonoured cheque
(B) A debit transfer
(C) A standing order
(D) A bank error.

MC52 Which of the following are not true? A bank reconciliation statement is:
(i) Drawn up by the bank monthly
(ii) Not part of the double entry system
(iii) Part of the double entry system
(iv) Drawn up by our cashier.

(A) (i) and (ii)
(B) (i) and (iii)
(C) (ii) and (iv)
(D) (iii) and (iv).

MC53 The journal is:
(A) Part of the double entry system
(B) A form of sales day book
(C) A form of diary
(D) A supplement to the balance sheet.

MC54 Given a desired cash float of £700, if £541 is spent in the period and the opening cash float has been £700, how much will be reimbursed at the end of the period?
(A) £541
(B) £700
(C) £159
(D) None of the above.

MC55 A petty cash book:
(A) Is used only in limited companies
(B) Is used when there is a bank overdraft
(C) Is used for small cheque payments
(D) Will keep down the number of entries in the general ledger.

Set No 3: Questions MC56–MC82

MC56 The straight line method of depreciation consists of:
- (A) Unequal amounts of depreciation each year
- (B) Increasing amounts of depreciation each year
- (C) Reducing amounts of depreciation each year
- (D) Equal amounts of depreciation each year.

MC57 Depreciation is:
- (A) The cost of a current asset wearing away
- (B) The cost of a replacement for a fixed asset
- (C) The salvage value of a fixed asset plus its original cost
- (D) The part of the cost of the fixed asset consumed during its period of use by the firm.

MC58 A firm bought a machine for £50,000. It is expected to be used for 6 years, then sold for £5,000. What is the annual amount of depreciation if the straight line method is used?
- (A) £7,000
- (B) £8,000
- (C) £7,500
- (D) £6,750.

MC59 When a separate provision for depreciation account is in use, then book-keeping entries for the year's depreciation are:
- (A) Debit profit and loss: Credit the balance sheet
- (B) Debit profit and loss: Credit asset account
- (C) Debit asset account: Credit provision for depreciation account
- (D) Debit profit and loss: Credit provision for depreciation account.

MC60 In a trial balance, the balance on the provision for depreciation account is:
- (A) Shown as a credit item
- (B) Not shown, as it is part of depreciation
- (C) Shown as a debit item
- (D) Sometimes shown as a credit, sometimes as a debit.

MC61 If a provision for depreciation account is not in use, then the entries for the year's depreciation would be:
- (A) Debit asset account, credit profit and loss account
- (B) Credit asset account, debit provision for depreciation account
- (C) Credit profit and loss account, debit provision for depreciation account
- (D) None of the above.

MC62 A provision for bad debts is created:
- (A) When debtors become bankrupt
- (B) When debtors cease to be in business
- (C) To provide for possible bad debts
- (D) To write off bad debts.

MC63 When final accounts are prepared, the bad debts account is closed by a transfer to the:

(A) Balance sheet
(B) Profit and loss account
(C) Trading account
(D) Provision for bad debts account.

MC64 These questions relate to the following assets and liabilities:

	£		£
Stock	1,000	Machinery	750
Cash at bank	750	Debtors	750
Cash in hand	50	Fixtures	250
Creditors	500	Motor vehicle	750
Capital	3,800		

(i) The balance sheet totals are (use the vertical presentation):
(A) £4,800. (B) £3,800. (C) £4,000. (D) £4,500.

(ii) Current liabilities are:
(A) £1,750. (B) £500. (C) £3,800. (D) £2,550.

(iii) Working capital is:
(A) £3,050. (B) £2,050. (C) £500. (D) £800.

Pitman Qualifications

MC65 If we take goods for own use, we should:

(A) Debit drawings account: Credit purchases account
(B) Debit purchases account: Credit drawings account
(C) Debit drawings account: Credit stock account
(D) Debit sales account: Credit stock account.

MC66 A debit balance brought down on a packing materials account means:

(A) We owe for packing materials
(B) We have no stock of packing materials
(C) We have lost money on packing materials
(D) We have a stock of packing materials unused.

MC67 A credit balance brought down on a rent account means:

(A) We owe that rent at that date
(B) We have paid that rent in advance at that date
(C) We have paid too much rent
(D) We have paid too little in rent.

MC68 Working capital is a term meaning:

(A) The amount of capital invested by the proprietor
(B) The excess of the current assets over the current liabilities
(C) The capital less drawings
(D) The total of fixed assets + current assets.

MC69 In the trading account, the returns inwards should be:

(A) Added to cost of goods sold
(B) Deducted from purchases
(C) Deducted from sales
(D) Added to sales.

MC70 If £750 was added to rent instead of being added to a fixed asset:

(A) Gross profit would not be affected
(B) Gross profit would be affected
(C) Both gross and net profits would be affected
(D) Just the balance sheet items would be affected.

MC71 Of the following, which should *not* be entered in the journal?

(i) Cash payments for wages
(ii) Bad debts written off
(iii) Credit purchases of goods
(iv) Sale of fixed assets.

(A) (i) and (ii)
(B) (i) and (iii)
(C) (ii) and (iii)
(D) (iii) and (iv).

MC72 Which of the following do *not* affect trial balance agreement?

(i) Purchases £585 from C Owens completely omitted from the books
(ii) Sales £99 to R Morgan entered in his account as £90
(iii) Rent account added up to be £100 too much
(iv) Error on sales invoice of £14 being entered in the books.

(A) (i) and (iv)
(B) (i) and (ii)
(C) (i) and (iii)
(D) (iii) and (iv).

MC73 Which of the following *are* errors of principle?

(i) Rent entered in buildings account
(ii) Purchases £150 completely omitted from books
(iii) Sale of machinery £500 entered in sales account
(iv) Cheque payment to R Kago entered only in cash book.

(A) (ii) and (iii)
(B) (iii) and (iv)
(C) (i) and (ii)
(D) (i) and (iii).

MC74 When trial balance totals do not agree, the difference is entered in:

(A) The balance account
(B) A suspense account
(C) An errors account
(D) The profit and loss account.

MC75 Which of these errors would be disclosed by the trial balance?
- (A) Error on a purchase invoice
- (B) Purchases from T Morgan entered in C Morgan's account
- (C) Carriage outwards debited to sales account
- (D) Overcast of total on sales account.

MC76 All these questions refer to the following trading and profit and loss account.

Trading Account and Profit and Loss Account			
		£	£
Sales			24,770
Less Returns inwards			270
			24,500
Less Cost of goods sold:			
Opening stock		700	
Add Purchases	18,615		
Less Returns outwards	280		
	18,335		
Add Carriage Inwards	320	18,655	
		19,355	
Less Closing Stock		980	18,375
Gross Profit			6,125
Less Expenses:			
Wages		1,420	
Rent (360 + 90)		450	
General expenses		220	
Carriage outwards		360	?
Net Profit			?

(i) The missing net profit figure should be:
(A) £1,675. (B) £21,675. (C) £3,675. (D) £4,675.

(ii) Total expenses were:
(A) £210. (B) £2,450. (C) £810. (D) £2,575.

(iii) The cost of goods sold totalled:
(A) £18,375. (B) £19,500. (C) £24,500. (D) £24,770.

(iv) The expense item of Rent totalled:
(A) £360. (B) £270. (C) £90. (D) £450.

(v) The turnover is:
(A) £24,770. (B) £24,500. (C) £19,355. (D) £18,375.

(vi) The net cost of purchases is:
(A) £18,615. (B) £18,335. (C) £18,655. (D) £18,375.

(vii) Purchases returned totalled:
(A) £360. (B) £320. (C) £280. (D) £270.

(viii) Gross profit as a percentage on net sales is:
(A) 20%. (B) 30%. (C) 25%. (D) $33\frac{1}{3}$%.

(ix) Net profit as a percentage on net sales is:
(A) 10%. (B) 20%. (C) 25%. (D) 15%.

(x) The value of unsold goods was:
(A) £980. (B) £24,500. (C) £6,125. (D) £19,355.
Pitman Qualification

MC77 Answer the following questions using the following trial balance and the information given below:

Trial Balance as at 31 December

	£	£
Capital		5,600
Furniture and fittings	5,880	
Stock January 1	700	
Drawings	1,200	
Bank overdraft		1,260
Salaries	3,560	
General expenses	190	
Purchases/sales	4,020	9,840
Discount all'd/rec'd	150	130
Rent and rates	820	
Returns in/out	90	80
Trade debtors/creditors	1,500	1,070
Bad debt provision		130
	£18,110	£18,110

Notes:
(*a*) Salaries owing at 31 December - £140
(*b*) Rent and rates paid in advance - £220
(*c*) Depreciate furniture and fittings by 10% p.a.
(*d*) Closing stock valuation - £800
(*e*) Increase the bad debt provision to bring it up to 10% of debtors' balances.

(i) What will be the yearly depreciation charge?
(A) £5,292. (B) £,6468. (C) £588. (D) £5,886.
(ii) What will be the salaries figure shown on the profit and loss account?
(A) £140. (B) £3,700. (C) £3,420. (D) £3,560.
(iii) The rent and rates figure shown on the profit and loss account will be:
(A) £600. (B) £820. (C) £220. (D) £1,040.
(iv) The new bad debt provision will be:
(A) £1,650. (B) £1,450. (C) £150. (D) £110.
(v) What will be the gross profit on the trading account?
(A) £5,910. (B) £5,830. (C) £4,630. (D) £4,430.
(vi) The net profit on the profit and loss account will be:
(A) £1,420. (B) £792. (C) £1,400. (D) £812.
(vii) The book value of furniture and fittings on the balance sheet will be:
(A) £5,292. (B) £6,000. (C) £6,368. (D) £5,880.
(viii) What will be the turnover for the year?
(A) £9,840. (B) £3,840. (C) £9,750. (D) £4,640.
(ix) Using the adjusted sales figure, the stock turnover for the year will be:
(A) 10. (B) 11. (C) 12. (D) None of these.

(x) What will be the capital figure at end of year?
(A) £4,100. (B) £5,600. (C) £5,192. (D) £6,392.

Pitman Qualifications

MC78 Given last year's capital as £57,500, this year's capital as £64,300, and drawings as £11,800, then profit must have been:
(A) £18,600
(B) £18,100
(C) £16,600
(D) £19,600.

MC79 Given last year's capital as £74,500, closing capital as £46,200, and drawings of £13,400, then:
(A) Profit for the year was £14,900
(B) Loss for the year was £14,900
(C) Loss for the year was £15,900
(D) Profit for the year was £16,800.

MC80 Given this year's closing capital as £29,360, the year's net profit as £8,460 and drawings as £5,320, what was the capital at the beginning of the year?
(A) £29,360
(B) £26,220
(C) £34,680
(D) None of the above.

MC81 In a commercial firm, an 'accumulated fund' would be known as:
(A) Fixed assets
(B) Total assets
(C) Net current assets
(D) Capital.

MC82 A receipts and payments account does not show:
(A) Cheques paid out during the year
(B) The accumulated fund
(C) Receipts from sales of assets
(D) Bank balances.

APPENDIX D

Answers to multiple-choice questions

Set 1

1	B	2	C	3	B	4	C	5	A
6	C	7	D	8	A	9	D	10	C
11	C	12	B	13	D	14	A	15	C
16	D	17	C	18	C	19	C	20	D

Set 2

21	D	22	C	23	A	24	D	25	C
26	A	27	B	28	D	29	B	30	D
31	A	32	D	33	D	34	B	35	B
36	B	37	C	38	A	39	D	40	B
41	C	42	B	43	D	44	C	45	C
46	A	47	A	48	A	49	D	50	C
51	A	52	B	53	C	54	A	55	D

Set 3

56	D	57	D	58	C	59	D	60	A
61	D	62	C	63	B	64 (i)	B (ii) B (iii) B	65	A
66	D	67	A	68	B	69	C	70	A
71	B	72	A	73	D	74	B	75	D
76 (i) C (ii) B (iii) A (iv) D (v) B (vi) B (vii) C (viii) C (ix) D (x) A									
77 (i) C (ii) B (iii) A (iv) C (v) A (vi) B (vii) A (viii) C (ix) D (x) D									
78	A	79	B	80	B	81	D	82	B

APPENDIX E

Answers to exercises

Set out in this Appendix are the answers to the Exercises at the end of each chapter, ***excluding*** *those with suffix 'X' in the Exercise number.*

Chapter 1

No questions.

Chapter 2

2.1 (*a*) £26,373
(*b*) £62,486
(*c*) £77,100
(*d*) £986,763
(*e*) £10,265
(*f*) £404,903

2.3 (*a*) Asset
(*b*) Asset
(*c*) Liability
(*d*) Asset
(*e*) Liability
(*f*) Asset

2.5 Wrong: Assets - Creditors, Loan from C Shaw
Liabilities - Debtors, Stock of Goods

2.7

Assets		£
Shop premises		50,000
Motor vehicle		10,000
Stock of goods		5,000
Cash at bank		7,000
Cash in hand		100
		72,100
Less Liabilities		
Loan from Uncle	30,000	
Owed for stock	2,100	32,100
CAPITAL INTRODUCED		40,000

2.9

Balance Sheet of T Lymer as at 31 December 2007

Fixed assets:	£	£	£
Office furniture			8,640
Delivery van			12,000
			20,640
Current assets:			
Stock	4,220		
Debtors	10,892		
Cash at Bank	11,722	26,834	
Less Current liabilities:			
Creditors	12,651	12,651	
Net current assets			14,183
			£34,823
Financed by:			
Capital			34,823
			£34,823

2.11

	Assets	Liabilities	Capital
(a)	- Cash	- Creditors	
(b)	- Bank		
	+ Fixtures		
(c)	+Stock	+ Creditors	
(d)	+ Cash		+ Capital
(e)	+ Cash	+ Loan from J Walker	
(f)	+ Bank		
	- Debtors		
(g)	- Stock	- Creditors	
(h)	+ Premises		
	- Bank		

Chapter 3

3.1

	Account to be debited	Account to be credited
(a)	Motor van	Cash
(b)	Office machinery	J Grant & Son
(c)	Cash	Capital
(d)	Bank	J Beach
(e)	A Barrett	Cash

3.3

Bank

(1) Capital	2,500	(2) Office F	150
		(5) Motor van	600
		(15) Planers Ltd	750
		(31) Machinery	280

Capital

		(1) Bank	2,500

Office Furniture

(2) Bank	150	(8) J Walker & Sons	60

Machinery

(3) Planers Ltd	750		
(31) Bank	280		

Cash

(23) J Walker	60		

Planers Ltd

(15) Bank	750	(3) Machinery	750

Motor Van

(5) Bank	600		

J Walker & Sons

(8) Office F	60	(23) Cash	60

3.5

Bank

(1) Capital	5,000	(2) Motor van	1,200
(25) Cash	800	(12) Cash	100
		(19) Super Motors	800
		(30) Office fixtures	300

Office Fixtures

(5) Young Ltd	400		
(15) Cash	60		
(30) Bank	300		

Capital

		(1) Bank	5,000

Cash

(12) Bank	100	(15) Office fixtures	60
(21) Loan: Jarvis	1,000	(25) Bank	800

Motor Van

(2) Bank	1,200		
(8) Super Motors	800		

Young Ltd

		(5) Office fixtures	400

Super Motors

(19) Bank	800	(8) Motor van	800

Loan from Jarvis

		(21) Cash	1,000

Chapter 4

4.1

	Account to be debited	Account to be credited
(a)	Purchases	J Reid
(b)	B Perkins	Sales
(c)	Motor van	H Thomas
(d)	Bank	Sales
(e)	Cash	Sales
(f)	H Hardy	Returns outwards
(g)	Cash	Machinery
(h)	Returns inwards	J Nelson
(i)	Purchases	D Simpson
(j)	H Forbes	Returns outwards

4.3

Cash

(1) Capital	500	(3) Purchases	85
(10) Sales	42	(25) E Morgan	88
(31) A Knight	55		

Returns Outwards

		(14) E Morgan	28
		(21) A Moses	19

A Knight

(24) Sales	55	(31) Cash	55

Purchases

(3) Cash	85		
(7) E Morgan	116		
(18) A Moses	98		

Sales

		(10) Cash	42
		(24) A Knight	55

E Morgan

(14) Returns outwards	28	(7) Purchases	116
(25) Cash	88		

A Moses

(21) Returns outwards	19	(18) Purchases	98

Capital

		(1) Cash	500

4.4

Cash

(1) Capital	1,000	(2) Bank	900
(19) Sales	28	(7) Purchases	55

Purchases

(4) S Holmes	78		
(7) Cash	55		

Returns Outwards

		(12) S Holmes	18

S Holmes

(12) Returns	18	(4) Purchases	78
(29) Bank	60		

D Moore

(10) Sales	98		

Bank

(2) Cash	900	(5) Motor van	500
(24) D Watson (Loan)	100	(29) S Holmes	60
		(31) Kingston Equipment	150

Sales

		(10) D Moore	98
		(19) Cash	28

Fixtures

(22) Kingston Equipment	150		

Motor Van

(5) Bank	500		

D Watson (Loan)

		(24) Bank	100

Kingston Equipment

(31) Bank	150	(22) Fixtures	150

Capital

		(1) Cash	1,000

Chapter 5

5.1

	Account to be debited	*Account to be credited*
(*a*)	Rent	Cash
(*b*)	Purchases	Cash
(*c*)	Bank	Rates
(*d*)	General exps	Bank
(*e*)	Cash	Commissions recd
(*f*)	T Jones	Returns outwards
(*g*)	Cash	Sales
(*h*)	Office fixtures	Bank
(*i*)	Wages	Cash
(*j*)	Drawings	Cash

5.3

Bank

		£			£
Jan 1	Capital	20,000	Jan 3	Rent	1,000
Jan 25	Sales	800	Jan 4	Motor van	5,000
			Jan 19	Insurance	220
			Jan 31	Electricity	78

Capital

					£
			Jan 1	Bank	20,000

Rent

		£			
Jan 3	Bank	1,000			

Motor Van

		£			
Jan 4	Bank	5,000			

Cash

		£			£
Jan 5	Sales	1,005	Jan 10	Motor expenses	75
			Jan 12	Wages	120
			Jan 31	Wages	135

Motor Expenses

		£			
Jan 10	Cash	75			

Wages

		£			
Jan 12	Cash	120			
Jan 31	Cash	135			

Insurance

		£			
Jan 19	Bank	220			

Electricity

		£			
Jan 31	Bank	78			

Purchases

		£			
Jan 4	M Parkin	580			
Jan 4	J Kane	2,400			
Jan 17	M Parkin	670			

Sales

					£
			Jan 5	Cash	1,005
			Jan 25	Bank	800

M Parkin

					£
			Jan 4	Purchases	580
			Jan 17	Purchases	670

J Kane

					£
			Jan 4	Purchases	2,400

5.5

Bank

		£			£
Jul 1	Capital	8,000	Jul 2	Rent	375
			Jul 3	Shop Fittings	800
			Jul 6	Insurance	130
			Jul 13	Printing & Stationery	120
			Jul 30	High Lane Motors	5,000

Capital

					£
			Jul 1	Bank	8,000

Rent

		£			
Jul 2	Bank	375			

Shop Fittings

		£			
Jul 3	Bank	800			

Insurance

		£			
Jul 6	Bank	130			

Motor Van

		£			
Jul 7	High Lane Motors	5,000			

Cash

		£			£
Jul 11	Sales	1,500	Jul 15	Wages	200
Jul 21	Sales	780	Jul 25	Motor Expenses	89
			Jul 31	Wages	300
			Jul 31	Stationery	45

Printing and Stationery

		£			
Jul 13	Bank	120			
Jul 31	Cash	45			

Wages

		£			
Jul 15	Cash	200			
Jul 31	Cash	300			

Motor Expenses

		£			
Jul 25	Cash	89			

Purchases

		£			
Jul 5	A Jackson	450			
Jul 5	D Hill	675			
Jul 5	E Frudd	1,490			
Jul 18	A Jackson	890			

Sales

					£
			Jul 11	Cash	1,500
			Jul 21	Cash	780

A Jackson

					£
			Jul 5	Purchases	450
			Jul 18	Purchases	890

D Hill

					£
			Jul 5	Purchases	675

E Frudd

					£
			Jul 5	Purchases	1,490

High Lane Motors

		£			£
Jul 30	Bank	5,000	Jul 7	Motor van	5,000

Chapter 6

6.1

H Harvey

(1) Sales	690	(10) Returns	40
(4) Sales	66	(24) Cash	300
		(31) Balance c/d	416
	756		756
(1) Balance b/d	416		

N Morgan

(1) Sales	153	(18) Bank	153

J Lindo

(1) Sales	420	(10) Returns	20
		(20) Bank	400
	420		420

L Masters

(4) Sales	418	(31) Balance c/d	621
(31) Sales	203		
	621		621
(1) Balance b/d	621		

6.2

J Young

(10) Returns	55	(1) Purchases	458
(28) Cash	250	(15) Purchases	80
(30) Balance c/d	233		
	538		538
		(1) Balance b/d	233

L Williams

(30) Returns	17	(1) Purchases	120
(30) Balance c/d	180	(3) Purchases	77
	197		197
		(1) Balance b/d	180

G Norman

(10) Returns	22	(1) Purchases	708
(30) Balance c/d	686		
	708		708
		(1) Balance b/d	686

T Harris

(19) Bank	880	(3) Purchases	880

6.3

H Harvey

2008			*Dr*	*Cr*	Balance
May	1	Sales	690		690 Dr
May	4	Sales	66		756 Dr
May	10	Returns		40	716 Dr
May	24	Cash		300	416 Dr

N Morgan

2008			Dr	Cr	Balance
May	1	Sales	153		153 Dr
May	18	Bank		153	0

J Lindo

2008			Dr	Cr	Balance
May	1	Sales	420		420 Dr
May	10	Returns		20	400 Dr
May	20	Bank		400	0

L Masters

2008			Dr	Cr	Balance
May	4	Sales	418		418 Dr
May	31	Sales	203		621 Dr

6.5

D Williams

(1)	Sales	458	(24)	Bank	300
			(28)	Cash	100
			(30)	Balance c/d	58
		458			458
(1)	Balance b/d	58			

J Moore

(1)	Sales	235	(12)	Returns	26
(8)	Sales	444	(20)	Balance c/d	653
		679			679
(1)	Balance b/d	653			

G Grant

(1)	Sales	98	(12)	Returns	9
			(30)	Balance c/d	89
		98			98
(1)	Balance b/d	89			

F Franklin

(8)	Sales	249	(30)	Bank	249

A White

(20)	Bank	77	(2)	Purchases	77

H Samuels

(17)	Returns	24	(2)	Purchases	231
(30)	Balance c/d	219	(10)	Purchases	12
		243			243
			(1)	Balance b/d	219

P Owen

			(2)	Purchases	65

O Oliver

(17)	Returns	12	(10)	Purchases	222
(26)	Cash	210			
		222			222

Debtors: D Williams, J Moore and G Grant.
Creditors: H Samuels and P Owen.

Chapter 7

7.1

Capital

								£
				May	1	Bank		2,500

Bank

			£				£
May	1	Capital	2,500	May 12		K Gibson	76
May	9	C Bailey	250	May 12		D Ellis	370
May	10	H Spencer	150	May 31		C Mendez	87
				May 31		Balance c/d	2,367
			2,900				2,900
Jun	1	Balance b/d	2,367				

Cash

			£			£
May	8	Sales	500	May 6	Rent	120
				May 15	Stationery	60
				May 19	Rent	120
				May 31	Balance c/d	200
			500			500
Jun	1	Balance b/d	200			

Rent

			£			£
May	6	Cash	120	May 31	Balance c/d	240
,,	19	Cash	120			
			240			240
Jun	1	Balance b/d	240			

Stationery

			£		
May	15	Cash	60		

Purchases

		£			£
May 2	D Ellis	540	May 31	Balance c/d	1,082
May 2	C Mendez	87			
May 2	K Gibson	76			
May 18	D Ellis	145			
May 18	C Mendez	234			
		1,082			1,082
Jun 1	Balance b/d	1,082			

Sales

		£			£
May 31	Balance c/d	1,496	May 4	C Bailey	430
			May 4	B Hughes	62
			May 4	H Spencer	176
			May 8	Cash	500
			May 25	C Bailey	90
			May 25	B Hughes	110
			May 25	H Spencer	128
		1,496			1,496
			Jun 1	Balance b/d	1,496

H Spencer

		£			£
May 4	Sales	176	May 10	Bank	150
May 25	Sales	128	May 31	Balance c/d	154
		304			304
Jun 1	Balance b/d	154			

D Ellis

		£			£
May 12	Bank	370	May 2	Purchases	540
May 31	Balance c/d	315	May 18	Purchases	145
		685			685
			Jun 1	Balance b/d	315

C Mendez

		£			£
May 31	Bank	87	May 2	Purchases	87
May 31	Balance c/d	234	May 18	C Mendez	234
		234			234
			Jun 1	Balance b/d	234

K Gibson

		£			£
May 12	Bank	76	May 2	Purchases	76

C Bailey

		£			£
May 4	Sales	430	May 9	Bank	250
May 25	Sales	90	May 31	Balance c/d	270
		520			520
Jun 1	Balance b/d	270			

B Hughes

		£			£
May 4	Sales	62	May 31	Balance c/d	172
May 25	Sales	110			
		172			172
Jun 1	Balance b/d	172			

Trial Balance as at 31 May 2004

	Dr £	*Cr* £
Capital		2,500
Bank	2,367	
Cash	200	
Rent	240	
Stationery	60	
Purchases	1,082	
Sales		1,496
H Spencer	154	
D Ellis		315
C Mendez		234
C Bailey	270	
B Hughes	172	
	4,545	4,545

7.2

Bank

		£			£
Mar 1	Capital	8,000	Mar 17	M Hyatt	84
Mar 24	J Carlton	95	Mar 21	Betta Ltd	500
			Mar 31	Motor van	4,000
			Mar 31	Balance c/d	3,511
		8,095			8,095
Apr 1	Balance b/d	3,511			

Cash

		£			£
Mar 5	Sales	870	Mar 6	Wages	140
Mar 30	J King (Loan)	600	Mar 9	Purchases	46
			Mar 12	Wages	140
			Mar 31	Balance c/d	1,144
		1,470			1,470
Apr 1	Balance b/d	1,144			

Capital

					£
			Mar 1	Bank	8,000

Motor Van

		£			
Mar 31	Bank	4,000			

Returns Outwards

		£			£
Mar 31	Balance c/d	44	Mar 18	T Braham	20
			Mar 27	K Henriques	24
		44			44
			Apr 1	Balance b/d	44

Wages

		£			£
Mar 6	Cash	140	Mar 31	Balance c/d	280
Mar 12	Cash	140			
		280			280
Apr 1	Balance b/d	280			

Purchases

		£			£
Mar 2	K Henriques	76	Mar 31	Balance c/d	864
Mar 2	M Hyatt	27			
Mar 2	T Braham	560			
Mar 9	Cash	46			
Mar 10	M Hyatt	57			
Mar 10	T Braham	98			
		864			864
Apr 1	Balance b/d	864			

Sales

		£			£
Mar 31	Balance c/d	1,074	Mar 5	Cash	870
			Mar 7	H Elliott	35
			Mar 7	L Lane	42
			Mar 7	J Carlton	72
			Mar 13	L Lane	32
			Mar 13	J Carlton	23
		1,074			1,074
			Apr 1	Balance b/d	1,074

Shop Fixtures

		£			
Mar 15	Betta Ltd	500			

J King (Loan)

					£
			Mar 30	Cash	600

H Elliott

		£			
Mar 7	Sales	35			

L Lane

		£			£
Mar 7	Sales	42	Mar 31	Balance c/d	74
Mar 13	Sales	32			
		74			74
Apr 1	Balance b/d	74			

J Carlton

		£			£
Mar 7	Sales	72	Mar 24	Bank	95
Mar 13	Sales	23			
		95			95

K Henriques

		£			£
Mar 27	Returns	24	Mar 2	Purchases	76
Mar 31	Balance c/d	52			
		76			76
			Apr 1	Balance b/d	52

M Hyatt

		£			£
Mar 17	Bank	84	Mar 2	Purchases	27
			Mar 10	Purchases	57
		84			84

T Braham

		£			£
Mar 18	Returns	20	Mar 2	Purchases	560
Mar 31	Balance c/d	638	Mar 10	Purchases	98
		658			658
			Apr 1	Balance b/d	638

Betta Ltd

		£			£
Mar 21	Bank	500	Mar 15	Shop Fixtures	500

Trial Balance as at 31 March 2004

	Dr £	*Cr* £
Bank	3,511	
Cash	1,144	
Capital		8,000
Motor van	4,000	
Returns Outwards		44
Wages	280	
Purchases	864	
Sales		1,074
Shop Fixtures	500	
J King (Loan)		600
H Elliott	35	
L Lane	74	
K Henriques		52
J Braham		638
	10,408	10,408

7.5 **Trial Balance of P Brown as at 31 May 2006**

	Dr £	*Cr* £
Capital		20,000
Drawings	7,000	
General expenses	500	
Sales		38,500
Purchases	29,000	
Debtors	6,800	
Creditors		9,000
Bank	15,100	
Cash	200	
Plant and equipment	5,000	
Heating and lighting	1,500	
Rent	2,400	
	67,500	67,500

7.6 Trial Balance of S Higton as at 30 June 2005

	Dr £	Cr £
Capital		19,956
Sales		119,439
Stationery	1,200	
General expenses	2,745	
Motor expenses	4,476	
Cash at bank	1,950	
Stock 1 July 2004	7,668	
Wages and salaries	9,492	
Rent and rates	10,500	
Office equipment	6,000	
Purchases	81,753	
Heating and lighting	2,208	
Rent received		2,139
Debtors	10,353	
Drawings	4,200	
Creditors		10,230
Motor vehicle	7,500	
Interest received		1,725
Insurance	3,444	
	153,489	153,489

Chapter 8

8.1 L Simpson
Trading and Profit and Loss Account
for the year ended 31 December 2008

	£	£
Sales		38,220
Less *Cost of goods sold:*		
Purchases	24,190	
less Closing stock	4,310	19,880
Gross Profit		18,340
Less *Expenses:*		
Rent	4,170	
Wages and salaries	5,390	
Postage and stationery	840	
Electricity expenses	710	
General expenses	370	11,480
Net Profit		6,860

8.3 C Worth
Trading and Profit and Loss Account for the year ended 30 June 2004

	£	£
Sales		28,794
Less Cost of goods sold		
Purchases	23,803	
Less Closing stock	4,166	19,637
Gross profit c/d		9,157
Less Expenses		
Salaries	3,164	
Rent and rates	854	
Lighting expenses	422	
Insurance	105	
Motor running expenses	1,133	
Trade expenses	506	6,184
Net profit		2,973

8.5 Mrs P Stewart
Trial Balance as at 31 March 2008

	Dr £	Cr £
Sales		24,765
Purchases	13,545	
Staff wages	2,100	
Drawings	5,500	
Rent and rates	1,580	
Electricity	565	
Motor expenses	845	
Insurance	345	
General expenses	245	
Cash in hand	135	
Cash at bank	2,675	
Creditors		3,285
Vehicle	5,875	
Fixtures and fittings	1,495	
Capital		6,855
	34,905	34,905

Closing stock £2,345

Mrs P Stewart
Trading and Profit and Loss Account for the year ended 31 March 2008

	£	£
Sales		24,765
Less Cost of goods sold		
Purchases	13,545	
Less Closing stock	2,345	
		11,200
Gross profit		13,565
Less Overheads		
Staff wages	2,100	
Rent and rates	1,580	
Electricity	565	
Motor expenses	845	
Insurance	345	
General expenses	245	
		5,680
Net profit		7,885

Chapter 9

9.1

C Worth
Balance Sheet as at 30 June 2004

Fixed Assets	£	£	£
Buildings		50,000	
Fixtures		1,000	
Motor vans		5,500	56,500
Current Assets			
Stock	4,166		
Debtors	3,166		
Bank	3,847		
	11,179		
Less Current Liabilities			
Creditors	1,206		
Net current assets			9,973
			66,473
Capital			
Balance at 1.7.2003		65,900	
Add Net profit		2,973	
		68,873	
Less Drawings		2,400	66,473

9.3

Mrs P Stewart
Balance Sheet as at 31 March 2008

	£	£	£
Fixed Assets			
Fixtures and fittings			1,495
Motor car			5,875
			7,370
Current Assets			
Stock	2,345		
Debtors	-		
Bank	2,675		
Cash	135	5,155	
Less Current Liabilities			
Creditors	3,285	3,285	
Net current assets			1,870
Total net assets			9,240
Financed by			
Capital			6,855
Add Net profit			7,885
			14,740
Less Drawings			5,500
			9,240

9.4

Miss V Holland
Balance Sheet as at 30 June 2008

	£	£	£
Fixed Assets			
Equipment			2,885
Van			3,400
			6,285
Current assets			
Stock in hand	1,465		
Trade debtors	2,375		
Cash in hand	150		
		3,990	
Current Liabilities			
Trade creditors	4,565		
Bank overdraft	1,785		
		6,350	
Net current liabilities			(2,360)
			3,925
Long-term Liabilities			
Loan from mother			2,000
Net assets			1,925
Financed by			
Capital account			
Cash introduced			2,000
Net profit			2,525
			4,525
Drawings			2,600
			1,925

Chapter 10

10.1 **Trading Account for the year ended 31 December 2007**

	£	£
Sales		38,742
Less cost of goods sold		
Opening stock	6,924	
Add Purchases	26,409	
Add Carriage inwards	670	
	34,003	
Less Closing stock	7,489	26,514
Gross profit		12,228

10.3

T Mann
Trading and Profit and Loss Account
for the year ended 31 December 2006

	£	£	£
Sales		52,790	
Less Returns inwards		490	52,300
Less cost of goods sold			
Opening stock		5,690	
Add Purchases	31,000		
Carriage inwards	1,700		
	32,700		
Less Returns outwards	560	32,140	
		37,830	
Less Closing stock		4,230	33,600
Gross Profit			18,700
Less Expenses:			
Rent		1,460	
Salaries and wages		5,010	
Motor expenses		3,120	
Carriage outwards		790	
General expenses		420	10,800
Net profit			7,900

10.5

S Makin
Trading and Profit and Loss Account for the year ended 30 September 2006

	£	£	£
Sales		18,600	
Less Returns inwards		205	18,395
Less cost of goods sold			
Opening stock		2,368	
Add Purchases	11,874		
Less Returns outwards	322	11,552	
Add Carriage inwards		310	
		14,230	
Less Closing stock		2,946	11,284
Gross profit			7,111
Less Expenses:			
Salaries and wages		3,862	
Rent and rates		304	
Carriage outwards		200	
Insurance		78	
Motor expenses		664	
Office expenses		216	
Lighting and heating expenses		166	
General expenses		314	5,804
Net profit			1,307

S Makin
Balance Sheet as at 30 September 2006

	£	£
Fixed Assets		
Premises	15,000	
Fixtures and fittings	350	
Motor vehicles	1,800	17,150
Current Assets		
Stock	2,946	
Debtors	3,896	
Bank	482	
	7,324	
Less Current Liabilities		
Creditors	1,731	
Net current assets		5,593
		22,743
Financed by:		
Capital		
Balance at 1.10.2005		22,636
Add Net profit		1,307
		23,943
Less Drawings		1,200
		22,743

10.8

J Smailes
Trading and Profit and Loss Account for the year ended 31 March 2007

	£	£	£
Sales			92,340
Less cost of goods sold			
Opening stock		18,160	
Add Purchases	69,185		
Less Returns outwards	640	68,545	
Carriage inwards		420	
		87,125	
Less Closing stock		22,390	64,735
Gross profit			27,605
Less Expenses			
Wages and salaries		10,240	
Carriage outwards		1,570	
Rent and rates		3,015	
Communication expenses		624	
Commissions payable		216	
Insurance		405	
Sundry expenses		318	16,388
Net profit			11,217

J Smailes
Balance Sheet as at 31 March 2007

Fixed Assets	£	£
Buildings	20,000	
Fixtures	2,850	22,850
Current Assets		
Stock	22,390	
Debtors	14,320	
Bank	2,970	
Cash	115	
	39,795	
Less Current Liabilities		
Creditors	8,160	
Net current assets		31,635
		54,485
Less Long-term liabilities		
Loan		10,000
		44,485
Capital		
Balance at 1.4.2006		40,888
Add Net profit		11,217
		52,105
Less Drawings		7,620
		44,485

Chapter 11

11.1 (*a*) Materiality
(*b*) Business entity
(*c*) Prudence
(*d*) Cost
(*e*) Money measurement
(*f*) Accrual
(*g*) Realisation
(*h*) Going concern
(*i*) Consistency
(*j*) Materiality.

11.4 The *cost concept* is an accounting concept whereby the assets of a business are recorded in the accounts at cost price. Refer to text, Sections 11.2 and 11.4.

Advantages of using the cost method of valuation are that the assets can easily be verified since there will be an invoice available for checking the purchase price; and, also, no valuations need be carried out on assets whose value may be subjective. Refer to text, Sections 11.2 and 11.4.

Chapter 12

12.1 (*a*) Sales day books/sales ledger/personal account
(*b*) Cash book/general ledger/nominal ledger
(*c*) Purchases day book/purchases ledger/personal account
(*d*) Cash book/general ledger/nominal account
(*e*) Sales day book/sales ledger/personal account
(*f*) Returns inwards day book/sales ledger/personal account
(*g*) Returns outwards day book/purchases ledger/personal account
(*h*) General journal/general ledger/real account.

12.3

Name of account	Personal	Nominal	Real
(*a*) Stock			✓
(*b*) Wages		✓	
(*c*) Bank		✓	
(*d*) Debtor	✓		
(*e*) Office equipment			✓
(*f*) Purchases		✓	
(*g*) Rent received		✓	

NEAB (GCSE)

Chapter 13

13.1

Petty Cash Book

Receipts	Date	Details	Total	Motor expenses	Post and stationery	Cleaning	Sundry expenses	Ledger
£			£	£	£	£	£	£
1,000	(1)	Balance b/d						
	(1)	Cleaning	36			36		
	(3)	Speedy Garage	24	24				
	(4)	Postage	55		55			
	(5)	Envelopes	17		17			
	(6)	Poison licence	18				18	
	(8)	Unique Garage	57	57				
	(9)	Corner Garage	64	64				
	(11)	Postage	58		58			
	(12)	F Lee	99					99
	(13)	H Norman	44					44
	(15)	Sweeping brush	23			23		
	(16)	Bends Garage	77	77				
	(17)	K King	65		65			
	(19)	Driving licences	11	11				
	(21)	C Hope	72					72
	(25)	Cleaning	68			68		
	(27)	Dog licence	12				12	
	(28)	Guard dog food	29				29	
	(31)	Corner Garage	54	54				
			883	287	195	127	59	215
	(31)	Balance c/d	117					
1,000			1,000					
117	(1)	Balance b/d						
883	(1)	Cash						

13.2

Petty Cash Book

Receipts	Date	Details	Total	Office expenses	Motor expenses	Cleaning expenses	Casual labour
£			£	£	£	£	£
500	(1)	Balance b/d					
	(1)	H Sangster	13				13
	(2)	Letterheaded stationery	22	22			
	(2)	Unique Motors	30		30		
	(3)	Cleaning materials	16			16	
	(6)	Envelopes	14	14			
	(8)	Petrol	28		28		
	(11)	J Hogan	15				15
	(12)	Paper-clips	12	12			
	(12)	Mrs Bell	27			27	
	(14)	Petrol	11		11		
	(16)	Computer discs	31	31			
	(16)	Petrol	29		29		
	(21)	Motor vehicle repair	50		50		
	(22)	T Cooke	21				21
	(23)	Mrs Bell	10			10	
	(24)	P King	19				19
	(25)	Stationery	27	27			
	(26)	Flat Cars	21		21		
	(29)	Petrol	12		12		
	(30)	J Young	16				16
			424	106	181	53	84
	(30)	Balance c/d	76				
500			500				
76	(1)	Balance b/d					
424	(1)	Cash					

General Ledger
Motor Expenses

(30) Petty cash 181	

General Ledger
Office Expenses

(30) Petty cash 106	

13.4

(a)

Petty Cash Book – S Dickinson (Estate Agents)

Receipts £	Date 2009		Details	Voucher no	Total payment £	Travelling £	Postage £	Stationery £	Office expenses £	VAT £	Ledger postings £
120.00	Mar	1	Cash	CB1							
		2	Postage Stamps	1	6.50		6.50				
		3	Rail Fare	2	23.00	23.00					
		7	Parcel	3	4.00		4.00				
		9	Window Cleaning	4	8.00				8.00		
		12	Envelopes	5	3.10			2.64		0.46	
		14	Office Tea, etc.	6	6.40				6.40		
		16	Petrol	7	10.00	8.51				1.49	
		19	Disks – Computer	8	13.00				11.06	1.94	
		20	Dusters and Polish	9	1.73				1.47	0.26	
		23	Postage Stamps	10	2.40		2.40				
		27	Ledger a/c J Cheetham	11	7.30						7.30
		31	Magazine	12	6.40				6.40		
					91.83	31.51	12.90	2.64	33.33	4.15	7.30
			Balance c/d		28.17						
120.00					120.00						
28.17	Apr	1	Balance b/d			GL1	GL2	GL3	GL4	GL5	
91.83	Apr	1	Cash	CB1							

(b)

General Ledger

Travelling Expenses Account GL1

2009					
Mar 31	Petty Cash	PCB1	31.51		

Postage Account GL2

2009					
Mar 31	Petty Cash	PCB1	12.90		

Stationery Account GL3

2009					
Mar 31	Petty Cash	PCB1	2.64		

Office Expenses Account GL4

2009					
Mar 31	Petty Cash	PCB1	33.33		

VAT Account GL5

2009					
Mar 31	Petty Cash	PCB1	4.15		

Cash Book (Bank Column Only) CB1

				2009			
				Mar 31	Petty Cash	PCB1	91.83

Purchase Ledger
J Cheetham Account C44

2009				2009			
Mar 31	Petty Cash	PCB1	7.30	Feb 1	Balance b/d		7.30

(c)

MEMORANDUM

To Ms S Dickinson Ref
From Student's Name Date 31 March 2009
Subject Petty Cash Imprest System

Advantages of Imprest System:

1. *Control*: The petty cash can be checked easily at any time because cash in hand plus vouchers paid out for the period should always equal the amount of the 'float'.
2. *Responsibility*: It is an ideal opportunity to appoint junior staff and give them some responsibility and test their honesty.
3. *Efficiency*: It relieves the accountant by dealing with numerous small cash payments and reduces the posting to the general ledger.

Chapter 14

14.1 Refer to text, Section 14.2.

14.2 *Drawer:* the person making out a cheque and using it for payment.
Payee: the person to whom the cheque is paid.

14.4 *(a)* Special crossing: refer to text, Section 14.4.
(b) Refer to text, Section 14.4.

14.5 Standing order/direct debit comparison: refer to text, Section 14.8.

Chapter 15

15.1

Cash Book

Dr		Cash	Bank			Cash	Bank Cr
(1)	Capital	100		(2)	Rent	10	
(3)	F Lake (Loan)		500	(4)	B McKenzie		65
(5)	Sales	98		(9)	B Burton	22	
(7)	N Miller		62	(16)	Bank C	50	
(11)	Sales		53	(19)	F Lake (Loan)		100
(15)	G Moores	65		(26)	Motor expenses		12
(16)	Cash C		50	(30)	Cash C		100
(22)	Sales		66	(31)	Wages	97	
(30)	Bank C	100		(31)	Balances c/d	184	454
		363	731			363	731

15.4

Cash Book

Dr			Cash	Bank				Cash	Bank Cr
2005					2005				
May	1	Balance b/d	14.72		May	1	Balance b/d		820.54
	3	P Wrench		432.36		2	Stationery	10.00	
	3	R Whitworth		634.34		6	SW Rail		37.50
	3	J Summers		341.00		9	Fabulous Fabrics Ltd		450.80
	12	Sales	76.00			11	Mellors Mfg. Co		348.32
	17	Trentham Traders		32.81		14	Inland Revenue		221.30
	24	Sales	350.00			20	Foreign Currency		250.00
	26	Cash C		300.00		20	Bank Charges		3.20
	31	J Summers		1,231.00		26	Bank C	300.00	
	31	Bradnop Mfg. Co		725.00		27	Salaries		5,720.00
	31	Taylors		2,330.50		31	Balance c/d	130.72	
	31	Balance c/d		1,824.65					
			440.72	7,851.66				440.72	7,851.66
June	1	Balance b/d	130.72		June	1	Balance b/d		1,824.65

Chapter 16

16.1

Cash Book

Dr		Disct	Cash	Bank			Disct	Cash	Bank Cr
(1)	Capital			6,000	(1)	Fixtures			950
(3)	Sales		407		(2)	Purchases			1,240
(5)	N Morgan	10		210	(4)	Rent		200	
(9)	S Cooper	20		380	(7)	S Thompson & Co	4		76
(14)	L Curtis			115	(12)	Rates			410
(20)	P Exeter	2		78	(16)	M Monroe	6	114	
(31)	Sales			88	(31)	Balances c/d		93	4,195
		32	407	6,871			10	407	6,871

General Ledger

Discounts Allowed

Dr					Cr
(31)	Cash Book	32			

Discounts Received

Dr					Cr
			(31)	Cash Book	10

16.2

Cash Book

Dr		Disct	Cash	Bank			Disct	Cash	Bank Cr
(1)	Balances b/d		211	3,984	(2)	T Adams	4		76
(4)	C Potts			98	(2)	C Bibby	13		247
(6)	Sales			49	(2)	D Clarke	22		418
(9)	R Smiley	4		156	(7)	Insurance		65	
(9)	J Turner	16		624	(12)	Motor expenses		100	
(9)	R Pimlott	13		507	(21)	Salaries			120
(18)	Sales		98		(23)	Rent		60	
(28)	R Godfrey (Loan)			500	(31)	Stationery			27
					(31)	Balances c/d		84	5,030
		33	309	5,918			39	309	5,918

General Ledger

Discounts Allowed

Dr					Cr
(31)	Cash Book	33			

Discounts Received

Dr					Cr
			(31)	Cash Book	39

Chapter 17

Note: Both in theory and in practice you can start with the cash book balance working to the bank statement balance, or you can reverse this method. Many teachers and lecturers have their preferences, but this is a personal matter only. Examiners sometimes ask for them using one way, sometimes the other. Students should therefore be able to tackle them both ways.

17.1
(*a*)

Cash Book

		£			£
2005	(Totals so far)	2,328	2005	(Totals so far)	497
Dec 31	J Walters	54	Dec 31	Bank charges	22
			Dec 31	Balance c/d	1,863
		2,382			2,382

(*b*) **Bank Reconciliation Statement as at 31 December 2005**

	£
Balance per cash book	1,863
Add Unpresented cheque	115
	1,978
Less Bankings not yet on bank statement (249 + 178)	427
Balance per bank statement	1,551

OR

Bank Reconciliation Statement as at 31 December 2005

	£
Balance per bank statement	1,551
Add Bankings not yet on bank statement (249 + 178)	427
	1,978
Less Unpresented cheque	115
Balance per cash book	1,863

17.3 (*a*)

Cash Book – James Baxter

Dr		£			*Cr* £
2006			2006		
Mar 31	Credit transfer – A May	929	Mar 31	Balance b/d	2,804
Mar 31	Balance c/d	2,003	Mar 31	Standing order – Oak plc	100
			Mar 31	Bank charges	28
		2,932			2,932

(*b*)

James Baxter
Bank Reconciliation Statement as at 31 March 2006

		£
Bank overdraft per cash book		2,003
Add	Banking not entered on bank statement	160
		2,163
Less	Unpresented cheque	490
Bank overdraft per bank statement		1,673

OR

James Baxter
Bank Reconciliation Statement as at 31 March 2006

	£
Balance per bank statement	1,673 O/D
Less Banking not entered on bank statement	160
	1,513 O/D
Add Unpresented cheque	490
Balance per cash book	2,003 O/D

17.5 (*a*)

Cash Book – K Talbot

Dr	£		*Cr* £
Balance b/d	4,500	RB Insurance	600
Bank interest received	720	Bank charges	90
KB Ltd	780	Dishonoured cheque: C Hill	210
Bank deposit account	4,200	Balance c/d	9,300
	10,200		10,200

(*b*)

K Talbot
Bank Reconciliation Statement as at 31 December 2006

	£
Balance per cash book	9,300
Add Unpresented cheques (750 + 870)	1,620
	10,920
Less Banking not recorded	2,070
Balance per bank statement	8,850

OR

K Talbot
Bank Reconciliation Statement as at 31 December 2006

	£
Balance per bank statement	8,850
Add Cash not yet credited	2,070
	10,920
Less Unpresented cheques (750 + 870)	1,620
Balance per cash book	9,300

Chapter 18

18.1 Capital: *(a) (c) (d) (f) (j) (l)*
Revenue: *(b) (e) (g) (h) (i) (k)*.

18.4

T Taylor
Revised Profits Year to 31 December 2008

	£
Gross profit before corrections	95,620
Add (a) Purchases overstated	311
	95,931
Less (c) Sale of building	10,000
Revised gross profit	85,931
Net profit before corrections	28,910
Less Gross profit overstated (10,000 – 311)	9,689
	19,221
Add (d) Loan interest overstated	500
Revised net profit	19,721

Error (b) does not affect gross profit or net profit calculations.

Chapter 19

19.1

Sales Day Book

(1) J Gordon	187
(3) G Abrahams	166
(6) V White	12
(10) J Gordon	55
(17) F Williams	289
(19) C Richards	66
(27) V Wood	28
(31) L Simes	78
	881

Sales Ledger

J Gordon

(1) Sales	187		
(10) Sales	55		

G Abrahams

(3) Sales	166		

V White

(6) Sales	12		

F Williams

(17) Sales	289		

C Richards

(19) Sales	66		

V Wood

(27) Sales	28		

L Simes

(31) Sales	78		

General Ledger

Sales Account

		(31) Sales day book	881

19.3

Workings of invoices:

(1) F Gray	3 rolls white tape × 10 =	30		
	5 sheets blue cotton × 6 =	30		
	1 dress length × 20 =	20	80	
	Less trade discount 25%		20	60
(4) A Gray	6 rolls white tape × 10 =	60		
	30 metres green baize × 4 =	120	180	
	Less trade discount × 33⅓%		60	120
(8) E Hines	1 dress length black silk × 20 =			20
(20) M Allen	10 rolls white tape × 10 =	100		
	6 sheets blue cotton × 6 =	36		
	3 dress lengths black silk × 20 =	60		
	11 metres green baize × 4 =	44	240	
	Less trade discount × 25%		60	180
(31) B Cooper	12 rolls white tape × 10 =	120		
	14 sheets blue cotton × 6 =	84		
	9 metres green baize × 4 =	36	240	
	Less trade discount 33⅓%		80	160

Sales Day Book

(1)	F Gray	60
(4)	A Gray	120
(8)	E Hines	20
(20)	M Allen	180
(31)	B Cooper	160
		540

Sales Ledger

F Gray

(1) Sales	60			

A Gray

(4) Sales	120			

E Hines

(8) Sales	20			

M Allen

(20) Sales	180			

B Cooper

(31) Sales	160			

General Ledger

Sales Account

		(31) Sales day book	540

19.6 See text, Section 19.13.

19.7 See text, Section 19.14.

Chapter 20

20.1

Workings of purchases invoices

(1) K King	4 radios × 30 =	120		
	3 music centres × 160 =	480	600	
	Less trade discount 25%		150	450
(3) A Bell	2 washing machines × 200 =	400		
	5 vacuum cleaners × 60 =	300		
	2 dish dryers × 150 =	300	1,000	
	Less trade discount 20%		200	800
(15) J Kelly	1 music centre × 300 =	300		
	2 washing machines × 250 =	500	800	
	Less trade discount 25%		200	600
(20) B Powell	6 radios × 70 =		420	
	Less trade discount 33$^1/_3$%		140	280
(30) B Lewis	4 dish dryers × 200 =		800	
	Less trade discount 20%		160	640

(*a*) *Purchases Day Book*

(1)	K King	450
(3)	A Bell	800
(15)	J Kelly	600
(20)	B Powell	280
(30)	B Lewis	640
		2,770

(*b*) **Purchases Ledger**

K King

		(1) Purchases	450

A Bell

		(3) Purchases	800

J Kelly

		(15) Purchases	600

B Powell

		(20) Purchases	280

B Lewis

		(30) Purchases	640

(*c*) **General Ledger**

Purchases Account

(31) Purchases day book	2,770		

20.3 (*a*)

Purchases Day Book

(1)	Smith Stores	90
(23)	C Kelly	105
(31)	J Hamilton	180
		375

Sales Day Book

(8)	A Grantley	72
(15)	A Henry	240
(24)	D Sangster	81
		393

(*b*) *Purchases Ledger*

Smith Stores

		(1) Purchases	90

C Kelly

		(23) Purchases	105

J Hamilton

		(31) Purchases	180

Sales Ledger

A Grantley

(8) Sales	72		

A Henry

(15) Sales	240		

D Sangster

(24) Sales	81		

(*c*) **General Ledger**

Sales Account

		(31) Sales day book	393

Purchases Account

(31) Purchases day book	375		

Chapter 21

21.1

Purchases Day Book

(1)	H Lloyd	119
(4)	D Scott	98
(4)	A Simpson	114
(4)	A Williams	25
(4)	S Wood	56
(10)	A Simpson	59
(18)	M White	89
(18)	J Wong	67
(18)	H Miller	196
(18)	H Lewis	119
(31)	A Williams	56
(31)	C Cooper	98
		1,096

Returns Outwards Day Book

(7)	H Lloyd	16
(7)	D Scott	14
(25)	J Wong	5
(25)	A Simpson	11
		46

General Ledger

Purchases Account

(31) Purchases day book	1,096		

Returns Outwards Account

		(31) Returns outwards day book	46

Purchases Ledger

H Lloyd

(7) Returns	16	(1) Purchases	119

D Scott

(7) Returns	14	(4) Purchases	98

A Simpson

(25) Returns	11	(4) Purchases	114
		(10) Purchases	59

A Williams

		(4) Purchases	25
		(31) Purchases	56

S Wood

		(4) Purchases	56

M White

		(18) Purchases	89

J Wong

(25) Returns	5	(18) Purchases	67

H Miller

		(18) Purchases	196

H Lewis

		(18) Purchases	119

C Cooper

		(31) Purchases	98

21.3 (*a*) *Sales Day Book*

(2) K King	119
(11) AB Ltd	99
(14) K King	720
	938

(*b*) *Purchases Day Book*

(4) S Todd	200
(17) T Jay	142
(20) K Fisher	180
	522

(*c*) *Returns Inwards Day Book*

(15) AB Ltd	19
(24) K King	39
	58

(*d*) *Returns Outwards Day Book*

(8) W Mears	40
(22) K Fisher	49
	89

(*e*) *Cash Book (extracts)*

	Disct.	*Cash*	*Bank*		*Disct.*	*Cash*	*Bank*
(6) C Cook	12		228	(19) W Mears	24		456
(27) K King	68		1,292	(28) S Todd	16	304	

(*f*) **Sales Ledger**

C Cook

(1) Balance b/d	240	(6) Bank	228
		(6) Discount allowed	12
	240		240

K King

(1) Balance b/d	560	(24) Returns inwards	39
(2) Sales	119	(27) Bank	1,292
(14) Sales	720	(27) Discount allowed	68
	1,399		1,399

AB Ltd

(1) Balance b/d	40	(15) Returns inwards	19
(11) Sales	99	(31) Balance c/d	120
	139		139
(1) Balance b/d	120		

(*g*) **Purchases Ledger**

S Todd

(28) Cash	304	(1) Balance b/d	120
(28) Discount received	16	(4) Purchases	200
	320		320

W Mears

(8) Returns outwards	40	(1) Balance b/d	520
(19) Bank	456		
(19) Discount received	24		
	520		520

K Fisher

(22) Returns outwards	49	(1) Balance b/d	280
(31) Balance c/d	411	(20) Purchases	180
	460		460
		(1) Balance b/d	411

T Jay

(31) Balance c/d	142	(17) Purchases	142
		(1) Balance b/d	142

(*h*) **General Ledger**

Sales

		Sales day book	938

Purchases

Purchases day book	522		

Returns Inwards

Returns inwards day book	58		

Returns Outwards

		Returns outwards day book	89

Discounts Allowed

Cash Book	80		

Discounts Received

		Cash Book	40

Chapter 22

22.1 (*a*)
Style of invoice will vary. Invoice number to be 10586

Calculations:

	£
3 sets of Boy Michael golf clubs × £240	720
150 Watson golf balls at £8 per 10 balls	120
4 Faldo golf bags at £30	120
	960
Less trade discount 33 1/3%	320
	640
Add VAT 17 1/2%	112
	752

(*b*)

D Wilson Ltd Ledger

G Christie & Sons

Dr					Cr
2005					
May 1	Sales	752			

G Christie & Son Ledger

D Wilson Ltd

Dr					Cr
			2005		
			May 1	Purchases	752

22.2

Sales Day Book

2006			*Total*	*Net*	*VAT*
Aug	1	M Sinclair & Co	188	160	28
Aug	8	M Brown & Associates	282	240	42
Aug	19	A Axton Ltd	94	80	14
Aug	31	T Christie	47	40	7
			611	520	91

Sales Ledger

M Sinclair & Co

(1) Sales	188		

M Brown & Associates

(8) Sales	282		

A Axton Ltd

(19) Sales	94		

T Christie

(31) Sales	47		

General Ledger

Sales

		(31) Credit sales for the month	520

Value Added Tax

		(31) Sales book: VAT content	91

22.3

Sales Day Book – R Colman Ltd

		Total	*Net*	*VAT*
(1)	B Davies & Co	188	160	28
(4)	C Grant Ltd	235	200	35
(16)	C Grant Ltd	141	120	21
(31)	B Karloff	94	80	14
		658	560	~~98~~

Purchases Day Book – R Colman Ltd

		Total	*Net*	*VAT*
(10)	G Cooper & Son	470	400	70
(10)	J Wayne Ltd	282	240	42
(14)	B Lugosi	47	40	7
(23)	S Hayward	47	40	7
		846	720	126

Sales Ledger

B Davies & Co

(1) Sales	188		

C Grant Ltd

(4) Sales	235		
(16) Sales	141		

B Karloff

(31) Sales	94		

Purchases Ledger

G Cooper & Son

		(10) Purchases	470

J Wayne Ltd

		(10) Purchases	282

B Lugosi

		(14) Purchases	47

S Hayward

		(23) Purchases	47

General Ledger

Sales

		(31) Sales day book	560

Purchases

(31) Purchases day book	720		

Value Added Tax

(31) VAT content in purchase book	126	(31) VAT content in sales book	98
		(31) Balance c/d	28
	126		126

22.5 (*a*) Trade discount £200.
(*b*) Cash discount £90.
(*c*) VAT £299.25.

22.6 VAT payable to HM Customs & Excise:

Manufacturer	35
Wholesaler (49 – 35)	14
Retailer (56 – 49)	7
	56

22.7 (*a*) Debited
(*b*) Six years
(*c*) Yes
(*d*)

Debit – Sales returns/Returns inwards	80
Debit – VAT	14
Credit – Bank/cash	94

AAT (Central Assessment)

Chapter 23

23.1
(*a*)

Curtain Design Company
Sales Day Book

Date	Details	Folio	Total	Ready-made	Custom-made	VAT
2006			£	£	£	£
Nov 1	Jarvis Arms Hotel	SL1	2,702.50		2,300.00	402.50
Nov 8	Springs Nursing Home	SL2	1,175.00	1,000.00		175.00
Nov 15	J P Morten	SL3	258.50	220.00		38.50
Nov 17	Queen's Hotel	SL4	1,762.50		1,500.00	262.50
Nov 30	W Blackshaw	SL5	105.75	90.00		15.75
			6,004.25	1,310.00	3,800.00	894.25
				GL1	GL2	GL3

(*b*)

Sales Ledger

Jarvis Arms Hotel Account *SL1*

Dr			Cr
Nov 1 Sales	2,702.50		

Spring's Nursing Home Account *SL2*

Dr			Cr
Nov 8 Sales	1,175.00		

J P Morten Account *SL3*

Dr			Cr
Nov 15 Sales	258.50		

Queen's Hotel Account *SL4*

Dr			Cr
Nov 17 Sales	1,762.50		

W Blackshaw Account *SL5*

Dr			Cr
Nov 30 Sales	105.75		

(*c*)

General Ledger

Sales – Ready-Made Account *GL1*

Dr			Cr
		Nov 30 Day book	1,310.00

Sales – Custom-Made Account *GL2*

Dr			Cr
		Nov 30 Day book	3,800.00

Value Added Tax Account *GL3*

Dr			Cr
		Nov 30 VAT on sales	894.25

23.2
(*a*)

Hall Engineering Co
Purchases Day Book

Date	Details	Folio	Total	Engineering parts	Printing and stationery	Motor expenses	VAT
2004			£	£	£	£	£
May 1	Black's Engineering Co	PL1	611.00	520.00			91.00
May 3	Ace Printing Co	PL2	170.37		145.00		25.37
May 24	Morgan's Garage	PL3	141.00			120.00	21.00
May 26	Martin's Foundry	PL4	822.50	700.00			122.50
May 28	Office Supplies	PL5	148.05		126.00		22.05
May 29	Black's Engineering Co	PL1	258.50	220.00			38.50
			2,151.42	1,440.00	271.00	120.00	320.42
				GL1	GL2	GL3	GL4

(*b*)

Purchases Ledger

Black's Engineering — *PL1*

Dr				*Cr*	
			May 1	Purchases	611.00
			May 29	Purchases	258.50

Ace Printing Co — *PL2*

Dr				*Cr*	
			May 3	Purchases	170.37

Morgan's Garage — *PL3*

Dr				*Cr*	
			May 24	Purchases	141.00

Martin's Foundry — *PL4*

Dr				*Cr*	
			May 26	Purchases	822.50

Office Supplies — *PL5*

Dr				*Cr*	
			May 28	Purchases	148.05

(*c*)

General Ledger

Purchases – Engineering Parts — *GL1*

Dr				*Cr*	
May 31	Day book	1,440.00			

Printing and Stationery — *GL2*

Dr				*Cr*	
May 31	Day book	271.00			

Motor Expenses — *GL3*

Dr				*Cr*	
May 31	Day book	120.00			

VAT — *GL4*

Dr				*Cr*	
May 31	VAT on Purchases	320.42			

23.3

Sales day book – Smart Campers

Date 2002	*Name of Customer*	*Invoice Total*	*Horsforth*	*Moortown*	*Otley*	*VAT*
May 2	Outdoor Centre	326.04		296.40		29.64
May 8	Premier Leisure	980.55	891.41			89.14
May 16	Airedale Sport	223.17			202.88	20.29
May 28	Empire Products	1,075.43		977.67		97.76
		2,605.19	891.41	1,274.07	202.88	236.83

Smart Campers: Workings:

			£	£
May 2		Outdoor Centre/Moortown		
	12	Flair cool boxes at £15.90 each	190.80	
	6	Camping stoves at £29.95 each	179.70	
			370.50	
		Less Trade discount 20%	74.10	296.40
		Add VAT at 10%		29.64
				326.04
May 8		Premier Leisure/Horsforth	£	£
	10	Explorer rucksacks at £34.99 each	349.90	
		Less Trade discount 20%	69.98	279.92
	12	Trekker ridge tents at £59.95 each	719.40	
		Less Trade discount 15%	107.91	611.49
				891.41
		Add VAT at 10%		89.14
				980.55
May 16		Airedale Sport/Otley	£	£
	8	Palma cool bags at £7.85 each	62.80	
	12	Flair cool boxes at £15.90 each	190.80	
			253.60	
		Less Trade discount 20%	50.72	202.88
		Add VAT at 10%		20.29
				223.17
May 28		Empire Products/Moortown	£	£
	14	Dome tents at £47.90 each	670.60	
	8	Trekker ridge tents at £59.95 each	479.60	
			1,150.20	
		Less Trade discount 15%	172.53	977.67
		Add VAT at 10%		97.76
				1,075.43

Chapter 24

24.1 **Sales Ledger Control Account**

Dr			Cr
(1) Balance b/d	4,560	(31) Returns inwards	460
(31) Sales day book	10,870	(31) Cheques and cash	9,615
		(31) Discounts allowed	305
		(31) Balances c/d	5,050
	15,430		15,430

24.2 **Sales Ledger Control Account**

Dr			Cr
(1) Balances b/d	6,708	(31) Discounts	300
(31) Sales day book	11,500	(31) Cash and cheques	8,970
		(31) Bad debts	115
		(31) Returns inwards	210
		(31) Balances c/d	8,613
	18,208		18,208

24.4 **Sales Ledger Control Account**

2005		£	2005		£
May 1	Balances b/d	6,420	May 31	Cash and bank	10,370
May 31	Sales	12,800	May 31	Discounts allowed	395
May 31	Balance c/d	50	May 31	Set-offs: purchases ledger	145
			May 31	Balances c/d	8,360
		19,270			19,270

24.6 (*a*) **Sales Ledger – Shery Tatupu**

L Barker

2004		£	2004		£
Mar 31	Credit sales	18,642	Jan 1	Balance b/d	62
			Mar 31	Bank	15,023
			Mar 31	Discount	142
			Mar 31	Balance c/d	3,415
		18,642			18,642

D Blackhurst

2004		£	2004		£
Jan 1	Balance b/d	1,466	Mar 31	Sales returns	88
Mar 31	Credit sales	16,428	Mar 31	Bank	16,009
			Mar 31	Balance c/d	1,797
		17,894			17,894

H Brackenbridge

2004		£	2004		£
Mar 31	Credit sales	19,886	Jan 1	Balance b/d	58
			Mar 31	Bank	17,332
			Mar 31	Discount	227
			Mar 31	Balance c/d	2,269
		19,886			19,886

(*b*) **Sales Ledger Control Account?**

2004		£	2004		£
Jan 1	Balance b/d	1,346	Mar 31	Sales returns	88
Mar 31	Credit sales	54,956	Mar 31	Bank	48,364
			Mar 31	Discounts	369
			Mar 31	Balance c/d	7,481
		56,302			56,302

(*c*) **Sales Ledger Outstanding Balances at 31 March 2004**

	£
L Barker	3,415
D Blackhurst	1,797
H Brackenbridge	2,269
	7,481
Balance per Sales Ledger Control Account	7,481

Pitman Qualifications

Chapter 25

25.1

(*a*)	Motor vehicles	Dr	6,790	:	Kingston Garage	Cr	6,790
(*b*)	Bad debts	Dr	34	:	H Newman	Cr	34
(*c*)	Unique Offices	Dr	490	:	Office furniture	Cr	490
(*d*) (i)	Bank	Dr	39	:	W Charles	Cr	39
(ii)	Bad debts	Dr	111	:	W Charles	Cr	111
(*e*)	Drawings	Dr	45	:	Purchases	Cr	45
(*f*)	Drawings	Dr	76	:	Insurance	Cr	76
(*g*)	Machinery	Dr	980	:	Systems Accelerated	Cr	980

25.3 (*a*)

The Journal as at 1 May 2008

	Dr	*Cr*
Bank	2,910	
Cash	160	
Equipment	5,900	
Premises	25,000	
Debtor: J Carnegie	540	
Creditors: R Smith		890
T Thomas		610
Loan: J Higgins		4,000
Capital		29,010
	34,510	34,510

(*b*)

Cash Book

	Cash	*Bank*		*Cash*	*Bank*
(1) Balances b/d	160	2,910	(5) R Smith		500
(31) Sales	8,560		(12) J Higgins		1,000
(31) Cash C		8,000	(31) Bank C	8,000	
			(31) Loan interest		200
			(31) Balance c/d	720	9,210
	8,720	10,910		8,720	10,910

Equipment

(1) Balance b/d	5,900		

Premises

(1) Balance b/d	25,000		

R Smith

(5) Bank	500	(1) Balance b/d	890

J Carnegie

(1) Balance b/d	540	(31) Returns	400
(24) Sales	2,220		

T Thomas

		(1) Balance b/d	610
		(2) Purchases	2,100

J Higgins (Loan)

(12) Bank	1,000	(1) Balance b/d	4,000

Loan Interest

(31) Bank	200		

Capital

		(1) Capital	29,010

Returns Inwards

(31) J Carnegie	400		

Sales

		(24) J Carnegie	2,220
		(31) Cash	8,560

Purchases

(2) T Thomas	2,100		

J Green

Trial Balance as at 31 May 2008

	Dr £	*Cr* £
Cash	720	
Bank	9,210	
Equipment	5,900	
Premises	25,000	
R Smith		390
J Carnegie	2,360	
T Thomas		2,710
J Higgins		3,000
Loan interest	200	
Capital		29,010
Sales		10,780
Purchases	2,100	
Returns inwards	400	
	45,890	45,890

Chapter 26

26.1

Straight Line			*Reducing Balance*		
Cost		4,000	Cost		4,000
Yr 1	Depreciation	700	Yr 1	Depn 40% of 4,000	1,600
		3,300			2,400
Yr 2	Depreciation	700	Yr 2	Depn 40% of 2,400	960
		2,600			1,440
Yr 3	Depreciation	700	Yr 3	Depn 40% of 1,440	576
		1,900			864
Yr 4	Depreciation	700	Yr 4	Depn 40% of 864	346
		1,200			518
Yr 5	Depreciation	700	Yr 5	Depn 40% of 518	207
		500			311

4,000 – 500 = 3,500 ÷ 5 = 700

26.2

(*a*) *Straight Line*			(*b*) *Reducing Balance*		
Cost		12,500	Cost		12,500
Yr 1	Depreciation	1,845	Yr 1	Depn 20% of 12,500	2,500
		10,655			10,000
Yr 2	Depreciation	1,845	Yr 2	Depn 20% of 10,000	2,000
		8,810			8,000
Yr 3	Depreciation	1,845	Yr 3	Depn 20% of 8,000	1,600
		6,965			6,400
Yr 4	Depreciation	1,845	Yr 4	Depn 20% of 6,400	1,280
		5,120			5,120

$$\frac{12{,}500 - 5{,}120}{4} = 1{,}845$$

26.3

(a) Reducing Balance			(b) Straight Line		
Cost		6,400	Cost		6,400
Yr 1	Depn 50% of 6,400	3,200	Yr 1	Depreciation	1,240
		3,200			5,160
Yr 2	Depn 50% of 3,200	1,600	Yr 2	Depreciation	1,240
		1,600			3,920
Yr 3	Depn 50% of 1,600	800	Yr 3	Depreciation	1,240
		800			2,680
Yr 4	Depn 50% of 800	400	Yr 4	Depreciation	1,240
		400			1,440
Yr 5	Depn 50% of 400	200	Yr 5	Depreciation	1,240
		200			200

$$\frac{6{,}400 - 200}{5} = 1{,}240$$

Chapter 27

27.1

(a) *Motor Cars*

2002							
Jan 1	Bank	12,500					

(b) *Provision for Depreciation: Motor Cars*

			2002		
			Dec 31	Profit and loss	2,500
2003			2003		
Dec 31	Balance c/d	4,500	Dec 31	Profit and loss	2,000
		4,500			4,500
2004			2004		
Dec 31	Balance c/d	6,100	Jan 1	Balance b/d	4,500
			Dec 31	Profit and loss	1,600
		6,100			6,100

(c) *Profit and Loss Account (extracts) – A White*

(2002)	Provision for depreciation: Motors	2,500	
(2003)	Provision for depreciation	2,000	
(2004)	Provision for depreciation	1,600	

(d) *Balance Sheets (extracts) – A White*

	2002	2003	2004
Motor car at cost	12,500	12,500	12,500
Less Depreciation to date	2,500	4,500	6,100
Net book value	10,000	8,000	6,400

27.3

(a) *Computer*

2005			2005		
Jan 1	Balance b/d	9,500	Jan 1	Computer disposals	9,500

(b) *Provision for Depreciation: Computer*

2002			2002		
Dec 31	Balance c/d	1,900	Dec 31	Profit and loss	1,900
2003			2003		
Dec 31	Balance c/d	3,800	Jan 1	Balance b/d	1,900
			Dec 31	Profit and loss	1,900
		3,800			3,800
2004			2004		
Dec 31	Balance c/d	5,700	Jan 1	Balance b/d	3,800
			Dec 31	Profit and loss	1,900
		5,700			5,700
2005			2005		
Jan 1	Computer disposals	5,700	Jan 1	Balance b/d	5,700

(c) *Computer Disposals*

2005			2005		
Jan 1	Computer	9,500	Jan 1	Depreciation	5,700
Dec 31	Profit and loss	450	,, 1	Bank	4,250
		9,950			9,950

(d) *Profit and Loss Account (extracts)*

(2002)	Provision for depreciation	1,900			
(2003)	Provision for depreciation	1,900			
(2004)	Provision for depreciation	1,900			
			(2005)	Profit on sale of computer	450

(e) *Balance Sheets (extracts)*

	2002	2003	2004
Computer at cost	9,500	9,500	9,500
Less Depreciation to date	1,900	3,800	5,700
Net book value	7,600	5,700	3,800

27.4 (a) *Motor Van Disposals*

Motor van	12,000	Provision for depreciation	9,700
		Bank	1,850
		Profit and loss: loss on sale	450
	12,000		12,000

(b) *Machinery Disposals*

Machinery	27,900	Provision for depreciation	19,400
Profit and loss: profit on sale	2,770	Bank	11,270
	30,670		30,670

(c) *Fixtures Disposals*

Fixtures	8,420	Provision for depreciation	7,135
		Bank	50
		Profit and loss: loss on sale	1,235
	8,420		8,420

(d) *Buildings Disposals*

Buildings	200,000	Provision for depreciation	110,000
Profit and loss: profit on sale	59,000	Bank	149,000
	259,000		259,000

Chapter 28

28.1 **Data Computer Services**

(a) *Bad Debts Account*

Dr			Cr		
2004		£	2004		£
Apr 30	H Gordon	1,110	Dec 31	Profit and loss	1,870
Aug 31	D Bellamy	640			
Oct 31	J Alderton	120			
		1,870			1,870

Provision for Bad Debts Account

Dr			Cr		
			2004		£
			Dec 31	Profit and loss	2,200

(b) *Profit and Loss Account*
for the year ended 31 December 2004 (extracts)

Gross profit		xxx
Less Expenses:		
Bad debts written off	1,870	
Provision for bad debts	2,200	4,070

(c) *Balance Sheet as at 31 December 2004 (extract)*

Debtors	68,500	
Less Provision for bad debts	2,200	66,300

28.2 (a) *Bad Debts Account*

Dr			Cr		
2003			2003		
Dec 31	Various debts	540	Dec 31	Profit and loss	540

(b) *Provision for Bad Debts Account*

Dr			Cr		
2003			2003		
Dec 31	Balance c/d	3,100	Jan 1	Balance b/f	2,600
			Dec 31	Profit and loss	500
		3,100			3,100
			2004		
			Jan 1	Balance b/d	3,100

(c) *Profit and Loss Account*
for the year ended 31 December 2003 (extract)

Gross profit		xxx
Less Expenses:		
Bad debts written off	540	
Increase in provision for bad debts	500	1,040

(d) *Balance Sheet as at 31 December 2003 (extract)*

Debtors	62,000	
Less Provision for bad debts	3,100	58,900

28.3 *(a)*

Bad Debts Account

Dr				*Cr*		
2006				2006		
Aug 31	W Best	85		Dec 31	Profit and loss	225
Sep 30	S Avon	140				
		225				225
2007				2007		
Feb 28	L J Friend	180		Dec 31	Profit and loss	490
Aug 31	N Kelly	60				
Nov 30	A Oliver	250				
		490				490

Provision for Bad Debts Account

Dr			*Cr*		
2006			2006		
Dec 31	Balance c/d	550	Dec 31	Profit and loss	550
2007			2007		
Dec 31	Balance c/d	600	Jan 1	Balance b/d	550
			Dec 31	Profit and loss	50
		600			600

(b) *Balance Sheet (extracts) as at 31 December*

	2006		2007	
Debtors	40,500		47,300	
Less Provision for bad debts	550	39,950	600	46,700

Chapter 29

29.1

(a) *Motor Expenses Account*

Dr			*Cr*		
2008			2008		
Dec 31	Cash & Bank	744	Dec 31	Profit and loss	772
Dec 31	Owing c/d	28			
		772			772

(b) *Insurance Account*

Dr			*Cr*		
2008			2008		
Dec 31	Cash & Bank	420	Dec 31	Prepaid c/d	35
			Dec 31	Profit and loss	385
		420			420

(c) *Stationery Account*

Dr			*Cr*		
2008			2008		
Dec 31	Cash & Bank	1,800	Jan 1	Owing b/f	250
Dec 31	Owing c/d	490	Dec 31	Profit and loss	2,040
		2,290			2,290

(d) *Rent Account*

Dr			*Cr*		
2008			2008		
Jan 1	Prepaid b/f	220	Dec 31	Prepaid c/d	290
Dec 31	Cash & Bank	950	Dec 31	Profit and loss	880
		1,170			1,170

(e) *Rent Received Account*

Dr			*Cr*		
2008			2008		
Jan 1	Owing b/f	180	Dec 31	Cash & Bank	550
Dec 31	Profit & Loss	580	Dec 31	Owing c/d	210
		760			760

29.2

J Smailes
Trading and Profit and Loss Account for the year ended 31 March 2007

	£	£	£
Sales			92,340
Less Cost of goods sold			
Opening stock		18,160	
Add Purchases	69,185		
Less Returns out	640	68,545	
Carriage inwards		420	
		87,125	
Less Closing stock		22,390	64,735
Gross profit			27,605
Less Expenses			
Wages and salaries		10,240	
Carriage outwards		1,570	
Rent and rates		3,015	
Communication expenses		624	
Commissions payable		216	
Insurance		405	
Sundry expenses		318	16,388
Net profit			11,217

Balance Sheet as at 31 March 2007

	£	£
Fixed Assets		
Buildings	20,000	
Fixtures	2,850	22,850
Current Assets		
Stock	22,390	
Debtors	14,320	
Bank	2,970	
Cash	115	
	39,795	
Less Current Liabilities		
Creditors	8,160	
Net current assets		31,635
		54,485
Less Long-term liabilities		
Loan		10,000
		44,485
Capital		
Balance at 1.4.2006		40,888
Add Net profit		11,217
		52,105
Less Drawings		7,620
		44,485

29.4

C Cainen
Trading and Profit and Loss Account
for the year ended 31 December 2008

Sales		18,590
Less Cost of goods sold:		
Opening stock	2,050	
Add Purchases	11,170	
	13,220	
Less Closing stock	3,910	
		9,310
Gross profit		9,280
Less Expenses:		
Rent (640 – 160)	480	
Wages and salaries (2,140 + 290)	2,430	
Insurance (590 – 190)	400	
Bad debts	270	
Telephone (300 + 110)	410	
General expenses	180	4,170
Net profit		5,110

29.6

J Sears
Trading and Profit and Loss Account
for the year ended 31 December 2007

Sales		80,000	
Less Returns inwards		1,000	79,000
Less Cost of goods sold:			
Opening stock		20,000	
Add Purchases	70,000		
Less Returns outwards	1,240	68,760	
		88,760	
Less Closing stock		24,000	64,760
Gross profit			14,240
Less Expenses:			
Wages and salaries (7,200 + 450)		7,650	
Telephone (200 – 20)		180	
Bad debts		40	
Provision for bad debts (1,960 × 10% – 160)		36	
Depreciation:			
Store fittings		800	
Motor van		1,200	9,906
Net profit			4,334

J Sears
Balance Sheet as at 31 December 2007

Fixed Assets			
Store fittings		8,000	
Less Depreciation to date		800	7,200
Motor van		6,000	
Less Depreciation to date		1,200	4,800
			12,000
Current Assets			
Stock		24,000	
Debtors	1,960		
Less Provision for bad debts	196	1,764	
Prepaid expenses		20	
Bank		600	
		26,384	
Less Current Liabilities			
Creditors	1,400		
Expenses owing	450	1,850	
Net current assets			24,534
			36,534
Financed by:			
Capital			
Balance 1.1.2007			35,800
Add Net profit			4,334
			40,134
Less Drawings			3,600
			36,534

Chapter 30

30.1 (*a*) (i) FIFO 6 × £13 = £78 stock valuation at 31 December 2007.
(ii) LIFO

2007	*Received*	*Issued*	*Stock*	*£*	*£*
Jan	24 × £10		24 × £10		240
April	16 × £12.50		24 × £10 16 × £12.50	240 200	440
June		14 × £10 16 × £12.50	10 × £10		100
Oct	30 × £13		10 × £10 30 × £13	100 390	490
Nov		4 × £10 30 × £13	6 × £10		60

Closing stock would be valued at £60 on a LIFO basis.

(iii) AVCO

2007	*Received*	*Issued*	*Average cost per unit*	*No. of units units in stock*	*Total value of stock*
Jan	24 × £10		£10.00	24	£240
April	16 × £12.50		£11.00	40	£440
June		30	£11.00	10	£110
Oct	30 × £13		£12.50	40	£500
Nov		34	£12.50	6	£75

Closing stock would be valued at £75 on an average cost basis.

(*b*) *Trading Accounts for the year ended 31 December 2007*

	FIFO		*LIFO*		*AVCO*	
Sales		1,092		1,092		1,092
Less Cost of goods sold						
Purchases	830		830		830	
Less Closing stock	78	752	60	770	75	755
Gross Profit		340		322		337

30.3

Item no. 24 *Date*		*Ref.*	*In*	*Out*	*Balance*
2009			No.	No.	No.
May	1	Opening balance			500
May	2	Starlight Co Ltd	300		800
May	8	740		173	627
May	8	Moonbeam & Sons	200		827
May	10	810		294	533
May	14	976		104	429
May	24	Starlight Co Ltd	350		779
May	28	981		206	573

30.5

DC Ltd

Stock Valuation as on 31 December 2008

		£	£
Value at 8 January 2009			50,850
Add (*a*)	Error in calculation (1,600 – 160)	1,440	
(*b*)	Sales at cost (500 – 100)	400	
(*d*)	Casting error (4,299 – 2,499)	1,800	3,640
			54,490
Less (*c*)	Reduce to NRV (560 – 425)		135
Corrected value of stock at 31 December 2008			54,355

30.6

Chung Ltd

Computation of Stock as at 31 December 2008

Total per stock sheets				198,444
Add (*b*)	Sales to 11 January 2009	6,960		
	Less profit 33⅓%	2,320	4,640	
(*c*)	Undercast		50	4,690
				203,134
Less (*c*)	Overcast		1,000	
(*d*)	Incorrect extension 560 – 528		32	
(*e*)	Goods on approval		3,000	
(*f*)	Incorrect total carried forward 106,850 – 105,680		1,170	5,202
				197,932

Chapter 31

(To economise on space, all narratives for journal entries in these answers are omitted.)

31.1

(*a*)	J Harkness	Dr	678	J Harker	Cr	678
(*b*)	Machinery	Dr	4,390	L Pearson	Cr	4,390
(*c*)	Motor van	Dr	3,800	Motor expenses	Cr	3,800
(*d*)	E Fletcher	Dr	9	Sales	Cr	9
(*e*)	Sales	Dr	257	Commissions received	Cr	257

31.3 (*a*)

Trial Balance as at 30 April 2009

	Dr	*Cr*
	£	£
Capital		15,000
Drawings	1,500	
Sales		27,250
Purchases	13,225	
Motor expenses	790	
Rent received		285
General expenses	2,190	
Wages	6,320	
Motor vehicles	6,000	
Premises	27,000	
Bank (overdrawn)		13,164
Suspense		*1,326
	57,025	57,025

**Figure of £1,326 is required to make the columns balance.*

(*b*) Refer to Chapter 7, Section 7.6 'Steps to take if the Trial Balance doesn't balance'.

31.4 Workings:

(*a*)	Sales	15,863	+	392	=	16,255
	Debtors	3,738	+	392	=	4,130
(*b*)	Bank overdraft	372	–	545	=	173
	Debtors (see above)	4,130	–	545	=	3,585
(*c*)	Purchases	7,590	–	196	=	7,394
	Creditors	2,095	–	196	=	1,899
(*d*)	Bank balance (see above)	173	–	150	=	23
	Drawings	1,420	+	150	=	1,570

Elaine Rowe
Corrected Trial Balance as at 31 May 2008

	Dr	*Cr*
	£	£
Equipment	9,750	
General expenses	1,394	
Sales		16,255
Purchases	7,394	
Sales returns	426	
Purchases returns		674
Creditors		1,899
Drawings	1,570	
Debtors	3,585	
Bank	23	
Capital		5,314
	24,142	24,142

Chapter 32

32.1

The Journal

	Dr	*Cr*
	£	£
(*a*) T. Thomas	900	
Bank		900
(*b*) C. Charles	35	
Discounts allowed		35
(*c*) Office equipment	6,000	
Motor vehicles		6,000
(*d*) J. Graham	715	
Sales		715
(*e*) Wages	210	
Drawings	210	
Suspense		420

32.2 (*a*) **The Journal (narratives omitted)**

		Dr	*Cr*
(i)	Suspense	100	
	Sales		100
(ii)	K Hart	250	
	K Hartley		250
(iii)	Rent	70	
	Suspense		70
(iv)	Suspense	300	
	Discounts received		300
(v)	Sales	360	
	Motors		360

(*b*) **Suspense Account**

Sales	100	Balance b/f	330
Discounts received	300	Rent	70
	400		400

(*c*) *Net profit per accounts*

				7,900
Add	(i)	Sales undercast	100	
	(iv)	Discounts undercast	300	400
				8,300
Less	(iii)	Rent undercast	70	
	(v)	Reduction in sales	360	430
Corrected net profit				7,870

32.5 (*a*) **Suspense**

	Balance as per T.B.	1,134	(i)	Sales over-cast	350
(iv)	Creditor	166	(ii)	Discounts under-cast	100
			(iii)	Fixtures omitted	850
		1,300			1,300

(*b*)

K Woodburn
Trial Balance as at 30 June 2008

	Dr	*Cr*
Sales (87,050 – 350)		86,700
Purchases	62,400	
Discounts allowed and received	405	410
Salaries and wages	3,168	
General expenses	595	
Fixtures (10,000 + 850)	10,850	
Stock 1 July 2007	12,490	
Debtors and creditors	8,120	4,721
Bank	6,790	
Drawings (4,520 – 490)	4,030	
Capital		17,017
	108,848	108,848

Note: Discounts allowed 305 + (ii) 100 = 405
Creditors 5,045 + (iv) 166 – (v) 490 = 4,721

32.7

The Journal

	Dr	*Cr*
(*a*) Suspense Sales *Correction of error sales day book undercast by £3,000*	3,000	3,000
(*b*) Purchases Dawson & Co. *Goods purchased on credit from Dawson & Co.*	1,147	1,147
(*c*) Motor repairs Motor vehicles *Motor repairs posted in error to motor vehicles account*	585	585
(*d*) J Greenway J Green *Goods sold on credit to J Greenway posted in error to J Green's account*	675	675
(*e*) Suspense Electricity *Payment of electricity account incorrectly debited £150 too much*	150	150
(*f*) Suspense Teape Ltd *Payment of £2,250 received from Teape Ltd not credited to their account*	2,250	2,250

Philip Hogan
Suspense Account

	£		£
Sales (*a*)	3,000	Balance b/d	5,400
Electricity (*e*)	150		
Teape Ltd (*f*)	2,250		
	5,400		5,400

Note that items (b), (c) and (d) do not pass through the suspense account, as they do not affect the balancing of the books.

Chapter 33

33.1 (*a*)

Total Debtors

Balances b/d	2,760	Cash	14,610
Sales (difference)	14,940	Balances c/d	3,090
	17,700		17,700

Total Creditors

Cash	9,390	Balances b/d	1,080
Balances c/d	1,320	Purchases (difference)	9,630
	10,710		10,710

(*b*)

K Rogers
Trading Account for the year ended 31 October 2006

	£	£
Sales		14,940
Less Cost of Goods Sold		
Opening Stock	2,010	
Add Purchases	9,630	
	11,640	
Less Closing Stock	2,160	9,480
Gross Profit		5,460

33.3 (*a*) Capital is £6,000.

(*b*)

D Lewinski
Balance Sheet as at 30 June 2006

	£	£
Fixed assets		
Plant		3,600
Fixtures		360
		3,960
Current assets		
Stock	1,350	
Debtors	930	
Bank	600	
Cash	135	
	3,015	
Less Current liabilities		
Creditors	720	
Net current assets		2,295
		6,255
Financed by:		
Capital		
Cash introduced		(*a*) 6,000
Add Net profit		1,855
		7,855
Less Drawings		1,600
		6,255

33.4

J Marcano
Statement of Affairs as at 31 August 2006

	£	£
Fixed assets		
Fixtures		3,500
Motor van		3,500
		7,000
Current assets		
Stock	16,740	
Debtors	11,890	
Bank	2,209	
Cash	115	
	30,954	
Less Current liabilities		
Creditors	9,952	21,002
		28,002

Statement of Affairs as at 31 August 2007

	£	£	£
Fixed assets			
Fixtures		5,500	
Less Depreciation		300	5,200
Motor van		3,500	
Less Depreciation		700	2,800
			8,000
Current assets			
Stock		24,891	
Debtors		15,821	
Prepaid expenses		72	
Cash		84	
		40,868	
Less Current liabilities			
Trade creditors	6,002		
Expenses owing	236		
Bank overdraft	165	6,403	
Net current assets			34,465
			42,465
Capital			
Balance as at 31.8.2006			28,002
Add Cash introduced			12,800
Add Net profit		(C)	9,223
		(B)	50,025
Less Drawings			7,560
		(A)	42,465

(A) Found as the figure to make balance sheet totals agree 42,465.
(B) Less 7,560 = (A) 42,465, therefore (B) is 50,025.
(C) Missing figure to total 50,025 = 9,223.

33.6

Workings:

Purchases		Sales	
Bank	29,487	Banked	37,936
Cash	2,994	Cash	9,630
	32,481		47,566
– Creditors 31.12.2006	5,624	– Debtors 31.12.2006	9,031
	26,857		38,535
+ Creditors 31.12.2007	7,389	+ Debtors 31.12.2007	8,624
Purchases for 2007	34,246	Sales for 2007	47,159

Opening Capital

Bank	405	
Stock	13,862	
Debtors	9,031	
Rates prepaid	210	
Fixtures	2,500	26,008
Less Creditors	5,624	
Rent owing	150	5,774
		20,234

P Kelly
Trading and Profit and Loss Account
For the year ended 31 December 2007

	£	£
Sales		47,159
Less Cost of goods sold:		
Opening stock	13,862	
Add Purchases	34,246	
	48,108	
Less Closing stock	15,144	32,964
Gross profit		14,195
Less Expenses:		
Wages	5,472	
Rent (1,650 – 150)	1,500	
Rates (890 + 210 – 225)	875	
Sundry expenses	375	
Depreciation: Fixtures	250	8,472
Net profit		5,723

P Kelly
Balance Sheet as at 31 December 2007

		£	£
Fixed assets			
Fixtures at valuation		2,500	
Less Depreciation		250	2,250
Current assets			
Stock		15,144	
Debtors		8,624	
Prepayments		225	
		23,993	
Less Current liabilities			
Trade creditors	7,389		
Bank overdraft	602	7,991	
Net current assets			16,002
			18,252
Capital			
Balance at 1.1.2007			20,234
Add Net profit			5,723
			25,957
Less Drawings (1,164 + 6,541)			7,705
			18,252

Chapter 34

34.1 (*a*)

Horton Hockey Club
Receipts and Payments Account for the year ended 30 June 2008

Receipts		*Payments*	
Bank balance b/f	2,715	Teams' travel expenses	1,598
Subscriptions	8,570	Groundsman's wages	3,891
Donations	1,500	Postage and stationery	392
Receipts from raffles	3,816	Rent of pitches and club house	4,800
		General expenses	419
		Prizes for raffles	624
		Bank balance c/f	4,877
	16,601		16,601

(b) *Horton Hockey Club*
Income and Expenditure Account for the year ended 30 June 2008

Income:		
Subscriptions (8,570 + 160)		8,730
Donations		1,500
Profit on raffles (3,816 – 624)		3,192
		13,422
Less Expenditure:		
Teams' travel expenses	1,598	
Groundsman's wages (3,891 + 75)	3,966	
Postage and stationery	392	
Rent of pitches and club house (4,800 + 400)	5,200	
General expenses	419	11,575
Surplus of income over expenditure		1,847

34.3 (*a*) Accumulated fund as at 1 June 2007:

Bar stocks	88
Equipment	340
Bank	286
	714

(*b*) *Down Town Sports and Social Club*
Income and Expenditure Account for the year ended 31 May 2008

Income	£	£	£
Subscriptions			149
Net proceeds of jumble sale			91
Net proceeds of dance			122
Contribution from Bar:			
Bar takings		463	
Less Cost of supplies:			
Opening Stock	88		
Add Purchases	397		
	485		
Less Closing stock	101	384	79
			441
Less Expenditure			
Wages		198	
Hire of rooms		64	
Loss on equipment		12	
Depreciation		30	304
Surplus of income over expenditure			137

34.6 *Amateur Dramatic Society*
Subscriptions Account

Dr	£		*Cr* £
In arrears b/d	235	In advance b/d	220
In advance c/d	140	Bank	2,600
Income and expenditure	2,630	In arrears c/d	185
	3,005		3,005
In arrears b/d	185	In advance b/d	140

Chapter 35

35.1 *E Smith*
Manufacturing and Trading Account for the year ended 31 March 2008

	£	£
Stock of raw material 1.4.2007		2,400
Add Purchases		21,340
Carriage inwards		321
		24,061
Less Stock of raw materials 31.3.2008		2,620
Cost of raw materials consumed		21,441
Manufacturing wages		13,280
Prime cost		34,721
Add Factory overhead expenses:		
Rent and rates	2,300	
Power	6,220	
Other expenses	1,430	9,950
		44,671
Add Work in progress 1.4.2007		955
		45,626
Less Work in progress 31.3.2008		870
Production cost of goods completed c/d		44,756
Sales		69,830
Less Cost of goods sold		
Stock finished goods 1.4.2007	6,724	
Add Production cost of goods completed b/d	44,756	
	51,480	
Less Stock finished goods 31.3.2008	7,230	44,250
Gross profit		25,580

Chapter 36

36.1 (*a*)

Stead and Jackson
Appropriation Account for the year ended 31 December 2002

			£
Net profit			45,000
Less Salary: Jackson			5,000
			40,000
Balance of profits shared:			
Stead	½	20,000	
Jackson	½	20,000	40,000

(*b*)

Capital Accounts

	Stead £	*Jackson* £		*Stead* £	*Jackson* £
			2002		
			Dec 31 Balance b/d	24,000	16,000

Current Accounts

	Stead £	*Jackson* £		*Stead* £	*Jackson* £
2002			2002		
Dec 31 Drawings	15,000	19,000	Dec 31 Balance b/d	2,300	3,500
Dec 31 Balances c/d	7,300	9,500	Dec 31 Salary		5,000
			Dec 31 Share of profits	20,000	20,000
	22,300	28,500		22,300	28,500
			2003		
			Jan 1 Balance b/d	7,300	9,500

36.4

Simpson and Young
Trading and Profit and Loss Appropriation Account
for the year ended 30 June 2003

		£	£
Sales			254,520
Less Cost of sales:			
Opening stock		18,000	
Add Purchases		184,980	
		202,980	
Less Closing stock		19,000	183,980
Gross profit			70,540
Less Expenses:			
Wages and salaries (32,700 + 500)		33,200	
Rent, rates and insurance (3,550 – 250)		3,300	
Electricity		980	
Stationery and printing		420	
Motor expenses		3,480	
General office expenses		1,700	
Depreciation: Motor van (20% of 16,000)		3,200	
Office equipment (10% of 5,600)		560	46,840
Net profit			23,700
Less Interest on capital:			
Simpson	(10% of 50,000)	5,000	
Young	(10% of 20,000)	2,000	7,000
			16,700
Share of profits:			
Simpson	3/5ths	10,020	
Young	2/5ths	6,680	16,700

Simpson and Young
Balance Sheet as at 30 June 2003

	Cost	Accumulated Depreciation		Net Book Value
Fixed assets	£	£		£
Premises	28,000	–		28,000
Office equipment	8,400	3,360	(W1)	5,040
Motor vans	16,000	8,200	(W2)	7,800
	52,400	11,560		40,840
Current assets				
Stock	19,000			
Debtors	28,000			
Prepayments	250			
Cash at bank	7,250	54,500		
Less Current liabilities				
Creditors	15,200			
Accruals	500	15,700		
Net current assets				38,800
				79,640
Financed by:				
Capital accounts	*Simpson*	*Young*		*Total*
Balance b/f	50,000	20,000		70,000
Current accounts				
Balance b/f	640	300		
Add Share of profit	10,020	6,680		
Add Interest on capital	5,000	2,000		
	15,660	8,980		
Less Drawings	10,000	5,000		
	5,660	3,980		9,640
				79,640

(W1) Provision for depreciation on office equipment:
8,400 – 5,600 + 560 = 3,360

(W2) Provision for depreciation on motor vans:
16,000 – 11,000 + 3,200 = 8,200

Chapter 37

37.1

LMT Ltd
Balance Sheet as at 31 December 2004

	Cost	Aggregate depreciation	Net book value
Fixed Assets			
Premises	45,000	18,000	27,000
Machinery	24,000	7,200	16,800
Fixtures	12,000	4,800	7,200
	81,000	30,000	51,000
Current Assets			
Stock		18,000	
Debtors		9,000	
Bank		6,000	
		33,000	
Less Current Liabilities			
Creditors	9,000		
Proposed dividend	3,000	12,000	
Net current assets			21,000
			72,000
Less Long-term Liabilities			
10% Debentures			18,000
			54,000
Financed by:			
Share Capital			
Authorised 60,000 ordinary shares at £1 each			60,000
Issued 36,000 ordinary shares at £1 each			36,000
Reserves			
General reserve		15,000	
Retained profits as per profit and loss account		(C)?	(B)?
			(A)?

(A) is the figure needed to make balance sheet total agree, i.e. 54,000.
(B) is the figure needed to add up to 54,000; therefore B = 54,000 – 36,000 = 18,000
(C) + 15,000 = B. (C) must be the missing figure of 3,000.

37.3

CA Company Ltd.
Profit and Loss Appropriation Account
for the year ended 31 December 2002

Net profit b/d		210,000
Add Retained profits from last year		17,000
		227,000
Less Transfer to general reserve	30,000	
Transfer to foreign exchange reserve	16,000	
Preference dividend paid (250,000 × £1 × 10%)	25,000	
Proposed ordinary dividend 10% (500,000 × £2 × 10%)	100,000	171,000
Retained profits carried forward to next year		56,000

37.4

Chang Ltd
Trading and Profit and Loss Account for the year ended 31 December 2004

Sales		316,810
Less Cost of goods sold:		
Opening stock	25,689	
Add Purchases	201,698	
	227,387	
Less Closing stock	29,142	198,245
Gross profit		118,565
Less Expenses:		
Wages and salaries (54,207 + 581)	54,788	
Rent (4,300 – 300)	4,000	
Lighting expenses	1,549	
Bad debts	748	
Provision for bad debts (938 – 861)	77	
General expenses	32,168	
Depreciation: Machinery (55,000 × 10%)	5,500	98,830
Net profit		19,735
Add Unappropriated profits from last year		34,280
		54,015
Less Proposed dividend		10,000
Unappropriated profits carried to next year		44,015

Chang Ltd
Balance Sheet as at 31 December 2004

Fixed Assets			
Premises			65,000
Machinery		55,000	
Less Aggregate depreciation (15,800 + 5,500)		21,300	33,700
			98,700
Current Assets			
Stock		29,142	
Debtors	21,784		
Less Provision for bad debts	938	20,846	
Prepayments		300	
Bank		23,101	
		73,389	
Less Current Liabilities			
Proposed dividend	10,000		
Creditors	17,493		
Expenses owing	581	28,074	
Net current assets			45,315
			144,015
Financed by:			
Authorised & issued capital			100,000
Revenue reserves:			
Profit and loss account			44,015
			144,015

37.6 (*a*)

Jaspa West Ltd
Profit and Loss Appropriation Account
for the year ended 31 December 2006

	£	£
Net profit		80,000
Add Unappropriated profits from last year		92,000
		172,000
Less Appropriations:		
General reserve (40% × 80,000)	32,000	
Proposed dividends		
Preference shares (8% × 80,000)	6,400	
Ordinary shares (4% × 150,000)	6,000	44,400
Unappropriated profits carried forward		127,600

(*b*)

Jaspa West Ltd
Balance Sheet as at 31 December 2006

	Cost £	*Depreciation to date* £	*Net Book Value* £
Fixed assets			
Premises	270,600	–	270,600
Machinery	72,600	18,400	54,200
	343,200	18,400	324,800
Current assets			
Stock	56,000		
Debtors (80,000 + 3,800)	83,800	139,800	
Creditors: Amounts falling due within one year			
Creditors (37,000 + 4,200)	41,200		
Bank	21,400		
Dividends owing (6,400 + 6,000)	12,400	75,000	
Net current assets			64,800
			389,600
Financed by:			
Share capital	*Authorised*	*Issued*	
Preference shares	100,000	80,000	
Ordinary shares	200,000	150,000	230,000
	300,000		
Reserves			
General reserve		32,000	
Profit and loss		127,600	159,600
			389,600

Pitman Qualifications

Chapter 38

38.1 (*a*) (i) Mark-up = 25%
(ii) Margin = 20%
(*b*) Margin = 25%
(*c*) Mark-up = 20%

38.3 First, draw up a trading account and insert the figures given in the question. The gross profit can now be calculated. Since mark-up is 25%, therefore margin is 20%. Consequently, gross profit is 20% of £30,000 = £6,000.
Cost of Goods Sold = Sales − Gross Profit = £30,000 − £6,000 = £24,000. Purchases can now be found arithmetically.

K Young
Trading Account for the year ended 31 July 2003

	£	£
Sales		30,000
Less Cost of goods sold (*a*)		
Opening stock	4,936	
Add Purchases (*b*)	25,374	
	30,310	
Less Closing stock	6,310	24,000
Gross profit (*c*)		6,000

38.4 (*a*) Average stock value = £4,000

Therefore $\frac{£2{,}000 + (a)}{2}$ = £4,000 and (a) is found to be £6,000.

Cost of goods sold is then calculated as £14,000. Mark-up is 50%, so sales = £14,000 + (£14,000 × 50%) = £21,000.

(*b*) *T Rigby*
Trading Account for the year ended 31 August 2009

	£	£
Sales		21,000
Less Cost of sales:		
Opening stock	2,000	
Add Purchases	18,000	
	20,000	
Less Closing stock	(a) 6,000	14,000
Gross profit		7,000

(*c*) If net profit on sales is not to be less than 10% of sales (= £2,100), this means that Rigby can afford up to £4,900 in expenses (i.e. Gross profit £7,000 − £4,900 expenses = £2,100 net profit).

38.5 (*a*)

	M Ltd	*N Ltd*
(i) *Current ratio*	$\frac{£200{,}000}{£50{,}000} = 4:1$	$\frac{£130{,}000}{£65{,}000} = 2:1$
(ii) *Acid test ratio*	$\frac{£60{,}000 + £40{,}000}{£50{,}000} = 2$	$\frac{£62{,}500 + £3{,}500}{£65{,}000} = 1.0$
(iii) *Stockturn*	$\frac{£288{,}000}{£120{,}000 + £100{,}000 \div 2}$ = 2.6 times	$\frac{£187{,}500}{£60{,}000 + £64{,}000 \div 2}$ = 3.0 times
(iv) *Debtors : Sales ratio*	$\frac{£60{,}000}{£360{,}000} \times$ 12 months = 2 months	$\frac{£62{,}500}{£250{,}000} \times$ 12 months = 3 months
(v) *Creditors : Purchases ratio*	$\frac{£50{,}000}{£268{,}000} \times$ 12 months = 2.2 months	$\frac{£65{,}000}{£191{,}500} \times$ 12 months = 4.1 months
(vi) *Gross profit %*	$\frac{£72{,}000}{£360{,}000} \times 100\% = 20\%$	$\frac{£62{,}500}{£250{,}000} \times 100\% = 25\%$
(vii) *Net profit %*	$\frac{£43{,}200}{£360{,}000} \times 100\% = 12\%$	$\frac{£35{,}000}{£250{,}000} \times 100\% = 14\%$
(viii) *Rate of return on shareholders' funds*	$\frac{£43{,}200}{£350{,}000} \times 100\% = 12.3\%$	$\frac{£35{,}000}{£255{,}000} \times 100\% = 13.7\%$

(*b*) Briefly N Ltd gives a better return to shareholders because of (viii) above.

Reasons include:

- M Ltd's current ratio is higher. This indicates that M Ltd is in a better liquidity position.
- N Ltd's stock turnover is higher than that of M Ltd. This shows that N Ltd manages its sales performance more effectively.
- The gross profit percentage of N Ltd is 5% higher than that of M Ltd. This is due to better purchasing and selling prices. Net profit margins differ by a smaller margin of 2%, suggesting, that M Ltd has tighter control of its overhead expenses when compared with its sales volume (8% compared with 11%).

Chapter 39

39.1 *Kevin Chandler*:

40 hrs at £7.50		300.00
Less deductions		
Income tax	55.00	
NIC (6% of 300.00)	18.00	73.00
Net pay		227.00

39.2 (*a*) *Michael Ford*:

40 hrs at £7.20		288.00
10 hrs × 1.5 = 15 hrs at £7.20		108.00
Gross pay		396.00
(*b*) *Less deductions*		
Income tax 22% (396–80)	69.52	
NIC (6% of 396)	23.76	
Pension (8% of 288)	23.04	
Union subscription	2.00	118.32
(*c*) Net pay		277.68

39.3 *Andrew Hill*:

		£
Basic 37 hours × £7.90		292.30
Overtime 6 hours × $1^1/2$ = 9 hours × £7.90		71.10
Overtime 4 hours × 2 = 8 hours × £7.90		63.20
Gross pay		426.60
Less Deductions:		
Income tax	95.50	
NIC (8% × 426.61)	34.13	
Pension (5% × 292.30)	14.62	
Social club	3.00	147.25
		279.35

39.8

Employee		£	*Gross Pay* £
A Taylor	35 hrs × £5.20 =	182.00	
	30 hrs × £0.75 =	22.50	204.50
S McKenzie	42 hrs × £5.20 =	218.40	
	40 hrs × £0.75 =	30.00	248.40
R Brindley	40 hrs × £5.20 =	208.00	
	36 hrs × £0.75 =	27.00	235.00
W Baseley	44 hrs × £5.20 =	228.80	
	36 hrs × £0.75 =	27.00	255.80
W Warburton	45 hrs × £5.20 =	234.00	
	52 hrs × £0.75 =	39.00	273.00
			£1,216.70

APPENDIX F

Specimen examination papers

GCSE style of examination

There are many examining bodies issuing their own syllabuses and assessment criteria for the General Certificate of Secondary Education. The authors of this book have written one general paper that covers all aspects of the syllabuses of the various bodies. They have devised questions that follow the style of the GCSE papers to help students gain practice and competence. It is, however, important for lecturers and students to refer to the actual specimen papers available from the examining body whose syllabus they are studying.

(TIME ALLOWED: 3.5 hours)

Paper 1, 1.5 hours (40%)
Paper 2, 2 hours (60%)

Marks will be awarded for clarity of expression and neatness of presentation. All workings are to be shown.

PAPER 1

Section A. Answer all 30 multiple-choice questions. Only *one* answer from (A)–(D) is in each case correct.

1 A firm bought a machine for £50,000. It is expected to last for six years and then be sold for £5,000. What is the annual amount of depreciation if the straight line method is used?

(A) £7,000
(B) £8,000
(C) £7,500
(D) £6,750.

2 Direct materials + direct labour + direct expenses + works overhead equals:

(A) Prime cost
(B) Total cost
(C) Production cost
(D) Variable cost.

3 Which of the following is *not* a liquidity ratio?

(A) Debtor: Creditor ratio
(B) Return on capital employed
(C) Current ratio
(D) Acid test ratio (Quick ratio).

4 Which of these would *not* be entered in the purchases ledger?

(*i*) Advice notes.
(*ii*) Discounts received.
(*iii*) Small accounts settled by petty cash.
(*iv*) Payments on accounts outstanding more than one year.

(A) (*iii*) only (B) (*iii*) and (*iv*) (C) (*i*) and (*iii*) (D) (*i*) only

5 Howells Ltd owes Beet & Co for goods bought a few days ago. Howells Ltd are paying the invoice early by cheque and are getting a cash discount. What is the correct double entry in Howells Ltd's books?

(A) Debit Beet & Co; Credit Bank; Credit Discount received.
(B) Debit Bank; Debit Discount allowed; Credit Beet & Co.
(C) Debit Beet & Co; Credit Bank; Credit Discount allowed.
(D) Debit Howells Ltd; Credit Bank; Credit Discount received.

6 Andrew's cash book shows that he has £1,595 in his bank account on 31 December. His bank statement, received the same day, shows otherwise. In fact, there were two unpresented cheques for £177 and £205. Not yet entered in the cash book were the following items: a standing order for £2,075, bank charges £115 and bank interest received £12. What balance was shown on his bank statement?

(A) £201 cash at bank (B) £87 overdraft
(c) £3,390 overdraft (D) £201 overdraft

7 Donald owns a small retail food store. He wants to know which of the following are fixed assets, and you are to advise him.

(*i*) Scales and weighing equipment.
(*ii*) Debtors.
(*iii*) Motor van.
(*iv*) Stock of food stuffs.

(A) (*i*) (*ii*) and (*iii*) (B) (*iii*) only (C) (*i*) and (*iii*) (D) (*i*) and (*ii*)

8 What would be the totals on a trial balance given the following balances: Loan from uncle £2,000; Stock £3,955; Bank overdraft £368; Debtors £3,092; Fixtures £5,500; Petty cash balance £121; Creditors £2,766; Motor vehicles £3,900; Capital?

(A) £11,494 (B) £14,628 (C) £16,568 (D) £16,996

9 What errors are shown in the following creditors control account?

Dr			*Creditors Control Account*		*Cr*
Balances b/f	(*i*)	307	Balances b/f	(*ii*)	18,526
Trade discounts	(*iii*)	1,311	Discounts received	(*iv*)	236
Bank	(*v*)	16,170	Purchases	(*vi*)	19,990
Balances c/d	(*vii*)	22,220	Bad debts	(*viii*)	58
			Balances c/d	(*ix*)	417

(A) (*iii*) and (*viii*) (B) (*iii*), (*iv*) and (*viii*)
(C) (*ii*), (*iii*) and (*vii*) (D) (*i*), (*iv*) and (*viii*)

10 The following figures have been extracted from a firm's balance sheet:

	£
Trade Debtors	15,000
Bank Overdraft	20,000
Stock	45,000
Trade Creditors	10,000

From the above figures the current ratio is:

(A) 3 : 1
(B) 1 : 1
(C) 4 : 1
(D) 2 : 1

11 A, B and C are in partnership but have not drawn up a Partnership Agreement. At the end of their financial year how should profits and losses be shared?

(A) In proportion to the amount of capital invested.
(B) By payment of a dividend.
(C) Equally.
(D) Only to partners active in the business.

12 The following information relates to Metal Ltd.

	£
Purchases	120,000
Sales	215,000
Creditors	20,000
Debtors	30,000

What is the creditors' payment period?

(A) 2 months
(B) 2.8 months
(C) 1 month
(D) 3 months

13 The correct title for the Statement of Affairs of Bradnop Youth Club on 31 March 2004 is:

(A) Statement of Affairs on 31 March 2004
(B) Bradnop Youth Club Statement of Affairs for the year ended 31 March 2004
(C) Statement of Affairs of Bradnop Youth Club as at 31 March 2004
(D) Statement of Affairs of Bradnop Youth Club for the year ended 31 March 2004

14 Which of the following are incorrect?

		Account debited	*Account credited*
(*i*)	Refund of part of insurance premium by cash	Cash	Insurance
(*ii*)	Cheque cashed for petty cash purposes	Bank	Petty cash
(*iii*)	Building new car park, paid by cheque	Motor expenses	Bank
(*iv*)	Sale of old fixtures for cash	Cash	Fixtures

(A) (*ii*),(*iii*) and (*iv*) (B) (*iii*) and (*iv*)
(C) (*ii*) and (*iii*) (D) (*ii*) and (*iv*)

15 When Howard is paying Susan by giro credit, which of the following must be shown on the bank giro form?

(*i*) Title of Susan's account.
(*ii*) Name of Howard's bank.
(*iii*) Name of Susan's bank.
(*iv*) Code number of Susan's account.

(A) All of them (B) (*i*), (*iii*) and (*iv*)
(C) (*i*), (*ii*) and (*iii*) (D) (*iii*) and (*iv*)

16 If the payer completes and signs a mandate form instructing the payee's bank to take funds from the payer's bank account, then this is known as:

(A) A standing order.
(B) A bank giro credit.
(C) A direct debit.
(D) The BACS system.

17 If Scott lent his friend Clarke £5,000 in cash, then the entries in Clarke's books would be:

(A) Debit Cash; Credit Creditors.
(B) Debit Loan from Scott; Credit Cash.
(C) Debit Capital; Credit Loan from Scott.
(D) Debit Cash; Credit Loan from Scott.

18 Moore Ltd keeps a bank cash book plus a petty cash book. Only cheques are banked. Oakley, a customer, pays Moore Ltd the balance on his account of £11 in cash. What double-entry records should be made?

(A) Debit Petty cash; Credit Oakley.
(B) Debit Cash sales; Credit Oakley.
(C) No Debit needed; Credit Oakley.
(D) Debit Oakley, Credit Petty cash.

19 Which of the following do not affect trial balance agreement?

(*i*) Purchases of £210 from P Cook entered in C Cook's account.
(*ii*) Sales £890 to J Lowe entered in both accounts as £809.
(*iii*) Cheque payment to R Noble of £155 entered only in cash book.
(*iv*) Motor vehicle purchased £5,000 entered in motor expenses account.

(A) (*i*) and (*ii*) (B) (*ii*) only (C) (*ii*) and (*iv*) (D) (*i*), (*ii*) and (*iv*)

20 In the books of Lee, a supplier, our account shows a debit balance of £2,190. Taking into account the following, what would be the balance on Lee's account in our books at that date?

(*i*) Cheque £950 sent by us but not received by him.
(*ii*) Goods £377 sent by him but not received by us.
(*iii*) Returns from us of £55 not received by him.

(A) £808 debit balance (B) £1,672 credit balance
(C) £808 credit balance (D) £2,708 credit balance

21 Debenture interest in a limited company's final accounts is charged in the:

(A) Trading Account.
(B) Profit and Loss Account.
(C) Profit and Loss Appropriation Account.
(D) Can be either B or C.

22 Stock should be valued at:

(A) Cost.
(B) Selling price less selling expenses.
(C) Net realisable value.
(D) Lower of cost or net realisable value.

23 Bagshaws Ltd sends out a document to a credit customer on a monthly basis, summarising the transactions that have taken place during the month and showing the amount owed by the customer. What is the name of the document?

(A) Remittance advice (B) Quotation
(C) Statement of account (D) Invoice

24 The closing balances in a sales ledger:

(A) Are always debit balances.
(B) Are always credit balances.
(C) Can be both debit and credit balances.
(D) Must be shown on the creditors control account.

25 Which is the best definition of 'real accounts'.

(A) The accounts which show the real value of a business.
(B) Account kept secret by the proprietors.
(C) Accounts in which errors or items of fraud have been corrected.
(D) Accounts for property of all kinds.

26 Which of the following columns should *not* be found in a columnar sales day book?

(*i*) Folio column
(*ii*) Trade discount column
(*iii*) VAT column
(*iv*) Sales returns column

(A) (*i*) and (*iii*) (B) (*ii*), (*iii*) and (*iv*) (C) (*ii*) and (*iv*) (D) (*i*), (*ii*) and (*iv*)

27 A new machine is bought for £5,600. During the first year of ownership the following expenditure occurs: repair broken shaft £205; fix new attachment £370; electricity used £497; wages of machine operator £3,920; instal new safety rails £217; costs of legal action when operator is injured £250. After the above, what would be the balance on the machinery account?

(A) £6,187 (B) £5,970 (C) £5,817 (D) £6,437

28 What ledger entries would need to be made by the business to record cash taken by the proprietor for his personal use?

(A) Debit Bank; Credit Drawings.
(B) Debit Cash; Credit Capital.
(C) Debit Drawings; Credit Capital.
(D) Debit Drawings; Credit Cash.

29 Which one of the following transactions should be treated as capital expenditure in the accounts of a computer sales company?

(A) Purchase of ten new computers for stock.
(B) Installation of new security system for the building.
(C) Decoration of the accounts office.
(D) Drawings by the company director to buy a new colour television.

30 Malcolm makes the following expenditure on his lorry. How much of it is capital expenditure?

(*i*) Repairs to bodywork £4,500, of which £300 is for an additional safety alarm system.
(*ii*) Motor insurance £790.
(*iii*) Fix a towing bar £190 to enable the lorry to tow a trailer.
(*iv*) Replacement engine £1,400.

(A) £300 (B) £190 (C) £490 (D) £4,990

Section B. Answer all 10 short-answer questions.

1 Describe *three* causes of depreciation, giving examples as appropriate.

2 If a business mistakenly overvalues its stock at the end of its financial year by £5,000 and the error is not discovered, state what the effect would be on:

(*a*) This year's profit.
(*b*) Next year's profit.

3 Brayshaw & Co purchase a new computer costing £2,500 on credit from Computer Office Supplies Ltd. The invoice is correctly posted to the Computer Office Supplies Ltd account, but unfortunately it is debited to the Stationery account instead of the Computer Equipment account. What effect will this error have on the profit of the business and the final accounts?

4 Outline *two* circumstances when a credit note would be issued.

5 State whether the following ledger accounts should be classed as expense, revenue, asset or liability.

(*a*) Interest Received
(*b*) Directors Remuneration
(*c*) Bank Overdraft
(*d*) Office Furniture.

6 Name *four* books of prime entry.

7 Rewrite the following trial balance, making the necessary corrections.

	Dr	*Cr*
Capital		18,936
Cash	146	
Bank Overdraft	1,279	
Stock	3,690	
Debtors		6,873
Creditors	3,594	
Fixtures	6,000	
Motor Vehicles	9,100	
Loan from uncle	2,000	
	25,809	25,809

8 Given the following, what is the amount of creditors?

Fixtures £450; Capital £15,700; Bank Overdraft £675; Cash Balance £97; Building £10,000; Debtors ledger - debit balances £3,175; Credit balances £66; Stock £5,170; Creditors?

9 Markham has an overdraft of £7,200 at the start of May. The following four transactions take place during May. Markham allows his customers 14 days to pay their invoices, and if they do so they are allowed 5 per cent cash discount.

May	4	Goods sold to Howe for £12,000 on credit. Howe pays within the time limit.
May	8	Markham buys goods on credit from Skermer for £1,400.
May	12	Markham sells goods worth £4,400 to King, who pays by cheque after two days, Markham allowing him a 10 per cent trade discount.
May	26	Jones, who is closing down his business, settles his account by giving Markham a cheque for £295 plus a photocopier valued at £180.

Calculate the balance in Markham's account at the bank of 31 May.

10 The petty cash balance at 1 June was £79, and the float was restored to £300 on that day. During June, items paid were: Stationery £44; Travel expenses £115; Sundries £45; and J Clayton a creditor £38. It was decided to reduce the float to £260. How much did the petty cashier then receive on 30 June using imprest system methods?

PAPER 2

Answer all five questions.

1 Kerr and Co keeps its petty cash records using the imprest system. The amount of the imprest is £600, and on 31 May 2007 the petty cash box contained £177. During June 2007, the following petty cash transactions occurred:

2007		£
June 1	Cash received to restore imprest	?
June 2	Train fares of staff	58
June 3	Letter-headings bought	42
June 5	Note books	13
June 7	Train fares of staff	23
June 9	D Rogers - casual labour	77
June 13	Window cleaning materials	11
June 15	Postages: Airmail parcel	84
June 17	K Tonge - casual labour	49
June 19	Staff train fares	31
June 21	Postage stamps	25
June 24	Electric light bulbs	22
June 29	Copying paper	38
July 1	Cash received to restore the imprest	?

The company analyses petty cash under the headings: travel expenses; stationery; casual labour; postage; and sundry expenses. Ignore VAT.

Required:

(*a*) Show the above transactions in an analysis petty cash book for the month of June 2007. Balance the petty cash book at 30 June and bring down the balance.

(*b*) On 1 July 2007 the petty cashier received an amount of cash from the cashier to restore the imprest. Enter this transaction in the Petty Cash Book.

(*c*) Open the ledger accounts to complete the double entry for travel expenses and stationery only.

(*d*) Explain the reason for keeping the petty cash book separate from the main cash book.

20 marks

2 The Hall Engineering Company manufactures small engineering components for the motor-car industry. It operates a columnar purchases day book in which the purchases invoices are recorded.

During May 2000, the following invoices were received:

				£
May	1	Black's Engineering Co	Engineering goods	520
May	3	Ace Printing Co	Printing catalogues	145
May	24	Morgan's Garage	Petrol account	120
May	26	Martin's Foundry	Engineering parts	700
May	28	Office Supplies	Stationery	126
May	29	Black's Engineering Co	Engineering parts	220

All goods are subject to VAT at 17.5 per cent. Ignore folio numbers.

Required:

(*a*) Enter the purchases invoices in a columnar purchases day book using the following analysis columns:

- Engineering parts
- Printing and stationery
- Motor expenses
- VAT.

(*b*) Post the transactions to the personal accounts in the purchases ledger.

(*c*) Post the totals to the appropriate accounts in the general ledger.

20 marks

3 T Fraser's cash book on 30 June 2004 showed a balance at the bank of £6,245. It was not an overdraft. Fraser obtained a bank statement from the bank showing a difference on that date. The following information is available to you:

		£
(1) On 29 June 2004 Fraser had banked an amount that the bank had not yet credited		1,061
(2) A standing order paid to J Tong & Co on 27 June 2004 has not yet been entered in Fraser's cash book		410
(3) The following cheques paid by him had not been presented for payment:		
26 June 2004	C Clark	205
27 June 2004	T Mayall	166
28 June 2004	K Worrall	429
(4) Bank charges not yet entered in cash book		115
(5) A customer, C Fern, had paid his account by credit transfer on 25 June 2004, but this had not been recorded in the cash book.		1,244

Required:

(*a*) Fraser's cash book is to be written up to date by entering the appropriate items.

(*b*) Beginning with the revised cash book balance in (*a*), you are to prepare a bank reconciliation statement at 30 June 2004.

(*c*) What figure should appear as 'cash at bank' in Fraser's balance sheet as at 30 June 2004?

20 marks

4 K Moon is a sole trader. He extracted the following list of balances from the books of his business on 31 March 2003:

	Dr	*Cr*
	£	£
Purchases/Sales	45,380	80,650
Returns inwards/Returns outwards	510	930
Discounts	1,120	390
Stock at 1 April 2002	12,460	
Motor van, at cost	12,500	
Fixtures at cost	9,600	
Provision for depreciation of motor van 1 April 2002		3,800
Provision for depreciation of fixtures 1 April 2002		2,150
Salaries & wages	17,620	
Motor van running expenses	3,910	
Sundry expenses	1,140	
Rent & rates	3,200	
Bad debts	375	
Provision for bad debts 1 April 2002		320
Debtors and creditors	12,870	9,100
Bank	8,040	
Cash	60	
Drawings	7,000	
Capital		38,445
	135,785	135,785

This additional information is available at 31 March 2003:

(1) Stock was valued at £20,100.
(2) Salaries & wages of £490 are to be accrued.
(3) The following have been prepaid: rent £550; rates £240.
(4) An additional £270 is to be written off as bad debts, and the provision for bad debts is to be adjusted to 2 per cent of debtors.
(5) Goods taken by Moon for his private use during the year amounted at cost to £370. No record of this has yet been made in the books.
(6) Depreciation is to be written off as follows: motor van £2,000; fixtures at 15 per cent using the straight line method.

Required:
Prepare for K Moon:
(*a*) A trading and profit and loss account for the year ended 31 March 2003.
(*b*) A balance sheet as at 31 March 2003.

20 marks

5 R King has drawn up her final accounts for the year ended 31 May 2003, showing a gross profit of £75,200 and a net profit of £31,740.

She asked you to check her accounts, and you found the following items that need adjusting:

(1) A credit sale to T Wood of £150 was completely omitted from the books.
(2) Motor vehicle running expenses of £370 had been debited to the motor vehicles account.
(3) Included in insurance is a private insurance policy with a premium paid of £76.
(4) A cash discount of £44, which should have been given to a credit customer named C. Sharp, had not been entered in the books.
(5) King had taken goods costing £314 for her own use but had made no adjustment for this.
(6) Because of item number (2) above, the depreciation provision for the year had been overstated by £74.

Required:

(*a*) Show the journal entries necessary to correct the above items.
(*b*) Calculate the revised figure of gross profit for the year.
(*c*) Calculate the revised figure of net profit for the year.

20 marks

Pitman, OCR and other examining bodies' style of examination

The paper set out below has been written to cover the other examining bodies' assessment criteria. It has been devised to help students gain practice and competence prior to taking their examination. Again, it is important for lecturers and students to refer to the actual specimen papers available from the examining body whose syllabus they are studying.

The time allowed is 2 hours, plus 15 minutes reading time. The marks allocated to each question are shown in brackets. Marks will be awarded for presentation and legibility. All workings should be shown.

Attempt all five questions

1 (*a*) The following trial balance was prepared by your junior assistant. On examination of the figures, you realise that it has been drawn up incorrectly. You are required to reconstruct the trial balance after making the necessary corrections.

Trial Balance of R Ainsworth as at 30 September 2004

	Dr	*Cr*
	£	£
Capital	59,550	
Sales		298,598
Advertising	3,000	
Computer equipment	15,000	
Motor vehicles	18,750	
Insurance		8,610
Purchases	223,553	
Cash at Bank	4,875	
Wages and salaries		23,730
Drawings		10,500
Creditors		25,575
Debtors	25,882	
Rent and rates	26,250	
General expenses	6,863	
Motor expenses		11,190
Heating and lighting		5,520
	383,723	383,723

(*b*) Briefly discuss *two* errors that would not affect the balancing of a trial balance.

25 marks

2 The following extracts are from the Cash Book and Bank Statement of Paul Richards and Co for the month ended June 2005:

Dr *Cash Book* *Cr*

			Bank				Cheque No.	Bank
2005			£	2005				£
June	1	Balance b/d	10,500	June	3	K Ward	121508	475
June	7	Sales	1,225	June	6	A Parker	121509	553
June	12	H Bolton	375	June	9	Stationery	121510	115
June	16	Sales	1,075	June	12	Insurance	121511	700
June	16	Sales	1,450	June	16	M Mellor	121512	950
June	23	D Straw	808	June	20	Petty cash	121513	218
June	28	Sales	995	June	26	Salaries	121514	3,137
				June	30	S/O Loan		625
				June	30	Balance c/d		9,655
			16,428					16,428

Bank Statement

				Dr	Cr	Balance
				£	£	£
2005						
June	1	Balance b/f				10,500
June	4	Cheque	121508	475		10,025
June	8	Deposit			1,225	11,250
June	11	S/O Pensions		600		10,650
June	14	Cheque	121511	700		9,950
June	15	Direct Debit - HP		950		9,000
June	15	Cheque	121510	115		8,885
June	18	Credit Transfer			225	9,110
June	18	Deposit			375	9,485
June	20	Deposit			2,525	12,010
June	21	Cheque	121512	950		11,060
June	23	Cheque	121513	218		10,842
June	24	Deposit			808	11,650
June	30	S/O Loan		625		11,025

Using the information given above, you are required to:

(*a*) bring the cash book up to date to show the correct balance
(*b*) prepare a bank reconciliation statement as at 30 June 2005
(*c*) distinguish between a direct debit and a standing order.

25 marks

3 (*a*) From the details listed below, you are required to calculate the working capital:

	£
Fixed Assets	30,552
Capital	63,000
Current Liabilities	23,724
Loan	15,000
Current Assets	71,172

(*b*) Briefly explain what you understand by the term 'working capital', and state its importance. Illustrate your answer with reference to (*a*) above.

12 marks

4 The following information is extracted from the books of Hazel Grove Printers:

2005			£
May	1	Sales ledger - debit balances	22,512
May	31	Transactions for the month:	
		Cheques received	126,222
		Cash received	3,366
		Sales	149,508
		Bad debts written off	258
		Discounts allowed	321
		Returns inwards	2,436
		Dishonoured cheque	150
		Purchase ledger contra	756

Required:

(*a*) From the details above, write up the Sales Ledger Control Account for the month ended 31 May 2005.

(*b*) List *two* advantages of using control accounts.

13 marks

5 The following trial balance was extracted from the books of Jordon & Co:

Trial Balance of Jordon & Co as at 31 December 2003

	Dr	*Cr*
	£	£
Purchases	73,936	
Sales		101,230
Carriage inwards	245	
Carriage outwards	703	
Returns inwards and outwards	212	1,140
Stock 1 January 2003	4,910	
Wages and salaries	14,975	
Rent, rates and insurance	2,950	
Heating and lighting	627	
Motor vehicle	4,500	
Motor expenses	1,250	
Capital 1 January 2003		18,948
Bank overdraft		2,819
Furniture and fittings	3,200	
Drawings	13,950	
Debtors	11,600	
Creditors		8,921
	133,058	133,058

Notes:

(i) Stock at 31 December 2003 was valued at £6,021.
(ii) Rent owing at 31 December 2003 was £220.
(iii) Rates paid in advance amounted to £180.
(iv) Depreciate the motor vehicle at 20% on cost.

You are required to prepare the Trading and Profit and Loss Account for the year ended 31 December 2003 and a Balance Sheet as at that date.

25 marks

Index

account 17, 25
  balancing off 48–54
  impersonal accounts 122,123
  nominal accounts 122, 123
  personal accounts 122, 123, 124
  real accounts 122, 124
  'T' accounts 19, 25
accounting
  accounting cycle 274, 275
  accounting ratios 450–5
  communicating information 4, 103–4
  definition 3, 5
  equation 6, 9, 12
  importance/need 3–4
  principles, concepts and conventions 110–15
  users of accounting information 3–4
accounting cycle 274, 275
accumulated fund 378, 383
accrual concept 113, 116
accruals (*see* accrued expenses) 309–15, 318
accrued expenses 309–15, 318
acid test ratio 453–4, 460, 461
acknowledgement letters 199
administrative expenses 389, 390
advice note 198, 203
ageing debtors schedule 299
aims of a business 2–3
analytical day books 243–7
  purchases 243–7
  sales 244–5
analytical petty cash book 128–9
annual general meeting 424, 440
appendices 485–579
  answers (appendix E) 522–64
  answers to multiple choice questions (appendix D) 521
  glossary (appendix A) 485–98
  multiple-choice questions (appendix C) 506–20
  specimen examination papers 565–79
  step-by-step guides (appendix B) 499–505
assets 6, 12, 89–91
  current 12, 89–90, 91
  fixed 12, 89–90, 91
  intangible 316, 318
  net current assets 88, 91
authorised share capital 424, 440
AVCO (average cost) 326, 331

bad debts 269, 296-305
provisions 297-304
recovered 304, 305
writing off 269, 296
balance sheet 7, 12 87-91, 99
definition 12
horizontal presentation 11, 12
vertical presentation 11, 12, 88, 99
balancing off accounts 48-54
bank/banking 140-6
bank cash book 131
bank giro credits 144, 146
Banker's Automated Clearing Services (BACS) 144, 146
cash book 121, 123
cheques 140, 141, 146
credit transfer 144, 172, 178
current account 140, 146
deposit account 140, 146
direct debit 145, 146
dishonoured cheque 176
drawer 141, 146
overdraft 141, 146, 163, 174
payee 141, 143, 146
paying-in book 140, 146
paying-in slip 143, 146
reconciliation statements 169-78
standing order 145, 146
statements 148, 153, 175
unpresented cheque 178
bank cash book 131
bank giro credits 144, 146
bank reconciliation statements 169-78
bank statements 148, 153, 175
Banker's Automated Clearing Services (BACS) 144, 146
book-keeping 4, 5
double entry system 16-25, 28-34, 38-44
books of original entry 120-3
business entity concept 112, 116

capital 6, 12, 90-1
account 76-7, 80, 90-1
authorised 424, 440
called-up capital 424, 440
calls in arrear 424, 440
definition 6, 12
employed 316, 318, 451-2, 455, 456, 458
invested 316, 318
issued 424, 440
loan 431, 440
paid-up capital 424, 440
reserve 428, 440
uncalled capital 424, 441
working capital (net current assets) 316, 318
capital employed 316, 318, 451-2, 455-6, 458
capital expenditure 187-9
capital and revenue expenditure 187-9
capital expenditure 187-9

capital and revenue expenditure *(continued)*
capital and revenue receipts 189
joint expenditure 188–9
revenue expenditure 188–9
carriage inwards 94, 104
carriage outwards 94, 104
carriage paid 202
cash analysis 478
cash book 121, 123
analytical cash book 164–6
bank cash book 131
contra items 151, 153
three-column 157–67
two-column 148–53
cash discounts 157, 167, 197, 235
cash on delivery (COD) 202
casting 343
overcasting 343
undercasting 343
cheques (*see* bank/banking) 140, 141, 146
club and society accounts 376–83
accumulated fund 378, 383
donations 382, 383
income and expenditure accounts 377–82
life membership 382, 383
receipts and payments accounts 376–7, 383
subscriptions 380–2, 383
treasurer's responsibilities 383
Companies Acts 422
computers 123
accounts 52–4
concepts of accounting 110–16
conservatism 115, 116
consistency concept 115, 116
contra items 151
control accounts 251
contra items (set-offs) 258–9
memorandum accounts 261–3
purchase ledger control account 255–7
sales ledger control account 252–5
cost concept 112
cost of goods sold 73, 74, 77, 82
credit card 222
credit control 200
credit notes 215–16, 223
credit transfers 144, 172, 178
creditor 8, 12
creditors' ratio 455, 461
current account 140, 146
current ratio 453, 460, 461

debentures 425, 440
debit notes 218, 223
debtor 8, 12
debtors' ratio 454, 461
delivery note 199, 203
deposit account 140, 146

depreciation 280–6
  amortisation 282, 286
  appreciation 283, 286
  causes of depreciation 281
  depletion 282, 286
  inadequacy 282–6
  lease 282, 286
  obsolescence 281, 286
  provisions 288–91, 294
  recording 288–91
  reducing balance method 284–6
  straight line method 284–6
despatch notes 199
direct costs 390, 399
direct debits 145, 146
directors 426, 440
discounts
  allowed 157, 167, 317
  cash discount 157, 167, 197, 235
  received 157, 167, 317
  trade discount 196–8, 203
discounts allowed 157, 167, 317
discounts received 157, 167, 317
dishonoured cheque 176, 178
disposal of assets 291–4
dividends 425–40
division of the ledger 120–3
donations 382, 383
double entry book-keeping 16–25, 28–34, 38–44
  balancing off accounts 48–54
  control accounts and double entry 260–4
  'in' and 'out' approach 18, 41
  purchases 208–10
  returns inward and returns outward 220
  rules 17–18
  sales 193–5
drawer 141, 146
drawings 43, 44, 80
dual aspect concept 113, 116

E & OE (errors & omissions excepted) 202
employee 468, 479
employer 469, 479
equity 7, 12
errors 334–43, 347–56
  commission 35, 343
  compensating 340, 343
  complete reversal 341–2
  correction 334–43, 347–56
  omission 339, 343
  original entry 338, 343
  principle 337, 343
  suspense account 347–56
ex works 202
exempt supplies (VAT) 228, 240
exempted firms (VAT) 236–7, 240
expenses 38, 40, 44, 281

expenses owing (*see* accrued expenses) 309-15

factoring 201, 203
FIFO (first in first out) 325, 331
final accounts 99, 104
  adjustments 308-18
  model layout 503-4
  preparation of 318
  services sector 317
financial statements 3, 72-82, 87-91, 93-104
folio columns 152, 153

general journal 121, 123
general ledger 121, 123
glossary (appendix A) 485-98
going concern concept 112, 116
goods for own use 240, 315
goodwill 315, 318
gross loss 82
gross profit 73, 74, 82
gross profit percentage 450-1, 460, 461

income and expenditure accounts 377-82
indirect costs 390
impersonal accounts 122, 123
imprest system 127, 131
incomplete records (*see* single entry) 362-71
input VAT 227, 240
intangible fixed asset 316, 318
interpretation of accounts 449
investments 431
invoice 193, 230, 233
  coding 211-12
  E & OE (errors & omissions excepted) 202
  ex works 202
  internal checks 200-1
  purchases 208, 212, 233
  sales 192-3, 203
  slip system 201-2, 203
issued share capital 424, 440

journal 266-75
  journal entries and examination questions 267, 273
  narrative 267, 275
  uses of the journal 267-75

lease 282, 286
ledgers
  general 121, 123
  nominal 121, 123, 124
  private 123, 124
  purchases 121, 124
  sales 121, 124
liabilities 6, 12, 90
  current 90, 91
  long-term 90, 91
life membership 382, 383

LIFO (last in first out) 325, 331
limited companies 422–41
  accounts 427–30, 431–9
  annual general meeting 424, 440
  authorised share capital 424, 440
  capital (*see* capital) 424, 440
  capital reserve 428, 440
  Companies Acts 422
  debentures 425, 440
  directors' remuneration 426, 440
  dividends 425, 440
  issued share capital 424, 440
  limited liability 423, 440
  private limited company 423
  public limited company 423, 440
  revenue reserve 428, 440
  shareholder 423, 441
  shares 423, 425, 441
limited liability 423, 440
limited partners 404, 417
liquidity 450, 461
  liquidity ratios 453, 461
loan capital 431, 440
loan interest 189
loss 38, 40, 44, 101–2

manufacturer's recommended retail price 200
manufacturing accounts 389–99
  administrative expenses 389, 390
  direct costs 390, 399
  indirect costs 390
  overhead expenses 389, 390, 399
  prime cost 389, 399
  production cost 389, 399
  selling and distribution expenses 389, 390
  stock of finished goods 391
  work in progress 392, 393, 399
margin 445–56, 448–9, 460, 461
mark-up 445–56, 448–9, 461
materiality 114, 116
memorandum accounts 261–3
model layout of final accounts 503–4
money measurement concept 112
multiple choice questions (appendix C) 506–20

narrative 267, 275
net book value 284, 286
net current assets 88, 91, 316, 318
net loss 101–2
net monthly 202
net profit 73, 75, 82
net profit percentage 450, 460
net realisable value 327, 331
net worth 7, 12
nominal accounts 122, 123
nominal ledger 121, 123, 124
non-trading organisation 5, 376, 383

objectivity 111, 116
organisations 5
  types of 5
original books of entry 120–3
output VAT 227, 240
overcasting 343
overdraft 141, 146, 163, 174
overhead expenses 389, 390, 399

partnership 5, 413–17
partnership accounts 403–17
  accounts 408–16
  agreements 404, 417
  balance sheet 412–13, 416
  interest on capital 405, 417
  interest on drawings 406, 417
  limited 404, 417
  Partnership Act 1890 403–4
  salaries 407, 417
payee 141, 143, 146
paying-in book 140, 146
paying-in slip 143, 146
personal accounts 122, 123, 124
personnel department 469, 480
petty cash book 126–31
  analytical petty cash book 128–9
  imprest system 127, 131
  petty cash voucher 127, 131
posting 151, 153
preliminary expenses 427, 440
prepaid expenses 310–15, 318
prime cost 389, 399
private ledger 123, 124
private limited company 5, 423
production cost 389, 399
profit 38, 40, 44
profit and loss account
  (*see* trading and profit and loss account) 73
profitability 450, 461
  profitability ratios 450, 461
provisions for bad debts 297–304, 305
  creation 298–9
  increasing 300–4
  reducing 301–4
prudence 114, 116
public limited company 5, 423
purchases
  account 28, 33, 35, 75
  analytical purchases day book 243
  credit card 222
  day book 121, 124, 208–10, 233, 245
  invoices 208, 212, 233
  orders 207–8, 212
  purchases ledger 121, 124, 209, 233–4, 246
  purchases ledger control account 255–7
purchases day book 121, 124, 208–10, 233, 245
purchases ledger 121, 124, 209, 233–4, 246

purchases ledger control account 255-7

quantifiability 115, 116

ratio analysis 449
real accounts 122, 124
realisation concept 112, 116
receipt 152, 153
receipts and payments accounts 376-7, 383
reconciliation of ledger accounts 177-8
recovered debts 304, 305
reducing balance method of depreciation 284-6
return on capital employed (ROCE) 451-2, 460, 462
returns inwards
  credit notes 215-16, 223
  day book 121, 124, 216-17
  definition 31, 35
  returns inwards account 28
  treatments in final accounts 100-1
returns inwards day book 121, 124, 216-17
returns outwards
  day book 121, 124, 218-20
  debit notes 218, 223
  definition 31, 35
  returns outwards account 28
  treatments in final accounts 100-1
returns outwards day book 121, 124, 218-20
revenue 38, 44
revenue expenditure 188-9

sales
  account 28, 33, 35, 75
  analytical sales day book 244
  cash sales 30, 34, 192
  credit card 222
  credit sales 20, 34, 192
  day book 121, 124, 193-5, 231, 244
  definition 33, 35
sales day book 121, 124, 193-5, 231, 244
sales invoices 192-3, 203, 230
sales ledger 121, 124, 193-5, 217, 231, 244
sales ledger control accounts 252-5
selling and distribution expenses 389, 390
services sector final accounts 317
shares 423, 425, 440, 441
  ordinary 425, 440
  preference 425, 440
single entry and incomplete records 362-71
  statement of affairs 363, 364, 366, 371
slip system 201-2, 203
specimen examination papers 565-79
  GCSE style 565-75
  Pitman, OCR and other examination bodies' style 576-9
sole trader 5
standing order 145, 146
statement of account 178, 221-2, 223
statement of affairs 363, 364, 366, 371

statutory deductions 475–6, 480
step-by-step guides (appendix B) 499–505
  dealing with adjustments in final accounts 500–1
  model layout of final accounts 503–4
  preparation of final accounts 499
  preparation of final accounts for incomplete records 501–2
  preparation of manufacturing accounts 505
stock 8, 12, 28–35, 77, 95–7, 324–31
  AVCO (average cost) 326, 331
  FIFO (first in first out) 325, 331
  of finished goods 391
  goods for own use 240, 315
  LIFO (last in first out) 325, 331
  net realisable value 327, 331
  records 329–30
  sale or return 327, 331
  stocktaking 328
stock turnover ratio 452, 460, 462
straight line method of depreciation 284–6
subjectivity 111, 116
subscriptions 380–2, 383
suspense account 347–56

trade discount 196–203
trading account
  (*see* trading and profit and loss account)
trading and profit and loss account 72–82, 94
  horizontal presentation 73, 76
  preparation of 73–6
  vertical presentation 73, 81, 94
transactions 16, 25
treasurer's responsibilities 383
trial balance 57–65
  definition 65
  skeleton trial balance 63–4
  steps to take when wrong 62–3
  uses of trial balance 62

undercasting 343
unpresented cheque 178

Value Added Tax (VAT) 226–40
  exempt supplies 228, 240
  exempted firms 236–7, 240
  on fixed assets 238
  included in the gross amount 237
  input VAT 227, 240
  output VAT 227, 240
  partly exempt traders 229
  purchases invoices 232–3
  rate 227
  taxable firms 229–35
  VAT and cash discounts 235
  VAT records 238
  VAT return forms 239
  zero-rated firms 235, 240
  zero-rated supplies 226, 228, 240

VAT records 238
voluntary deductions 476, 480

wages
  bonus 468, 479
  calculating pay 470–2
  cash analysis 478
  clock cards 472–3, 479
  commission 472, 479
  computerised card systems 475, 479
  employee 468, 479
  employer 469, 479
  flexitime 475, 479
  gross pay 469–70, 479
  net pay 469–70, 479
  payroll functions 468–9
  pension fund/superannuation 478, 479
  piece rate 471–2
  remuneration 469, 480
  salaries 468, 480
  statutory deductions 475–6, 480
  time rate 470–1, 480
  time sheets 473–4, 480
  voluntary deductions 476, 480
wages book 477
work in progress 392, 393, 399
working capital (net current assets) 91, 316, 456–7, 462

zero-rated firms 235, 240
zero-rated supplies 226, 228, 240